LIFE APPLICATION® BIBLE COMMENTARY

LUKE

Bruce B. Barton, D.Min.
Dave Veerman, M.Div.
Linda K. Taylor

General Editor: Grant Osborne, Ph.D.
Series Editor: Philip Comfort, Ph.D.

Tyndale House Publishers, Inc.
WHEATON, ILLINOIS

Visit Tyndale's exciting Web site at www.tyndale.com

Contributing Editors: James C. Galvin, Ed.D., and Ronald A. Beers
Life Application is a registered trademark of Tyndale House Publishers, Inc.

Library of Congress Cataloging-in-Publication Data

Barton, Bruce B.
    Luke / Bruce B. Barton, Dave Veerman, Linda Taylor ; general editor, Grant Osborne.
        p.   cm. — (Life application Bible commentary)
    Includes bibliographical references and index.
    ISBN 0-8423-2852-1 (sc : alk. paper)
    1. Bible. N.T. Luke—Commentaries.   2. Bible. N.T. Luke—Devotional
literature. I. Veerman, David. II. Taylor, Linda Chaffee, date.   III. Osborne, Grant R.
IV. Title. V. Series.
BS2595.3.B32   1998   97-27767
226.4′077—dc21

Printed in the United States of America
05 04 03 02 01
7 6 5 4 3

CONTENTS

Gospels

MATTHEW
MARK: betweer
LUKE

ACTS
Paul's Epistles

ROMANS: about 57
1 CORINTHIANS: about 55
2 CORINTHIANS: about 56–57
GALATIANS: about 49

EPHESIANS:
PHILIPPIANS:
COLOSSIANS:
1 THESSALONIANS: about 51
2 THESSALONIANS: about 51–52
1 TIMOTHY:
2 TIMOTHY:
TITUS:
PHILEMON:

General Epistles

JAMES: about 49

1 PETER:
2 PETER:

JUDE:

NEW TESTAMENT

AD 30	40	50	60
The church begins (Acts 1)		*Jerusalem Council and Paul's second journey* (Acts 15)	64 *Rome burns*
35 *Paul's conversion* (Acts 9)	46 *Paul's first missionary journey* (Acts 13)	54 *Paul's third journey* (Acts 18) *Nero becomes emperor*	58 *Paul arrested* (Acts 21)
			61–63 *Paul's Roman imprison- ment* (Acts 28)

etween 60–65
5–65
about 60

JOHN: probably 80–85

about 63–65

about 61
about 62
about 61

about 64
about 66–67
about 64
about 61

HEBREWS: probably before 70

about 62–64
about 67

1 JOHN: between 85–90
2 JOHN: about 90
3 JOHN: about 90

about 65

REVELATION: about 95

T·I·M·E·L·I·N·E

70	80	90	100

67–68
*Paul and
Peter
executed*

*Jerusalem
destroyed*

79 *Mt. Vesuvius
erupts in Italy*

68
*Essenes hide
their library
of Bible
manuscripts
in a cave
in Qumran
by the
Dead Sea*

About 75
*John begins
ministry in
Ephesus*

75
*Rome begins
construction
of Colosseum*

About 98
*John's
death
at Ephesus*

FOREWORD

The *Life Application Bible* Commentary series provides verse-by-verse explanation, background, and application for every verse in the New Testament. In addition, it gives personal help, teaching notes, and sermon ideas that will address needs, answer questions, and provide insight for applying the Word of God to life today. The content is highlighted so that particular verses and phrases are easy to find.

Each volume contains three sections: introduction, commentary, and reference. The introduction includes an overview of the book, the book's historical context, a time line, cultural background information, major themes, an overview map, and an explanation about the author and audience.

The commentary section includes running commentary on the Bible text with reference to several modern versions, especially the New International Version, the New Revised Standard Version, and the New Living Translation, accompanied by life applications interspersed throughout. Additional elements include charts, diagrams, maps, and illustrations. There are also insightful quotes from church leaders and theologians such as John Calvin, Martin Luther, John Wesley, and A. W. Tozer. These features are designed to help you quickly grasp the biblical information and be prepared to communicate it to others. The reference section includes an index and a bibliography.

INTRODUCTION

Precision. Accuracy. Truth.

Certain men and women make it their business to deal only with the facts. No hearsay. No speculation. No rumor.

Scientists belong in this category. Checking the data and conducting experiments, they test theories and draw conclusions. Detectives, too, work hard to discover the truth. Carefully gathering and analyzing evidence, they follow the clues to solve the crime. Add to the mix judges who weigh testimony, hear arguments, and consider the law before rendering just verdicts. Historians also strive to be accurate—to know precisely what happened at a certain time and place. And surely doctors stand with this group. With informative tests and diagnostic expertise, they examine patients, draw conclusions, and prescribe cures.

Luke wanted only the truth. As a historian, Luke's research would be meticulous, interviewing reliable witnesses and primary sources. As a doctor, a man of science, he would carefully consider all the facts before rendering an opinion. That is exactly what he did. Addressing Theophilus, Luke wrote, "Having carefully investigated all of these accounts from the beginning, I have decided to write a careful summary for you, to reassure you of the truth of all you were taught" (1:3-4 NLT). To "reassure" his friend and other believers who never had the opportunity to see Jesus themselves, Luke's investigation included reading "accounts about the events" (1:1) and analyzing "reports . . . from the early disciples and other eyewitnesses" (1:2). Thus, Luke sought and found the truth. Then he recorded it to affirm this truth in writing and to point his readers to the Truth, Jesus Christ.

As you read Luke's Gospel, *carefully investigate* for yourself. Analyze the evidence presented, follow the clues, and render your judgment. No doubt, you too will discover that Jesus is Christ, the Savior, God's Son.

AUTHOR

Luke: doctor, Gentile Christian, traveling companion of Paul, and writer of the book of Acts.

Although the texts of this Gospel and Acts make no mention of

Luke, early church fathers, without dispute or exception, identified him as the author. Justin Martyr (c. A.D. 100–165), Irenaeus (c. A.D. 175–195), and Tertullian (c. A.D. 160–230) all agree. Even the Muratorian Canon (c. A.D. 170–180), an early list of biblical books considered as inspired by God, includes Luke. One of the oldest copies of this Gospel (Bodmer Papyrus XIV), dated to around A.D. 200, includes Luke in the title as the author.

What makes this unanimous testimony so remarkable is that Luke was a relatively unknown figure in the writings of the early church. Paul only mentions Luke three times, in the greetings portion of three of his letters:

- "Dear Doctor Luke sends his greetings, and so does Demas." (Colossians 4:14 NLT)
- "Only Luke is with me. Bring Mark with you when you come, for he will be helpful to me." (2 Timothy 4:11 NLT)
- "So do Mark, Aristarchus, Demas, and Luke, my co-workers." (Philemon 24 NLT).

Most significant is the fact that Luke was not an original disciple, an eyewitness follower of Christ. This fact is freely admitted at the outset of the Gospel, as the author explains the necessity of relying on eyewitnesses for his investigation about Jesus' life (1:2-4). Assuming that Luke is the author, his close relationship to the apostle Paul and other church leaders undoubtedly would have given him access to a wealth of evidence about the life of Christ (see Acts 20:5-15; 27:1–28:16).

In addition to the testimony of the early church, the argument for Lukan authorship includes the following:

- *The author of Acts was one of Paul's traveling companions.* In Acts 16:10-17; 20:5-15; 21:1-18; and 27:1–28:16, the author uses the pronoun "we" in describing Paul's ministry experiences. This seems to indicate that the author was traveling with Paul. Although some have seen this pronoun as merely a Greek literary device to give the impression of being an eyewitness, most scholars understand the use of "we" as reflecting the time when the author of Acts joined Paul in his travels.

A careful study of the "we" sections of Acts reveals that the author was with Paul when he established the church at Philippi and when he returned to Jerusalem. Perhaps in Jerusalem, the author had the opportunity to meet many of the apostles and hear their stories about Jesus, providing the eyewitness accounts needed for compiling the Gospel. Finally the author accompanied Paul to his trial in Rome. These details about the author's life fit well with what is known about Luke. His presence with Paul during his imprisonment is well attested in three of Paul's prison letters (Colossians 4:14; 2 Timothy 4:11; Philemon 24, all quoted above).

- *The author of Acts also wrote the Gospel of Luke.* This seems clear from the opening to Acts: "Dear Theophilus: In my first book I told you about everything Jesus began to do and teach until the day he ascended to heaven after giving his chosen apostles further instructions from the Holy Spirit" (Acts 1:1-2 NLT). Certainly the "first book," also addressed to Theophilus, is the Gospel.
- *Thus, the author of the Gospel of Luke would have been one of Paul's traveling companions.* Paul's letters name some of his traveling companions: Mark, Aristarchus, Demas, and Luke (Colossians 4:14; Philemon 24). Other names could be added to this list: Barnabas, Silas, Timothy, Titus, and Epaphras. It is likely that the author of the Gospel is included in this list.
- *Of all these potential authors, Doctor Luke seems to fit the profile the best.* The style of Greek, the Gentile sensitivities, and the attention to detail all seem to point to Luke as the author.

This evidence, along with the unanimous agreement of early church fathers, makes it difficult to doubt Luke's authorship of this Gospel.

In addition to being one of Paul's traveling companions, the following important facts are known about Luke:

Doctor. Colossians 4:14 uses the title of "doctor" for Luke. Many have attempted to prove Luke's authorship of this Gospel by identifying medical terminology in it. In a few places, Luke presents more exact descriptions of diseases than Matthew or Mark. For instance, a fever is said to be "high" (4:38—compare this with Mark 1:30 in the Greek), and an advanced case of leprosy is described (5:12). Also, only this Gospel mentions a woman spending all of her money on doctors (8:43). Although most Greek scholars have concluded that the literary style and terminology of Luke cannot prove that the author was a doctor (primarily because there wasn't a body of technical medical terminology in the first century as there is today), the literary style of this Gospel suggests a well-educated author. The Greek style of Luke does not prove that the author was a physician, but it does not disprove it and certainly seems consistent with what a doctor would write.

Gentile. Luke is not included among the Jews in Paul's final greetings in Colossians (see Colossians 4:11, 14). From this omission, many have concluded that Luke was a Gentile, probably the only Gentile author of a New Testament book. Another clue to a Gentile identity is Acts 1:19. Here Luke took the trouble to translate an Aramaic place name, and he commented on the Aramaic as "their" language, implying that Aramaic was a different language than his own. A careful study of the Greek style of both Luke and Acts agrees with the conclusion that the author, Luke, was a Gentile. These books consistently avoid Aramaic expressions, such as *rabbi,* and include, instead, words that would be more familiar to Gentiles, such as *teacher.*

Historian. Although Luke's historical accuracy has been called into question by critical scholars on certain points (especially the census of Quirinius in 2:1-2 and references to the priesthoods of Annas and Caiaphas in 3:2), it is clear that Luke, more so than Matthew and Mark, took great pains to verify the historical accuracy of the accounts that he was retelling. In fact, the first few sentences present this as his express purpose: "Having carefully investigated all of these accounts from the beginning, I have decided to write a careful summary for you" (1:3 NLT). Historical references abound in the Gospel. For example, Luke dated Jesus' birth by mentioning the reigning Roman emperor and the local governor (2:1); he even dated the beginning of John the Baptist's ministry in the same way (3:1). This Gospel, along with the numerous details in Acts, reveals the careful and diligent research of a precise historian.

Companion. Clearly Luke was a close friend and traveling companion of Paul, but Scripture gives no specific details about how they met. The circumstances described in Acts, however, seem to point to their meeting in Troas during Paul's second missionary journey.

Paul and his companions had been traveling through Asia Minor (present-day Turkey) visiting the churches that Paul had established on his first missionary journey. After visiting Derbe and Lystra, they began heading north, attempting to spread the Good News of salvation to the people in that region (Acts 16:1-7). But the Spirit of Jesus said, "No!" (Acts 16:7). Frustrated and baffled, the group went to Troas, where Paul saw a vision: a Macedonian man pleading with Paul to come and help them (Acts

16:8-9). This is where Luke seems to have joined Paul, for "we" begins to be used to refer to Paul and company.

This energized group had a clear purpose and direction: God had called them to preach the Good News to an entirely new group of people, the Greeks in Macedonia. Obeying this leading of the Holy Spirit, Paul changed his plans and headed directly to Macedonia (Acts 16:10-12). As they sailed across the Aegean Sea, they could not help but wonder what God had awaiting them in those cities and villages nestled in the mountains of Macedonia.

Their first opportunity for ministry came in Philippi. Not enough Jews lived in this city for a synagogue to be constructed, so Paul and his companions searched the riverbank for a group that regularly met to pray. The women who gathered at the river included Lydia, a godly woman who worshiped God. As she listened to Paul, the Lord opened her heart, and she was baptized. Afterward, Lydia asked Paul and the others to be her guests so that she might learn more about Jesus (Acts 16:13-15).

Lydia's transformation was only the beginning. The simple gospel message turned Philippi, the most affluent city of Macedonia, upside down. The exorcism of a demon-possessed fortune-teller was followed by a riot and a severe beating. Bruised and bloody, Paul and Silas were thrown into the inner dungeon of the Philippian jail (Acts 16:16-24). A great earthquake rocked the entire city that night, leaving the prison in ruins (Acts 16:26). This miraculous event led to the salvation of the Philippian jailer and his household and to the Philippian judges fearfully pleading with Paul and Silas to leave town, before anything else would happen to disturb the city's peace (Acts 16:27-36).

It is unclear whether Luke continued with Paul on the rest of this journey—to Amphipolis, Apollonia, Thessalonica, Corinth, and Antioch (Acts 17:1–18:28)—because the text no longer uses "we" to describe Paul and his party. It is clear, however, that Luke joined Paul again on his third missionary journey (Acts 20:13), accompanying him to Jerusalem, where Paul was arrested (Acts 20:14–22:23). Even though Paul was in chains, Luke stayed with him, finally accompanying him to Rome where Paul was to be tried. Luke courageously faced a hurricane and a shipwreck in order to stay with Paul and serve him (Acts 22:24–28:31).

Although not much is known about Luke, it is evident that he was Paul's loyal and faithful friend. He quietly supported Paul, both when he was valiantly preaching the Good News and when he was sitting in prison. Toward the end of Paul's life, when everyone else had deserted him, Luke was by his side, encouraging and supporting the apostle during his last days (2 Timothy

4:11). Perhaps during these long hours at Paul's side, Luke quietly took up a pen and started writing down the results of his meticulous research of Jesus' life.

As you read Luke, watch for the accuracy and precision with which Luke presents the teaching and ministry of Jesus. But also look beyond this to the Jesus whom Luke presents. Luke's careful research uncovered a person with a revolutionary message, a person who expressed love and compassion that could only come from God. Convinced of the truth of Jesus' message, Luke dedicated all his talents to furthering that message. What is your response to Jesus and his teachings? What can you do to spread the Good News?

DATE AND SETTING

Probably written from Caesarea, around A.D. 60–61.

The best clue to the date for this Gospel is the last recorded event in the book of Acts, Paul's first Roman imprisonment. Acts ends on an unexpected note, with Paul a prisoner in Rome, awaiting his trial. It is an abrupt ending, with no mention of the trial's results and subsequent events. This seems to indicate that Luke was writing Acts right up to the present. If that is so, then Acts was probably written around A.D. 61–62 because Paul's first imprisonment is usually dated A.D. 62 and his second imprisonment and subsequent execution, much later. Clearly identifying his Gospel as the first of his two books (Acts 1:1), Luke probably wrote it around A.D. 60–61, perhaps when he was staying with Paul during his imprisonments in Caesarea (Acts 23:33) and Rome (Acts 28:14-16).

After accompanying Paul on parts of his second and third missionary journeys, Luke remained with him when Paul was arrested in Jerusalem (Acts 21). Luke did not abandon Paul even when he was brought to Caesarea under heavy Roman guard (to protect him from his Jewish accusers, Acts 23:23-35). Also, Luke most likely endured, with Paul, the treacherous sea journey to Rome (Acts 27–28). It was during those long months, as Paul awaited trial, first before Felix (Acts 24:1-27), then Festus (Acts 25:1-22), then Agrippa (Acts 25:23–26:32), and finally Caesar himself (Acts 28:15-31), that Luke probably wrote this Gospel (and the book of Acts). Especially during the imprisonment at Rome, Paul enjoyed a measure of freedom. He lived in his own rented house, under the constant watch of a Roman guard, and welcomed guests and friends to tell them about the Good News concerning Jesus Christ and salvation (Acts 28:30-31). During this somewhat mild imprisonment, it appears that Luke stayed with Paul (Paul mentions Luke in the letters he wrote during that time—see Colossians 4:14 and Philemon 24).

In addition to staying with Paul and supporting him, Luke was diligently compiling the facts relating to Jesus' life—the testimonies of eyewitnesses, the written histories, and the stories of the Messiah's life that Paul had employed in his preaching. Luke wrote a history of Jesus' life that would become more influential than the Roman Empire itself. Luke's history would survive the fall of that powerful empire and would help establish the truth about Christ.

This date (A.D. 60–61) is fairly close to the time that the other two synoptic Gospels were written—Mark being the first, around A.D. 55–60, and Matthew following, around A.D. 60. Because of this proximity, some critics have maintained a later date for Luke and Acts—in the mid-eighties. Their reasons, however, are far from persuasive. The common assumption of these critics, that Luke would not have access to Mark's Gospel until several decades after Mark wrote it, is very doubtful because Paul mentioned in both Philemon 24 and 2 Timothy 4:11 that Luke and Mark were together. (Philemon was written in A.D. 60, and 2 Timothy was written in A.D. 66 or 67.)

In addition, Acts makes no mention of the destruction of Jerusalem, which occurred in A.D. 70. Surely this catastrophic event would have been included in any history of the early church. In fact, Luke reported Jesus' predictions that Jerusalem would be utterly demolished (19:41-44; 21:20-24). Mentioning the fulfillment of Jesus' prophecy would have been especially appropriate since Luke wrote of Stephen's martyrdom (Acts 6:8–7:60) and Paul's arrest (Acts 21:26-36), both events having occurred in Jerusalem. Note also that Luke wrote of the fulfillment of Agabus's prophecy (Acts 11:28). Certainly the omission in Acts of the destruction of Jerusalem points to an earlier date for the Gospel.

Most likely, Luke took advantage of the prolonged imprisonment of Paul in both Casearea and Rome to collect information relating to Jesus' life and to record Paul's memories of his four missionary journeys that had spanned the previous decade.

AUDIENCE

Theophilus ("one who loves God"), Gentiles, and people everywhere.

Luke addressed both of his books—the Gospel and the book of Acts—to Theophilus (1:1; Acts 1:1). Because "Theophilus" literally means "one who loves God" or "friend of God," some have speculated that the name does not refer to an actual person but, rather, to all people who love God. "Most excellent" or "honorable" (the words preceding the name), however, was a title often used in addressing a Roman official. For example, it is used in the address to Felix (Acts 23:26; 24:2). This has led most scholars to conclude that Theophilus was an actual person, probably someone of rank in Roman society. Beyond that brief mention in Luke and Acts, however, nothing else is known of Theophilus. The name appears nowhere else in Scripture.

The name, "Theophilus," suggests a Gentile. This is consistent with the content of both Luke and Acts, which seem to be written to a predominately Gentile audience. As discussed above (see "Author"), Luke typically avoided Jewish expressions, such as *scribe* and *rabbi,* and replaced them with common Greek expressions, such as *lawyer* and *master* (compare 9:33; 11:52 with Mark 9:5; 12:28 NRSV). He translated the Hebrew word *Golgotha* into the Greek *Kranion,* meaning "Skull" (compare 23:33 with Mark 15:22). Luke also took the trouble to explain common Jewish customs, such as the Passover, to his readers, who were apparently Gentiles (see 22:1-7). In addition, Luke omitted the teachings of Jesus that involved the intricacies of Mosaic law and Jewish customs, such as divorce regulations (see Mark 10:1-12), customs surrounding oaths (see Matthew 5:33-37), praying (see Matthew 6:5-6), and fasting (see Matthew 6:16-18). On the other hand, Luke underscored Jesus' mission to the Gentiles (2:32; 24:47) by tracing his genealogy back to Adam instead of just to Abraham (compare 3:23-38 with Matthew 1:1-17) and by highlighting the centurion's remarkable faith (7:1-10). Luke's concern for Gentile inclusion into the community of faith becomes even more clear in the book of Acts, where he charted the spread of the gospel among the Gentiles (Acts 10:1–11:18; 13:46-48).

Some have suggested that Theophilus may have been an unbeliever whom Luke was trying to evangelize, but it is apparent that Luke was assuming a cursory knowledge of the gospel and Old Testament history. The book is liberally sprinkled with quotations from the Old Testament throughout (3:4-6; 4:18-19; 7:27; 8:10; 20:42-43; Acts 2:17-28; 28:26-27) and does not explain common Christian expressions like the "Son of Man" (5:24; 6:5).

In conclusion, Luke seems to be addressing a Gentile Christian who was questioning his faith. It is possible that Theophilus had come to faith in Jesus Christ as a God-fearer, a Jewish proselyte (God-fearers are mentioned in 1:50; 7:2-6; Acts 10:1-2; 13:16, 26). By joining the Christian community, he found himself in a persecuted sect of Judaism. Many of the Jewish people with whom he had formerly worshiped were probably rejecting him because of his commitment to Christianity. In addition, his Gentile friends did not understand his fascination with this one Jew, Jesus Christ. Theophilus may have been wondering if Jesus was merely a religious teacher for the Jews, if Christianity was just an obscure sect of Judaism, if Jesus actually was the Son of God, and if Jesus really had come to earth to save him.

Although written to a specific individual, Luke probably also had a larger audience in mind. Certainly a new Christian questioning his or her faith would gain much from reading this Gospel. Jews and Jewish Christians would benefit from seeing that despite numerous invitations by God to participate in the New Covenant, Israel had rejected God's invitations and their Messiah. Gentiles, especially, would benefit from this Gospel, especially those feeling out of place in what originally was a Jewish movement. Growing numbers of Gentiles were coming to Christ in Asia Minor and Greece, evangelized, for the most part, by Paul (as described in Acts). Luke offered reassurance that they belonged, as Christ's followers and God's people. Clearly, through Luke, God was communicating his message to *all* "who love God."

What tensions do you face in your faith? What doubts about Jesus and the Christian faith nibble at the edges of your mind? Apparently Theophilus did not cover up his questions; instead, he went to his trusted and knowledgeable friend and asked for information and answers. Luke responded to Theophilus with two books, filled with the results of his careful research about Jesus. As you read, dive into this God-inspired history of Jesus with your hard questions. You will find answers.

OCCASION AND PURPOSE

To present an accurate account of the life of Christ and to present Christ as the perfect man and Savior.

Luke's purpose for writing is stated in his preface to the book. He wanted to provide Theophilus with a "carefully investigated" and "orderly account" of the life of Jesus (1:3 NIV). In short, Luke wrote this account to provide Theophilus with a history of Jesus that could hold up to the standards of historical investigation. Luke had sifted through the evidence, the eyewitness accounts, and the writings describing Jesus' life, assuring that the stories did not contradict each other. Moreover, he put Jesus' life within a historical framework, placing markers along the way to solidly anchor Jesus' life in history (see, for example, 2:1 and 3:1).

Luke knew that his account of Jesus' life must do more than

report the Master's words and deeds. Jesus' actions certainly
could speak for themselves. Healing the sick (5:12-16), exorcising thousands of demons (8:26-39), calming the waves (8:22-25),
and raising people from the dead (8:40-56) surely could not be
attributed to a mere human being. Only God could possess that
type of control over nature, diseases, the spirit world, and even
death. Yet Luke did not stop there. He connected Old Testament
Scriptures with Jesus' actions, showing how Jesus fulfilled the
prophecies concerning the Messiah (3:4-6; 7:22-23; 20:17). Jesus
was the one about whom the prophets had spoken.

Luke did not leave Theophilus wondering how he should
respond to Jesus. He described the various reactions of those who
saw and heard Jesus—from amazement, joy, and wholehearted
belief to fear, skepticism, and coldhearted rejection (compare 4:16-
30 and 9:18-20). Luke highlighted the appropriate responses: fervent belief in Jesus as the Son of God (9:18-20) and willingness to
sacrifice everything to follow him (9:23-27). *Anyone* who
responded to the gospel message, repenting of sin and trusting in
Christ, could become a member of the community of faith.

With two well-researched volumes, Luke answered Theophilus's hard questions about Christian faith. By retelling the life
and teachings of Jesus, Luke presented Jesus as a real man, an
extraordinary Jewish teacher in his own right. By recounting the
miracles and the prophecies connected to Jesus' life, Luke portrayed him as a divine being, the Messiah sent by God. By tracing the growth of the Christian church throughout the known
world at that time, Luke presented the good news of salvation,
applicable to every person—from the lowliest slave to the most
respected nobleman, from Orthodox Jews to pagan Greeks and
Romans. When you sit down to read Luke, don't let your familiarity with the Gospel stories rob the freshness and vividness of
Luke's account. Like Theophilus, approach Luke with questions.
Who is Jesus? Why should I care about a Jewish teacher? Let
Jesus' words speak directly to you, challenging you to repent and
believe.

RELATIONSHIP TO THE OTHER GOSPELS

It is commonly accepted that Luke had access to Mark's Gospel
when he was composing his account, for he seems to have
adapted Mark's material in large blocks (see chapters 4, 5, 8, 9,
19-21; compare 18:15-17 and Mark 10:13-16 for the similar
wording of the two Gospels). Parts of the rest of Luke's narrative
have close affinities with portions of Matthew, but the striking dif-

ferences at times suggest that Luke may not have had direct access to Matthew's Gospel. Around 30 percent of the Gospel is entirely unique. Most of this is parables:

Parables Unique to Luke:
Two debtors—7:41-50
The Good Samaritan—10:25-37
The persistent friend—11:5-10
The rich fool—12:13-21
The barren fig tree—13:6-9
The foolish builder—14:28-30
The foolish king—14:31-33
The lost sheep—15:1-7
The lost coin—15:8-10
The lost son—15:11-32
The shrewd manager—16:1-8
The rich man and Lazarus—16:19-31
The humble servant—17:7-10
The persistent widow—18:1-8
The Pharisee and the tax collector—18:9-14

A theme emerges in a study of the parables unique to Luke: the emphasis on the spiritual importance of prayer and generosity. The parables of the persistent friend, the persistent widow, and the Pharisee and the tax collector all teach the power of prayer. Prayer is highlighted throughout Jesus' ministry—from his baptism (3:21) to his choosing of the disciples (6:12-13) to the night he was betrayed (22:40-46).

The parables of the rich man and Lazarus, the rich fool, the two debtors, the shrewd manager, and the Good Samaritan emphasize the importance of generosity. Luke drives this point home by recording Jesus' straightforward confrontation of a rich man's spiritual arrogance: "Sell everything you have and give to the poor, and you will have treasure in heaven. Then come, follow me" (18:22 NIV).

Among all of the Gospel writers, Luke highlighted the high ethical demands Jesus made on his followers. Jesus did not mince words, commanding anyone who wanted to follow him to "take up his cross daily" (9:23 NIV). This means dedicating all of one's talents and possessions to furthering God's kingdom. As you read Luke, consider whether you are committed to taking up your cross each day. Do you dedicate time to God, praising him and praying for his will for your life? Have you committed all your resources to his purposes?

MESSAGE

Jesus Christ, the Savior; History; People/Women; Social Concern; Holy Spirit.

Jesus Christ, the Savior (1:26-38; 2:1-52; 3:21-23; 4:1-44; 5:1-39; 6:1-11, 46-49; 7:1-50; 8:22-56; 9:18-45, 57-62; 10:16, 21-24; 11:14-32; 12:8-12, 35-59; 13:31-35; 14:15-35; 17:20-37; 18:18-34; 19:28-48; 20:1-47; 21:25-36; 22:14-71; 23:1-56; 24:1-53). Luke's Gospel describes how God entered human history. Jesus, the sinless Son of God, was born of a virgin (2:1-7), grew and matured as a human boy and young man (2:52), resisted Satan's temptations (4:1-13), taught and ministered among the people (4:14–21:38), was betrayed by Judas and deserted by his closest followers (22:1-62), was convicted and executed as a common criminal (22:63–23:56), rose from the dead (24:1-49), and ascended into heaven (24:50-51). Jesus is an exemplar for all people. After a perfect ministry, he provided a perfect sacrifice for our sin so that men and women of all races and nations could be saved.

Importance for today. Jesus is the unique Son of God, humanity's perfect leader and only Savior. He offers forgiveness to all who will accept him as Lord of their lives and who believe that what he says is true. Christians know this profound truth. Christ has changed their lives, forever. They also have the great responsibility to share the Good News with others. The world is lost, with millions heading for eternal separation from God. These men, women, and children need to meet and know the Savior.

You know the truth about the Truth, your Lord and Savior Jesus Christ. What are you doing to share the gospel with others?

History (1:1-4; 2:1-3; 3:1-2, 23-38; 13:1-4; 23:6-7). Luke was a medical doctor and historian. He put great emphasis on dates and details, connecting Jesus to events and people in history. Luke made sure that what he was writing was historically accurate, in every detail. He wanted believers, especially Theophilus, to be confident and secure in their faith. Inspired by the Holy Spirit, Luke faithfully recorded God's message for his first-century audience and for believers throughout the ages.

Importance for today. Christians today can believe in the reliability of Luke's history of Jesus' life. Even if approached as a secular document, this Gospel presents solid evidence for its historicity and accuracy. What is most important, however, is that the historical facts point to the divinity of Christ.

When assailed by questions or doubts about your faith, return to Luke. You can believe with certainty that Jesus is God.

People/Women (4:42-44; 5:5-11, 27-32; 6:13-15, 27-42; 7:18-

28, 36-50; 8:1-3, 19-21; 9:10-17, 47-48; 10:38-41; 12:1, 22-34; 18:15-17; 19:1-10; 21:5-24, 37-38; 23:42-43; 24:13-52). Jesus was deeply interested in relationships. He treated people with care and concern, not merely as potential converts. Jesus enjoyed strong friendships with his disciples, other followers, and special families (for example, Mary, Martha, and Lazarus, 10:38-42). He reached out to all types of people: outcasts such as lepers (17:12-19), alienated Samaritans (9:52), despised tax collectors (5:27; 19:1-10), women (8:1-3), and children (18:16). He showed warm concern for his followers and friends.

Of special note is Jesus' friendships with women. Luke seems to have made a point of highlighting this aspect of the Lord's ministry. Luke 8:1-3, for example, lists several women as close followers and supporters. This fits, of course, with Greek and Roman culture where women were active participants in busi- · ness, politics, and household management (see, for example, Acts 16:13-15; 17:4, 12). It would have been almost scandalous, however, in Jewish culture where men and women were separated in the synagogue and only men could be taught by the rabbis.

Importance for today. Jesus' love for people is good news for everyone. His message is for all people in every nation, and each person has the opportunity to respond to him in faith. In addition, Jesus' example teaches that his followers should love people, regardless of their sex, race, age, or worldly status. Christians should be known by their love.

You may feel as if you are a second-class citizen in your community or neighborhood, but not in Jesus' eyes. Regardless of your status in society, know that you are important to him.

Also, as you relate to neighbors, coworkers, and others, think of how you can show genuine concern and care for them and their families. Determine to reflect Christ in your life, to be known as a person of love.

Social Concern (4:31-41; 5:12-26; 6:6-10, 17-19; 7:1-17; 8:28-39, 41-56; 9:1-2; 10:25-37; 13:10-17; 14:1-6; 16:19-31; 17:11-19; 18:35-43; 22:50-51). As a perfect human, Jesus showed tender sympathy to the poor, the despised, the hurt, and the sinful. No one was rejected or ignored by him. Jesus healed the sick, diseased, and crippled. His compassion reached across racial lines and broke with convention (for example, healing on the Sabbath, 6:6-10).

Luke paid special attention to Jesus' treatment of the poor and his teachings about poverty and wealth. Jesus pointed out the dangers of wealth and the impossibility of serving both God and money ("woe" to the rich, 6:24-25; the parable of the rich fool,

12:16-21; the parable of the rich man and Lazarus, 16:19-31; the rich young man, 18:18-30; the Zacchaeus narrative, 19:1-10). Jesus also emphasized God's special interest in the poor ("God blesses you who are poor," 6:20; giving to those in need, 12:32-34; inviting the poor, crippled, lame, and blind to the banquet, 14:21). And he commanded his followers to help the poor (4:18; 12:33; 14:13).

Importance for today. Obeying his teachings, Christ's followers should check their lives for materialism and love of money. Is financial security the focus of your life? Do you think more about what you can *get* or what you can *give?*

Also, as they emulate their leader, Christ's followers should reach out to the hurting and disenfranchised in society, offering loving care, emotional support, and material assistance. What poor or infirm people can you help? Consider how you can "sell what you have and give to the poor," using your resources to make a difference in their lives.

Finally, Jesus' compassion shows that he is more than an idea or teacher; he tenderly cares for each person. Know that only his kind of deep love can satisfy you. Whatever your need, bring it to the Savior.

Holy Spirit (1:15, 35, 41, 67-79; 2:25-32; 3:16, 22; 4:1, 14; 10:21; 11:12). The Holy Spirit was present at Jesus' birth, baptism, ministry, and resurrection. Jesus lived in dependence on the Holy Spirit. This emphasis is carried over into Luke's sequel, the book of Acts, where we see Christians thoroughly immersed and motivated by the Holy Spirit.

Importance for today. The Holy Spirit was sent by God as confirmation of Jesus' authority. The Holy Spirit is given to enable people to live for Christ. By faith, believers can have the Holy Spirit's presence and power to witness and to serve. Don't try to live the Christian life in your own strength. Just as you trusted Christ to save you, rely on the Holy Spirit to give you the power to live for him.

VITAL STATISTICS

Purpose: To present an accurate account of the life of Christ and to present Christ as the perfect human and Savior

Author: Luke—a doctor (Colossians 4:14), Greek, and a Christian. He is the only known Gentile author in the New Testament. Luke was a close friend and companion of Paul. He also wrote Acts, and the two books go together.

To Whom Written: Theophilus ("one who loves God"), Gentiles, and people everywhere

Date Written: About A.D. 60

Setting: Luke wrote from Rome or possibly from Caesarea.

Key Verses: "Jesus said to him, 'Today salvation has come to this house, because this man, too, is a son of Abraham. For the Son of Man came to seek and to save what was lost'" (19:9-10 NIV).

Key People: Jesus, Elizabeth, Zechariah, John the Baptist, Mary, the disciples, Herod the Great, Pilate, Mary Magdalene

Key Places: Bethlehem, Galilee, Judea, Jerusalem

Special Features: This is the most comprehensive Gospel. The general vocabulary and diction show that the author was educated. He makes frequent references to illnesses and diagnoses. Luke stresses Jesus' relationships with people; emphasizes prayer, miracles, and angels; records inspired hymns of praise; and gives a prominent place to women. Most of 9:51–18:35 is not found in any other Gospel.

OUTLINE

A. Birth and Preparation of Jesus, the Savior (1:1–4:13)
B. Message and Ministry of Jesus, the Savior (4:14–21:38)
  1. Jesus' ministry in Galilee
  2. Jesus' ministry on the way to Jerusalem
  3. Jesus' ministry in Jerusalem
C. Death and Resurrection of Jesus, the Savior (22:1–24:53)

Luke begins his account in the temple in Jerusalem, giving us the background for the birth of John the Baptist, then moves on to the town of Nazareth and the story of Mary, chosen to be Jesus' mother (1:26). As a result of Caesar's call for a census, Mary and Joseph had to travel to Bethlehem, where Jesus was born in fulfillment of prophecy (2:1ff.). Jesus grew up in Nazareth and began his earthly ministry by being baptized by John (3:21-22) and tempted by Satan (4:1ff.). Much of his ministry focused on Galilee—he set up his "home" in Capernaum (4:31) and from there he taught throughout the region (8:1ff.). Later he visited the Gerasene region, where he healed a demon-possessed man (8:36ff.). He fed more than five thousand people with one lunch on the shores of the Sea of Galilee near Bethsaida (9:10ff.). Jesus always traveled to Jerusalem for the major festivals, and he enjoyed visiting friends in nearby Bethany (10:38ff.). He healed ten men with leprosy on the border between Galilee and Samaria (17:11) and helped a dishonest tax collector in Jericho turn his life around (19:1ff.). The little villages of Bethphage and Bethany on the Mount of Olives were Jesus' resting places during his last days on earth. He was crucified outside Jerusalem's walls, but he would rise again. Two men on the road leading to Emmaus were among the first to see the resurrected Christ (24:13ff.).

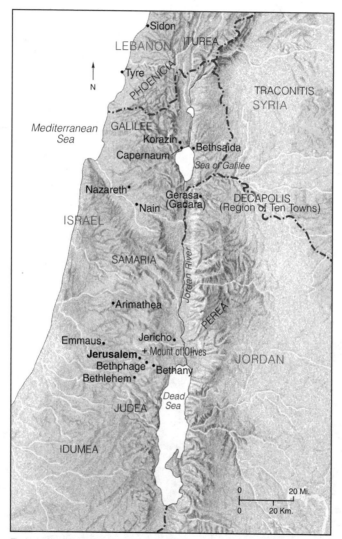

Sidon

LEBANON   ITUREA

Tyre
PHOENICIA

N

TRACONITIS
SYRIA

Mediterranean
Sea

GALILEE

Korazin
Bethsaida

Capernaum

Sea of Galilee

Nazareth

Gerasa
(Gadara)

DECAPOLIS
(Region of Ten Towns)

Nain

ISRAEL

SAMARIA

Jordan River

Arimathea

PEREA

Emmaus

Jericho

Jerusalem

+ Mount of Olives

JORDAN

Bethphage

Bethany

Bethlehem

JUDEA

Dead
Sea

IDUMEA

0   20 Mi.
0   20 Km.

The broken lines (—·—·) indicate modern boundaries.

LUKE 1

The author of this Gospel account, Luke, was a doctor, a Greek, and a Gentile Christian. His Gospel was directed to a Gentile audience, and the very first sentences of his letter reflect this. Matthew begins with a genealogy; Mark opens with a concise statement that moves into the gospel story immediately; John gives a theological treatise. Luke, however, begins with a few words to justify his writing and to assure the reader of the reliability and accuracy of his account. This follows the pattern of the great Greek and Hellenistic historians, who would explain their work in a short preface. Luke's opening verses prove that he truly believed that he, along with the other evangelists, was recording history.

Luke opens his Gospel with the explanation that, though he was not himself an eyewitness of Jesus' ministry, he wanted the eyewitness accounts to be preserved accurately and the foundations of Christian belief transmitted intact to the next generations. As a traveling companion of Paul, Luke would have had the opportunity to meet many of the disciples and ask them what Jesus had done and said while on this earth. Evidently Luke, as an educated doctor, dedicated himself to this task, becoming a meticulous and thorough student of Jesus' life. This is evident in his Gospel, for 30 percent of it is new information—not contained in the other three Gospels. As you read this Gospel, watch the way Luke carefully presents all the evidence surrounding Jesus' life, death, and resurrection to Theophilus—a Gentile Christian who was filled with questions about his faith. As you read this accurate account of what Jesus did and said during his ministry in Galilee and Judea, recommit yourself to following in his footsteps.

1:1 Since many have undertaken to set down an orderly account of the events that have been fulfilled among us.^{NRSV} The first four verses of the Gospel of Luke are one sentence in Greek, serving as a preface. Luke's sophisticated Greek writing style, revealed in this preface, set his work apart from the other three

Gospels. The Gospels of Matthew and Mark were written at about the same time as Luke, and apparently *many* other witnesses and writers had also *undertaken to set down an orderly account of the events* of Jesus' life and ministry. Luke did not criticize the other works; instead, he appealed to their importance as precedents for his own work. Luke perceived a need to put the facts from these other written sources into an account written especially for a Gentile believer who needed to understand Jesus' story. Thus, Luke tells Jesus' story from Luke's unique perspective of a Gentile, a physician, and the first historian of the early church. Luke wrote to Gentiles, presenting Jesus Christ as the perfect human and Savior of all people.

The words "events that have been fulfilled" point to the theme of the book—Jesus Christ who fulfilled God's plan and purposes through his ministry, his death, and his resurrection. This "fulfillment" has eternal significance for all who read the words Luke wrote in his Gospel.

DECIDE FOR YOURSELF
At the time that Luke wrote this letter to Theophilus, there was a lot of interest in Jesus and in this movement called Christianity. Many people had written firsthand accounts about Jesus. Luke used these and all other available resources as material for an accurate and complete account of Jesus' life, teachings, and ministry. Because truth was important to Luke, he relied heavily on eyewitnesses. Christianity doesn't say, "Close your eyes and believe," but rather, "Check it out for yourself" (John 1:46; 21:24; Acts 17:11-12). No halfhearted investigation will do, however. Approach the life and impact of Jesus with expectation and intensity. Thoroughly investigate the Bible's claims about Jesus because your conclusion about him is a life-and-death matter.

1:2 Just as they were handed on to us by those who from the beginning were eyewitnesses and servants of the word.^{NRSV}
Many had "set down" written accounts; many others had been *eyewitnesses and servants of the word.* This refers to people who had seen Jesus' life and ministry and who were actively spreading the gospel message—most certainly the apostles and perhaps other loyal followers. The apostle Peter later wrote:

> *For we were not making up clever stories when we told you about the power of our Lord Jesus Christ and his coming again. We have seen his majestic splendor with our own eyes. And he received honor and glory from God the Father when God's glorious, majestic voice called down from heaven, "This*

is my beloved Son; I am fully pleased with him." We ourselves
heard the voice when we were there with him on the holy
mountain. (2 Peter 1:16-18 NLT)

These eyewitnesses reported what they had seen and heard—
"handed on to us" refers to oral transmission. These were not
myths. Believers today owe the Gospels and the book of Acts to
writers who, like Luke, took the carefully preserved oral information from eyewitnesses and wrote it down. These events were not
mythological or hearsay—actual people gave factual reports.
Doctor Luke, a man whose very living depended on knowing and
diagnosing the facts, took the facts of Jesus' life gained from writings and eyewitness reports and prepared this document for his
friend.

IT'S TRUE!
As a medical doctor, Luke knew the importance of being
thorough. He used his skills in observation and analysis to
thoroughly investigate the stories about Jesus. His diagnosis?
The gospel of Jesus Christ is true! You can read Luke's
account of Jesus' life with confidence that it was written by a
clear thinker and a thoughtful researcher. Because the gospel
is founded on historical truth, our spiritual growth must involve
careful, disciplined, and thorough investigation of God's Word
so that we can understand how God has acted in history. If this
kind of study is not part of your life, find a pastor, teacher, or
even a book to help you get started and to guide you in this
important part of Christian growth. (You might want to read
Mere Christianity by C. S. Lewis or *More Than a Carpenter* by
Josh McDowell.) In this day of accepting the diversity of many
religious points of view, we need the reassurance that comes
from studying the life of Christ.

1:3-4 **I too decided, after investigating everything carefully from**
the very first, to write an orderly account for you, most excel-
lent Theophilus, so that you may know the truth concerning
the things about which you have been instructed.NRSV These
words, in the tradition of Greek historians, were meant to inspire
confidence in Luke's readers. Even though other accounts of
Jesus' life existed, Luke *too decided* to write an account. Luke, as
an educated Gentile believer and a medical doctor, would certainly pay attention to details: *investigating everything carefully,*
writing a full account that would cover events *from the very first,*
making his account *orderly* (although not necessarily chronological), and giving his readers *the truth.*

"Theophilus" literally means "one who loves God." While

this may be a general term for all believers, it is a proper name and with the title, *most excellent,* indicates a person of some rank or distinction. The book of Acts, also written by Luke, is likewise addressed to Theophilus (Acts 1:1). Theophilus may have been Luke's patron who helped to finance the book's writing. More likely, Theophilus was a Roman acquaintance of Luke's with a strong interest in the new Christian religion. Luke wanted to assure Theophilus of the truth *concerning the things about which [he] had been instructed.* Theophilus had learned some of the facts about the gospel via oral teaching, but he desired further clarification in writing. Luke set out to explain the entire gospel story to Theophilus, from the story of the birth of John the Baptist until the ascension of Christ. In Acts, Luke continued the story of the spread of the gospel until Paul brought it to Rome.

We can thank Theophilus for his concerns. Without his questions, we would not today have this Gospel, with its story of Jesus' birth and childhood and its record of many of Jesus' parables (most of 9:51–18:35 is not in any other Gospel).

AN ANGEL PROMISES THE BIRTH OF JOHN TO ZECHARIAH / 1:5-25 / 4

Sitting down to read a biography, a person typically will turn to page 1 of chapter 1 and expect to read about the beginning—usually about the person's birth, or at least, his or her youth. The same was true of ancient Greco-Roman biographies: an infancy narrative would begin the biography and build the foundation of the entire work. Luke follows this well-known pattern by starting in "the beginning" (1:3 NIV). But for Jesus' life, the beginning is not his birth, but instead the announcement of the birth of John the Baptist—the person who would prepare the way for Jesus.

In contrast to the secular Greek tone of the preceding section (1:1-4), this section has a Hebraic tone, demonstrating the close association of Luke's narrative with the Old Testament, the Hebrew Bible. The announcement of a child to a childless older couple parallels other stories in the Old Testament: the three men who visited Abraham and Sarah (Genesis 18) and the angel of the Lord who visited Manoah and his wife (Judges 13). Moreover, the angel's words to Zechariah recall the words of the prophet Malachi (Malachi 4:5-6): "And he will go on before the Lord, in the spirit and power of Elijah, to turn the hearts of the fathers to their children and the disobedient to the wisdom of the righteous—to make ready a people prepared for the Lord" (1:17 NIV). Luke's presentation of the announcement of John the Baptist's birth makes it clear that everything he is recounting—from John the Baptist's birth to all of Jesus' life—is a continuation, or more accurately, a fulfillment of Old Testament prophecies (see 1:1).

When God fulfills his promises and acts on behalf of his people, it is an occasion to rejoice in God's goodness. Not only could Zechariah and Elizabeth rejoice that God was answering their prayer for a child, but the people gathered around the temple could rejoice over the announcement of John's birth because he would prepare the way for the promised Messiah. This was a time to rejoice, but tragically Zechariah did not believe the angel's word. We do not know why he did not believe. Perhaps he was tired of waiting on God; perhaps he had lost hope that God would ever answer his persistent prayers for a child. In any case, this story is a clear warning: we shouldn't let unbelief ruin our joyful walk with God. Instead, we should anticipate God working in our lives; we should pray that he will accomplish his will in our lives; we should look for occasions to praise him for what he is doing.

1:5 **In the days of King Herod of Judea, there was a priest named Zechariah, who belonged to the priestly order of Abijah. His wife was a descendant of Aaron, and her name was Elizabeth.**^{NRSV} As a good historian should, Luke gave his readers the historical setting. The story begins *in the days of King Herod of Judea.* This was Herod the Great, confirmed by the Roman Senate as king of the Jews but never accepted by the Jewish people as their king (although half-Jewish, Herod was not part of the royal line of David). For the Jews living in Judea, this was a time of oppression. Although they were not in slavery, they were not completely self-governing either. Herod had expanded and beautified the Jerusalem temple, but he had placed a Roman eagle over the entrance and also had built pagan temples. When he helped the Jews, it was for political purposes and not because he cared about them or their God. Evil and ruthless, Herod the Great later ordered a massacre of infants in a futile attempt to kill the infant Jesus, whom some were calling the new "king of the Jews" (Matthew 2:1-2). Herod the Great ruled from 37 to 4 B.C.

After mentioning the king of Judea, Luke moved to a heretofore unknown *priest named Zechariah, who belonged to the priestly order of Abijah.* A Jewish priest was a minister of God who worked at the temple managing its upkeep, teaching the people the Scriptures, and directing the worship services. At this time there were about twenty thousand priests throughout the country—far too many to minister in the temple at one time. Therefore the priests were divided into twenty-four separate groups of about one thousand each, according to David's instructions (1 Chronicles 24:3-19). Zechariah was a member of the order (or division) of Abijah. Each division served in the Jerusalem temple twice each year for one week.

Zechariah's wife, *Elizabeth, was a descendant of Aaron.* Elizabeth descended directly from Aaron, brother of Moses and Israel's first high priest (Exodus 28:1). As a priest, Zechariah would have been required to marry a virgin Israelite, but not necessarily one from a priestly family. Zechariah was especially blessed to have a wife with such a background. These were quality people, not only by descent, but also by their character (1:6). Both were known for their personal holiness.

1:6-7 **Both of them were righteous before God, living blamelessly according to all the commandments and regulations of the Lord. But they had no children, because Elizabeth was barren, and both were getting on in years.**^NRSV These verses reveal two important details about Zechariah and Elizabeth. First, they both *were righteous before God.* To say they lived *blamelessly* does not mean that they were sinless, but that they loved God and obeyed him, living *according to all the commandments and regulations.* Second, *they had no children.* To ancient readers, this would have seemed like a contradiction. Children were considered to be God's greatest blessings. Certainly such God-fearing and God-honoring people as Zechariah and Elizabeth should have been blessed with children. But *Elizabeth was barren.* Not only that, but Luke adds the detail that they *both were getting on in years,* meaning that they could not expect any change in their situation. In societies like Israel, in which a woman's value was largely measured by her ability to bear children, to be aging and without children often led to personal hardship and public shame. For Elizabeth, a childless old age was a painful and lonely time, but during this time she remained faithful to God.

BLAMELESS
Zechariah and Elizabeth didn't merely go through the motions in following God's laws; they backed up their outward compliance with inward obedience. Unlike the religious leaders whom Jesus called hypocrites, Zechariah and Elizabeth did not stop with the letter of the law. Their obedience was from the heart, and that is why God viewed them as *righteous.* Does your life reflect careful obedience and high regard for God's will? As your life shows your love for God, others will be drawn to him.

COUPLES AND CHILDREN

Zechariah and Elizabeth were by no means alone in their strong desire to have children, as well as in their inability to do so. The Bible records the stories of other couples who desperately wanted to be parents. Some remained faithful to God through the pain (as did Elizabeth); others used other methods to obtain children—methods that led only to sorrow (as did Sarah).

Abraham and Sarah . . . . Genesis 11:30; 15:1–17:27; 21:1-7

Isaac and Rebekah . . . . Genesis 25:21-24

Jacob and Rachel . . . . Genesis 29:31–30:20; 35:1-20

Manoah and his wife . . . . Judges 13:1-25

Elkanah and Hannah . . . . 1 Samuel 1:1-20

1:8-9 Once when he was serving as priest before God and his section was on duty, he was chosen by lot, according to the custom of the priesthood, to enter the sanctuary of the Lord and offer incense.[NRSV] Zechariah's division of priests was serving in the temple during this particular week (see 1:5). Each morning, one of the priests would enter the Holy Place in the temple *(the sanctuary)* to *offer incense.* Incense was burned in the temple twice daily. Lots were cast to decide who would enter the sacred room, and one day during that week Zechariah *was chosen by lot.* Offering the incense before the Lord was considered a great privilege. A priest was only allowed to do so once in his lifetime; many priests never had the opportunity. But it was not by chance that Zechariah was on duty and that he was chosen that day to enter the Holy Place. God was guiding the events of history to prepare the way for Jesus to come to earth.

1:10 And when the time for the burning of incense came, all the assembled worshipers were praying outside.[NIV] The other priests and people would wait outside for the chosen priest to offer the incense and pray on behalf of the nation. When the people would see the smoke from the burning incense, they would pray. The smoke drifting heavenward symbolized their prayers ascending to God's throne. These *assembled worshipers* were the faithful in Israel who were waiting and praying for deliverance. Faithful believers had been doing this since their captivity in Babylon six centuries before. This time, their prayers received a very special answer.

1:11 Then an angel of the Lord appeared to him, standing at the right side of the altar of incense.[NIV] As Zechariah discharged his duty in the Holy Place, *an angel of the Lord appeared to him.*

GOD'S UNUSUAL METHODS

One of the best ways to understand God's willingness to communicate to people is to note the various methods, some of them quite unexpected, that he has used to give his message. Following is a sample of his methods and the people he contacted.

Person/Group	Method	Reference
Jacob, Zechariah, Mary, shepherds	Angels	Genesis 32:22-32; Luke 1:13, 30; 2:10
Jacob, Joseph, a baker, a cup-bearer, Pharaoh, Isaiah, Joseph, the magi	Dreams	Genesis 28:10-22; 37:5-10; 40:5; 41:7-8; Isaiah 1:1; Matthew 1:20; 2:12-13
Belshazzar	Writing on the wall	Daniel 5:5-9
Balaam	Talking donkey	Numbers 22:21-35
People of Israel	Pillar of cloud and fire	Exodus 13:21-22
Jonah	Being swallowed by a fish	Jonah 2
Abraham, Moses, Jesus at his baptism, Paul	Verbal	Genesis 12:1-4; Exodus 7:8; Matthew 3:13-17; Acts 18:9
Moses	Fire	Exodus 3:2
Us	God's Son	Hebrews 1:1-2

The *right side* indicates a position of favor or blessing, perhaps indicating that the message was good, not foreboding. The exact location where the angel stood is a detail passed along by Zechariah himself and kept intact by writers (1:1-3). Only two angels are mentioned by name in Scripture—Michael and Gabriel—but many angels act as God's messengers. Here, Gabriel (1:19) delivered a special message to Zechariah. This was not a dream or a vision; the angel was a royal herald of God. The angel appeared in visible form and spoke audible words to the priest. (For two other significant revelations that occurred at the temple, see 1 Samuel 3:4-14; Isaiah 6:1-13.)

1:12-13 When Zechariah saw him, he was terrified; and fear overwhelmed him. But the angel said to him, "Do not be afraid, Zechariah, for your prayer has been heard. Your wife Elizabeth will bear you a son, and you will name him John."[NRSV] Confronted by a supernatural, heavenly being, Zechariah *was terrified.* We learn later that this angelic visitor was Gabriel (1:19), who also appears in the Old Testament (Daniel 8:16; 9:21).

Angels are powerful beings, certainly awesome in their appearance. No wonder *fear overwhelmed* Zechariah. Yet the angel's
first words to him were *do not be afraid.* The angel had come to
deliver an important message.

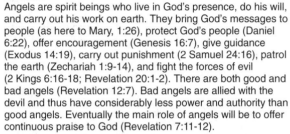

ANGELS
Angels are spirit beings who live in God's presence, do his will,
and carry out his work on earth. They bring God's messages to
people (as here to Mary, 1:26), protect God's people (Daniel
6:22), offer encouragement (Genesis 16:7), give guidance
(Exodus 14:19), carry out punishment (2 Samuel 24:16), patrol
the earth (Zechariah 1:9-14), and fight the forces of evil
(2 Kings 6:16-18; Revelation 20:1-2). There are both good and
bad angels (Revelation 12:7). Bad angels are allied with the
devil and thus have considerably less power and authority than
good angels. Eventually the main role of angels will be to offer
continuous praise to God (Revelation 7:11-12).

While Zechariah had been burning incense on the altar, he had
also been praying, most likely for Israel's deliverance and for the
coming of the Messiah. The angel's awesome words must have
astounded him: *Your prayer has been heard.* Then the angel made
a seemingly unrelated statement: *Your wife Elizabeth will bear
you a son.* The angel even told Zechariah what to name the baby.
John means "the LORD is gracious." Through the birth of this
son, God was gracious to Zechariah and Elizabeth and ultimately
to all people, for this son would prepare people's hearts for the
Messiah.

That the Lord hears our prayers is a common theme in the
Psalms, as the following verses illustrate (quoted from NRSV):

- Psalm 6:8-9, "Depart from me, all you workers of evil, for the
  LORD has heard the sound of my weeping. The LORD has heard
  my supplication; the LORD accepts my prayer."
- Psalm 18:6, "In my distress I called upon the LORD; to my God
  I cried for help. From his temple he heard my voice, and my
  cry to him reached his ears."
- Psalm 28:6, "Blessed be the LORD, for he has heard the sound
  of my pleadings."
- Psalm 31:22, "I had said in my alarm, 'I am driven far from
  your sight.' But you heard my supplications when I cried out to
  you for help."
- Psalm 34:6, "This poor soul cried, and was heard by the LORD,
  and was saved from every trouble."
- Psalm 34:17, "When the righteous cry for help, the LORD
  hears, and rescues them from all their troubles."

- Psalm 40:1, "I waited patiently for the LORD; he inclined to me and heard my cry."
- Psalm 55:17, "Evening and morning and at noon I utter my complaint and moan, and he will hear my voice."
- Psalm 66:19, "But truly God has listened; he has given heed to the words of my prayer."
- Psalm 116:1, "I love the LORD, because he has heard my voice and my supplications."
- Psalm 145:19, "He fulfills the desire of all who fear him; he also hears their cry, and saves them."
- Proverbs 15:29, "The LORD is far from the wicked, but he hears the prayer of the righteous."

GOD'S TIMING
God answers prayer in his own way and in his own time. He worked in an "impossible" situation—Elizabeth's barrenness—to bring about the fulfillment of all the prophecies concerning the Messiah. If you want to have your prayers answered, you must be open to what God can do in impossible situations. And you must wait for God to work in his way and in his time.

1:14-15 **"You will have great joy and gladness, and many will rejoice with you at his birth, for he will be great in the eyes of the Lord. He must never touch wine or hard liquor, and he will be filled with the Holy Spirit, even before his birth."**NLT The special son to be born to Zechariah and Elizabeth would fulfill a predetermined purpose before God. Not only would his parents and their friends *rejoice . . . at his birth,* but he would be *great in the eyes of the Lord* as well. John was to be set apart for special service to God. He may have been forbidden to drink wine as part of the Nazirite vow, an ancient vow of consecration to God (see Numbers 6:1-8). Samson (Judges 13) was under the Nazirite vow, and Samuel may have been also (1 Samuel 1:11).

This is Luke's first mention of the *Holy Spirit,* the third person of the Trinity. Luke refers to the Holy Spirit more than any other Gospel writer; it is a major theme for him (see 1:35, 41). Luke was thoroughly attuned to the work of the Holy Spirit, as seen in the book of Acts. Luke recognized and emphasized the Holy Spirit's work in directing the founding of Christianity and in guiding the early church. The presence of the Spirit is God's gift given to the entire church at Pentecost. Prior to that, the Holy Spirit was given to the faithful for special tasks. That John would be *filled* with the Holy Spirit, *even before his birth,* indicates a special choice of this child.

This also signals the restoration of the prophetic work of the Holy Spirit that had not been present in Israel for over four hundred years (since the days of the prophet Malachi).

1:16-17 **"Many of the people of Israel will he bring back to the Lord their God. And he will go on before the Lord, in the spirit and power of Elijah, to turn the hearts of the fathers to their children and the disobedient to the wisdom of the righteous—to make ready a people prepared for the Lord."**^{NIV} John's role was to be almost identical to that of an Old Testament prophet—to encourage people to turn away from sin and *back to the Lord their God.* The angel explained to Zechariah that John would go before God *in the spirit and power of Elijah,* a great prophet who was known for not mincing words and for standing up to evil rulers (1 Kings 17–19; 2 Kings 2:9, 15; see also Matthew 11:14; 17:10-13).

HEART TRANSPLANT
In preparing people for the Messiah's arrival, John would "turn people's hearts"—in effect, he would do "heart transplants." Through John's words, God would take stony hearts and exchange them for hearts that were soft, pliable, trusting, and open to change. (See Ezekiel 11:19-20 and 36:25-29 for more on "heart transplants.") Are you as open and receptive to God as you should be? Or do you need a change of heart?

John's mission would be *to turn the hearts of the fathers to their children and the disobedient to the wisdom of the righteous.* The first part of this phrase comes directly from the prophecy of the Messiah's forerunner found in Malachi 4:5-6, "See, I will send you the prophet Elijah before that great and dreadful day of the LORD comes. He will turn the hearts of the fathers to their children, and the hearts of the children to their fathers; or else I will come and strike the land with a curse" (NIV). Elijah was one of the greatest prophets who ever lived. With Malachi's death, the voice of God's prophets would be silent for four hundred years. Then a prophet would come, like Elijah, to herald Christ's coming. This prophet was John the Baptist (Matthew 17:10-13; Luke 1:17). John prepared people's hearts for Jesus by urging people to repent of their sins (see also Isaiah 49:5). Christ's coming would bring unity and peace, but also judgment on those who refused to turn from their sins.

The meaning of the phrase "turn the hearts of the fathers to their children" is not immediately clear, but some meanings have been suggested. It may mean that John's messages of repentance

DOUBTERS IN THE BIBLE

Many of the people God used to accomplish great things started out as real doubters. With all of them, God showed great patience. Honest doubt was not a bad starting point as long as the doubters were willing to move from doubt to belief. How great a part does doubt have in your willingness to trust God?

Doubter	Doubtful Moment	Reference
Abraham	When God told him he would be a father in old age	Genesis 17:17
Sarah	When she heard she would be a mother in old age	Genesis 18:12
Moses	When God told him to return to Egypt to lead the people	Exodus 3:10-15
Israelites	Whenever they faced difficulties in the desert	Exodus 16:1-3
Gideon	When told he would be a judge and leader	Judges 6:14-23
Zechariah	When told he would be a father in old age	Luke 1:18
Thomas	When told Jesus had risen from the dead	John 20:24-25

would unify broken family relationships, help fathers in their parental responsibilities, or change the lives of disobedient children so that their fathers would approve of them. In light of the Malachi reference, "fathers" may refer to the patriarchs, great men of faith who would be greatly displeased with their descendants' faithlessness toward God. John's call to repentance would turn the *disobedient to the wisdom of the righteous,* bringing many of his contemporaries back to God. This would please those faithful ancestors. Those who listened to and obeyed John's message would become *a people prepared for the Lord.* They would be ready for their Messiah.

1:18 Zechariah said to the angel, "How can I know this will happen? I'm an old man now, and my wife is also well along in years."NLT Zechariah's response to the angel's word came perilously close to doubt. Zechariah wanted more than the word of this heavenly visitor; he wanted a sign: *How can I know this will happen?* Zechariah saw only the obstacle—he and Elizabeth were both past childbearing years, so he reminded the angel of this fact as if it had somehow been overlooked. Contrast his response with that of Mary, who saw the opportunity and merely asked how God would perform the miracle (1:34).

GABRIEL'S MISSIONS

Gabriel appeared in the Old Testament to Daniel and brought announcements regarding the end times. Compare Daniel's experience with that of Zechariah in the chart below (quotations from NIV):

Daniel	Zechariah
"While I was speaking and praying, confessing my sin and the sin of my people Israel and making my request to the LORD my God for his holy hill—while I was still in prayer, Gabriel, the man I had seen in the earlier vision, came to me in swift flight about the time of the evening sacrifice" (Daniel 9:20-21).	"And when the time for the burning of incense came, all the assembled worshipers were praying outside. . . . But the angel said to him: 'Do not be afraid, Zechariah; your prayer has been heard'" (Luke 1:10, 13).
"As he came near the place where I was standing, I was terrified and fell prostrate. 'Son of man,' he said to me, 'understand that the vision concerns the time of the end.' . . . I, Daniel, was the only one who saw the vision; the men with me did not see it, but such terror overwhelmed them that they fled and hid themselves" (Daniel 8:17; 10:7).	"When Zechariah saw him, he was startled and was gripped with fear" (Luke 1:12).
"In the third year of Cyrus king of Persia, a revelation was given to Daniel (who was called Belteshazzar). Its message was true and it concerned a great war. The understanding of the message came to him in a vision" (Daniel 10:1).	"When he came out, he could not speak to them. They realized he had seen a vision in the temple, for he kept making signs to them but remained unable to speak" (Luke 1:22).
"While he was saying this to me, I bowed with my face toward the ground and was speechless" (Daniel 10:15).	"'And now you will be silent and not able to speak until the day this happens, because you did not believe my words, which will come true at their proper time'" (Luke 1:20).

1:19 **Then the angel said, "I am Gabriel! I stand in the very presence of God. It was he who sent me to bring you this good news!"**[NLT] Zechariah asked for some kind of sign so he would believe the angel's words (1:18); the angel explained that he himself ought to be sign enough *I am Gabriel,* he exclaimed, *I stand in the very presence of God.* Zechariah would have remembered that it was also Gabriel who had appeared to Daniel (see chart, "Gabriel's Missions"). Obviously Gabriel had come with an extremely important message—Gabriel himself described it as *good news.* Gabriel had come from *the very presence of God* to speak to Zechariah. The old priest ought not have doubted anything the angel said. For a pious Jew, and for believers today, a word from God should be the ultimate assurance.

1:20 **"And now, since you didn't believe what I said, you won't be able to speak until the child is born. For my words will certainly come true at the proper time."**^{NLT} Unbelief ultimately results in punishment. In this case, Zechariah, who should have known better, doubted an angel's words. Zechariah asked for a sign, and received it in the form of his own punishment. He would be unable to speak *until the child is born* (in light of 1:62, it appears that he was deaf as well as mute). The angel's words would *certainly come true at the proper time* whether Zechariah believed or not. God's plan had been set in motion, and nothing could stop it.

1:21-22 **Meanwhile, the people were waiting for Zechariah to come out, wondering why he was taking so long. When he finally did come out, he couldn't speak to them. Then they realized from his gestures that he must have seen a vision in the Temple sanctuary.**^{NLT} *The people were waiting* outside (1:10) for Zechariah to come out and pronounce the customary blessing upon them as found in Numbers 6:24-26. It seemed that the priest was taking an unusually long time in the Holy Place, so they became anxious, *wondering why he was taking so long.* Finally, Zechariah appeared, but he could not pronounce the blessing because he could not speak. The angel's words had already begun to come true; the sign of fulfillment had taken place right in Zechariah's life. Apparently he made *gestures* to them, and they *realized . . . that he must have seen a vision in the Temple sanctuary.* In Jewish tradition, the silent gestures indicated that God had acted in a special way. But Zechariah could not tell anyone about it. Zechariah alone knew that God was moving forward in his plans to bring the Messiah to his people. But Zechariah would remain silent until his promised and longed-for son arrived.

1:23-24 **He stayed at the Temple until his term of service was over, and then he returned home. Soon afterward his wife, Elizabeth, became pregnant and went into seclusion for five months.**^{NLT} Zechariah completed *his term of service* (a week) *and then he returned home* to the hill country (see 1:39) south of Jerusalem. The promise of a son to Zechariah and Elizabeth came even before this child was conceived. But, true to the angel's words, Elizabeth *became pregnant.* She may have gone into *seclusion* until her condition would be obvious to others.

THAT'S IMPOSSIBLE!
When told he would have a son, Zechariah doubted the angel's word. As a pious Jew and priest of God's law, he should have known better. From Zechariah's human perspective, his doubts were understandable—but with God, anything is possible. Although Zechariah and Elizabeth were past the age of childbearing, God gave them a child. It is easy to doubt or misunderstand what God wants to do in our lives. Even God's people sometimes make the mistake of trusting their intellect or experience rather than God. When tempted to think that one of God's promises is impossible, remember his work throughout history. God's power is not confined by narrow perspective or bound by human limitations. Trust him completely.

1:25 **"The Lord has done this for me," she said. "In these days he has shown his favor and taken away my disgrace among the people."**[NIV] Zechariah and Elizabeth were both faithful people, yet they had been suffering. Some Jews at that time did not believe in a bodily resurrection, so their hope of immortality was in their children. In addition, children cared for their parents in their old age and added to the family's financial security and social status. Children were considered a blessing, and childlessness was seen as a curse. Zechariah and Elizabeth had been childless for many years, but God was waiting for the right time to encourage them and take away their disgrace. Elizabeth realized that, in this impossible pregnancy, God had performed a miracle. She praised God for showing his *favor* on her and taking away her *disgrace among the people* (see also Genesis 21:1-7; 30:23 for the experiences of Sarah and Rachel).

AN ANGEL PROMISES THE BIRTH OF JESUS TO MARY / 1:26-38 / **5**

Luke places the story of the announcement of Jesus' birth right after the announcement of John's birth. By doing so, he highlights the similarities and differences between the two births. The announcement of John the Baptist's birth shows the Lord answering the prayer of an elderly couple by blessing the barren womb of Elizabeth with a healthy child. The announcement was public (in the temple), to an important official (the priest Zechariah), and an occasion for public rejoicing. In contrast, the announcement of Jesus' birth was in private, to a person of low social station in ancient Israel (a young woman), and an occasion for Mary to recommit herself to God's will. Where John the Baptist was described by Gabriel as "great in the eyes of the Lord,"

Jesus was described as "very great," "the Son of the Most High," and an heir to an everlasting kingdom. Where John the Baptist's birth was remarkable because of the advanced age of Zechariah and Elizabeth, Jesus' birth was miraculous because Mary was a virgin (a fact Luke emphasized by describing Mary as a virgin twice in this short passage).

The clearest contrast between the two narratives is the different ways Zechariah and Mary responded to the angel. Unlike Zechariah, Mary did not doubt the angel's message. While Zechariah asked how he could be certain that his wife would bear a child, Mary simply believed and submitted herself to the Lord's will with these words: "I am the Lord's servant" (1:38 NLT). She not only took Gabriel's statement "Nothing is impossible with God" as her confession of faith, she also anticipated the Lord working out his will in her life: "May everything you have said come true." With these words, Mary committed herself to facing the hardships that obeying God would entail—the ridicule and disgrace she would inevitably face for carrying a baby whose father was unknown.

WAIT FOR THE LORD

Zechariah thought it unbelievable that he and his wife, at their old age, could conceive a child. But what God promises, he delivers. And God delivers on time! You can have complete confidence that God will keep his word. His promises may not be fulfilled the next day, but they will be "at the proper time." If you are waiting for God to answer some request or to fill some need, remain patient and "wait for the Lord" (Psalm 27:14; Isaiah 40:31). No matter how impossible God's promises may seem, what he has said in his Word will come true at the right time.

Unfortunately, believers often follow Zechariah's example instead of Mary's, doubting the truth of God's Word, asking for proofs (1:18). Instead, follow Mary's simple demonstration of faith. Believe in the God for whom nothing is *impossible* and humbly submit to his will, even if it means facing hardship. Any hardship is worth enduring with God on your side (see 1:28).

1:26-27 In the sixth month of Elizabeth's pregnancy, God sent the angel Gabriel to Nazareth, a village in Galilee, to a virgin named Mary. She was engaged to be married to a man named Joseph, a descendant of King David.NLT Six months after Gabriel delivered God's message to Zechariah (1:11-20), God sent the angel with another message, this time *to a virgin named Mary* who lived in *Nazareth, a village in Galilee.* The angel

Gabriel had also appeared to the prophet Daniel more than five hundred years earlier (Daniel 8:15-17; 9:21). Each time Gabriel appeared, he brought important messages from God. This time was no exception.

Nazareth in Galilee, Joseph's and Mary's hometown, was a long way from Jerusalem, the center of Jewish life and worship. Located on a major trade route, Nazareth was frequently visited by Gentile merchants and Roman soldiers. Jesus was born in Bethlehem but grew up in Nazareth. Nevertheless, the people of Nazareth would reject him as the Messiah (4:22-30).

> In order that the body of Christ might be shown to be a real body, he was born of a woman; but in order that his Godhead might be made clear he was born of a virgin.
>
> *Thomas Aquinas*

Mary was not a prophet or a priest; she was not in God's temple performing acts of service. Instead, she was simply a young woman who was living at home and planning her wedding, for *she was engaged to be married to a man named Joseph.* In ancient Jewish marriages, the word "engaged" (or "betrothed") had a different meaning than today. First, the two families would agree to the union and negotiate the betrothal, including a price for the bride that would be paid to the bride's father. Next, a public announcement would be made. At this point, the couple was "pledged." This is similar to engagement today, except that it was much more binding. At this point, even though the couple was not officially married, their relationship could be broken only through death or divorce. Sexual relations were not yet permitted. This second step lasted for a year. During that time, the couple would live separately, with their parents. This waiting period would demonstrate the bride's purity. If she were found to be pregnant during that time, the marriage could be annulled. After this waiting time, the couple would be married and begin living together. What Mary was about to hear from the angel would have significant impact on her engagement.

GOD'S CHOICES

Mary was young, poor, female—all characteristics that, to the people of her day, would make her seem unusable by God for any major task. But God chose Mary for one of the most important acts of obedience he has ever demanded of anyone. You may feel that your ability, experience, or education makes you an unlikely candidate for God's service. Don't limit God's choices. He can use you if you trust him. Take him at his word.

That Joseph was *a descendant of King David* is important for
the movement of Joseph to Bethlehem (2:1-4) and for the fact
that Jesus would be born into the royal line of David. (Although
Joseph was not his father, Jesus would be considered in the royal
line through the rights of adoption.)

1:28-29 **Gabriel appeared to her and said, "Greetings, favored
woman! The Lord is with you!" Confused and disturbed,
Mary tried to think what the angel could mean.**^{NLT} When
Gabriel appeared to Mary, he called her a *favored woman.* She
was favored because she would be a special recipient of God's
grace. That the Lord was *with* Mary indicates that God would
give her his help in the privilege and responsibility she was about
to receive. While Zechariah had been terrified at Gabriel's very
appearance (1:12), Mary was more fearful at the words Gabriel
spoke. This young maiden from a small town was *confused and
disturbed* as to why she was being greeted in such a way by this
heavenly visitor.

1:30-33 **Then the angel said to her, "Do not be afraid, Mary, for you
have found favor with God. And behold, you will conceive
in your womb and bring forth a Son, and shall call His
name JESUS. He will be great, and will be called the Son of
the Highest."**^{NKJV} Gabriel repeated to Mary that she had *found
favor with God* (see "favored woman" in previous verse). The
words meant that Mary had become the recipient of favor
bestowed on her by a superior—in this case, by God himself.
It did not point out any special virtue in Mary—she was not sinless. Some have suggested that Mary was favored because of
what she was in herself, that she had grace to bestow on others,
and that she remained a virgin forever. However Scripture
gives the opposite understanding. God chose Mary, blessed her,
and she humbly accepted his call to be the mother of Jesus.
Then she went on to have other children (8:19; Matthew 13:55-
56; Mark 6:3).

The result of this favor came in God's choice of Mary to be
the mother of Jesus. Gabriel explained that this child would
grow in her womb, be born as all human children are born, and
be named Jesus. This son *will be great, and will be called the
Son of the Highest.* The word "Son" was a designation of the
Messiah. God would miraculously create a human child who
would actually be *his* Son, the long-awaited Savior (Genesis
49:10; 2 Samuel 7:9-16; Psalm 2:7; Isaiah 7:14; 9:1-7; 11:1-3).

Jesus, a Greek form of the Hebrew name Joshua, was a common
name meaning "Yahweh saves." Just as Joshua had led Israel into
the Promised Land (see Joshua 1:1-2), so Jesus would lead his

people into eternal life. The symbolism of Jesus' name was not lost on the people of his day, who took names seriously and saw them as a source of power. In Jesus' name people would be healed, demons would be banished, and sins would be forgiven.

FAVOR WITH GOD
God's favor does not automatically bring instant success or fame. His blessing on Mary, the honor of being the mother of the Messiah, would lead to much pain: her peers would ridicule her; her fiancé would consider leaving her; her son would be rejected and murdered. But through her son would come the world's only hope, and this is why Mary has been praised by countless generations as the young girl who "found favor with God." Mary's submission was part of God's plan to bring about salvation. If sorrow weighs you down and dims your hope, think of Mary and wait patiently for God to finish working out his plan.

"And the Lord God will give Him the throne of His father David. And He will reign over the house of Jacob forever, and of His kingdom there will be no end."NKJV Centuries earlier, God had promised David that his kingdom would last forever: "And your house and your kingdom shall be established forever before you. Your throne shall be established forever" (2 Samuel 7:16 NKJV). This promise was fulfilled in the coming of Jesus, a direct descendant of David (1:27). "His father David" also means "his ancestor David." Jesus was born in the line of David and thus could be a king to *reign over the house of Jacob* (referring to God's people—initially understood to be the twelve tribes, but later revealed to be much more). His will be an eternal kingdom, a kingdom with *no end*. God had promised to continue the house (or dynasty) of David forever. David's earthly dynasty ended four centuries after his reign, but Jesus Christ, a direct descendant of David, was the ultimate fulfillment of this promise (Acts 2:22-36). Christ will reign for eternity—now in his spiritual kingdom and in heaven, and later, on earth, in the new Jerusalem (Luke 1:30-33; Revelation 21).

1:34 Mary asked the angel, "But how can I have a baby? I am a virgin."NLT Unlike Zechariah, who desired a sign as proof of the angel's words (1:18), Mary's question displayed her faith. She merely asked how this miraculous event could occur because she was a *virgin*. She was engaged to be married and probably planned on having children. Engagements usually occurred when girls were in their early teens. Mary may have been as young as thirteen when this event took place. Her question reveals spiritual sensitivity—Mary understood that Gabriel was referring to a miracle child to be born while she was still a virgin, prior to her marriage to Joseph. She naturally wondered how this was going to occur.

The birth of Jesus to a virgin is a miracle that many people find difficult to believe. Some have said that the concept of a virgin birth was picked up from other ancient sources. However, this concept has no precedent in either Jewish or pagan stories. That Jesus would be conceived without sexual activity between a man and a woman, that he would be conceived by God's power, was never imagined—until it happened. Even the often-quoted Old Testament prophecy in Isaiah 7:14, referring to a virgin giving birth, was interpreted as referring to a young woman of marriageable age who had never had children.

Others say that the reference to the Virgin Birth in Scripture is merely theological, not historical. But if the believers had intentionally made this up, they also caused all kinds of problems to go along with it, such as inviting the charge that Jesus was an illegitimate child.

Given such information, Luke would have been far better off *not* giving this information if he had been making it up. It would be too unbelievable. Luke reported it because it was true. Note these three facts: (1) Luke was a medical doctor, and he knew perfectly well how babies are made. It would have been just as hard for him to believe in a virgin birth as it is for people today, and yet he reported it as fact. (2) Luke was a painstaking researcher who based his Gospel on eyewitness accounts. Tradition holds that he talked with Mary about the events that he recorded in the first two chapters. This is Mary's story, not a fictional invention. (3) Christians and Jews, who worship God as the Creator of the universe, should believe that God has the power to create a child in a virgin's womb.

JESUS UNDERSTANDS

Why is the Virgin Birth important to the Christian faith? Jesus Christ, God's Son, had to be free from the sinful nature passed on to all other human beings by Adam. Because Jesus was born of a woman, he was a human being; but as the Son of God, Jesus was born without any trace of human sin. Jesus is both fully human and fully divine. Because Jesus lived as a man, human beings know that he fully understands their experiences and struggles (Hebrews 4:15-16). Because he is God, he has the power and authority to deliver people from sin (Colossians 2:13-15). People can tell Jesus all their thoughts, feelings, and needs. He has been where they are, and he has the ability to help.

Jesus' miracles, transfiguration, and resurrection were all actual, historical events that defy explanation. They were acts of God in a human world. Jesus' birth was no exception. Christians' faith, however, rests not on the Virgin Birth—indeed two of the four Gospels don't even mention it. Faith rests on the death and resurrection of Jesus Christ, not on his virgin birth. Paul explained, "And if Christ has not been raised, our preaching is useless and so is your faith" (1 Corinthians 15:14 NIV). However, the Virgin Birth reveals two important facts: (1) In Jesus, God began a "new creation," for through Jesus' life, death, and resurrection, sin's power would be broken. In Jesus, people can come to God for a personal relationship and be freed from the power of sin. (2) Jesus was God's Son before he was even conceived in Mary's womb. He did not become God's Son at a later time. He was not accepted as God's Son because of good behavior or obedience. He was not a man promoted to that position. God's Son was born God's Son. In the birth of Jesus, God himself became human and entered the world—for fallen human beings! Therein lies the miracle! People are not meant to explain it, prove it, or ignore it—they are meant to believe it and worship God, who made it happen.

1:35 **The angel replied, "The Holy Spirit will come upon you, and the power of the Most High will overshadow you. So the baby born to you will be holy, and he will be called the Son of God."**[NLT] Gabriel explained how Mary would become pregnant and yet remain a virgin. *The Holy Spirit will come upon you, and the power of the Most High will overshadow you*—these words picture the powerful presence of God (the same word is used in the Transfiguration accounts to describe the overshadowing cloud, see 9:34; Matthew 17:5; Mark 9:7). This would indeed be a special baby, for he *will be holy*. Jesus was born without the sin that had entered the world through Adam. He was born holy, just as Adam had been created sinless. Believers must be careful not to explain that Jesus was sinless simply because he did not have a human father. To do so would mean that Mary would have been sinless, which she was not. Jesus' sinlessness rests not on his miraculous birth to a virgin girl but on the basis of his position with God. Through the birth of Jesus, God himself entered the world in human form. This is the miracle!

> If Jesus Christ were not true God, how could he *help* us? If he is not true man, how could he help *us?* *Dietrich Bonhoeffer*

In 1:32, the angel said Jesus would be called "the Son of the Highest"; here he adds that *he will be called the Son of God.* This passage is very key to the theology of who Jesus was. The title "Son of God" shows that he has a special role in God's purpose and that he is the true Son of David, the expected Messiah. The mention of the Holy Spirit gives the name greater significance, showing that God, through the Spirit, has a special role in creating this child. The connection of "Son of God" to Son of the Most High states Jesus' divinity. In contrast to Adam, who disobeyed God, Jesus would completely obey his Father, enabling him to face sin's consequences in sinners' place and make them acceptable to God (Romans 5:14-19). This Son would be born totally because of God's initiative and by his grace. Jesus came as a gift from God.

1:36-37 **"Even Elizabeth your relative is going to have a child in her old age, and she who was said to be barren is in her sixth month. For nothing is impossible with God."**[NIV] Mary did not ask for a sign, but it seems that Gabriel gave her one by explaining that Mary's relative Elizabeth was also pregnant as the result of God's grace. Gabriel gave Mary a person to whom she could go for support during what could prove to be a difficult time for Mary as she humbly fulfilled God's will. This also illustrated for Mary the fact that *nothing is impossible with God.* God took a barren woman who was past childbearing age and caused her to become pregnant. God took a virgin and caused a child to grow in her womb. With God, nothing is impossible (see 18:27; Genesis 18:14; Jeremiah 32:17, 27; Matthew 17:20; 19:26; Mark 10:27).

1:38 **Then Mary said, "Here am I, the servant of the Lord; let it be with me according to your word." Then the angel departed from her.**[NRSV] God's announcement of a child to be born was met with various responses throughout Scripture. Sarah, Abraham's wife, laughed (Genesis 18:9-15). Zechariah doubted (1:18). By contrast, Mary submitted, knowing that she was merely *the servant of the Lord.* She believed the angel's words and agreed to bear the child, even under humanly impossible circumstances, even with difficult social consequences. A young unmarried girl who became pregnant risked disaster. Unless the father of the child agreed to marry her, she would probably remain unmarried for life. If her own father rejected her, she could be forced into begging or prostitution in order to earn her living. She risked losing Joseph, her family, and her reputation. And her story about being made pregnant by the Holy Spirit risked her being considered crazy as well. Still Mary said, despite the risks, *"Let it be with me according to your word."* When Mary said that, she didn't know about the tremendous opportunity she would have.

She took the risk of faith; she didn't consult with anyone else; she didn't take time to weigh the pros and cons. She only knew that God was asking her to serve him, and she willingly obeyed. Believers need Mary's kind of trust and responsiveness. Too many wait to see the bottom line before offering themselves to God. God wants willing servants.

MARY VISITS ELIZABETH / 1:39-56 / *6*

Mary is the type of woman who puts her faith into action. She not only says, "Lord, your will be done" (see 1:38), but she also "hurries" to see God at work in the life of her relative Elizabeth. The journey to Judea that Mary undertook was not a simple drive to the next town; it was a difficult journey that would have taken at least three days at that time. Mary did not let that stop her from going to Elizabeth, rejoicing with her, and praising the Lord for fulfilling his promises.

In his description of the meeting of Mary and Elizabeth, Luke continued to highlight the superiority of Jesus over John. Even in the womb, John leaped for joy, for he was already pointing to the Lord's Anointed—to Jesus.

Mary's response—a song of praise for God's mercy—echoes Hannah's song (1 Samuel 2:1) and models the way all believers should respond to God's work in their lives: with gratitude and praise. In the first half of her song (1:46-49), Mary acknowledged her humble position before the Almighty and praised him for working in her life. Although commentators have debated whether the last part of Mary's song (1:50-55) praises the Lord for his deliverance of the Israelites in the past or prophesies of the deliverance God would provide through Jesus Christ in the future, it is clear that Mary was praising God for showing mercy to his people in general. Today, believers can join Mary in singing God's praises, by recounting God's mercy to people today and to spiritual forebears—from Abraham and Sarah to the apostle Paul.

1:39-40 **A few days later Mary hurried to the hill country of Judea, to the town where Zechariah lived. She entered the house and greeted Elizabeth.**[NLT] Elizabeth and Mary were related (1:36). Perhaps Mary felt the need to take her news to someone who would understand. So Mary left Nazareth and *hurried to the hill country of Judea,* although *the town where Zechariah lived* is unknown. The trip from Nazareth to the hill country was probably fifty to seventy miles—a major trip for a young woman alone and on foot.

1:41 **When Elizabeth heard Mary's greeting, the child leaped in
her womb. And Elizabeth was filled with the Holy Spirit.**^{NRSV}
Gabriel had told Mary of Elizabeth's pregnancy (1:36), which, at
this time, was in its sixth month. Luke records that *when Elizabeth heard Mary's greeting . . . Elizabeth was filled with the Holy
Spirit.* The visit from Mary no doubt came as a surprise, but the
Holy Spirit made Elizabeth suddenly aware of both Mary's pregnancy and the identity of Mary's baby. (For more on the theme of
the Holy Spirit in Luke, see 1:14-15.) The beautiful interweaving
of the lives of Elizabeth and Mary before their children were
born is a touching picture of God's grace upon his servants. Mary
stayed with Elizabeth for three months (1:56). How they must
have talked, wondering at what God was doing in their lives and
what he was planning for their very special children.

 FILLED WITH THE SPIRIT
Christians are urged to be filled with the Spirit as part of normal
growth in the Lord (see Ephesians 5:18), but the filling
Elizabeth experienced was different, spontaneous, entirely
God-given, much like that of Peter in Acts 4:8. This filling
captures the emotions with a God-centered joy and creates in
the heart an excited sense of God's loving purpose in your life.
This filling makes you want to sing, pray, shout, and dance.
When God moves your heart this way, let it show.

1:42-45 **In a loud voice she exclaimed: "Blessed are you among
women, and blessed is the child you will bear! But why am I
so favored, that the mother of my Lord should come to me?
As soon as the sound of your greeting reached my ears, the
baby in my womb leaped for joy. Blessed is she who has
believed that what the Lord has said to her will be accomplished!"**^{NIV} Elizabeth had not even yet been told that Mary was
pregnant. Elizabeth spoke words given to her by the Spirit (1:41)
as she recognized Mary's *blessed* state, knowing that Mary was
"blessed" because she had been specially chosen by God, much
as Elizabeth had. As Mary had rushed off to visit her relative, she
must have been wondering whether the events of the last few
days were real. Elizabeth's greeting surely strengthened her faith.
Mary's pregnancy may have seemed impossible, but her wise relative believed in the Lord's faithfulness and rejoiced in Mary's
blessed condition. The Spirit also showed Elizabeth the identity
of Mary's child, for she knew that this child was *blessed*—God's
Son, the promised Messiah, with a unique identity and role to fulfill. Mary would be *the mother of [the] Lord.* As in Psalm 110:1,
the word "Lord" is an exalted title, used many times by Luke in

his Gospel (twenty-five in the first two chapters in some versions). Only the Holy Spirit could have revealed this to Elizabeth. Mary and Elizabeth (and Zechariah—although he had been stricken deaf and mute, 1:20) were the first people on earth to see God's hand moving to fulfill hundreds of years of promises.

Under inspiration of the Spirit, Elizabeth interpreted the movement in her womb as the child's *joy* at hearing Mary's *greeting.* Even though she herself was pregnant with a long-awaited son, Elizabeth could have envied Mary, whose son would be even greater than her own. Instead she was filled with joy that the mother of her Lord would visit her. Elizabeth repeated that Mary was *blessed* because she *believed* that what God had said to her would *be accomplished.*

That Mary "believed" is really quite remarkable. Her pregnancy was unprecedented. Her pregnancy was controversial, not established by a long tradition in a particular supportive community. Her pregnancy needed to be a quasi-secret—if she told everyone all that had actually occurred, they would have put her away as being crazy. The facts that she was asked to believe required admirable trust, discernment, and patience. But as Gabriel told Mary, "The Lord is with you" (1:28). Mary believed *that,* and it made all the difference.

MOTHER OF MY LORD
The veneration of Mary has been a hallmark of Roman Catholic worship since the seventh century and a major dividing line with Protestants, who regard such veneration as tantamount to making Mary the Savior. Many stereotypes and caricatures have created costly misunderstandings and made genuine discussion difficult. Catholics are bewildered at Protestants' cold shoulder to such a warm biblical character. Protestants see Jesus' role threatened when Mary is idolized.

The Bible helps here. Jesus is the Savior, and no one else. Mary is the blessed mother of Jesus, and her unique blessing was a gift from God. With Elizabeth, believers can rejoice for God's work in Mary's life. With Elizabeth and Mary, believers can praise God for the salvation won by Jesus' death and guaranteed by his resurrection.

1:46-50 And Mary said: "My soul magnifies the Lord, and my spirit has rejoiced in God my Savior. For He has regarded the lowly state of His maidservant."[NKJV] This song is often called the "Magnificat," the first word in the Latin translation of this passage. Mary's song has often been used as the basis for choral music and hymns. Like Hannah, the mother of Samuel (1 Samuel 2:1-10), Mary glorified God in song for what he was going to do for the world through her. Notice that in both songs, God is pictured as a champion of the poor, the oppressed, and the despised.

Some have wondered how this young woman managed to speak these insightful words. We can take this beautiful song as coming from the lips of a woman who deeply loved God and to whom God gave special understanding of what he was doing. Just as the Holy Spirit gave Elizabeth insight, so Mary received it as well. As Mary journeyed from Nazareth to visit her relatives, she had much time to think about what she had heard from the angel and what she understood about God's plan for the Jewish people. When she arrived and Elizabeth spoke to her, Mary's joy overflowed and she could say with her whole heart, *"My soul magnifies the Lord, and my spirit has rejoiced in God my Savior."* The tense of "magnifies" indicates a habitual act; the tense of "has rejoiced" points to a special act of rejoicing, presumably when the angel gave her God's message. Mary humbly understood that she was just a *maidservant* chosen by God. "Lowly state" most likely refers to her low social class in an occupied country. She recognized that God had honored her; she recognized that what he was doing in her life would have a profound impact on the world and future generations: **"Surely, from now on all generations will call me blessed; for the Mighty One has done great things for me, and holy is his name. His mercy is for those who fear him from generation to generation."**[NRSV] Mary focused on God's power, holiness, and mercy. Her insight into God's character formed the basis for her confidence in him. Her words echo the Old Testament:

- For God as "the Mighty One," see Genesis 49:24; Joshua 22:22; Psalms 50:1; 132:2, 5; Isaiah 1:24; 9:6; 49:26; 60:16; Zephaniah 3:17.
- For God as "holy," see Leviticus 11:44; 19:2; 20:26; 21:8; Joshua 24:19; Psalms 89:18; 99:3; 111:9; Isaiah 5:16.
- For God doing many "great things" for Israel, see Deuteronomy 11:7; Judges 2:7; Job 37:5; Psalms 71:19; 126:2-3; Joel 2:20-21.
- For God's "mercy," see Exodus 33:19; 1 Chronicles 21:13; Psalms 25:6; 103:17; Isaiah 55:7; Micah 7:18.

1:51-53 **"He has shown strength with his arm; he has scattered the proud in the thoughts of their hearts. He has brought down the powerful from their thrones, and lifted up the lowly; he has filled the hungry with good things, and sent the rich away empty."**[NRSV] The *arm* of God is used in the Old Testament to describe his *strength* and power (see, for example, Exodus 6:6; Isaiah 51:5). Mary pictured God's strength being revealed to the sinful world as he scatters *the proud,* brings down *the powerful,* and sends *the rich away empty.* By contrast, God's power shows in his mercy to his own—lifting up *the lowly* and filling *the hungry with good things.* The tense of the verbs indicates that, while yet future, Mary was speaking prophetically of these events so certain to occur that they could be spoken of as having already happened.

PRIVILEGED POSITION
When Mary said, "From now on all generations will call me blessed," was she being proud? No, she was recognizing and accepting the gift God had given her. If Mary had denied her privileged position, she would have been throwing God's blessing back at him. Pride is refusing to accept God's gifts or taking credit for what God has done; humility is accepting the gifts and using them to praise and serve God. Don't deny, belittle, or ignore your gifts. Thank God for them and use them to his glory.

Mary's song shows that what is seen is not all that it seems. God takes the world's values and expectations and turns them upside down. God himself would come to earth and face rejection by the proud, the powerful, and the rich. He would lift the lowly and fill the hungry. And God continues to do that today. God is mighty and merciful, ruthless against pride and injustice but sensitive to individual needs. God knows humanity's sinful, stubborn nature, and he sent his Son to redeem sinful human beings.

Mary's song breaks all the stereotypes of her as a young, self-absorbed mother, too naive to know about the political climate around her and too centered on her pregnancy to care. Here Mary speaks in the highest Old Testament prophetic voice, echoing all the great Old Testament themes of redemption, freedom, and justice. She was revolutionary for her time, probably for this time too. She exhibited a large vision of God, a sense of God's grand purpose, and the heart of God for oppressed people. This is a very strong message of resolute faith in a God who wills to act in a sinful world, to save it, and to redeem it. This message of salvation continues throughout Luke's Gospel, but takes on a different sense than what all of Israel was expecting. Instead of salvation bringing deliverance from Roman oppression, Jesus' salvation brings deliverance from the oppressions of sin, sickness, and materialism—all greater enemies to humanity's soul than a foreign political power.

1:54-55 **"He has helped his servant Israel, in remembrance of his mercy, according to the promise he made to our ancestors, to Abraham and to his descendants forever."**[NRSV] The words "he has helped . . . Israel" are in the same verb tense as the previous verses—this is a future event so certain that it is mentioned in the past tense. This "help" for Israel is the Messiah, who will come *according to the promise [God] made to our ancestors.* God kept his promise to *Abraham* to be merciful to God's people forever (Genesis 22:16-18). Jesus' birth fulfilled the promise, and Mary understood this as the Spirit revealed it to her. Some of God's promises to Israel are found in 2 Samuel 22:50-51; Psalms 89:2-4; 103:17-18; Micah 7:18-20.

1:56 Mary stayed with Elizabeth about three months and then went back to her own home.[NLT] Because travel was not easy, long visits were customary. Mary must have been a great help to Elizabeth, who was experiencing the discomforts of being pregnant in her old age. In addition, Elizabeth certainly helped Mary. During these *three months,* Mary surely discussed with Elizabeth how to handle what would be an extremely difficult social predicament. She would have to return home and explain her pregnancy to her family and her fiancé. Hopefully, when Mary *went back to her own home,* three months pregnant, she was even more strengthened in her faith by Elizabeth's faith (1:6), ready to face all that the future would hold. Mary does not appear in the following section about John's birth. Evidently she returned home just before Elizabeth's baby was born.

JOHN THE BAPTIST IS BORN / 1:57-80 / 7

In this section, Luke returns to the story of John's birth. Zechariah has changed (compare 1:5-23). No longer does he face God's miraculous hand in his life with skepticism and unbelief. Instead he has humbly learned from his past mistakes, repented of his unbelief, and submitted to God's will. Zechariah demonstrated his obedient attitude to all by obeying the angel's word to him and naming his son John. His obedience brought unparalleled joy: he burst out in a song of praise.

Luke consciously placed Zechariah's song close to Mary's, for throughout this chapter he has compared the birth of John the Baptist with Jesus' birth. While Mary praised God in a general way, highlighting how he had shown mercy to her; Zechariah prophesied about the coming Messiah—Jesus. He was the Promised One from David's royal household, the one who would provide salvation for all of God's people. Zechariah's son, John, would be the one who would prepare the way for Jesus, the Lord's Anointed (1:76).

It is fitting that this chapter ends with a joyous song from

Zechariah's lips, for the entire chapter speaks of the joy that comes from watching God fulfill his promises: Gabriel spoke of that joy in his appearance to Zechariah (1:14); as a baby in Elizabeth's womb, John expressed that joy (1:44); and Mary spoke of her joy in her song of praise (1:47). In this section, Elizabeth's neighbors rejoiced over the birth of John the Baptist, an indication of God's blessing on her life (1:58). By highlighting the joyous responses of Mary, Zechariah, and others at the beginning of his Gospel, Luke demonstrated to his readers the appropriate response to the entire gospel story—the story of Jesus' life. In addition to believing in Jesus, believers should rejoice in the fulfillment of God's promises in Jesus' life, death, and resurrection.

1:57-58 **Now the time came for Elizabeth to give birth, and she bore a son. Her neighbors and relatives heard that the Lord had shown his great mercy to her, and they rejoiced with her.**^{NRSV} Elizabeth gave birth to a *son,* just as the angel had said (1:13). From the wording of this verse, it seems that no one had known about Elizabeth's pregnancy. So when the *neighbors and relatives heard that the Lord had shown his great mercy to her, . . . they rejoiced.* News that Elizabeth, an old woman who had been childless all her life, had given birth would have astounded everyone. They would have considered this God's mercy on her because children were considered to be blessings from the Lord. In her old age, God had taken away Elizabeth's barrenness and had given her a son. This was indeed cause for great rejoicing.

MERCY
It seems like such an old word—mercy. Old quality, too. Like a store owner handing a crying kid a piece of counter candy—before the strip-mall era. Or a doctor taking time to talk to a patient—before the HMO era. Today, efficiency is the keynote, mercy the forgotten quality.

But where God is worshiped and honored, mercy may still be found—in the close call that could have been tragic, in the phone call that lifted your spirit, or as for Elizabeth here, in the fulfillment of a dream.

Look around today for moments of God's mercy to you. Be God's channel of mercy for someone else. Surprise someone with a quality all but forgotten in the rush to get more done.

1:59-60 **When the baby was eight days old, all the relatives and friends came for the circumcision ceremony. They wanted to name him Zechariah, after his father. But Elizabeth said, "No! His name is John!"**^{NLT} In observance of the law, *when the baby was eight days old,* he was circumcised. God had commanded circumcision when he was beginning to form his holy nation (Genesis 17:4-14), and he had reaffirmed it through Moses (Leviticus 12:1-3). The *circumcision ceremony* was an important event for the family of a Jewish baby boy. This ceremony was a time of joy when *relatives and friends came* to celebrate the baby's becoming part of God's covenant nation.

The day of circumcision was also the day when parents would formally announce the child's name. Family lines and family names were important to the Jews. The people naturally assumed the child would receive Zechariah's name or at least a family name. Thus they were surprised that Elizabeth wanted to name the boy *John.* Apparently Zechariah had communicated to Elizabeth all that the angel had told him, so she knew what the child's name was to be (1:13). Zechariah and Elizabeth knew what family and friends did not know—that John had been given his name by God and that he had a God-given mission to fulfill.

CONVICTION
Stubbornness wants its own way at any price. It's the quality of someone who will not listen to a better idea, who acts simply in order to exert the power of his or her will.

Conviction is the settled confidence that God is leading and you intend to follow, come what may. Conviction isn't your will against the sound advice of others; it's your will surrendered to God's will in a way that other Christians verify as good. Elizabeth had a conviction to name her son John.

Stubbornness compensates for a feeling of weakness. It's an "I'll show you" strategy of empowering the self. Conviction—Elizabeth's quality in the naming of her son—is the courage to depend on God's strength alone, the confidence that God has said, "I'll show you the way." Trade your stubbornness for God-guided conviction.

1:61-63 **"What?" they exclaimed. "There is no one in all your family by that name." So they asked the baby's father, communicating to him by making gestures. He motioned for a writing tablet, and to everyone's surprise he wrote, "His name is John!"**[NLT] After Elizabeth gave the surprising name to her son, the relatives and friends took the situation to the head of the household, who had been unable to speak since the day he had seen the vision in the temple (1:20). It was customary to name a child after his father or grandfather, especially when they were esteemed men. The people could not believe that Elizabeth would choose a name that no one in the family had ever had. Apparently Zechariah had been stricken deaf as well because they had to communicate to him *by making gestures,* asking him to name the child. In writing, Zechariah agreed with his wife, expressing in no uncertain terms, *"His name is John!"*

1:64 Instantly Zechariah could speak again, and he began praising God.^{NLT} After fulfilling God's command spoken through the angel that he name the child John, *instantly Zechariah could speak again.* With his first words, *he began praising God.* The last words Zechariah had spoken months before had been words of doubt; his first words when all was being fulfilled, even the name of the child, were words of praise to God for all God had done and all he would do through this special child.

1:65-66 The neighbors were all filled with awe, and throughout the hill country of Judea people were talking about all these things. Everyone who heard this wondered about it, asking, "What then is this child going to be?" For the Lord's hand was with him.^{NIV} This baby's birth to an elderly couple, their strange insistence on an unusual name, the supernatural muteness and then instantaneous cure—all combined to fill the *neighbors . . . with awe.* Unusual news travels fast, and as the story spread, everyone talked *about all these things.* Certainly this was a special child with a special destiny. It was obvious to everyone that *the Lord's hand was with him.*

1:67-68 His father Zechariah was filled with the Holy Spirit and prophesied: "Praise be to the Lord, the God of Israel, because he has come and has redeemed his people."^{NIV} Zechariah praised God with his first words after months of silence. In a song that is often called the "Benedictus" after the first words in the Latin translation of this passage, Zechariah, *filled with the Holy Spirit* (see also 1:41), *prophesied* the coming of a Savior who would redeem his people. All the Old Testament prophecies were coming true—no wonder Zechariah praised *the Lord, the God of Israel.* These words were a common way to introduce a thanksgiving (see 1 Kings 1:48; 1 Chronicles 16:36; Psalms 41:13; 72:18; 106:48); thus Zechariah's words offered thanksgiving to God. Like Mary, Zechariah spoke of the coming redemption of Israel as though it were occurring: God *has come and has redeemed his people.* Indeed, the Messiah was already on the way—although few people knew it. In Zechariah's song is a reminder that Jesus came as the fulfillment of all God's purposes and promises in the Old Testament.

The words "has come" (or "has visited") are key to this passage. In the Old Testament, these words usually indicate God seeing his people and coming to deal with them—either in grace or in judgment, such as in Israel's escape from Egypt ("the LORD had visited the children of Israel," Exodus 4:31 NKJV); or when Naomi returned to Israel because "the LORD had visited His people by giving them bread" (Ruth 1:6 NKJV). The Lord would come—in the flesh—but, tragically, few would recognize him when he arrived (19:44).

The words "has redeemed" literally mean "accomplished redemption." Psalm 111:9 states, "He provided redemption for his people; he ordained his covenant forever—holy and awesome is his name" (NIV). In the Old Testament, "redemption" pictured the rescue by God of the Israelites from Egypt and their return from captivity in Babylon (see Deuteronomy 7:8; Jeremiah 31:11). "Redemption" means recovery of something or someone upon payment of a ransom. The climate of Israel in the first century was again a "captivity," for the Jews were subject to the Romans. The Jews were looking for a political Messiah to "redeem" them once again. But Messiah's redemption would be different from current expectations. Jesus would bring redemption from sin.

1:69-71 **"He has raised up a horn of salvation for us in the house of his servant David (as he said through his holy prophets of long ago), salvation from our enemies and from the hand of all who hate us."**NIV Zechariah praised God because he *has raised up a horn of salvation for us in the house of his servant David*. Again, Zechariah was speaking in the past tense about an event still future, albeit in the near future. The Messiah was already being "raised up," for God had begun to set his plan into motion. The "horn" was a common Old Testament metaphor for strength and power (2 Samuel 22:3; Psalms 18:2; 89:24; 132:17; Ezekiel 29:21). Deuteronomy 33:17 refers to the powerful horns of an ox. Psalm 75:4-5 refers to a warrior with a horned helmet. Thus, the "horn" is often a military metaphor for God's intervening to deliver. This will be a powerful Savior. "The house of . . . David" refers to the ancestral line of David, through whom the Messiah was to come, as God had *said through his holy prophets* (see, for example, 2 Samuel 7:11-13, 26; Psalms 89; 132:17; Ezekiel 34:23-24; Amos 9:11-12; Hebrews 1:1). All this would occur as part of God's plan, prophesied *long ago*. Zechariah was revealing that the ancient prophecies were beginning to be fulfilled.

The words "salvation from our enemies and from the hand of all who hate us" clearly indicate what was happening in that society. Zechariah prophesied that the Messiah would bring deliverance. The Jews were eagerly awaiting the Messiah, but they thought he would come to save them from the powerful Roman Empire. They were ready for a military Savior, but not for a

peaceful Messiah who would conquer sin. Zechariah's words
would come true, but in a different manner than most expected.
Thirty years later, when Jesus began his public ministry, he
would be misunderstood and rejected for not being the mighty
warrior for whom the Jews had been hoping.

1:72-75 **"Thus he has shown the mercy promised to our ancestors,**
and has remembered his holy covenant, the oath that he
swore to our ancestor Abraham, to grant us that we, being
rescued from the hands of our enemies, might serve him with-
out fear, in holiness and righteous-
ness before him all our days."[NRSV]

Through the coming Savior, God *has*
shown the mercy promised to our ances-
tors and he also *has remembered his*
holy covenant, specifically the covenant
that he swore to our ancestor Abraham.
Recorded in Genesis 22:16-18, the oath
to Abraham promised that the enemies
of Abraham's descendants would be
subdued and that blessing to his descendants would result from Abraham's obedience. God keeps his promises (see
Micah 7:20). Yet the fulfillment of
these promises means opportunity for
God's people—that they *might serve*
him without fear, in holiness and righ-
teousness before him.

> It is wholesome to apply
> the song to ourselves and
> ask how far we have
> participated in these great
> blessings. Are we
> experiencing this daily
> salvation from our
> spiritual enemies who
> hate us? Do we serve
> God without the slavish
> fear of the serf, and with
> the loyal allegiance of the
> child? Are all our days
> characterized by holiness
> toward God and
> righteousness toward
> man? Has the "dayspring
> from on high" visited our
> hearts, and are our feet
> walking in the way of
> peace?   *F. B. Meyer*

Zechariah must have thought that
God would now rescue his people from
the hands of the oppressors in Israel.
Luke, in his Gospel and in the book of
Acts, will show how God has in mind
to carry out this promise to his people.
Zechariah knew the purpose of God's
rescue—so that people might truly serve him. Our purpose
should be as true as Zechariah's—to serve God both in our worship of him and in our daily obedience!

1:76-77 **"And you, child, will be called the prophet of the Most High;**
for you will go before the Lord to prepare his ways, to give
knowledge of salvation to his people by the forgiveness of
their sins."[NRSV] After recalling hundreds of years of God's sovereign work in history, beginning with Abraham and going on into
eternity, Zechariah personalized the story. His son had been chosen for a key role in the drama of the ages. Although God has

unlimited power, he chooses to work through frail humans who begin as helpless babies. Believers must never minimize what God can do through those who are faithful to him. Zechariah proclaimed what the angel had told him (1:16-17), words that Zechariah had at first doubted. John *will be called the prophet of the Most High.* Zechariah speaks these same amazing words in a land where the voice of prophecy had been silent for over four hundred years. John would *go before the Lord to prepare his ways,* as had been predicted by Israel's last prophet, Malachi (Malachi 3:1; 4:5-6). John would *give knowledge of salvation to his people by the forgiveness of their sins.* The "salvation" referred to in 1:69-71 is here spelled out as "forgiveness of sins." John would explain this to people as he prepared the way for the Messiah. His message would be "repent," for only through repentance can sinners find forgiveness (see 3:3-18).

A PARENT'S PRAYER
As Zechariah looked at his baby son, so full of potential and promise, could he see what John would become—how John would challenge Roman immorality, how John would die in prison? No, Zechariah could see none of that—only John's little life to be blessed and used by God.

Every Christian parent can echo Zechariah's dreams. Before Jesus comes again, many prophets (preachers, teachers, enablers) will tell the world about God's salvation. Will your child endure hardship along the way? Don't worry, God is in control. Pray that your child will prepare the way of the Lord, helping many find God's mercy and eternal life.

1:78-79 **"By the tender mercy of our God, the dawn from on high will break upon us, to give light to those who sit in darkness and in the shadow of death, to guide our feet into the way of peace."**[NRSV] "The dawn from on high" refers to that visitation of God to humanity in the form of the Messiah. These words echo the Old Testament promises: "The people walking in darkness have seen a great light; on those living in the land of the shadow of death a light has dawned" (Isaiah 9:2-3 NIV). This message of *light to those who sit in darkness and . . . death* was fulfilled in the birth of Christ and the establishment of his eternal kingdom. He came to deliver all people from their slavery to sin. (See also Isaiah 58:8, 10; 60:1-3.) He will also *guide our feet into the way of peace.* This peace would not merely be political, but spiritual. All of this would occur because of God's *tender mercy* and compassion on sinful humankind.

John would prepare the way, but the Savior himself would

come to forgive sins (1:77; Matthew 9:6; 26:28), offer light (John 8:12), and bring peace (John 14:27).

1:80 John grew up and became strong in spirit. Then he lived out in the wilderness until he began his public ministry to Israel.NLT Luke, always interested in people, briefly gave a glimpse of John's growing-up years. "Became strong in spirit" could refer to moral development but could also refer to strengthening in God's Spirit. That John lived out in the wilderness refers to his isolation from people as he prepared for ministry. His parents, already old when he was conceived, presumably did not live very long into his growing-up years. John would have been on his own. Some scholars have suggested that John may have joined the community of the Essenes after his parents passed away. While possible, there is no direct evidence to support this.

LUKE 2

As a historian, Luke identified the time period of Jesus' birth by naming the Roman emperor and the local governor. The contrast between Jesus, the divine King of kings, and Augustus, the first Roman emperor, would have been striking to Luke's first readers. Octavian, who had been renamed Augustus (meaning "reverend") by the Roman Senate, was the first Roman emperor, ruling all of the vast Roman Empire under his sole authority. The month of August was named after him—to honor him. In contrast, Jesus was born into humble circumstances, even having a livestock's trough as his cradle. Jesus, the beloved Son of God, did not shrink from coming to this earth to the most modest of circumstances. Augustus is the emperor who began the worldwide Pax Romana (Roman Peace), but only Jesus brings true peace with God. Jesus did not come as a conquering king but as a servant; and he calls people to follow him, in denying themselves and finding ways to serve others (9:23-27; 22:25-30; Philippians 2:5-11).

2:1-3 In those days Caesar Augustus issued a decree that a census should be taken of the entire Roman world. (This was the first census that took place while Quirinius was governor of Syria.)^{NIV} Luke is the only Gospel writer who related the events he recorded to world history. His account was addressed to a predominantly Greek audience that would have been interested in and familiar with the political situation. The Romans ruled Palestine; Emperor *Caesar Augustus,* the first Roman emperor, was one of the greatest of all Roman rulers. He was a good administrator and was fastidious about the financial accounting of his empire. Augustus ended the civil war in the land and brought peace and prosperity throughout the Empire. He reigned from 27 B.C. to A.D. 14. The Roman rulers, considered to be like gods, contrasted greatly with the tiny baby in a manger who truly was God in the flesh.

A Roman *census* (registration) was taken to aid military conscription or tax collection. The Jews didn't have to serve in the Roman army, but they could not avoid paying taxes. Augustus's decree went out in God's perfect timing and according to God's perfect plan to bring his Son into the world. No one had a choice about participating in the census. Thus **all went to their own towns to be registered.**NRSV

There has been much debate over the facts presented by Luke in chapter 2. There are four key issues:

1. Did Augustus order an empirewide census during the time that Luke reports?
2. Why did Joseph go to Bethlehem since a Roman census did not require people to go to their hometowns?
3. Why did Mary have to go with Joseph?
4. How do we date this particular census with the birth of Jesus because there is no record of a census during the days of Quirinius until A.D. 6?

The questions will be answered in order. First, did Augustus order an empire-wide census during the time that Luke reports? There is no record of a single empire-wide census by Augustus (who ruled from 27 B.C. to A.D. 14). However, there was an empire-wide policy for periodic census-taking and the resultant taxation. Luke was probably reflecting Augustus's policy as it was acted out regionally.

Second, why did Joseph go to Bethlehem since a Roman census did not require people to go to their hometowns? The normal Roman procedure only required subjects to register where they were living. However, Roman policy often allowed exceptions for local practices. Traditional Jewish practice required registering in one's place of birth. So Joseph went to Bethlehem.

Third, why did Mary have to go with Joseph? Normally the Romans did not require women to be part of the poll tax as was the policy in Egypt, but they probably required women to be accounted for in the Syrian region. It could also be possible that Mary and Joseph desired to be together since they both knew the special significance of this baby's birth.

Finally, how do we date this particular census with the birth of Jesus because there is no record of a census during the days of Quirinius until A.D. 6? In A.D. 6, when Quirinius became governor, Syria annexed Judea to itself as part of the Roman province. A very unpopular census was taken as recorded by Josephus and mentioned in Acts 5:37. Quirinius is nowhere listed as governor during the time of Herod, who died in 4 B.C. It may be possible, however, that Quirinius was the administrator of this census before he officially became governor. Censuses took time to complete, and the actual taxation could have come much later.

WHO'S IN CHARGE?
The Romans ruled the civilized world at this time. By contrast, Joseph controlled very little. Against his better judgment and political convictions he complied with the Roman order and traveled with Mary to Bethlehem. Often people feel like Joseph, caught by forces larger than they are.

 The Romans were in control insofar as human authority can get its way by exerting human power. But the Romans did not recognize their limitations. In reality, God controls the world. In all times and places, he works his will. God did not write Roman law, but judged it. God did not soften Joseph's bumpy road, but strengthened him. God is in charge of your life too. He will guide you and provide all you need. Like Joseph, live each day by faith, trusting that God is in charge.

2:4 Joseph also went from the town of Nazareth in Galilee to Judea, to the city of David called Bethlehem, because he was descended from the house and family of David.^{NRSV} Certainly Joseph would not have chosen to travel either with or without his pregnant wife just as she was ready to deliver, but he had no choice. Rome was far too powerful for anyone to resist. Most Jews hated taking part in a census because they viewed it as sacrilegious. God alone was to number his people. When David attempted to number Israel, he brought great calamity on the nation because of his rash decision (2 Samuel 24; 1 Chronicles 21). So Joseph had two reasons to be angry about the census. Joseph *also went from the town of Nazareth in Galilee to Judea, to the city of David called Bethlehem,* a journey of about seventy or eighty miles (see map). In the Old Testament, the "city of David" generally referred to Jerusalem (2 Samuel 5:7, 9), but Bethlehem was where David grew up (1 Samuel 16; 17:12; 20:6).

 God controls all history. By the decree of Emperor Augustus, Jesus was born in the very town prophesied for his birth (Micah 5:2), even

THE JOURNEY TO BETHLEHEM
Caesar's decree for a census of the entire Roman Empire made it necessary for Joseph and Mary to leave their hometown, Nazareth, and journey the 70 or 80 miles to the Judean village of Bethlehem. This village was about 5 miles from Jerusalem.

though his parents did not live there. Joseph and Mary went to Bethlehem because Joseph *was descended from the house and family of David.* In fact, both Joseph and Mary were descendants of David. Old Testament prophets predicted often that the Messiah would be born in David's royal line (see, for example, Isaiah 11:1; Jeremiah 33:15; Ezekiel 37:24; Hosea 3:5).

2:5 **He went to be registered with Mary, to whom he was engaged and who was expecting a child.**[NRSV] Luke does not explain why Mary made this difficult trip with Joseph. Some suggest that she was needed for the census—unlike the policy in Egypt, women in Syria were subject to the poll tax. Certainly Joseph did not want to leave Mary alone. She probably had already faced painful gossip because of her premarriage pregnancy and preferred to stay with Joseph. Or perhaps they simply both saw the outworkings of God's plan and traveled to Bethlehem where the promised child was to be born (Micah 5:2). At this point, Joseph and Mary were *engaged.* The two were living together, but they abstained from sexual relations. Matthew 1:24-25 explains that an angel spoke to Joseph in a dream about Mary's condition: "When Joseph awoke from sleep, he did as the angel of the Lord commanded him; he took her as his wife, but had no marital relations with her until she had borne a son; and he named him Jesus" (NRSV).

COMFORT ZONES
The government forced Joseph to make a long trip just to pay his taxes. His fiancée, who had to go with him, was going to have a baby any moment. But when they arrived in Bethlehem, they couldn't even find a place to stay. Doing God's will often takes people out of their comfort zones. Jesus' life began in poverty. Later, Jesus would stress to his disciples what it meant to have no place to lay one's head (9:58). Those who do God's will are not guaranteed comfortable lives. But they are promised that everything, even their discomfort, has meaning in God's plan.

2:6-7 **So it was, that while they were there, the days were completed for her to be delivered. And she brought forth her firstborn Son, and wrapped Him in swaddling cloths, and laid Him in a manger, because there was no room for them in the inn.**[NKJV] In simple, direct language, Luke presented the Christmas story: no trees or lights, just a *manger* and animals and a too-crowded inn. It isn't surprising that there was *no room for them in the inn* considering the number of travelers flocking to various cities during the time of this census.

At some time during their visit in Bethlehem, *the days were completed* and the promised child was born. Of course, he was *her firstborn Son*—Mary had had no previous children (indeed, she was a virgin), and the angel had promised that the child would be "Son of the Most High" (1:32). Mary wrapped the baby in *swaddling cloths,* bands of cloth that were used to keep a baby warm and give it a sense of security. These cloths were believed to protect its internal organs. This custom of wrapping infants is still practiced in many Mideastern countries. Apparently Mary and Joseph accomplished the delivery themselves; otherwise, a midwife would have wrapped the child.

After the birth and after the child had been cleaned and wrapped, Mary *laid Him in a manger,* an animal's feeding trough. She may have filled the manger with hay to make a soft bed. This mention of the manger is the basis for the traditional belief that Jesus was born in a stable. Stables were often caves with feeding troughs (mangers) carved into the rock walls. Despite popular Christmas card pictures, the surroundings were dark and dirty. Everything pointed to obscurity, poverty, and even rejection. Luke showed the King of kings born into poor and humble circumstances—born as a human, born to serve.

> The twist in the story is, of course, that it is the very pagan authorities who are responsible for bringing Jesus to Bethlehem. Caesar, like Cyrus before him, unknowingly becomes the servant of God's purpose. The promise is fulfilled through the actions of the unlikeliest of people. For God is Lord of all the earth and there is no power not under his authority, no poverty to which he turns a blind eye of indifference.
> *June Osborne*

SHEPHERDS VISIT JESUS / 2:8-20 / **10**

The angel Gabriel had announced the coming births of John and Jesus (1:5-20, 26-38); here a host of angels announced the "good news" of Jesus' birth and broke out into exuberant praise. The angels called the baby Jesus the promised Messiah—the Savior. Such an announcement was a typical proclamation of the birth of a child to the royal family—for Augustus himself had been called a "savior" at his birth. But while the announcement of Augustus's birth would have been first delivered to the members of the Roman Senate and other dignitaries, the privilege of hearing about Jesus' birth *first* was given to ordinary shepherds.

MANGER SCENE
Although our first picture of Jesus is as a baby in a manger, it must not be our last. The Christ child in the manger has been made into a beautiful Christmas scene, but we cannot leave him there. This tiny, helpless baby lived an amazing life, died for sinners, ascended to heaven, and will come back to this earth as King of kings. Christ will rule the world and judge all people according to their decisions about him. Do you still picture Jesus as a baby in a manger—or is he your Lord? Don't underestimate Jesus. Let him grow up in your life.

The angels also gave the shepherds a sign. They would find their Savior in "a manger"—a sign of not only Jesus' identity but also his humble circumstances. By highlighting the modest character of Jesus' birth, Luke set the stage for the bulk of his narrative: a story describing how Jesus gathered twelve common Israelite men to help him minister to the ordinary people of Israel. The shepherds' response to the angels' announcement is similar to Mary's: they "hurried off" to see what God was accomplishing and returned, praising him (1:39, 46-56; 2:16, 20 NIV). God still breaks into ordinary lives, even yours. Follow his instructions, praising him for using you to accomplish his will.

2:8 And there were shepherds living out in the fields nearby, keeping watch over their flocks at night.[NIV] From the dirty manger, Luke moved to *the fields nearby,* outside the village. It was *night. Shepherds* were there, *keeping watch over their flocks.* Among the occupations, shepherding had a lowly place. They were outcasts, not allowed in the city and not trusted by the general public, for often they were thieves. Luke gave this story about the shepherds for a reason. Jesus would come, not to the proud and powerful, but to the outcasts, the humble, those considered "last" on the social lists. To these men God brought the first news of his Son's arrival.

Shepherds also have other implications in this story of the Messiah's birth. King David, from whom this new king is descended, had been a shepherd most of his life. God had called him from that occupation to become a "shepherd" over the nation of Israel (2 Samuel 7:8). Scripture often uses shepherds to symbolize all who care for God's people, including God himself (Psalm 23:1; Isaiah 40:11; Jeremiah 23:1-4; Ezekiel 34:23; Hebrews 13:20; 1 Peter 2:25; 5:2).

2:9-10 And behold, an angel of the Lord stood before them, and the glory of the Lord shone around them, and they were greatly afraid. Then the angel said to them, "Do not be afraid, for

**behold, I bring you good tidings of great joy which will be to
all people.**"ᴺᴷᴶⱽ As these shepherds were living in the fields
under the sky, suddenly a bright light broke through the darkness.
*An angel of the Lord stood before them, and the glory of the Lord
shone around them.* They recognized that this was a supernatural
being because of the dazzling light, "the glory of the Lord" that
was shining all around them. "Glory" refers to the majesty and
splendor accompanying God's presence (see also Exodus 16:7;
24:17; Psalm 63:2; Isaiah 40:5).

JUST AS YOU ARE
The greatest event in history had just occurred! The Messiah
had been born! For ages the Jews had waited for this, and
when it finally happened, the announcement came to humble
shepherds. The good news about Jesus is that he comes to all
types of people, including the plain, the ordinary, and the
outcasts of society. He comes to anyone with a heart humble
enough to accept him. Whoever you are, whatever you do, you
can have Jesus in your life. Don't think that you need
extraordinary qualifications—Jesus accepts you as you are.

The stunning display of God's glory and the appearance of the
angel naturally terrified these shepherds. This may have been
Gabriel, who had also appeared to Zechariah (1:19) and to Mary
(1:26). Both Zechariah and Mary were encouraged when Gabriel
said, "Do not be afraid" (1:13; 1:30);
the angel here also encouraged the shepherds, *Do not be afraid.* He had come
with *good tidings of great joy* for *all
people.* "Good tidings" or "good news"
became another way of describing the

> The hinge of history is on
> the door of a Bethlehem
> stable. *Ralph W. Sockman*

gospel message itself; Luke used this phrase as the name for the
gospel throughout the book of Acts (for a sampling of verses, see
Acts 5:42; 8:12; 10:36; 14:15). At the very hour of Jesus' birth,
the good news was already being spread supernaturally by an
angel. This good news would bring *great joy,* for it comprised
everything for which the Jews had been hoping and waiting—the
Savior had come. The "all people" to whom this news came was
first the people of Israel (the Greek word used here, *laos,* referred
to Israelites, not to people in general). While the "good tidings"
would one day bring great joy to people of every land across the
globe, it came first of all to God's covenant people.

Some of the Jews were waiting for a savior to deliver them from
Roman rule; others hoped that the Christ (Messiah) would deliver
them from physical ailments. But Jesus, while healing their

TO FEAR OR NOT TO FEAR

People in the Bible who were confronted by God or his angels all had one consistent response—fear. To each of them, God's response was always the same—don't be afraid. As soon as they sensed God accepted them and wanted to communicate with them, their fear subsided. He had given them freedom to be his friends. He has given you the same freedom.

Person	Reference
Abraham	Genesis 15:1
Moses	Numbers 21:34; Deuteronomy 3:2
Joshua	Joshua 8:1
Jeremiah	Lamentations 3:57
Daniel	Daniel 10:12, 19
Zechariah	Luke 1:13
Mary	Luke 1:30
Shepherds	Luke 2:10
Peter	Luke 5:10
Paul	Acts 27:23-24
John	Revelation 1:17-18

illnesses and establishing a spiritual kingdom, delivered them from sin. His work is more far-reaching than anyone could imagine. Christ paid the price for sin and opened the way to peace with God. He offers us more than temporary political or physical changes—he offers us new hearts that will last for eternity.

2:11 "For there is born to you this day in the city of David a Savior, who is Christ the Lord."NKJV The angel explained the substance of the "good news" that he brought: *There is born to you this day in the city of David a Savior, who is Christ the Lord.* A child had just been born. The site of his birth was the "city of David," Bethlehem (see commentary on 2:4).

The child is the *Savior.* The word "Savior" is used to refer to Jesus only two times in the Gospels: here as the angels proclaimed his birth, and in John 4:42 by the Samaritans who came to believe in Jesus as "the Savior of the world." In the Old Testament, the same word (sometimes translated "deliverer" in some versions) is used for certain individuals, as well as for God (Judges 3:9, 15; 1 Samuel 10:19; 2 Samuel 22:2-3; 2 Kings 13:5; Isaiah 19:20). For the Greeks and Romans, the word "savior" could be applied to their gods as well as to great military or political leaders. Julius Caesar was called a "savior." The basic meaning of the word was readily understood by Jews as well as Gentiles.

The title *Christ the Lord* is found only here in the New Testament, although the understanding of Christ as the Lord appears elsewhere (Acts 2:36; 2 Corinthians 4:5; Philippians 2:11). The word "Christ" is Greek for "Anointed One"; the word "Messiah" comes from the Hebrew term with the same meaning. To be anointed meant to be set apart for some special purpose. Moses anointed Aaron and his sons as the first priests of Israel (Exodus 28:41); the prophet Samuel anointed both Saul and David as kings of Israel (1 Samuel 10:1; 16:3). The title was applied to that future one whom God would raise up. The Jews were awaiting this special deliverer, one who would be the Anointed One of God, the Messiah, the Christ.

The word "Lord" refers here to deity. That this tiny baby was the "Lord" means that God had arrived in human form. Thus the angel gave no doubt as to the identity of this child. He was the one for whom all Israel had been waiting.

2:12 **"And this will be the sign to you: You will find a Babe wrapped in swaddling cloths, lying in a manger."**[NKJV] The shepherds did not ask for a *sign* (as had Zechariah, 1:18), but they received one. The angel apparently expected the shepherds to immediately go looking for this child, so he told them what to look for. The baby would be *wrapped in swaddling cloths* and *lying in a manger.* Not only would this sign help the shepherds find the right baby, it would also attest to the truth of the angel's words to the last detail. While there might be other newborn babies in Bethlehem wrapped in strips of cloth, there would be only one "lying in a manger."

The shepherds were not told to look in a palace or in a wealthy home—indeed, they would not have gotten past the gates if they had. But they could go to the poor stable, receive acceptance from a poor couple, and discover the miracle baby.

> A man can no more diminish God's glory by refusing to worship him than a lunatic can put out the sun by scribbling "darkness" on the walls of his cell.   *C. S. Lewis*

2:13-14 **Suddenly, the angel was joined by a vast host of others—the armies of heaven—praising God: "Glory to God in the highest heaven, and peace on earth to all whom God favors."**[NLT] After the angel gave the great news of God's arrival on earth, *suddenly* all heaven broke into praise, for *the angel was joined by a vast host of others—the armies of heaven.* John's vision of heaven recorded in Revelation reveals that there are innumerable

angels in heaven: "Then I looked and heard the voice of many
angels, numbering thousands upon thousands, and ten thousand
times ten thousand" (Revelation 5:11 NIV). One of the angels'
key roles is to offer continuous praise to God. The arrival of
God's Son on earth caused the "armies of heaven" to join in an
anthem of praise to God. Rarely did more than one angel come;
at this great event, however, all the angels joined together, praising God. The "armies of heaven" or "heavenly host" refers to a
select group of angels that serve God (see 1 Kings 22:19; Daniel
7:10). The story of Jesus' birth resounds with music that has
inspired composers for two thousand years. The angels' song is
an all-time favorite. Often called the "Gloria" after its first word
in the Latin translation, it is the basis of modern choral works,
traditional Christmas carols, and ancient liturgical chants. "Glory
to God" focuses the praise on the one who set these events in
motion, the one who controls all events on earth. He is "in the
highest heaven" and is sending *peace on earth to all whom [he]*
favors. The peace referred to is the peace that only the Messiah
can bring—not peace after war or conflict, but peace between
sinful humanity and the holy God. Those whom God favors are
those to whom he will graciously reveal his truth. The emphasis
is on God—he is to be glorified, and he will bring peace to those
whom he chooses. The entire "good news," brought to humanity
through the birth of Jesus, came by God's decision and grace
alone.

SPREAD THE WORD
What a birth announcement! The shepherds were terrified, but
their fear turned to joy as the angels announced the Messiah's
birth. First the shepherds ran to see the baby; then they spread
the word. Jesus is *your* Messiah, *your* Savior. Praise for God
and gratitude for what he has done should motivate you to
witness to others. Have you discovered a Lord so wonderful
that you can't help sharing your joy with your friends?

2:15-16 When the angels had left them and gone into heaven, the
shepherds said to one another, "Let us go now to Bethlehem
and see this thing that has taken place, which the Lord has
made known to us." So they went with haste and found Mary
and Joseph, and the child lying in the manger.NRSV After their
anthem of praise, the angels went back *into heaven* (see also
24:51; Acts 1:11), and the shepherds wanted to go and *see this*
thing that has taken place. Obviously *the Lord* (through his
angels) had given them a special message, *so they went with*
haste into the village of Bethlehem to find a baby "wrapped in

swaddling cloths, lying in a manger" (2:12). They were not disappointed, for they *found Mary and Joseph, and the child lying in the manger,* just as the angel had said.

2:17-18   Then the shepherds told everyone what had happened and what the angel had said to them about this child. All who heard the shepherds' story were astonished.ᴺᴸᵀ The *shepherds told everyone what had happened and what the angel had said*—thus becoming the first witnesses of the gospel message. They told about the child and all that the angels had said about him, and *all who heard . . . were astonished.* Most likely, "everyone" and "all" refer to the people at the inn. Everyone was astonished at the shepherds' story.

TELLING ALL YOU KNOW
These shepherds told everyone who would listen all that they had heard and seen. Often people who try to tell all that they know are politely avoided. It can be boring to listen to someone who never stops to take a breath.

But in the shepherds' case, people listened, because:
- Shepherds were not supposed to know much, and these shepherds had startling information.
- The message was revolutionary, breathtaking, and transformative. It changed listeners' lives.
- The shepherds spoke from the heart, and their words connected to the deepest needs of others.

When you tell about Jesus, start with what you know best: your life experience. Tell the story of God in your life. You don't need to embellish, but don't hold back either. Your words will change many, and God will use you to change the world.

2:19   But Mary treasured all these words and pondered them in her heart.ᴺᴿˢⱽ Surely the shepherds told Mary and Joseph what the angels had said in order to explain why they were intruding on the couple with their baby. When they left they spread the story, and those who heard it were "astonished" (2:18). In contrast, *Mary treasured all these words and pondered them in her heart.* "Treasured" means deep reflection, keeping in mind or safely storing up; "pondering in the heart" refers to mulling over, seeking to understand and interpret. Mary had a lot to think about as she gazed into the face of her tiny child. Gabriel had told her that the little boy would reign forever (1:31-33); the shepherds reported the angel's words—he is the Savior, Christ the Lord (2:11). As Mary held this tiny baby, she must have wondered at all that God was doing, and who her son would grow up to become.

2:20 The shepherds returned, glorifying and praising God for all they had heard and seen, as it had been told them.^{NRSV} The shepherds had to get back to the fields before their sheep wandered off into the night. So they *returned,* but as they did so, they were *glorifying and praising God.* They knew that they had received a special message and had been privileged to be the first to see the promised child.

MARY AND JOSEPH BRING JESUS TO THE TEMPLE / 2:21-40 / **11**

Just as the story of John the Baptist's birth began in the temple (1:5-25), so the story of Jesus' birth culminates in the temple. In obedience to the dictates of Jewish law, Mary and Joseph presented Jesus to God (see Exodus 13:2-16) and offered a sacrifice for the ritual purification of Mary (see Leviticus 12:2-6).

In the temple, Simeon approached Jesus and delivered a prophecy, describing Jesus as "the Savior" (2:30 NLT). Anna joined in, praising God for the baby Jesus. Their testimony confirmed at least seven different prophecies surrounding Jesus' birth (1:17, 31-33, 42-45, 68-76; 2:10-14, 28-32, 38). These prophecies, one after another, proclaim Jesus their Savior, Deliverer, and Lord. Like Anna, believers should join their voices with these witnesses, praising God for providing salvation through his beloved Son, Jesus.

2:21-24 After eight days had passed, it was time to circumcise the child; and he was called Jesus, the name given by the angel before he was conceived in the womb. When the time came for their purification according to the law of Moses, they brought him up to Jerusalem to present him to the Lord (as it is written in the law of the Lord, "Every firstborn male shall be designated as holy to the Lord"), and they offered a sacrifice according to what is stated in the law of the Lord, "a pair of turtledoves or two young pigeons."^{NRSV} To understand these times and ceremonies, it will help to understand the background. Jewish families went through several ceremonies soon after a baby's birth:

1. Circumcision. Every Jewish boy was circumcised and named on the eighth day after birth (Leviticus 12:3; Luke 1:59-60). Circumcision symbolized the Jews' separation from Gentiles and their unique relationship with God (Genesis 17:9-14). So *after eight days had passed,* Mary and Joseph took the child to be circumcised. They named him Jesus, *the name given by the angel before he was conceived in the womb* (1:31). They did not go to

Jerusalem for this ceremony; instead, a local priest most likely performed it.

2. Redemption of the firstborn. A firstborn son was presented to God one month after birth (Exodus 13:2, 11-16; Numbers 18:15-16). The ceremony included buying back—"redeeming"— the child from God through an offering. Through this, the parents would acknowledge that the child belonged to God, who alone has the power to give life. Luke explained for his Gentile audience that this command came from *the law of the Lord, "Every firstborn male shall be designated as holy to the Lord"* as taken from Exodus 13:2, 12, 15 and Numbers 18:15. So Mary and Joseph *brought him up to Jerusalem to present him to the Lord.*

3. Purification of the mother. For forty days after the birth of a son and eighty days after the birth of a daughter, the mother was ceremonially unclean and could not enter the temple. So *when the time came for their purification,* that is, at the end of Mary's time of separation, they went to the temple to present Jesus to the Lord (#2 above) and to offer *a sacrifice according to what is stated in the law* (as part of #3). Mary and Joseph were to bring an offering—a lamb for a burnt offering and a dove or pigeon for a sin offering. The priest would sacrifice these animals and declare the woman to be clean. If a lamb was too expensive, the parents could bring a second dove or pigeon instead. This is what Mary and Joseph did.

2:25-26 Now there was a man in Jerusalem whose name was Simeon; this man was righteous and devout, looking forward to the consolation of Israel, and the Holy Spirit rested on him. It had been revealed to him by the Holy Spirit that he would not see death before he had seen the Lord's Messiah.[NRSV] Luke introduced another person who would be divinely told of the Messiah's arrival and who would confirm the baby's identity. His name is *Simeon.* He was spiritually in tune with God: *righteous, devout, looking forward to the consolation of Israel,* with the *Holy Spirit* resting on him. His occupation is unknown. He had all his life held on to God's promise of a coming deliverer, so through the Holy Spirit, God promised that Simeon would not die before seeing *the Lord's Messiah.* The "consolation of Israel" was another way of describing the Messiah. See Anna's prophecy in 2:38 where the faithful are called those waiting for "the redemption of Jerusalem." "Consolation" refers to the restoration of Israel as a nation; the word comes from Isaiah 40:1; 49:13; 51:3; 57:18; 66:10-11. Simeon, a righteous, devout, and Spirit-filled man who hoped in the future God had promised, stands forever in Scripture as a model of devotion and faithfulness to God.

SIMEON'S HOPE
Simeon was old and had much to ponder. No doubt he had
disappointments in his life to worry over, much to bemoan, lots
to regret. Rather than dwelling on life's rough ride, Simeon,
even in old age, looked to God's future with brightness and
hope. Simeon's secret was in his worship and expectation for
God. Worship and praise were natural to him; they were the
center of his life.

Nothing is so bleak as a day without tomorrow. With God,
however, every day has hope and good cheer. Neither old age
nor grim circumstances should keep you from God's comfort,
sufficient for your needs today. Take Simeon's example and
look ahead to God's great plan for you and the world.

2:27-32 **Moved by the Spirit, he went into the temple courts. When
the parents brought in the child Jesus to do for him what the
custom of the Law required, Simeon took him in his arms and
praised God, saying: "Sovereign Lord, as you have promised,
you now dismiss your servant in peace. For my eyes have seen
your salvation, which you have prepared in the sight of all
people, a light for revelation to the Gentiles and for glory to
your people Israel."**NIV When Mary and Joseph brought Jesus to
the temple to present him to the Lord (2:22), Simeon also *went
into the temple courts,* having been *moved by the Spirit* to be
there on this particular day. God was ordaining this meeting, in
keeping with his promise to Simeon (2:26).

Mary and Joseph arrived in the temple *to do for [Jesus] what
the custom of the Law required.* This obedience to the Old Testament law is mentioned several times in Luke. It points out Jesus'
credentials as one who obeyed the law, even from birth, because
his parents did exactly as they were commanded. At the temple,
Mary and Joseph met an old man who took the baby Jesus *in his
arms and praised God.* The Spirit led Simeon to recognize this
baby as the "consolation of Israel . . . the Lord's Messiah" (2:25-
26).

Simeon's song is often called the "Nunc Dimittis," the first
words of its Latin translation. Simeon praised God that he had
done what he promised and could *dismiss your servant* (meaning
himself) *in peace.* In other words, Simeon was now ready to die
in peace because he had seen God's *salvation.* To see Jesus is to
see salvation. This salvation has been *prepared in the sight of all
people, a light for revelation to the Gentiles and for glory to your
people Israel.* Jesus Christ is the fullest manifestation of God's
"glory" that his people had ever seen. Luke, writing to Gentiles,
pointed out that from the very beginning God's plan was to offer

salvation to Gentiles as well as to Jews. The mission to the Gentiles is a key theme in Luke and Acts. Even the prophets had predicted this (see, for example, Isaiah 42:6; 49:6; 52:10; 60:1-2). The Jews were well acquainted with

> If you want to know what God has to say to you, see what Christ was and is.   *C. H. Spurgeon*

the Old Testament prophecies that spoke of the Messiah's blessings to their nation. They did not always give equal attention to the prophecies saying that he would bring salvation to the entire world, not just the Jews. Many thought that Christ had come to save only his own people. Luke made sure his Greek audience understood that Jesus had come to save all who believe, Gentiles as well as Jews.

JESUS THE LIGHT
Simeon referred to Jesus as "a light for revelation." Few metaphors capture Jesus' mission as well. Light makes the stillness come alive; light settles fear; light reveals mystery; light enables relationships. Jesus is God in the flesh, eternal light breaking into a spiritually dark world.

Jesus is your light. He is not a distant sun, remote and driven by physics' laws. Jesus is the light of your life—your courage, your enabler. Start each day by turning on the light—a moment of meditation on God's Word, a prayer of dedication to live for God all day.

2:33-35 **The child's father and mother marveled at what was said about him. Then Simeon blessed them and said to Mary, his mother: "This child is destined to cause the falling and rising of many in Israel, and to be a sign that will be spoken against, so that the thoughts of many hearts will be revealed. And a sword will pierce your own soul too."**[NIV] Here Joseph and Mary are called *the child's father and mother,* which they were, although Joseph was not technically the father (as the genealogy in chapter 3 will clarify, and as the reader already knows). They *marveled* (were amazed) that this stranger in the temple recognized their small son and prophesied his coming as a light to all nations, not just the Jews. Simeon *blessed* Mary and Joseph and then prophesied that Jesus would have a paradoxical effect on Israel. He would bring light and salvation, but his coming could also cause division. Some would "fall" because of him (see Isaiah 8:14-15), while others would "rise" (see Malachi 4:2). There would not be overwhelming acceptance of the promised Messiah—in fact, many would not recognize him and would reject him altogether. With Jesus, there would be no neutral ground: people would either joyfully accept him or totally reject him. He would indeed be a *sign,* but he would *be spoken against* by many, thus revealing what was inside *many* people's *hearts.* This would have surprised and saddened Mary. Simeon told Mary that a *sword* would *pierce* her *soul.* As Jesus' mother, Mary would be grieved by the widespread rejection he would face; she would experience great pain when he died. Although she could not have known it and Simeon had only a hint of it, Mary would be the only person on earth who would witness both his birth and his death. He was God's Son, but she would always be his mother and she would love him as dearly as any mother loves a son. The sorrow and horror he would face would affect her deeply.

OLDER AND WISER
Although Simeon and Anna were very old, they had never lost their hope that they would see the Messiah. Led by the Holy Spirit, they were among the first to bear witness to Jesus. In the Jewish culture, elders were respected; thus, because of Simeon's and Anna's age, their prophecies carried extra weight. Contemporary society values youthfulness over wisdom, and potential contributions by the elderly are often ignored. Christians should reverse those values wherever they can. Encourage older people to share their wisdom and experience. Listen carefully when they speak. Offer them your friendship and help them find ways to continue to serve God.

2:36-37 Anna, a prophet, was also there in the Temple. She was the daughter of Phanuel, of the tribe of Asher, and was very old. She was a widow, for her husband had died when they had been married only seven years. She was now eighty-four years old. She never left the Temple but stayed there day and night, worshiping God with fasting and prayer.[NLT] Another person who recognized this special baby arrived on the scene as Simeon was giving his words of prophecy to Joseph and Mary. This was *Anna.* While we know nothing of Simeon's occupation, we are told that Anna was *a prophet,* indicating that she was unusually close to God. Prophets did not necessarily predict the future. Their main role was to speak for God, proclaiming his truth. While the *tribe of Asher* does not stand out in Old Testament history (see Genesis 30:12-13; 35:26) and nothing is known of *Phanuel,* her father, apparently these details were important in establishing her credentials and her Jewishness. Anna had been a *widow* for most of her life, never remarrying but instead focusing her attention on *worshiping God with fasting and prayer.* That "she never left the Temple" means that she made her life occupation to be at worship whenever the doors of the temple were open (see 24:53). Most likely she did not sleep there as there was no place to stay. Her lifestyle of worshiping, fasting, and praying indicates a woman of faith and strict devotion.

2:38 At that moment she came, and began to praise God and to speak about the child to all who were looking for the redemption of Jerusalem.NRSV While Luke did not record any exact words spoken by Anna, he wrote that she *began to praise God and to speak about the child to all who were looking for the redemption of Jerusalem.* As a second witness to the identity of this child, Anna praised God as she perceived that this baby would provide "redemption" for the nation (echoing Isaiah 52:9). This "redemption" was another way of saying that Anna was looking forward to the Messiah's arrival. Like Simeon, she, in her old age, was privileged to see the Messiah.

PRAISING GOD
To praise God is to . . .
- Set aside all your problems and complaints in order to celebrate God's generosity.
- Thank God for his marvelous provision for your daily needs.
- Take time from business and leisure to focus on God's magnificent power and love.
- Rehearse the splendid surprise of eternal life through faith in Jesus Christ.
- Reorient your heart around God's message and priorities.

2:39 When Joseph and Mary had done everything required by the Law of the Lord, they returned to Galilee to their own town of Nazareth.NIV Luke again mentioned the fact that Joseph and Mary had done *everything required by the Law* (see 2:22-24). Jesus may have been the Son of God, but his earthly parents had fulfilled everything that God's law required regarding the birth of firstborn sons.

Luke wrote that *they returned to Galilee to their own town of Nazareth,* from where they had come to register for the census (2:4). Did Mary and Joseph return immediately to Nazareth, or did they remain in Bethlehem for a time (as implied in Matthew 2)? Apparently there is a gap of several years between verses 38 and 39—ample time for them to find a place to live in Bethlehem, flee to Egypt to escape Herod's wrath (Matthew 2:1-18), and return to Nazareth when it was safe to do so (after Herod had died, Matthew 2:19-23).

The small town of Nazareth rested in the hilly area of southern

PRAISING GOD

The Bible speaks often of people praising God and encourages continual praise. What does it mean to praise God? Why should we do it? How should we do it? The Bible gives us answers to those questions.

Verse	Explanation
"I will thank you, LORD, with all my heart; I will tell of all the marvelous things you have done. I will be filled with joy because of you. I will sing praises to your name, O Most High" (Psalm 9:1-2 NLT).	**PRAISE IS GIVING THANKS TO GOD FOR WHO HE IS.** Praise is saying thank you for each aspect of his divine nature and for all the marvelous works that God has done. One's inward attitude becomes outward expression. When people praise God, they expand their awareness of who he is.
"Praise the LORD. Praise the LORD, O my soul. I will praise the LORD all my life; I will sing praise to my God as long as I live" (Psalm 146:1-2 NIV).	**PRAISE IS FOCUSING ONE'S HEART ON GOD.** The last five psalms (146–150) are filled with praise. Each begins and ends with "Praise the Lord!" What does praise do? (1) Praise takes people's minds off their problems and shortcomings and focuses them on God; (2) Praise leads from individual meditation to corporate worship; (3) Praise causes believers to consider and appreciate God's character; (4) Praise lifts one's perspective from the earthly to the heavenly.
"Praise the LORD, I tell myself, and never forget the good things he does for me" (Psalm 103:2 NLT).	**PRAISE IS THANKING GOD FOR HIS MANY GRACIOUS GIFTS.** It is easy to complain about life, but there is much for which to praise God—he forgives sins, heals diseases, redeems from death, crowns with love and compassion, satisfies

Galilee near the crossroads of great caravan trade routes. The town housed the Roman garrison in charge of Galilee. The people of Nazareth had constant contact with people from all over the world. When faced with the prospect of meeting Jesus, a man from Nazareth, Nathanael, later commented, "Nazareth! Can anything good come from there?" (John 1:46 NIV).

2:40 The child grew and became strong, filled with wisdom; and the favor of God was upon him.NRSV Jesus' life gave the evidence of being filled with the Spirit. He *grew* (*euxanen,* refers to his physical growth), *became strong* (*ekrataiouto,* refers to his spiritual growth), was *filled with wisdom* (refers to his intellectual growth), and was an object of *the favor of God* (refers to his growth in perception of God's will). Wisdom and God's favor indicated the presence of the Holy Spirit in his life. Jesus,

Verse (con't)	Explanation (con't)
	desires, and gives righteousness and justice. Believers receive all of these without deserving any of them. No matter how difficult your life's journey, you can always count your blessings—past, present, and future.
"For it is by grace you have been saved, through faith— and this not from yourselves, it is the gift of God— not by works, so that no one can boast" (Ephesians 2:8-9 NIV).	**PRAISE IS THANKING GOD FOR SALVATION.** When someone gives you a gift, do you say, "That's very nice—now how much do I owe you?" No, the appropriate response to a gift is, "Thank you." Yet, often Christians, even after they have been given the gift of salvation, feel obligated to try to work their way to God. Because salvation and even faith are gifts, believers should respond with gratitude, praise, and joy.
"Through Jesus, therefore, let us continually offer to God a sacrifice of praise— the fruit of lips that confess his name" (Hebrews 13:15 NIV).	**PRAISE IS A SPIRITUAL OFFERING.** Jewish Christians, because of their witness to the Messiah, no longer worshiped with other Jews. So praise and acts of service became their sacrifices—ones they could offer anywhere, anytime. The prophet Hosea wrote, "Forgive all our sins and receive us graciously, that we may offer the fruit of our lips" (Hosea 14:2). A "sacrifice of praise" today would include thanking Christ for his sacrifice on the cross and telling others about it. Acts of kindness and sharing are particularly pleasing to God, even when they go unnoticed.

like any child, developed from an infant to a toddler to a young child. He learned to crawl, sit up, walk, and finally to run. He learned to eat and talk. In many ways he was probably a typical child. Yet he was sinless in nature and certainly had uncanny wisdom for his years, as the next section reveals. For more on Jesus' growth, see 2:52.

JESUS SPEAKS WITH THE RELIGIOUS TEACHERS / 2:41-52 / **15**

In first-century Israel, the age of twelve was considered the time when a child was beginning to reach adulthood. This section of Luke contains an incident at this crucial juncture in Jesus' childhood to give readers an indication of what Jesus' life would center on: the teachings of God, his true Father. Jesus' own testimony of his purpose, "I had to be in my Father's house" (2:49 NIV), concludes the infancy narratives (1:1–2:52). Luke is the only Gospel writer to offer this quick glimpse into Jesus' childhood. This story not only reflects Luke's thorough research of Jesus' life but also reveals a youth who, at an early age, understood his special connection to God and dedicated himself to studying God's law. Sit back in amazement, just like those who heard the boy Jesus speak during that Passover season long ago, and rededicate yourself to following Jesus' example, diligently studying the Scripture to learn more about God your Father.

2:41-42 Every year Jesus' parents went to Jerusalem for the Passover festival. When Jesus was twelve years old, they attended the festival as usual.^{NLT} According to God's law, every male was required to go to Jerusalem three times a year for the great festivals (Exodus 23:14-17; Deuteronomy 16:16). In the spring, the Passover was celebrated, followed immediately by the weeklong Festival of Unleavened Bread. Passover commemorated the night of the Jews' escape from Egypt when God had killed the Egyptian firstborn but had passed over Israelite homes (see Exodus 12:21-36). Passover was the most important of the three annual festivals. *Every year,* along with other Jewish families, Jesus and his *parents* (referring to Joseph and Mary, his earthly parents) *went to Jerusalem for the Passover festival.* Again there is attention to the law—Jesus grew up in a home where God's laws were obeyed and annual festivals observed. So, the year when *Jesus was twelve years old* was no different, and the family set off for the festival *as usual.*

REGULAR HABITS
Jesus' parents, like most devout Jews, went to Jerusalem each year. Jesus' family had the right priorities. Families that establish regular habits of worship are less likely to have their spiritual life deflected by alternative attractions. Keep worship on top of your family's agenda. Putting God first is a great example to children, who quickly learn what parents care about by observing how they plan and spend time.

2:43-44 When the festival was ended and they started to return, the boy Jesus stayed behind in Jerusalem, but his parents did not know it. Assuming that he was in the group of travelers, they went a day's journey. Then they started to look for him among their relatives and friends.^{NRSV} At age twelve, Jesus was considered almost an adult, so he probably didn't spend a lot of time with his parents during the feast. Those who attended these feasts usually traveled in caravans for protection from robbers along the Palestine roads. It was customary for the women and children to travel at the front of the caravan, with the men bringing up the rear. A twelve-year-old boy conceivably could have been in either group, and both Mary and Joseph assumed Jesus was with the other one. Their caravan probably included a large number of people. So it was not until they had gone *a day's journey* and were ready to strike camp that Mary and Joseph checked for Jesus among all their *relatives and friends,* only to discover that he was not in the crowd but had *stayed behind in Jerusalem.*

2:45-47 When they did not find him, they returned to Jerusalem to search for him. After three days they found him in the temple, sitting among the teachers, listening to them and asking them questions. And all who heard him were amazed at his understanding and his answers.NRSV When Mary and Joseph discovered that Jesus was not among the travelers, *they returned to Jerusalem to search for him.* The *three days* that elapsed probably involves one day in travel away from the city, one day for them to return, then finding him on the third day. Certainly to their great relief, *they found him in the temple.*

The temple courts were famous throughout Judea as places of learning. The apostle Paul studied in Jerusalem, perhaps in the temple courts, under Gamaliel, one of its foremost teachers (Acts 22:3). At the time of the Passover, the greatest rabbis of the land would assemble to teach and to discuss great truths among themselves. The coming Messiah would no doubt have been a popular discussion topic, for everyone was expecting him. Jesus would have been eager to listen and to ask probing questions. It was not his youth, but the depth of his wisdom, that *amazed* these teachers.

2:48 His parents didn't know what to think. "Son!" his mother said to him. "Why have you done this to us? Your father and I have been frantic, searching for you everywhere."NLT Mary and Joseph knew the true identity of their son, yet that did not keep them from being typical concerned parents. Their son had been gone from them for three days, yet that seems not to have bothered him at all. Jesus was absorbed in discussions at the temple and did not seem to have wondered about his parents or his connection with the caravan back to Nazareth. Mary was worried, anxious, and overwhelmed by what had happened and her frustrating search for Jesus. Mary's words indicate a hint of scolding: *Why have you done this to us?* She explained that they had been *frantic* ever since he turned up missing, *searching* through the city to find him. They did not understand how Jesus could have treated them so casually.

2:49-50 **He said to them, "Why were you searching for me? Did you not know that I must be in my Father's house?" But they did not understand what he said to them.**^{NRSV} Jesus couldn't understand why Mary and Joseph got so frantic in their search for him. He surely felt bad that he had caused them distress, but it made perfect sense to him that he would be in his *Father's house,* that is, in the temple. This is the first mention of Jesus' awareness that he was God's Son (he called God "my Father") and that he had special work to do (he said I "must" be here). His relationship with his Father in heaven superseded his human family and even his human home. While he probably went to school and studied along with other boys in the synagogue in Nazareth, to be in the temple with many learned teachers was a great opportunity for Jesus. He took full advantage of his time there, and it seems that he thought his parents would know where he would be.

Jesus' parents *did not understand* what he meant about his Father's house. They didn't realize that he was making a distinction between his earthly father and his heavenly Father. Jesus knew that he had a unique relationship with God. Although Mary and Joseph knew he was God's Son, they didn't understand what his mission would involve. Besides, they had to rear him, along with his brothers and sisters (Matthew 13:55-56), as a normal child. They knew Jesus was unique, but they did not know what was going on in his mind. They had to learn and observe the complex outworkings of Jesus' special identity and calling even as he lived in their family.

2:51 **Then he returned to Nazareth with them and was obedient to them; and his mother stored all these things in her heart.**^{NLT} Although Jesus had been in his Father's house, and although he did not understand his parents' concern, Luke explained that Jesus *returned to Nazareth . . . and was obedient.* Jesus understood his identity with God but also was not yet supposed to go about his earthly ministry (that did not happen until he was thirty years old). Jesus' behavior was not disobedient but precociously acting out his true identity, which he would one day fulfill. In the meantime, Jesus lived a human life, obeying his parents, growing up, studying, and learning. As she had with the words of the shepherds at Jesus' birth (2:19), Mary *stored all these things in her heart.* She did not completely understand her son, but she remembered these events, thought them over, and sought to find their meaning. One day, it all would be clear. One day her son would become her Savior, and she would understand.

BEING YOUNG
If you are twelve years old, one of your hardest jobs in life is obeying the adults who run your home. They are called parents, and they always think they know best. It's very tough for a twelve-year-old to keep from taking over the family and running it according to intelligent twelve-year-old standards. But when the temptation strikes, remember Jesus. . . . Even though he knew his real Father, he did not reject his earthly parents. He went back to Nazareth with them and lived under their authority for another eighteen years. God's people do not despise human relationships or family responsibilities. If the Son of God obeyed his human parents, how much more should you honor your family members!

2:52 So Jesus grew both in height and in wisdom, and he was loved by God and by all who knew him.[NLT] This wording is similar to 1 Samuel 2:21, 26. The Bible does not record any events of the next eighteen years of Jesus' life, but Jesus undoubtedly was learning and maturing. As the oldest in a large family, he assisted Joseph in his carpentry work. Joseph may have died during this time, leaving Jesus to provide for the family. The normal routines of daily life gave Jesus a solid understanding of the Judean people.

The second chapter of Luke shows us that although Jesus was unique, he had a normal childhood and adolescence. In terms of development, he went through the same progression we do. He grew physically *(in height)* and mentally *(in wisdom)*, he related to other people *(loved . . . by all who knew him),* and he was *loved by God.* A full human life is balanced. It was important to Jesus—and it should be important to all believers—to develop fully and harmoniously in each of these key areas: physical, mental, social, and spiritual.

LUKE 3

JOHN THE BAPTIST PREPARES THE WAY FOR
JESUS / 3:1-18 / **16**

When John began preaching in the wilderness, a group of eager
listeners gathered around him. The Israelites considered John to
be a great prophet. God had not sent a prophet to Israel for
around four hundred years, so people noticed John. Some whispered: Has the Messiah come, the promised Deliverer of Israel?
Indeed, he had. But he was not John; he was the quiet carpenter
of Nazareth, watching and waiting for God's appointed time.
When that time came, that carpenter, Jesus, would announce a
new era, with a brand-new covenant—the kingdom of God had
come!

Meanwhile, John the Baptist shouted in the barren wilderness,
speaking like the prophets of old, exhorting the people to turn
from their sin to avoid punishment and turn to God to experience
his mercy. This is a message for all times and places, but John
spoke it with particular urgency: he was preparing the people for
the coming Messiah. His ministry was a fulfillment of Isaiah's
prophecy of "a voice shouting in the wilderness" (3:4 NLT) to prepare the coming of the Lord. The calling for believers today is
similar to John's, for they too should prepare the way for others
to come to Jesus. And sometimes, they have to muster the courage to call people, even though a moral and spiritual wilderness
surrounds them. How much urgency do you feel for those who
still need to hear the message?

**3:1-2 In the fifteenth year of the reign of Emperor Tiberius, when
Pontius Pilate was governor of Judea, and Herod was ruler of
Galilee, and his brother Philip ruler of the region of Ituraea
and Trachonitis, and Lysanias ruler of Abilene.**NRSV Once
again Luke gave his Roman audience a historical context for his
narrative (as in 2:1-2). This would be like writing "during Abraham Lincoln's administration." *Tiberius,* the Roman emperor,
ruled from A.D. 14 to 37. He began his reign in August of A.D. 14
when Caesar Augustus died. Thus, Tiberius's *fifteenth year* would
have been from August A.D. 28 to the following August.

Pontius Pilate was the Roman *governor* responsible for the province of *Judea* from A.D. 26 to 36. The term "governor" is quite general. According to history, Pilate was actually *praefectus Iudaeae,* a military title of a commander of auxiliary troops. Originally, Archelaus, son of Herod the Great, had been assigned this portion to rule after his father died, but he ruled so poorly that his subjects petitioned for him to be removed. The Romans installed a governor in A.D. 6, and eventually Pilate held this post. Pilate was greedy, inflexible, and cruel. He was always at odds with the Jews. At one point, he brought Roman standards bearing the figure of the emperor into Jerusalem. The Jews protested and Pilate eventually removed them.

Herod, ruler of Galilee, was Herod Antipas. Herod and his *brother* (actually, half brother) *Philip* were both sons of the cruel Herod the Great, who had been dead more than twenty years. Herod Antipas was in power from 4 B.C. to A.D. 39. Philip ruled *the region of Itureaea and Trachonitis* from 4 B.C. to A.D. 33 or 34. *Lysanias ruler of Abilene* is otherwise unknown. The region of Abilene was north of the other regions mentioned. Herod Antipas, Philip, Pilate, and Lysanias apparently had equal powers in governing their separate territories. All were subject to Rome and responsible for keeping peace in their respective lands.

During the high priesthood of Annas and Caiaphas.[NRSV] Under Jewish law there was only one high priest. He was to be appointed from Aaron's line, and he would hold his position for life. By this time, however, the religious system had been corrupted, and the Roman government was appointing its own religious leaders to maintain greater control over the Jews. Apparently the Roman authorities had deposed the Jewish-appointed *Annas* (who ruled from A.D. 6 to 15). Five of Annas's sons became high priest; *Caiaphas* was his son-in-law, who held the *high priesthood* from A.D. 18 to 36. Caiaphas, therefore, actually held the office, but Annas retained his title (see Acts 4:6) and probably much of the power and influence it carried. Because the Jews believed the high priest's position to be for life, they would have continued to call Annas their high priest.

The word of God came to John son of Zechariah in the wilderness.[NRSV] This "John" refers to John the Baptist, *son of Zechariah* the priest, whose birth story is told in chapter 1. The words Luke used here to describe John's call are reminiscent of the Old Testament prophets. Dating a prophet's call with reference to political and religious authorities was also common in the Old Testament. Thus, Luke was placing John in the category of the Old Testament prophets (see 7:24-28; 1 Samuel 15:10; 2 Samuel

7:4; 1 Kings 17:2; Isaiah 6:1; 38:4; Jeremiah 1:1-3; 2:1; 13:3; Ezekiel 1:1-3; Daniel 7:1; Hosea 1:1). There had not been a prophet in Israel for more than four hundred years. It was widely believed that when the Messiah would come, prophecy would reappear (Joel 2:28-29; Malachi 3:1; 4:5). With the arrival of John, prophecy returned to Israel, and this was a sign to the people. For more on the wilderness theme, see 3:4.

"The word of God came to John" means that God gave John his message, and from that point, John brought that message to the people. The narrative here picks up from 1:80, which explains that John lived *in the wilderness* until he began his preaching. That preaching began only after God gave John the message he was to proclaim.

MEASURE OF GREATNESS
Powerful religious and political leaders like Pilate, Annas, and Caiaphas ruled in Palestine, but they were upstaged by a desert prophet from rural Judea. God chose to speak through the loner, John the Baptist, who has gone down in history as greater than any of the rulers of his day. How often people judge others by the superficial standards of power, wealth, and beauty, and miss the truly great people through whom God works! Greatness is measured not by what a person has but by his or her faith in God. Like John, give yourself entirely to God, so that his power can work through you.

3:3 He went into all the region around the Jordan, proclaiming a baptism of repentance for the forgiveness of sins.^{NRSV} The word of God came to John in the wilderness, and apparently he stayed in the wilderness with the people coming out to hear him (3:7). There had been no prophecy in Israel for hundreds of years; news that a prophet had burst onto the scene excited the people. So John went from place to place *into all the region around the Jordan,* taking the message that God had given him (3:2).

John proclaimed to those who came to hear him *a baptism of repentance for the forgiveness of sins.* "Baptism," "repentance," and "forgiveness" go hand in hand. To "repent" means to con-

> It would tire the hands of an angel to write down all the pardons God bestows upon true penitent believers. *William Bates*

fess sin and then to turn away from sin and toward God. It is, in effect, an inner cleansing. So John used an act to symbolize that cleansing from sin: "baptism."

The origins of John's baptism are difficult to trace. Some have claimed that his baptism modeled that practiced by those at

Qumran; others have urged that his baptism modeled that practiced by Jews when initiating proselytes to Judaism. The members of the Qumran community viewed themselves as the covenant community of the last days and so dwelt in the desert, living an ascetic life and immersing themselves daily in acts of ceremonial cleansing. At the same time they taught that internal repentance must accompany the external act. Its sacramental nature is seen in the fact that only a full member of the community could practice it, and then only after two probationary years. Converts from pagan religions were admitted to Judaism only after fulfilling certain obligations, which included the study of the Torah, circumcision, and a ritual bath to wash away the impurities of the Gentile background.

John's baptism both parallels and differs with these forms of baptism. His baptism was new in that he was asking the Jews themselves to be baptized as a sign of repentance. They considered themselves "clean" as descendants of Abraham; only "unclean" Gentiles needed baptism. But John explained that sin makes everyone "unclean," and they all needed cleansing and forgiveness. Forgiveness from God is available, but there can be no forgiveness without repentance.

TURN AROUND!
Every now and then in a football or basketball game, some poor player gets totally turned around and begins running toward the wrong goal. When that happens, his coaches and teammates don't stand by passively and politely suggest that he rethink his plan. They scream and yell in the most impassioned tones and terms for him to stop and turn around—NOW!

John the Baptist's message was very similar: you are heading the wrong way, and if you don't do a "180," you will meet with disaster. There was very little concern for subtlety or social protocol in John's preaching. He let people know in no uncertain terms that if they continued on their present course, no matter how well or how skillfully they proceeded, they were on a collision course with judgment. John called for true repentance—nothing less than a complete change of mind, heart, and behavior, the kind of radical change that only God can enable. Have you experienced this kind of change in your life? Do you need to repent of anything—actions, thoughts, attitudes, omissions—now?

For baptism, John needed water, so he remained in the region around the Jordan River. This seventy-mile-long river stretches between the Sea of Galilee and the Dead Sea. Jerusalem lies about twenty miles west of the Jordan. Many significant events in the

nation's history took place by the Jordan River. For example, there
the Israelites renewed their covenant with God before entering the
Promised Land (Joshua 1–5). In the Old Testament, "repent" means
the radical return to God of those who have broken the covenant
with him (Ezekiel 18:21, 30). So this prophet burst onto the scene
at the Jordan River, calling the people back to God—this time
through repenting, turning from sin, and being baptized.

**3:4 As it is written in the book of the words of Isaiah the prophet,
saying: "The voice of one crying in the wilderness: 'Prepare
the way of the LORD; make His paths straight.'"**^{NKJV} In John's
day, before a king took a trip, messengers would tell those he was
planning to visit to prepare the roads for him. Similarly John told
his listeners to make their lives ready so the Lord could come to
them.

Isaiah the prophet also called his people to repentance. The
second half of the book of Isaiah focuses on the promise of salvation—the coming of the Messiah and the arrival of a man who
would announce this coming (Isaiah 40:3). John the Baptist was,
in fact, that *voice . . . crying in the wilderness.* The Greek word
for "crying" is *boao,* meaning "to cry out with great feeling."
Why did this voice come from the "wilderness"? The word "wilderness," also translated "desert," refers more to a lonely, unin-
habited place than to a sandy desert. Isaiah's use of the word
"wilderness" alludes to the wilderness experience of the children
of Israel on their exodus from Egypt to Canaan. The "wilderness"
represents the place where God would once again act to rescue
his people and bring them back to him.

John was merely God's "voice" for the important message that
God was sending to his people (3:2). What was that message? *Prepare the way of the LORD.* "Prepare" refers to making something
ready; "way" could also be translated "road." Thus, part of "preparing the way" is to *make His paths straight.* John's audience, the
people in Israel who came to see this prophet in the wilderness,
were faced with a life-changing message. If they would prepare
themselves—clear away the spiritual debris and straighten any
"crooked" moral paths—the way would be ready for their King and
Messiah to come. Those who accepted John's status as a true
prophet from God understood these words as God's message to
them, humbled themselves, repented, received baptism, and opened
the "way" for their Messiah to take hold of their lives.

**3:5-6 "'Every valley shall be filled and every mountain and hill
brought low; the crooked places shall be made straight and
the rough ways smooth; and all flesh shall see the salvation of
God.'"**^{NKJV} While both Matthew and Mark quoted from Isaiah

40:3, Luke also quoted the two following verses, Isaiah 40:4-5. As the "way" is being prepared (3:4), seemingly impossible tasks must be done—such as valleys filled in and mountains leveled, crooked places straightened and rough ways smoothed. The images of these words reflect a powerful construction force grinding up everything in its path. God's highway will roll over every obstacle of unbelief or idolatry. As people prepare for the King, they will "straighten out" their lives through repentance from sin. The important words quoted from Isaiah *(and all flesh shall see the salvation of God)* showed Luke's non-Jewish audience that salvation was for all people, not just the Jews (see also Isaiah 52:10). John the Baptist called all humankind to prepare to meet Jesus. As Simeon said, "My eyes have seen your salvation" (2:30), so one day "all flesh" shall see God's salvation, for it will be made available to everyone.

FEAR OR FAITH?
What motivates your faith—fear of the future, or a desire to be a better person in a better world? Some people wanted to be baptized by John so they could escape eternal punishment, but they didn't turn to God for salvation. John had harsh words for such people. He knew that God values reformation above ritual. Is your faith motivated by a desire for a new, changed life, or is it only like a vaccination or insurance policy against possible disaster?

3:7 Here is a sample of John's preaching to the crowds that came for baptism: "You brood of snakes! Who warned you to flee God's coming judgment?"NLT John was the first prophet Israel had heard in over four hundred years. When news spread that a prophet was preaching in the wilderness, *crowds* came out to hear him, and apparently many also believed his message and *came for baptism.* This baptism represented repentance from sin (3:3). This sample of his *preaching* sounds harsh; Matthew tells us that John spoke these words specifically to "Pharisees and Sadducees," distinguished men who had come to John not to be baptized but simply to find out what was going on (Matthew 3:7). John called them a *brood of snakes* (Jesus also used this term, see Matthew 12:34; 23:33), conveying how dangerous and cunning these religious leaders were and suggesting that they were Satan's offspring (see Genesis 3; John 8:44). John asked them, *"Who warned you to flee God's coming judgment?"* The Jews, and especially their self-righteous religious leaders, applied God's judgment to the Gentiles; John warned that judgment was coming on them. John's astonishing frankness made him popular with the people but unpopular with the religious establishment. Anyone, religious leader or member of the crowd, who was open to John's message found repentance, baptism, and readiness for the coming Messiah. Those who rejected him faced stunning accusation for their hard-heartedness.

3:8 **"Bear fruits worthy of repentance. Do not begin to say to yourselves, 'We have Abraham as our ancestor'; for I tell you, God is able from these stones to raise up children to Abraham."**[NRSV] Confession of sins and a changed life are inseparable. Faith without deeds is dead (James 2:14-26). Repentance must be tied to action, or it isn't real. John's message is very similar to both that of Amos and James in showing God's ethical and social demands flowing from salvation (see, for example, Amos 5:4-15; James 2:14-25). Those who believe must also *bear fruits worthy of repentance*—they must truly turn from sin and live for God.

The Jews thought that, as descendants of Abraham, they were guaranteed God's blessings and that the promise given to the patriarchs was guaranteed to all their descendants, no matter how they acted or what they believed. John explained, however, that relying on Abraham as their ancestor would not qualify them for God's kingdom. John probably pointed at stones nearby and said, *"God is able from these stones to raise up children to Abraham."* John may have used a play on the Aramaic words for "stone" and "children" in making his point that God can make a nation for himself from whomever he chooses. Only those who "produce fruit in keeping with repentance" would be ready for God's coming kingdom. The apostle Paul would later explain this to the Romans: "Not all who are descended from Israel are Israel. Nor because they are his descendants are they all Abraham's children. . . . It is not the natural children who are God's children, but it is the children of the promise who are regarded as Abraham's offspring" (Romans 9:6-8 NIV).

NO HAND-ME-DOWNS
Many of John's hearers were shocked when he said that being Abraham's descendants was not enough for God. The religious leaders relied more on their family lines than on their faith or their standing with God. For them, religion was inherited. But a personal relationship with God is not handed down from parents to children. Everyone has to commit to it on his or her own. Don't rely on someone else's faith for your salvation. If you profess to having a life renewed and changed by Jesus, then make sure your actions truly show it.

3:9 "The ax is already at the root of the trees, and every tree that does not produce good fruit will be cut down and thrown into the fire."[NIV] God's message hasn't changed since the Old Testament—people will be judged for their unproductive lives. Just as a fruit tree is expected to bear fruit, God's people should produce a crop of good deeds (3:8). John said that people who claim to believe God but don't live for God are like unproductive trees that will be cut down. *The ax is already at the root of the trees,* poised and ready to do its work, cutting down those trees that do not bear good fruit (see Psalm 74:5-6; Jeremiah 46:22). Not only will the trees be *cut down,* but they will be *thrown into the fire,* signifying complete destruction.

IN NAME ONLY
We know people by their fruits, their lives. God has no use for people who call themselves Christians but do nothing about it. Like many in John's day who were God's people in name only, people are of no value if they are Christians in name only. If others can't see someone's faith in the way that person treats them, he or she may not be God's person at all. So how are believers to bear good fruit? God calls them to be "active" in their obedience. To be productive for God means obeying his teachings, resisting temptation, actively serving others, and sharing the faith.

3:10-11 And the crowds asked him, "What then should we do?" In reply he said to them, "Whoever has two coats must share with anyone who has none; and whoever has food must do likewise."[NRSV] John's preaching elicited responses from the crowd. Many asked, *"What then should we do* in order to 'bear fruit'?"* (3:8; see also Galatians 5:22-23). To the mixed *crowds,* John responded that they could readily show compassion, such as sharing food and clothing with people in need. The word for "coats" is actually "tunic," referring to a short garment worn for extra warmth under the longer robe. The person with two tunics ought to *share with anyone who has none.* The same with extra food, so that no one is hungry.

3:12-13 Tax collectors also came to be baptized. "Teacher," they asked, "what should we do?" "Don't collect any more than you are required to," he told them.[NIV] *Tax collectors* were notorious for their dishonesty. Romans gathered funds for their government by farming out the collection privilege. Tax collectors earned their own living by adding a sizable sum—whatever they could get away with—to the total and keeping this money for themselves. Unless the people revolted and risked Roman retaliation, they had to pay whatever was demanded. Obviously they hated the tax collectors, who were generally dishonest, greedy, and ready to betray their own countrymen for cold cash. Yet, said John, God would accept even these men; God desires to pour out mercy on those who confess, and then to give strength to live changed lives. So when these men *also came to be baptized,* they too asked what they should do to act on their repentance. John told them to tax appropriately: *Don't collect any more than you are required to.* They had to stop enriching themselves at the expense of their countrymen. John did not ask them to quit their jobs, only to do them honestly. Both Matthew and Zacchaeus were tax collectors (5:27-28; 19:2).

WHAT SHOULD WE DO?
John's message demanded at least three specific responses:
1. Share what you have with those who need it.
2. Whatever your job is, do it well and with fairness.
3. Be content with what you are earning.
John had no time to give comforting messages to those who lived careless or selfish lives—he was calling the people to right living. What changes can you make in sharing what you have, doing your work honestly and well, and being content?

3:14 "What should we do?" asked some soldiers. John replied, "Don't extort money, and don't accuse people of things you know they didn't do. And be content with your pay."[NLT] John's powerful message even reached *soldiers.* Luke does not specify, but most scholars agree that these were not Roman soldiers but Jewish soldiers who served to help keep the peace (similar to police officers). Like the tax collectors, they stood in a separate and privileged position over the common people, capable of using their power for good or for taking advantage of people. So when the soldiers asked what they should do, John told them to quit some of their activities—such as extorting money from people and accusing people of things they didn't do. As with the tax collectors, they were told to control their greed by being *content* with their pay.

John's message took root in unexpected places—among the poor, the dishonest, and even hardened soldiers. These people were painfully aware of their needs. Too often respectability is confused with right living. They are not the same. Respectability can even hinder right living if it keeps a person from seeing his or her need for God. If you had to choose, would you protect your character or your reputation?

TRUE RELIGION
Have you ever heard someone describe another person's religious commitment by saying, "Well, she talks a good game"? Obviously, there is a difference in talking about faith and actually living it. When some soldiers—gruff, hardened, experienced military men—came to John and asked what they needed to do to get their lives right with God, he didn't tell them to start singing in the choir or giving their testimonies. He told them to change the way they lived. John promoted an aggressive, outgoing, action-oriented way of life, not a "shelter-in-the-time-of-storm" mentality. True repentance, true religion, does not consist of changing the vocabulary as much as changing the lifestyle. Talk is cheap; true religion is not. What has yours cost you lately?

3:15 Everyone was expecting the Messiah to come soon, and they were eager to know whether John might be the Messiah.^{NLT} There had not been a prophet in Israel for more than four hundred years. It was widely believed that when the Messiah came, prophecy would reappear (Joel 2:28, 29; Malachi 3:1; 4:5). When John burst onto the scene, the people were excited. He was obviously a great prophet, and they were sure that the eagerly awaited age of the Messiah had arrived. Some, in fact, *were eager to know whether John might be the Messiah.* Even after his death, some of John's disciples considered him to be the Messiah (see Acts 18:25; 19:1-7). John spoke like the prophets of old, saying that the people must turn from their sin to avoid punishment and turn to God to experience his mercy and approval. This is a message for all times and places, but John spoke it with particular urgency—he was preparing the people for the coming Messiah.

3:16 John answered them all, "I baptize you with water. But one more powerful than I will come, the thongs of whose sandals I am not worthy to untie. He will baptize you with the Holy Spirit and with fire."^{NIV} John's baptism with water symbolized the washing away of sins. His baptism coordinated with his message of repentance and reformation. Baptism was an "outward" sign of commitment. To be effective, it had to be accompanied by an "inward" change of attitude leading to a changed life. John's baptism did not give salvation; it prepared a person to welcome the coming Messiah and receive *his* message and *his* baptism.

Although John was the first genuine prophet in four hundred years, Jesus the Messiah would be infinitely greater than he. John was pointing out how insignificant he was compared to the *one more powerful* who was coming. In Oriental households, a lowly slave would untie the sandals of guests and then wash their feet.

John saw himself as even lower than that slave in comparison to the coming Messiah. John was not even worthy of doing the most menial tasks for him, like untying his sandals.

> He who has the Holy Spirit in his heart and the Scriptures in his hands has all he needs.
>
> *Alexander MacLaren*

The coming of the Spirit had been prophesied as part of the Messiah's arrival. *He will baptize you with the Holy Spirit and with fire* revealed the identity of the promised Messiah:

- I will pour out my Spirit on your offspring, and my blessing on your descendants. (Isaiah 44:3 NIV)
- The time is coming. . . . I will put my law in their minds and write it on their hearts. I will be their God, and they will be my people. . . . For I will forgive their wickedness and will remember their sins no more. (Jeremiah 31:31-34 NIV)
- I will give you a new heart and put a new spirit in you; I will remove from you your heart of stone and give you a heart of flesh. And I will put my Spirit in you and move you to follow my decrees and be careful to keep my laws. (Ezekiel 36:26-27 NIV)
- And afterward, I will pour out my Spirit on all people. Your sons and daughters will prophesy, your old men will dream dreams, your young men will see visions. Even on my servants, both men and women, I will pour out my Spirit in those days. (Joel 2:28-29 NIV)

FIRED UP!
In describing the baptism that Jesus brings, John links the ministry of the Holy Spirit with fire. Fire can give light, warm us, and cook our food. Fire can also purify. The Holy Spirit, like fire, purifies believers in a number of ways. He shines light on their hearts and in their minds, disclosing areas that need to be confessed, repented, and brought under the lordship of Christ. He uses the heat of conviction from God's Word to prompt them to deal with their sins. He illuminates the path before believers, guiding them into all truth. Like a laser in the hands of a skillful surgeon, the Holy Spirit helps bring healing and wholeness to the believer. Have you taken time lately to let him examine you and do any necessary treatment?

The Old Testament promised a time when God would demonstrate his purifying power among people (Isaiah 32:15; Ezekiel 39:29). The prophets also looked forward to a purifying fire (Isaiah 4:4; Malachi 3:2). This looked ahead to Pentecost (Acts

2), when the Holy Spirit would be sent by Jesus in the form of tongues of fire, empowering his followers to proclaim Jesus' resurrection in many languages. The baptism with fire also symbolizes the work of the Holy Spirit in bringing God's judgment on those who refuse to repent. The experience would not necessarily be like that recorded in Acts 2, but the outcome would be the same. This baptism would purify and refine each believer. When Jesus would baptize with the Holy Spirit, the entire person would be refined by the Spirit's fire. For those who believe, "the fire" is positive; but for unbelievers, "the fire" brings awful judgment, as is described in the next verse.

3:17-18 **"His winnowing fork is in his hand to clear his threshing floor and to gather the wheat into his barn, but he will burn up the chaff with unquenchable fire." And with many other words John exhorted the people and preached the good news to them.**[NIV] Threshing was the process of separating the grains of wheat from the useless outer shell called chaff. This was normally done in a large area called a *threshing floor,* often on a hill, where the wind could blow away the lighter chaff when the farmer tossed the beaten wheat into the air. A *winnowing fork* is a pitchfork used to toss wheat in the air in order to separate wheat from chaff. The *wheat* is the part of the plant that is useful; *chaff* is the worthless outer shell. Chaff is burned because it is useless; wheat, however, is gathered.

"Winnowing" is often used in the Bible to picture God's judgment. Jesus used the same analogy in a parable (Matthew 13:24-30). John spoke of repentance, but he also spoke of judgment upon those who refused to repent. Those who refuse to live for God are chaff, the useless outer husk of the grain. By contrast, those who repent and reform their lives are like wheat. Those who refuse to be used by God will be discarded because they have no value in furthering God's work. Those who repent and believe, however, hold great value in God's eyes because they are beginning a new life of productive service for him.

The warnings coupled with John's announcement of *the good news* made John's message all that much more riveting.

HEROD PUTS JOHN IN PRISON / 3:19-20 / *26*

Unlike any other Gospel writer, Luke told the entire story of John the Baptist's ministry all at once (cf. Matthew 14:3-5; Mark 6:17-20): John's courageous ministry in the wilderness led to his imprisonment and eventually his execution.

The different responses to John's call to repentance are instruc-

tive. While the crowd asked, "What should we do?" (3:10 NLT),
Herod tried to silence John. How do you react to a word of exhortation, especially from the Bible? Do you rationalize away your
actions? Or do you admit your wrongs and humbly turn to God,
asking him for the power to change?

3:19-20 **John also publicly criticized Herod Antipas, ruler of Galilee,
for marrying Herodias, his brother's wife, and for many
other wrongs he had done. So Herod put John in prison, adding this sin to his many others.**ᴺᴸᵀ While John proclaimed the
Good News and warnings of judgment, he also apparently had a
no-nonsense attitude toward the morality of the day. He *also publicly criticized Herod Antipas, ruler of Galilee,* who was in power
from 4 B.C. to A.D. 39 (see 3:2). John criticized Herod because he
had married *Herodias, his brother's wife.* Besides being his brother's wife, Herodias was also Herod's own niece. So Herod was
committing both adultery and incest. John publicly protested
these sins, as well as *many other wrongs [Herod] had done,* so he
greatly angered both Herod and Herodias. Herod *put John in
prison,* presumably to silence him. The Herods were renowned
for their cruelty and evil (Herod the Great had ordered the murder of the babies in Bethlehem, Matthew 2:16). Putting John in
prison was simply *adding this sin to . . . many others.* The imprisonment of John the Baptist was only one evil act in a family
filled with incest, deceit, and murder. (The full story is told in
Matthew 14:1-12.)

Rebuking a tyrannical Roman official who could imprison and
execute him was extremely dangerous, yet that is what John did.
Herod seemingly had the last word, but the story was not finished. At the Last Judgment, Herod, not John, will be the one in
danger.

JOHN BAPTIZES JESUS / 3:21-22 / 17

God's words at Jesus' baptism clearly identified who Jesus was:
God's beloved Son (3:22). What Jesus was doing, including his
baptism by John, totally pleased God. Jesus was in no way
becoming God's Son at his baptism; instead, his true nature was
being revealed. Jesus' baptism showed that he was identifying
with sinful men and women, without implying that he himself
was a sinner. Luke further underscored this point with his record
of the story of Jesus' temptation soon after—another example of
Jesus' identifying with sinners without committing sin. Because
Jesus went through everything human beings have to go through,

people can be confident that he can sympathize with their weaknesses, when they attempt to follow his perfect example.

3:21-22 **When all the people were being baptized, Jesus was baptized too. And as he was praying, heaven was opened and the Holy Spirit descended on him in bodily form like a dove. And a voice came from heaven: "You are my Son, whom I love; with you I am well pleased."**NIV The words in 3:20, recording that Herod put John in prison, explained what would happen later in John's ministry as a result of his willingness to denounce sin where he saw it. In these verses, he was still out in the wilderness, preaching and baptizing (3:16). One day, *when all the people were being baptized,* Jesus came for baptism too.

Luke emphasized Jesus' human nature. Jesus was born to humble parents, a birth unannounced except to shepherds and foreigners. This baptism recorded here was the first public declaration of Jesus' ministry. Instead of going to Jerusalem and identifying with the established religious leaders, Jesus went to a river and identified himself with those who were repenting of sin. When Jesus, at age twelve, visited the temple, he understood his mission (2:49). Eighteen years later, at his baptism, he began carrying it out. And as Jesus prayed, God spoke and confirmed his decision to act. God was breaking into human history through Jesus the Christ.

If John's baptism was for repentance from sin, why was Jesus baptized? While even the greatest prophets (Isaiah, Jeremiah, Ezekiel) had to confess their sinfulness and need for repentance, Jesus didn't need to admit sin—he was sinless (John 8:46; 2 Corinthians 5:21; Hebrews 4:15; 1 John 3:5). Although Jesus didn't need forgiveness, he was baptized for the following reasons: (1) to confess sin on behalf of the nation, as Isaiah, Ezra, and Nehemiah had done (see Isaiah 6:5; Ezra 9:2; Nehemiah 1:6; 9:1ff.); (2) to fulfill all righteousness (Matthew 3:15) in order to accomplish God's mission and advance God's work in the world; (3) to inaugurate his public ministry to bring the message of salvation to all people; (4) to show support for John's ministry; (5) to identify with the penitent people of God, thus with humanness and sin; and (6) to give an example to follow. John's baptism for repentance was different from Christian baptism in the church. Paul had John's followers baptized again (see Acts 19:2-5).

Jesus, the perfect human being, didn't need baptism for sin, but he accepted baptism in obedient service to the Father. God showed his approval, for *as he was praying, heaven was opened.* Most likely, only Jesus saw heaven opened (see Matthew 3:16). The opening of the heavens is a powerful metaphor for the in-

breaking of God's kingdom into this world through Jesus (see
Ezekiel 1:1; John 1:51; Acts 7:56; Revelation 19:11). It was as if
the heavens rolled back to reveal the throne of God (Isaiah 63:19–
64:2).

After the heavens opened, *the Holy Spirit descended on
[Jesus] in bodily form like a dove*. According to John 1:29-34,
the act of the Holy Spirit coming down from heaven like a dove
revealed to John the Baptist that Jesus was the Messiah. This signaled that Jesus was the Messiah and that the age of the Spirit predicted by the prophets was formally beginning (Isaiah 61:1). John
knew that the Messiah would come, but
it is uncertain when he knew that his
cousin, Jesus, was the one. The church
uses the dove as a symbol for the Holy
Spirit; however, the bird itself was not
important. The descent of the Spirit
"like" (or "in the form of") a dove
emphasized the way the Holy Spirit

> Remember, Christ was
> not a deified man, neither
> was he a humanized God.
> He was perfectly God and
> at the same time perfectly
> man.   *C. H. Spurgeon*

related to Jesus. The descending Spirit portrayed a gentle, peaceful, but active presence coming to anoint Jesus. It was not that
Jesus needed to be filled with the Spirit (as if there were any lack
in him) because he was "from the Holy Spirit" (1:35) since his
conception. Rather, this was Jesus' royal anointing (see Isaiah
11:2; 42:1). The Holy Spirit's appearance in the form of a dove
showed that God's plan for salvation was centered in Jesus. He
was the perfect human who didn't need baptism for repentance,
but he was baptized anyway.

The Spirit descended and *a voice came from heaven* proclaiming the Father's approval of Jesus as his divine Son: *You are my
Son, whom I love*. In Greek, the literal translation of this is, "As
for you, you are my Son, the beloved one." While all believers
would eventually be called "sons of God" (or "children of God"),
Jesus Christ has a different, unique relationship with the Father;
he is the one unique Son of God. The words "with you I am well
pleased" mean that the Father takes great pleasure in the Son.
The verb in Greek conveys that God's pleasure in the Son is constant. He has always taken pleasure in his Son.

The words spoken by the voice from heaven echo two Old Testament passages. First, Psalm 2:7, "He said to me, 'You are my Son'"
(NIV). Psalm 2 is a messianic psalm that describes the coronation of
Christ, the eternal King. The rule of Christ described in the psalm
will begin after his crucifixion and resurrection and will be fulfilled
when he comes to set up his kingdom on earth. Second, Isaiah 42:1,
"Here is my servant, whom I uphold, my chosen one in whom I
delight" (NIV). Isaiah 42:1-17 describes the Servant-Messiah who

would suffer and die as he served God and fulfilled his mission of atoning for sin on behalf of humanity. Thus, in the two phrases spoken, the voice from the throne of heaven described both Jesus' status as the Servant who would suffer and die for all people, and as the King who would reign forever.

Jesus did not *become* the Son or the Messiah at this baptism. Jesus already had his divinity from eternity past. The opened heavens, the dove, and the voice revealed to John the Baptist (and to readers of this story) that Jesus was God's Son, come to earth as the promised Messiah to fulfill prophecy and bring salvation to all who believe.

In 3:21-22, all three persons of the Trinity are named as present and active. The doctrine of the Trinity, which was developed much later in church history, teaches that God is three persons and yet one in essence. God the Father speaks; God the Son is baptized; God the Holy Spirit descends on Jesus. God is one, yet in three persons at the same time. This is one of God's incomprehensible mysteries. Other Bible references that speak of the Father, Son, and Holy Spirit are Matthew 28:19; John 15:26; 1 Corinthians 12:4-13; 2 Corinthians 13:13; Ephesians 2:18; 1 Thessalonians 1:2-5; and 1 Peter 1:2.

TWO IN ONE

Theologians have long been troubled by Jesus' allowing himself to be baptized by John. After all, baptism was for sinners. Why did Jesus agree to undergo baptism? He did it because he is both God and man—in identifying with people, he underwent their baptism; in his role as God, he both gives the Holy Spirit and receives the anointing of the Spirit as the one and only Son, in whom the Father is well pleased. God and man, two natures in one Person. He gives the Holy Spirit and life, as only God can; he undergoes baptism and even death, as only a human can. He represents the sacrifice for sins before the Father, and he communicates the Father's love. When you are hurting, depressed, broken, remember: you have a Savior who understands your humanity. When you sin, remember: He has paid the price for your disobedience.

THE ANCESTORS OF JESUS / 3:23-38 / 3

Although many Bible readers either skip over the extensive genealogies in the Bible or read through them quickly (Genesis 4–5; 1 Chronicles 1–9), it is important to pause at these genealogies and recognize their significance. Unlike Matthew, who provides a genealogy to Abraham (Matthew 1:1-17), Luke provides a genealogy that reaches back to the beginning of human history—to Adam himself (3:38). This is the point: Jesus is not only the fulfillment of the promises given to Abraham (3:34) and to King David (3:31) but also the embodiment of perfect humanity. This point would have been significant to Luke's Gentile reader, Theophilus (1:1), and is highlighted in the next section, the temptation of Jesus. Yet at the same time, Luke accurately wrote that Jesus was more than Joseph's son: people "thought" Jesus was the son of Joseph, when actually he was God's "Son" (3:22-23). Luke skillfully placed the two ideas right next to each other, confronting readers with the truth that Jesus is completely divine and completely human—a perfect exemplar for all people.

3:23 **Now Jesus himself was about thirty years old when he began his ministry.**[NIV] Jesus *began his ministry* at the time when he was baptized by John (3:21-22). He was *about thirty years old* at that time. Thirty was the prescribed age for priests to begin their ministry (Numbers 4:3). Joseph was thirty years old when he began serving the king of Egypt (Genesis 41:46), and David was thirty years old when he began to reign over Judah (2 Samuel 5:4). Age thirty, then, was a good time to begin an important task in the Jewish culture.

WAITING ON GOD
Imagine the Savior of the world working in a small-town carpenter's shop until he was thirty years old! It seems incredible that Jesus would have been content to remain in Nazareth all that time, but he patiently trusted the Father's timing for his life and ministry. Like Jesus, believers need to resist the temptation to jump ahead before receiving the Spirit's direction. Are you waiting and wondering what your next step should be? Don't jump ahead—trust God's timing. In the meantime, do what he wants you to do, right where you are.

He was the son, so it was thought, of Joseph, the son of Heli.[NIV] The Old Testament contains several genealogies: See Genesis 5; Ruth 4:18-22; and 1 Chronicles 1–9. Matthew included a genealogy of Jesus at the very beginning of his Gospel because his Jewish audience would have wanted to know Jesus' heritage. A person's family line proved his or her standing as one of God's chosen people, so Matthew showed that Jesus was a descendant of Abraham, the father of all Jews, and a direct descendant of David, fulfilling Old Testament prophecies about the Messiah's line.

There appear to be differences between Luke's and Matthew's genealogies. Some differences can be explained by Matthew's omitting names in order to achieve a symmetry of three sets of fourteen generations (see Matthew commentary for explanation). Not every single person had to be included in a genealogy—the words "son of" could also mean "descendant of." Luke most likely was tracing Jesus' natural human ancestry through Joseph, while Matthew was focusing on the legal and royal names to emphasize the succession of the throne of David and Jesus' arrival as the promised King. Matthew stressed Israelite history. Luke's longer genealogy traced Jesus' ancestry through David's son, Nathan, not through Solomon, as Matthew did. Matthew also included the names of four women, which Luke did not. Matthew's genealogy begins with Abraham and moves forward to Jesus, showing that Jesus is related to all Jews (Matthew 1). Luke's genealogy begins with Jesus and goes backward to Adam, showing that Jesus is related to all human beings.

Why does Luke give a genealogy at all? To his Gentile audience, it would have had little significance—not nearly as important as to the Jews to whom Matthew was writing. Luke probably included his genealogy to show that Jesus was a man, not a god or a demigod. His story is unlike those of the Greek and Roman gods of mythology. Luke presented a human, descended from the first human, who came to be by God's will alone. This is consistent with Luke's picture of Jesus as the Savior of the whole world.

While it is impossible to completely harmonize the genealogies recorded by Matthew and Luke, believers can trust, as they can with all Scripture, that this is factual information obtained from different sources. Luke would have had no reason to include a false genealogy, for it would have been refuted quickly and would have ruined his purpose to give a "carefully investigated" and "orderly account" of Jesus' life (1:3 NIV). If there had been no information on Jesus' heritage other than what Matthew wrote, Luke would have been content to do without a genealogy. While most of Matthew's names can be found in the Old Testament, Luke's names came from other sources, perhaps personal interviews or written registries of the day.

Luke's genealogy begins by saying that Jesus *was the son, so it was thought, of Joseph, the son of Heli.* Genealogies were always traced through the fathers, so Luke begins with the man who was "thought" to be Jesus' father, Joseph. Although God was Jesus' Father, God had a reason for placing him in this particular line with Mary as his mother and Joseph as his legal father.

According to Matthew 1:16, Joseph's father was Jacob. The

answer to this apparent discrepancy may lie in the ancient custom of "levirate marriage" by which the widow of a childless man could marry his brother. A son born to that union would be considered the son of the deceased man. Heli and Jacob may have been half brothers—same mother but different fathers. One may have died and the other married his widow. So depending on which line of the genealogy was to be followed, the name of the actual or legal father would be used.

3:24-25 The son of Matthat, the son of Levi, the son of Melki, the son of Jannai, the son of Joseph, the son of Mattathias, the son of Amos, the son of Nahum, the son of Esli, the son of Naggai.[NIV] Nothing is known of these persons. They should not be confused with Old Testament people with the same names.

3:26-27 The son of Maath, the son of Mattathias, the son of Semein, the son of Josech, the son of Joda, the son of Joanan, the son of Rhesa, the son of Zerubbabel, the son of Shealtiel, the son of Neri.[NIV] There is Old Testament information on *Zerubbabel,* who was born in Babylon during the Jewish captivity there and then returned to Judah under the decree of Cyrus (Ezra 1:1–2:2). He led the first group of Jewish exiles back to Jerusalem and oversaw the rebuilding of God's temple. The Old Testament often lists him as Zerubbabel, *son of Shealtiel* (see, for example, Ezra 3:2, 8; 5:2; Nehemiah 12:1).

3:28-29 The son of Melki, the son of Addi, the son of Cosam, the son of Elmadam, the son of Er, the son of Joshua, the son of Eliezer, the son of Jorim, the son of Matthat, the son of Levi.[NIV] Nothing is known of any of these people. They should not be confused with Old Testament people with the same names.

3:30-31 The son of Simeon, the son of Judah, the son of Joseph, the son of Jonam, the son of Eliakim, the son of Melea, the son of Menna, the son of Mattatha, the son of Nathan, the son of David.[NIV] The mention of *David* brings the line of Jesus Christ directly back to the great king of Israel to whom the promise of an eternal kingdom had been made: "Your house and your kingdom will endure forever before me; your throne will be established forever" (2 Samuel 7:16 NIV). David's story is recorded in 1 Samuel 16—1 Kings 2 (also 1 Chronicles 11–29). David himself was seen as an archetype of the coming Messiah-King (Isaiah 9:6-7; 11:1-2; Ezekiel 34:23-24; 37:24-25). David's most famous son, Solomon, who sat on the throne, is referenced in Matthew's genealogy. Luke, however, has been tracing, up to this point, David's line through his third son, *Nathan.*

3:32-33 **The son of Jesse, the son of Obed, the son of Boaz, the son of Salmon, the son of Nahshon, the son of Amminadab, the son of Ram, the son of Hezron, the son of Perez, the son of Judah.**[NIV] *Jesse* had several sons, one of whom had been anointed by the prophet Samuel to be the next king of Israel after King Saul (see 1 Samuel 16:5-13). The book of Ruth tells the story of *Boaz* and a young woman named Ruth, who had come to Israel from the nearby nation of Moab. Boaz married Ruth, and they became the parents of *Obed* (Ruth 4:13-17). Obed later became the father of Jesse (Ruth 4:21-22). See also 1 Chronicles 2:12.

Salmon is mentioned again only in the genealogy in Ruth 4:18-22. *Nahshon* and *Amminadab* are mentioned in Exodus 6:23—Amminadab's daughter and Nahshon's sister, Elisheba, married Aaron, who became Israel's high priest. Mentioned in Numbers 1:7, Nahshon was chosen to help Aaron number the men of Israel who could fight in the army. Then in Numbers 2:3, Nahshon is called "the leader of the people of Judah," meaning that he was in charge of that tribe. He also was in charge of bringing an offering for the dedication of the altar in God's tabernacle—and he brought his offering on the first day (Numbers 7:12-17). These men are also listed in 1 Chronicles 2:10-11.

Not much is known about *Ram* and *Hezron.* Hezron is mentioned in Genesis 46:12; Numbers 26:21; and 1 Chronicles 2:5. Ram (or Aram) is mentioned in Ruth 4:19; 1 Chronicles 2:9-10.

Judah, one of Jacob's sons, was patriarch of the tribe of Judah. His story is told in Genesis 29:35–50:26. He actually had twin sons named *Perez* and Zerah (see also 1 Chronicles 2:4). Matthew records the name of their mother, Tamar, to whom Judah was not married. Judah's sons were borne by Tamar, who had prostituted herself to her father-in-law (she had been the wife of one of Judah's sons). The story of Judah and Tamar is told in Genesis 38—an intriguing tale of evil, judgment, lies, deceit, and ultimate vindication. The line tracing Perez to King David is also recorded in Ruth 4:12, 18-22. Despite Judah's character flaws, God had promised that the royal line would continue through him. In Jacob's blessing upon Judah, he had said, "The scepter shall not depart from Judah, nor the ruler's staff from between his feet" (Genesis 49:10 NRSV). King David was from the tribe of Judah (2 Samuel 2:4; 1 Chronicles 28:4).

3:34-35 **The son of Jacob, the son of Isaac, the son of Abraham, the son of Terah, the son of Nahor, the son of Serug, the son of Reu, the son of Peleg, the son of Eber, the son of Shelah.**[NIV] Judah had been one of the twelve sons of *Jacob.* Jacob had many

sons by his wives Rachel and Leah, including Joseph, whose coat
of many colors caused great envy among his older brothers.
Jacob's twelve sons became the twelve tribes of Israel (see Genesis 49:1-28). Jacob's story is told in Genesis 25–50.

Jacob was *the son of Isaac.* He had been the miracle child,
born to Abraham and Sarah in their old age, through whom God
had promised Abraham, "I will make you into a great nation . . .
and all peoples on earth will be blessed through you" (Genesis
12:2-3 NIV). The line of Jesus would naturally go back through
Isaac, this promised son. Jesus would ultimately fulfill God's
promise to Abraham. Isaac's story is told in Genesis 17:15–35:29.

Abraham was the recognized father of the Jewish nation. Abraham was called by God, received God's covenant promises, and
believed the Lord—so "the LORD reckoned it to him as righteousness" (Genesis 15:6 NRSV). His story is told in Genesis 11–25.
(He is also mentioned in Exodus 2:24; Acts 7:2-8; Romans 4;
Galatians 3; Hebrews 2; 6–7; 11.)

These three men—Abraham, Isaac, and Jacob—are often
named together as the "patriarchs," fathers of the nation and
receivers of God's covenant (see 13:28; Genesis 50:24; Exodus
3:16; 33:1; Numbers 32:11; Deuteronomy 1:8; 6:10; 9:5, 27;
29:13; 30:20; 34:4; 2 Kings 13:23; Jeremiah 33:26; Matthew
8:11; Acts 3:13; 7:32).

For the names listed from *Terah* through *Arphaxad* (3:36),
Luke seems to have drawn upon Genesis 11:10-26 and 1 Chronicles 1:24-27. Terah, father of Abraham, first took his family to
Haran. There, God had called Abraham to travel to the land that
would be given to his descendants. Apart from the listing of these
names in the Old Testament passages noted above, nothing else is
known of these men.

**3:36-37 The son of Cainan, the son of Arphaxad, the son of Shem, the
son of Noah, the son of Lamech, the son of Methuselah, the
son of Enoch, the son of Jared, the son of Mahalalel, the son
of Kenan.**[NIV] *Cainan* and *Arphaxad,* as noted in 3:34-35, are
known only from the Old Testament passages that list their
names. Arphaxad was the third *son of Shem.* Shem was one of the
three sons of Noah from whom the Jews were descended. *Noah,*
by his righteousness, spared his family from the Flood that
destroyed the earth (see Genesis 6–9). His sons and their wives
repopulated the earth after the Flood. Noah's father was *Lamech*
(see Genesis 5:25, 28; 1 Chronicles 1:3). *Methuselah* reportedly
lived 969 years, the longest anyone has ever lived (see Genesis
5:27; 1 Chronicles 1:3). *Enoch* was a righteous man who did not
die but was taken up to heaven after walking with God for 365

img_1Icon showing a pine tree with a sunburst below it

years (Genesis 5:23-24; Jude 14). For *Jared,* see Genesis 5:15;
1 Chronicles 1:2. *Mahalalel* is also mentioned in Genesis 5:13
and 1 Chronicles 1:2. For *Kenan,* see Genesis 5:9; 1 Chronicles
1:2.

**3:38 The son of Enosh, the son of Seth, the son of Adam, the son of
God.**[NIV] For the record of *Enosh,* see Genesis 4:26; 5:6; and
1 Chronicles 1:1. *Seth* was born to Adam and Eve after Cain
killed Abel (Genesis 4:25). *Adam,* the first man, fathered the
entire human race. Luke called him *the son of God.* While Jesus
is God's true and only Son, all of the human race are considered
sons of God because they were created by him and owe their
very existence to his divine will.

Luke accomplished his goal for this genealogy—to establish
for his Gentile readers Jesus' direct connection, not only with the
promises recorded in the Jewish Scriptures, but also with the
entire human race. Jesus came for all people.

THE REAL THING
Why would Luke take this much space in a document of this
length to talk about Jesus' ancestry? Several competing ideas
have been suggested, but one thing seems clear: Luke, the
careful historian, was anchoring Jesus in history. He (Jesus)
was not some mystical figure who appeared on the scene for a
while, said and did some remarkable things, and then faded
into the mist. He was a Jew, born in Bethlehem of Judea to a
Jewish couple, Joseph and Mary. He was born "when the
fullness of time had come" (Galatians 4:4 NRSV), and he died
very publicly one Friday outside Jerusalem. The Christian
Messiah is not merely a literary or philosophical character. He
is a real person, a real man, someone who understands what it
is like to be human. When you pray, you don't have to wonder
whether or not he understands. He does.

LUKE 4

The purpose of this section was to prove that Jesus was the Son of God by defeating Satan in open combat. No argument or temptation could daunt the Lord Jesus. This temptation by Satan also reveals that though Jesus was human and subject to human temptations, he was perfect because he overcame all the temptations that Satan presented to him. The story of Jesus' temptation is an important demonstration of his power and sinlessness. He faced temptation and did not give in. His followers should trust in him as they face temptations that will test their faithfulness to God.

Studying this account of Jesus' temptation can help believers better understand their temptations and how to overcome them. Note that this episode began with the Spirit's guidance. God's leading does not always guarantee safe circumstances, free from all temptations. God's Spirit will lead believers, as he led Jesus, into the places that will test and stretch their faith. Through these crucibles of life, believers' character and faith in God will be refined so that God can use them more effectively to advance the cause of Christ here on earth. As God's Spirit leads them, believers can fully expect to be tempted by Satan and to be exposed to the wilderness of the world with both its wonders and its dangers.

4:1-2 Then Jesus, full of the Holy Spirit, left the Jordan River. He was led by the Spirit to go out into the wilderness, where the Devil tempted him for forty days. He ate nothing all that time and was very hungry.^NLT The word "then" picks up the story from 3:22. The *Holy Spirit* sent Jesus to be baptized by John in the Jordan River. Jesus *left the Jordan River . . . to go out into the wilderness.* Jesus took the offensive against the enemy, *the Devil,* by going into the wilderness to face temptation. In the Old Testament, the "wilderness" (or "desert") was a desolate and danger-

> Temptation is not sin; it is the call to battle.
> *Frederick P. Wood*

ous place where wild animals lived (see, for example, Isaiah 13:20-22; 34:8-15).

The word "Devil" in Greek means "accuser"; in Hebrew, the

word "Satan" means the same. The devil, who tempted Adam and Eve in the Garden, also tempted Jesus in the wilderness. Satan is a real being, a created yet rebellious fallen angel, and not a symbol or an idea. He constantly fights against God and those who follow and obey God. Satan is not omnipresent, nor is he all-powerful. Through the evil spirits under his dominion, Satan works everywhere, attempting to draw people away from God and into his own darkness. His power and his goals should not be taken lightly, yet believers are already assured of victory. Jesus' dealings with Satan in these temptations provide insight into how to deal with Satan's proddings.

Satan had succeeded in getting Adam and Eve to sin, and he hoped to succeed with Jesus too. The verb "to be tempted" describes continuous action, and Jesus was tempted constantly during the forty days. The word "tempted" means "to put to the test to see what good or evil, strengths or weaknesses, exist in a person." The Spirit compelled Jesus into the wilderness where God put Jesus to the test—not to see if Jesus was ready, but to *show* that he was ready for his mission. Satan, however, had other plans; he hoped to thwart Jesus' mission by tempting him to do evil. Satan tried to get Jesus to declare his kingship prematurely, to take his messianic power into his own hands, and to forsake his Father's will. If Jesus had given in, his mission on earth—to die for sin and give people the opportunity to have eternal life—would have been lost. For more on Satan, see 10:18; 1 Chronicles 21:1; Job 1–2; Zechariah 3:1-2; Revelation 20.

Why was it necessary for Jesus to be tempted? First, temptation is part of the human experience. For Jesus to be fully human, he had to face temptation (see Hebrews 4:15). Second, Jesus had to undo Adam's work. Adam, though created perfect, gave in to temptation and passed sin on to the whole human race. Jesus, by contrast, resisted Satan. His victory offers salvation to Adam's descendants (see Romans 5:12-19).

The devil's temptations focused on three crucial areas: (1) physical needs and desires, (2) possessions and power, and (3) pride (see 1 John 2:15-16 for a similar list). This temptation by the devil shows that Jesus was human, and it gave Jesus the opportunity to reaffirm God's plan for his ministry. It also provides an example to follow during temptation. Jesus' temptation was an important demonstration of his sinlessness. He faced temptation and did not give in.

This temptation lasted *for forty days*. The number forty, significant in Scripture, brings to mind the forty days of rain in the great Flood (Genesis 7:17), the forty days Moses spent on Mount Sinai (Exodus 24:18), the forty years of Israel's wandering in the wil-

derness (Deuteronomy 29:5), the forty days of Goliath's taunting
of Israel prior to David's victory (1 Samuel 17:16), and the forty
days of Elijah's time of fear in the wilderness (1 Kings 19:8). In
all those situations, God worked in his people, preparing them for
special tasks.

During those forty days, Jesus *ate nothing.* So at the end of this
forty-day fast, Jesus obviously would have been *very hungry.*
Jesus' status as God's Son did not make this fast any easier; his
physical body suffered the severe hunger and pain of going without sustenance. The three temptations recorded here occurred
when Jesus was at his most physically weakened state. But Satan
could not weaken Jesus spiritually.

THE HOLY SPIRIT'S LEADING
Some Christians feel that the Holy Spirit will lead them always
"beside quiet waters" (Psalm 23:2 NIV). But that is not
necessarily true. He led Jesus into the wilderness for a long
and difficult time of testing, and he may also lead believers into
difficult situations. When facing trials, first make sure you
haven't brought them on yourself through sin or unwise
choices. If you find no sin to confess or unwise behavior to
change, then ask God to strengthen you for your test. Finally,
faithfully follow wherever the Holy Spirit leads.

**4:3 The devil said to him, "If you are the Son of God, command
this stone to become a loaf of bread."**NRSV On the surface, this
might seem to be a fairly harmless act, even a compassionate suggestion on the devil's part. Jesus was very hungry, so why not use
the resources at his command and make himself a loaf of bread
from a stone? In this case, however, the sin was not in the act but
in the reason behind it. The devil was trying to get Jesus to take a
shortcut, to solve his immediate problem at the expense of his
long-range goals, to seek comfort at the sacrifice of his discipline. Satan often works that way—persuading people to take
action, even right action, for the wrong reason or at the wrong
time. The fact that something is not wrong in itself does not mean
that it is good for someone at a given time. Many people sin by
attempting to fulfill legitimate desires outside of God's will or
ahead of his timetable.

Satan phrased his temptation in an interesting manner. He said,
"If you are the Son of God." The word "if" did not imply doubt;
both Jesus and Satan knew the truth. Instead, Satan was tempting
Jesus with his own power. If indeed Jesus was the Son of the one
true, all-powerful God, then Jesus certainly could *command this
stone to become a loaf of bread* if he so chose in order to satisfy

his hunger. "God's powerful Son ought not go hungry," Satan suggested. Satan did not doubt Jesus' sonship or his ability to turn stones to bread. Instead, he wanted Jesus to use his power in the wrong way at the wrong time—to use his position to meet his own needs rather than to fulfill his God-given mission. In later miracles Jesus did supply baskets full of bread, but he supplied them for a hungry crowd, not to satisfy himself. And he did the miracles according to God's perfect timing for God's purposes as part of his mission (see 9:10-17).

DILEMMA OF DOUBT
Satan may tempt believers to doubt Christ's true identity. He knows that once they begin to question whether or not Jesus is God, it's far easier to get them to do what he wants. Times of questioning can help believers sort out their beliefs and strengthen their faith, but those times can also be dangerous. If you are dealing with doubt, realize that you are especially vulnerable to temptation. Even as you search for answers, protect yourself by meditating on the unshakable truths of God's Word.

4:4 Jesus answered him, "It is written, 'One does not live by bread alone.'"NRSV *Jesus answered* Satan with what *is written* in Scripture. The words in Deuteronomy describe God's lesson to the nation of Israel:

> *Remember the long way that the LORD your God has led you these forty years in the wilderness, in order to humble you, testing you to know what was in your heart, whether or not you would keep his commandments. He humbled you by letting you hunger, then by feeding you with manna, with which neither you nor your ancestors were acquainted, in order to make you understand that one does not live by bread alone, but by every word that comes from the mouth of the LORD. (Deuteronomy 8:2-3 NRSV)*

In all three quotes from Deuteronomy, found in Luke 4:4, 8, and 12, the context shows that Israel failed each test each time. Jesus showed Satan that while the test may have caused Israel to fail, it would not work with him. Jesus had come to earth to accomplish the Father's mission. Everything he said and did worked toward that goal; nothing could deter or distract him. Jesus understood that obedience to the Father's mission was more important than food. To truly accomplish his mission, Jesus had to be completely humbled, totally self-abased. Making himself bread would have shown that he had not quite set aside all his powers, had not humbled himself, and had not identified completely with the human race. But Jesus refused, showing that he would use his powers only in submission to God's plan and that he would depend on God for his daily needs. Jesus lived not *by bread alone.*

ON THE OFFENSIVE
Knowing and obeying God's Word is an effective weapon against temptation, the only "offensive" weapon provided in the Christian's "armor" (Ephesians 6:17). Jesus used Scripture to counter Satan's attacks, and you can too. But to use it effectively you must have faith in God's promises because Satan also knows Scripture and is adept at twisting it to suit his purpose. Obeying the Scriptures is more important than simply having a verse to quote, so read them daily and apply them to your life. Then your "sword" will always be sharp.

4:5-7 The devil led him up to a high place and showed him in an instant all the kingdoms of the world. And he said to him, "I will give you all their authority and splendor, for it has been given to me, and I can give it to anyone I want to. So if you worship me, it will all be yours."[NIV] The devil arrogantly hoped to succeed in his rebellion against God by diverting Jesus from his mission and winning his worship. "This world is mine, not God's," he was saying, "and if you hope to do anything worthwhile here, you had better recognize that fact." Jesus didn't argue with Satan about who owned the world, but Jesus refused to validate Satan's claim by worshiping him. Jesus knew that he would redeem the world through giving up his life on the cross, not through making an alliance with a corrupt angel.

In Matthew, the order of the second and third temptations is reversed. Matthew has the pinnacle of the temple before this "high place" temptation. The reason for this is unknown.

Satan tempted Jesus to take the world as an earthly kingdom right then, without carrying out the plan to save the world from sin. For Jesus, that meant obtaining his promised dominion over the world without experiencing the suffering and death of the cross. Satan offered a painless shortcut. But Satan didn't understand that suffering and death were a part of God's plan that Jesus had chosen to obey. Satan hoped to distort Jesus' perspective by making him focus on worldly power, not on fulfilling God's plans. In addition, Jesus would have to denounce his loyalty to the Father in order to worship Satan. Satan's goal always has been to replace God as the object of worship.

The obvious impossibility of being able to see *all the kingdoms of the world* from one mountaintop makes little difference to this story, but it supports the view that this experience may have been visionary. The focus is not on the mountain but on those kingdoms that were (and are) under Satan's dominion. Presently, Satan is "ruler of this world" (John 12:31 NRSV). The devil explained, *"I will give you all their authority and splendor, for it has been given to me, and I can give it to anyone I want to."* Satan offered to "give" dominion over the world to Jesus. Satan knew that one day Jesus Christ would rule over the earth (see Philippians 2:9-11). The offer wasn't evil, but it challenged Jesus' obedience to God's timing and will. Satan's temptation was, in essence, "Why wait? I can give this to you *now!"* Of course, he would never really give them away because the offer had a catch: *If you worship me, it will all be yours.*

> If Satan dared to use Scripture for the temptation of our Lord, he will not scruple to use it for the delusion of men.
> *Donald MacLeod*

4:8 Jesus answered him, "It is written, 'Worship the Lord your God, and serve only him.'"NRSV Again, *Jesus answered* Satan with what *is written* in Scripture. For Jesus to gain rule over the world by worshiping Satan would not only be a contradiction (Satan would still be in control), but it would also break the first commandment: "Hear, O Israel: The LORD our God, the LORD is one! You shall love the LORD your God with all your heart, with all your soul, and with all your strength. . . . You shall fear the LORD your God and serve Him" (Deuteronomy 6:4-5, 13 NKJV). To accomplish his mission of bringing salvation to the world, Jesus would take the path of submission to God. He would *worship* and *serve* the Lord alone.

THE PRICE IS WRONG
What would it take for you to "sell out"? What is there in life that would cause you to compromise your faith? Whatever it is—sexual temptation, financial inducement, fear of alienating or offending someone—it will be placed in your path at some point. The enemy wants to destroy believers or at least neutralize them through sin, shame, and guilt. When that temptation rears its seductive head, do what Jesus did: rely on the Word of God, and stand fast in your commitment to worship God, and God alone, above all else. No matter the cost or the sacrifice, no matter how appealing the come-on, believers dare not put anything or anyone in his place.

4:9-11 Then the devil took him to Jerusalem, and placed him on the pinnacle of the temple, saying to him, "If you are the Son of

God, throw yourself down from here, for it is written, 'He will command his angels concerning you, to protect you,' and 'On their hands they will bear you up, so that you will not dash your foot against a stone.'"NRSV Jerusalem was the religious and political seat of Palestine. The *temple* was the tallest building in the area, and this *pinnacle* was probably the corner wall that jutted out of the hillside, overlooking the valley below. The historian Josephus wrote about the enormous height from the top of the temple to the bottom of the ravine below. From this spot, Jesus could see all of Jerusalem behind him and the country for miles in front of him. Whether the devil physically *took* Jesus to Jerusalem, or whether this occurred in a vision is unclear. In any case, Satan was setting the stage for his next temptation.

Jesus had quoted Scripture in response to Satan's other temptations. Here Satan tried the same tactic with Jesus: he used Scripture to try to convince Jesus to sin! Again Satan began with *"If you are the Son of God."* As in 4:3, Satan was not suggesting doubt, but rather he was saying, "If you're God's Son, then certainly God will want to protect you from harm. Thus, *throw yourself down* from this pinnacle so that God will send his angels to protect you." Satan was quoting from Psalm 91:11-12 to support his request. The psalm describes God's protection for those who trust him. Psalm 91:11 begins, "He shall give His angels charge over you"; verse 12 continues, "In their hands they shall bear you up, lest you dash your foot against a stone" (NKJV). Obviously Satan was misinterpreting Scripture, making it sound as though God protects even through sin, removing the natural consequences of sinful acts. Jumping

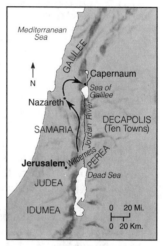

JESUS' TEMPTATION AND RETURN TO GALILEE
Jesus was tempted by Satan in the rough Judean wilderness before returning to his boyhood home, Nazareth. John's Gospel tells of Jesus' journeys in Galilee, Samaria, and Judea (see John 1–4) before he moved to Capernaum to set up his base of operations (see Matthew 4:12-13).

from the roof in order to test God's promises would not have been part of God's will for Jesus. In context, the psalm promises God's protection for those who, while being in his will and serving him, find themselves in danger. It does not promise protection for artificially created crises in which Christians call to God in order to test his love and care. We should not test God, as Jesus will explain (see the following verse).

DANGEROUS KNOWLEDGE
What a sobering thought that Satan knows Scripture and knows how to use it for his own purposes! Sometimes friends or associates will present attractive and convincing reasons why you should try something that you believe is wrong. They may even find Bible verses that seem to support their viewpoint. Study the Bible carefully, especially the broader contexts of specific verses, so that you understand God's principles for living and what he wants for your life. Only if you really understand what the whole Bible says will you be able to recognize errors of interpretation when people take verses out of context to make them say what they want them to say. Choose your Bible teachers carefully. Believers have much to learn from others. Capable and wise teachers often present the broader context to help stimulate growth in Bible knowledge.

4:12 Jesus answered him, "It is said, 'Do not put the Lord your God to the test.'"NRSV Jesus *answered* from Scripture again; however, he used Scripture with an understanding of the true meaning. No matter what the words that Satan quoted may have *sounded* like (that is, they seemed to say that no matter what Jesus did, God would protect him), the facts were that while God promises to protect his people, he also requires that they not put him *to the test.*

Quoting for the third time from Deuteronomy, Jesus explained, *"It is said, 'Do not put the LORD your God to the test, as you tested him at Massah'"* (Deuteronomy 6:16 NRSV). In this passage, Moses was referring to an incident during Israel's wilderness wanderings, recorded in Exodus 17:1-7. The people were thirsty and ready to mutiny against Moses and return to Egypt if he did not provide them with water. God supplied the water, but only after the people had "quarreled and tested the LORD, saying, 'Is the LORD among us or not?'" (NRSV).

Jesus could have jumped from the pinnacle of the temple; God could have sent angels to bring him safely to the ground. But for Jesus to jump from the pinnacle of the temple would have been a ridiculous test of God's power, and it would have been out of God's will. Jesus knew that his Father could protect him; he also understood that all his actions were to be focused on fulfilling his Father's mission.

4:13 When the devil had finished all this tempting, he left him until an opportune time.NIV This would only be the first of many encounters that Jesus would have with Satan's power. Jesus' personal victory over Satan at the very outset of his ministry set the stage for his command over demons throughout his ministry, but it did not dissuade Satan from continuing to try to ruin Jesus' mission. His defeat of the devil in the desert was decisive but not final, for the devil *left him until an opportune time.* Throughout his ministry, Jesus would confront Satan in many forms.

KNOW THE WORD
Jesus was able to resist all of the devil's temptations because he not only knew Scripture, but he also obeyed it. Ephesians 6:17 says that God's Word is a sword to use in spiritual combat. Knowing Bible verses is an important step in helping believers resist the devil's attacks, but they must also obey the Bible. Note that Satan knew the Scriptures, but he failed to obey them. Knowing and obeying the Bible helps you follow God's desires rather than the devil's.

JESUS PREACHES IN GALILEE / 4:14-15 / **30**

Just as God's Spirit had led Jesus into the desert to be tempted (4:1), next the Spirit led Jesus to begin his teaching ministry among the people of Galilee. Throughout this Gospel and the sequel, the book of Acts, Luke pointed out that Jesus and his followers were submitting to the leading of God's Spirit. That submission to God's will and the Spirit's guidance should characterize believers' lives today.

4:14-15 Then Jesus, filled with the power of the Spirit, returned to Galilee, and a report about him spread through all the surrounding country. He began to teach in their synagogues and was praised by everyone.NRSV After the temptation narrative, Jesus, *filled with the power of the Spirit* and freshly victorious over Satan, returned to Galilee, where *a report about him [had] spread.* Luke did not yet mention anything that Jesus did in his ministry, but the other Gospels reveal much that had happened

> There is no freedom from temptation in this life. There was not for Jesus and there is not for us.
> *Leon Morris*

in the interim. Jesus already had his followers, he had turned water into wine (John 2:1-12), and he cleared the temple (John 2:12-25). He had ministered in Samaria (John 4:1-42) and had *returned to Galilee.* No wonder reports had spread.

Jesus spoke often in Jewish *synagogues.* These gathering places for worship grew up during the Exile when the Jews no

longer had their temple. Synagogues were established as places
of worship on the Sabbath and as schools for young boys during
the week. They continued to exist even after the temple was
rebuilt. Any town with at least ten Jewish families could have a
synagogue. The synagogue was administered by one leader and
an assistant. Often the leader would invite a visiting rabbi to read
from the Scriptures and to teach. Thus Jesus, traveling from town
to town, teaching, preaching, and doing miracles, would be a popular person to invite into a town's synagogue. Everyone praised
this new rabbi. His teaching was fresh—as Matthew recorded,
"He taught as one who had authority, and not as their teachers of
the law" (Matthew 7:29 NIV).

JESUS IS REJECTED AT NAZARETH / 4:16-30 / **32**

Jesus' cruel rejection by the people of his hometown in Nazareth
is highlighted to characterize Jesus' initial teaching ministry in
Galilee. Isaiah 61, the passage Jesus read in the synagogue of
Nazareth, speaks of the anointing of the Spirit on a prophet who
would preach the good news of salvation to the poor. Luke has
already described Jesus as being empowered by the Spirit twice
(4:1, 14), so it should be no surprise that the prophet about whom
Isaiah prophesied would be Jesus himself. This inaugural sermon
at Nazareth is not recorded in the other Gospels. Luke begins his
portrayal of Jesus' ministry with this account. It sets the tone for
the importance of social concerns as found in the rest of Luke.

But the announcement of his mission to proclaim the year of
the Lord's favor—an idea reminiscent of the Year of Jubilee, in
which debts were canceled, fields were left unplanted, and slaves
were freed—was met with unbelief. The people not only rejected
Jesus but also tried to kill him, an appropriate response to a false
prophet but not to God's Son (see Deuteronomy 13:5-9).

Jesus accepted the cold skepticism of his hometown friends as
the fate of true prophets—a fate similar to Elijah and Elisha.
Instead of joining the mob in angrily rejecting Jesus, join the few
who believe in Jesus and work to carry out his mission.

4:16 **When he came to the village of Nazareth, his boyhood home,**
he went as usual to the synagogue on the Sabbath and stood
up to read the Scriptures.^NLT Jesus had been on a preaching tour
of Galilee (4:14-15), and at last *came to the village of Nazareth,*
his boyhood home. Although Jesus had been born in Bethlehem
(2:4-7), his parents had fled to Egypt to protect their son from
King Herod (Matthew 2:7-18). After King Herod's death, Joseph

had brought his family back to Israel, to the district of Galilee, to live in a town called Nazareth (Matthew 2:22-23).

The village of Nazareth sat in the hilly area of southern Galilee near the crossroads of great caravan trade routes. The town itself was rather small. The Roman garrison in charge of Galilee was housed there. The people of Nazareth had constant contact with people from all over the world, so world news reached them quickly. The people had surely heard about what Jesus was doing (see 4:14-15).

Jesus *went as usual to the synagogue on the Sabbath.* Even though he was the perfect Son of God, Jesus attended services every week. As a visiting rabbi, Jesus was invited to *read the Scriptures.*

> You can be perfectly free to go to your Bible with assurance that you will find Jesus Christ everywhere in its pages.
> *A. W. Tozer*

The synagogue service usually included recitation of the Shema (Numbers 15:37-41; Deuteronomy 6:4-9; 11:13-21), benedictions, a psalm, a priestly blessing (Numbers 6:24-26), prayers, a reading from the Law (the Torah, Genesis through Deuteronomy) and then from the Prophets, and then an interpretation of the reading. Because there were no permanent rabbis, visiting teachers would often be invited to preach. (The apostle Paul would later benefit from this custom.)

CHURCH INVOLVEMENT

"I don't get anything out of it." "The sermon's too long." "The music's too old." "The building is too cold (or too hot)." How many of these criticisms of the worship service have you heard? How many have you said? These criticisms may have validity, but involvement in worship is not an option for God's people. Luke 4:16 reveals that Jesus was in the habit of attending synagogue services. He was faithful in his participation in worship. Whatever your excuses for not being involved, they are only that: excuses. Find a church you can support with your presence, your gifts, your money, and your time. Make participation in the life of that church as much a part of your life as it was for Jesus in the synagogue.

4:17-21 **The scroll of the prophet Isaiah was handed to him. Unrolling it, he found the place where it is written: "The Spirit of the Lord is on me, because he has anointed me to preach good news to the poor. He has sent me to proclaim freedom for the prisoners and recovery of sight for the blind, to release the oppressed, to proclaim the year of the Lord's favor."**NIV This key passage sets the tone for a key theme in Luke. Jesus was concerned for both the spiritual restoration of people and their actual physical needs. Several parts of the service had already been performed while Jesus sat and worshiped (see commentary on 4:16). After the Law had been read, Jesus was asked to read from the Prophets. Thus, *the scroll of the prophet Isaiah was handed to him.* Scrolls were ancient "books" made of papyrus sewn together to make a long strip that was then wound around sticks at each end. Some scrolls were only a few feet long; others might be thirty-five feet long with writing on both sides. Thus Jesus had to unroll the book by *unrolling* one side and rolling the other side until *he found the place* from which he wanted to read. It is unclear whether Jesus asked for this particular scroll, or whether it was handed to him and then he chose the reading. But the ancient words of hope and restoration came to life on the lips of the one about whom those words had prophesied.

Jesus read from Isaiah 61:1-2. Isaiah's words pictured the deliverance of Israel from exile in Babylon as a Year of Jubilee when all debts were to be canceled, all slaves freed, and all property returned to original owners (Leviticus 25). But the release from Babylonian exile had not brought the fulfillment that the people had expected; they were still a conquered and oppressed people. Isaiah was prophesying a future messianic age, a time when one would come in *the Spirit of the Lord, . . . anointed to preach good news to the poor . . . freedom for the prisoners and recovery of sight for the blind, to release the oppressed, to proclaim the year of the Lord's favor.* This passage offered great expectations to an oppressed people.

The Jews wondered about this passage and what it meant for them. So after reading, **he rolled up the scroll, gave it back to the attendant and sat down. The eyes of everyone in the synagogue were fastened on him, and he began by saying to them, "Today this scripture is fulfilled in your hearing."**NIV As Jesus read this passage from Isaiah to the people in the synagogue, he stopped in the middle of 61:2 after the words "to proclaim the year of the Lord's favor." Rolling up the scroll, he *sat down.* To show respect for Scripture, he had stood as he read; then he sat down, the traditional pose for teaching. Jesus' words shocked his hearers. Commenting on this passage in Isaiah, he said, *"Today this scripture is fulfilled in your hearing."* (The next phrase in Isaiah 61:2, however, is "and the day of vengeance of our God." This will not be fulfilled until Jesus returns to earth again. We are now under God's favor; his wrath is yet to come.)

When Jesus spoke these words, he was proclaiming himself as the one who would bring this good news to pass. He was the "Anointed" One, a king in the line of David, the King through

whom the promises to David would be fulfilled. Jesus had come
to evangelize the poor, proclaim freedom, give sight to the blind,
and release the oppressed. We must not spiritualize away Jesus'
concerns for the poor and physically needy. Neither may we collapse all his words into the single desire for social restoration.
Jesus' ministry, as the promised Messiah, would focus on calling
people back to God—those who saw their need, such as the poor,
the outcasts, the disabled, and the Gentiles. Jesus fulfilled every
prophecy about him, but in a way that many of the Jews were
unable to grasp. They pictured their Messiah as a conqueror who
would free them from Rome. Instead, Jesus was a conqueror who
would free them from sin—the sin that had caused their captivity
and oppression in the first place—and restore them to wholeness.

EXCUSES, EXCUSES
Here are eight common excuses for not helping the poor:
1. They don't deserve help. They got themselves into
   poverty; let them get themselves out.
2. God's call to help the poor applies to another time.
3. We don't know any poor people.
4. I have my own needs.
5. Any money I give will be wasted, stolen, or spent on other
   things. The poor will never see it.
6. I may become a victim myself.
7. I don't know where to start, and I don't have the time.
8. My little bit won't make any difference.
Instead of making lame excuses, ask what can be done to
help the poor. Does your church have programs that help the
needy? Could you volunteer to work with a community group
that fights poverty? As one individual, you may not be able to
accomplish much, but join up with similarly motivated people,
and watch mountains begin to move.

**4:22 All spoke well of him and were amazed at the gracious words
that came from his mouth. They said, "Is not this Joseph's
son?"**[NRSV] The listeners in the synagogue that day were
impressed by Jesus. All that they had heard about him was true
(4:14-15). They *spoke well of him,* meaning that at first they were
impressed at his manner and his teaching. The text also says that
they *were amazed at the gracious words that came from his
mouth.* Jesus' ministry was characterized by grace. His words
were both kind and wise; they were not mere winsome words,
but they were words of God's favor and kindness bestowed upon
his people. Jesus probably said more than just the single sentence
that Luke recorded in 4:21, yet the nature of those words surprised these people, many of whom had known him since he was

a child. Their question, *"Is not this Joseph's son?"* reveals their amazement that this man who had grown up among them was making such claims. This amazement, however, did not give way to faith, as seen in the following verses.

4:23-24 **Then he said, "Probably you will quote me that proverb, 'Physician, heal yourself'—meaning, 'Why don't you do miracles here in your hometown like those you did in Capernaum?' But the truth is, no prophet is accepted in his own hometown."**[NLT] Jesus understood what the people were thinking, so he quoted *that proverb, "Physician, heal yourself."* Nazareth was Jesus' hometown; shouldn't he most certainly take care of all the needs there—even before he did so in other cities? Jesus was right in thinking that the people wanted him to do miracles in Nazareth *like those [he] did in Capernaum.* What had Jesus done in Capernaum? The word had spread around Galilee about Jesus as he visited various towns. He had already healed a government official's son who lived in Capernaum (John 4:46-54). Apparently Jesus had already been through that city and done miracles, just as he soon would do more miracles there (4:33-41). If he were going to have the audacity to say that he was the one about whom Isaiah wrote—recovery of sight, releasing of oppression—then he ought to do so for them.

However, Jesus had not come to Nazareth to put on a show for all his friends and neighbors. In fact, his purpose was quite the opposite, for he understood *the truth* that *no prophet is accepted in his own hometown.* This was certainly true of many Old Testament prophets. Isaiah, Jeremiah, Ezekiel, Micah, and Amos suffered martyrdom. Jesus would illustrate Israel's refusal to accept prophets in his message to follow.

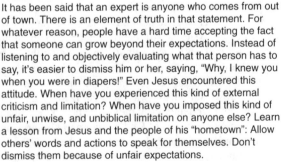

FAMILIARITY BREEDS DISRESPECT
It has been said that an expert is anyone who comes from out of town. There is an element of truth in that statement. For whatever reason, people have a hard time accepting the fact that someone can grow beyond their expectations. Instead of listening to and objectively evaluating what that person has to say, it's easier to dismiss him or her, saying, "Why, I knew you when you were in diapers!" Even Jesus encountered this attitude. When have you experienced this kind of external criticism and limitation? When have you imposed this kind of unfair, unwise, and unbiblical limitation on anyone else? Learn a lesson from Jesus and the people of his "hometown": Allow others' words and actions to speak for themselves. Don't dismiss them because of unfair expectations.

4:25-26 "Certainly there were many widows in Israel who needed
help in Elijah's time, when there was no rain for three and a
half years and hunger stalked the land. Yet Elijah was not
sent to any of them. He was sent instead to a widow of Zarephath—a foreigner in the land of Sidon."NLT Jesus stood in a
long line of people sent by God specifically to Gentiles and
rejected by their own countrymen. Jesus cited the experience of
the prophet Elijah, who was sent, not to any of the Israelite widows, but instead to *a widow of Zarephath—a foreigner in the
land of Sidon.* Jesus' mission to the Gentiles is reemphasized
here. The story is recorded in 1 Kings 17:8-16. When the widow
of Zarephath met Elijah, she thought she was preparing her last
meal. But her simple act of faith produced a miracle. She trusted
Elijah and gave all her food to him. Faith is the step between
promise and assurance. She had faith and received an endless supply of food in time of famine.

GOD USES THE UNLIKELY
Whenever a person with great talents or gifts declares his or
her intention to "go into the ministry," or to use those gifts
somehow in God's service, people are pleased and excited.
They may even say, "What a great impact someone like that
can have for the Lord!" But when another person with lesser
gifts, a less-pleasing personality, or even a checkered past
announces that he or she feels called to serve God, the
response is likely to be less enthusiastic. God, however, seems
to delight in using the unlikely to accomplish his purposes.
Jesus reminded his listeners (in Luke 4:27) that the only leper
healed in Israel at the time of the prophet Elisha was a
detested Syrian; they were outraged. By their response, they
revealed their racist attitude and arrogance. Are there people,
or groups, that you believe are unworthy of being used by
God? The truth is, no one is worthy, but God sees fit to use
people anyway. Don't be too quick to dismiss others because of
their perceived unlikeliness as God's servants.

4:27 "And there were many in Israel with leprosy in the time of
Elisha the prophet, yet not one of them was cleansed—only
Naaman the Syrian."NIV Elijah's successor, Elisha, met with similar guidance from God in one particular instance. While *there
were many in Israel with leprosy,* God sent Elisha to cleanse only
one person, *Naaman the Syrian,* a hated Gentile. Syria was Israel's neighbor to the north. In Elisha's day, Syria was growing in
power and frequently conducted raids on Israel, trying to frustrate
the people and bring about political confusion. Syria had op-

pressed Israel, yet God had done a miracle for a commander in their army. The story is recorded in 2 Kings 5.

Jesus' message to the people was shocking. He did his work through lepers, Gentiles, and women just as Elisha did. Elijah and Elisha condemned Israel for their lack of faith; Jesus, too, confronted their unbelieving hearts. Israel often rejected the prophets, and they were about to reject Jesus. Here Jesus implied that his work would be done outside his homeland among those who believe.

REACTIONS TO JESUS
"How many responses did you have?" People often ask this or questions like it after someone has preached an evangelistic sermon or given an invitation to receive Christ at an outreach event. What they usually mean is, how many people received Christ as Savior? But notice here in Luke 4:28-30 that people can respond to Jesus and to the gospel message in a number of ways, some positive, some not. The people of Nazareth were "filled with rage" when they heard Jesus' message. If someone had asked Jesus, "How many responses did you have?" he would have said, "They all responded!" Be careful about equating "salvation decisions" with ministry success. By that standard, Jesus would have often been considered an abject failure. But by the standards of faithfulness, honesty, integrity, love for the lost, he was the greatest success the world has ever seen. How are you evaluating your own and others' effectiveness in ministry?

4:28-30 **When they heard this, all in the synagogue were filled with rage. They got up, drove him out of the town, and led him to the brow of the hill on which their town was built, so that they might hurl him off the cliff. But he passed through the midst of them and went on his way.**[NRSV] Why did the people of Nazareth react this way? Jesus words *filled* them *with rage* because he was saying that God would reach out to Gentiles as well as to Jews. The Jews expected their Messiah to come and minister to them—free them from oppression, heal them, usher in a glorious kingdom. They also expected that with his coming, the evil Gentiles would be vanquished. Instead, Jesus, who had just claimed to be the Messiah about whom Isaiah prophesied, illustrated his mission by way of the prophets who had shown kindness to Gentiles. Jesus' words implied that his hearers were as unbelieving as the citizens of the northern kingdom of Israel in the days of Elijah and Elisha, a time notorious for great wickedness. People became so angry that they *got up, drove him out of the town . . . so that they might hurl him off the cliff.* They wanted to kill him, but it was not yet Jesus' time to die, so he simply *passed through the midst of them and went on his way.* There is no record that Jesus ever returned to Nazareth. They rejected him; he rejected them.

JESUS TEACHES WITH GREAT AUTHORITY / 4:31-37 / **34**

In this second snapshot of Jesus' ministry in Galilee (the first being 4:14-30), the Gospel presents a glimpse of the cosmic battle that was occurring. A demon challenges Jesus. But Jesus—unruffled—commands the demon to leave. Jesus' teaching style was clearly different than the rabbis, who cited past religious teachers to bolster and support their various interpretations of Scripture. In contrast, Jesus taught straight from Scripture, applying it directly to his listeners' own lives. There was no need to cite past religious authorities because he possessed his own authority, as the Son of God. His fearless confrontation of demonic powers demonstrated his authority and left the crowd questioning: "What is this teaching?" (4:36).

Our familiarity with the words of Jesus should never lull us into thinking that they have lost their power and significance. Jesus is alive, at the right hand of God the Father. He remains as powerful today as ever, and his words—recorded in the Bible—demand complete obedience just as much as they did on that Sabbath day in Capernaum.

4:31 Then he went down to Capernaum, a town in Galilee, and on the Sabbath began to teach the people.^NIV Jesus left his home in Nazareth for good and *went down to Capernaum,* about twenty miles farther north (going "down" in elevation; Nazareth was in the hills, and Capernaum was a fishing town on the Sea of Galilee). Capernaum became Jesus' home base during his ministry in the northernmost region of Palestine, *Galilee.* Jesus had already been in Capernaum (as suggested in 4:23). He probably moved there to get away from intense opposition in Nazareth, as well as to have an impact on the greatest number of people. Capernaum was a thriving town. Because many Roman troops were headquartered in Capernaum, the city contained heathen influences from all over the Roman Empire. Capernaum was a needy place for Jesus to challenge both Jews and Gentiles with the gospel of God's kingdom.

It has already been established that Jesus' custom was to go to the synagogue on the Sabbath (4:16). This was probably the case here, for *on the Sabbath [he] began to teach the people.* The setting was probably much the same as it had been in Nazareth. He would be invited to read a portion of the Scripture and then teach on it. The fact that this was a Sabbath day is important to the event to follow.

AUTHORITY
How many people do you know whom you take absolutely at face value? When they tell you something, you accept it without reservation, right on the spot? Probably not many. People who speak with that kind of credibility are rare today. They were rare in Jesus' time too. When the people in Capernaum heard Jesus speak, they knew they were hearing someone with the authority that comes from that kind of complete honesty and integrity, and their response showed it. They were amazed. People may not respond in amazement when you speak about your faith, but you should strive for that kind of honesty and integrity, knowing that you speak in the name of the one who has absolute authority.

4:32 **There, too, the people were amazed at the things he said, because he spoke with authority.**^{NLT} The people were completely amazed by Jesus' authority in his teaching. The Jewish teachers whom the people were used to hearing usually quoted from well-known rabbis or gave the opinions of predecessors in order to give their words more authority. Jesus did not merely give his opinion; he proclaimed his authority. Jesus answered the questions John the Baptist raised by saying that his miracles showed his authority (7:22-23). In 4:35-37, Jesus rebuked the demon with his word of authority. The people had been without a true prophet of God since Malachi (430 B.C.) and recognized Jesus' intrinsic power displayed in his words and deeds. Because Jesus was the Son of God, he knew exactly what the Scriptures said and meant. He could speak *with authority* because he was the ultimate authority and would use God's Word itself. The people had never heard such teaching, so they *were amazed at the things he said.*

4:33-34 **In the synagogue there was a man possessed by a demon, an evil spirit. He cried out at the top of his voice, "Ha! What do you want with us, Jesus of Nazareth? Have you come to destroy us? I know who you are—the Holy One of God!"**^{NIV} In these verses (4:33-37), Luke portrays Jesus' great battle with Satan and shows Jesus as the victor. This is the first of Jesus' miracles that Luke recorded. Jesus was teaching the people *in the synagogue* on the Sabbath (4:31). *A man possessed by a demon* had also made his way into the synagogue. Jesus' authoritative teaching and the astonishment of the people prompted an outburst by this man, who had *an evil spirit.* Evil (unclean) spirits, or demons, are ruled by Satan. They work to tempt people to sin. They were not created by Satan because God is the Creator of all. Rather, evil spirits and demons are fallen angels who joined Satan in his rebellion and thus became perverted and evil. The evil spirit had entered the man's body, had taken up residence, and controlled him. Though not all disease comes from Satan, sometimes demons can cause a person to become mute, deaf, blind, or insane. In every case where demons confronted Jesus, however, they lost their power. God limits what evil spirits can do. During Jesus' life on earth, demons were allowed to be very active to demonstrate once and for all Christ's power and authority over them.

God's power present in Jesus confronted the power of Satan. The Jews believed that the Messiah would crush Satan and destroy his power. That the spirits feared Jesus demonstrated his power over them. In this showdown, Luke established Jesus' credentials by showing that even the evil spirits recognized Jesus as Messiah. Luke emphasized Jesus' conflict with evil powers to show his superiority over them, so he recorded many stories about Jesus driving out evil spirits. Jesus didn't have to conduct an elaborate exorcism ritual. His word was enough to send out the demons. This shows that Jesus was far more than just a teacher. Jesus' power over demons reveals his absolute power over Satan, even in a world that seems to be in Satan's control. Satan is presently under God's authority; when God chooses to command, Satan must obey. Satan's workings are only within God's prescribed limits; he can do no more evil than God allows. In the end, Satan and all his demons will be tormented in the lake of fire forever (Revelation 20:10).

This demon inside the man *cried out at the top of his voice.* The evil spirit knew two facts—that Jesus had indeed come to *destroy* them (and their power) and that Jesus was *the Holy One of God.* All demons, and Satan himself, knew that Jesus was the Messiah. While the people in the synagogue were astounded at Jesus' teaching and wondered who this man could be, the demon knew. At this time, people believed that to know a person's precise hidden name was to be able to gain control over the person. Thus the demon's first attempt against Jesus was to state his name in public. Their master, Satan, had tried and failed—the demons would try and fail as well.

4:35 But Jesus rebuked him, saying, "Be silent, and come out of him!" When the demon had thrown him down before them, he came out of him without having done him any harm.NRSV

Jesus did not respond to the demon's comment, except to rebuke him by telling him to *be silent.* The word in Greek means "to muzzle." A modern alternative would be "Shut up!"—a colloquial translation that also gives Jesus' attitude toward Satan. Why would Jesus want the demon to be silent (the demon knew more about who he was than the rest of Jesus' audience did)? The demon spoke the truth: Jesus had come to destroy evil, and he was the Holy One of God. Two explanations may help us understand why Jesus commanded the demon to "be silent":

1. Jesus wanted to restrain any enthusiasm for a political messiah. He did not wish to be the people's king in the way they desired, nor did he want to be a military leader.
2. To confess Jesus' deity without a proper understanding of his crucifixion would be partial and invalid. Jesus did not want people to wildly proclaim him to be God's Son unless they understood the meaning of his death for them on the cross. Even Jesus' disciples lacked understanding until his resurrection.

To silence the demon was not enough, for Jesus wanted to free the man possessed by the demon. Jesus commanded the demon to *come out of him.* Jesus didn't need incantations or magic words; his power and authority over Satan and his demons were enough. He simply had to tell the demon to leave, and the demon had no choice. As if to get in the last "word," however, the demon threw the man *down before them.* Mark describes this event, saying, "The evil spirit shook the man violently and came out of him with a shriek" (Mark 1:26 NIV). The demon went, but not quietly. This could have been a severe spasm or a blow that thrust the man to the ground. This behavior reveals the true purpose of demons in their possession of people. Demons want only to do violence and destroy anything made in God's image.

Many psychologists dismiss any account of demon possession as a primitive way to describe mental illness. Throughout history, mental illness has often been wrongly diagnosed as demon possession, but clearly a hostile outside force controlled the man described here.

4:36-37 Amazed, the people exclaimed, "What authority and power this man's words possess! Even evil spirits obey him and flee at his command!" The story of what he had done spread like wildfire throughout the whole region.NLT Jesus displayed power that no one had ever experienced before. No one could perform an exorcism with a simple word. He had *authority and power* so that with his words alone he could make a demon flee in fear.

(For more on Jesus' authority, see 4:32.) This *amazed* the people in the synagogue that day. Jesus' display of his authority in the showdown with a demon caused amazement and even terror in the people who witnessed it.

BACKING IT UP
Imagine you were in your home one day, and a man you didn't know came and said, "You must leave your house at once." You would undoubtedly be suspicious of the person. "Who are you to tell me to leave my own home?" you probably would ask. If he then produced a badge showing that he was an FBI agent, you would be much more likely to comply. You would know that he had the authority to order you to leave. Jesus possessed exactly this kind of authority over the spiritual realm. Luke 4:35 reports him as ordering the demon to be quiet and come out of a man. The demon obeyed, causing great amazement and even fear among the people. Jesus is Lord, even over those who have no love for him at all. Submit your life—every thought, word, action, attitude, relationship—to him. Do what he commands.

Their amazement became headline news as the people left the synagogue, and *the story of what he had done spread like wildfire throughout the whole region.* This captivating new teacher possessed unheard-of power. If they had only ceased being amazed long enough to listen to Jesus' teaching and to understand the Scriptures about him (as the Isaiah passage he had read in Nazareth, 4:17-21), they might have realized exactly who Jesus was and not been so surprised at his power.

JESUS HEALS PETER'S MOTHER-IN-LAW AND MANY OTHERS / 4:38-41 / **35**

After his clash with the demon in Capernaum, Jesus demonstrated his supernatural power to heal the sick by healing Simon's mother-in-law of a fever. Thus, by evening, the sick and demon possessed crowded Jesus, seeking his attention. Almost as an afterthought, Luke noted that Jesus was commanding the demons not to identify him. His goal was not to draw attention to himself but to meet the real needs of others. Your service should be just as genuine as Jesus'. Instead of looking for ways to elevate yourself and receive praise, you should look for ways to empower those in need.

4:38 After leaving the synagogue that day, Jesus went to Simon's home, where he found Simon's mother-in-law very sick with a high fever. "Please heal her," everyone begged.NLT Jesus left the synagogue and *went to Simon's home.* Simon was another name for Peter. Obviously Jesus had met some of the men who would be his disciples. Luke did not write of the meeting, but Matthew and Mark recorded Jesus' call of the first four disciples (Matthew 4:18-22; Mark 1:16-20). This story of Jesus healing Peter's mother-in-law is in all three synoptic Gospels. Mark explains that Jesus, along with James, John, Simon Peter, and Andrew, arrived at Peter's home, where he was living with his wife (mentioned in 1 Corinthians 9:5), his *mother-in-law,* and his brother Andrew. Peter and Andrew had lived in Bethsaida (John 1:44) but must have moved to Capernaum, where they continued their occupation as fishermen.

HEALING
Why did Jesus demonstrate his authority in these different areas—in teaching, over demons, and over disease? There are a number of reasons, including his love for people and his desire to present his "credentials" as Messiah. The case of healing Simon's mother-in-law gives another reason. Jesus healed her in order to enable her to serve others. If you know Jesus and he has truly come into your heart, he has healed you. He has not, however, healed you just to make you whole; he has also healed you so that you might extend his healing touch to others. How is that taking place in your life? What specific ways do you serve? Remember: God has not healed you solely for your own benefit. He has healed you so that you might be a benefit to others.

Simon Peter's mother-in-law was *very sick with a high fever.* There is no mention of a specific illness, but a malaria-type of fever was common to this region because of marshes near the mouth of the Jordan River. The Greek word for "fever" in the noun form is also the word for "fire"; thus, she was burning with a severe fever. Jesus' reputation for healing had spread so much that the people with him knew just what to do. They *begged* Jesus, *"Please heal her."* Jesus had a reputation for miracles involving healing, so they asked him to do this for the sick woman.

4:39 So he bent over her and rebuked the fever, and it left her. She got up at once and began to wait on them.[NIV] Each Gospel presents a slightly different perspective; thus comparable stories in the Gospels often highlight different details. Matthew states that Jesus touched the woman's hand. In Mark, he helped her up. In Luke, *he bent over her and rebuked the fever.* The accounts do not conflict. Each writer chose to emphasize different details of the story in order to emphasize a certain characteristic of Jesus.

In this case, Luke had just recorded the incident where Jesus had "rebuked" a demon, and the demon had left the man at Jesus' command (4:35). Here Jesus "rebuked" the fever, and it too *left her* at his command. Jesus' power and authority were again emphasized as Luke pointed out what Jesus did with only a word.

Jesus healed Simon's (Peter's) mother-in-law so completely that not only did the fever leave, but her strength was restored, and *she got up at once and began to wait on them.* Her healing was so complete it was as if she had never been ill. In fact, she went about serving the meal as she had probably planned. What a beautiful attitude of service she demonstrated! God gives health in order that his people will serve others.

4:40 As the sun went down that evening, people throughout the village brought sick family members to Jesus. No matter what their diseases were, the touch of his hand healed every one.[NLT] The people came to Jesus *as the sun went down* because this was the Sabbath (4:31), their day of rest. Sabbath lasted from sunset on Friday to sunset on Saturday. The people didn't want to break the law that prohibited travel on the Sabbath, so they waited until the Sabbath hours were over before coming to Jesus.

TOUCH
Think of the loneliest, darkest points in your life: an illness . . . the loss of a loved one . . . a broken relationship. During those times, what helped you get through it? Perhaps it was a word of comfort or sympathy. More likely, it was not words at all but just the presence of a friend and his or her human touch. A hug, an arm around your shoulder, or even just a hand laid gently on top of yours—these simple, wordless gestures often are the most meaningful expressions of kindness and compassion. In healing the sick and the demon possessed, Jesus had already demonstrated that he could heal with just a word (Luke 4:39). But Luke 4:40 explains that in Capernaum, Jesus laid hands on all those who came to him for healing. Why? Why not just speak a word and heal the whole crowd at once? Why go to all the trouble of treating each person individually, face-to-face? There must be something very important about human touch, important enough that God would put on flesh and reach out, person to person. Who in your life needs a touch of friendship, understanding, compassion? Go to that person today and touch him or her like Jesus would.

News had spread quickly about Jesus' healing powers, so the people *brought sick family members to Jesus.* The Greek word for "brought," *phero,* means "to carry a burden or to move by carrying." Since there were no ambulance services, many people literally carried the ill to Peter's home so Jesus could heal them. That was another part of the reason for waiting until the end of the Sabbath—it was against the law to carry burdens on the Sabbath. The verb is in the imperfect tense, signifying continuous action. A steady stream of sick and demon-possessed people (4:41) were being carried to Jesus. Luke, the doctor, noted that *no matter what their diseases were,* they came to Jesus, and *the touch of his hand healed every one.* No sickness stumped him; no disease was beyond his ability to cure; no sickness was too disgusting for the touch of his hand.

4:41 **Demons also came out of many, shouting, "You are the Son of God!" But he rebuked them and would not allow them to speak, because they knew that he was the Messiah.**NRSV Jesus healed the sick as well as those who were demon possessed. The *demons also came out of many,* again getting in the "last word" by *shouting* what they knew about Jesus. While their words were true, Jesus *rebuked them and would not allow them to speak, because they knew that he was the Messiah.* There were good reasons for this command to silence: (1) Jesus commanded them to remain silent to show his authority over them. (2) Jesus wanted his listeners to believe he was the Messiah because of his words, not because of the demons' words. (3) Jesus was going to reveal his identity according to God's timetable, and he would not be pushed by Satan's evil plans. The demons called Jesus "Son of God" or "the Holy One of God" (4:34) because they knew he was the Christ. But Jesus was going to show himself to be the suffering Servant before he became the great King. To reveal his identity as King too soon would stir up the crowds with the wrong expectations of what he had come to do.

The knowledge of the demons would soon become an ironic contrast to the misunderstanding of Jesus' own disciples, the fickleness of the crowds, and the stubborn blindness of Israel's own religious leaders.

JESUS PREACHES THROUGHOUT GALILEE / 4:42-44 / 36

Jesus had just spent a Sabbath day in feverish activity—healing the sick and exorcising demons. He had done practically everything except rest. Early in the morning of the next day, he set aside a time of prayer, by himself. He was careful to spend time maintaining his intimate fellowship with his Father. By the time the people found him, he was ready to face the next challenge.

Believers should follow Christ's example by carving out time in their busy schedules for worship and prayer. Ability to serve will be hindered if believers neglect times of spiritual replenishment.

4:42 Early the next morning Jesus went out into the wilderness. The crowds searched everywhere for him, and when they finally found him, they begged him not to leave them.[NLT] "Early the next morning" refers to the hours before the sun had come up because Mark wrote that it was still dark (Mark 1:35). Jesus *went out into the wilderness,* the same kind of place where he had met Satan's temptations (4:1). Luke didn't write this, but Mark recorded that he went alone to a deserted place to pray. During his ministry on earth, Jesus was in constant contact with the Father. Jesus had to get up very early just to get some time alone. If Jesus needed solitude for prayer and refreshment, how much more is this true

> I think the devil has made it his business to monopolize on three elements: noise, hurry, crowds. . . . Satan is quite aware of the power of silence.   *Jim Elliot*

for Christians today? Believers must not become so busy that life turns into a flurry of activity leaving no room for quiet fellowship alone with God. No matter how much you have to do, always make time for prayer.

Apparently the people in Capernaum continued to arrive at Simon Peter's house the next morning hoping to hear more of Jesus' teaching and see him perform more miracles. When Jesus didn't appear, *the crowds searched everywhere for him.* Jesus was the man of the hour, and had done wonderful things in Capernaum. So when the people finally tracked him down, *they begged him not to leave them.* Who would want to lose this kind man who could heal any sickness with just a word or a touch?

PRAYER
Any student of military history will explain that no war has ever been won without sending in the ground troops. But it is also true that air support makes a tremendous difference to the troops on the ground. In the spiritual battle, prayer is like the air support. Why would anyone ever go into battle without that covering? Jesus didn't. Luke 4:42 says that after all the healings in Capernaum, Jesus went out to a place in the wilderness, no doubt to pray and be alone with his Father. It was just as difficult for Jesus to spare the time as it is for you, and just as essential. If you are going to be involved in spiritual warfare—and the Bible teaches that you will be (see Ephesians 6)—then you need your air support.

4:43-44 But he said to them, "I must proclaim the good news of the kingdom of God to the other cities also; for I was sent for this purpose." So he continued proclaiming the message in the synagogues of Judea.^{NRSV} Jesus had been persecuted in Capernaum, but he refused to be deterred from his mission to preach the Good News to as many people as possible. Three key terms describe Jesus' understanding of his mission on earth: *must, kingdom of God,* and *sent.* The sentence Jesus spoke here is unique to Luke; it explains that Jesus' primary mission was to bring people to a place of decision to have faith in God, not merely to remove their pain.

1. The word "must" conveys Jesus' sense of call and urgency.
2. The "kingdom of God" was the core of Jesus' teaching. This is the kingdom where God reigns—it is a present reality and a future hope. Today Jesus Christ reigns in the hearts of believers, but the kingdom of God will not be fully realized until all evil in the world is judged and removed. Jesus came to earth first as a suffering Servant; he will come again as King and Judge to rule victoriously over all the earth. The nature of this kingdom, and those who would become its inhabitants, were key themes in Jesus' messages. The kingdom of God was good news! It was good news to the Jews because they had been awaiting the coming of the promised Messiah ever since the Babylonian captivity. It is good news for people today as well because it means freedom from slavery to sin and selfishness. The kingdom of God is here and now because the Holy Spirit lives in the hearts of believers. Yet it is also in the future because Jesus will return to reign over a perfect kingdom where sin and evil no longer exist.
3. The word "sent" stresses Jesus' understanding of who was in charge. The Father, to whom he had just been talking in the wilderness, had sent him *for this purpose.*

Thus Jesus could not remain in Capernaum healing people. *So he continued proclaiming the message in the synagogues of Judea.* Jesus had the call and the message; he had the power and authority. Knowing exactly what he was to accomplish in his short time on earth, he continued with that "purpose." Wherever Jesus went, he also healed many people and cast out many demons, as he had in Capernaum. These miracles revealed Jesus to be the Messiah for whom the Jews had been waiting. The miracles also demonstrated Jesus' compassion for hurting people. Many people needed to hear Jesus proclaim the good news of the kingdom of God.

According to the parallel account in Mark's Gospel, Jesus left

Capernaum and "traveled throughout Galilee" (Mark 1:39 NIV).
Here Luke wrote that he traveled and taught in Judea. The
Romans had divided the land of Israel into three separate regions:
Galilee, Samaria, and Judea. Galilee was the northernmost
region, an area about sixty miles long and thirty miles wide.
Jesus did much of his ministry in this area, an ideal place for him
to teach because over 250 towns were concentrated there. Judea,
the southern region, included the city of Jerusalem, and John
recorded some of Jesus' ministry in that area. The term "Judea,"
however, could also be used for the entire country (the "land of
the Jews"), and it could be in that general sense that Luke applied
the term here.

LUKE 5

Simon had spent all night casting out nets into the still lake
waters and pulling them back. No fish—time . . . after time . . .
after time. By morning, Simon was tired and frustrated—angrily
washing the nets that had brought in nothing all night.

At this most inopportune time, Jesus called Simon: first asking
to borrow his boat, then instructing him to cast out his nets, and
finally calling him to be a fisher of men. Simon's simple obedience brought abundant blessing—a boat overflowing with fish.
Instead of getting caught up in the details of securing the fish,
Simon realized that he needed more than fish: he needed spiritual
nourishment to restore his sinful soul. Simon was just the type of
person Jesus wanted. A broken spirit and a willingness to obey
gave Jesus the opportunity to mold Simon so that he could be
used effectively by God. Are you facing troubles and difficulties?
Does your hard work never seem to pay off? Let these experiences humble you before God; then, pray that you will allow God
to mold you into a servant for him.

Some scholars consider this incident to be the same as that
which is in Matthew 4:18-22 and Mark 1:16-20, which record
Jesus' first encounter with the fishermen—Peter, Andrew, James,
and John—at the Sea of Galilee. Matthew and Mark then
describe how Jesus called them to follow him. However, other
scholars see Luke as giving an account of Jesus' second call to
these disciples because there are several differences in the
accounts. In Matthew and Mark (1) Peter and Andrew were not
fishing from a boat; (2) Jesus did not enter a boat; and (3) there is
no mention of a great catch of fish. If Luke was recording a second call, the disciples must have gone back to their occupation of
fishing in the interim. Some of the disciples did the same after
Jesus' crucifixion and resurrection (see John 21:1-14).

**5:1 One day as Jesus was preaching on the shore of the Sea of
Galilee, great crowds pressed in on him to listen to the word
of God.**NLT Jesus continued his teaching tour and *one day . . . was*

preaching on the shore of the Sea of Galilee. Word about Jesus
had spread everywhere (4:14), so *great crowds pressed in on him
to listen to the word of God.* The Sea of Galilee (located in the
region of Galilee) is a very large lake of freshwater—650 feet
below sea level, 150 feet deep, and surrounded by hills. It was 13
miles long and 7 miles wide. Jesus could stand on the shore, and
the people could sit on the hillsides to listen. On this occasion,
the crowds were pushing in and around him, eager to hear the
word of God.

**5:2 He noticed two empty boats at the water's edge, for the fisher-
men had left them and were washing their nets.**^{NLT} With the
crowds pressing in, Jesus would be backed right into the lake!
When *he noticed two empty boats,* he had an idea. The text
explains that the reason the boats were empty was that *the fishermen had left them and were washing their nets.* Fishermen on the
Sea of Galilee used nets, often bell-shaped with lead weights
around the edges. Nets had to be kept in good condition, so they
were washed to remove weeds and then mended in preparation
for the next fishing expedition.

The normal fishing boat was not very large—usually sixteen to
twenty feet long—and carried a crew of four men comfortably.
The sail was a large triangle attached to a central mast, enabling
the boat to be operated by the sail or just by oars. Two men usually steered the boat while the other two worked with the nets.
Because the boats were small, they were vulnerable in a storm.

**5:3 He got into one of the boats, the one belonging to Simon, and
asked him to put out a little way from the shore. Then he sat
down and taught the crowds from the boat.**^{NRSV} These fishermen
who were cleaning their nets were probably right next to their boats
on the shore. So when Jesus *got into one of the boats,* he called to
its owner, *Simon* (Peter), *and asked him to put out a little way from
the shore.* From this position, Jesus *sat down and taught the crowds
from the boat.* This allowed Jesus to continue to speak and be heard
as his voice could carry across the water. Sitting down was the preferred teaching position of the rabbis (4:20).

**5:4-5 When he had finished speaking, he said to Simon, "Put out into
the deep water and let down your nets for a catch."**^{NRSV} Jesus
finished the lesson to the crowds and then spoke to Simon, the
owner of the boat. Simon had not yet officially become a disciple
of Jesus (that would happen after this incident, see 5:10-11), but he
knew Jesus. Simon had spoken with Jesus and had even been called
to be a follower (Matthew 4:18-22; Mark 1:16-20), and he had seen
Jesus perform great miracles. Even Simon's own family had bene-

fitted from Jesus' compassion and power (4:38-41). So when Jesus suggested that they *put out into the deep water and let down [their] nets for a catch,* Simon was inclined to take Jesus seriously. Yet Simon was probably bone tired, so he explained, **"Master, we have worked all night long but have caught noth-ing."**[NRSV] Night fishing was very common on the Sea of Galilee. Fishing was usually best during the night while the fish were active and feeding closer to the surface. Also, fish go deeper in the water when the sun gets high, and a net would be of no apparent use. These expert fishermen had *worked all night long* but had returned with empty nets. When Jesus had first met Simon (and Andrew), Jesus was walking along the sea, and they were "casting a net into the lake" (Mark 1:16). At that time, they were in the shallow water and would have been using a circular casting net about fifteen feet in diameter. The fishermen would wade about chest high into the water and throw the net flat onto the water. Lead weights around the edge of the net would cause it to sink around the fish. Then the fishermen would pull on a cord, drawing the net around the fish.

> The Lord always supersedes us. He superseded Peter in his command of the boat, which he had navigated since he was a lad. There is always a testing-point for the soul. Will you surrender the command and let Christ be captain? If so, in the teeth of great difficulties for fish are not caught generally in the glare of day he will fill your boat to the water's edge. He does beyond all we asked or thought.
>
> *F. B. Meyer*

DEEP WATER
Picture the scene: Simon and other experienced, career fishermen have been trying all night to catch fish. They know the lake, and they know their trade, yet they have caught nothing. Jesus, a carpenter, tells them to move out into the deeper water and try again. Simon and the others must have felt like telling Jesus he should stick to building furniture and leave the fishing to the experts . . . but they didn't. Instead, they obeyed him. Have you ever been in a situation where you felt that Jesus couldn't possibly understand your needs? Many acts of service and enterprises for God require moving out into deeper water. Learn a lesson from a bunch of fishermen: Listen to Jesus and obey his commands, however difficult they may be to do.

Simon and his partners had been out all night in the deep water, using a different type of net called a dragnet. This net was about three hundred feet long and eight feet wide. One side had corks to keep it afloat; the other side had lead sinkers. Sometimes the net would be stretched between two boats; then the fishermen would row in a circle to bring the ends of the net together. Other fishermen on the boat would work at drawing in the cord at the bottom and top of the net in order to trap the fish inside. If Simon and the others had been doing this over and over all night long and had *caught nothing,* surely they were tired and frustrated. So for Simon to answer Jesus, **"Yet if you say so, I will let down the nets"**^{NRSV} shows deference to Jesus and budding faith in what Jesus could do.

COMMANDER IN CHIEF
What a sight this must have been—Simon and the other fishermen, rolling their eyes and thinking they were only humoring Jesus. Suddenly they found their boats sinking under the weight of all the fish they caught! When Simon gave Jesus command of his boat, the rewards exceeded his expectations—*two* boats were overflowing with fish.

Following Jesus does not always result in such immediate rewards. But whether the rewards are immediate or eternal, the course of action is clear: unquestioned obedience. What specific areas in your life do not match with God's will? Acknowledge them, confess and repent of them, and ask Christ's help in bringing them in line with his purposes. Give Jesus command of your boat. The rewards may surprise you.

5:6 When they had done so, they caught such a large number of fish that their nets began to break.^{NIV} The last thing Simon had wanted to do was row back out onto the lake and send the net down again, but he had obeyed Jesus. Certainly Simon's instruction to go back out on the lake caused a few grunts, groans, and muffled anger from some of those who had been hoping for breakfast and sleep. The words "when they had done so" occurred after Simon had rounded up his partners and other workers ("they" indicates more than one, see 5:9-10), had put the huge net they had been cleaning (5:2) back into the boat, had rowed out to the deeper water, had spread the net, and then had begun to row and draw the net together. Nevertheless, they had followed Simon's instructions (Simon, in turn, had been obeying Jesus), and "when they had done" all of the above and had drawn the net tight, *they caught such a large number of fish that their nets began to break.*

5:7 A shout for help brought their partners in the other boat, and soon both boats were filled with fish and on the verge of sinking.^{NLT} Simon and his workers began to haul in the catch of fish, but the weight of the nets was too much. So they shouted for help from *their partners in the other boat,* and pulling together they began to dump the fish into the boats. *Soon both boats were filled with fish and on the verge of sinking.* Obviously this was not an ordinary catch by any standards, judging from Peter's response in the following verse.

5:8 But when Simon Peter saw it, he fell down at Jesus' knees, saying, "Go away from me, Lord, for I am a sinful man!"^{NRSV}

Simon had seen people cured and had heard Jesus' teachings, but this miracle reached directly into his life and grabbed him. Simon had been fishing all his life. When he saw what Jesus did in supplying such a huge haul of fish, he recognized Jesus as the Messiah. He had

> The broken spirit and the contrite heart are the abiding marks of the believing soul.
>
> *John Murray*

called him "Master" in 5:5, but here he called him *Lord.* When Isaiah saw a vision of God, he exclaimed, "Woe to me! . . . I am ruined! For I am a man of unclean lips, and I live among a people of unclean lips, and my eyes have seen the King, the LORD Almighty" (Isaiah 6:5 NIV). Simon saw no vision; he saw the living Christ. Recognizing Jesus' identity and thus his inherent holiness made Simon painfully aware of his own sinfulness. Simon knew he was looking at the Messiah, and his sin and unworthiness caused him to fall at Jesus' feet and ask him to leave.

THE FIRST STEP
Simon Peter was awestruck by this miracle, and his first response was to feel his own insignificance in comparison to this man's greatness. Simon knew that Jesus had healed the sick and had driven out demons, but he was amazed that Jesus cared about his day-to-day routine and understood his needs. God is interested not only in saving you but also in helping you in your daily activities. But your first step must be to relinquish command to him.

5:9-11 For he was awestruck by the size of their catch, as were the others with him. His partners, James and John, the sons of Zebedee, were also amazed. Jesus replied to Simon, "Don't be afraid! From now on you'll be fishing for people!" As soon as they landed, they left everything and followed Jesus.^{NLT} Simon's request that Jesus "go away" (5:8) is explained as the reaction to being *awestruck by the size of their catch.* Simon realized that he had witnessed a true miracle and did not feel worthy to be in Jesus' presence or to be the recipient of Jesus' special favor. *The others* *with him* included those who helped on the fishing boats, as well as Simon's *partners, James and John, the sons of Zebedee* (see Mark 1:19, 29). Jesus spoke reassuringly to Simon. Indeed, the central focus of this story is not so much the miraculous catch as it is the picture it gives of Jesus' call to Simon to be his disciple and begin *fishing for people.* While James and John also followed, Luke focused on Simon, as he did in much of this Gospel, most likely because Simon Peter figured prominently in the early church (Luke's second volume is the book of Acts) and because his Gentile readers would have been familiar with him.

When the fishing party landed, *they left* behind the biggest catch they had ever seen *and followed Jesus.* Jesus had not come along with them to give them a good catch and a good day's wage; Jesus had come to change their professions and priorities forever. They understood the picture he had given them of what he was calling them to do, and they left their ships and nets behind and followed.

While Jesus did not require all his followers to leave everything behind, some he called for special purposes. Jesus does require every believer to make him the center of his or her life and rearrange every priority to serve him. It may mean some will leave their professions to follow; others will stay where they are. After knowing Jesus, no one may hold tightly to their possessions. Everything must be made available to his use.

LEFT BEHIND
These fishermen had seen Jesus establish his authority in the synagogue, heal the sick, and drive out demons. With this miraculous catch of fish, he also established his authority in their lives—he met them on their level and helped them in their work. So they left their nets and remained with Jesus. There are two requirements for coming to God. First is recognition of one's sinfulness. Second is the realization of the impossibility of saving oneself. Those who know that they need help and that Jesus is the only one who can help them are ready to leave everything and follow him. Following Jesus means more than just acknowledging him as Savior. It means leaving the past behind and committing the future to him.

JESUS HEALS A MAN WITH LEPROSY / 5:12-16 / 38

After recording the story of Simon's call, Luke placed a story of another person—this time, a leper—who with a spirit of brokenness ran to the mercy of Jesus, literally falling at his feet (5:8, 12).

This story reveals the limitations of Jesus' earthly ministry. Perhaps the greatest handicap that Jesus accepted in coming to earth was to limit his divine nature to space, to time, and to a human body. Jesus was a single individual with divine power in a sea of human needs. Even those he helped, like this man cured of leprosy, hampered Jesus by insisting on telling everyone of Jesus' miraculous power. By so doing, the leper drew attention to the sensational and miraculous aspect of Jesus' ministry and away from the need for repentance and faith that leads to a life of service.

5:12 **While Jesus was in one of the towns, a man came along who was covered with leprosy. When he saw Jesus, he fell with his face to the ground and begged him, "Lord, if you are willing, you can make me clean."**[NIV] This man took a great risk when he *came* near to Jesus because he was *covered with leprosy.* Leprosy was a feared disease because there was no known cure for it, and some forms of it were highly contagious. Leprosy had a similar emotional impact and terror associated with it as AIDS does today. (Sometimes called Hansen's disease, leprosy still exists today in a less contagious form that can be treated.) If a person contracted the contagious type, a priest declared him a leper and banished him from his home and city. This also excluded him from participating in any social or religious activities (according to the law in Leviticus 13–14). The leper went to live in a community with other lepers until the disease went into remission or he or she died. Quarantine was the only way the people knew to contain the spread of the contagious forms of leprosy. Even the mention of the name of this disabling disease terrified people because they were afraid of catching it. Because leprosy destroys the nerve endings, lepers often would unknowingly damage their fingers, toes, and noses. This man with leprosy had an advanced case (he was "covered"), so he undoubtedly had lost much bodily tissue. It was against the law for lepers to enter a town, so either this man met Jesus outside, or he ignored the law and entered the town in order to find Jesus.

Along with being outcasts from society, lepers were also considered "unclean," meaning that they were unfit to participate in any religious or social activity. Because the law said that contact with any unclean person made that person unclean too, lepers were required to call out "Unclean" to keep people away (Leviticus 13:45). People did not want to become ceremonially unclean through any contact with lepers, otherwise they would be unable to worship until the correct cleansing ceremonies had been performed.

That the man *fell with his face to the ground* reveals his desperation and his humility. He believed that Jesus could heal every trace of the disease; he only wondered if Jesus was *willing.* This man wanted to be made *clean*. He wanted to become a person again, to be reunited with his family and community, to be able to worship in the synagogue and temple.

5:13 **Jesus reached out his hand and touched the man. "I am willing," he said. "Be clean!" And immediately the leprosy left him.**[NIV] Lepers were considered untouchable because people feared contracting their disease. Yet Jesus *reached out his hand and touched* the man who was covered with leprosy. Jesus first touched the man. Next he assured the leper that he was *willing* to heal him. Then he spoke the words, *"Be clean."* That Jesus' touch precedes his pronouncement of healing indicates his sovereignty over the Jewish law not to touch a leper (Leviticus 5:3; 13:1-46; Numbers 5:2). In touching the leper, Jesus became "unclean," but he did not worry about becoming ritually unclean when he could reassure this social outcast. Jesus also exposed himself to the disease. Most likely no one had touched this man in years. Jesus' touch showed great compassion. When Jesus spoke the words, *immediately the leprosy left* the man. When Jesus spoke, the man's health was restored completely and instantly. The disease did not go into a type of "remission"—it was gone. The man's becoming "clean" meant that he had his life back. He could return to his community, to his family, and to worshiping in the synagogue.

BEYOND THE LAW
Certain people who are diseased or disabled are considered untouchable or repulsive. Believers must not be afraid to reach out and touch them with God's love. In Jesus' time, the word "leprosy" was used to describe a number of diseases, all of which disfigured the person. Since many of the diseases were contagious, the law of Moses forbade touching a person with "leprosy." But Jesus, confronted with a leper's request for healing, not only granted the request, but actually touched the man. In so doing, he went beyond what the law prescribed. When you are in a situation where the law of God seems to collide with the love of God, do what Jesus did: obey the law of love. In other words, when in doubt, err on the side of compassion.

5:14 **Then Jesus ordered him, "Don't tell anyone, but go, show yourself to the priest and offer the sacrifices that Moses commanded for your cleansing, as a testimony to them."**[NIV] Jesus healed the man but also gave him a warning: *don't tell anyone*. Why would Jesus ask this man not to tell anyone about his healing? Jesus' mission was to preach the good news of the kingdom of God. He did not want the crowds descending on him to see miracles or to benefit from his power. He also may have wanted the cleansed man to not be distracted by talking to people until he followed the law and went to the priest.

The law required a priest to examine a healed leper (Leviticus 14). Then the healed leper was to give an offering at the temple, called the "guilt offering" in Leviticus 14:12. Jesus adhered to these laws by telling the man to *show* himself *to the priest,* thereby demonstrating high regard for God's law. Jesus wanted this man to give his story firsthand to the priest to prove that his leprosy was completely gone. This would allow him to be restored to his family and community. Next the man was to *offer the sacrifices that Moses commanded for your cleansing.* The Mosaic offering was a pair of birds; one was killed over running water while the other, after being dipped in the mingled blood and water, was set free (Leviticus 14:2-32).

The reason? These acts would be *a testimony to them.* Some think that "them" refers to the priest to whom the man would go to show himself. However, there has been no mention of Jesus' disagreement with the religious establishment, so Jesus may have intended this to be a positive testimony to the people who witnessed the healing. The man was not to proclaim his healing, but the priest's pronouncement would testify to everyone that the man had been healed. Most important, however, the testimony would reveal that the one who heals lepers had come. People believed that healing leprosy was a sign of the Messiah's arrival (see Matthew 11:5).

5:15-16 Yet despite Jesus' instructions, the report of his power spread even faster, and vast crowds came to hear him preach and to be healed of their diseases. But Jesus often withdrew to the wilderness for prayer.^{NLT} Mark recorded that the man disobeyed Jesus' warning and "went out and began to talk freely, spreading the news. As a result, Jesus could no longer enter a town openly but stayed outside in lonely places" (Mark 1:45 NIV). Thus, *the report of [Jesus'] power spread even faster.* The healed man's disobedience to Jesus' command, even if from good motives, hindered Jesus' work because the publicity Jesus received severely hampered his ministry in the synagogues. *Vast crowds came to hear him preach and to be healed of their diseases;* Jesus' notoriety as a healer made it impossible for him to teach and speak because people pressed on him, seeking special favors. Instead of enjoying his newfound fame and success (at least according to the world's standards), *Jesus often withdrew to the wilderness for prayer.*

Prayer is a major theme in Luke, which records many instances of Jesus taking time out to pray. He prayed when he was baptized (3:21), when he dealt with the crowds (5:16), and when he was transfigured (9:29). Before choosing the twelve disciples, Jesus spent the night praying to God (6:12). In great times of active ministry and before key events or conflicts, Jesus prayed (23:46). He also taught about prayer in the Lord's Prayer (11:1-4). Jesus taught his followers to make their requests to God in confident trust (11:9-13). Prayers should not be pretentious or hypocritical (18:9-14). Believers should persist in prayer, relying on him, not giving up easily (11:5-8). Believers should also thank God for providing food (9:16).

WITHDRAW TO THE WILDERNESS
Many things clamor for attention, and people often run themselves ragged attending to them. Jesus took time to withdraw to a quiet and deserted place to pray. When facing conflict or troubled times, follow Jesus' clear example. Strength comes from God, and you can only be strengthened by spending time with him.

JESUS HEALS A PARALYZED MAN / 5:17-26 / **39**

The religious leaders, accustomed to giving lip service to the idea of a coming Messiah, found that Jesus threatened their power and prestige. Jesus challenged their authority, questioned their teachings, and trampled on their way of hypocritically practicing religion.

Jesus could have easily focused just on healing and feeding people. There were plenty of diseases to heal and mouths to feed. But Jesus made it clear that healing and feeding were the means, not the ends, of his ministry on earth. He chose a paralyzed man to make his point. Presented with an obvious physical need, Jesus responded by forgiving the man's sins. The religious leaders regarded Jesus' claim as blasphemy because it was commonly known that only God could forgive sins.

Before they could publicly challenge him, Jesus made a second claim: he would heal the paralyzed man instantly. When the invalid leaped to his feet, the people were amazed. They were stunned by what they had seen, but missed what they had heard. The Pharisees were quiet for the moment, but certainly far from silenced.

Now, as then, those who approach Jesus with the demand that he fit their preconceived notions will be disappointed. He did not come to be your ally, but your Lord. What you believe must be conformed to his will, for he will never conform to your beliefs.

5:17 One day as he was teaching, Pharisees and teachers of the law, who had come from every village of Galilee and from Judea and Jerusalem, were sitting there. And the power of the Lord was present for him to heal the sick.^{NIV} This is the first record in Luke of Jesus' interplay with the Jewish religious leaders of the day. Jesus was making headline news in ancient Israel, so obviously those in religious power wanted to see him for themselves. So they came *from every village of Galilee* and from as far away as *Judea and Jerusalem* to listen to Jesus and see if everything they heard about him was true. Mark wrote that this event took place in Capernaum (Mark 2:1).

Two main groups of religious leaders, the Pharisees and the Sadducees, unofficially ran the religious affairs of the country. Although Palestine was occupied by Rome, the Jews had a certain amount of self-government, especially regarding their religion. By far the most influential, the *Pharisees* zealously followed the Old Testament laws, as well as their own religious traditions. They were highly respected in the community. The ancient historian Josephus wrote that there were about six thousand Pharisees. The Pharisees taught the Scriptures and the law to the people, but unfortunately many became so proud of their "righteousness" that they felt set apart from the common people (even their name means "the separated ones"). They pledged to obey every minute detail, not only of God's law, but also of all the traditions and rules for life (over six hundred of these details came to be as important or more important than the word of God in the Torah). Traditions and interpretations often began to take a backseat to the Torah. Jesus attacked the Pharisees' self-righteous attitudes and their hypocrisy in knowing but not living the Scriptures. They looked forward to the Messiah's coming, believing that if all Jews would dedicate themselves to obeying the laws and oral traditions, God would send his Messiah to deliver Israel. But when Jesus came, they could not accept him as the Promised One. Jesus fulfilled every prophecy about the Messiah, but he did not fit the Pharisees' expectations. They became Jesus' chief enemies (and later, Christianity's chief early opposition).

The *teachers of the law* (also called "scribes") were the legal specialists of the day. Many teachers of the law were also Pharisees. They often handled correspondence for people or managed their financial accounts. By the time of Jesus, they had become a fairly powerful class.

These religious leaders spent much time defining and discussing the huge body of religious tradition that had been accumulating for more than four hundred years since the Jews' return from exile. They were so concerned with these human traditions, in

fact, that they often lost sight of Scripture. At this time, these
leaders felt threatened because Jesus challenged their authority—
the people were flocking to him. Matthew recorded the comparison the people made: "When Jesus had finished saying these
things, the crowds were amazed at his teaching, because he
taught as one who had authority, and not as their teachers of the
law" (Matthew 7:28-29 NIV). Jesus had a new and exciting message. He did not despise the common people, as did many of
these religious leaders; he even compassionately touched those
sick and in need while the religious leaders stayed away so as not
to become ceremonially unclean. Jesus was different, and these
religious leaders were trying to find out why.

Pharisees and teachers of the law had arrived to check out Jesus,
and Luke immediately moved to the central point of this narrative,
a healing. *The power of the Lord was present for him to heal the
sick* (for more on Jesus' power, see 4:14; 6:19; 8:44-46). Through
the Holy Spirit, who had been given to Jesus, the power of God
resided in him, which could flow out to those whom Jesus touched.
Jesus would not deny a person who came to him in need. Healing
was supposed to be one of the key signs of the Messiah (4:18-21;
Isaiah 61:1-2). Jesus healed and these religious leaders saw it with
their own eyes, but they refused to believe.

BRING THEM TO HIM
It wasn't the paralytic's faith that impressed Jesus, but the faith
of his friends. Jesus responded to their faith and healed the
man. For better or worse, a person's faith affects others. No
one can make another person a Christian, but a person's
words, actions, and love will give people a chance to respond.
Look for opportunities to bring your friends to the living Christ. It
will often require the same initiative, creativity, and courage to
step out that was shown by these friends.

**5:18 Just then some men came, carrying a paralyzed man on a bed.
They were trying to bring him in and lay him before Jesus.**NRSV
Jesus was teaching (we will soon find out that he was in a building,
5:19) and the building was filled to capacity, with people standing
outside (Mark 2:2). Suddenly there was a rustling at the edge of the
crowd. *Some men* had come, undoubtedly having heard of Jesus'
healing power, *carrying a paralyzed man on a bed* ("bed" being
more like a stretcher). This may have been a small group of men,
more than four, because Mark wrote that some men came, bringing
a paralyzed man who was being carried by four of them. *They were
trying to bring him in and lay him before Jesus.* The men knew that

Jesus could answer their friend's need, and they wanted to gain access to Jesus so he could touch him.

PERSISTENCE
How important is it to you to see your lost friends and family members come to Christ? Most Christians would say it's very important, and they probably pray for them regularly and look for ways to influence them to receive Christ. Luke 5:18-19 tells of some men who were very persistent in bringing a friend to Jesus. They actually took off a section of a roof and lowered their friend through it to where Jesus was. What would you do to introduce someone to Christ? Would you tell your friend about your faith? invite him or her to a worship service or Bible study? pray for him or her daily? How important is it to you to help that person meet Jesus?

5:19 When they could not find a way to do this because of the crowd, they went up on the roof and lowered him on his mat through the tiles into the middle of the crowd, right in front of Jesus.[NIV] The crowd surrounding Jesus was too thick, and *they could not find a way* to get through it and to Jesus. So ingenuity and creativity proved to be the answer. One can picture this group of men standing together trying to figure out plan B. Someone had an idea, so up onto the roof they went. In Bible times, houses were built of stone and had flat roofs made of mud mixed with straw. In addition, some homes had stone slabs underneath the mortar mixture—this was probably the case here, for the text mentions "tiles." Outside stairways led to the roof. These men carried their friend up the stairs to the roof where they took apart as much of the mud and straw mixture and pried up as many tiles as was necessary. Somebody else got some rope and attached lengths of it to each corner of the pallet. Then they *lowered him on his mat through the tiles into the middle of the crowd, right in front of Jesus.* Mission accomplished.

> Faith is a living, daring confidence in God's grace. It is so sure and certain that a man could stake his life on it a thousand times.
> *Martin Luther*

5:20 When he saw their faith, he said, "Friend, your sins are forgiven you."[NRSV] Silence probably filled the room as the first sounds of digging and tile pulling came from above. For several minutes, the crowd probably watched the hole in the roof become larger. This determination to get near Jesus must have surely astonished the religious leaders who had been there that day. These men working on the roof had one mission in mind—to get their friend within Jesus' touch. Certainly Jesus could have healed from a distance, and in other cases he did so. But these men of Capernaum didn't know that. They had seen Jesus' touch heal many of their townsfolk, so they naturally assumed that the way for their friend to be healed was to be touched by Jesus. They acted on that understanding. Yet they would hardly have gone to so much trouble if there had been any doubt in their minds.

Jesus *saw their faith* acted out in their determination. He saw "their" faith, the faith of all the men who came, but he spoke directly to the paralyzed man, saying, *"Friend, your sins are forgiven you."* Jesus spoke first to the man's spiritual condition. All sickness and death are the result of evil and sin in the world. That does not mean that a person's spiritual health can be measured by looking at his or her physical health. It means that every person is sinful and that every person, whether healthy, sick, or paralyzed, needs forgiveness of sins. A healthy spiritual life with God is always far more important than a perfectly healthy body. The man needed spiritual healing, so Jesus forgave his sins. Both the man's body and spirit were paralyzed; he could not walk, and he was not yet one of Jesus' disciples. The man's spiritual state was Jesus' first concern. If Jesus had only forgiven the man's sins and sent him back through the roof, that would have been enough. However, if Jesus had healed his body and had not dealt with his sinful condition, the man would have been ultimately worse off. If God does not heal you or someone you love, remember that physical healing is not Christ's only concern. All believers will be completely healed in Christ's coming kingdom.

TRUE FORGIVENESS

God offers the same forgiveness given to the paralytic to all who believe. The Greek word *aphiemi,* translated "forgiven," means to leave or let go, to give up a debt, to send away from oneself. Forgiveness means that a relationship has been renewed despite a wrong that has been done. But the act cannot be erased or changed. The notion of *aphiemi,* however, goes far beyond human forgiveness, for it includes the "putting away" of sin in two ways: (1) The law and justice are satisfied because Jesus paid the penalty that sin deserved; thus, sins can no longer be held against a believer. (2) The guilt caused by sin is removed and replaced with Christ's righteousness. Believers are so forgiven that, in God's eyes, it is as if they had never sinned. Do you carry a heavy burden for sins you have committed? Confess all to Christ and receive his forgiveness.

He can cleanse your conscience from guilt. He puts away those sins and remembers them no more. Neither should you.

5:21 "Who does this man think he is?" the Pharisees and teachers of religious law said to each other. "This is blasphemy! Who but God can forgive sins?"^{NLT} When the religious leadership, *the Pharisees and teachers of religious law,* heard Jesus tell the paralyzed man that his sins were forgiven, they were shocked. *"Who does this man think he is?"* they asked incredulously. *"This is blasphemy!"* Blasphemy is the act of claiming to be God or to do what only God can do, as well as to curse, revile, or insult the name of God. In Jewish law, blasphemy was punishable by death (Leviticus 24:16). People in Jesus' day took blasphemy very seriously. Even an unproven accusation of blasphemy could prove life-threatening. Innocent persons could be accused, convicted, and killed without having a chance to defend themselves. In such a climate, the charge of blasphemy worked almost as well as a contract for murder.

WHO IS THIS MAN?
The Pharisees—making their first appearance in Luke in this story—are often thought of as the bad guys in the Gospels. And usually they are seen in opposition to Jesus. But one thing can be said in their defense: they took God and their beliefs about him very seriously. When they heard Jesus say the paralytic's sins were forgiven, they understood full well that Jesus was claiming to be able to do what only God could do. They knew he was claiming equality with God—and thus they wondered who would dare to speak such blasphemies. The question was the right one; unfortunately, their answer was dead wrong. They saw the miracle Jesus performed but missed the importance of it. Do you ever get sidetracked or distracted by theological arguments or doctrinal disputes? Theology is important. Doctrine is critical. But the real issue is: Do you believe Jesus is the Christ?

Forgiveness of sins was a sign that the messianic age had come (Isaiah 40:2; Joel 2:32; Micah 7:18-19; Zechariah 13:1), and these lifetime students of God's Word should have known this. In labeling Jesus' claim to forgive sins as blasphemous, the religious leaders showed they did not understand that Jesus is God and that he has God's power to heal both the body and the soul. The offense of blasphemy was a subject of scholarly debate in the first century. Some said that a person had to use the divine name to be accused. These scribes, however, took the assumption of divine prerogatives (*"Who but God can forgive sins?"*) as also constituting blasphemy.

The religious leaders were correct in their statement that only God can forgive sins (Exodus 34:6-7; Psalm 103:3; Isaiah 43:25; Daniel 9:9). Therefore, because only God can forgive sins, Jesus was claiming to be God. Unfortunately, these religious leaders' reaction was anger and hatred, instead of honestly considering that perhaps this man was indeed their Messiah.

5:22-23 **When Jesus perceived their questionings, he answered them, "Why do you raise such questions in your hearts? Which is easier, to say, 'Your sins are forgiven you,' or to say, 'Stand up and walk'?"**NRSV Apparently the religious leaders didn't shout out the questions raised in 5:21, but instead muttered them back and forth among themselves. Jesus did not hear them, but he *perceived their questionings.* This perception was part of his divine nature. While Jesus walked as a human on this earth, he never ceased to be God. When Jesus was born, God became a man. Jesus was not part man and part God; he was completely human and completely divine, the perfect expression of God in human form. As a man, Jesus was subject to place, time, and other human limitations. He did not give up his eternal power when he became human, but he did set aside his glory and his rights. In response to the Father's will, he limited his power and knowledge. When Jesus became human, he restrained the full use of his powers, yet he could still see each person's thoughts, intents, and motives. So Jesus asked them point-blank, *"Why do you raise such questions in your hearts?"*

The teachers of the law knew about Jesus' ability to heal, and they probably had expected Jesus to immediately heal the paralyzed man. Instead, Jesus forgave the man's sins. To the teachers, this sounded like blasphemy, and it also sounded like an easy out. Anyone can just *say* someone's sins are forgiven, but it would take someone with great power and authority to heal a paralyzed person. Jesus asked them the question that they were asking themselves, *"Which is easier, to say, 'Your sins are forgiven you,' or to say, 'Stand up and walk'?"* Jesus would show that he had the power to forgive sins by also showing that he had the power to make a paralyzed person "stand up and walk" (in Greek, "start walking and keep on walking," indicating a complete and permanent cure). Jesus was offering to do an easier task (healing the man) as public evidence that the more difficult, "secret" task (forgiveness of sin) also had been accomplished.

5:24-25 **"But that you may know that the Son of Man has authority on earth to forgive sins. . . ." He said to the paralyzed man, "I tell you, get up, take your mat and go home." Immediately he stood up in front of them, took what he had been lying on and**

went home praising God.^{NIV} The implied answer to the question Jesus asked in 5:23 is that it would certainly be far easier to just say to someone, "Your sins are forgiven" (who would know whether it had happened or not?) than to perform a miraculous healing in public view. So to prove that he had power to forgive sins, Jesus showed them his power to heal. Speaking to the religious leaders, Jesus said, *"That you may know that the Son of Man has authority on earth to forgive sins."* Jesus here offered them an outright sign of his power (something they would later ask for, 11:16), as well as using the messianic title "Son of Man" (Daniel 7:13). There could be absolutely no doubt of Jesus' power or of who he claimed to be.

Turning back to the paralyzed man still lying on the mat in front of him, Jesus said, *"I tell you, get up, take your mat and go home."* It did not even take a moment—*immediately he stood up . . . took what he had been lying on and went home praising God.* The healing unmistakably revealed Jesus' power and authority. The religious leaders who had questioned Jesus' ability to forgive sins saw the formerly paralyzed man get up and walk. Such a healing would have been impossible apart from God's power. There could be no mistaking the connection—Jesus had the power to make the paralyzed man walk; thus, he also had the authority to forgive his sins. If only these leaders had responded in jubilant praise as the healed man did (and probably his friends who had been watching the proceedings through the hole in the roof!). The man returned home, living proof of Jesus' power and authority. More than that, his sins had been forgiven, and more than physical restoration had occurred. No wonder he praised God!

BACKING IT UP
Any religious huckster can go around handing out "forgiveness" and dispensing God's favors to the gullible. It's like the man who says he can dunk a basketball or play piano on a concert level . . . but never "feels like" demonstrating his skills and abilities. How do you know he can back up his talk unless he shows some proof? That was the situation confronting Jesus in this episode with the paralyzed man and the religious leaders. He said the man's sins were forgiven, but anyone could say that. How would the Pharisees, or the paralytic himself for that matter, know that what Jesus claimed was true? Jesus offered this as proof: The paralyzed man would stand up and walk, a pretty convincing bit of evidence that Jesus spoke with authority. You don't have that kind of miracle-working, sin-forgiving authority, but you follow the one who does. Therefore, your life should be consistent with your words. Your actions should back up your claims to belong to him.

5:26 **Everyone was gripped with great wonder and awe. And they praised God, saying over and over again, "We have seen amazing things today."**^{NLT} The phrase "everyone was gripped with great wonder and awe" refers to the crowd in the house and implies amazement as well as fear. Such awe was appropriate in the presence of one who displayed the authority to heal and to forgive sins. As a result, the people *praised God,* recognizing that Jesus had indeed done *amazing things.*

JESUS EATS WITH SINNERS AT MATTHEW'S HOUSE / 5:27-32 / **40**

The next clash between Jesus and the religious leaders revolved around the company he kept. Not only was Jesus not separating himself from distasteful characters, he was seeking them out. Jesus wasn't accused of accepting sinners as his friends; he was charged with befriending sinners.

What a mystifying man Jesus was. He called Levi (also called "Matthew," 6:15) to follow him, and then he visited Levi in his own home. Jesus met Levi in Levi's world. The Pharisees, who were carefully scrutinizing Jesus, believed that he couldn't possibly affiliate with the *world* without being sullied by such contact. Jesus responded by saying that precisely the opposite was true; contact with him could change the world. In order to accomplish his mission, he had to be with those who needed a Savior and a Physician. Jesus still enters sinful lives to rescue people from their sins.

5:27 **After this he went out and saw a tax collector named Levi, sitting at the tax booth; and he said to him, "Follow me."**^{NRSV} In Mark and Luke, Matthew is called Levi. Most people in this day had two or three names: a Jewish name, a Roman name, and possibly a Greek name. Levi was his Jewish name, Matthew his Roman name. *Levi* was a Jew who worked for the Romans (specifically for Herod Antipas) as the area's *tax collector.* He collected taxes from the citizens as well as from merchants passing through town. Capernaum was a customs post on the caravan route between Damascus to the northeast and the Mediterranean Sea to the west. Most Jews hated tax collectors because of their reputation for cheating, their support of Rome, and their constant contact with "unclean" Gentiles. Tax collectors took a commission on the taxes they collected, so most of them overcharged the people and kept the profits. When tax collectors had asked John the Baptist what they needed to do, John had told them, "Don't collect any more than you are required to" (3:13 NIV). Jews who became tax collectors shamed their family and friends and were excommunicated from the synagogue.

Everyone in Capernaum knew Matthew, and anyone passing through the city who had to pay taxes could find him easily, for he sat at the *tax booth,* an elevated platform or bench. This would not have been the first time that Jesus had seen Matthew, for Jesus had often walked along the shore of the Sea of Galilee. Certainly Matthew had seen Jesus before and, with the crowds, probably had been impressed and intrigued with this man. So one day when Jesus walked right up to Matthew's booth and said two simple words: *"Follow me,"* Matthew lost no time in responding. This was not a request, but a command; not an invitation, but a call to discipleship. Jesus called Matthew to "follow"—that is, to walk the same road.

Luke's Gospel has much to say about taxes and tax collectors. Jesus' parents went to Bethlehem as a result of taxation (2:1-7); John the Baptist spoke specifically to tax collectors (3:12-13); this incident occurred with Levi, followed by a feast with his tax-collecting friends (5:27-32); Jesus told a parable contrasting a Pharisee and a tax collector (with the tax collector coming out ahead! 18:10-14); Luke alone told the story of Zacchaeus, a tax collector in Jericho (19:1-10); along with Matthew and Mark, Luke recorded the religious leaders' question to Jesus regarding paying taxes (20:20-26). Perhaps the appointment of Levi to the group of disciples caused a stir among other outcast tax collectors who came to listen to Jesus (7:29, 34; 15:1).

5:28 So Levi got up, left everything, and followed him.[NLT] Levi responded as Jesus would want all his followers to do—he *got up, left everything, and followed him.* Levi left a lucrative, though probably dishonest, tax-collecting business to follow the Lord. Jesus broke Levi's bondage to money. That Levi "left everything" was no small matter. Matthew was probably very wealthy—tax collecting was a lucrative occupation; so when he walked away from his booth, he left behind a lifetime of potentially great wealth. Several of the other disciples could always return to fishing, but Matthew could never turn back.

> Sinners cannot obey the gospel, any more than the law, without renewal of heart.   *J. I. Packer*

5:29 Then Levi gave Him a great feast in his own house. And there were a great number of tax collectors and others who sat down with them.[NKJV] Levi lost no time. He called his friends together to meet Jesus too. Matthew *gave [Jesus] a great feast in his own house* (this, incidentally, gives us an idea of his wealth) so that his fellow *tax collectors and others* could meet Jesus. This was a

crowd that Jesus could not reach in the synagogues, for they had
been excommunicated because their profession was seen as traitorous against their countrymen. Many of the tax collectors may have
loved money more than anything, so that was a small price to pay.
Still Jesus loved them and had a message for them too—the good
news of the kingdom of God. These people gathered at Levi's
house where they knew they had a welcome, and they *sat down*
with Jesus and listened to his message.

FRIENDS IN LOW PLACES
People who are involved with Alcoholics Anonymous say the
group is at a turning point of sorts. In many chapters, people
would be scandalized if a "sloppy drunk" walked into a meeting
and made a scene. Those chapters have apparently become
too respectable for such behavior. Imagine—an organization
dedicated to helping alcoholics, offended by drunken behavior!
And yet the church faces a similar dilemma. What would
happen if a hard-core "sinner" came to your fellowship and
made a spectacle of himself, sobbing, crying out for
forgiveness, interrupting the routine?
    Jesus associated with the "wrong" people—sinners, tax
gatherers, undesirables—and was criticized harshly for it. He
offered them God's love and forgiveness regardless of their
social status. Could anyone criticize you or your church for
hanging out with the "wrong crowd"? If not, make it a matter of
prayer for God to move you into the lives of one or two people
who really need to experience his grace and mercy.

**5:30 But the Pharisees and the teachers of the law who belonged to
their sect complained to his disciples, "Why do you eat and
drink with tax collectors and 'sinners'?"**[NIV] The religious leaders
had apparently continued to follow Jesus like a pack of reporters
following a hot story. They had seen him heal a paralyzed man;
then they had seen him speak to a notorious outcast and ask him to
become a disciple! After this turn of events, they trailed Jesus all
the way to Matthew's house and watched the feast. According to
the *Pharisees and the teachers of the law who belonged to their
sect* (many of the teachers of the law, or scribes, were also Pharisees), contact with *tax collectors and 'sinners'* made a Jew unclean.
The term "sinners" referred not only to immoral and pagan people
but also to the common people, who were not learned in the law
and did not abide by the rigid standards of the Pharisees. The Pharisees regarded these people as wicked and opposed to the will of
God because they did not observe the rituals for purity that enabled
them to eat with others. Thus, to *eat and drink* with such people
was particularly heinous. Sharing fellowship around a meal indi-

cated close association and identification. The Pharisees would have nothing to do with such people. But not so with Jesus.

That Jesus would stoop to the level of the poor, unlearned, common people made him appear to be no rabbi, and certainly no Messiah! The Pharisees, separatists who believed that they could be saved only by perfect obedience and staying away from impurity and impure people, *complained to [Jesus'] disciples.* How could Jesus make the claims he did and hang out with the worst element of society?

5:31-32 **Jesus answered and said to them, "Those who are well have no need of a physician, but those who are sick. I have not come to call the righteous, but sinners, to repentance."**NKJV The disciples, perhaps wondering about this themselves, brought the question to Jesus. The first part of Jesus' answer was from a common proverb on the healthy and the sick. *Those who are well have no need of a physician;* the physician's waiting room is filled with *those who are sick.* They recognize their need and come to the one who can make them well. The Pharisees were appalled that Jesus ate with sinners and outcasts. Their love of principle and position motivated them to drive a wedge between God's law and common people. But no human can block God's grace, love, and forgiveness. They are available to all.

Jesus carried the proverb a step further and explained his messianic mission: *I have not come to call the righteous, but sinners, to repentance.* The word "righteous" was used ironically— referring to those who think they are righteous, like these religious leaders who dared to question Jesus' choice of dinner companions. Jesus was saying, "I am here because these are the people who realize their need and welcome me." This was Jesus' audience. Jesus, the Great Physician, healed people of physical illnesses, but he knew that all people are spiritually sick and in need of salvation. He was not lowering the standards; he was reaching out to seeking souls in order to bring them the salvation for which they sought. He had come to call them "to repentance." Later Jesus described his mission this way: "For the Son of Man came to seek out and to save the lost" (19:10 NRSV). Incidentally, he said this after another tax collector had come to faith in him.

RELIGIOUS LEADERS ASK JESUS ABOUT FASTING / 5:33-39 / 41

By this time, the Pharisees were constantly skirmishing with Jesus. Two confrontations have preceded this section: one over Jesus' authority to forgive sins (5:17-26) and the other over Jesus'

friendship with "sinners" (5:27-31). While this exchange probably did not happen at Levi's party, the holy freedom exercised by
Jesus and the restrictive views of the religious leaders create an
effective literary contrast.

At every turn, Jesus challenged the Pharisees' way of looking
at life. They lived by appearance; he challenged their motives.
They developed conspicuous habits that showed off their "holiness"; Jesus taught that good actions done for the wrong reasons
are useless.

In response to their questions about fasting, Jesus turned
the discussion from outward behavior to the reasons for fasting. Jesus made it clear that fasting was not a self-justifying
action. It was right in its proper place, but there was also a
proper place for feasting and joy. To further underscore this
truth, Jesus added two other analogies (clothing repair and
the care of wineskins). A worn item of clothing cannot be
repaired with a new piece of cloth that shrinks when washed.
When an old, well-stretched wineskin is filled with new wine,
it will expand and burst when the wine ferments. So also the
new spiritual age brought by Christ would burst the confines
of the old religious system, providing the freedom to serve
God wholeheartedly.

**5:33 Then they said to him, "John's disciples, like the disciples of
the Pharisees, frequently fast and pray, but your disciples
eat and drink."**NRSV "John's disciples" refers to the remaining
disciples of John the Baptist; *the disciples of the Pharisees*
were probably Pharisees-in-training who would observe the
older men and attempt to also practice all the rules and regulations. The Pharisees wanted to know why their own followers,
as well as those of John the Baptist, would *frequently fast and
pray.* "Fasting" refers to going without food in order to spend
time in prayer. The Old Testament law set aside only one day
a year as a required day of fasting for all Jews—the Day of
Atonement (Leviticus 16:29). The Pharisees, however, fasted
on Mondays and Thursdays (see 18:12) as an act of piety, so
their followers did the same. Jesus' disciples, however, were
out of step. Although the statement focused on the disciples, it
indirectly criticized their leader, who should have been fasting
and praying for Israel's deliverance as the Pharisees did.
Instead, Jesus and his disciples were eating and drinking. The
tense of the verb indicates that the feast at Levi's house happened at the very time that the Pharisees were fasting, apparently on one of the weekly fasting days.

FASTING
What should be believers' attitude toward fasting—going
without food in order to spend time in prayer? Fasting needs to
be done for the right reasons. It gives believers time to pray,
teaches self-discipline, reminds them that they can live with a
lot less, and helps them to focus on and appreciate God's gifts.
Fasting was mandatory for the Jewish people once a year, on
the Day of Atonement, and the Pharisees voluntarily fasted
twice a week to impress people with their "holiness." Jesus
commended acts of self-sacrifice done quietly and sincerely.
He wanted people to adopt spiritual disciplines for the right
reasons, not from a selfish desire for praise.

Fasting presents a physical example of the painstaking
aspects of spiritual growth. This kind of discipline humbles
believers because going without food is a reminder of their
complete dependence on God. It also gives them more time to
pray and meditate on God. Being willing to devote a mealtime
or set aside other major activities to devote time to prayer can
be a great exercise of faith.

**5:34-35 Jesus answered, "Can you make the guests of the bridegroom
fast while he is with them? But the time will come when the
bridegroom will be taken from them; in those days they will
fast."**[NIV] In the Old Testament, people would fast in times of
disaster and as a sign of their humility and repentance. Fasting
represented mourning. During that time, the people approached
God with humility and sorrow for sin (see, for example, Judges
20:26; 1 Kings 21:27; Ezra 8:21; Joel 1:14; Jonah 3:5). In the
New Testament, the Pharisees fasted as a show of piety; the disciples of John the Baptist fasted as a sign of mourning for sin and
to prepare for the Messiah's coming. Jesus' disciples, however,
did not need to fast because the Messiah was with them!

Jesus compared himself to a *bridegroom* and his time on earth as
a time of feasting and celebration. His *guests* (those who had come
to believe in him) did not need to fast while he was with them. Jesus
did not condemn fasting—he himself fasted (4:2). He emphasized
that fasting must be done at the right time for the right reasons.

Jesus also knew that *the time will come when the bridegroom
will be taken from them,* referring to his death. *In those days they
will fast,* for fasting will be in order then. At that time they will
grieve. Although Jesus was fully human, he knew he was God
and why he had come—to die, paying the penalty for sin.

**5:36 He also told them a parable: "No one tears a piece from a
new garment and sews it on an old garment; otherwise the
new will be torn, and the piece from the new will not match
the old."**[NRSV] Jesus then told the questioning Pharisees a para-

ble—a short story that uses familiar scenes and everyday objects and relationships to explain spiritual truths. A parable compares something familiar to something unfamiliar. In this parable, Jesus compared his message first to mending and then to storing wine (5:37-38).

Jesus' arrival on earth ushered in a new covenant between God and people. The new covenant called for a new way of expressing personal faith. The newness of the gospel could not be combined with the legalism of the Pharisees any more than *a piece from a new garment* should be used as a patch *on an old garment.* When the garment was washed, the patch would shrink, pull away from the old garment, and leave a worse tear than before.

Jesus did not come to patch up the old religious system of Judaism with its rules and traditions. His purpose was to fulfill the law and start something new, though it had been prophesied for centuries. The "new" cannot fit with the "old" patterns of thought. Jesus Christ, God's Son, came to earth to offer people forgiveness of sins and reconciliation with God. The gospel did not fit into the old rigid legalistic system of religion. The gospel offered grace; Judaism offered law and rule keeping. The parables of the cloth and the wineskins (5:37-38) apply to more than just fasting or to the Pharisees; they speak of Jesus' entire mission and the new era he inaugurated by his entrance into human history.

5:37-38 **"And no one puts new wine into old wineskins; otherwise the new wine will burst the skins and will be spilled, and the skins will be destroyed. But new wine must be put into fresh wineskins."**NRSV In Bible times, people would store wine in goatskins sewn around the edges to form watertight bags (called "wineskins"). New wine expands as it ferments; thus *new wine must be put into fresh wineskins.* Old wineskins would become brittle and wouldn't stretch anymore; thus, if someone put new wine into an old wineskin, the old wineskin would *burst* and spill the wine.

There are several interpretations of the "old versus the new":

- *Law versus grace.* The old cloth and old wineskins represent people under the Old Testament law, and the new cloth and new wineskins represent people under grace. This view, preserved by dispensationalists, stresses the complete break of the Old Testament view of obedience with the New Testament.
- *Old covenant versus new covenant.* The old cloth and old wineskins represent the older and partial understanding of God's will. The new covenant would reflect a new way of understanding what true faithfulness to the law would be under Christ's authority. This view does justice to "both are preserved" (5:38 NKJV) because it sees the revealed will of

God as present in both old and new. But limiting Jesus' words to apply to time in history alone misses his point.

- *Old system of spirituality versus new system.* This view sees continuity in the revealed will of God, both in the Old Testament Scripture and in the New Testament message of Christ. The old cloth and wineskins referred to the old system of application of the law (rigid, legalistic) as typified by the worst teaching of the Pharisees. The old forms and traditions were characterized by the sorrow of fasting. The new attitude of spirituality is characterized by the joy of feasting as seen in Christ and his disciples. New attitudes and methods would be needed. When new attitudes are present, both the understanding of the will of God in Scripture and the new forms will be preserved.

The Christian church was never meant to be a sect or adaptation of Judaism. Instead, Christ fulfills the intent of the Old Testament Scripture. The law reveals the nature and will of God; Jesus Christ reveals the nature and will of God. But while the law could only point out sin and condemn people, Jesus Christ gave his life to bring forgiveness of sin and salvation. These parables speak of Jesus' entire mission and the new era he inaugurated by his entrance into human history.

TRADITION
Someone has said that the seven last words of a church are: "We've never done it that way before." How do you react to change? Do you welcome it, fear it, embrace it, run away from it? The church is an institution with a tremendous heritage and tradition, much of it going all the way back to Jesus and the apostles, and some of it going back beyond that to the Old Testament forebears. These traditions should be respected but not worshiped. Jesus said as much in Luke 5:36-38, when he said that new wine must be put into new wineskins. Give yourself a quick mental examination: How often do you say things like "That will never work" or "Our last pastor never did it that way"? If those words sound familiar, you may need to ask God to help you stop idolizing tradition and start allowing him to work in your life and the life of your church in new and fresh ways.

The "new wine" was the newness of the gospel as exemplified in the person of Jesus Christ (John 2:1-11). Like old wineskins, the Pharisees and indeed the entire religious system of Judaism had become too rigid to accept Jesus, who could not be contained in their traditions or rules. Their understanding of faithfulness to the law had become unsuitable for the fresh, dynamic power of Christ's message. They were the self-appointed guardians of the "old garment" and the "old wineskins."

5:39 **"And no one after drinking old wine desires new wine, but says, 'The old is good.'"**NRSV Jesus could have quoted another well-known parable for our day: "You can't teach an old dog new tricks." Jesus realized that many people are so content with the *old wine* that they don't even want to try the new wine. *"The old is good,"* they say. Many tragically stick with the good when God wants to give them the best. Many of the Pharisees would investigate Jesus' teaching but cling to the old traditions. Many who check out Christianity will reject it, preferring their old ways. Loyalty to the old life may prevent people from believing and certainly will keep them from growing.

FAMILIARITY
Have you ever watched a young child encounter some new aspect of life—a first-time experience with ocean waves, or nuzzling a puppy, or a new taste sensation like a sour fruit? It can be comical to watch, but for the child, it can also seem overwhelming. Often he or she will run quickly back to the safety and security of Mommy's or Daddy's arms. There is something in people that is both attracted to, and at the same time afraid of, the new and the novel. Jesus understood that, as evidenced by his words in Luke 5:39. He knew that people tend to gravitate toward the familiar and the comfortable. But those who only allow those kinds of experiences into their world rob themselves of the rich variety of experiences that God intends for them to have. Consider the child who lets fear of the unknown keep him from enjoying the ocean or puppies or sour fruits . . . and then, with God's help, commit to being open to whatever he sends your way, even if it is new, novel, and unknown.

LUKE 6

Jewish life in Jesus' day revolved around the Sabbath. Elaborate
laws had been designed so that everyone knew exactly how *to*
keep the Sabbath. This is the first of the two clashes recorded in
Luke between Jesus and the religious leaders about the Sabbath
(see 6:6-10). Jesus and his disciples were taking a Sabbath afternoon stroll, pausing to eat grain in a farmer's field along the way.
On any other day, this would have been acceptable (Deuteronomy 23:25). But on the Sabbath, Jewish religious teachers had
prohibited this type of activity because it was considered reaping
and threshing. In other words, it was work. Although not doing
that kind of work, the Pharisees were clearly on the job, confronting Jesus about his disciples' behavior. They must have expected
to put Jesus on the defensive. Instead, he refuted their specific
accusation and their whole interpretation of the Sabbath.

To modern Christians, the Pharisees' reaction to Jesus seems
overstated. But by imposing a bewildering system of Sabbath
laws, the religious leaders had, in fact, made themselves lords of
the Sabbath and thus lords over the people. By claiming the title
of the Lord of the Sabbath, Jesus was stating his divinity and confronting the position of the religious leaders. By remaking the
Sabbath into a day of refreshment, worship, and healing, he pried
open the tightfisted control the Pharisees held on the people.

6:1-2 One Sabbath day as Jesus was walking through some grain-
fields, his disciples broke off heads of wheat, rubbed off the
husks in their hands, and ate the grains.^{NLT} The end of chapter
5 has the parables of the unshrunk cloth and the new wine. These
were Jesus' explanation of how the mes-
sage of the Good News could not be
confined within the rigid rules and traditions of the Pharisees. This chapter
shows this conflict escalating. Not only

> Legalism is bound to
> produce pride of heart.
> *Watchman Nee*

had Jesus been associating with "undesirables" (5:27-32) and
neglecting the rules of fasting that the religious leaders observed

(5:33-35), he did not keep the Sabbath as they required. This is illustrated in the following story.

As these leaders continued to follow Jesus, they observed him *one Sabbath day as [he] was walking through some grainfields.* The fields were not fenced off but separated by stones set at intervals (Deuteronomy 19:14). Roads often went right though the fields. The disciples *broke off heads of wheat, rubbed off the husks in their hands, and ate the grains.* On any other day but the Sabbath, this would have been acceptable. God's law said that farmers were to leave the edges of their fields unplowed so travelers and the poor could eat (Deuteronomy 23:25). This day was a problem, however, because the religious leadership had set up strict laws regarding how to observe the Sabbath. They had set up thirty-nine categories of forbidden activities—and harvesting was one of them. The teachers of the law even went so far as to describe different methods of harvesting. Luke alone wrote that the disciples "rubbed off the husks in their hands." This was considered "threshing" and was against their narrow laws about what constituted "work" on the Sabbath. Thus **some of the Pharisees asked, "Why are you doing what is unlawful on the Sabbath?"**[NIV] These Pharisees had a skewed view of what was truly *unlawful.* Farmers were not allowed to reap grain on the Sabbath because they would be engaging in their daily work on a day of rest (Exodus 34:21). The disciples, however, were merely picking grain to satisfy their hunger (see Matthew 12:1); this was not their regular profession. According to the religious leaders, however, the disciples were technically "harvesting" because they were picking wheat and rubbing it in their hands. The disciples were not breaking God's law as recorded by Moses. Instead, they were only violating one of the Pharisees' many rules.

ALL THE ANSWERS
The Pharisees thought their religious system had all the answers. They could not accept Jesus because he did not fit into their system. Religious people today could miss Christ for the same reason. Beware of thinking that you or your church has all the answers. No religious system is big enough to contain Christ completely or to fulfill perfectly all his desires for the world.

6:3-4 Jesus answered, "Have you not read what David did when he and his companions were hungry? He entered the house of God and took and ate the bread of the Presence, which it is not lawful for any but the priests to eat, and gave some to his companions?"[NRSV] The Pharisees would have been taken aback by Jesus' question (*"Have you not read . . ."*). Of course they had read this story about what *David did when he and his companions were hungry.* But they probably read it only as a historical account devoid of any present application. Jesus, then, explained his disciples' action on the grounds that they were hungry and that their need superseded the technicalities of ceremonial law.

The story is recorded in 1 Samuel 21:1-6. Each week twelve consecrated loaves of bread, representing the twelve tribes of Israel, would be placed on a table in the *house of God,* the tabernacle. This bread was called the *bread of the Presence* (or showbread). At the end of the week, the bread would be replaced with fresh loaves, and the old loaves would be eaten by the priests (Leviticus 24:9). On one occasion, the high priest gave this consecrated bread to David and his men to eat as they were fleeing from Saul. The priest understood that their need was more important than ceremonial regulations. The loaves given to David were the old loaves that had just been replaced with fresh ones. Although the priests were the only ones allowed to eat this bread, God did not punish David because his need for food was more important than the priestly regulations.

By comparing himself and his disciples to David and his men, Jesus was saying, in effect, "If you condemn me, you must also condemn David." Jesus was not condoning disobedience to God's laws. Instead, he was emphasizing discernment and compassion in enforcing the ceremonial laws, something the self-righteous Pharisees did not comprehend. People's needs are more important than technicalities.

6:5 Then Jesus said to them, "The Son of Man is Lord of the Sabbath."[NIV] When Jesus said that he, calling himself *Son of Man,* was *Lord of the Sabbath,* he was claiming to be greater than the law and above the law. Jesus meant that he had the authority to overrule the Pharisees' traditions and regulations because he had created the Sabbath—and the Creator is always greater than the creation. Jesus claimed the authority to correctly interpret the meaning of the Sabbath and all the laws pertaining to it. Who created the Sabbath? God did. Therefore, because Jesus, the Son of Man, is God's Son, given authority and power by God himself, then he is also Lord of the Sabbath.

The new kingdom brought an entirely new relationship between God and people, an attitude of joy and fulfillment, not burdensome restrictions. The ceremonial Sabbath rules simply did not apply when held against the needs of people. Christ brought something entirely new, and he had the power to decide when the rules could be overturned.

TRADITIONALISM
History says that John Calvin wore a hat when he preached. He did so because his health was frail, and church buildings were drafty and full of pigeons. Long after Calvin, preachers who admired the great reformer also wore hats when they preached, even though his reasons for wearing one no longer applied. Someone has defined tradition as "the living faith of those now dead," whereas traditionalism is "the dead faith of those now living." Jesus' critics in Luke 6:5 were locked into traditionalism. They had long since forgotten the reason behind the Sabbath observance: honoring the Lord. Instead, they focused solely on the mindless rule keeping that is the empty soul of legalism. Do you observe the Sabbath? Why—or why not? If someone were to ask you to explain what you do or don't do on Sunday, could you? Beware of falling into legalism: simplistic, unthinking obedience to rules and regulations. Christianity is based not on rules but on love—love for people and love for God.

JESUS HEALS A MAN'S HAND ON THE SABBATH / 6:6-11 / 46

This healing is the last in a series of five confrontations with the Pharisees in this section. The Pharisees had already objected to Jesus forgiving sins (5:17-26), associating with "sinners" (5:29-32), and challenging their traditions involving fasting (5:33-39) and the Sabbath (6:1-5).

This last confrontation recorded by Luke sums up the difference between the approaches of Jesus and the Pharisees to religion: "I ask you, which is lawful on the Sabbath: to do good or to do evil, to save life or to destroy it?" (6:9 NIV). Jesus understood the essence of the law: to promote a love of God and others. In contrast, the Pharisees were perverting the purpose of the law, using it to exalt themselves over others and hold them in contempt. Jesus, who knew the heart, saw through their hypocrisy. They were using the law and the human traditions that had developed around the law to justify their hatred of others, a hatred that led them to plot how they could murder Jesus (6:11). People become like the Pharisees when they use religion to judge and condemn others instead of reaching out to them with loving concern and the truth of the gospel.

6:6-7 **On another Sabbath day, a man with a deformed right hand was in the synagogue while Jesus was teaching. The teachers of religious law and the Pharisees watched closely to see whether Jesus would heal the man on the Sabbath, because**

they were eager to find some legal charge to bring against him.^{NLT} The ongoing debate about the Sabbath would continue to escalate as Jesus continued with his mission, regardless of the day of the week. Obviously Jesus taught and healed throughout the week, but the Gospel writers present several incidents that occurred on the Sabbath in order to highlight the animosity of the religious leaders.

So *on another Sabbath day,* we find Jesus *in the synagogue . . . teaching.* Apparently the religious leaders had not let up on their scrutiny of Jesus' ministry. They followed him out into the fields (6:1-5); here they are back in the synagogue, not to worship, but to watch Jesus closely. At this particular time, *a man with a deformed right hand* came into the synagogue. (Note Luke's attention to physical details: it was the "right" hand.) The man may have been born with this defect or may have acquired it through an accident or disease. Whatever the cause, his hand was useless.

There seems to be no question that Jesus could heal the man. The Pharisees were concerned only *to see whether Jesus would heal the man on the Sabbath.* What difference should that make? Luke explains that *they were eager to find some legal charge to bring against him.* How unfortunate that they could not rejoice in a healing; instead, they hoped to use the healing to bring a charge against Jesus. It was more important for them to protect their laws than to free a person from suffering. God's law prohibited work on the seventh day of the week (Exodus 31:14-17); thus, the religious leaders allowed no healing to be done on the Sabbath unless a person's life was in danger. Healing, they argued, was practicing medicine, and they had a law that a person could not practice this profession on the Sabbath.

The man's condition was not life-threatening. Jesus could have avoided conflict by waiting until the next day to heal the man. But Jesus, as Lord of the Sabbath, had the authority to overrule the Pharisees' traditions and regulations. If he had waited another day, he would have been submitting to the Pharisees and showing that their made-up rules were indeed equal to God's law. But God's law for the Sabbath was never meant to keep people in bondage. When Jesus saw a need, he filled it, regardless of the day or time. Healing the man not only revealed Jesus' authority over the Sabbath but also showed that, in the new kingdom, every day is holy and that salvation and healing can come to anyone on any day. The Sabbath, while an important day given to God's people as a day of rest and worship, was also a day for people to be merciful and kind to those in need. And that is exactly what Jesus intended to show the Pharisees when he spoke to the man.

LEGALISM
The religious leaders' tradition said that there was to be no healing done on the Sabbath. Healing, they said, was practicing medicine, and a person could not practice his profession on the, Sabbath. For those leaders, protecting their tradition was more important than alleviating human suffering. Jesus, on the other hand, was far more concerned with the person than petty human-made regulations. The religious leaders were more concerned with negatives; that is, what rules should not be broken, what activities should not be done on the Sabbath. Jesus was proactive, positive, concerned with doing good and helping others.

Which would an objective observer say is more characteristic of your Christianity—the positives or the negatives? Are you more concerned with opposing certain sins and cultural movements or in advancing the kingdom of God and proclaiming his love for men and women? Christianity is the most positive force to ever hit planet earth. Make sure you don't let it degenerate into a negative religion.

6:8 But Jesus knew their thoughts. He said to the man with the deformed hand, "Come and stand here where everyone can see." So the man came forward.ᴺᴸᵀ Again the text reveals the divine perception that Jesus retained while on earth: he *knew their thoughts* (see also 5:22). Luke did not record what the Pharisees had been thinking, but he focused on the fact that they were watching him to see if he would heal so they could bring a charge against him (6:7). Jesus' adversaries wanted a confrontation; they wanted something to bring against Jesus, and Jesus would not disappoint them. He would make a public display of this healing, so *he said to the man with the deformed hand, "Come and stand here where everyone can see."* Jesus would make the important point that he could not and would not be bound by the Pharisees' burdensome laws. As the Son of God and Lord of the Sabbath, he would perform an act of kindness and healing, even on the Sabbath. Neither the Pharisees nor anyone in the crowd would miss what Jesus was about to do.

6:9 Then Jesus said to them, "I will ask you one thing: Is it lawful on the Sabbath to do good or to do evil, to save life or to destroy?"ᴺᴷᴶⱽ Jesus had perceived the religious leaders' thoughts and so turned to them to *ask . . . one thing.* The question should be obvious—even to these religious leaders: *"Is it lawful on the Sabbath to do good or to do evil, to save life or to destroy?"* In Matthew, the Pharisees ask this question, and Jesus answers by saying, "Suppose one of you has only one sheep and it falls into a pit on the sabbath; will you not lay hold of it and lift it out? How much more valuable is a human being than a sheep! So it is lawful to do good on the sabbath" (Matthew 12:11-12 NRSV). The Pharisees' own laws allowed people to do good and to save life on the Sabbath—a farmer could rescue a sheep from a pit on that day, even though such an act would clearly be considered "work." How absurd, then, to refuse to allow a person to do good to another person on the Sabbath simply because it violated a rule. Refusing to do good means doing evil—there is no middle ground. Refusing to save life means to destroy it. For Jesus to have done nothing—thereby refusing to do good and save life, he would be, by default, doing evil and destroying life. And that would be impossible for Jesus.

6:10 **After looking around at all of them, he said to him, "Stretch out your hand." He did so, and his hand was restored.**NRSV Jesus did not receive an answer to his question recorded in 6:9. Mark wrote that the Pharisees remained silent (Mark 3:4). So *after looking around at all of them,* with sorrow at their stubbornness (see Mark 3:5), Jesus turned his attention back to the man. Jesus told him to *stretch out* his hand. When the man did so, *his hand was restored.* "Restored" means that it became like it had been before. As with the leper (5:12-13) and the paralyzed man (5:24-25), Jesus gave this new life.

RESTORATION
If you have ever lost something valuable, thinking it was gone forever, and then gotten it back, you know how much you appreciate the recovered object. In some ways it means even more to you than it did before. Luke didn't record what caused this man to lose the use of his hand, but he did write that Jesus restored it and made it useful again. Certainly the man appreciated having two good hands again. Take a moment to think of the good things God has given you: health, a loving family, a job, a home, a church, freedom, the ability to read these words. Now think what life would be like if you lost any of them . . . and then thank God for his goodness to you, and resolve to use those gifts for his glory and the benefit of others.

6:11 **At this, the enemies of Jesus were wild with rage and began to discuss what to do with him.**NLT No particular action of Jesus is recorded; he told the man to move, and with that movement, healing arrived. Jesus did nothing that could be called "work," but the Pharisees would not be swayed from their purpose. This blatant act was too much for them to take, so they became *wild with* *rage.* Jesus had looked them in the eyes and then had flouted their laws, overruled their authority, and exposed the hatred in their hearts to the entire crowd in the synagogue. They were so jealous of Jesus' popularity, his miracles, and the authority in his teaching and actions that they missed who he was—the Messiah for whom they had been waiting. They refused to acknowledge Jesus because they were not willing to give up their treasured position and power. When Jesus exposed their attitudes, he became their enemy, and they began looking for ways to destroy him.

Luke wrote that they *began to discuss what to do with him.* Matthew and Mark state that their discussion focused on how they might kill Jesus (Matthew 12:14; Mark 3:6). Ironically, their hatred, combined with their zeal for the law, was driving them to plot murder—an act that was clearly against the law.

JESUS SELECTS THE TWELVE DISCIPLES / 6:12-16 / 48

After a night dedicated to prayer, Jesus chose twelve men to be his apostles—his representatives. Whatever Jesus' specific reasons for choosing each disciple, as a group they were often hot-tempered, unbelieving, and "clueless" about the spiritual realities behind Jesus' ministry. One became a traitor, and all of them abandoned Jesus when following him meant sacrifice and hardship. The apostles proved the truth of Jesus' words: "You did not choose me, but I chose you and appointed you to go and bear fruit—fruit that will last" (John 15:16 NIV).

The better that Christians come to know the weaknesses of the disciples, the more they can see that God has freely chosen them, also. God's grace can overcome any human trait that can mar believers' effectiveness—even the sin that so horribly corrupts them. Believers who are aware of their unworthiness to merit God's mercy and love are in the best position to experience what he can do for them and through them.

6:12 One of those days Jesus went out to a mountainside to pray, and spent the night praying to God.[NIV] Luke continued his narrative without giving exact reference to time frames—*one of those days.* Jesus' enemies had revealed their stubborn hearts and refusal to see him for who he was; his ministry was increasing as people crowded in to hear him. Jesus knew that he would not be long on the earth, so the continuing task of spreading the good news of the kingdom would be entrusted to a group of human beings whom he must choose. This was a daunting task and Jesus needed the Father's help. So *Jesus went to a mountainside to pray, and spent the night praying to God.* This was not a quick call for help while Jesus followed his instincts; this was an intense conversation as Jesus sought his Father's guidance in this supremely important task. (For more on Luke's theology of prayer, see the commentary on 5:16.)

PRAY FIRST
Jesus never wrote any books. He never led any church-growth conferences or revival meetings. He left no organizational charts for us to follow. His one and only method for founding and building up his church was the men whom he called to follow him. These men were his legacy, his "organization." There was no plan B. No wonder he spent an extended period of time in prayer before choosing them. What a contrast to the way that Christians operate so much of the time, making decisions and then asking God to bless them. How much better the decisions would be, how much more effective the work and healthy the churches, if believers would follow Jesus' model: pray first—really pray—and then act. Do you have a major decision (or several) on the horizon? Commit your decisions to the Lord in prayer.

6:13-14 **At daybreak he called together all of his disciples and chose twelve of them to be apostles.**[NLT] *At daybreak,* after his night of prayer, Jesus *called together all of his disciples.* Of the many who were following him at this time, he *chose twelve of them to be apostles.* Jesus did not take volunteers; he chose those whom God had directed him to choose.

The choice of twelve men is highly symbolic. The number twelve corresponds to the twelve tribes of Israel (Matthew 19:28), showing the continuity between the old religious system and the new one based on Jesus' message. Jesus looked upon this as the gathering of the true people of God. These men were the righteous remnant who would carry on the work the twelve tribes were chosen to do—to build the community of God (see 22:28-30). The Gospels and Epistles stress the ministry of the twelve men together and its significance. The number was so important that when Judas Iscariot killed himself, another man was chosen to replace him (see Acts 1:15-26). The apostles formed Jesus' inner circle. He gave them intense training and sent them out with his own authority. These were the men who started the Christian church. In the Gospels, these twelve men are usually called the disciples, but in the book of Acts they are called apostles. This is a rare instance of the term "apostles" in the Gospels.

Here are their names: Simon (he also called him Peter), Andrew (Peter's brother), James, John, Philip, Bartholomew.^{NLT} The first name recorded was *Simon,* whom Jesus also called *Peter* (see John 1:42). Jesus had given Simon a new name. Sometimes Peter is referred to as Cephas. "Peter" is the Greek equivalent of the Aramaic *Cephas*—a word meaning "stone" or "rock." Simon was a fisherman for whom Jesus had provided a miraculous catch of fish. Then Jesus had called him to be a follower (5:1-11). The Gospel of Luke follows Peter very closely, as noted in the commentary on 5:9-11. He became one of three in Jesus' core group among the disciples, and he recognized that Jesus was the Messiah (9:18-20). Although Peter would deny ever knowing Jesus, this Gospel alone has Jesus' prayer on behalf of Peter that his faith would not fail (22:31-32). The risen Christ made a special appearance to Peter (24:34). He would become a leader in the Jerusalem church, write two letters that appear in the Bible (1 and 2 Peter), and be crucified for his faith.

ONENESS IN JESUS
Jesus selected ordinary men with a mixture of backgrounds and personalities to be his disciples. Jesus did not choose these twelve to be his disciples because of their faith—it often faltered. He didn't choose them because of their talent and ability—no one stood out with unusual ability. The disciples represented a wide range of backgrounds and life experiences, and apparently they may have had no more leadership potential than those who were not chosen. The one characteristic they all shared was their willingness to obey Jesus.

Today, God calls ordinary people together to build his church, teach salvation's message, and serve others out of love. Individual Christians may feel unqualified to serve Christ effectively, but with other believers, they make up a group strong enough to serve God in any way. Remember that it is the oneness that believers have in Jesus that holds them together. Without that, all the congregations would break apart. Ask for patience to accept the diversity of people in your church, and for wisdom to see their gifts and abilities. Build on the variety of strengths represented in your group.

Andrew was *Peter's brother* and also a fisherman (Matthew 4:18). Andrew had been a disciple of John the Baptist and had accepted John the Baptist's testimony that Jesus was "the Lamb of God." He had left John to follow Jesus and then had brought his brother Simon to Jesus (John 1:35-42).

James and *John* had also been fishermen and, incidentally, Peter and Andrew's business partners (5:10). Along with Peter,

the three of them became Jesus' inner circle, witnessing certain
miracles (8:51) and Jesus' transfiguration (9:28-29). James would
become the first martyr for the Christian faith (Acts 12:2). John
would write the Gospel of John, the letters of 1, 2, and 3 John,
and the book of Revelation. These two men may have been Jesus'
distant cousins; thus, at one point, they requested special places
in Christ's kingdom (Mark 10:35, 37). Scripture gives glimpses
of these men, revealing that they were somewhat short-tempered
and judgmental; for example, they wanted to call fire down from
heaven on an inhospitable Samaritan village (9:52-56). Jesus
called them "Sons of Thunder."

John wrote about *Philip*, "The next day Jesus decided to leave
for Galilee. Finding Philip, he said to him, 'Follow me'" (John
1:43 NIV). Philip then brought *Bartholomew* (also called Nathanael) as recorded in John 1:45. In the list of disciples here and in
Matthew, Philip and Bartholomew are listed together (Matthew
10:3; Mark 3:18); in John's Gospel, Philip and Nathanael are
paired up (John 1:45). It seems reasonable to conclude, then, that
since Bartholomew is not mentioned in John, and Nathanael is
not mentioned in the other Gospels, Nathanael and Bartholomew
must be the same person.

Philip probably knew Andrew and Peter because they were
from the same town, Bethsaida (John 1:44). Bartholomew was an
honest man; indeed, Jesus' first words to him were, "Here is a
true Israelite, in whom there is nothing false" (John 1:47 NIV).
Bartholomew at first rejected Jesus because Jesus was from Nazareth. But upon meeting Jesus, his attitude changed and he
exclaimed, "Rabbi, you are the Son of God! You are the King of
Israel!" (John 1:49 NRSV). (This is not the same Philip mentioned
in Acts 7.)

**6:15 Matthew, Thomas, James (son of Alphaeus), Simon (the
Zealot).**^{NLT} *Matthew* was also known as Levi. He had been a tax
collector who, at Jesus' call, had given up everything in order to
follow him (5:27-28). Then he had invited all his tax collector
friends to also meet Jesus (5:29). He would later write the Gospel
of Matthew.

Thomas is often remembered as "Doubting Thomas" because
he doubted Jesus' resurrection (John 20:24-25). Thomas had not
been with the disciples at Jesus' first appearance, so when the
other disciples said that Jesus was alive, he didn't believe them.
However, when Thomas saw and touched the living Christ, he
readily believed. Thomas loved Jesus and understood what Jesus'
mission entailed, for when Jesus determined to return to Judea

and enemy territory, Thomas said to the disciples, "Let us also go, that we may die with him" (John 11:16 NIV).

This *James* was called *son of Alphaeus* to differentiate him from James the son of Zebedee (and brother of John) in 6:14.

Simon the Zealot is also called, in some versions of Scripture, Simon the Canaanite. Simon was probably not a member of the party of Zealots, for that political party was not identified as such until A.D. 68. Most likely the word "Zealot" used here indicates zeal for God's honor and fervent nationalism that characterized Simon before he followed Jesus. Most likely, it was an affectionate nickname.

6:16 Judas (son of James), Judas Iscariot (who later betrayed him).[NLT] *Judas (son of James)* is also called Thaddaeus (Mark 3:18). He is also mentioned in Acts 1:13.

Rounding out the list is *Judas Iscariot,* with the footnote that he is the one *who later betrayed* Jesus. The name "Iscariot" is probably a compound word meaning "the man from Kerioth." Thus, Judas's hometown was Kerioth in southern Judea (see Joshua 15:25), making him the only one of the Twelve who was not from Galilee. It might seem strange that Jesus would spend an entire night in prayer to pick this group, then end up choosing Judas. Did Jesus make a mistake? No. Did God? No. The plan had been set in motion from the beginning of time, and this was part of the plan that would eventually come to its final conclusion in Judas's betrayal of Jesus and suicide. The betrayal fulfilled prophecy and helped to bring Jesus to the cross. There was no mistake. That was the way of salvation.

JESUS GIVES THE BEATITUDES / 6:17-26 / *49*

Luke's Sermon on the Plain (6:17-49) is similar to Matthew's Sermon on the Mount (Matthew 5–7). It has been widely debated whether the two are the same sermon or different ones. It is very likely that Jesus taught the same truths twice, if not more. Luke's account does not cover as much material as Matthew's does, either because Luke's sources lacked it or because it had Jewish legalistic characteristics that Luke thought were not necessary to include for his Gentile audience.

This simple and short sermon of Jesus has spawned a number of interpretations, some complementary and some contradictory. Five of the main interpretations are as follows:

1. *Perfectionist legalism.* This view was developed during medieval times and teaches that the standards here are high because they are for *disciples* (clergy and the monastic orders).

It teaches that true followers should live on a level of righteousness above normal Christians. The problem with this, however, is that Jesus' sermon does not teach two different standards for Christians, and we must not read into the sermon salvation by works.

2. *Impossible ideal.* Widely accepted after the time of Martin Luther (who promoted this concept), this view states that the sermon functions like the Old Testament law, forcing people to realize their sinfulness and helplessness and so turn to God. Some scholars see the use of hyperbole (overstatement to make a point, as in "If your right hand causes you to sin, cut it off" in Matthew 5:30) as an accepted teaching method during Jesus' time to stress moral urgency.

3. *Only for Jesus' disciples.* Albert Schweitzer said that this teaching was only for the Twelve, who thought that Jesus would return in their lifetime, and that these moral demands were not for all time. The problem with this view is that Jesus makes no reference to the end of the world or to his return in this sermon.

4. *Kingdom age.* Dispensationalism teaches that these laws are for the kingdom age (the Millennium) and are only an example for our day. Jesus offered the kingdom to the Jews, but they rejected it. Thus the reality was postponed until his second coming. The problem with this view is that nothing in Jesus' teaching ever exempted the disciples then or now from these principles.

5. *Social gospel.* Protestant liberals have used the ethics of the sermon as a mandate for the church, so that they can usher in the kingdom of God by means of reforming society. The problem with this view is that the teachings of Jesus here cannot be isolated from all his other teachings, especially his command to believe in him and preach the gospel message to others.

There is another way to understand this sermon in light of a double-pronged interpretation. The kingdom has been inaugurated (begun) but has not yet been realized (completed). So there remains a tension between the *already* and the *not yet* aspects of the kingdom. Those who obey Jesus now experience, in a partial way, the wonderful benefits that he describes in this sermon. So then, the Beatitudes (1) present a standard of conduct for all believers, (2) contrast kingdom values (which are eternal) with worldly values (which are temporary), (3) contrast the superficial "faith" of the Pharisees with the real faith that Christ wants, and (4) show how the future kingdom will fulfill Old Testament prophecies.

It is important to note that the Beatitudes of the Sermon on the

Plain are slightly different than the ones in Matthew. The Beatitudes recorded in Luke seem to speak more of the literal "poor," instead of merely the "poor in spirit" (Matthew 5:3). The contrasting *woes* in Luke (6:24-26), which are conspicuously absent in Matthew's account, reinforce this point, condemning the wealthy and self-satisfied. The "woes" exactly parallel the Beatitudes. Although the rich can come to salvation, Jesus seems to be issuing a severe warning here that the kind of attitudes—pride, greed, and selfishness—that naturally flow from riches are antithetical to the values of the kingdom of God. In contrast, the attitudes that poverty tends to cultivate—a genuine humility and a willingness to depend on God—will propel a person to the feet of the Savior, begging for mercy. Without a doubt, Jesus, in this concise sermon, exposes hypocrisy, self-centeredness, and greed. Believers need to make sure that they don't harden their hearts like the rich but humble themselves before God, admitting their utter sinfulness and recommitting themselves to live for him.

6:17-19 **He came down with them and stood on a level place, with a great crowd of his disciples and a great multitude of people from all Judea, Jerusalem, and the coast of Tyre and Sidon. They had come to hear him and to be healed of their diseases; and those who were troubled with unclean spirits were cured.**[NRSV] Jesus had been up on a mountainside praying through the night (6:12) before he had chosen his twelve disciples to whom he would give special training to carry on his work. Then *he came down with them and stood on a level place* from which he could continue to teach. Jesus' popularity had continued to grow, for there is not only a *great crowd of his disciples* (referring to all who were following him) but also a *great multitude.* People had come from *Judea* (the southernmost region of Israel), *Jerusalem* (the key city of Israel, in Judea), and *the coast of Tyre and Sidon* (Gentile cities to the far north on the coast of the Mediterranean Sea). Word of Jesus' authoritative teaching and healing power had spread, so they had come *to hear him.* Many others also had come *to be healed of their diseases.* This Gospel has already shown Jesus healing all manner of sickness and demon possession. Jesus did not disappoint those who came—*those who were troubled with unclean spirits were cured.* Luke the doctor gives us the detail that **all in the crowd were trying to touch him, for power came out from him and healed all of them.**[NRSV] Luke distinguished between those with physical illness and those possessed by demons. This Gospel also emphasizes Jesus' *power,* and explains here that when he healed, *power came out from him.* (For more on power, see 4:14, 36; 5:17; 8:46; 9:1; 10:19; 21:27; 24:49.) No one went away disappointed; he *healed all of them.*

6:20 Then He lifted up His eyes toward His disciples, and said: "Blessed are you poor, for yours is the kingdom of God."NKJV Jesus *lifted up His eyes toward His disciples.* Some believe that the word "disciples" refers to the large crowd of disciples that have come to Jesus (6:17). Others think this refers specifically to the Twelve, whom Jesus had just chosen. Most likely, Jesus gave these teachings primarily to the disciples, with the crowds listening in. Jesus' newly chosen disciples, the twelve men who would be his closest associates, might have become tempted to feel proud and important. After all, Jesus' popularity continued to grow, as seen in the multitude with them at that moment. The disciples, riding on the wave of Jesus' popularity, needed to first understand the priorities of God's kingdom. In addition, many of these disciples were confused about what exactly Jesus was going to do. The Gospels present a group of men who, while believing, never quite understood Jesus' coming death and resurrection until they witnessed it for themselves. In the meantime, they could be found arguing about their places in the kingdom (9:46). So Jesus told them here, in no uncertain terms, that they should not expect fame and fortune in this world, for that is not what Jesus came to bring. They would indeed be "blessed," but by a different kingdom's standards.

These verses are called the Beatitudes, from the Latin word meaning "blessing." They describe what it means to be Christ's follower; they are standards of conduct; they contrast kingdom values with worldly values, showing what Christ's followers can expect from the world and what God will give them; they contrast fake piety with true humility; they show how Old Testament expectations are fulfilled in God's kingdom.

The word "blessed" means more than happiness; it means favored and approved by God. According to worldly standards, the types of people whom Jesus describes as "blessed" don't seem to be so. However, God's way of living usually contradicts the world's. In God's kingdom, a person who is "blessed" experiences hope and joy, independent of his or her outward circumstances.

The first "blessed" is reserved for *you [who are] poor.* Matthew captures the meaning with the words "poor in spirit." These are the people who have nothing but God on whom to depend. They realize that they have nothing of their own to give to God and therefore must depend on his mercy. The rich always have their money and financial security to fall back on—Jesus later explained how difficult it is for rich people to enter the kingdom.

Their riches can become a stumbling block (18:18-25). Those who are humbly dependent upon God receive the kingdom. Jesus says, *"Yours is the kingdom of God."* Notice that he does not say, yours "will be," but yours "is." Accepting Jesus into one's heart brings that person into the kingdom, even as he or she lives on earth.

Jesus was not exalting poverty; instead, he was clarifying that these are the results of discipleship and that the disciples would ultimately be blessed because they could count on Jesus, the Son of Man. In these Beatitudes, Jesus was not cursing all that is part of life—such as laughter, fun, happiness, money, food—but if these become the focus of life without regard to God, then a person cannot be "blessed" by God.

6:21 **"Blessed are you who hunger now, for you shall be filled."**^{NKJV} The hunger about which Jesus spoke is a hunger based on poverty. See the contrasting "woe" to those who are well fed (6:25). This applies to those who face poverty because of their lot in life or for taking their stand with Christ. The word "hunger" pictures an intense longing that needs to be satisfied; people who do not get food will eventually die of hunger. Jesus' promise to those with this kind of hunger is *you shall be filled.* Jesus will completely satisfy those with spiritual hunger.

Luke focused on Jesus' ability to meet every need. In a nation where riches were regarded as a sign of God's favor, Jesus startled his hearers by pronouncing blessings on the hungry. In doing so, however, he was in line with an ancient tradition. The Old Testament is filled with texts proclaiming God's concern for the poor and needy. See, for example, 1 Samuel 2:5; Psalm 146:7; Isaiah 58:6-7; and Jesus' own mother's prayer in Luke 1:53.

"Blessed are you who weep now, for you shall laugh."^{NKJV} Jesus promises that those *who weep now . . . shall laugh.* Scholars differ on the exact nature of this "weeping." Jesus may have been referring to the nation of Israel weeping for its sins; others interpret this more personally, explaining that it refers to those who weep for their own sins or even for personal grief or oppression. Still other scholars see in the word "weep" a picture of God's people who suffer because of their faith in him. Most likely it refers to people who are sensitive to the world's sin and resultant suffering. While their pain is real, they can know the end of the story and laugh. Later, the apostle John would see a vision of heaven where "God will wipe away every tear from their eyes" (Revelation 7:17 NIV). Jesus explained to his disciples that following him would not involve fame, popularity, and wealth. Instead, it could very well mean sorrow, weeping, and suffering. But they would always know that God would be their comfort.

6:22-23 **"Blessed are you when people hate you, and when they exclude you, revile you, and defame you on account of the Son of Man. Rejoice in that day and leap for joy, for surely your reward is great in heaven; for that is what their ancestors did to the prophets."**^{NRSV} To be surrounded by hateful people would hardly make a person feel like the object of blessing. But kingdom values are the opposite of this world's values. Jesus explained to his disciples that not only would they, like anyone else, experience poverty and sorrow in this life, but they also would be actively persecuted. People would *hate* them, *exclude* them, *revile* them, and *defame* them—the one common factor would be that this would occur *on account of the Son of Man.* Because they believed in Jesus, they would face persecution.

Surely this must have sounded strange to the disciples on the mountainside, surrounded by literally a multitude of people desiring to get close to Jesus. He would be hated? And they would be hated because of their association with him? Yet Jesus saw what the future held, and he warned them accordingly.

GOD'S FAMILY VALUES
Being a Christian may bring you into conflict with others, simply because your values and theirs are radically different. Someone has described this world, and especially contemporary culture, as being like a display window in a department store, full of various objects of all shapes, sizes, and prices. During the night, a mischievous little boy breaks in and switches all the price tags. The next day, people pass by and look in the window, never realizing that all the values have been rearranged. The Christian knows that the world's values are grossly distorted and out of touch with reality—but try telling the world! When believers do, Jesus says, the world will not thank them for their trouble. In fact, it will hate them. But they can persevere and even smile, because they know the truth. Don't compromise your beliefs or your values just because the world can't handle them.

Jesus also comforted them by saying that when they faced persecution, they were to *rejoice* and *leap for joy.* Why? Because no matter what those who hate Jesus attempt to do to his followers on earth, a great *reward* awaits those followers in heaven. When God judges the world, the persecution will pale in comparison to the great reward that awaits. Jesus placed his disciples in a long line of God's followers who lived righteously and spoke truthfully—only to suffer for it. The Jews held the ancient prophets of God in high esteem; to be placed among them was a great honor. Jesus explained that to live and speak for God in the face of unjust persecution, as did the ancient prophets, would bring great reward in heaven.

6:24 "But woe to you who are rich, for you have already received your comfort."[NIV] The next three verses contain "woes" that give the flip side of the "blesseds" in the previous verses. The word "woe" expresses regret and sorrow. While most in the world see riches as desirable and as a sign of God's blessing, Jesus says the opposite. He pronounces, *"Woe to you who are rich."* Jesus probably addressed these comments to his audience at large. Jesus does not decry riches themselves but their effect on people. Riches cause people to feel self-sufficient and to feel that they have found the happiness for which they were seeking. Those who choose present comfort over God's way *have already received [their] comfort.* Those who try to find fulfillment through wealth will find that wealth is the only reward they will ever get and that it does not last. Believers should not seek comfort now at the expense of eternal life.

TRUE RICHES
Jesus' message of "woe" on the rich doesn't mean that everyone should be poor, hungry, and miserable. Instead, it means that those who make happiness in this life their goal may very well get it . . . but that is all they will get. There is a higher law, a higher ethic, a higher reality. Pursue it, and God may be kind enough to grant you some of the world's riches also. Maybe not. But if you pursue only the world's riches, the world's happiness, you are guaranteed to miss the higher ones. Jim Elliot, martyred missionary to the Auca tribe in Ecuador, wrote shortly before his death: "He is no fool who gives what he cannot keep to gain what he cannot lose." In the tug-of-war between the world's riches and God's, which side has the stronger grip on your heart?

6:25 "Woe to you who are full now, for you will be hungry."[NRSV] The phrase "who are full now" refers to those who have everything that this world offers. They lack nothing. Their material possessions and financial "security" cause them to think that they have no need for God. One day, however, they *will be hungry.* This may not occur in this life, but they will find that for eternity, when it really matters, they will be the ones who suffer. The Gospel later records a parable of a rich man and a poor man that illustrates this point (see 16:19-31).

"Woe to you who are laughing now, for you will mourn and weep."^{NRSV} In much the same way, those *who are laughing now* will one day *mourn and weep*—and that will last for eternity. Jesus was not against laughter—indeed, laughter is one of the greatest gifts God has given to his people. Jesus was pointing at the same attitude carried by those who are rich and self-satisfied in this life and give superficial laughter at any mention of God or of eternity. They will find that they were wrong, and they will mourn and weep forever.

6:26 **"Woe to you when all speak well of you, for that is what their ancestors did to the false prophets."**^{NRSV} Jesus points out a serious problem when *all speak well of you.* The key word is "all." While being spoken well of is certainly a worthy goal, rarely can a person be spoken well of by everyone and have everyone completely agree with him or her on every topic. One cannot be pleasing to everyone in that way without sacrificing some principle here or another there. Such a person must waffle in all areas of life so everyone will like him or her.

One group in the Old Testament was well thought of by everyone, from the king to the common people—they were the *false prophets.* The *ancestors* of these Israelites listening to Jesus had spoken well of the false prophets. They were praised by kings and crowds because their predictions—personal prosperity and victory in war—were exactly what the people wanted to hear. Unfortunately, their words were shown to be lies as the nations of Israel and later Judah lost their freedom and their homeland when they were taken into captivity. Popularity is no guarantee of a person's truthfulness; human flattery does not bring God's approval. Sadness lies ahead for those who chase after the crowd's praise rather than God's truth.

JESUS TEACHES ABOUT LOVING ENEMIES / 6:27-36 / 57

By telling Christians not to retaliate and not to hate their enemies, Jesus is calling them to an unnatural type of love. The natural reaction to personal injustices is to get even. But Jesus wants us to demonstrate a higher type of love. By delaying judgment and providing for everyone's needs on a daily basis, God demonstrates an abundance of love and mercy, even to his enemies day after day. Believers are to imitate this type of divine love. By loving and praying for their enemies, believers display God's love in an unlovely world and overcome evil with good.

6:27-28 **"But if you are willing to listen, I say, love your enemies. Do good to those who hate you. Pray for the happiness of those who curse you. Pray for those who hurt you."**[NLT] Jesus explained to his disciples that they must live by a higher standard than the world's. While the Pharisees sought Jesus' death because he refused to keep their regulations regarding cleanliness and the Sabbath observance, Jesus was teaching standards of living that were far higher than anything the Pharisees could imagine. The difference was that the Pharisees were performing their acts in order to be good enough for God; Jesus knew the standards were impossible to reach on human strength alone. Jesus did not ask people to act this way in order to be good enough for God. But people who have accepted Christ as Savior have the Holy Spirit's help to accomplish what would otherwise be impossible.

Jesus taught that love must not be selective. His followers are to love all people, regardless of how unlovely or even hostile they may be. They also must act on that love by being willing to do good when it is in their power to do it. There are several words for love in Greek: *storge,* referring to natural affection; *eros,* meaning romantic love; *philia,* meaning the love between friends. The word used here, however, is *agape,* meaning the kind of love that is willed by the person loving. *Agape* love is shown even when the one loved has no merit for that love. It is love that must be chosen and willed.

LOVE YOUR ENEMIES
The Jews despised the Romans because they oppressed God's people, but Jesus told the people to love these enemies who provoked and angered them. Such words turned many away from Christ. But Jesus wasn't talking about having affection for enemies; he was talking about an act of the will. You can't "fall into" this kind of love—it takes conscious effort. Loving your enemies means acting in their best interests. You can pray for them and think of ways to help them. Jesus loved the whole world, even though the world was in rebellion against God. Jesus asks believers to follow his example by loving their enemies (see also 6:35). Grant your enemies the same respect and rights you desire for yourself.

All people have experienced *agape* from God. "God so loved the world" even while people were sinful and rebellious. God willed to love his people and sent his Son to die for them, not because they deserved it or had any merit, but only because of God's love. Those who have experienced God's love understand what it means to be loved undeservedly. People who were once enemies of God and have joined his family can understand what it means to *love your enemies.* Only with the help of God's Spirit can his people *do good to those who hate* them, *pray for the happiness of those who curse* them, and *pray for those who hurt* them (see Romans 12:14-21). When believers are hated, cursed, and hurt, they are to respond with love.

6:29-30 **"If someone slaps you on one cheek, turn the other cheek. If someone demands your coat, offer your shirt also. Give what you have to anyone who asks you for it; and when things are taken away from you, don't try to get them back."**NLT Jesus says to respond in love when faced with hatred, cursing, and physical abuse. The context of Jesus' instruction to the Christian community probably implies

> If God should have no more mercy on us than we have charity one to another, what would become of us?
>
> *Thomas Fuller*

religious persecution of Christians, not the actions of a criminal. The action of praying for enemies, even "loving" them, might seem easy enough if just left at that. But what about responding in love—how can anyone do that? Jesus offered a couple of examples. If you get slapped, *turn the other cheek.* The word for "cheek" is *siagon,* which really means the jaw; this probably refers to a punch on the jaw. The normal response would be to punch back as hard as possible. But Jesus offers another option—the attitude that says, "I will not seek revenge. In fact, if need be, I am ready to take another blow." The attitude is not so much to offer to be hit again as it is to offer forgiveness.

The same attitude is illustrated regarding the *coat* and the *shirt.* The word for "coat" referred to the outer garment; "shirt" to the undergarment. If someone demanded the one, offer the other as well. The point is not so much being passive when being robbed, as it is being compassionate for another's need. If someone needs to steal a coat, then perhaps that person also needs your shirt.

In fact, the more general principle could be stated: *Give what you have to anyone who asks you for it; and when things are taken away from you, don't try to get them back.* Such an attitude completely confounds the world. It doesn't understand nonretaliation, forgiveness, and a loose hold on possessions. But believers, citizens of a future heavenly kingdom, don't need to retaliate, hold a grudge, or hang on to every item they own. They are freed to forgive and to give. The point is not that giving is always the correct answer but that believers' actions are rooted first in love, not in regard for honor or possessions.

6:31 **"Do to others as you would have them do to you."**^{NRSV} In this verse we see how Jesus took the law and applied it at even a higher level than the Pharisees. This is commonly known as the Golden Rule. Many religions teach a negative version of this statement. Confucius said, "What you do not want done to yourself, do not do to others." The well-known Rabbi Hillel, when challenged to teach the entire Law while standing on one foot, said, "Whatever angers you when you suffer it at the hands of others, do not do it to others, this is the whole law." But Jesus stated this in a positive manner, making it even more powerful. While it may be possible to not do evil to others, it is much more difficult to take the initiative to actually do good. A person may be able to keep the negative form of the law by avoiding sin, but to keep the positive form requires action. This is the key to the radical discipleship that Jesus wants. The Golden Rule is the foundation of active goodness and mercy—the kind of love God shows to people every day.

6:32-34 **"Do you think you deserve credit merely for loving those who love you? Even the sinners do that! And if you do good only to those who do good to you, is that so wonderful? Even sinners do that much! And if you lend money only to those who can repay you, what good is that? Even sinners will lend to their own kind for a full return."**^{NLT} In these short statements, Jesus explained his commands that he had just given by showing how his followers must be different from *sinners,* that is, those who do not believe in him. How would God's people be any different from the world if they only loved people who love them? How would they be any different from the world if they only did good to people who could do good to them in return? *Even the sinners do that!* Sinners love, sinners do good, sinners lend money—the difference is that God's people are willing to love, do good, and lend even when there is no promise of return, even when it results in abuse. Such actions will mark Jesus' followers as different—different from the world, different even from the religious leadership.

GOD'S WAY
Jesus said that love means action. One way to put love to work is to take the initiative in meeting specific needs. This is easy to do with people who love you, people whom you trust. But love means doing this even to those who dislike you or plan to hurt you. The money you give others should be considered a gift, not a high-interest loan that will help you more than them. Give as though you are giving to God.

6:35 **"But love your enemies, do good to them, and lend to them without expecting to get anything back. Then your reward will be great, and you will be sons of the Most High, because he is kind to the ungrateful and wicked."**[NIV] Because his followers are to be different, Jesus sums up their actions as *love your enemies, do good to them, and lend to them.* To make them different from the world, God's people will do those actions *without expecting to get anything back.* Their lives reflect the attitude of God himself; thus their *reward will be great,* and they *will be sons of the Most High.* God's people do these actions not so that they can *be* God's people but because they *are* God's people. Their attitudes and values reflect God's attitudes and values—because God himself *is kind to the ungrateful and wicked,* so should his followers be.

> You can give without loving, but you cannot love without giving.
> *Amy Carmichael*

GOD'S LOVE
Probably no single teaching of Jesus' is more challenging than that Christians should love their enemies (6:32-35). How can they do that? It not only seems impossible, it is. But God specializes in doing what seems impossible. He can give believers the power to love their enemies because he himself loves his enemies. Outside of Christ, all are rebels, enemies of God, yet he "demonstrates his own love for us in this: While we were still sinners [enemies of God], Christ died for us" (Romans 5:8 NIV). If God loves you that way, can you do any less than ask him to give you that kind of love for your enemies?

6:36 **"Therefore be merciful, just as your Father also is merci-ful."**[NKJV] Matthew reported Jesus' command to "be perfect, there-fore, as your heavenly Father is perfect" (Matthew 5:48 NIV). But Matthew also included much of Jesus' discussion regarding the Pharisees and law keeping, which was of great interest to his Jew-ish audience. Luke, as he recorded portions of Jesus' sermon, omitted that part, which would have been of less interest to his Gentile readers, and included the above discussion of kindness to all in need, regardless of their friendliness or ability to return the favor. The words of Jesus that Luke included here focus on God's mercy and the fact that believers are to show that kind of mercy in their dealings with others.

To *be merciful* means to refuse to inflict just vengeance, as well as to show compassion. See the chart, "As God Is Merciful," on page 160.

AS GOD IS MERCIFUL

The Old Testament records over 130 references to God the Father's mercy on people. Many references also say that his people are to follow his example. Below is a sampling of some of these verses (quoted from NIV, italics added):

Reference:	*How God shows mercy:*
Genesis 19:16	"When [Lot] hesitated, the men grasped his hand and the hands of his wife and of his two daughters and led them safely out of the city, for the LORD was *merciful* to them."
Deuteronomy 4:31	"For the LORD your God is a *merciful* God; he will not abandon or destroy you or forget the covenant with your forefathers, which he confirmed to them by oath."
2 Samuel 24:14	"David said to Gad, 'I am in deep distress. Let us fall into the hands of the LORD, for his *mercy* is great; but do not let me fall into the hands of men.'"
Nehemiah 9:31	"But in your great *mercy* you did not put an end to them or abandon them, for you are a gracious and *merciful* God."
Isaiah 55:7	"Let the wicked forsake his way and the evil man his thoughts. Let him turn to the LORD, and he will have *mercy* on him, and to our God, for he will freely pardon."
Daniel 9:9	"The Lord our God is *merciful* and forgiving, even though we have rebelled against him."
Titus 3:5	"He saved us, not because of righteous things we had done, but because of his *mercy*. He saved us through the washing of rebirth and renewal by the Holy Spirit."
Hebrews 4:16	"Let us then approach the throne of grace with confidence, so that we may receive *mercy* and find grace to help us in our time of need."

Reference:	*How believers are to show mercy:*
Hosea 6:6	"For I desire *mercy*, not sacrifice, and acknowledgment of God rather than burnt offerings."
Micah 6:8	"He has showed you, O man, what is good. And what does the LORD require of you? To act justly and to love *mercy* and to walk humbly with your God."
Zechariah 7:9	"This is what the LORD Almighty says: 'Administer true justice; show *mercy* and compassion to one another.'"
James 3:17	"But the wisdom that comes from heaven is first of all pure; then peace-loving, considerate, submissive, full of *mercy* and good fruit, impartial and sincere."
Jude 1:22-23	"Be *merciful* to those who doubt; snatch others from the fire and save them; to others show *mercy*, mixed with fear—hating even the clothing stained by corrupted flesh."

MERCY

Has there ever been a time in your life as a Christian when you really blew it? You sinned so grievously, you made such a mess of things, that you thought you could never call yourself a Christian again? If they are honest, most people would admit that they have been through a time (or times) like that. If you have, think back and ask yourself: Who was the person who helped you most as you got up off the spiritual floor? Was that person characterized by a judgmental and critical spirit, a severe and self-righteous manner . . . or was he or she a person of mercy? The answer is obvious. In times of crisis and outright failure, a person doesn't need someone else to act as judge or critic. Instead, the person needs someone who can remind him or her of the mercy of God. Jesus says that his followers are to be merciful, just as the Father is. And when they fail—which they will, repeatedly—they can thank God that he deals with them mercifully too.

JESUS TEACHES ABOUT CRITICIZING OTHERS / 6:37-42 / **63**

Jesus not only commanded his disciples to be loving and merci- ful, he also went on to explain to them what true love entails. First he emphasized that true love does not judge others or with- hold forgiveness. Jesus, the communicator par excellence, drove home the point with a graphic illustration: a comparison of a per- son with a speck of sawdust in the eye with a person with a plank in the eye. Jesus took the analogy to an extreme to emphasize how repulsive it is to God for a sinner to judge another sinner. Only God, the Perfect One, can judge in justice. Believers need to be slow to condemn others and allow God to judge another per- son's motives. If a church community must censure a person, it needs to examine itself thoroughly before confronting the person (see Matthew 18:15-17).

6:37 **"Do not judge, and you will not be judged; do not condemn, and you will not be condemned. Forgive, and you will be for- given."**NRSV Jesus continued to speak about the attitudes that would charac- terize his followers. Jesus explained that his people must not *judge* or *con- demn* but that they should be willing to *forgive*.

> In judging and censuring our brethren, we meddle with that which does not belong to us.
> *Matthew Henry*

While the word "judge" (Greek, *krino*) can mean to evaluate or analyze, Jesus did not mean his people should refuse to think critically or make decisions, nor was he attempting to abolish the legal system or disciplinary measures. Believers must be discerning and make certain judgments. For example, Jesus said to expose false teachers (Matthew 7:15-23) and to admonish others in order to help them (Matthew 18:15). Paul taught that we should exercise church discipline (1 Corinthians 5:1-5). Jesus was referring to the judgmental attitude that focuses on others' faults, tearing them down. Harsh judgment often leads to an attitude of condemnation, and this also must not characterize Jesus' followers. One cannot love and have a judgmental, condemnatory spirit (see Galatians 6:1; Hebrews 3:13).

Believers' special position with Christ does not give them license to take God's place as judge. Those who judge in that manner will find themselves *judged* likewise by God. Neither should they condemn, otherwise they will *be condemned.* This judgment and condemnation could refer to this world or the world to come. Those who refuse to judge and condemn others usually find that people will return the favor. Likewise when they forgive.

The practice of forgiveness leads also to forgiveness by God. Those who refuse to forgive show that they do not understand what God has done for them. God's children must be ready and willing to forgive, just as God has forgiven them.

JUDGING OTHERS

If you were caught in some notorious sin—unquestionably, publicly, humiliatingly—would you run to the church, or away? Unfortunately, many, if not most, people probably would run away. How ironic, how tragic! The church exists to proclaim the mercies of God. The church exists to let people know that God is indeed the righteous judge, that he does not laugh at sin or treat it lightly . . . but also that he has made a way of atonement and redemption for those who deserve his wrath. Yet the church is often thought of as the first place a person would go to be judged for his or her sins.

You may not be able to change your whole church, but you can take a bold, unblinking look at your own attitudes. When you hear of another Christian being involved in some scandalous behavior, how do you react? With smugness, superiority, self-righteousness? Or is your heart grieved for that person, knowing that you are capable of committing the same sins, or worse? When you are tempted to act as someone else's judge, remember what God has done so that you can be pardoned before him. Then extend that same grace to your fallen brother or sister.

6:38 **"Give, and it will be given to you. A good measure, pressed down, shaken together and running over, will be poured into your lap. For with the measure you use, it will be measured to**

you."^{NIV} Generosity in giving, both material goods as well as love, compassion, and forgiveness of others, will result in returned generosity. The Jewish rabbis pictured God as having two scales—one called justice, the other mercy. If believers, having been forgiven (measured by the mercy scale), withhold mercy to others, God will judge them by his scale of justice. How easy it is for people to want strict and harsh justice measured to others while expecting mercy for themselves. Jesus wants his disciples to be merciful and loving, not selfish or spiteful. He does away with retaliation and the concept of demanding an eye-for-an-eye recompense for wrongdoing. The picture is of blessings being returned in a bushel basket, filled to the brim, *pressed down* and *shaken together* to make room for more, then *running over* so that you have to hold up your shirt like a basket in *your lap* to catch the rest. *With the measure you use, it will be measured to you.* In Palestine, it was required that the bushel used to purchase grain would be used to deliver it; this was to prevent fraud. Jesus wants our measure of mercy to overflow. Those who give easily will find goodness coming back to them. Those who are stingy and reluctant givers will receive in the same way.

RUNNING OVER
A forgiving spirit demonstrates that a person has received God's forgiveness. Jesus used the picture of measuring grain in a basket to ensure the full amount. Those who are critical rather than compassionate will also receive criticism. Those who treat others generously, graciously, and compassionately, however, will receive the qualities in full measure. God will use the same method to judge people (exacting or generous) that they use to judge others. Taking a stand against sin is important, but Jesus' teaching is that believers are to be generous in their giving and that their mercy must supersede their desire to condemn the guilty. Give your love—generously, unhesitatingly, running over.

6:39-40 He also told them a parable: "Can a blind person guide a blind person? Will not both fall into a pit? A disciple is not above the teacher, but everyone who is fully qualified will be like the teacher."^{NRSV} In this parable, Jesus explained that, while his followers are to give, love, and refuse to be judgmental, they must also be discerning and careful whom they follow. Obviously, the first question here demands a negative answer—no, a blind person cannot lead a blind person because *both* of them will end up in *a pit*. Then Jesus explained what he meant: *a disciple is not above the teacher*. Those who lead others must have clear

vision, willingness to learn and understand, and no arrogance or
self-righteousness. Such a standard would disqualify the Pharisees, who, in this instance, were the blind guides leading people
into disaster. Jesus explained that his disciples should not go
beyond what they learned from him; instead, they should aim to
be like him. They should not ignore any of his commands; they
should not use their own "insight" in order to skirt certain commands, believing themselves to be "beyond" them. Jesus' disciples would need to watch out for spiritual blindness or a loveless
atttitude. Both would blind them and cause them to lead others
astray. Watch out whom you follow. No matter how many human
teachers you may have, your ultimate authority must be Christ
and his Word.

BLINDNESS
Be careful whom you follow. Some people, because of their
age, experience, and track record, are wonderful guides and
mentors. They can lead the way because they have been there
themselves, and they know the right paths to take. They have
learned from both their successes and their failures. Other
people merely repeat their mistakes over and over. These
people are "blind," as Jesus said (6:39), and they lead others
down the wrong road with them. Do you have a mentor,
someone who willingly shares his or her insights and experience with you? The right role model or mentor can bring
tremendous benefits to your life. The wrong one can bring grief
and sorrow. Be careful whom you follow.

6:41-42 **"And why worry about a speck in your friend's eye when you
have a log in your own? How can you think of saying,
'Friend, let me help you get rid of that speck in your eye,'
when you can't see past the log in your own eye? Hypocrite!
First get rid of the log from your own eye; then perhaps you
will see well enough to deal with the speck in your friend's
eye!"**NLT How well Jesus understood human nature. He knew that
human beings find it easy to *worry about a speck in [a] friend's
eye when [they] have a log in [their] own.* It is easy for people to
overlook their own sins yet easily spot sin in others. It's true that
the sin that people most clearly see in others is also present in
them. Sometimes they may offer help by saying, *"Friend, let me
help you get rid of that speck in your eye."* But there is a crucial
flaw, for they will do great damage when they *can't see past the
log* still lodged in their eye. Jesus used hyperbole to show that
someone attempting to help a brother or sister with a "speck"
when that person is carrying around a "log" makes him or her a

hypocrite. The person has criticized and found fault in another without applying the same standards to himself. Before that person can be of any assistance, he must *first get rid of the log* that is in his own eye, and then maybe he can *see well enough to deal with the speck* in the other person's eye.

The word "speck" also has been translated "splinter"; "log" also has been translated "plank" or "beam." Many have taken this metaphor to mean that Christians should never correct anyone— one's personal sins before God are too great to even consider dealing with others' sins. However, Jesus' point was that while all people have sin in their lives (some as small as a speck; some as large as a log), they are responsible to deal with their own sins first and then help others. James wrote, "My brothers and sisters, if anyone among you wanders from the truth and is brought back by another, you should know that whoever brings back a sinner from wandering will save the sinner's soul from death and will cover a multitude of sins" (James 5:19-20 NRSV). However, while the person with the "speck" may certainly need help, that help must come from one who can "see clearly" to take out that speck. Paul wrote to the Galatians, "My friends, if anyone is detected in a transgression, you who have received the Spirit should restore such a one in a spirit of gentleness. Take care that you yourselves are not tempted" (Galatians 6:1 NRSV). Only those who are spiritually mature can discern when and how to confront sin in others.

Believers should not be so afraid of the label "hypocrite" that they stand still in the Christian life, hiding their faith and making no attempts to grow. A person who tries to do right but often fails is not a hypocrite. Neither are those who fulfill their duty even when they don't feel like doing it—it is often necessary and good to set aside one's desires in order to do what needs to be done. It is not hypocrisy to be weak in faith. A hypocrite is a person who puts on religious behavior in order to gain attention, approval, acceptance, or admiration from others.

MOVE THE LOGS
In these words about the speck or log in one's eye—Jesus did not mean that Christians should ignore wrongdoing but that they should not be so worried about others' sins that they overlook their own. People often rationalize their sins by pointing out the same mistakes in others. What kinds of specks in others' eyes are the easiest for you to criticize? Remember your own "logs" when you feel like criticizing, and you may find that you have less to say.

JESUS TEACHES ABOUT FRUIT IN PEOPLE'S LIVES / 6:43-45 / **66**

With a couple of proverbs derived from the agricultural setting of ancient Israel, Jesus showed his audience why hypocritically judging others (6:41-42) is foolish. Just as a good tree will eventually bear good fruit, so a person's heart will eventually bear fruit—a good heart producing good works and an evil heart bringing forth evil. Everyone's heart will eventually be exposed for what it is, and a strong indicator of the character of a person's heart is what one says. With these simple proverbs, Jesus demands much more from his followers than external obedience to a list of rules. He demands a changed heart—one that is centered on God and not on self, that delights in good and not evil. His demands are great, but the power he gives to live a godly life is even greater.

6:43-45 **"A good tree can't produce bad fruit, and a bad tree can't produce good fruit. A tree is identified by the kind of fruit it produces. Figs never grow on thornbushes or grapes on bramble bushes."**NLT *Figs* and *grapes* were two of the main agricultural products of Israel; no one would misunderstand Jesus' meaning. A person knows a tree by its fruit. Fruit is good or bad depending on the health of the tree. A *good* (or healthy) *tree can't produce bad fruit,* and likewise, a *bad* (or unhealthy) *tree can't produce good fruit.* (The positive and negative repetition of the teaching in these verses was a common Jewish teaching method.) In Matthew this teaching follows directly after Jesus' warning to "watch out for false prophets" (Matthew 7:15 NIV). While Luke did not include Jesus' comments about false prophets here, he has been writing about the characteristics of Jesus' followers from their attitudes toward enemies to their generosity of spirit. Jesus had explained that "a student is not greater than the teacher" (6:40 NLT). "Fruit" is a Jewish metaphor for both character and conduct. Jesus' followers would be able to discern falseness in teachers, prophets, and fellow believers by looking at their lives and conduct.

Claims are easier to make or fake than results. Even Jesus' claims would have been ludicrous if he hadn't backed them up with results. He understood the relationship between claim and proof. And he pointed out that the principle applies universally: You can tell a lot about a tree from its fruit! Jesus warned that people are like trees: Examine their "fruit" closely. Bad characters frequently attempt to pass as believers. Some can cover it up so well that they become teachers and leaders. Eventually, however, their "fruit" will make them known: **"A good person produces good deeds from a good**

heart, and an evil person produces evil deeds from an evil heart. Whatever is in your heart determines what you say."ᴺᴸᵀ Jesus reminded his listeners that their *deeds* and speech (what they *say*) would reveal their true underlying beliefs, attitudes, and motivations. The good impressions people try to make cannot last if their hearts are deceptive. What is in the heart will come out in a person's speech and behavior.

HEART, SOUL, AND MOUTH
"Pay no attention to that man behind the curtain!" Everyone who has seen *The Wizard of Oz* remembers that scene from near the end of the movie. The great, fire-breathing "wizard" was nothing more than a normal man, standing behind a curtain, working a machine. In spite of all his attempts to fool people, the truth came out. It's the same with people's words and actions. They can put up a good show for a while, but sooner or later, the real "person behind the curtain" shows through. What does your language and your behavior reveal about the real you? If you find that your words and actions are disproportionately angry, depressed, and hopeless, then take them to the Lord and ask him to transform them—from the inside out.

JESUS TEACHES ABOUT THOSE WHO BUILD HOUSES ON ROCK AND SAND / 6:46-49 / **67**

The Sermon on the Plain ends with a clear warning from Jesus to put his words into action. Jesus was not content with letting his audience ponder his profound thoughts. His teaching is not meant for academic discussion and debate. Instead Christians should build their entire lives around his teachings, applying them to every facet of life. If they don't, they will not be able to withstand the pressures and temptations of this world and will be swept away to their destruction. Jesus calls believers to take the time they have now—before the floodwaters come—to reevaluate the way they live in light of his teachings.

6:46-47 **"So why do you call me 'Lord,' when you won't obey me? I will show you what it's like when someone comes to me, listens to my teaching, and then obeys me."**ᴺᴸᵀ People who choose to follow Jesus will find a change in their attitudes and behavior, as Jesus has just described. Those who are false followers will be found out by the "fruit" they produce (6:43-45). To call Jesus *Lord* means to have committed oneself to following him and his teaching. Why would someone call Jesus "Lord" and then refuse to obey his teachings? Jesus' true followers not only hear his words, but they act on his words, allowing his message to make a difference in their lives. The following parable will *show* Jesus' listeners *what it's like* when a person *comes, listens, and then obeys.*

COME, LISTEN, OBEY
You go to the doctor. She diagnoses your problem and gives you a prescription, telling you to take the medication daily and check in with her in a week. The week passes; you go in for the follow-up appointment. "Have you been taking the medication?" she asks.

"No," you say, "I decided I didn't really need to."

"Then why are you coming to me for treatment?" she asks, reasonably enough. "Why ask my advice? Why bother having a doctor at all?"

It's doubtful that anyone would do that. And yet how often do we Christians profess Jesus as our Lord, then ignore his clear commands? We call him Lord, yet do not do what he tells us to do. It's as foolish as seeing a doctor and then disregarding her instructions. The Lord's commands are clear and relatively few: Love God. Love one another. Treat others as you want to be treated. Be forgiving with the offender and compassionate with the weak and oppressed. Are there areas of your life that need to be brought under his lordship? Ask him to enable you to do so by his grace today.

6:48 **"It is like a person who builds a house on a strong foundation laid upon the underlying rock. When the floodwaters rise and break against the house, it stands firm because it is well built."**ᴺᴸᵀ Jesus explained that his true followers, by coming, listening, and obeying (6:46-47) were *like a person who builds a house on a strong foundation laid upon the underlying rock.* The one who builds "on rock" is a hearing, responding disciple, not a superficial one. Practicing obedience builds on the solid foundation of Jesus' words to weather the storms of life. Jesus pictured Palestine's climate in these words. There were few rainfalls all year, but during the rainy season, heavy rains with excessive flooding could wash away poorly grounded homes. But those houses with their foundations on solid rock would be unaffected by the rising waters and beating winds—*when the floodwaters rise and break against the house, it stands firm because it is well built.* When the "storms of life" come (perhaps the hatred and persecution Jesus warned his followers to expect) only the person who builds his or her life on the "strong foundation" of Jesus Christ will be able to "stand firm." When life is calm, the foundation doesn't seem to matter. But when crises come, the foundation is tested. Be sure your life is built on the solid foundation of knowing and trusting Jesus Christ.

6:49 **"But anyone who listens and doesn't obey is like a person who builds a house without a foundation. When the floods sweep down against that house, it will crumble into a heap of ruins."**[NLT] In contrast to the one who comes, listens, and obeys is the person who *listens and doesn't obey.* While both of these people may have built houses that looked identical, the crucial difference was in the foundation. The person who won't listen to Jesus will be *like a person who builds a house without a foundation.* When the floodwaters *sweep down against that house,* it cannot stand firm. The sand beneath the house will be driven away, and the house *will crumble into a heap of ruins.* As character is revealed by fruit (6:43-45), so faith is revealed by storms. The wise person, seeking to act upon God's Word, builds to withstand anything. It will be the foundation, not the house, that will determine what happens on the Day of judgment.

SETTLING FOR SAND
Why would people build a house without a foundation? Perhaps they want to save time and avoid the hard work of preparing a stone foundation. Possibly because the waterfront scenery is more attractive or because beach houses have higher social status than cliff houses. Perhaps because they want to join their friends who have already settled in sandy areas. For some reason people who build their lives on weak foundations assume that disaster can't happen to them. When God judges each person's life, only those who have built on Jesus and his teaching will stand the test. Obedience is the only flood insurance you need.

LUKE 7

The story of the centurion's extraordinary faith in Jesus reiterates a dominant theme in Luke's writings (this Gospel and the book of Acts): the inclusion of the Gentiles in the family of faith. One of Luke's major purposes for writing was to demonstrate to Theophilus, a Gentile convert to Christianity (1:1; Acts 1:1), that Jesus had come to save both the Jews and the Gentiles. This theme can be seen in this Gospel in the fact that Luke traced Jesus' genealogy back to Adam (3:38), that he recorded the songs of Mary and Simeon, which both allude to the extension of salvation to the Gentiles (1:50; 2:32), and that he emphasized Jesus' association with the Samaritans (a group held in contempt by Jews because they were a "mixed race" contaminated by Gentile blood, see 10:33; 17:16). This passage tells of Jesus extending his healing ministry to a Gentile and commending the centurion for his genuine faith (which rivaled the faith of Israelites). In the first sermon that Luke records, Jesus had already compared the faith of Gentiles to the unbelief of the Israelites (in the time of Elijah and Elisha, see 4:24-26). The faith of this centurion foreshadows the faith of another centurion, Cornelius, the first Gentile convert to Christianity (see Acts 10).

For those connected to a predominantly Gentile church, these distinctions between Jew and Gentile appear antiquated, a part of a church debate that has no relevance. Nothing could be farther from the truth. Jesus excludes no one. He has commissioned believers to proclaim the Good News to all—from the people of a remote village to the "annoying" neighbor next door (24:46-49; Matthew 28:18-20).

7:1 **When Jesus had finished saying all this, he went back to Capernaum.**^{NLT} *Capernaum* had become Jesus' "home base" while he was in Galilee. Located on the northwestern shore of the Sea of Galilee, Capernaum was the largest of the many cities surrounding the lake. Far more than just a fishing village, it was the economic center of Galilee and sat near a major trade route and thus was a wealthy city. The city housed a contingent of Roman soldiers even though Galilee was not under Roman occupation until after the death of Herod Agrippa in A.D. 44. Because Capernaum had the headquarters for Roman troops, the city was filled with heathen influences from all over the Roman Empire. The Gospels do not explain why Jesus chose this city, although it must have offered good possibilities for ministry such as (1) it was farther away from the intense opposition of the Pharisees in Nazareth; (2) it was a busy place, so Jesus' message could reach many people and spread quickly; and (3) it was home to several of the disciples and could provide extra resources and support for his ministry.

7:2-3 **A centurion there had a slave whom he valued highly, and who was ill and close to death. When he heard about Jesus, he sent some Jewish elders to him, asking him to come and heal his servant.**[NRSV] A *centurion* was a Roman army officer in charge of one hundred men. Often the sons of Roman senators or powerful figures would begin their careers at this level.

This centurion *had a slave whom he valued highly* and whom he wanted to be healed. Why so much concern about a slave? The Jewish historian Josephus wrote that Roman soldiers had many slaves who actually trained and fought with them. So this slave may have been the centurion's personal attendant with whom he felt a close bond. Thus, this centurion made an appeal on behalf of his servant *who was ill and close to death.* (Matthew 8:6 tells us that the servant was paralyzed and suffering terribly.)

BREAKING DOWN BARRIERS
This passage marks a turning point in Luke's account of Jesus' ministry. Up until this point, Jesus has dealt exclusively with the Jews; here he begins to include the Gentiles. Notice who the main characters are in this short drama: the Jewish elders, a Roman centurion, and the centurion's slave. The elders were part of God's chosen nation, Israel, but they are generally not well spoken of in Scripture. Centurions are generally regarded positively by the Gospel writers but were obviously not part of the chosen people. And slaves were regarded at that time as human chattel, little more than mere property. Jesus broke through all those barriers, all the way to the sick man's need. The gospel travels well across ethnic, racial, national, and religious barriers. Are you willing to work through them as well? Do you have friends, Christian or non-Christian, from other racial and ethnic backgrounds? Jesus was no respecter of such artificial divisions. Reach out to those whom Jesus came to save.

The centurion had *heard about Jesus,* so he certainly knew of Jesus' healing power. So he sent a request for healing to Jesus apparently because he believed Jesus was sent from God. He may have known about the healing of the Roman official's son (which probably occurred earlier, see John 4:46-54). He knew that Jesus had the power to heal his slave.

Matthew 8:5 says the Roman centurion visited Jesus himself, while Luke says he sent Jewish *elders* to present his request to Jesus. In those days, dealing with a person's messengers was considered the same as dealing with the one who had sent them. Thus, in dealing with the messengers, Jesus was dealing with the centurion. For his Jewish audience, Matthew emphasized the man's faith. For his Gentile audience, Luke highlighted the good relationship between the Jewish elders and the Roman centurion. As an army captain, he daily delegated work and sent groups on missions, so this was how he chose to get his message to Jesus.

7:4-5 **When they came to Jesus, they appealed to him earnestly, saying, "He is worthy of having you do this for him, for he loves our people, and it is he who built our synagogue for us."**[NRSV] The animosity between the Jews and the Romans was no secret. The Jews hated the occupation army; the Romans, in turn, hated the Jews. Yet in this story we find a different sort of Roman soldier—a man who seems to have been a God-fearing man. He loved the Jewish people, and he built their synagogue (meaning that he funded it and certainly had genuine interest in it and the God worshiped there). That this centurion could request a favor of these Jewish elders and have them respond so willingly would normally come as a surprise. That the elders *appealed to [Jesus] earnestly* on behalf of this centurion was even more out of character with normal Jewish/Roman relations. The elders appealed to Jesus, saying that this centurion was *worthy* of having Jesus heal his slave.

A WORD FROM JESUS
It's difficult to find people who can be taken absolutely at their word. In spite of good intentions, many people are not completely reliable and trustworthy. What a treasure when we meet reliable people! We respect and admire them. The centurion who sent for Jesus' help somehow knew that Jesus was completely dependable. And, what's more, he knew Jesus was capable of doing what he said he would do. Hence the soldier's confession of faith: "Say the word, and my servant will be healed." His trust in Jesus serves as an excellent model for ours. We should strive to obey Jesus and take him at his word.

7:6-7 **So Jesus went with them. He was not far from the house when the centurion sent friends to say to him: "Lord, don't trouble yourself, for I do not deserve to have you come under my roof. That is why I did not even consider myself worthy to come to you. But say the word, and my servant will be healed."**[NIV] Jesus responded to the request brought by the Jewish elders and *went with them* to the centurion's home. Surely the centurion knew of the Jewish policy of not entering Gentile homes and may have realized, on second thought, his presumption in asking this Jewish teacher to come. So when Jesus and the Jewish elders were *not far from the house,* the centurion sent another message by way of some friends: *"Lord, don't trouble yourself, for I do not deserve to have you come under my roof."* He understood that since he was a Gentile, he was considered unclean by the Jews. He may also have felt himself unworthy to have Jesus enter his home, and he *did not even consider [himself] worthy to come to* meet Jesus. The centurion showed that he had the true attitude of a disciple (see Peter's response in 5:8). He called Jesus "Lord," indicating his respect for Jesus. This Gentile understood more than most of the Jews of Jesus' day; he saw Jesus' superiority. He saw that Jesus' authority was greater than his own and that Jesus did not have to personally visit his home. The centurion understood that Jesus needed only to *say the word* to heal the servant (see Psalm 107:20). Most of the people who came to Jesus sought to get close enough to touch him in order to be healed, but this centurion knew that Jesus could also heal without touch. His word would be enough.

AUTHORITY
A private does not ponder the wisdom of his sergeant's orders before carrying them out. A captain doesn't debate with a colonel the merits of his decisions. Soldiers respond to and obey orders from their commanding officers. Otherwise, the military would collapse in chaos and never be able to defend itself against another army. Any good military person, like this centurion, understands this implicitly. That is probably why the centurion was able to grasp so profoundly the authority that Jesus possessed over even diseases. When you read God's commands in the Bible, or sense his leading in prayer, do you respond as automatically as a soldier under someone else's authority? Do you carry out the Lord's instructions as faithfully and unquestioningly as this centurion? Do you regard yourself as a person under God's authority?

7:8 **"For I also am a man set under authority, with soldiers under me; and I say to one, 'Go,' and he goes, and to another, 'Come,' and he comes, and to my slave, 'Do this,' and the**

slave does it."^{NRSV} The centurion had authority by virtue of his position. He had soldiers under him who had been trained to respond unquestioningly. He was *a man set under authority* because final authority rested with the Roman emperor. The emperor delegated responsibility to various officials such as this centurion. The centurion was accustomed both to obeying and to being obeyed. He may have understood that Jesus' power and authority came from God. When Jesus spoke, God spoke. Jesus did not need rituals or medicines or even his touch or presence to accomplish a healing. The centurion applied his understanding of authority to Jesus. Just as this officer did not need to be present to have his orders carried out, so Jesus didn't need to be present to heal. The centurion had absolutely no doubt that Jesus could merely speak the word and heal the servant.

FAITH LIKE THIS
Everybody loves to see the underdog come through. It's become a movie cliché—the poor kid with nothing going for him except his own heart and determination wins against the wealthy, privileged kid whose parents and trainers have given him every material advantage. There's something about a man or woman who achieves against the odds and overcomes the obstacles. Spiritually, the Jews had every advantage: they had Abraham as their father, Moses had given them God's law, and they had the great written record of the kings and the prophets to instruct and inspire them. In spite of all that, they were still lacking something: courageous, unquestioning faith. This Gentile, on the other hand, this Roman centurion—who had none of the advantages God's people had enjoyed for hundreds and hundreds of years—had such a faith, and it astonished Jesus and, presumably, gave him great joy. The faith present in many who have been in church for many years would hardly astonish Jesus. Believers must keep their trust in Christ at full strength. Reading Christ's words and studying his amazing life will fortify your faith.

7:9 **When Jesus heard this, he was amazed. Turning to the crowd, he said, "I tell you, I haven't seen faith like this in all the land of Israel!"**^{NLT} This Roman centurion grasped the "big picture" about Jesus' authority. The Jews who had been looking for Jesus couldn't see him for who he was, yet this Gentile did. That's why Jesus *was amazed* and exclaimed to *the crowd* that he had not *seen faith like this in all the land of Israel.* This did not mean that no one in Israel had faith, but many did not accept the Good News (Romans 10:16). Without the benefit of growing up memorizing the Old Testament Scriptures and learning from esteemed Jewish leaders, this Gentile man understood the need to depend totally on Jesus' power. He knew, without a doubt, that Jesus could do what seemed impossible. Such faith both astonished and pleased Jesus.

7:10 **And when the captain's friends returned to his house, they found the slave completely healed.**NLT Luke did not even record another word spoken by Jesus, but emphasized that the centurion's faith had been well placed. The *captain's friends returned to his house* and *found the slave completely healed.* Matthew wrote that "his servant was healed at that very hour" (Matthew 8:13 NIV), meaning he was healed immediately.

JESUS RAISES A WIDOW'S SON FROM THE DEAD / 7:11-17 / **69**

With a touch and his word, Jesus gave life. He had already healed a number of maladies: demon possession (4:35), sin (5:20), and all kinds of diseases (5:13, 15). Here Jesus clearly demonstrated his power over death.

The people correctly perceived the implications: Jesus was a great prophet (similar to Elijah and Elisha; see 1 Kings 17:17-24; 2 Kings 4:8-37), and God had come "to help" them (7:16 NIV). God has also come today. In the Bible, he shows the way of life, and, through the leading of the Spirit, he guides us to the truth. The townspeople of Nain began praising God and telling others the good news about Jesus.

7:11-12 **Soon afterwards he went to a town called Nain, and his disciples and a large crowd went with him. As he approached the gate of the town, a man who had died was being carried out. He was his mother's only son, and she was a widow; and with her was a large crowd from the town.**NRSV The *town called Nain* was a few miles southeast of Nazareth (see map) and about a day's journey from Capernaum. Jesus continued his teaching ministry throughout the land, training *his disciples* and being followed by *a large crowd* of the curious that went from place to place. Upon approaching the *gate of the town* of Nain, they came upon a funeral procession. A woman led the procession, followed by the dead man being carried out and then a *large crowd from the town.*

In contrast to Jesus' crowd, this crowd would have been a group of mourners. Honoring the dead was important in Jewish tradition. A funeral procession—the relatives of the dead person following the body that was wrapped and carried on a kind of stretcher— would make its way through town. The burial ground was usually outside the town, and the body was on its way to the burial site. As the procession passed, bystanders would be expected to join. In addition, hired mourners would cry aloud and draw attention to the procession. The family's mourning would continue for thirty days. What made this funeral especially sad was that the dead young man *was his mother's only son, and she was a widow.*

7:13 When the Lord saw her, his heart went out to her and he said, "Don't cry."^{NIV} This woman had already lost her husband, and here her only son was dead—her last means of support. The crowd of mourners would go home, and she would be left penni-

less and alone. The widow was probably past the age of childbearing and would not marry again. Unless a relative would come to her aid, her future was bleak. In the first century, it was very difficult for a woman to earn her own living. Without anyone to provide for the widow, she would be an easy prey for swindlers, and she would likely be reduced to begging for food. No wonder *when the Lord saw* this sad sight and the tearful woman, *his heart went out to her.* In fact, as Luke repeatedly emphasized, Jesus cares about people's deepest needs. As Jesus' crowd met the crowd of mourners, Jesus went to the woman and gently said, *"Don't cry."* This would be a meaningless request under most circumstances; however, Jesus, Lord over death itself, was going to change the circumstances. Jesus has the power to bring hope out of any tragedy.

JESUS RAISES A WIDOW'S SON
Jesus traveled to Nain and met a funeral procession leaving the village. A widow's only son had died, leaving her virtually helpless, but Jesus brought the young man back to life. This miracle, recorded only in Luke, reveals Jesus' compassion for people's needs.

7:14 Then he came forward and touched the bier, and the bearers stood still. And he said, "Young man, I say to you, rise!"^{NRSV} Jesus again reached out to someone in need with compassion, risking becoming unclean. To touch even the bier would have made him unclean. Yet this time *he came forward.* No one came to him; no one asked him for anything, but Jesus wanted to relieve this woman's suffering. Risking ceremonial defilement according to the law (Numbers 19:11-22), Jesus *touched the bier,* the frame on which the corpse, usually wrapped in shrouds, was laid to be carried out for burial. Jesus' approaching the procession and touching the bier was highly unusual, so *the bearers stood still.* Jesus may have asked them to stop. Then he spoke directly to the body that lay on the bier, *"Young man, I say to you, rise!"*

COMPASSION
How do you react when you see a funeral procession? Sadness, grief, indifference, even anger or annoyance . . . different people have different responses to others' grief. Luke 7:13-14 shows us Jesus' response to such a situation. The text does not reveal if Jesus knew the bereaved mother or her son, but he felt compassion for her. Perhaps Jesus was thinking ahead to the time when his own mother would have to endure the loss of her son. Whatever the reason, we know that Jesus reached out to this woman in empathy and compassion in her time of grief. When you are confronted by human suffering, grief, pain, need, you have a choice: you can walk away, hiding behind social, pragmatic, or even religious excuses; or you can emulate Jesus and reach out in compassion to others in his name.

7:15 Then the dead boy sat up and began to talk to those around him! And Jesus gave him back to his mother.[NLT] Imagine the surprise of the crowd—Jesus' followers, the mourners, the mother, and those carrying the bier! Suddenly the boy who had been dead *sat up and began to talk.* What he said is left to our imagination, but the important point is that *Jesus gave him back to his mother.* Jesus did the ultimate act of compassion—he did what no human being could have done. These words are almost identical to 1 Kings 17:23 when the great Old Testament prophet Elijah brought a widow's only son back to life. After doing so, "he gave him to his mother" (NIV).

7:16 They were all filled with awe and praised God. "A great prophet has appeared among us," they said. "God has come to help his people."[NIV] The miracle of raising a widow's son to life brought to the people's minds the story of Elijah and the widow of Zarephath. While John the Baptist was like Elijah as forerunner (Malachi 4:5), Luke pictures Jesus as Elijah the prophet because of his miraculous works. When Elijah brought back the widow's son, she exclaimed, "Now I know that you are a man of God and that the word of the LORD from your mouth is the truth" (1 Kings 17:24 NIV). The people in this story likewise were *filled with awe, praised God,* and exclaimed that *a great prophet [had] appeared among [them].* The people thought of Jesus as a prophet because, like the Old Testament prophets, he

RAISED FROM THE DEAD

There are many comparisons to this story and the one recorded in 1 Kings 17:8-24. The location and the nature of the miracle caused the townspeople to recognize that a "great prophet" was among them.

Elijah/Elisha	*Jesus*
Elijah raised the son of a widow in Zarephath. He first met the widow at the town gate (1 Kings 17:10).	Jesus met the woman as he approached the town gate (Luke 7:12).
The boy who died was the son of a widow (1 Kings 17:9, 17).	The boy who died was the son of a widow (Luke 7:12).
The expression is that Elijah "gave" the boy back to his mother (1 Kings 17:23).	The expression is repeated that Jesus "gave him back to his mother" (Luke 7:15).
The recognition that a man of God had done the miracle (1 Kings 17:24).	The recognition that "a great prophet has appeared among us" (Luke 7:16).
Elisha also raised a boy from the dead, the only child of a woman in Shunem (2 Kings 4:8, 32-37).	Jesus raised a boy from the dead, the only son of a widow in Nain (Luke 7:11). Scholars place Nain on the other side of the hill of Moreh from Shunem, thus placing this miracle in the same general location as Elisha's. The people would have remembered this from Scripture and the life of the great prophet Elisha.
However: Elijah had to cry out to the Lord and stretch himself on the boy three times (1 Kings 17:20-21).	*However:* Jesus merely had to speak a word of command. Jesus spoke and the boy came back to life. Jesus clearly had superior power than all the greatest OT prophets.
Elisha prayed and stretched himself out on the boy (2 Kings 4:32-35).	

boldly proclaimed God's message and performed great miracles. Both Elijah and Elisha had raised children from the dead (1 Kings 17:17-24; 2 Kings 4:8-37). The people were correct in thinking that Jesus was a prophet, but he was much more—he was God himself. That they recognized that *God has come to help his people* probably does not mean that they recognized Jesus as God. Instead, they were using an Old Testament expression that often denoted blessing (as in Ruth 1:6; 1 Samuel 2:21).

7:17 This news about Jesus spread throughout Judea and the surrounding country.[NIV] The obvious result of Jesus' miraculous act of raising a dead person to life meant that the *news . . . spread throughout Judea and the surrounding country.* The town of Nain is actually in the region of Galilee, so the word "Judea" is used here not for the region but for the entire "land of the Jews" (as in 4:44). Word about Jesus went all over the country and beyond.

JESUS EASES JOHN'S DOUBT / 7:18-35 / **70**

"Are you the Messiah we've been expecting?" (7:19 NLT). Luke used John the Baptist's simple question as a springboard for exploring Jesus' identity. He was not merely a prophet (as the people recognized in the preceding section; 7:16); he was the Prophet, the promised Messiah. Jesus' response to John the Baptist's question made this clear: "the blind see," "the dead are raised," and "the gospel is preached to the poor"—all signs of the glorious day of God's salvation in the prophecy of Isaiah (Isaiah 26:18-19; 35:5-6; 61:1). The answer to John's question is an implicit "yes." Yes—Jesus is the Messiah!

But not everyone recognizes this. Luke noted that those who submitted to John's baptism of repentance believed in Jesus, but those who refused (the Pharisees) also rejected and ridiculed the Lord Jesus. Jesus compared the Pharisees' rejection of him to the foolishness of a selfish child who refuses to play because he cannot have everything his way. All too often people imitate the silliness of the Pharisees, demanding that God act like they want him to. They get mad at God—for not giving success in their careers, for not delivering them from difficult situations, for not giving a little more money. Instead, believers should imitate the tax collectors, who not only recognized that God's ways were right but also submitted to the Lord's will for them.

7:18-20 **John's disciples told him about all these things. Calling two of them, he sent them to the Lord to ask, "Are you the one who was to come, or should we expect someone else?" When the men came to Jesus, they said, "John the Baptist sent us to you to ask, 'Are you the one who was to come, or should we expect someone else?'"**[NIV] At this time, John the Baptist was in prison (see 3:19-20). King Herod, also known as Herod Antipas, had married his own sister-in-law, and John the Baptist had publicly rebuked Herod's blatant sin. In an attempt to quiet him, Herod had imprisoned him (see also Matthew 4:12; 14:1-5).

John the Baptist had his own *disciples* who apparently were keeping in touch with him during his imprisonment. They *told him about all these things,* referring to Jesus and his activities—healing people, raising some from the dead, and teaching about a

coming kingdom. This caused John to
wonder, so he called two of his disciples and sent them back to Jesus with a
question: *"Are you the one who was to
come, or should we expect someone
else?"* The "one who was to come"
referred to the promised Messiah. This
statement provides a glimpse of John's
human side. He had baptized Jesus, had
seen the heavens open, and had heard
the voice of God (3:21-22), yet something caused him to doubt.

> Christ distinguished
> between doubt and
> unbelief. Doubt says,
> "I can't believe." Unbelief
> says, "I won't believe."
> Doubt is honest. Unbelief
> is obstinate.
>   *Henry Drummond*

Perhaps John was wondering why Jesus brought blessing but
little judgment, for John had preached that Jesus would baptize
with the Holy Spirit and fire and separate the "wheat" from the
"chaff" (3:15-17). Jesus' peaceful teaching and healing ministry
may not have seemed to measure up. Maybe John wondered that
if Jesus was the promised Messiah, why he didn't just say so.
John, like the rest of the Jews, expected Jesus to be the conquering Messiah-King. What did all the parables and veiled teachings
mean? Was Jesus really "the one," or was he another prophet and
they should *expect someone else?*

**7:21 Jesus had just then cured many people of diseases, plagues,
and evil spirits, and had given sight to many who were
blind.**NRSV The acts listed here that Jesus *had just then* done consist of observable deeds, not theories—actions that Jesus' contemporaries had seen and have reported for people to read today. The
prophets had said that the Messiah would do these very acts (see
Isaiah 35:5-6; 61:1). These physical proofs helped John—and
will help people today—to recognize who Jesus is.

**7:22-23 Then he told John's disciples, "Go back to John and tell
him what you have seen and heard—the blind see, the lame
walk, the lepers are cured, the deaf hear, the dead are
raised to life, and the Good News is being preached to the
poor. And tell him, 'God blesses those who are not offended
by me.'"**NLT Jesus answered John's doubts by telling John's disciples to *go back to John and tell him what you have seen and
heard.* Jesus gave specific examples of miracles he had done—
some are recorded in the Gospels, probably many more are not.
The various places where such miracles occurred in the Gospels are noted in the chart on 342 (some of these healings happened after this conversation with John's disciples). Even more
important, the prophet Isaiah had prophesied that the "one to
come" would do such miracles:

Then will the eyes of the blind be opened and the ears of the deaf unstopped. Then will the lame leap like a deer, and the mute tongue shout for joy. Water will gush forth in the wilderness and streams in the desert. . . . The Spirit of the Sovereign LORD is on me, because the LORD has anointed me to preach good news to the poor. He has sent me to bind up the brokenhearted, to proclaim freedom for the captives and release from darkness for the prisoners. (Isaiah 35:5-6; 61:1 NIV)

Jesus' actions revealed who he was—and Jesus knew that by telling the messengers to say this, John would come to the right conclusion. Then, as if in a postscript, Jesus told the messengers to tell John, *"God blesses those who are not offended by me."* The word for "offended" suggests closing a trap. God's blessing would come to those who accepted Jesus' credentials and believed in him rather than being "caught and trapped" by their false expectations and thus missing him completely.

LOOK FOR ANSWERS
John was confused because the reports he received about Jesus were unexpected and incomplete. John's doubts were natural, and Jesus didn't rebuke him for them. Instead, Jesus responded in a way that John would understand: Jesus explained that he had accomplished what the Messiah was supposed to accomplish. God can handle all doubts, and he welcomes all questions. Do you have questions about Jesus— about who he is or what he expects of you? Admit them to yourself and to God, and begin looking for answers. Only as you face your doubts honestly can you begin to resolve them.

7:24 **When John's messengers had gone, Jesus began to speak to the crowds about John: "What did you go out into the wilderness to look at? A reed shaken by the wind?"**[NRSV] *John's messengers* returned to John with Jesus' words. When they *had gone,* Jesus turned *to speak to the crowds* that were always following him. In case anyone got the wrong impression of John or thought that Jesus was rebuking him, Jesus set the record straight by explaining John's ministry. In the following verses, Jesus asks three questions and gives three answers. When John the Baptist began his ministry, he was preaching out in the wilderness, and people went out to see and hear him (3:3). Jesus asked if the people had gone into the wilderness to see *a reed shaken by the wind.* A "reed" is the canelike grass that grows on the banks of the Jordan River. To compare a person to a reed was to say that the person was without moral fiber or courage, easily tossed about by various opinions, never taking a stand on anything. In addition, reeds were everywhere; they were commonplace. Obviously, the people did not flock into the wilderness to see something commonplace, nor did they go to see a weak and fearful person. Instead, the people were attracted by John's

> The Old Testament Scriptures are intelligible only when understood as predicting and prefiguring Christ.
>
> *Charles Hodge*

fiery preaching and willingness to speak out against sin.

7:25 **"Or were you expecting to see a man dressed in expensive clothes? No, people who wear beautiful clothes and live in luxury are found in palaces, not in the wilderness."**[NLT] In a second question, Jesus asked if the people had trekked out into the wilderness *expecting to see a man dressed in expensive clothes.* Again, Jesus gave the answer—John's rough attire made of camel's hair (Matthew 3:4) was hardly expensive or *beautiful.* Someone dressed like that would be found in *palaces, not in the wilderness.*

7:26-27 **"But what did you go out to see? A prophet? Yes, I say to you, and more than a prophet."**[NKJV] In this third question, Jesus pinpointed the reason that the people had gone into the wilderness—they went out to see *a prophet.* The people realized that John's tough message and rough clothing signified that something was about to happen. They knew he was a prophet, for many of the Old Testament prophets had come with such messages and such austere lifestyles. They went out to see a prophet and had seen one; in fact, they had seen, Jesus said, *more than a prophet.* Jesus described John as "more" because John alone had inaugurated the messianic age and had announced the coming kingdom of God. More than being a prophet, John had been the subject of prophecy, fulfilling Malachi 3:1. **"This is the one about whom it is written: 'I will send my messenger ahead of you, who will prepare your way before you.'"**[NIV] Jesus changed the words "before me" to "before you," showing that the wording refers to Jesus as the Messiah. John was the last to function like the Old Testament prophets, the last to prepare the people for the coming messianic age. John came to announce the arrival of the kingdom; with Jesus Christ, the kingdom arrived.

7:28 **"I tell you, among those born of women there is no one greater than John; yet the one who is least in the kingdom of God is greater than he."**[NIV] Of all people, no one fulfilled his God-given purpose better than John the Baptist. His role as forerunner of the Messiah put him in a position of great privilege,

described as "more than a prophet" (7:26) with *no one greater.*
Yet in God's kingdom, all who come after John have a greater
spiritual heritage because they have clearer knowledge of the purpose of Jesus' death and resurrection. The *least in the kingdom of
God* are those of the faithful followers who participate in the
kingdom. John would die before Jesus would be crucified and
rise again to inaugurate his kingdom. Because they will witness
the kingdom's reality, Jesus' followers will have privilege and
place greater than John's. Jesus was not contrasting the man John
with individual Christians; he was contrasting life before Christ
with life in the fullness of Christ's kingdom.

TRUE GREATNESS
Anyone who reads the Bible even casually can tell that John
the Baptist was a great man, a man of tremendous courage
and faithfulness to God. He clearly proclaimed Jesus (John
1:29). He clearly preached the need for repentance and
salvation (Luke 3:3-9). He clearly magnified and exalted Jesus
and humbled himself (John 3:30). He preferred a faithful death
to an unfaithful life (Matthew 14:1-12). Jesus himself said no
one in the world was greater than John . . . yet the least citizen
of the kingdom of God is greater than John. That should put
Christians' ideas of greatness in a new light—and give a new
appreciation for the great privilege they have to be part of
God's kingdom! Thank God for this incredible privilege, and ask
his grace to live as befits a citizen of his kingdom.

7:29-30 **(All the people, even the tax collectors, when they heard
Jesus' words, acknowledged that God's way was right,
because they had been baptized by John. But the Pharisees
and experts in the law rejected God's purpose for themselves,
because they had not been baptized by John.)**[NIV] The obvious
contrast here cannot be missed. The words are simple but their
significance is profound. "All the people," referring to the
crowds, and *even the tax collectors* had come to understand an
important truth. The tax collectors were so hated and ostracized
that Luke mentioned them separately and almost with a hint of
surprise (Luke took special interest in tax collectors, as noted in
commentary on 5:27). When these common, ordinary people and
these evil, self-serving tax collectors *heard Jesus' words,* they
acknowledged that God's way was right. Certainly John had done
his job—these people were ready to accept Jesus because they
had been prepared. They had listened to John's preaching
(3:7-18) and *had been baptized by* him.

But the group who should have been most ready and most
accepting *had not been baptized by John.* They had refused the

repentance and confession that John had required (probably because they felt themselves already righteous and did not need to do so). *The Pharisees and experts in the law* had rejected the forerunner of Jesus; the obvious result was that they also had rejected their own Messiah. Luke explained that in so doing, they had *rejected God's purpose for themselves.* While they may have understood God's law, they had missed his purpose. These tragic words set the stage for the continuing animosity the Pharisees and legal experts felt toward Jesus until they finally succeeded in putting him to death. Missing God's purpose can be a step-by-step process. At any point they could have asked God to open their eyes, but they remained stubborn and self-assured. They continued down the steep path until these experts in the law found themselves planning a murder—and breaking the law in the process.

DISCOVER THE PLAN
The tax collectors (who embodied evil in most people's minds) and common people heard John's message and repented. In contrast, the Pharisees and experts in the law—religious leaders—rejected his words. Wanting to live their own way, they justified their own point of view and refused to listen to other ideas. Rather than trying to force your plans on God, try to discover his plan for you.

7:31-32 **"To what then will I compare the people of this generation, and what are they like? They are like children sitting in the marketplace and calling to one another, 'We played the flute for you, and you did not dance; we wailed, and you did not weep.'"**NRSV The phrase "to what then will I compare" was a common rabbinic introduction to a metaphor. "This generation" referred to the people, many of whom were the religious leaders (7:30), who had rejected John the Baptist and so also rejected Jesus. With these words, Jesus condemned their attitudes. No matter what Jesus said or did, they took the opposite view. They were cynical and skeptical because Jesus challenged their comfortable, secure, and self-centered lives. Jesus compared them to *children sitting in the marketplace,* the central part of town where the town's business was conducted. These children played games, perhaps copying adults in either celebrating as at a wedding dance or wailing as at a funeral. Some wanted to play "wedding" and so were playing the *flute* and calling out to others to join them and *dance,* but their companions ignored their invitation and didn't want to play. Then the children suggested playing "funeral," so they *wailed,* and the others would not *weep* but again refused to play. Nothing they did could get their friends to join them; neither extreme pleased them. Jesus' generation, like the children in the square, did not respond to the calls issued by John the Baptist and by Jesus. Based on 7:33-34, some have identified Jesus' ministry with the wedding dance because he celebrated with his disciples (5:33-34), and John is identified with the funeral dirge because of his ascetic ministry.

CHILDLIKE OR CHILDISH?
Children at play can be a joy to watch. Their free, uninhibited laughter and total abandonment to the pursuit of having fun are beautiful to see. But a child who is sulking and withdrawn can be equally exasperating; nothing makes him happy, nothing will cheer him up, nothing is any good at all. Jesus said believers are to be childlike in their faith (Matthew 18:1-4)—free, trusting, joyful. But he had harsh words for those whose behavior was childish. To them he basically said, "Nothing is good enough for you. Nothing makes you happy." Would an impartial observer describe your Christian walk as childlike or childish? Believers should enjoy the Lord and his people rather than constantly feeling unhappy, critical, looking for reasons to withdraw from brothers and sisters who may be slightly different. Do you change churches often, criticizing various pastors, music and worship leaders, or programs? Take a few minutes to examine your heart to see if you need a more mature approach to your Christian faith.

7:33-34 **"For John the Baptist has come eating no bread and drinking no wine, and you say, 'He has a demon'; the Son of Man has come eating and drinking, and you say, 'Look, a glutton and a drunkard, a friend of tax collectors and sinners!'"**NRSV The religious leaders hated anyone who spoke the truth and exposed their hypocrisy. They criticized John the Baptist because he fasted and drank no wine. He came *eating no bread and drinking no wine,* yet that did not satisfy the Jews. John was an ascetic; he did not seek out social occasions. Because he was so different, the religious leaders assumed that he had *a demon* (Matthew 11:18).

By contrast, Jesus (here calling himself *the Son of Man*) came *eating and drinking.* He joined in social occasions, and his diet was like other people's. But that did not satisfy the Jews either. They simply labeled him as a *glutton and a drunkard* who hung out with the lowest sort of people. They also accused Jesus of possessing a demon (John 10:20). Many of the Jews in Jesus' generation, including most of the religious establishment, simply refused to listen to either John or Jesus. Neither John's asceticism

nor Jesus' enjoyment of life could please the stubborn people
who chose not to believe, no matter what was offered.

RELIGION VS. RELIGIOSITY
What comes to your mind when you hear someone described
as "religious"? A man wearing a dark suit and narrow tie, or a
woman with a frumpy dress and long face? Unfortunately,
contemporary culture has made the word "religious" synonymous with "boring," "rigid," and "no fun." And yet what a
contrast Jesus presents—someone who enjoyed life, lived with
gusto, and brought joy to the most downcast and rejected people.
He enjoyed himself and others. Christians should acknowledge
that they often fit the narrow, stuffy stereotype so often portrayed
on TV and in the movies. Then they should look at their vibrant,
life-loving Lord and repent, asking him for the grace to live the
abundant life he himself lived and died to give them.

7:35 "But wisdom is proved right by all her children."[NIV] Here *wisdom* is personified as a woman. (See also Proverbs 1:20; 4:6; 7:4;
8:1 for more verses personifying wisdom.) God's wisdom is seen in
Jesus' deeds. People could see the kingdom's power through Jesus'
miracles. These miracles *proved right* (justified) Jesus' teaching.
People might reject both the miracles and the teaching, but that will
not change their truth nor will it hinder the kingdom's arrival. Wisdom's *children* were the followers of Jesus and John. These followers lived changed lives. Their righteous living demonstrated the
validity of the wisdom that Jesus and John taught.

A SINFUL WOMAN ANOINTS JESUS' FEET / 7:36-50 / 72

In this section, Luke continued to explore the two radically different reactions to Jesus' ministry (see 7:29, 30). In this passage, the
silly arrogance of the Pharisees and the wise humility of a sinful
woman stand side by side. The contrast is striking. Simon
remains seated; the sinful woman is at Jesus' feet, wiping them
with her hair. Simon waits to be served, while the woman throws
herself in the service of Jesus. The other guests, and presumably
Simon, doubt Jesus' authority to forgive sin; the woman places
her faith in Jesus and receives forgiveness of her sins. Her love
for Jesus is obvious, while Simon remains strangely aloof, showing his contempt not only for the sinful woman but also for Jesus.

Although Christians are quick to dissociate themselves from the
actions and attitudes of the Pharisees, many just as rapidly fall into
similar habits. How many times have they said, "I am not perfect,

but I am not as bad as . . ." Believers are quick to judge the weaknesses of others, to compare themselves with others, and to justify their own sins by pointing the finger at someone else. By doing this—instead of humbly confessing their own sins and committing themselves to serving Jesus—they take their place right next to Simon, sitting arrogantly in the presence of the Lord and Savior.

This is a different woman and different incident from the one that would occur later in Jesus' ministry (see Matthew 26:6-13; Mark 14:3-9; John 12:1-11).

7:36 Now one of the Pharisees invited Jesus to have dinner with him, so he went to the Pharisee's house and reclined at the table.^{NIV} While Jesus did dine with tax collectors and others whom the religious elite thought to be "sinners" (5:29-30; 7:34), he also would share a meal with a Pharisee (see also 11:37; 14:1). This Pharisee was named Simon (7:40). Jesus went to his house *and reclined at the table.* This was a customary position at a formal meal. Dinner guests would lie on couches with their heads near the table, propping themselves up on one elbow and stretching their feet out behind them. Generally, guests would remove their sandals; then their feet would be washed by servants before they reclined at the table.

7:37 When a woman who had lived a sinful life in that town learned that Jesus was eating at the Pharisee's house, she brought an alabaster jar of perfume.^{NIV} This *woman,* who may have been a prostitute, *learned that Jesus was eating* at the home of a certain Pharisee, so she went there. A meal such as this was not a private affair; people could come in, sit around the edges, watch what went on, and listen to the conversation. Thus, this woman could have gotten in, although her reputation would proceed her and she would not necessarily be welcome among this company of people. So it probably took great courage. The woman *brought an alabaster jar of perfume.* Alabaster jars were carved, expensive, and beautiful. Such jars were made from a translucent, compact gypsum, carved with a long neck that was to be broken off when the contents were poured out. This jar held an expensive perfume. Many Jewish women wore a small perfume flask on a cord around their neck. This jar of perfume would have been valued very highly by this woman.

7:38 Then she knelt behind him at his feet, weeping. Her tears fell on his feet, and she wiped them off with her hair. Then she kept kissing his feet and putting perfume on them.^{NLT} Although the woman was not an invited guest, she entered the house anyway and *knelt behind [Jesus] at his feet.* Because these people were reclining as they ate (7:36), the woman could easily anoint Jesus' feet without approaching the table. She came intending to anoint Jesus with her perfume, but she began *weeping,* and as *her tears fell on his feet . . . she wiped them off with her hair.* This woman understood that Jesus was very special. Perhaps she, as a sinner, had come to Jesus with great sorrow for her sin. Or it could be that her sins were behind her and that though she "had lived a sinful life" (7:37), she had found forgiveness. Perhaps she had followed John the Baptist and had confessed her sins. She may have been in the crowds that had been following Jesus and had come to believe in him. She may have come to Jesus grateful for being forgiven and so offering him the gift of her valuable perfume. Despite this woman's reputation, she came publicly to Jesus and *kept kissing his feet and putting perfume on them.* Usually perfume was used to anoint the head, but she did not want to get any closer to the table. To wash Jesus' feet was a sign of deep humility—it was the job of a slave.

7:39 Now when the Pharisee who had invited him saw it, he said to himself, "If this man were a prophet, he would have known who and what kind of woman this is who is touching him—that she is a sinner."NRSV Simon the Pharisee (his name is revealed in 7:40) looked over from his meal and *saw it*—that is, he saw this woman with a notorious reputation in his house, near his table, weeping and pouring perfume on the feet of his guest. Any self-respecting rabbi would have realized this woman's sinful nature and recoiled at being touched by her—for to be touched by a sinner would make Jesus unclean, and the Pharisees avoided any contact with "uncleanness." This Pharisee concluded that *if this man were a prophet, he would have known who and what kind of woman this is* and would have told her to go away.

This religious leader had no concern for this woman's plight, no desire to lift her from her sinful life or to help her become a better Jewish woman. Instead, he judged her as a *sinner,* shoved her aside, and presumed that any other rabbi (and especially one who was a "prophet") would do the same. The religious establishment had become an esoteric group shut off from common people. No wonder Jesus' compassion and forgiveness gave a breath of fresh air to people such as this woman. Jesus cared when no one else bothered. Whether she knew it yet or not (see 7:50), Jesus held the only answer—complete forgiveness of sin.

7:40 Then Jesus spoke up and answered his thoughts. "Simon," he said to the Pharisee, "I have something to say to you."NLT While the words of 7:39 had not been spoken aloud, Jesus knew the Pharisee's thoughts and so *spoke up and answered* them (see also 5:22; 6:8). He asked for Simon's direct attention because he had *something to say to* him. Simon had already made a judgment of Jesus and probably felt morally superior to him as well. He probably was no longer interested in anything this self-styled prophet had to say. But Jesus had asked for his attention, so he acted like the good host. **"All right, Teacher," Simon replied, "go ahead."**NLT

---

* e·g^{'r}

SELF-RIGHTEOUSNESS
Have you ever badly overestimated your abilities in some area? Maybe you asked someone to play tennis or one-on-one basketball, only to get blown off the court. Or perhaps you volunteered to sing with a choral ensemble, and then found out the music was way beyond your abilities. It's a very humbling and enlightening experience. Simon the Pharisee had a similar experience with Jesus. Simon badly overestimated his own righteousness. He looked at the woman who anointed Jesus' feet with her perfume and her tears as someone of less value, morally inferior. Jesus had to show Simon his own sins—particularly the sins of ungraciousness and inhospitality—in order for him to understand his own need for forgiveness. When you see someone caught in some kind of notorious sin, how do you respond: "Thank God I'm not like that" or "Lord, have mercy on me, the sinner"? If you have understood God's forgiveness and personally experienced it, be willing to grant forgiveness to others.

7:41-43 **"A certain creditor had two debtors; one owed five hundred denarii, and the other fifty. When they could not pay, he canceled the debts for both of them. Now which of them will love him more?"**NRSV A denarius was the usual day's wage for a laborer. This *creditor* had one man who owed him *five hundred* day's worth of wages; the other owed him *fifty* day's worth of wages. It would not be difficult for Simon to see which debtor would *love* the kind creditor more. So **Simon answered, "I suppose the one for whom he canceled the larger debt."**NLT Simon's answer was grudging at best. Simon barely wanted to talk any longer to this guest who, Simon now believed, was hardly what he claimed to be. Jesus needed to teach a lesson, so he gave Simon the benefit of having given the right answer: **"That's right," Jesus said.**NLT

7:44-46 **Then turning toward the woman, he said to Simon, "Do you see this woman? I entered your house; you gave me no water for my feet, but she has bathed my feet with her tears and dried them with her hair. You gave me no kiss, but from the**

time I came in she has not stopped kissing my feet. You did not anoint my head with oil, but she has anointed my feet with ointment."NRSV Simon had committed several social errors in neglecting to wash Jesus' feet (a courtesy extended to guests because sandaled feet got very dirty), offer him the kiss of greeting, and anoint his head with oil. Did Simon perhaps feel that he was too good to treat Jesus as an equal? Simon may have thought that he had correct doctrine behind him, but he displayed an unloving, uncaring spirit. He was one of those who had rejected God's purpose for him (7:30). The sinful woman, by contrast, lavished tears, expensive ointment, and kisses on Jesus. In this story it is the grateful prostitute,, and not the self-righteous religious leader, whose sins were forgiven.

7:47 **"Therefore, I tell you, her many sins have been forgiven—for she loved much. But he who has been forgiven little loves little."**NIV This woman's act of humility and love shows that she had *been forgiven.* Jesus did not overlook her sins. He did, in fact, know that this woman was a sinner (7:39), and he knew that her sins were *many.* But the fact that her many sins were forgiven caused her to overflow with much love for Jesus. The woman's love did not cause her forgiveness, for no one can earn forgiveness. Her faith in Jesus, despite her many sins, saved her (7:50). By contrast, self-righteous people, like Simon, feel that they have no sins that need to be forgiven; therefore they also have little love to show for it.

GREAT FORGIVENESS
Overflowing love is the natural response to forgiveness and the appropriate consequence of faith. But only those who realize the depth of their sin can appreciate the complete forgiveness God offers them. Jesus has rescued all of his followers, whether they were once extremely wicked or conventionally good, from eternal death. Do you appreciate the wideness of God's mercy? Are you grateful for his forgiveness?

7:48 **Then He said to her, "Your sins are forgiven."**NKJV Although it is God's grace through faith that saves, and not acts of love or generosity, this woman's act demonstrated her true faith, and Jesus honored her faith by telling her in no uncertain terms, *"Your sins are forgiven."* Jesus supported this woman and treated her with dignity. Believers need to demonstrate Jesus' approach in dealing with people.

PERSPECTIVE
Simon saw the sin; Jesus saw the sinner. Simon saw her offenses; Jesus saw her need. Simon saw the depth of her depravity; Jesus saw the magnitude of her love. All people are sinners. That fact alone should keep anyone from feeling superior or self-righteous. People also are loved beyond measure. That should keep anyone from feeling worthless or hopeless. Is there someone whom you have been looking down upon, considering his or her sins as much more serious than your own? Do you need to repent of any self-righteous attitudes toward anyone? When you are confronted with the sins of others, remember Jesus' words of forgiveness for this woman. When you face the reality of your own sins, remember that God's mercy and forgiveness are just as real—and just as necessary—for you too.

7:49-50 **But those who were at the table with him began to say among themselves, "Who is this who even forgives sins?"**^{NRSV} Jesus' words of forgiveness to the woman provoked a discussion among the rest of *those who were at the table.* The Pharisees believed that only God could forgive sins, so they wondered why this man Jesus was saying that the woman's sins were forgiven. They asked each other, *"Who is this who even forgives sins?"* They did not grasp the fact that Jesus was God and therefore did have the authority to forgive sins. A similar discussion had occurred in 5:20-21. Jesus did not perform a miracle to back up his words as he had with the paralyzed man. Instead he simply looked at the woman and said, **"Your faith has saved you. Go in peace."**^{NKJV} This woman's humility did not save her, nor did her tears or her expensive perfume. It was her *faith,* her complete trust in the only one who could forgive her sins and save her. Ephesians 2:8-9 says, "For by grace you have been saved through faith, and this is not your own doing; it is the gift of God—not the result of works, so that no one may boast" (NRSV). When people trust Christ, he changes their lives, gives them freedom from sin, and allows them to *go in peace*—true peace, peace with God. Like so many whom Jesus had healed, this woman had a new life and a new reason for living. No wonder she wept with joy and love.

LUKE 8

In a culture where women played invisible roles, the fact that Luke
mentioned the support of three women—Mary Magdalene, Joanna,
and Susanna—is amazing. But it is clear why he did: these women
would witness Jesus' crucifixion, burial, and resurrection. The fact
that Luke highlighted a number of women in his Gospel—the
stories of Elizabeth (1:39-45), Mary (1:26-56), the prophetess Anna
(2:36-38), the widow of Nain (7:11-15)—indicates the interest
Luke took in showing how women were involved in Jesus' ministry.

**8:1 Not long afterward Jesus began a tour of the nearby cities
and villages to announce the Good News concerning the Kingdom of God. He took his twelve disciples with him.**^{NLT} The
Gospel again gives a vague time reference, only that *not long
afterward* (after the event with the sinful woman at the Pharisee's
house, 7:36-50), *Jesus began a tour of the nearby cities and villages.* Jesus' mission remained unchanged—he continued *to announce the Good News concerning the Kingdom of God* (see
4:43; 7:22). The *twelve disciples* (named in 6:13-16) traveled
with him—Jesus poured much of his ministry into them. As Jesus
traveled and preached the Good News, he was also training the
Twelve, preparing them for future ministry.

**8:2-3 along with some women he had healed and from whom he
had cast out evil spirits. Among them were Mary Magdalene,
from whom he had cast out seven demons; Joanna, the wife
of Chuza, Herod's business manager; Susanna; and many
others who were contributing from their own resources to
support Jesus and his disciples.**^{NLT} Luke gives more attention to
women than any other Gospel. Women played a special role in
the life and ministry of Jesus (see the chart, "Jesus and Women"
on page 194). Jesus' acceptance of women as disciples and as
participants in his ministry and teaching gave women a positive
place in the New Testament church (Acts 1:14). Women traveling
with Jesus and his disciples would have been completely unchc-
teristic of rabbis in ancient times. Rabbis refused to teach women

JESUS AND WOMEN

As a non-Jew recording the words and works of Jesus' life, Luke demonstrated a special sensitivity to other "outsiders" with whom Jesus came into contact. For instance, Luke recorded five events involving women that are not mentioned in the other Gospels. In first-century Jewish culture, women were usually treated as second-class citizens, enjoying few of the rights that men had. But Jesus crossed those barriers, and Luke showed the special care of Jesus for women. Jesus respected all people equally. The following passages tell of his encounters with women.

Jesus talks to a Samaritan woman at the well . . . . John 4:1-26

Jesus heals Peter's mother-in-law . . . . Luke 4:38-39

Jesus raises a widow's son from the dead . . . . Luke 7:11-17

A sinful woman anoints Jesus' feet . . . . Luke 7:36-50

The adulterous woman whom Jesus forgave . . . . John 8:1-11

Women travel with Jesus . . . . Luke 8:1-3

Jesus heals a diseased woman . . . . Luke 8:43-48

Jesus visits Mary and Martha . . . . Luke 10:38-42

Jesus heals a crippled woman . . . . Luke 13:10-17

Jesus heals the daughter of a Gentile woman . . . . Mark 7:24-30

Weeping women follow Jesus on his way to the cross . . . . Luke 23:27-31

Jesus' mother and other women gather at the cross . . . . . John 19:25-27

Jesus appears to Mary Magdalene . . . . Mark 16:9-11

Jesus appears to other women after his resurrection . . . Matthew 28:8-10

---

because they were generally considered to be inferior. Jesus, however, lifted women up from degradation and servitude to the joy of fellowship and service. By allowing these women to travel with him, Jesus was showing that all people are equal under God. These women supported Jesus' ministry with their own money. They owed a great debt to him because *he had healed* some of them and *had cast out evil spirits* from others.

The Gospel names three of the women. First, *Mary Magdalene* (from a town called Magdala or Magadan, see Matthew 15:39) *from whom he had cast out seven demons.* Apparently Mary Magdalene had lived a very sorry existence because demons were usually associated with mental or physical disorders. The number of demons indicates the severity of the possession from which Jesus freed her. Although some have suggested that Mary Magdalene was a prostitute, there is no biblical evidence to support this. Mary stayed at the cross, went to the tomb, and was the first person to see the resurrected Christ (24:10; Mark 15:40, 47; 16:1, 9;

John 19:25; 20:1, 18). Because she is always first in any list of
women indicates that she probably had a special leadership role.

The second woman named is *Joanna, the wife of Chuza,* who
was *Herod's business manager* (or steward). He may have been in
charge of one of Herod Antipas's estates. Joanna is also mentioned
in 24:10 as one of the women, along with Mary Magdalene, who
told the disciples the news of Jesus' resurrection. Otherwise, nothing else is known of her; Joanna's husband is mentioned only here.
Perhaps Luke's Gentile readers knew of this man and the exact
nature of the office that he held. Some have conjectured that this
may have been the man whose son was healed in Capernaum,
recorded in John 4:46-53, after which he allowed his wife to be a
part of Jesus' supporters. But this is uncertain.

Finally, Luke mentioned a woman named *Susanna* who is
found nowhere else in Scripture and about whom nothing is
known. Perhaps Luke highlighted these three women because
they would have been known to his readers.

WITH DIGNITY
It is common today to hear people criticize the Bible as a
male-dominated, patriarchal document. There is no question
that the major characters that populate the biblical landscape
are overwhelmingly men, although there are notable
exceptions. Ruth, Naomi, Queen Esther, and Deborah the
judge are a few of them. But Luke's Gospel in particular
highlights the positive role that women played in Jesus' public
ministry. Jesus never denigrated women, never acted in a
chauvinistic manner, never victimized women in any way. He
showed them great respect and compassion, as he did others
who were oppressed and downtrodden. When you meet those
who are different than you—minorities, people of different
economic levels, members of the opposite sex—show them the
same dignity and compassion Jesus did.

Besides these women there were *many others who were contributing from their own resources to support Jesus and his disciples.* This provides an insight into how Jesus and his disciples
met their basic needs. John 13:29 reveals that Jesus and the disciples had a common pool of money from which they bought food
and gave to the poor and that Judas Iscariot acted as treasurer.
This passage tells the origin of that pool of money. People, like
the women listed here, gave money to Jesus and the disciples out
of gratefulness for what Jesus had done for them. Note that, in
the Gospels, no women ever reject Christ or become his enemies,
only men. These women are models of the faith response that
Christ desires.

These same women also would witness Jesus' crucifixion (23:49) and see the empty tomb (24:10, 22, 24). Luke revealed that they had been with Jesus from the time of his ministry in Galilee. He also wrote that women stayed close to Jesus and would have influential roles in the church (Acts 1:14; 8:12; 16:13-15; 17:4, 12; 18:24-26).

JESUS TELLS THE PARABLE OF THE FOUR SOILS / 8:4-8 / 77

Jesus began teaching in parables to get his listeners to think. These parables hid the truth from those who had their minds made up, having already chosen to reject Jesus. On the other hand, those who truly wanted to know Jesus could listen carefully and learn more about the kingdom of God. Jesus ended this parable with a loud cry to all to listen. Jesus' words give life. Listening to him, by reading the Bible regularly, is a wise use of a believer's time.

8:4 While a large crowd was gathering and people were coming to Jesus from town after town, he told this parable.^{NIV} Jesus often taught in outdoor settings where *a large crowd* could gather from surrounding towns to listen to him. At this particular time, Jesus told a *parable.* Jesus often communicated spiritual truth through "parables"—short stories or descriptions that take a familiar object or situation and give it a startling new twist. By linking the known with the hidden and forcing listeners to think, parables would point to spiritual truths. Jesus' parables compelled listeners to discover the truth for themselves, and they concealed the truth from those too lazy or dull to understand. People must be careful not to read too much into Jesus' parables. Most of his parables have only one point and one meaning unless Jesus says otherwise. In this parable, the farmer represents Jesus, the soil represents Israel, and the seed represents the proclamation of the kingdom. The parable shows the contrast between the results of acceptance and rejection of the gospel message.

8:5 "A farmer went out to plant some seed. As he scattered it across his field, some seed fell on a footpath, where it was stepped on, and the birds came and ate it."^{NLT} In this parable, Jesus used a familiar picture to illustrate an important truth about the kingdom of heaven. In ancient times, when *a farmer went out to plant some seed,* he didn't lay it in neat rows. He would walk across the field and scatter handfuls of seed from a large bag slung across his shoulders. The farmer scattered the seed liberally—and *some seed fell on a footpath.* A "footpath" (a "walkway" in Bible times) often ran right through fields. The hard and compacted soil of the path meant that the seed did not sink into the ground, so it sat on top *where it was stepped on* and where *the birds came and ate it.* In 8:12 Jesus explains that the devil comes and takes away the gospel message from hard hearts so that those people cannot hear or be saved.

Jesus was speaking to the crowds about the kingdom, explaining through this parable that the religious leaders' rejection of the Messiah did not change the truth. Jesus and the gospel were truth; there was no problem with them as there was no problem with the farmer or his seed. The only variable was the land (or the hearts) where the seed (the message) fell.

A CARELESS SOWER?
In this story of the farmer and the seed, the farmer sows the seed on all kinds of soil, seemingly indiscriminately. No wise farmer would sow seed in thorns or on a path. Is he simply careless, wasteful, or perhaps unskilled? No—the farmer knows that some of the soil is unproductive, but he willingly scatters the seed on it anyway. God is like this farmer, allowing his words and his love to fall on many who will not receive them. And yet he is still willing to pour out his mercies upon them. God knows the high potential of this seed. Christians sometimes tend to pull back from those who are uninterested or even just different—but God doesn't. Seek to emulate his extravagant love for the seemingly unreceptive.

8:6 "Other seed fell on shallow soil with underlying rock. This seed began to grow, but soon it withered and died for lack of moisture."[NLT] Other handfuls of that same seed (the seed was all the same—it was the soil that differed) *fell on shallow soil with underlying rock.* The footpath had no soil at all. But on the shallow soil, the *seed began to grow.* This type of soil was probably found in every farmer's field—most of the land in Palestine is very rocky, filled with stones of all sizes. Soil on top of rocks traps the moisture so that plants can grow quickly, but the roots cannot go deep. The hot sun then dries up the water, causing the young plant to wither and die *for lack of moisture.* In 8:13, Jesus explains that those with hearts like this may hear the word and at first receive it with joy. But, like the crowds who followed, when the going gets tough, they fall away.

8:7 "Some fell among thorns, and the thorns grew with it and choked it."[NRSV] Other handfuls of seed *fell among thorns.* Thorns rob sprouts of nutrition, water, light, and space. Thus, when *the thorns grew* (weeds grow faster than wheat), the good seed was *choked* out and could not grow to maturity. In 8:14, Jesus explains that those with "thorny" hearts may receive the message but then find it choked out by "life's worries, riches and pleasures, and they do not mature" (NIV). The crowds who followed Jesus also fit this category.

SPREAD THE SEED
Why would a farmer allow precious seed to land on the path, on rocks, or among thorns? This is not an irresponsible farmer scattering seeds at random. He is using the acceptable method of hand-seeding a large field—tossing it by handfuls as he walks through the field. His goal is to get as much seed as possible to take root in good soil, but there is inevitable waste as some falls or is blown into less productive areas. That some of the seed produced no crop was not the fault of the faithful farmer or of the seed. The yield depended on the condition of the soil where the seed fell. It is the believers' responsibility to spread the seed (God's message), but they should not give up when some of their efforts fail. Remember, not every seed falls on good soil.

8:8 **"Still other seed fell on fertile soil. This seed grew and produced a crop one hundred times as much as had been planted."**NLT Some seed may be lost, but *other seed fell on fertile soil.* This soil had been plowed by the farmer, and the seed had ample sunlight, depth, and moisture to be able to grow. The seed *produced a crop one hundred times as much as had been planted.* Normal yield for good seed would be seven- to tenfold. Any farmer would be overjoyed at such a tremendous yield, for it would mean even more seed to plant and harvest during the next year. In 8:15 Jesus explains that "fertile soil" people are those disciples who hear the word, hold on to it, and share it with others.

When he had said this, he called out, "Anyone who is willing to hear should listen and understand."NLT Jesus understood that not everyone who has ears necessarily hears what has been said. Certainly all the people in the crowd had ears to hear the parable. But "listen and understand" refers to a different kind of hearing, a deep listening with the mind and heart that opens a person to spiritual understanding. Jesus purposely spoke in parables to weed out false followers from among the true ones. Jesus' words, like the farmer's seed, fell on various types of hearts. Those who truly heard and understood would become his followers. Those not ready for Jesus would not understand his words, would lose interest, and finally would either fade away or become his avowed enemies (as did most of the religious leaders).

JESUS EXPLAINS THE PARABLE OF THE FOUR SOILS / 8:9-18 / **78**

The disciples are the ones who respond to Jesus' command to "listen and understand"; they are the ones who are "willing to hear" (8:8 NLT). The meaning of the parable of the four soils reinforces Jesus' differentiation between those who are given the secrets of the kingdom and those who are not. The secrets of God's kingdom are for those whom God has prepared. They genuinely embrace the gospel message, obey God's Word, and tell others about the Good News. The blinded ones let the devil, trials, and cares of this life steal the truth from them.

"Be sure to pay attention" (8:18 NLT). Jesus' words of warning echo through the centuries. "Wake up! Wake up! Listen to what I'm saying and put it into practice." Deciding to block out all other distractions—the problems at work, the frenzied sights and sounds of television—in order to read and study God's Word is the best decision believers can make.

8:9-10 **His disciples asked him what this parable meant. He said, "The knowledge of the secrets of the kingdom of God has been given to you, but to others I speak in parables, so that, 'though seeing, they may not see; though hearing, they may not understand.'"**NIV This explanation probably occurred after Jesus and the disciples were away from the crowd. "Disciples" here probably refers to the Twelve and other true followers, such as the women described in 8:1-3. As soon as they were alone with Jesus, his followers *asked him what this parable* (told in 8:4-8) *meant.* Jesus' parables were not always easy to understand, even to those closest to Jesus. The disciples may have thought that they should have understood the parable without an explanation, so away from the crowds, they asked.

Jesus explained first that *knowledge of the secrets of the kingdom of God* comes as a gift of God to those he has chosen. That this knowledge is *given* reveals God's sovereignty. God had given this ability to understand to these disciples as a permanent possession, a distinguishing mark of discipleship. They understood, though only partially, the "secret" that God's kingdom had arrived among them in the person of Jesus. Those who have not been given this knowledge (the *others*) willfully reject the gospel message.

The word translated "secrets" is also translated "mysteries."

The Aramaic word *raz* was used in the intertestamental writings
to refer to the "hidden" revelation of God, unknown to the apos-
tates, but "given" to his true people at the proper time. In this context, they are the "secrets of the kingdom" given to the disciples
through Jesus' teaching. The kingdom of God was a mystery to
the prophets of the Old Testament—they wrote about it, but they
did not understand it (as Romans 16:25-26 explains). The believers received spiritual insight that illuminated the mystery so that
it was no longer a mystery to them.

HARD SOIL, HARDER HEARTS
Have you ever had the experience of trying to explain your faith
in Christ to another person, only to have that person look at
you as though you were from some other planet? You may not
have communicated very clearly what Jesus means to you. Or
perhaps the other person's heart was too hard to allow your
words to penetrate. Jesus said that some people's hearts are
like a packed-down, foot-trampled path, too hard to let God's
Word take root. Satan has great success with those who refuse
to listen. It is probably wise not to spend too much time and
effort on evangelizing that person at that time; your efforts may
only "trample the path" even more. Prayerfully wait until you
sense a more opportune time—perhaps when life has softened
these hearts a bit more through suffering, loss, or even great
blessing.

Why did so many people in the large crowds that followed
Jesus never gain a true understanding of what he was saying?
Jesus explained that it was because of their presence that he
spoke *in parables*. These people were not sincere seekers.
They followed Jesus to see his miracles or to see if he was the
military leader or political Messiah they had come to expect.
When speaking in parables, Jesus was not hiding truth from
sincere seekers, because those who were receptive to spiritual
truth understood what he was saying. To others they were only
stories without meaning. Those "others" (the religious leaders
and the vast majority of the crowd) would never see, hear, or
understand, for they would not come to God for the answers.
Choosing not to believe in Jesus as the Messiah, they would
not be able to understand the kingdom. Jesus would not explain
or speak clearly to these people; he would answer questions
about his parables with other parables. The soil of their heart
was hard; the seed would not grow; the parables would be
nothing more than strange stories to them. To the "rocky soil,
footpath, or thorn patch" people, the parables were stories without meanings.

The parables allowed Jesus to give spiritual food to those who hungered for it. Isaiah's prophecy explains the situation of the others. God told Isaiah that people would hear without understanding, and see without perceiving (Isaiah 6:9). That kind of reaction confronted Jesus. By quoting the prophet Isaiah, Jesus was telling his inner group of followers that the crowd resembled the Israelites about whom Isaiah had written. God had told Isaiah that the people would listen but not learn from his message because their hearts had hardened beyond repentance. Yet God still sent Isaiah with the message because, even though the nation itself would not repent and would reap judgment, some individuals *would* listen. Jesus came to the Israelites hundreds of years after Isaiah, but the words to Isaiah still applied. Most would not repent because their hearts were hardened; but a few would listen, turn from their sins, and believe.

SOLID OR SHALLOW?
Check the appropriate answer. Jesus is
   (a) A better high than drugs.
   (b) More fun than last weekend's party.
   (c) The solution to your loneliness.
   (d) All of the above.
   If you checked a, b, c, or d—watch out. You may be trying to grow your faith in shallow soil. Why? Isn't Jesus better than drugs, more fun than some superficial party, and "a friend who sticks closer than a brother" (Proverbs 18:24 NIV)? Yes, he is. But if you come to Jesus on these terms—simply expecting him to solve your problems or make your life more enjoyable—you have bought into a very watered-down imitation of Christianity.
   This may explain why some people latch on to the gospel with great enthusiasm at first, only to bail out when the initial excitement wears off. They are the people whose hearts are like the rocky soil, more shallow than solid. Is your faith the kind that will stand when "the thrill is gone"? Ask God to help you stand firm.

8:11-12 **"This is the meaning of the story: The seed is God's message. The seed that fell on the hard path represents those who hear the message, but then the Devil comes and steals it away and prevents them from believing and being saved."**[NLT] Jesus' closest followers may not have immediately understood the meaning of his parable, but that did not mean they were hard-hearted. They did perceive that Jesus' words had a deeper meaning, and they had come to the right source to find out what that meaning was. As they gained further spiritual insight, the parables would become clearer.

So Jesus gave them *the meaning of the story.* The *seed* that the farmer sowed represents *God's message* to the people—the good news of the kingdom. *The seed that fell on the hard path* represents those, like the religious leaders, who *hear,* but *the message* cannot penetrate their hearts. This was not a passive unbelief—the element of spiritual warfare is revealed here because *the Devil* himself *comes and steals* the message *and prevents them from believing and being saved.* "Footpath" people, like many of the religious leaders, refused to believe God's message. Satan locked their minds and hearts and threw away the key. Though not beyond God's reach, their hardness will make it very difficult for them to ever believe.

8:13 **"Those on the rock are the ones who receive the word with joy when they hear it, but they have no root. They believe for a while, but in the time of testing they fall away."**NIV Those who are like "rocky soil" *are the ones who receive the word with joy when they hear it.* Something in the gospel message hits a nerve, and they gladly accept what it offers. But they are not in it for the long haul, not ready to be a disciple *in the time of testing* if believing brings persecution. These people *believe for a while,* but Jesus explains that *they have no root,* so they *fall away.*

SEEDS AND WEEDS
An old story says that Satan called in one of his most effective demons for a chat. This demon had personally overseen the ruin of thousands upon thousands of souls. "What's your secret, little brother?" asked Satan. "I tell them to get serious about God," replied the demon. "I tell them they need to open their hearts to Christ. I tell them to repent of their sins and follow Jesus."

"You tell them what?!?" exploded old Slewfoot.

"I tell them they need to do all these things . . . tomorrow," he answered with a sly grin.

Take a moment and consider what seems so important to you right now. The things you work day and night for, the goals you try to attain—how meaningful are they in the context of eternity? Are they truly important, or are they merely "weeds" that choke out the priorities that really matter? Don't trade away what is truly significant for a bunch of weeds—no matter how pretty they look or how sweet they smell.

8:14 **"As for what fell among the thorns, these are the ones who hear; but as they go on their way, they are choked by the cares and riches and pleasures of life, and their fruit does not mature."**NRSV The same seed also *fell among the thorns.* These people *hear,* accept the Word, and allow it to take root in their hearts. But *as they go on their way,* something happens—*thorns* grow up and choke out the growing seed. Thorns rob nutrition, water, light, and space from newly sprouting seeds. Jesus described such people as being *choked by the cares and riches and pleasures of life.* Worldly cares (no matter how important or how minor), the false sense of security brought on (or merely promised) by riches, and the desire for pleasure and material possessions (including anything that serves to distract a person) plagued first-century disciples as they do believers today (for examples, see 10:41; 12:15, 19; 14:26; 16:19; 21:34). These distractions and conflicts rob new believers of growth—they do not spend time in God's Word or with God's people. So even though the seed has grown, it *does not mature.* Daily routines overcrowd and materialistic pursuits distract believers, choking out God's Word so that it yields nothing.

GOOD SOIL, GOOD SEED, GOOD SOWING
By now the point to Jesus' parable should be apparent. The seed is the gospel, the Word of God; the sower is Jesus, or those who represent him; the various kinds of soils are people's hearts. How can the type of soil in someone's heart be identified? By the fruit produced. Just like a person putting literal seeds in literal dirt, at first it's hard to tell what kind of seeds were planted and how fertile is the soil. But in time, it becomes evident. There's no faking this. Time will show what kind of seeds you have been sowing. If you want God's good and productive fruit in your life, read, study, and memorize God's Word.

8:15 **"But the seed on good soil stands for those with a noble and good heart, who hear the word, retain it, and by persevering produce a crop."**[NIV] Of course, some of the seed falls on *good soil* or the farmer would not plant in that area at all. Good soil can be found—hearts open to the gospel message wherever the seed of God's Word is sown. Those with hearts like "good soil" are those

> If you were arrested for being a Christian, would there be enough evidence to convict you?
> *David Otis Fuller*

who hear the word, retain it, and by persevering produce a crop. These people have truly believed and are willing to let Jesus make a difference in their lives. Because of this, they also "produce a crop" because they are willing to share what Jesus has done for them.

"Footpath" people, like many of the religious leaders,

refused to believe God's message. "Rocky" people, like many
in the crowds who followed Jesus, believed his message but
never got around to doing anything about it. "Thorny" people,
overcome by worries and the lure of materialism, left no room
in their lives for God. "Good soil" people, in contrast to all the
other groups, followed Jesus no matter what the cost.

Sometimes people's lives can represent several different
types of soil at once. A person may react like good soil to
God's teaching regarding one part of life, but be "thorny" in
another area. Believers are called to be like "good soil" all the
time in all areas of life. Then God can continue to teach them,
they can continue to mature, and they can share the message
with others.

8:16 **"No one after lighting a lamp hides it under a jar, or puts it
under a bed, but puts it on a lampstand, so that those who
enter may see the light."**^{NRSV} These listeners would have understood Jesus' reference to a *lamp* as being a lighted wick in a clay
bowl that was full of oil. People light lamps when it gets so dark
that they cannot see. It would be ludicrous to light a lamp and
then hide it *under a jar* (referring to a clay jar that hides the light
and snuffs it out). Nor would someone put the lamp *under a bed,*
again in an attempt to hide the light. Obviously, a lit lamp is put
on a lampstand to light up the room.

LET YOUR LIGHT SHINE
When the light of the truth about Jesus illuminates a person,
it is his or her duty to shine that light to help others. Witness
for Christ should be public, not hidden. Believers should not
keep the benefits for themselves, but pass them on to others.
To hide the truth is foolish and unproductive. We must not
blend so well with our non-Christian friends and neighbors that
our faith remains invisible to them. In order to be helpful,
Christians should be well placed. Take Christ's light out into the
world. Seek opportunities to be available when unbelievers
need help. Seek ways to let your light shine so that others may
see it.

The disciples may have begun to understand the mission to
which Jesus had called them. Like the farmer in the parable, they
would have the job of sowing the seed of the gospel in a largely
hostile world. The light of the truth about Jesus had illuminated
them, and it was their ministry to shine that light into a sin-darkened
world. Their witness for Christ would be public, not hidden. The
benefits of knowing Jesus and receiving salvation were not to be

kept to themselves but passed on to others. Their light would
shine *so that those who enter may see the light.*

In addition, Jesus was explaining his use of parables. He was
not deliberately trying to conceal truth; that would be like lighting a lamp and then hiding it. Instead, the parables were like
light, shining in and illuminating certain truths about the coming
kingdom that human minds cannot grasp. The parables take something understood and use it to explain a truth that is beyond
human understanding. Only those seeking to grapple with those
difficult truths will be able to understand the parables. Others
will find them to be no more than stories and will be unable to understand anything deeper.

**8:17 "For nothing is secret that will not be revealed, nor anything
hidden that will not be known and come to light."**[NKJV]
Although the truth may be *hidden* or kept *secret* for a while, it
will not remain so. One day the truth will be *known* and *come to
light.* Jesus was speaking of the days of his ministry as the time
of using parables and being rejected by many. The time of revelation and coming to light could refer either to Jesus' resurrection
and ascension (when his followers would fully understand his
words) or to the Second Coming. Jesus' followers did not understand everything about Jesus at that time, but one day all their
questions would be answered.

MUSCLE UP
Jesus encouraged his disciples to pay close attention to his
words. Applying God's Word helps Christians grow. A muscle,
when exercised, will grow stronger, but an unused muscle will
grow weak and flabby. If you are not growing stronger, you are
growing weaker; it is impossible for you to stand still. How are
you using what God has taught you?

**8:18 "Then pay attention to how you listen; for to those who have,
more will be given; and from those who do not have, even
what they seem to have will be taken away."**[NRSV] Because the
teachings in the parables were so important for his followers to
understand, Jesus warned them to *pay attention to how [they]
listen.* Were they acting like "rocky" people who didn't take the
truth to heart, or like "thorny" people who let the cares of this
world keep them from maturing? They needed to listen with understanding and then apply what Jesus said to their daily lives.
All believers must treasure the words of Jesus. The people who
listen and understand are *those who have.* They hear, understand,
and then share with others. Even then, *more will be given* because

their openness and perception of the kingdom message will bring
great rewards. They will continue to grow because they let God's
Word make a difference in their lives. Ultimately, of course, they
will receive eternal blessings.

Those who do not listen or understand *(those who do not
have)* will lose whatever they had—it *will be taken away.*
Jesus' words here may have been directed to the Jews who had
no understanding of Jesus and would lose even what they had—
that is, their privileged status as God's people. Or Jesus might
have meant that when people reject him, their hardness of heart
drives away or renders useless even the little understanding
they had.

JESUS DESCRIBES HIS TRUE FAMILY / 8:19-21 / **76**

Jesus' proverbial remark, that his true family members are those
who listen to God's Word and obey it, reinforces the point of the
preceding sections (8:8, 15, 18). Studying the Bible and applying
it to all aspects of our lives are important marks of faithful followers of Christ.

**8:19-20 Once when Jesus' mother and brothers came to see him, they
couldn't get to him because of the crowds. Someone told
Jesus, "Your mother and your brothers are outside, and they
want to see you."**NLT Jesus' *mother* was Mary (1:30-31), and his
brothers were the other children Mary and Joseph had after Jesus
(see also Mark 6:3-4). According to Mark, the reason Jesus'
mother and brothers *came to see him* was because "they went to
take charge of him, for they said, 'He is out of his mind'" (Mark
3:21 NIV). Jesus and his disciples were so swamped by the
crowds that they were not even able to take time to eat (Mark
3:20). We see here that his mother and brothers *couldn't get to
him because of the crowds.* Apparently Mary had gathered her
family, and they had gone to find Jesus. Mary was hoping to use
her personal relationship with Jesus to influence him. She saw
her son in a busy ministry that was taking its toll. Perhaps she
hoped to get him to come home; maybe she brought the brothers
along to pull Jesus away from the crowd if necessary. While
Mary may have understood the nature of Jesus' mission, she also
remained his mother and was concerned for him. Jesus' brothers,
meanwhile, had to be brought along because they did not believe
in him and were not among the crowds who followed (John 7:5).

Standing at the edge of the crowd, Mary and the brothers
relayed a message to Jesus. They thought that because of their
relationship with him, he would make his way out to see them.

8:21 He replied, "My mother and brothers are those who hear God's word and put it into practice."[NIV] Many years earlier, Jesus had told his frantic mother, "Why did you seek Me? Did you not know that I must be about My Father's business?" (2:49 NKJV). At that time, he was only twelve years old, so he had obediently left with his parents.

> Join hands, then,
>   brothers of the faith,
> Whate'er your race
>   may be!
> Who serves my Father as
>   a son
> Is surely kin to me.
>   *John Oxenham*

Here, however, Jesus was a man in the middle of a mission. He was indeed "about his Father's business." In these words, Jesus gave a respectful rebuke to his overly concerned mother; he was not severing ties with his earthly family. Through this incident, Jesus gave another lesson to his followers by explaining that spiritual relationships are as binding as physical ones. This would be the basis for the new community that Jesus was building—the Christian family. Therefore, Jesus told them that his *mother and brothers,* that is, those closest to him, *are those who hear God's word and put it into practice.* As Jesus loved his mother (see John 19:25-27), so he loves his followers. He offers people an intimate family relationship with him. The types of people who can have a relationship with Christ are those who do the Father's will. They listen, learn, believe, and follow. Obedience is the key to being part of God's family. Knowledge is not enough—the religious leaders had that and still missed Jesus. Following is not enough—the crowd did that but still didn't understand who Jesus was. Those who believe are brought into a family. In these words, Jesus was explaining that in his spiritual family, relationships are ultimately more important and longer lasting than those formed in one's physical family.

FAMILY TIES
What comes to mind when you hear the word "family"? For many, the word recalls happy memories. For others, the associations aren't so pleasant. Whatever your biological family is like, following Jesus means that you are part of the worldwide family of God. This family isn't perfect; brothers and sisters in Christ have their rough edges and idiosyncrasies. But it should give great comfort to know that this family, with God the Father as the head, God the Son as the elder brother, and God the Holy Spirit as the "family tie," will one day be perfected together. Until then, believers must try to keep family squabbles under control, lest they reflect badly on the Father who loved them enough to make them his adopted children.

JESUS CALMS THE STORM / 8:22-25 / **87**

Following a section emphasizing obedience and faith in God's Word, Luke placed a powerful demonstration of Jesus' supernatural power. Only God controls nature (Psalm 107:23-32), and here Jesus demonstrated his complete control over the wind and the sea, leaving his disciples thoroughly dumbfounded. Jesus' probing question, "Where is your faith?" (8:25 NLT), is the same question Jesus asks believers today when they are rocked back and forth by the storms of life. Just like the disciples, Christians need to cling to Jesus in the most trying times.

8:22 One day Jesus said to his disciples, "Let's cross over to the other side of the lake." So they got into a boat and started out.ᴺᴸᵀ Luke's vague time reference of *one day* shows again his focus not so much on chronology as on giving his readers information about Jesus that would help them believe. The previous events probably took place in Capernaum. Crowds continued to gather around Jesus (8:19-20), but he had to minister in other places as well. So he asked his disciples to *cross over to the other side of the lake.* Capernaum sat on the northwestern shore of the Sea of Galilee (also called a "lake" because it is inland). So Jesus and the disciples got into a boat (perhaps Peter's fishing boat) and began to cross to the eastern shore.

Jesus' ministry was never without purpose. He was crossing the lake in order to enter a new area of ministry. Along the way, the disciples would be taught an unforgettable lesson about his power.

8:23 As they sailed, he fell asleep. A squall came down on the lake, so that the boat was being swamped, and they were in great danger.ᴺᴵⱽ Mark explained that it was evening when they finally set sail (Mark 4:35). Setting sail in the evening was not unusual because Peter was used to fishing at night (see John 21:3). With the crowds and healing and teaching, Jesus certainly must have been exhausted. So as the boat set out, Jesus *fell asleep.* He probably lay down on the low bench in the stern where the helmsman (or pilot) would sit and then fell asleep on the leather cushion.

That *a squall came down on the lake* was not necessarily unusual. The Sea of Galilee is relatively small (13 miles long, 7 miles wide), 150 feet deep, and the shoreline is 680 feet below sea level. Storms appear suddenly over the surrounding mountains, stirring the water into violent twenty-foot waves. The disciples had not foolishly set out in a storm. They usually did not encounter storms at night and did not see this one coming. Even though several of these men were experienced fishermen and knew how to handle a boat, they had been caught without warning by this squall, *the boat was being swamped* by the waves, and *they were in great danger.*

That Jesus could sleep during this storm indicates his complete exhaustion. That the noise, the violent rocking of the boat, and the cold spray of the water did not awaken him gives us a glimpse of the physical fatigue of Jesus throughout his earthly ministry.

8:24 The disciples went and woke him, saying, "Master, Master, we're going to drown!" He got up and rebuked the wind and the raging waters; the storm subsided, and all was calm.^{NIV}

The disciples were in great danger, so they went to Jesus, waking him to tell him that they were all *going to drown!* Mark records their words as, "Don't you care if we drown?" (Mark 4:38 NIV). These words were spoken in frustration. After a long day Jesus had sent them off across the lake, he had gone to sleep, and the disciples had ended up fending off waves and attempting to save themselves from drowning. They knew that they needed Jesus' help, but they didn't know what to expect or even how to ask.

Jesus, roused out of his sleep not by the storm but by the cries of the disciples, *got up.* Then he *rebuked the wind and the raging waters.* The Gospel of Mark alone tells the words he said, "Quiet! Be still!" (Mark 4:39 NIV). The verb "rebuked" may indicate that there was an evil force behind the storm. The Greek word is the same as that used when Jesus cast out demons, telling them to be silent. It means "Be calm and remain calm." With his rebuke, *the storm subsided, and all was calm.* Jesus has complete power over nature, and he demonstrated this power to his frightened disciples.

HEALING A DEMON-POSSESSED MAN
As he traveled through Galilee, Jesus told many parables and met many people, as recorded in Matthew and Mark. Later, from Capernaum, Jesus and the disciples set out in a boat, only to encounter a fierce storm. Jesus calmed the storm and, when they landed, exorcised a "legion" of demons.

8:25 Then he asked them, "Where is your faith?" And they were filled with awe and amazement. They said to one another, "Who is this man, that even the winds and waves obey him?"^{NLT} Jesus' words to the disciples, floating in their boat on the now-quiet sea, were simply, *"Where is your faith?"* They ought not to have been afraid—they were with Jesus. If they had learned anything about him at all in their time with him, they should have understood that, as the Son of God, he has control over every aspect of creation. They had seen him heal people, but power over a furious storm may not have crossed their minds. But they should have readily made the connection and have come to Jesus in faith, not in fear. This demonstration of power *filled* them *with awe and amazement.*

WHO'S IN CHARGE?

All people want to be in control of their lives and circumstances. If they are in good health, making enough money to pay the bills, and their loved ones are happy and safe, people can sometimes feel as though they really *are* in charge of their destinies. And then . . . something happens that is totally beyond their control—an illness, an accident, a natural disaster, financial reversal—and they realize that any such notion of being in command is at best a fleeting illusion.

What should Christians do in a crisis? They should do what the disciples did: go to Jesus. He may not always "calm the storm" as he did for them, but he is in control. Christ is Lord over everything—including nature, life, finances, and all circumstances. Are there areas of your life you are trying to handle without him? Learn a lesson from a bunch of frightened fishermen: submit everything to him. He can handle it better than you can.

They asked the question to which they should have known the answer: *"Who is this man?"* This miracle clearly displayed Jesus' divine identity. Yet despite all that they had seen and heard thus far, and despite their love for Jesus, they still did not grasp that he was himself God and thus had power and authority over all of creation.

When the later believers in the early church read this story, they applied it to themselves in the seas of persecution that they faced. Just as the disciples had been surrounded by a sea that threatened to sink them, the church was surrounded by enemies who threatened to destroy it (first the Jews tried to undermine the Christian faith; then the Romans widely persecuted Christians). Storms will come, but followers of Christ have peace and faith with the knowledge that Jesus has power over all storms. He can quiet them if he chooses. Often the early Christians hoped for Jesus to quiet the storm of persecution, but he did not. So in the middle of the storm, they relied, instead, on their faith in the power of their Savior and the eternal rest promised to them.

When caught in the storms of life, it is easy to think that God has lost control and that you are at the mercy of the winds of fate. In reality, God is sovereign. He controls the history of the world as well as your personal destiny. Just as Jesus calmed the waves, he can calm whatever storm you may face.

STORM-READY FAITH
Almost anyone can sail a boat across a calm, glassy lake. But the Sea of Galilee was known for its sudden, fierce squalls. Several of the disciples were fishermen who had spent their lives on and around it, and they knew it could be treacherous. Still, they probably felt confident enough in transporting Jesus from one side to the other . . . until the wind and the waves knocked the courage out of them. It is easy to criticize the disciples for not trusting their Master at that point, but would your faith handle a seemingly life-threatening situation any better? Those crises will come; it's not a matter of *if,* but *when.* Is your faith ready for the storm? Resolve now that by God's grace, you will trust in him, not just when it's easy, but all the time.

JESUS SENDS THE DEMONS INTO A HERD OF PIGS / 8:26-39 / **88**

At Jesus' word, the winds and waves were calmed. At his command, thousands of demons fled. Previously, Jesus had loudly called people to listen to his words and obey them (see 8:8, 15, 18). The elements of nature and the evil beings of the spiritual world do not ignore his command, but people do. The Pharisees rejected God's plan (7:30), and the Gerasenes were more concerned about the economic loss of a herd of pigs. But all was not lost, for the man who had been liberated from the clutches of demons listened—intently. His soul was the "good soil" about which Jesus had spoken, the heart that listens to Jesus and heeds his command (8:15). Knowing this, Jesus commanded this man to stay in this Gentile region, testifying to God's goodness and producing an abundant harvest of faith.

Learn a simple lesson from the winds, the waves, even demons, and, most of all, from this healed man: Jesus' command must be obeyed. For demons it means judgment, but for those of us who humble ourselves at Jesus' feet it

> As he that fears God fears nothing else, so he that sees God sees nothing else.   *John Donne*

means eternal life. Jesus' command to this man, "Tell how much God has done for you," is also for you two thousand years later. Tell others what Jesus has done for you.

8:26 They sailed to the region of the Gerasenes, which is across the lake from Galilee.^{NIV} After Jesus had calmed the storm, the boat arrived at its intended destination, for Jesus wanted to go *to the region of the Gerasenes.* This region was *across the lake from Galilee,* a Gentile region probably southeast of the Sea of Galilee, home of the Decapolis, or the Ten Cities. These were Greek cities that belonged to no country and were self-governing. The exact location of this region is uncertain because this country (or region) is sometimes written as "Gerasenes," "Gergesenes," or "Gadarenes" in various manuscripts. Whatever the exact location of their landing, the point is that this was Gentile territory (there would not have been a herd of pigs in Jewish territory, for Jews considered pigs to be unclean, see 8:32 and Leviticus 11:7) and that Jesus had planned to go there. Luke would want to show his readers Jesus' desire to go into Gentile territory with his message.

8:27 As Jesus was climbing out of the boat, a man who was possessed by demons came out to meet him. Homeless and naked, he had lived in a cemetery for a long time.^{NLT} The boat landed in the region. Then, as soon as Jesus *was climbing out of the boat,* he met with demonic opposition. Matthew's account speaks of two demon-possessed men, while Mark and Luke refer only to one. Apparently Mark and Luke mention only the man who did the talking or the one who was the most severe (with a "legion" of demons, 8:30). This man *came out to meet him,* but not as a welcoming party, for he was *possessed by demons.* The demons probably wanted to scare away Jesus and the disciples.

Demons are fallen angels who had joined Satan in his rebellion against God and are now evil spirits under Satan's control. They help Satan tempt people to sin and have great destructive powers. Demon-possessed people are controlled by one or more demons. Although no one is sure why demon possession occurs, it is clear that evil spirits can use the human body to distort and destroy a person's relationship with God. Demons had entered this man's body and were controlling him, trying to destroy or distort God's image.

A demon-possessed person lived in isolation and agony. This man was *homeless.* (Mark's Gospel describes him as uncontrollable, so he could not live anywhere, see Mark 5:3-5.) He was *naked*—unable to take care of himself, not caring about physical comfort (Mark also says that he cut himself with stones, Mark 5:5). The man lived *in a cemetery.* In those days it was common for cemeteries to have many tombs carved into the hillside, making cave-like mausoleums. There was enough room for a person to live in such tombs. Tombs of wealthy people had more than one chamber for later family members to be buried, so there were empty cham-

bers available for shelter. Such cemeteries were often in remote areas. A demon-
possessed person, already shunned,
would also be considered unclean
because of living among the tombs.
Finally, the text says that he had been in
this condition *for a long time.*

> Satan has no constructive
> purpose of his own; his
> tactics are simply to
> thwart God and destroy
> men.   *J. I. Packer*

8:28-29 **When he saw Jesus, he fell down before him and shouted at
the top of his voice, "What have you to do with me, Jesus, Son
of the Most High God? I beg you, do not torment me"—for
Jesus had commanded the unclean spirit to come out of the
man.**NRSV The demon-possessed man had gone out to meet this
boat and its occupants, probably hoping to scare them away. But
then *he saw Jesus*—or rather, the demons saw Jesus and recognized him and his authority immediately. So the demons caused
the man to fall down before Jesus, not in worship, but in grudging submission to Jesus' superiority. The man *shouted at the top
of his voice*—a defensive move designed to scare these men, as
well as showing how angry the demons were.

The question "What have you to do with me?" is a request for
Jesus to leave them alone; it means literally "What to you and to
me?" or "What do we have in common?" In other words, the
demons were asking Jesus to go away because they had nothing
to do with each other. Such a question shows the demons' ultimate rebellion. Jesus and the demons were as far separated as
anything could be. Jesus' purpose was to heal and give life; the
demons' purpose was to kill and destroy. But Jesus would not
leave this man in such a condition.

Then, the demon used Jesus' divine name, *Jesus, Son of the
Most High God.* Compare this with 4:33-34 where the demon-
possessed man in the synagogue "cried out at the top of his
voice" and made a point of saying that he knew Jesus was "the
Holy One of God." Here the demon was again using Jesus' true
name, hoping to gain control over him (in ancient times, people
believed that to know a person's precise name could help one
gain control over that person). The words "Most High God"
appear in the Old Testament and often were used by Gentiles
when speaking of the superiority of Israel's God over any idol.
(See Melchizedek's words in Genesis 14:18-24; Balaam's words
in Numbers 24:16; Isaiah speaking of a heathen king—sometimes interpreted as Satan—in Isaiah 14:14; Nebuchadnezzar's
words in Daniel 3:26; 4:2.)

Next, while Luke did not record Jesus' exact words, the text
does say that Jesus *commanded the unclean spirit to come out*

of the man. Then the demon begged Jesus, saying, *"Do not torment me."* Demons recognize Jesus, understand who he is, know his power, and also seem to know their ultimate fate. Jesus has the power to "torment" them (see also 8:31), and even with all their shrieking and horrifying acts, they are reduced to begging before the one who is far more powerful than they or their leader Satan can even pretend to be. Their "torment" will be no more than the consequences for the rebellion (see Revelation 20:10).

The evil motives and power of the demon are revealed in these words: **(For many times it had seized him; he was kept under guard and bound with chains and shackles, but he would break the bonds and be driven by the demon into the wilds.)**[NRSV] These words ought to cause anyone to stop and consider who Satan is and what his army of demons attempts to do. This story shows their hatred of anything living or beautiful; they always seek to destroy and ruin. It also reveals their power. Although Satan is not as powerful as God, for he is a created being, he still exerts great power over this world. Satan's demons (there are more than one in this man) could cause this man to break iron shackles that were intended to hold him. Then the demons would drive him into the wilderness. Finally, the story also shows Satan's cruelty. For all that Satan might promise (see what he wanted to give Jesus, 4:6), he is a cruel and ruthless master. Those under his control face complete ruin under a master bent on destroying even those who serve him.

THE DESTROYER

There is an old fable about a scorpion and a frog. The scorpion asked the frog to carry him on his back across a creek. The frog said no, fearing the scorpion would sting him. The scorpion swore he would not, and so the frog warily allowed the scorpion to hop on, and started across the stream. Sure enough, when they were halfway across, the scorpion stung the frog. "Why did you do that?" yelled the frog. "Now I will die and you will drown, too!"

"I know," replied the scorpion. "It's just my nature to sting."

Satan is pictured several different ways in Scripture—Lucifer, the Accuser, a prowling lion—but they all have this in common: Satan's nature is to destroy. Luke 8:27-29 shows how demons were intent on destroying a man. When that plan was thwarted by Jesus, they settled for destroying a herd of pigs. Satan and his minions have one goal: to destroy. Don't make the same mistake the frog made. Avoid riding with the devil.

8:30 **"What is your name?" Jesus asked. "Legion," he replied—for
the man was filled with many demons.**^{NLT} Whether Jesus was
asking this poor man for his name or asking the demon for its
name is uncertain. But the demon answered, saying that its name
was *Legion.* A "legion" was the largest unit in the Roman army,
having between three thousand and six thousand soldiers. Thus
this man *was filled with many demons.* Jesus had cast out individual demons, but this time he would be taking on a whole army of
them. This man, possessed by many demons, was extremely dangerous. Certainly the disciples, standing in the background, must
have been frightened of him. But Jesus had authority, and this
legion of demons knew it.

8:31 **And they begged him repeatedly not to order them to go into
the Abyss.**^{NIV} The demons undoubtedly knew that Jesus planned
to free their prisoner—the human whom they possessed. Their
concern at this point was *where* Jesus would send them. They
knew where they did *not* want to go. They also knew that they
had no power over Jesus and would have to submit to him. When
the demons realized that they were face-to-face with Jesus himself, they *begged him repeatedly not to order them to go into the
Abyss.* Also mentioned in Revelation 9:1 and 20:1-3, the Abyss is
the place of confinement for Satan and his demons (this is sometimes called the "bottomless pit"). The demons obviously knew
about this place and didn't want to go there.

Why didn't Jesus just destroy these demons—or send them far
away? Matthew 8:29 says that the demons asked not to be sent to
the Abyss before the appointed time. They knew their ultimate fate,
but the time for such work had not yet come. Jesus healed many
people of the destructive effects of demon possession, but he did
not yet destroy demons. In this situation, Jesus wanted to show
Satan's destructive power and intent through what the demons did
to the two thousand pigs. The same question could be asked today:
Why doesn't Jesus stop all the evil in the world? His time for that
has not yet come. But it will come. The book of Revelation portrays the future victory of Jesus over Satan, his demons, and all evil.

8:32-33 **A large herd of pigs was feeding on the hillside nearby, and
the demons pleaded with him to let them enter into the pigs.
Jesus gave them permission. So the demons came out of the
man and entered the pigs, and the whole herd plunged down
the steep hillside into the lake, where they drowned.**^{NLT} The
Gospel of Mark reports that this *large herd of pigs* numbered
about two thousand (Mark 5:13). Why did the demons plead with
Jesus to *let them enter into the pigs?* Demons have a destructive
intent—to be sent away or into the Abyss would mean they

would be unable to torment anyone. They probably would have preferred to be sent into the city in order to find other people to inhabit, but apparently they knew Jesus would not allow that. But many physical animal hosts were on the hillside. Pigs were unclean animals according to God's law, so this was an appropriate place for these "unclean spirits" (8:29).

So *Jesus gave them permission.* Satan has no final authority but can do only what God "permits" for the short time that he is allowed to be "god of this world" (2 Corinthians 4:4 NRSV). Why Jesus gave them permission is as uncertain as why the demons wanted to enter the pigs. While Jesus could have sent them away, he did not because the time for final judgment had not yet come. Yet it is clear from this story that Jesus valued this one man far more than any number of pigs.

The demons' ultimate destructive intent cannot be missed in the picture of *the whole herd* (about two thousand pigs!) running headlong *down the steep hillside into the lake, where they drowned.* The sight must have been amazing. A rather peaceful herd of pigs suddenly became a stampeding horde that ran straight to its destruction. The demons wanted something to torment, and then immediately killed them.

While Jesus granted the demons' request to enter the swine and destroy the herd, he stopped their destructive work in this demon-possessed man, setting him free from the torment that had held him for so long (8:27). We're not told if the sea destroyed the demons, but very clearly Jesus was in control. Luke 11:24-26 presents the possibility that an exorcised demon can cause trouble later. Jesus' time for total destruction of demonic forces had not yet come.

AUTHORITY
If this incident were to take place today, Jesus would have been besieged by animal rights activists protesting that he had no right to let those demons destroy that herd of pigs. Many wonder why Jesus chose that particular means of casting demons out of this poor man; Luke didn't say. One insight should be very clear, however: Jesus has authority over unclean spirits, pigs, people, and everything else. He didn't ask permission of the pigs' owner before allowing his herd to be destroyed because he didn't need to. Jesus is Lord over all, whether people acknowledge his authority or not. You may never be confronted by a person possessed by a legion of demons, but you do have to face the daily struggle of submitting your will to God. What "unclean" areas in your life do you need to let him clean up or clean out? Take some time in prayer to let him point them out to you, and then ask his help to change.

8:34 When the herdsmen saw it, they fled to the nearby city and the surrounding countryside, spreading the news as they ran.NLT The *herdsmen* on the hill, responsible for the safety of the pigs, were astounded when their herd suddenly ran away, down the hill, and into the Sea of Galilee. Terrified, surprised, and afraid that they would somehow be blamed for the disaster, *they fled to the nearby city and the surrounding countryside, spreading the news as they ran.* Certainly those who heard the news had to go and see for themselves, so a crowd soon surrounded Jesus, the disciples, and the newly freed man.

8:35 Then they went out to see what had happened, and came to Jesus, and found the man from whom the demons had departed, sitting at the feet of Jesus, clothed and in his right mind. And they were afraid.NKJV One would think that the people would have rejoiced that this man who had terrorized them for so long had been completely cured. But when *they went out to see what had happened,* their response was quite different. They saw a boat on the shore, a couple thousand dead pigs floating in the water, a small group of men on the seashore, and the formerly demon-possessed man *sitting at the feet of Jesus, clothed and in his right mind.* But they did not respond in joy or relief or welcome—instead, *they were afraid.* Of what? At those moments when Jesus directly confronted the forces of evil in a contest of will and power, he may have struck a most intense and fearsome image. Maybe they realized Jesus' obvious power and wondered what he might want from them. His unconcern for this large herd of pigs may have appeared to be a threat to their financial security. In any case, these people, who had the author of true and eternal life standing among them with evidence of his love sitting at his feet, made a terrible mistake.

8:36-37 Those who had seen it told the people how the demon-possessed man had been cured. Then all the people of the region of the Gerasenes asked Jesus to leave them, because they were overcome with fear. So he got into the boat and left.NIV There could be no mistaking it, *the demon-possessed man had been cured,* but the operative word in the sentence is "how." Those who had seen what had happened correctly connected the healing of the man with the destruction of the pigs—although Jesus had not told the demons to destroy the pigs. But the people, *overcome with fear,* told Jesus that they wanted him to leave. If they were afraid because of the loss of their livestock, it was foolish for them to value possessions, investments, and even animals above human life. If they were afraid because of the miracle (as in the Transfiguration in 9:34), it was foolish for them to pass up an opportunity to witness God's miraculous power. Unfortunately for them, Jesus did as they asked—*he got into the boat and left.* And there is no biblical record that he ever returned. Sometimes the worst that can happen is for Jesus to answer a poorly considered request.

A MATTER OF PRIORITIES
Unbelievable! Jesus healed a man possessed by demons, and the local people asked Jesus to go away. Why? Why would they do such an obviously stupid and ungrateful thing? Some may have worried that Jesus might allow something similar to happen to their herds of livestock; some may have been uncomfortable with the idea of a former demon-possessed man reentering their community. Whatever the reason, the people were obviously afraid of Jesus and his ability to upset the status quo. How shortsighted of them, and yet, how typical. Have you ever heard someone in your church say (or said yourself),

- "I'm glad the church has a heart for evangelism, but all these new people make me uncomfortable."
- "Why do we need to sing these new songs? The old hymns are good enough for me."
- "Our last pastor didn't do that. . . ."

If so, you or your church may be unknowingly following in the footsteps of the people of the Gerasenes. Beware of letting your personal preferences or your attachment to the status quo take priority over Jesus and his work in people's lives.

8:38-39 **The man who had been demon possessed begged to go, too, but Jesus said, "No, go back to your family and tell them all the wonderful things God has done for you." So he went all through the city telling about the great thing Jesus had done for him.**[NLT] While the townspeople wanted Jesus gone, the formerly possessed man *begged to go* with Jesus, meaning that he wanted to become one of Jesus' followers. We don't know if this man was a Jew or a Gentile. We don't know his motive in asking to stay with Jesus. He may have wanted to be with Jesus out of adoration; he may have been afraid of being shunned by his people for indirectly causing the death of the pigs; he may have been afraid that the demons might return if Jesus went away. Although the man wanted to go with Jesus, Jesus had other plans for him, saying, *"No, go back to your family and tell them all the wonderful things God has done for you."* This man would be returning to his home in a Gentile region. Jesus knew that this man would be an effective witness to those who remembered his previous condition and could attest to the miraculous healing. Through him, Jesus' ministry would expand into this Gentile area. Jesus would not remain in the region, but he did not leave himself without a witness, for this man *went all through the city telling about the great thing Jesus had done for him.* The Gentiles may have sent Jesus away, but they could not send away his message or the irrefutable miracle evidenced by this healed man. Luke's Gentile audience would have been glad to know that although Jesus had been sent away from this Gentile region, Jesus still had compassion and a desire for their salvation by leaving behind this man to be his witness.

"GO BACK"
Often Jesus asked those he healed to be quiet about the healing, but he urged this man to return to his family and tell what God had done for him. Why the difference?

- Jesus knew the man would be an effective witness to those who knew his previous condition and could attest to the miraculous healing.
- Jesus wanted to expand his ministry by introducing his message into this Gentile area.
- Jesus knew that the Gentiles, since they were not expecting a Messiah, would not divert his ministry by trying to crown him king.

When God touches your life, share the wonderful events with your family and friends.

JESUS HEALS A BLEEDING WOMAN AND RESTORES A GIRL TO LIFE / 8:40-56 / **89**

In this story, Jesus is not battling thousands of demons or commanding the winds. Instead he is fighting on a much more uneven ground—the human heart with all its fears and doubts. Although witnessing the wind being stilled may be much more spectacular than watching a woman come to faith, the stakes in transforming a human heart are much higher and the victory much greater, prompting a celebration in the presence of God (15:10). Here Jesus took the timid faith of a woman and transformed her into a powerful, public testimony of him. Then he gently encouraged the grief-stricken Jairus to believe in him. Today, the more noticeable miracles—the healing of the woman's bleeding and the raising of Jairus's daughter from the dead—draw attention. But in the Gospels, Jesus always points away from the external aspects of his miracles to what takes place in the human soul—the faith of the person who has been healed.

Believers today have been called to adjust their vision as well (Romans 12:2)—to focus on the spiritual realities that all too often are obscured by the dazzling and hollow attractions of this world. For people who are customarily focused on the physical and material, this requires discipline, consciously deciding day after day to shine the revealing light of God's Word on their lives.

8:40 Now when Jesus returned, the crowd welcomed him, for they were all waiting for him.^{NRSV} *Jesus returned* across the Sea of Galilee, back to Jewish territory, probably landing at Capernaum. In contrast to the crowd on the eastern shore that had asked him to leave, here *the crowd welcomed him, for they were all waiting for him.* The people had seen Jesus leave, and they presumed that he would return to the same location. They were not disappointed.

DESByRATE FAITH
Would a respected leader of some mainline denomination—Southern Baptist, Methodist, Presbyterian—go to a tent pitched on the outskirts of town and ask for help from a traveling faith healer? Not likely. But if that respected person's son or daughter were dying and conventional medicine had been ineffective, then he or she might consider something unconventional. That's the situation in which Jairus, leader of the local synagogue, found himself when Jesus came to town. Jesus was an itinerant preacher from lowly Nazareth, a nobody from nowhere. But Jairus was a desperate man, and his desperation drove him to ask for help from this unlikely person. What is the great need or fear in your life? Are you desperate enough to do something radical or unconventional about it? Then take it to Jesus, just as Jairus did, and let him meet you at the point of your need.

8:41-42 And now a man named Jairus, a leader of the local synagogue, came and fell down at Jesus' feet, begging him to come home with him. His only child was dying, a little girl twelve years old. As Jesus went with him, he was surrounded by the crowds.^{NLT} A man in the crowd had apparently been waiting for Jesus to return. His name was *Jairus* and he was *a leader of the local synagogue.* A synagogue leader was highly visible and respected. The synagogue was the local center of worship, and Jairus was a lay person elected as one of the leaders (a synagogue could have more than one leader or ruler, see Acts 13:15). The synagogue leaders were responsible for supervising worship services, caring for the scrolls, running the daily school, keeping the congregation faithful to the law, distributing alms, administering the care of the building, and finding rabbis to teach on the Sabbath.

Despite his status, Jairus (whose name means "he will awaken") *came and fell down at Jesus' feet, begging him to come home with him.* This would have been an unusual scene, but Jairus was desperate because *his only child was dying, a little girl twelve years old.* Jairus's position as a loving father overshadowed his position as a leader. He put aside any concern for himself and went directly to the man whom he had seen heal so many (perhaps even in his own synagogue, 6:6-11). Jesus went with Jairus; as usual, *the crowds* went along.

8:43-44 **And a woman was there who had been subject to bleeding for twelve years, but no one could heal her. She came up behind him and touched the edge of his cloak, and immediately her bleeding stopped.**[NIV] The crowds followed Jesus and as they made their way through the streets, they pressed against one another (8:45). One woman also had been awaiting Jesus' return. Tradition says that she was from Caesarea Philippi, so she had traveled to Capernaum to find Jesus. Perhaps she had hoped to reach out to him when he came back and thus be healed. But Jairus got to Jesus first, and now they were walking away from her. Perhaps she thought this would be her only chance—she might not be able to talk to Jesus, but she knew she wanted to be healed.

RELEASE THE POWER
Many people were surrounding Jesus as he made his way toward Jairus's house. It was virtually impossible to get through the multitude, but one woman fought her way desperately through the crowd in order to touch Jesus. As soon as she did so, she was healed. What a difference there is between the crowds that are curious about Jesus and the few who reach out and touch him! Today, many people are vaguely familiar with Jesus, but nothing in their lives is changed or bettered by this passing acquaintance. It is only faith that releases God's healing power. Jesus must be more than a curiosity. Reach out to him in faith, knowing that his mercy will bring healing to your body, soul, and spirit.

Luke wrote that the woman *had been subject to bleeding for twelve years, but no one could heal her.* Many doctors had tried, but with no success (Mark 5:26). This was a type of painful hemorrhage (perhaps a menstrual or uterine disorder). The bleeding caused the woman to be in a constant condition of ceremonial uncleanness (see Leviticus 15:25-33). She could not worship in the synagogue (perhaps even Jairus had been the one to exclude her from worship), and she could not have normal social relationships, for under Jewish law, anyone who touched her also would become unclean. Thus, the woman had been treated almost as severely as a leper. That she was in the crowd at all was a courageous move on her part. If all those people bumping against her in the crowd had known her condition, she would have been in for some rough treatment.

Nevertheless, she also desperately needed Jesus. So she pressed her way through the crowd, *came up behind* Jesus, and *touched the edge of his cloak,* for she believed, as did many people, that the clothes of a holy man imparted spiritual and healing power (see Mark 6:56; Acts 19:11-12). She may also have feared that Jesus would not touch her if he knew her condition because she would make him unclean. And she certainly did not want the pressing crowd to know that she had ventured among them. So she hoped to touch Jesus and then get away as unobtrusively as possible.

The moment that she touched Jesus, *her bleeding stopped.* The text in Luke says that she was healed *immediately*—her pain was gone and she knew that she was healed. After twelve years of suffering, the bleeding vanished completely in an instant.

8:45 **"Who touched me?" Jesus asked. Everyone denied it, and Peter said, "Master, this whole crowd is pressing up against you."**[NLT] The woman had touched Jesus and probably had turned to go, hoping to disappear into the crowd. But Jesus knew about the healing the moment it happened. He asked the seemingly absurd question, *"Who touched me?"* While the *whole crowd* had been *pressing up against* him, no one close by had deliberately touched him, so of course *everyone denied it.* Then Peter pointed out the obvious, basically telling Jesus it was a strange question to ask in the middle of a crowd.

Why did it matter? Couldn't Jesus have let this woman go on her way? It wasn't that Jesus didn't know who had touched him. He wanted her to step forward and identify herself. Jesus wanted to teach her that his cloak did not contain magical properties but that her faith in him had healed her. He may also have wanted to teach the crowds a lesson. According to Jewish law, a man who touched a menstruating woman became ceremonially unclean (Leviticus 15:19-28). This was true whether her bleeding was normal or, as in this woman's case, the result of illness. To protect themselves from such defilement, Jewish men carefully avoided touching, speaking to, or even looking at women. By contrast, Jesus proclaimed to hundreds of people that this "unclean" woman had touched him—and then he healed her. In Jesus' mind, this suffering woman was not to be overlooked. As God's creation, she deserved attention and respect.

DON'T WAIT
Just as it was most unusual for a synagogue official to seek out a wandering rabbi, it was most inappropriate according to Jewish custom for a woman subject to bleeding to touch a man (see Leviticus 15:19-28). But if you had been seriously ill for twelve years with a disease that doctors could not cure, you might set aside such protocol as well. That's what this woman did. She put aside her pride, fear, and hopelessness and pushed her way through the crowd until she could touch Jesus. Would you have done that? Or would you have let doubt or vanity or worry over what others might think keep you back? Don't wait until you're desperate to take your problems to Jesus. Overcome your fear of what others might say and take your stand for him.

8:46 But Jesus said, "Someone touched me; I know that power has gone out from me."^{NIV} Jesus persisted. He stopped the entire crowd, determined to find out who touched him. *"Someone touched me,"* he said. Jesus was talking about a different kind of touch—not the press of a person in the crowd but the purposeful touch of someone who wanted to be healed. Jesus knew it because *power* had *gone out from* him. Probably Jesus knew who had touched him; it is doubtful that Jesus' power could just flow out to anyone at any time without his knowledge. But Jesus knew that the woman needed to identify herself and so receive more than physical healing. Jesus wanted to heal her spiritually as well. In addition, Jesus knew that for this woman to be able to return to normal social relations and worship, her cure would need to be known publicly.

8:47 When the woman saw that she could not remain hidden, she came trembling; and falling down before him, she declared in the presence of all the people why she had touched him, and how she had been immediately healed.^{NRSV} The woman realized that to try to slip away at that point would have been impossible; Jesus wanted an answer, and she realized that *she could not remain hidden.* The woman came forward, *trembling,* and fell down before Jesus. *She declared in the presence of all the people why she had touched him.* This was not a simple act, for she would have to explain how she—unclean and filled with a dreadful disease—had come in among the crowd, had reached out and touched a man (a rabbi) in her unclean state, and had hoped to slip away. All these were huge infractions of social laws and would have probably been grounds for anger from any other rabbi and any other crowd. But this was no ordinary rabbi, for she also explained how when she had touched Jesus, *she had been immediately healed.*

8:48 Then he said to her, "Daughter, your faith has healed you. Go in peace."NIV The woman may have been afraid of an angry backlash for her actions, but Jesus spoke to her in gentle words, calling her *daughter,* revealing a father-child relationship. She came for healing and received it, but she also received a relationship and peace with God himself because of her faith. Jesus explained that it was not his clothing that had healed her; rather, her *faith* in reaching out to the one Person who could heal her had allowed that healing to take place. Not only did the woman have faith, but she had also placed her faith in the right person.

The words "go in peace" are more literally "go into peace." With this healing, Jesus gave this woman her life. Her cure was permanent. Jesus wished her peace of both body and soul—renewed health for her body and eternal salvation for her soul.

FAITH OR SUPERSTITION
Superstitions are commonplace. For example, many athletes have certain rituals they go through before every game, such as eating a certain meal or not stepping on the sideline as they go onto the playing field. Most Christians would probably say they don't have any such superstitions, but . . . they sit in the exact same place every time for worship, or pray the same prayer every morning, or read only one translation of the Bible. The point is that none of these things really have anything to do with spirituality. What really counts is a person's relationship with and closeness to Jesus. The woman who had hemorrhaged for twelve years thought there was something magical about Jesus' robe; there wasn't. It was her faith that mattered. Take inventory of your spiritual practices and ask yourself if any of them have become merely superstitious. If so, get rid of them and put your trust in Jesus alone.

8:49 While he was still speaking to her, a messenger arrived from Jairus's home with the message, "Your little girl is dead. There's no use troubling the Teacher now."NLT During this interval, Jairus had been waiting. Jesus *was still speaking* to this woman who had interrupted his walk to Jairus's house when *a messenger arrived.* What Jairus feared most had happened. His dear little girl had died. It was too late for the *Teacher* to heal her, so there was no longer any reason to bring Jesus to his home. Apparently Jairus hadn't heard that Jesus could raise the dead (7:11-15)—or perhaps he thought it would be too much to ask.

8:50 **Hearing this, Jesus said to Jairus, "Don't be afraid; just believe, and she will be healed."**^{NIV} Upon hearing the news, Jairus surely reacted in great sorrow. It seemed that the delay had been too long, and it was now too late. Jairus had tried, but he had failed. Jesus, however, would not be put off. He turned to the grieving man and said, *"Don't be afraid; just believe."* In the presence of Jairus, the woman had been commended for her faith. Here in the presence of the woman, Jairus was told to have faith. The woman became a model of faith for Jairus. Using a woman to illustrate faith would have been unheard of in that time. What did Jesus want Jairus to believe? Perhaps he simply wanted him to hold on to the faith that had driven him to Jesus in the first place. He had believed that Jesus could heal his daughter; Jesus wanted him to continue to believe that *she will be healed.* The fact that the daughter had died did not change anything for Jesus.

In many ways, the woman and Jairus are similar. Both came to Jesus in desperate need, kneeling at his feet (8:41, 47); both had public problems (8:47, 51); both needed faith, which was the crucial step in their solution (8:48, 50). Faith had healed the desperate woman; faith could also heal Jairus's child. The fact that she had died made no difference to Jesus, who had power over death.

BELIEVING THE IMPOSSIBLE
Anyone with a child or children can readily put himself or herself emotionally in Jairus's place. His daughter, his only beloved daughter, had died while they were on the way home. Luke did not write this, but the poor man probably wept and cried out in his grief—the deepest, most painful grief anyone can experience. To a man in this kind of intense pain and anguish in his soul, Jesus said, "Don't be afraid; just believe." Again, Luke didn't record Jairus's reaction to these words, but Jairus must have had at least some flicker of hope because he did complete his mission in bringing Jesus to his house. When you experience intense grief over the loss of a loved one, breakup of a marriage, loss of a job, or rejection of a close friend, don't abandon hope. Don't turn away from the one Person who can help you. Do what Jairus did, and cling to the hope found only in our resurrected Lord, the one with power over life and death.

8:51 **When they arrived at the house, Jesus wouldn't let anyone go in with him except Peter, James, John, and the little girl's father and mother.**^{NLT} Apparently Jairus did continue to believe, for he led Jesus the rest of the way to his house. The crowd still followed, perhaps all the more curious, wondering what Jesus would do in this seemingly impossible situation. *When they arrived at the house,* however, Jesus took control and made everyone stay outside. The only people who entered with him were *Peter, James, John,* and the child's parents. These three particular disciples had become Jesus' inner circle to whom he gave special teaching and consideration (they were the only ones to see his transfiguration, see Matthew 17:1; also Mark 13:3; 14:33).

Jesus had required the sick woman to step forward and make her healing public (8:47). This helped her faith, as well as helped her back into society after having been an outcast. Her healing was not something obvious. Raising a dead child would be obvious enough, so in this miracle, Jesus wanted privacy for the child and her parents. He did not need the miracle-hungry throng filling the room.

8:52-53 The house was filled with people weeping and wailing, but he said, "Stop the weeping! She isn't dead; she is only asleep." But the crowd laughed at him because they all knew she had died.^{NLT} The house full of people probably included relatives and neighbors, as well as professional mourners who may have already arrived. Lack of *weeping and wailing* was the ultimate disgrace and disrespect. Jairus, the leader of the synagogue, was an important person in the town. Thus, at the death of his only daughter, the townspeople demonstrated their great love and respect for Jairus and his family by their intense grief. Yet their weeping turned to derisive laughter at Jesus' words that the girl was not dead, *only asleep.* The people assumed that Jesus was misinformed, had not yet heard the news, or was a rather ignorant rabbi to be unable to tell sleep from death. Before Jesus' resurrection, the idea of raising the dead seemed absurd (see Acts 17:32 where Luke records Paul's teaching on resurrection). *They all knew she had died.* She was indeed dead, but Jesus would bring her back to life, as if awakening her from sleep. Jesus used the image of sleep to indicate that the girl's condition was temporary and that she would be restored. For Jesus, death is nothing more than sleep, for he has power and authority over death.

8:54-55 But he took her by the hand and said, "My child, get up!" Her spirit returned, and at once she stood up. Then Jesus told them to give her something to eat.^{NIV} Jesus, the three chosen disciples, and the girl's parents entered the room where the body lay. Again Jesus went against all ceremonial law and *took* the dead girl *by the hand.* Touching a dead body would make a person unclean, but Jesus often would go past such laws in order to show compassion on those in need. He could have raised the girl without touching her (as he did Lazarus, John 11:43-44), but in this case, he chose to take her hand. Jesus' words were simple and direct: *"My child, get up!"* While Mark recorded the words in Aramaic (Mark 5:41), as Jesus most likely said them, Luke translated for his Gentile audience. With those words, *her spirit returned.* She had indeed been dead, but Jesus' words called back her spirit and *at once she stood up.* The little girl didn't come back to life in the sick state in which she had left; she came back well, whole, and able to walk around. She was even well enough to eat, for Jesus gave her parents instructions to *give her something to eat.*

HOPE THROUGH PAIN

What is the pain of death? Death is inevitable, so why do people react so powerfully at the loss of a loved one? Death means separation. It means no longer being able to enjoy the presence of the one who has been lost. But Jesus has the power to remove the sting of death. Jesus, who met death head-on and overcame it, assures those who believe in him that they also can overcome. They won't receive back loved ones who have died, but they can conquer the pain and fear of separation by the sure and certain hope that they will be reunited with the loved ones. Death is inevitable; loss of hope is not. Let hope in Christ answer the pain and heartache when death separates you from a loved one.

8:56 And her parents were astonished, but He charged them to tell no one what had happened.[NKJV] The young girl's parents *were astonished* and certainly overjoyed. Reversal of death is never expected—and only a few have ever received a dead loved one back to life. Jesus told the parents not to talk about their daughter's healing because he knew that the facts would speak for themselves. Jesus was not attempting to keep this a secret, for the crowd outside was waiting and would see what had happened. Jesus *charged them to tell no one* because he was concerned for his ministry. Jesus probably was asking them to keep to themselves the details of what he had done. He did not want to be known as just a miracle worker; he wanted people to listen to his words that would heal their broken spiritual lives. Jesus' mission was to preach the good news of the kingdom of God. If crowds descended on him to see dead people raised, they would not be coming with the attitude needed to hear and respond to the gospel.

LUKE 9

After giving examples of Jesus' pattern of preaching about the kingdom of God and of his power through all types of miracles, Luke reported how Jesus sent out the Twelve to continue this work. This begins two missionary trips (9:1; 10:1). Luke is the only Gospel writer who includes two trips, and the disciples probably were sent on other trips as well. Luke may have been introducing the theme of missionary journeys that became so prevalent in Acts.

All believers, from all walks of life, have a similar mission as the twelve disciples—to courageously tell others about the Good News. Even in the face of rejection, believers must be willing to continue to bring the message to a needy world.

9:1-2 **When Jesus had called the Twelve together, he gave them power and authority to drive out all demons and to cure diseases, and he sent them out to preach the kingdom of God and to heal the sick.**[NIV] Jesus had chosen twelve disciples for special training (6:13-16). The men had traveled with Jesus, observed him, and listened to his teaching as he traveled throughout Galilee. They had seen him heal numerous sick people, raise others from the dead, calm stormy seas, and set a dangerous demon-possessed man free from his

> Every man who is divinely called to the ministry is divinely equipped. *A. W. Pink*

legion of demons. Now they were to take a more active part in Jesus' ministry—themselves going out to *preach the kingdom of God.* More than that, Jesus also *gave them power and authority to drive out all demons and to cure diseases.* That was important because these miracles backed up the message. Jesus sent the Twelve out *to preach the kingdom of God and to heal the sick.* He gave them this power. The message of the Good News was of primary importance, but the healings showed God's great compassion and fulfilled the ancient prophecies of the Messiah's arrival (4:18-19).

Jesus announced his kingdom by both preaching and healing.

If he had limited himself to preaching, people may have seen his kingdom as spiritual only. On the other hand, if he had healed without preaching, people may not have realized the spiritual importance of his mission. Most of Jesus' listeners expected a Messiah who would bring wealth and power to their nation; they preferred material benefits to spiritual discernment. The truth about Jesus is that he is both God and man, both spiritual and physical; and the salvation that he offers is both for the soul and for the body. Christians' ministry should have an evangelistic message of word and action. People need to experience the whole message of God so that they will be restored in mind and body. Medical missions, feeding the hungry—these carry the impact of Christ's message by showing his love.

Jesus *sent them out;* the book of Mark says they went out in twos (Mark 6:7). Jesus gave the Twelve some instructions and then sent them on a "training mission." They would soon be the ones left to carry on Jesus' work after he was gone.

HIS METHOD
If you were given the task of carrying the good news about God's love to the whole world, how would you attempt to accomplish it? Mass communication, satellite uplinks, fax machines, the Internet? All of those technologies have been and continue to be used for evangelism and the building up of God's people. But Jesus relied on a more basic means of communication: people. He called his twelve key men together and entrusted them with the most important message the world has ever heard: the gospel of Jesus Christ. Technology is a wonderful tool, but there is no substitute for committed men and women who love God enough and care enough about their lost friends and neighbors to tell them about God's wonderful plan of salvation. If you know people who need to hear the Good News, pray for an opportunity to tell them. Be an active, willing part of Christ's strategy to tell the world.

9:3-4 **He said to them, "Take nothing for your journey, no staff, nor bag, nor bread, nor money—not even an extra tunic. Whatever house you enter, stay there, and leave from there."**[NRSV] The disciples were to travel light. The urgency of their task required that they not spend time preparing for the trip. Besides, it was to be a short trip after which they would come back and report to Jesus. As disciples sent by God, they were to depend on him and on the people to whom they ministered to meet their needs. Jesus told them not to take along any of the normal trappings that one might pack for a journey—*no staff* (for protection or for walking), *nor bag* (something in which to carry supplies;

some beggars carried bags, and the disciples were not to appear to be beggars or to accept money), *nor money* (obviously to buy food and shelter), *not even an extra tunic* (for extra warmth if sleeping outside at night).

Mark recorded that Jesus instructed the disciples to take nothing with them *except* staffs, while the accounts in Matthew and Luke say that Jesus told them *not* to take staffs. One explanation for this difference is that Matthew and Luke were referring to a club used for protection, whereas Mark was talking about a shepherd's crook used for walking. Another explanation is that according to Matthew and Luke, Jesus was forbidding them to acquire an *additional* staff or sandals, but instead to use what they already had. The point in all three accounts is the same: The disciples were to leave at once, without extensive preparation, trusting in God's care for all their needs.

TRAVELING (WITH THE) LIGHT
Different journeys call for different equipment. The gear you carry with you on a family ski vacation differs radically from what you take on a cross-country road rally. Jesus sent the disciples out on their preaching and healing mission without a lot of comforts or even supplies. That's because they weren't going out to enjoy the scenery or stay in any place for very long. They were going on a short-term mission to spread the gospel widely through the spoken word and the authoritative command over demons and diseases. That kind of ministry doesn't require much in the way of luggage, but it does require tremendous faith and reliance on the power of God. What kind of service are you involved in? Whatever it is—preaching, teaching, serving with medicine, working with youth, evangelizing—you undoubtedly have a list of equipment you'd love to have to be more effective. Next time you ask God to provide your needs, be sure to ask for his inner power and blessing on your work before you list your material needs.

In addition, *whatever house* the disciples entered (that is, whatever home showed them hospitality) was the house where they were to *stay* until they left that town. The disciples were not to offend their hosts by moving to a home that was more comfortable or socially prominent. To remain in one home was not a burden for the homeowner because there would only have been two together at a time and their stay in each community would be short.

The disciples were instructed to depend on others while they went from town to town preaching the gospel. This had a good effect: (1) it clearly showed that the Messiah had not come to offer wealth to his followers; (2) it forced the disciples to rely on

God's power and not on their own provision—they carried no outward symbols of authority, only the inward power that Christ gave them; and (3) it involved the villagers and made them more eager to hear the message. This was an excellent approach for the disciples' short-term mission; it was not intended, however, to be a permanent way of life for them. Jesus' instructions pertained only to this particular mission, so this would not be a command for missionaries today. Indeed, just after Jesus and the disciples ate the Last Supper, Jesus would ask them: "'When I sent you without purse, bag or sandals, did you lack anything?' 'Nothing,' they answered. He said to them, 'But now if you have a purse, take it, and also a bag; and if you don't have a sword, sell your cloak and buy one'" (Luke 22:35-36 NIV). Different times and situations would call for different measures, both then and now.

THE JOB: TO SHARE
Shaking off the dust of a place, Jesus said, would be a testimony against the people. The implications of this action were clear and had eternal consequences. It showed that the disciples had discharged their duty, had nothing further to say, and would leave the people to answer to God.

Believers should not stop ministering to others in a community if some reject the message. Jesus was saying that if the disciples were rejected by nonbelieving Jews, they should treat those Jews the same as nonbelieving Gentiles. By this statement, Jesus was making it clear that the listeners were responsible for what they did with the gospel. As long as the disciples had faithfully and carefully presented the message, they were not to blame if the townspeople rejected it. Likewise, believers are not responsible when others reject Christ's message of salvation if they have carefully and truthfully presented it. But they do have the responsibility to share the gospel clearly and faithfully. When the message is rejected, they should move on to others whom God desires to reach.

9:5 "Wherever they do not welcome you, as you are leaving that town shake the dust off your feet as a testimony against them."NRSV The disciples could be sure of finding hospitality from some people, but Jesus told them to also expect places where they would not be welcomed. Jesus' instructions for such a town was that as the disciples were leaving, they were to *shake the dust off [their] feet as a testimony against them.* Shaking the dust of unaccepting towns from their feet had deep cultural implications. Shaking off dust that had accumulated on one's sandals showed extreme contempt for an area and its people, as well as the determination not to have any further involvement with them.

Pious Jews would do this after passing through Gentile cities to show their separation from Gentile practices. If the disciples shook the dust of a *Jewish* town from their feet, it would show their separation from Jews who rejected their Messiah. This action also showed that the disciples were not responsible for how the people responded to their message.

9:6 So they began their circuit of the villages, preaching the Good News and healing the sick.^{NLT} Six teams of two *began their circuit of the villages*—perhaps going back to villages in which Jesus had already preached, or going where he did not have time to go (4:14-15, 43-44). They went with Jesus' authority and power—*preaching the Good News and healing the sick.*

HEROD KILLS JOHN THE BAPTIST / 9:7-9 / **95**

The ministry of Jesus and his disciples was effective. The gospel message even reached Herod, leaving him questioning: "Who is this man?" The same should be true of the church's ministry. Believers' eagerness to serve the poor and the sick, their straightforward presentation of God's truth, and their loyal love for each other should leave others asking: "Who are these people?"

9:7-8 Now Herod the tetrarch heard about all that was going on. And he was perplexed, because some were saying that John had been raised from the dead, others that Elijah had appeared, and still others that one of the prophets of long ago had come back to life.^{NIV} This was Herod Antipas, who, after his father (Herod the Great) died (in 4 B.C.), divided the kingdom among his four sons, naming each one a tetrarch—one of four rulers over the four districts of Palestine. (Herod the Great was the king who had ordered the killing of the babies in Bethlehem, Matthew 2:16.) Herod Antipas was the king who had imprisoned and executed John the Baptist, and he would later hear Jesus' case before the Crucifixion (23:6-12). The history of the Herod family is filled with lies, murder, treachery, and adultery. Herod Antipas was known for his insensitivity and debauchery. Though he was popular with his Roman superiors, his unbridled political ambitions eventually led to his exile in A.D. 39 by the Roman emperor Caligula, who removed him on the basis of charges by his nephew (Herod Agrippa I), the one who ruled Galilee after Herod Antipas.

> Surely those who know the great passionate heart of Jehovah must deny their own loves to share in the expression of his!
> *Jim Elliot*

What caused Herod to be *perplexed?* A man and his disciples

were traveling around doing miracles and teaching a message
that, once reported to Herod, sounded eerily like the message that
John the Baptist had taught. John the Baptist had been arrested
by Herod and put in prison for condemning Herod's sin of marrying his brother's wife (3:20; see also Mark 6:14-29). The arrest
marked the end of John's public ministry, and he was imprisoned
for some time prior to his death. At this point, John the Baptist
has already been executed. But this new teacher was causing a
stir among the people—*some were saying that John had been
raised from the dead.* Herod thought that John had come back to
life to trouble him some more; it worried him that the people said
that John had come back.

Others thought that *Elijah had appeared* (the great Old Testament prophet who did not die but had been taken to heaven in a
chariot of fire; 2 Kings 2:1-11). They applied the prophecy of Elijah's return in Malachi 4:5 to Jesus. Instead, they should have
applied the prophecy to John; then they would have realized
Jesus' identity. Jesus had explained to his disciples that John had
fulfilled Malachi's prophecy (Mark 9:13).

THE COST OF DISCIPLESHIP
When people receive Christ as Lord, they gain riches beyond
compare. Forgiveness, peace of mind, a new heart, a new
will, eternal life . . . the list of benefits is staggering. But the
demands of following Christ can also be formidable. For Jesus'
friend and colaborer, John the Baptist, following Jesus cost him
the ultimate: his very life. John was beheaded by Herod—the
other Gospels reveal that it was not for any criminal offense but
for boldly proclaiming God's truth. Believers today may not face
physical persecution and death—although that does still go on
in many places around the world—but the call and the cost are
still the same. Is your faith strong enough to regard imprisonment or even death as God's triumph?

Still others thought that *one of the prophets of long ago had
come back to life*—such as Moses, Isaiah, or Jeremiah. While
John the Baptist had been widely regarded as a prophet (and the
first prophet to the nation in over four hundred years), the people
had refused to listen to him.

Oddly enough, few people thought Jesus was their Messiah.
Because they would not accept Jesus as the Son of God, they
tried to come up with other solutions. For many people today, it
is still not easy to accept Jesus as the fully human yet fully divine
Son of God. People are still trying to find alternate explanations—a great prophet, a radical political leader, a self-deceived

rabble-rouser. None of these explanations can account for Jesus' miracles or, especially, his glorious resurrection—so these realities too have to be explained away. In the end, the attempts to explain away Jesus are far more difficult to believe than the truth. And when the truth is refused, people can only remain perplexed—like Herod and many of the Jews.

9:9 "I beheaded John," Herod said, "so who is this man about whom I hear such strange stories?" And he tried to see him.^{NLT} For the story of how Herod had *beheaded John,* see Matthew 14:1-12 and Mark 6:14-29. Herod may have had some guilty pangs, for he had beheaded an innocent man who had done no more than speak the truth. So it bothered Herod that this good man, considered by everyone to be a prophet, may have come back to life. This certainly caused Herod to think twice about this man and try *to see him*—perhaps Herod thought he might be able to recognize him or talk to him. Luke did not include the details surrounding John's death, focusing instead on Herod's question: *"Who is this man about whom I hear such strange stories?"* More stories and more proofs about the identity of "this man" would follow.

WHO DO YOU SAY THAT I AM?
"I can accept Jesus as a great teacher, but why do you insist that he's actually God?"

"I went to church when I was younger, but I've never actually read the Bible for myself. What does it really say about who Jesus is?"

"If Jesus were really the Son of God, why do so many today think the opposite?"

Perhaps you've heard these kinds of questions. Although the Bible is still the best-selling book in the world, year after year, and although the entire Western world was founded on biblical thought and principles, most people are "biblically illiterate." And where ignorance of the truth is widespread, opinions about Jesus multiply. Believers should encourage people to examine the Bible's claims about Jesus for themselves, instead of relying on vague memories of childhood Sunday school lessons or intellectual trends that change like the seasons. Herod's question "Who is this man?" is still the important question to answer. Be ready to help someone who sincerely wants to know the answer.

JESUS FEEDS FIVE THOUSAND / 9:10-17 / **96**

Apart from Jesus' resurrection, this is the only miracle that appears in all four Gospels, showing its importance to Jesus' ministry and to the early church (see also the commentary on 9:16).

While many people have tried to explain away the incident, it is clear that all the Gospel writers saw this as a marvelous miracle.

By connecting this miracle with the return of the apostles from ministering throughout the country, Luke highlighted the way Jesus was passing the mantle of service to his apostles. Here Jesus gave the disciples a simple command: "You feed them" (9:13 NLT). Overwhelmed by the needs of over five thousand people and faced with their own poverty, they responded with the timeless excuse: "We can't." But Jesus took the little that they had and transformed it into more than enough. All the disciples had to do was step out in faith, obeying Jesus' word. Many believers face overwhelming situations, just as the disciples did in that small town of Bethsaida. Finances may be in shambles; families may be in disorder. The odds may seem stacked against them. Like the disciples, believers must trust God for the power to conquer these problems, stepping out in faith day after day. If they do, they will eventually see that God was supplying more than enough all the way.

9:10 When the apostles returned, they reported to Jesus what they had done. Then he took them with him and they withdrew by themselves to a town called Bethsaida.^{NIV} The word "apostle" means "one sent" as a messenger, authorized agent, or missionary. The word became an accepted title for Jesus' twelve disciples after his death and resurrection (Acts 1:25-26; Ephesians 2:20). The disciples had completed their teaching mission (9:6) and thus were official "sent ones." They *returned* (apparently at a prearranged time) to Capernaum and *reported to Jesus what they had done.* Jesus wanted to hear how their training mission, their "student teaching," had gone. In order to do this, he needed to get them away from the crowds. So *they withdrew by themselves to a town called Bethsaida*—this must have been in the vicinity of Bethsaida, for when the crowds later found them, they were in the wilderness away from any towns. In this isolated place, Jesus could listen to his disciples' stories and answer their questions.

9:11 But the crowds found out where he was going, and they followed him. And he welcomed them, teaching them about the Kingdom of God and curing those who were ill.^{NLT} The disciples needed rest; Jesus wanted quiet teaching time with them, but this was not to be. *The crowds found out where he was going, and they followed him.* Matthew wrote that they had gone by boat, and the crowds went on foot and met Jesus when he landed (Matthew 14:13-14). Far from being upset by the interruption of their plans, Jesus *welcomed* the people, using the opportunity afforded by their interest to teach *them about the Kingdom of God.* Surely

there were always some in the crowd who were ill and had come
to be healed, and Jesus took care of them as well.

The kingdom of God was a focal point of Jesus' teaching. He
explained that it was not just a future kingdom; it was among
them, embodied in him, the Messiah. Even though the kingdom
will not be complete until Jesus comes again in glory, believers
do not have to wait to taste it. The kingdom of God begins in the
hearts of those who believe in Jesus. It is as present today as it
was in Judea almost two thousand years ago.

INTERRUPTIONS
Jesus had tried to slip quietly away from the crowds, but they
found out where he was going and followed him. Instead of
showing impatience at this interruption, Jesus welcomed the
people and ministered to their needs. How do you see people
who interrupt your schedule—as nuisances, or as the reason
for your life and ministry?

**9:12 The day was drawing to a close, and the twelve came to him
and said, "Send the crowd away, so that they may go into the
surrounding villages and countryside, to lodge and get provisions; for we are here in a deserted place."**NRSV Jesus' teaching
about the kingdom of God (9:11) lasted until the evening. As *the
day was drawing to a close,* the disciples certainly wondered
when they would have time alone with Jesus. So they went to
Jesus and suggested that he *send the crowd away* so they would
have time to get food and lodging in the *surrounding villages.*
The place where Jesus had been teaching was *deserted,* far from
any town or village. It was near Bethsaida, east of the lake about
four miles from Capernaum.

**9:13 But he said to them, "You give them something to eat."
They said, "We have no more than five loaves and two fish—
unless we are to go and buy food for all these people."**NRSV
These disciples, already tired, meant to be compassionate in
their request for Jesus to send the crowd away to get food
before nightfall. Jesus' response certainly surprised them, for
he said, *"You give them something to eat."* What could Jesus be
talking about? How were the disciples supposed to provide
food? A check of the resources had yielded *five loaves and two
fish*—John's Gospel explains that this was a small boy's lunch
(John 6:9), a lunch he was willing to share for Jesus' use. The
disciples had just come back from a teaching tour in which they
had used Jesus' authority to preach and heal. But apparently
they couldn't see past the obvious in this situation. Obviously

the little lunch would go nowhere among all those people, and the only other option was for them *to go and buy food for all these people.* Surely this was said ironically, for their resources would never meet the need. (John's Gospel explains that Philip calculated the need as about eight month's wages—far beyond the amount they had, see John 6:7.)

Why did Jesus bother to feed these people? He could just as easily have sent them on their way. But Jesus does not ignore needs. He is concerned with every aspect of life—the physical as well as the spiritual. As you work to bring wholeness to people's lives, remember that every person has both physical and spiritual needs. It is impossible to minister effectively to one type of need without considering the other.

RESOURCES
When the disciples expressed concern about where the crowd of thousands would eat, Jesus offered a surprising solution—"You give them something to eat." The disciples protested, focusing their attention on what they didn't have (food and money). Do you think God would ask you to do something that you and he together couldn't handle? Don't let your lack of resources blind you to seeing God's power. Use the resources you have at your disposal; let God stretch them to meet the need.

9:14-15 **For there were about five thousand men there.**^{NLT} No wonder the disciples were a little dismayed at Jesus' command to feed this crowd. Luke fills us in on the detail that *there were about five thousand men there.* The Greek word translated "men" is *andres,* meaning not "people" but "male individuals." Therefore, there were five thousand men in addition to the women and children. The total number of people Jesus fed could have been over ten thousand. The number of men was listed separately because in the Jewish culture of that day, men and women usually ate separately in public. The children ate with the women. It is not known if this was the case at this particular meal.

"Just tell them to sit down on the ground in groups of about fifty each," Jesus replied. So the people all sat down.^{NLT} The disciples didn't understand what Jesus wanted them to do, so he gave them a job and prepared to show them that little is much when God is in charge. The disciples followed Jesus' instructions to have everyone *sit down on the ground in groups of about fifty each.* We don't know why Jesus organized the people this way—it may have been to make food distribution more efficient. The men were probably separated from the women and children for the meal according to Jewish custom. So the disciples went through the crowd, organizing them and having them all take a seat. *The people*, perhaps realizing that this would be worth staying for, *all sat down.*

ALL YOU NEED
"Jesus is all you need!" That statement, or others very similar, is uttered in countless church services, Bible studies, and outreach meetings the world over. And committed Christians would no doubt agree. But have you ever actually been in a situation where Jesus was really all you had? If so, you know that it can be anxiety producing. Imagine how the disciples must have felt when Jesus told them to tell five thousand men (and presumably several thousand more women and children) to sit down on the grass to be fed—with five loaves of bread and two fish! But instead, Jesus was all that was necessary to accomplish this miracle. When you are in situations where you have no other resource than Jesus—relax. He's the best resource you could have, and the only one you need.

9:16 Taking the five loaves and the two fish and looking up to heaven, he gave thanks and broke them. Then he gave them to the disciples to set before the people.[NIV] The question of Jesus' identity had come up (8:25; 9:7-9). Soon Peter would witness to it (9:18-20). But this event demonstrated who Jesus was. All people in all nations and in all classes need and enjoy bread. For Jesus to use this setting to do a miracle shows the universal need all people have for God's love and power, and it shows how perfectly Christ satisfies that need as the Bread of Life. But people must come to him and accept his provision.

Jesus took the small lunch provided by the boy and *gave thanks* for it to God the Father. *Then he gave* the food *to the disciples to set before the people.* As Jesus broke the loaves, a miracle happened. The disciples began serving the groups of people, and the supply never diminished.

This miracle certainly helped a hungry crowd, but it had a higher purpose and theology. God, who multiplied the bread, was authenticating Jesus as his Son and portraying the munificent blessings of the kingdom. Just as God had provided manna to the Hebrews in the wilderness (Exodus 16), had multiplied oil and meal for Elijah and the widow at Zarephath (1 Kings 17:7-16) and for Elisha (2 Kings 4:1-7), and had multiplied twenty loaves to feed one hundred men (2 Kings 4:42-44), he was providing bread for the people on this day. This also points to the prophesied feast that the Messiah will abundantly provide for people in the wilderness (see also 13:29; 14:15-24; Isaiah 25:6, 9).

9:17 **They all ate as much as they wanted, and they picked up twelve baskets of leftovers!**[NLT] The disciples continued serving food, and the food continued to be supplied in abundance. Each person in the crowd did not receive a token piece of bread—which would have been a miracle in itself. Instead *they all ate as much as they wanted.* They ate their fill—they had a full meal (in ancient times, fish and bread would have constituted a basic but complete meal). Not only that, but there were enough leftovers to fill *twelve baskets.* The disciples collected the leftovers and may have taken them along for their own provision for a couple of days. While Jesus could have, he did not make a habit of supplying food out of nothing for himself and the disciples.

DOWN TO BASICS
Perhaps you've heard the expression "A hungry man has no ears." Obviously, it means that it's useless to try to talk to someone about other needs—including spiritual matters—while his or her basic physical needs go unmet. God created the whole person, spiritually, emotionally, intellectually, and physically, and he cares about needs in all those areas. Jesus gave ample proof of this in his miraculous feeding of the multitude. He not only satisfied the need for food, he went way above and beyond, providing enough to leave twelve baskets of leftovers. How do you respond to others' physical needs? Do you shrug it off, concentrating solely on their "spiritual" needs? Or do you emulate Jesus, going above and beyond, and address even basic needs like food and shelter?

PETER SAYS JESUS IS THE MESSIAH / 9:18-20 / **109**

Peter's confession that Jesus is the Christ, the promised Messiah, marks a turning point in this Gospel. Luke had been meticulously recording the reactions of people to Jesus and his message (4:42-44; 5:15, 25-26; 8:37, 56) and their questions revolving around Jesus' identity (4:14-30; 7:16; 8:25; 9:7-9). Finally Peter gave a clear answer to Jesus' identity: "You are the Messiah sent from God!" (9:20 NLT). This is the conclusion that everyone should come to, for who else—but God—has power over nature (8:22-25), thousands of demons (8:26-35), all kinds of diseases (5:12-15; 8:43-48), and death itself (8:51-56)? Who else can supernaturally supply food to thousands (9:13-17) and also give them the words that can bring eternal life (6:20-49)?

9:18 Once when Jesus was praying alone, with only the disciples near him, he asked them, "Who do the crowds say that I am?"NRSV Apparently the disciples and Jesus did at times get to be alone, for here we find Jesus and his disciples together, away from the crowds. Jesus *was praying.* That the Son of God often took time to pray was certainly an example to his disciples, as well as to all who follow him (see also 3:21; 6:12; 11:1).

Then he asked his disciples, *"Who do the crowds say that I am?"* What had the disciples heard—perhaps this information would come from what they had learned on their preaching tour (9:6).

9:19 They replied, "Some say John the Baptist; others say Elijah; and still others, that one of the prophets of long ago has come back to life."NIV The disciples' answer echoes what the crowds had been saying and what Herod had heard (9:8). This belief may have come from Deuteronomy 18:18, where God said he would raise up a prophet from among the people. (For the story of *John the Baptist,* see Mark 1:1-11; 6:14-29. For the story of *Elijah,* see 1 Kings 17–21 and 2 Kings 1–2.) All of these responses were incorrect, revealing that the people still didn't recognize Jesus' true identity. They didn't see that Jesus was the Messiah, the Son of God.

WHAT ABOUT YOU?
Great moral leader . . . enlightened master . . . political dissident . . . avatar . . . great teacher . . . prophet. In our pluralistic, no-tolerance-for-absolutes culture, people will apply all these labels to Jesus and be comfortable with them. To talk of Jesus as a great teacher or even a prophet isn't terribly unsettling or disturbing. There have been many prophets and teachers. But to declare him as the Messiah, the one and only Son of the living God, calls for a response. If Jesus is Messiah, then we must accept that as true and receive him as Lord. If he is not, then all of Christianity is based upon a lie. There is no middle ground. "Who do you say I am?" Jesus asked the disciples, and the question reverberates down through the centuries, into modern ears. What is your answer? Who do *you* say Jesus is?

9:20 "But what about you?" he asked. "Who do you say I am?" Peter answered, "The Christ of God."NIV The Christian faith goes beyond knowing what others believe. It requires individuals to hold their own beliefs. People may have had various opinions and ideas about Jesus' identity, but Jesus was concerned about what his chosen twelve believed about him. So he asked, *"Who* *do you say I am?"* The word "you" is plural; Jesus was asking the entire group. But Peter, who often acted as their spokesman, answered. Peter's ready answer reveals a deep insight into Jesus' identity, for he said, *"The Christ of God."* Peter, for all his blustery qualities and mistakes, had come to understand Jesus' identity, prior to the Cross, the Resurrection, and the Ascension. He did not understand the exact nature of Jesus' ministry, but he knew one fact for sure—Jesus was the Messiah, the Christ. The word "Christ" is Hebrew for "the Anointed One" (see Psalm 2:2; Isaiah 11:1-16; Daniel 9:25-26).

From this point on, Jesus would speak plainly and directly to his disciples about what it would mean that he was the Messiah. It would involve his death and resurrection. Jesus began to prepare the disciples for what was going to happen to him by telling them three times that he would soon suffer and die and then be raised back to life (9:21-27, 44-45; 18:31-34).

THE WHOLE TRUTH

When you received Christ and gave your heart to him, you may have enjoyed a honeymoon period following your conversion, when you experienced greater peace and fulfillment than you had ever known. But if you have followed Christ for any length of time, there inevitably came the day when you learned firsthand that being a Christian also includes certain costs. It may have been taking an unpopular moral stand, or refusing to cut an ethical corner in business, or walking away from an ungodly relationship. Whatever form it took—or is now taking—it is the universal experience of all those who profess Christ as Lord. Adjust your expectations. Prepare to live with desires unfulfilled. Jesus himself signaled that the way of discipleship can be difficult when he described his own suffering and death.

JESUS PREDICTS HIS DEATH THE FIRST TIME / 9:21-27 / 110

Jesus responded to Peter's confession that he was the Messiah with a prophecy of his own death and resurrection. Most Jews at this time were expecting a political messiah, a person who would deliver them from their subjection to the Romans. To correct these misperceptions of his disciples, Jesus depicted his suffering and death at the hands of the religious leaders (see 9:43-45). Jesus' path would be the way of the cross: he would have to face the rejection and suffering of a hardened criminal, even though he was completely innocent. Jesus didn't beat around the bush:

he made it crystal clear that anyone who followed him would have to trudge that same grueling path. Yet any rejection, any suffering they endure for the cause of Christ will produce eternal dividends (6:20-23). No type of ridicule or deprivation should sway people from Christ, for only he can give eternal life.

9:21-22 **He sternly ordered and commanded them not to tell anyone, saying, "The Son of Man must undergo great suffering, and be rejected by the elders, chief priests, and scribes, and be killed, and on the third day be raised."**NRSV Jesus *sternly ordered and commanded* his disciples *not to tell anyone* that he was the Christ because at this point they didn't fully understand the significance of that confession of faith. The Jews still expected their Messiah to come as a conquering king. If they had spread this message, Jesus would have had a following for the wrong reasons, and no one would have heard his words. Even though Jesus was the Messiah, he still had to *undergo great suffering, be rejected* by the Jewish religious leaders, and *be killed.* Jesus knew that he would be hated and killed by (1) the *elders*— they decided issues of religious and civil law and a group of them was included in the Jewish Council (Sanhedrin); (2) the *chief priests*—not just the ruling high priest but all those who formerly held the title and some of their family members; and (3) the *scribes*—also called teachers of the law, who were the legal experts. All three groups made up the Jewish supreme court that would sentence Jesus to die.

THE WAY OF THE CROSS
What does it mean to live for Christ? Luke 9:23 is one of the clearest and most challenging descriptions of the Christian life in all of the Bible. Jesus says that to be his disciple means: putting aside selfish desires, shouldering one's "cross" every day, following him. It is simple and yet so demanding. For the original twelve, this meant literal suffering and death. For believers today, it means understanding that they belong to him and that they live to serve his purposes. Consider this: Do you think of your relationship with God primarily in terms of what's in it for you (which is considerable) or in terms of what you can do for him? If your thoughts run more toward your own benefits, repent and ask God to give you grace to live a Luke 9:23 Christian life.

For most people's life stories, that would be the end, but Jesus added that after all those tragic events occurred, *on the third day* he would *be raised.* When the disciples saw all this happen to Jesus, they would understand what the Messiah had come to do and the kind of kingdom he was preparing. Jesus here called himself *Son of Man,* a title emphasizing that he had power and authority from God himself. The Son of Man was the figure prophesied by Daniel to come as God's agent to gather his people and to be their judge. Only then would they be equipped to share the gospel around the world.

This was the turning point in Jesus' instruction to his disciples. From then on he began teaching clearly and specifically what they could expect, so that they would not be surprised when it happened. He explained that he would not *now* be the conquering Messiah because he first had to suffer, die, and rise again. But one day he would return in great glory to set up his eternal kingdom.

9:23 Then he said to them all, "If any want to become my followers, let them deny themselves and take up their cross daily and follow me."^{NRSV} Jesus didn't make following him sound very easy. To his disciples who may have been hoping to have special positions in Jesus' earthly kingdom (22:24), these would have been hard words to hear. Denying one's personal desires and taking up a cross in order to follow this man was not what most of them had bargained for.

What does it mean that Jesus' followers must *deny themselves?* To deny oneself means a willingness to let go of selfish desires and earthly security. "Self" is no longer in charge; God is. Too often this has been interpreted to mean that believers should have no self-esteem. Some discipleship or "deeper life" strategies have advocated stripping oneself of all dignity or anything that contributes to a sense of self-worth. Jesus' view of denial was immediate and practical. They would need this attitude in the days ahead. They would need a willingness to set aside their own desires in order to spread the Good News.

THE WEIGHT OF THE CROSS
Christians follow their Lord by imitating his life and obeying his commands. To take up the cross meant to carry one's own cross to the place of death. Many Galileans had been executed that way by the Romans. Applied to the disciples, it meant to identify completely with Christ's message, even if it meant death. Christ's followers must deny selfish ambitions and selfish desires to use their time and money their own way. Following Christ is costly now, but in the long run, it is well worth the pain and effort. People are willing to pay a high price for something they value. Is it any surprise that Jesus would demand this much commitment from his followers? There are at least three conditions that must be met by people who want to follow Jesus. They must be willing to deny self, to take up the cross, and to follow him. Anything less is superficial.

What does it mean that believers must *take up their cross daily?* There is a double meaning in "take up their cross." It means to follow Jesus to the death if necessary. It also means to die to selfish desires and ambitions. Thus it further explains how to "deny yourself." When Jesus used this picture of his followers taking up their crosses, everyone knew what he meant. Death on a cross was a form of execution used by Rome for dangerous criminals. A prisoner would carry his own cross to the place of execution, signifying submission to Rome's power. Following Jesus, therefore, meant identifying with Jesus and his followers, facing social and political oppression and ostracism, and no turning back. And this would not be a once-for-all deal—believers would need to be willing to take up this cross "daily" as they faced new situations, new people, new problems.

What does it mean to *follow?* These words applied to the disciples and to all who would become disciples and enter his fellowship. Recognizing and confessing belief in Jesus as the Messiah is only the beginning of discipleship. Following Jesus doesn't mean walking behind him, but taking the same road of self-denial and self-sacrifice. Because Jesus walks ahead, he provides an example and stands with his followers as encourager, guide, and friend.

RISK IT
If this present life is most important to you, you will do everything you can to protect it. You will not want to do anything that might endanger your safety, health, or comfort. By contrast, if following Jesus is most important, you may find yourself in unsafe, unhealthy, and uncomfortable places. You will risk death, but you will not fear it because you know that Jesus will raise you to eternal life. Nothing material can compensate for the loss of eternal life. Jesus' disciples are not to use their lives on earth for their own pleasure—they should spend their lives serving God and people. Have you discovered the most fulfilling use of your life?

9:24 **"For those who want to save their life will lose it, and those who lose their life for my sake will save it."**[NRSV] As the Messiah must suffer and die (9:21-22), so his followers must realize that they must not grasp selfishly on to their own lives. *Those who want to save their life* identify the attitude of striving to get only the best for themselves. Thus it reflects a totally self-centered attitude toward life. Such people will try to hold on to earthly rewards and security only to find that in the end, they *lose.* By contrast, however, those who generously give their lives, willing to lose them if necessary for the sake of Jesus and the kingdom, *will save [them].* That person will have given up in order to gain, and what is gained is of greater value indeed for it is eternal. Nothing that a person can possess or accomplish on this earth can compare with eternal life with Christ.

The Greek word used here for "life" *(psuche)* means "self," referring to the whole person. Those who greedily grasp life, refusing to use it to help others, and focusing on satisfying their desires apart from God, will find that they have lost what they tried to keep. They lose eternal life and forfeit the spiritual fulfillment Christ can give. Those who invest their life for Christ and his kingdom will receive eternal life as well as the satisfaction of serving God on earth. Those who give up control to God find that he fills their lives with himself.

9:25 **"And how do you benefit if you gain the whole world but lose or forfeit your own soul in the process?"**[NLT] Many people are willing to turn away from Christ in order to stay in a relationship, hold on to a sin, or stay on a career path. Jesus explained, however, that even if someone could *gain the whole world,* it would be of no *benefit* if it means losing his or her *soul in the process.* The answer to Jesus' question, then, is that nothing is so valuable that it can be exchanged for one's soul. In order to gain the whole world, one would have to worship the ruler of this world—Satan—because this is the offer he made to Jesus (4:5-7). Even if a person could gain the whole world, that person would lose his or her soul—and the soul counts for eternity. No amount of money, power, or status can buy back a lost soul. Believers must be willing to make the pursuit of God more important than the selfish pursuit of pleasure. Those who follow Jesus will discover what it means to live abundantly now and to have eternal life later.

PRIORITIES
You've seen the bumper stickers: "He who dies with the most toys wins." Maybe you've seen the follow-up version: "He who dies with the most toys is dead." It's not hard to see through the emptiness and superficiality of materialism. The idea that the meaning of life is to be found in the things acquired, the trophies accumulated, and the amount of money made loses its credibility in the emergency room and the funeral parlor. As one wise older person once put it, "I've never heard anyone on his deathbed say, 'I sure wish I'd spent more time in the office.'"

What is it you are pushing so hard to acquire or accomplish? Is it truly important, or merely something to gratify your ego or impress your peers? Will it come at the expense of your family or your own relationship with God? How do you benefit if you gain the whole world but lose or forfeit your own soul?

9:26 "Those who are ashamed of me and of my words, of them the Son of Man will be ashamed when he comes in his glory and the glory of the Father and of the holy angels."[NRSV] Luke's Greek audience would have found it difficult to understand a God who could die, just as Jesus' Jewish audience would have been perplexed by a Messiah who would let himself be captured. Both would be ashamed of Jesus if they did not look past his death to his glorious resurrection and second coming. Then they would see Jesus as the Lord of the universe, who through his death, brought salvation to all people.

> You will never glory in God till first of all God has killed your glorying in yourself.
>
> *C. H. Spurgeon*

But Jesus here offered his listeners a choice. If they chose to be *ashamed* of him, he *will be ashamed* of them at his second coming (they would be rejected from eternal life with him). In the Bible, "ashamed" means more than embarrassment. It refers to the judgment of God: "[Idolmakers] will be put to shame" (Isaiah 44:11 NIV). It stands for deep and contrite repentance: "That they may be ashamed of their sins" (Ezekiel 43:10 NIV). It can mean submission before God: "Nations will see and be ashamed" (Micah 7:16 NIV). When Jesus judges unbelieving people, his "being ashamed of them" means that he will reject them *when he comes in his glory and the glory of the Father and of the holy angels.* This indicates the Second Coming—the time of future judgment when present life ceases and all people will be judged for their decisions about Jesus Christ.

THE GLORY AND THE SHAME
Jesus told his disciples to speak up for him without shame. You can tell a lot about a society by what it glorifies and what it considers shameful. Today some behaviors that once would have been considered scandalous are openly admired, and others that once were accepted as virtuous are criticized and condemned. Even Christians are often made to feel guilty or somehow inferior for holding to the belief that Jesus is the only true "way." And anyone with the audacity to state that belief in a public forum is considered ignorant and closed-minded. Believers must stand boldly for the Lord in a world that increasingly stands for nothing. When nonbelievers heap pressure, rejection, and humiliation on us, we must remain faithful to Christ.

9:27 "But I tell you truly, there are some standing here who shall not taste death till they see the kingdom of God."[NKJV] When Jesus said that some of those who were with him *shall not taste*

death till they see the kingdom of God, he may have been referring to (1) Peter, James, and John, who would witness the Transfiguration eight days later (as a preview of the *parousia*—the
Second Coming), or in a broader sense (2) all who would witness
the Resurrection and Ascension, or (3) all who would take part in
the spread of the church after Pentecost. Jesus' listeners would
not have to wait for another, future Messiah—the kingdom was
among them, and it would soon come in power. Jesus' transfiguration, which follows, previewed the kingdom of God.

JESUS IS TRANSFIGURED ON THE MOUNTAIN / 9:28-36 / 111

Drowsily, Peter, James, and John awoke to an extraordinary
sight—Moses and Elijah, with Jesus, standing together in a
moment of glorious heavenly splendor. Stunned—Peter blurted
out that he would build three shelters. Peter's instant reaction
was to commemorate this moment of glory, at this very site.
But God himself answered Peter. No shelters or monuments
were needed; instead the disciples needed to recognize Jesus'
unique identity—that he was God's Son—and obey what he
told them to do.

Many believers have the same response to God working in
their lives. They want to freeze the moment that they "feel" the
presence of God, by achieving that "feeling" again through a certain number of steps. In effect, what God was saying to Peter—
and by extension, to believers today—is that listening intently to
Jesus and following his example is more important than trying to
achieve a mountaintop experience with God. The Lord is seeking
out those who will take God's Word and apply it to the trouble-
some circumstances, in the trenches of life.

**9:28 About eight days later Jesus took Peter, James, and John to a
mountain to pray.**^NLT Three of Jesus' disciples did indeed get a
glimpse of the kingdom of God within days of Jesus' pronouncement (9:27). Matthew and Mark both recorded this event as "six
days later" rather than Luke's *eight days* (see Matthew 17:1;
Mark 9:2). Luke's was a more general reckoning, measuring partial days as whole days. Jesus singled out *Peter, James, and John*
for this special revelation of his glory and purity. These three disciples comprised the inner circle of the Twelve (see 8:51; Mark
14:33). Jesus took them with him and went *to a mountain to pray.*
This "mountain" is traditionally considered to have been either
Mount Hermon or Mount Tabor.

> **QUIET TIME**
> Jesus took three disciples away to pray. Times of conversation
> with God—and that is what prayer is—each require a time and
> place undisturbed by the rush of the day's traffic. Telephones,
> fax machines, televisions, and radios are wonderful tools, but
> poor help for sincere, concentrated times of prayer. Jesus didn't
> deal with these technological intrusions; he had thousands of
> people following him around, some of whom wanted him dead.
> That's why he often would withdraw to a remote, lonely place to
> pray. Where is your "prayer closet"? Where can you go and
> have uninterrupted time with God? If you have such a place,
> enjoy it and protect it. If not, make whatever arrangements
> necessary to find one. Jesus needed it, and so do you.

9:29 And as he was praying, the appearance of his face changed, and his clothing became dazzling white.NLT Jesus *was praying*—talking to his Father as he regularly did. What he was praying about is, of course, unknown, but perhaps he wanted to give his three disciples the glimpse of his glory that he had promised. So as he prayed, he was prepared for a meeting in the heavenly sphere with two men long since dead, but alive in heaven with God. Thus, *the appearance of his face changed, and his clothing became dazzling white.* This revealed Jesus' true glory and purity. While Luke avoided the word "transfiguration," what occurred was an outward change that came from within—he appeared glorious because he was divine. On earth, Jesus appeared as a man; at this time, he was transformed into the glorious radiance that he will have in heaven. The glory shone out from him, and the appearance of his face changed. This recalls Moses' experience recorded in Exodus 34:29-35. His clothing became dazzling white, a white that was not of this earth, a white that revealed supreme glory, purity, and holiness. These were the radiant robes of God, clothing "white as snow" (Daniel 7:9).

9:30-31 Two men, Moses and Elijah, appeared in glorious splendor, talking with Jesus. They spoke about his departure, which he was about to bring to fulfillment at Jerusalem.NIV *Two men . . . appeared in glorious splendor*—apparently looking much like Jesus looked. These men were already in heaven, having died hundreds of years before. But why, in particular, did *Moses and Elijah* appear to Jesus? Both of these men had, during their time on earth, met with God on a mountain (Exodus 24; 1 Kings 19). Both men also had departed from this earth in an unusual way—Elijah was taken up into heaven in a whirlwind (2 Kings 2:11); Moses was buried by the Lord (Deuteronomy 34:6), and the location of his body became a matter of great speculation (Jude 9). These men represented the

sweeping vista of God's plan of salvation across the ages. Moses
represented the Law, or the Old Covenant. He had written the Pentateuch and had predicted the coming of a great prophet (Deuteronomy 18:15-19). Elijah represented the prophets who had foretold
the coming of the Messiah (Malachi 4:5-6). Together they confirmed Jesus' mission: "Do not think that I have come to abolish
the Law or the Prophets; I have not come to abolish them but to fulfill them" (Matthew 5:17 NIV).

These men were *talking with Jesus . . . about his departure,*
which was about to happen in Jerusalem. The "departure"
referred to Jesus' death, but of course they saw death as departing
the earth and returning to heaven. The word for "departure" is
exodos, an unusual word to use for death, yet a helpful word picture. As Moses delivered Israel from bondage in Egypt through
their exodus from there, even more significantly, Jesus would
deliver people from bondage through his "exodus" from this life.
His death, which would happen on a dusty hill outside the walls
of Jerusalem, would accomplish true freedom for all people who
believe in him. It would happen according to God's divine plan
(see 1 Peter 1:19-20).

DEATH
Jesus' transfiguration provides many wonderful insights into his
life and ministry. It also points out the inevitability of death,
even for the Son of God, who would die as a fulfillment of
God's plan. The Bible says, "It is destined that each person
dies only once" (Hebrews 9:27 NLT). Common experience and
observation show that death is the inevitable end of every life.
And yet, how many people live as if they don't have to worry
about such unpleasantries, as if they will just continue forever
in their present state. Death calls for each person, who must
then give an account of his or her life to the Creator. If you died
today, could you say that you have lived the way God wanted?
If you live another fifty years, is your life headed in the direction
that God wants it to go? Death indeed comes for everyone. Are
you ready to die?

9:32-33 **Peter and his companions were very sleepy, but when they
became fully awake, they saw his glory and the two men
standing with him. As the men were leaving Jesus, Peter said
to him, "Master, it is good for us to be here. Let us put up
three shelters—one for you, one for Moses and one for Elijah." (He did not know what he was saying.)**[NIV] Apparently
Jesus had been spending a long time in prayer; Peter, John, and
James had become *very sleepy.* The display of dazzling glory
awakened them. When it seemed that Elijah and Moses were

going to leave, Peter spoke up and suggested putting up *three shelters—one for you, one for Moses and one for Elijah.* Peter may have been thinking of the Feast of Tabernacles, where shelters were set up to commemorate the Exodus, God's deliverance from slavery in Egypt (Leviticus 23:42-43). Peter wanted to keep Moses and Elijah with them. But this was not what God wanted. Peter's desire to build shelters for Jesus, Moses, and Elijah may also show his understanding that real faith is built on three cornerstones: the law, the prophets, and Jesus. But he seems to have misunderstood in his drowsy state, perhaps thinking that the kingdom had arrived. While these three disciples got a glimpse of Jesus' future glory, they had to realize that this did not erase Jesus' previous words of suffering and death for himself (9:21-22). Peter also mistakenly treated these three men as equals—he was missing Jesus' true identity as God himself. He called Jesus *Master* (meaning, Teacher) when this glorious display should have shown him that Jesus was far more. His words "it is good for us to be here" reveal a further lack of understanding. He wanted to prolong the experience, to keep Moses and Elijah there with them. But that was not the point of the experience nor the lesson to be learned by it. Luke's explanation gets Peter a bit off the hook: Peter *did not know what he was saying.* If Peter had thought about the situation or, better yet, kept his mouth shut, he might have understood more of what was happening. No shelters would be built; no one was going to stay. Moses and Elijah would return to glory; Jesus would walk back down the mountain and head toward Jerusalem. There would be no shortcuts.

MOUNTAINTOP EXPERIENCES
Peter, James, and John experienced a wonderful moment on the mountain, and they didn't want to leave. Sometimes believers have such an inspiring experience that they want to stay where they are—away from the reality and problems of daily life. Knowing that struggles await in the valley encourages them to linger on the mountaintop. Yet staying on top of a mountain prohibits ministry to others. Christians need times of retreat and renewal, but only so they can return to minister to the world. When you leave an inspiring mountaintop experience, be ready for the challenging real-life experiences in the valley. Your faith must make sense off the mountain as well as on it.

9:34-35 But even as he was saying this, a cloud came over them; and terror gripped them as it covered them. Then a voice from the cloud said, "This is my Son, my Chosen One. Listen to

him."^{NLT} Even as Peter was blurting out words that he shouldn't have been saying, *a cloud came over them* and *covered them.* This "cloud" was actually the glory of God—the same glory that had guided Israel out of Egypt (Exodus 13:21), had appeared to the people in the wilderness (Exodus 16:10; 24:15-18; 34:5; 40:34-38), had appeared to Moses (Exodus 19:9), and had filled the temple (1 Kings 8:10). No wonder *terror gripped* the three disciples. Then, as had happened at Jesus' baptism, *a voice* came *from the cloud—* the voice of God himself (3:22). God gave divine approval of his Son, separating him from Moses and Elijah by saying that Jesus was the *Son,* the *Chosen One,* and that the disciples must *listen to him.* The voice affirmed, both at the Baptism and at the Transfiguration, that Jesus was the one sent by God and the one whose authority came directly from God.

LISTEN TO HIM
God clearly identified Jesus as his Son before saying that Peter and the others were to listen to Jesus and not to their own ideas and desires. The ability to follow Jesus comes from confidence about who he is. People who say they believe Jesus is God's Son will want to do what he says. As God's Son, Jesus has God's power and authority; thus his words should be believers' final authority. If a person's teaching is true, it will agree with Jesus' teachings. Test everything you hear against Jesus' words, and you will not be led astray. Don't be hasty to seek advice and guidance from merely human sources and thereby neglect Christ's message.

9:36 **When the voice had spoken, they found that Jesus was alone. The disciples kept this to themselves, and told no one at that time what they had seen.**^{NIV} The glory disappeared, the cloud went away, the voice finished speaking, Moses and Elijah left, and Jesus looked once again like a traveling rabbi. The conversation with heaven over, *Jesus was alone* with his disciples. The mission had been talked about, the way to Jerusalem and the cross laid out. Jesus would return to glory, but he would first follow the path of suffering and seeming defeat on this earth. Only then could he fully accomplish the plan of salvation. Only by dying could he return to eternal life. Only by dying could he give us life.

The three disciples kept quiet about this entire experience, not telling anyone *at that time what they had seen.* Matthew and Mark wrote that Jesus ordered the disciples not to tell anyone about this until he had risen from the dead—then they could talk about it, presumably because then they would better understand it

(Matthew 17:9; Mark 9:9). Peter's outburst had shown that he and the other disciples did not yet comprehend, and probably would not until after Jesus had risen from the dead. Only then would they be able to see that only through dying could Jesus conquer death.

JESUS HEALS A DEMON-POSSESSED BOY / 9:37-43 / 112

Luke closely tied the Transfiguration to this healing of a demon-possessed boy. What is the connection? The ignorance and unbelief of the disciples were the same issues that God had spoken about on the mountain. He had commanded Peter, James, and John to "listen" to Jesus. There was no reason for the disciples to be defeated by any demon; all they needed to do was to believe in Jesus and dedicate themselves to prayer (see Matthew 17:20; Mark 9:29). They needed to express the same faith as the father of the demon-possessed boy: "I do believe; help me overcome my unbelief" (Mark 9:24 NIV). Is there something you think is unattainable? Is there some sin you think is impossible to conquer? Listen to Jesus and believe in him. If you only have "faith as small as a mustard seed," nothing—within the perfect will of God—will be impossible (see Matthew 17:20).

THE LITTLE PEOPLE
The Transfiguration was one of the key events of Jesus' life. Being human, it would have been understandable if Jesus had come down from the mountain a bit overwhelmed at what had just occurred—meeting with Moses and Elijah and hearing the voice of his Father. Instead of being carried away by the experience or his own importance or being distracted by the huge crowd that met him at the foot of the mountain, Jesus took the time to notice one man and his demon-possessed son. He cared enough about these seemingly insignificant people to listen and respond to their problem, even with the tremendous events of cosmic magnitude playing out around him. Do you notice "the little people"? Do you have a place in your heart and your schedule for the seemingly insignificant ones who desperately need to know that someone cares about them? Ask God if there is someone—even someone insignificant in the world's eyes—who needs your attention and compassion.

9:37 The next day, after they had come down the mountain, a huge crowd met Jesus.NLT *The next day* after the glorious Transfiguration (probably the next morning, as many scholars believe the Transfiguration occurred during the night), Jesus, Peter, James, and John came down from the mountain. As so often happened, *a huge crowd* met Jesus when he arrived. This crowd included the rest of Jesus' disciples, some teachers of the law, and a group of followers and onlookers. Mark wrote that the disciples and the religious leaders were in an argument (Mark 9:14), which probably focused on the fact that the disciples had tried and failed to cast out a demon (9:40). The religious leaders may have been questioning the disciples' power and authority.

9:38-39 **A man in the crowd called out, "Teacher, I beg you to look at my son, for he is my only child. A spirit seizes him and he suddenly screams; it throws him into convulsions so that he foams at the mouth. It scarcely ever leaves him and is destroying him."**^{NIV} Another man came in search of healing for a loved one. He brought his *only child,* who was possessed by *a spirit* (a demon). While the symptoms described by the father sound much like an epileptic convulsion, the destructive intent of the demon was described by the father—the demon was *destroying* his son. This was more than mere epilepsy; it was indeed a case of demon possession. Mark's Gospel reveals that the boy could neither speak nor hear (Mark 9:17, 25).

PREPARED FOR BATTLE
As the disciples came down from the mountain with Jesus, they passed from a reassuring experience of God's presence to a frightening experience of evil. The beauty and transcendence they had just witnessed must have made the ugliness of Satan's control over a young boy seem even uglier. Improved spiritual vision allows believers to see and understand God better; then they also see and understand the destruction of evil better. Believers would be overcome by its horror if they did not have Jesus to take them through it safely. Use your personal times of prayer with him to prepare you to face the enemy.

9:40 **"I begged your disciples to cast the spirit out, but they couldn't do it."**^{NLT} This desperate man wanted his child to be freed from the demon, so he brought his son to Jesus and his disciples (the disciples had been given authority to heal demon possession, 9:1). But the disciples *couldn't do it.* The text does not explain the reason for their failure. Matthew explained it as the disciples' lack of faith (Matthew 17:19-20), Mark as a need for prayer (Mark 9:28-29). It is good to denounce sin, but it takes God's power to remove it. The disciples certainly tried, but the demon did not respond.

9:41 **"O unbelieving and perverse generation," Jesus replied,**
"how long shall I stay with you and put up with you? Bring
your son here."^{NIV} Jesus saw the failure of the disciples to cast
out this demon as merely one more indication of the *unbelieving*
and perverse generation in which they were trying to minister.
They themselves were a representation of this unbelieving mind-
set, and it made Jesus angry. These words were much like those
of Moses, who served as an intercessor
between God and Israel, and who often
was exasperated by the people's stubborn faithlessness (Deuteronomy 32:5,
20). God also portrayed such frustration
(Numbers 14:11; Isaiah 63:8-10). The

> In the Gospels, Jesus
> often rebukes weak faith,
> but never rejects it.
> *John Berridge*

disciples were not singled out for rebuke, but they reflected an
attitude prevalent in their society. Jesus would not *stay* with them
forever; one day he would leave and the Spirit would come. The
Spirit could help soften stubborn hearts. In the meantime, Jesus
would battle this unbelief, but he would not leave this young boy
in his horrible condition, so Jesus told the father to bring his son.

9:42-43(a) **As the boy came forward, the demon knocked him to the**
ground and threw him into a violent convulsion. But Jesus
rebuked the evil spirit and healed the boy. Then he gave him
back to his father. Awe gripped the people as they saw this dis-
play of God's power.^{NLT} As if to show its anger that Jesus was
now involved, the demon *knocked* the boy *to the ground and*
threw him into a violent convulsion. It did not yell Jesus' name as
did other demons, for this one was mute (4:34; 8:28; Mark 9:17),
but it showed its displeasure. Jesus, however, simply *rebuked the*
evil spirit, and it had no choice but to obey. As the boy was
healed and returned to his father, the people realized that this was
a *display of God's power,* and they were filled with *awe.*

JESUS PREDICTS HIS DEATH THE SECOND TIME / 9:44-45 / **113**

While Jesus was still in the limelight, while the people were still
marveling over his recent exorcism, Jesus took time to reiterate
to his disciples that the path he was traveling was not leading to
fame, power, and prestige. Instead, his was the way of suffering—
the way of the cross (9:23-27). Jesus calls all his followers to that
path. He calls them to relinquish their false securities—possessions and finances—in order to put him first.

9:43(b)-44 **While everyone was amazed at all that he was doing, he said**
to his disciples, "Let these words sink into your ears: The Son

of Man is going to be betrayed into human hands."NRSV The
people were in awe and *amazed at all that [Jesus] was doing.*
But Jesus did not let this fill him with pride, for he knew that the
path ahead did not hold earthly glory and honor. As the crowd
murmured their wonder at Jesus, he turned *to his disciples* and
reminded them a second time (see 9:21-22 for the first) that he
was going to die. This time he added the element that he would
be betrayed.

**9:45 But they did not understand what this meant. It was hidden
from them, so that they did not grasp it, and they were afraid
to ask him about it.**NIV The disciples *did not understand* Jesus'
words about his death. As in 24:16, this means that God sover-
eignly kept them from understanding who Jesus really was until
the appointed time. They still thought of Jesus as only an earthly
king, and they were concerned about their places in the kingdom
that he would set up (9:46-48). If Jesus died, the kingdom as they
imagined it could not come. Consequently, they preferred not to
ask him about his predictions.

THE DISCIPLES ARGUE ABOUT WHO WOULD BE THE GREATEST / 9:46-48 / **115**

This argument among the disciples about who would be the greatest highlights how they did not understand Jesus' mission (9:45).
Jesus was trying to prepare these men for the suffering and rejection that would come. At the same time, however, the disciples
were enjoying all the attention and even disputing with each
other over who was the greatest. Their attention was elsewhere—
glory, fame, and honor. So Jesus called over a little child—considered the most lowly person in first-century society—to show
them their false priorities. Take time to evaluate your priorities.
Are you always striving to become the greatest or looking for
opportunities to serve?

**9:46 Then there was an argument among them as to which of them
would be the greatest.**NLT Apparently this argument among the
disciples was occurring away from Jesus, but they could not hide
it from him (9:47). The disciples, still not understanding the true
nature of Jesus' mission, were having *an argument . . . as to
which of them would be the greatest.* Either they ignored Jesus'
words about his death as they planned for the coming kingdom,
or they took his words to heart and wondered who would be in
charge after he had died. The argument may also have been
sparked by the fact that Peter, John, and James had been singled
out to be with Jesus alone on a few occasions (8:51; 9:28).

TRUE GREATNESS
Who are the people you know that you consider truly "great"?
Perhaps they are particularly wealthy, or well-known, or
influential, or talented. While these are wonderful qualities, they
are not, according to Jesus, the essence of greatness. When
the disciples argued about which of them would be the
greatest, Jesus did not rebuke them for wanting to be great. He
simply redefined "greatness" for them. True greatness, he said,
is anyone who welcomes a little child in his name, whoever
sincerely humbles himself. The world needs Jesus' kind of
greatness. Do you truly want to be great for God? Be a servant
even to the "least."

9:47-48 **But Jesus, aware of their inner thoughts, took a little child
and put it by his side, and said to them, "Whoever welcomes
this child in my name welcomes me, and whoever welcomes
me welcomes the one who sent me; for the least among all of
you is the greatest."**[NRSV] The disciples were probably ashamed
to have Jesus hear them argue, so they attempted to do so in private. They should have realized, however, that nothing could be
hidden from Jesus. He was *aware of their inner thoughts,* so he
used this as an opportunity to teach his disciples a lesson about
the "greatness" about which they were so concerned. So Jesus
took a little child and put the child by his side. This would have
been a visual aid. The disciples had two people before them. One
who had great value because of who he was and what he could
do; the other, a child, considered of not much importance in the
ancient world. Children would eventually become valuable, but
at this time they were not highly esteemed.

Jesus suggested that he and this child were peers—*"Whoever
welcomes this child in my name welcomes me."* Jesus equated the
attitude of welcoming children with a willingness to welcome
him. This was a new approach in a society where children were
usually treated as second-class citizens. Jesus equated the attitude
of receiving children with a willingness to receive him. Even
more important is the profound truth of Jesus' identity—*"Whoever welcomes me welcomes the one who sent me."* Jesus added
that to receive him is to receive the one who sent him, God the
Father. Jesus was saying that he and God the Father are one.

The disciples had become so preoccupied with the organization of Jesus' earthly kingdom that they had lost sight of its
divine purpose. Instead of seeking a place of service, they were
seeking positions of advantage. Jesus used a child to help his self-
centered disciples get the point. They were to have servant
attitudes, being not "childish" (arguing over petty issues) but

"childlike," with humble and sincere hearts. Greatness would be measured by attitude toward service—"For the least among all of you is the greatest." True greatness means to deny oneself, willingly serve others, and then follow and obey the Master.

REALLY GREAT
Your care for others is a measure of your greatness. How much concern do you show to others? This is a vital question that can accurately measure your greatness in God's eyes. How have you expressed your care for others lately, especially the helpless, the needy, the poor—those who can't return your love and concern? Your honest answer to that question will give you a good idea of your real greatness.

THE DISCIPLES FORBID ANOTHER TO USE JESUS' NAME / 9:49-50 / 116

Here the disciples displayed their tendency to become a closed group. By challenging the credentials of an outsider, they were attempting to funnel access to the power, teaching, and authority of Jesus through themselves. Yet Jesus rebuked their attempt to be exclusive. His ministry was to empower and encourage all those who do good, not to limit and restrict. Christians must welcome and encourage all who serve in the name of Christ. Having the same Lord should cover a multitude of differences.

9:49-50 **"Master," said John, "we saw a man driving out demons in your name and we tried to stop him, because he is not one of us." "Do not stop him," Jesus said, "for whoever is not against you is for you."**[NIV] *John* was one of the inner circle of three, along with his brother James and Peter. Apparently he needed to clear something with Jesus—he may have felt concerned that they had done wrong, especially after this illustration about greatness through serving. They had seen *a man driving out demons in [Jesus'] name,* and they had *tried to stop him.* This was not an evil man, for apparently God was blessing him—the man was having success (as opposed to the disciples, nine of whom had just failed, 9:40). But the disciples stopped the man for one reason—*"He is not one of us."*

Jesus explained that they should not stop such a person; instead, they should have been thrilled that there were other people through whom God was working, others who were on Jesus' side. Jesus made the point that with him there would be no middle ground—*"Whoever is not against you is for you."* The disciples had been wrong to stop the man from exorcising

demons in Jesus' name; and they were also wrong to think that
they alone had a monopoly on Jesus' power. Jesus explained that
no one would do such a miracle as exorcising a demon in Jesus'
name and then turn around and publicly speak against Jesus. The
man, whatever his motivation, had at least done a deed of mercy
for a possessed person and had stood against Satan in so doing.
(See Numbers 11:24-29 where Moses permitted two elders to
prophesy in the Spirit, even though they were not part of the
meeting.)

The disciples were jealous of a man who healed in Jesus' name
because they were more concerned about their own group's position than in helping to free those troubled by demons. We do the
same today when we refuse to participate in worthy causes
because (1) other people or groups are not affiliated with our
denomination; (2) these projects do not involve the kind of
people with whom we feel most comfortable; (3) others don't
operate the way we are used to; or (4) our efforts won't receive
enough recognition. Correct theology is important but should
never be an excuse to avoid helping people in need.

Matthew 12:30 records the same statement in the opposite,
"He who is not with Me is against Me" (NKJV). People who are
on Jesus' side have the common goal of building up the kingdom
of God, and they should not let their differences interfere with
this goal. Those who share a common faith in Christ should cooperate. Just as the man did not have to belong to the select group
of disciples to be God's servant, so people don't have to be just
like us to be following Jesus with us.

OPEN ARMS
The disciples were jealous. Nine of them together were unable
to drive out a single evil spirit (9:40), but when they saw a man
who was not one of their group driving out demons, they told
him to stop. A person's pride is hurt when someone else
succeeds where he or she has failed, but Jesus says there is
no room for such jealousy in the spiritual warfare of his
kingdom. Share Jesus' open-arms attitude to Christian workers
outside your group or denomination. Don't let possessiveness,
protectiveness, or divisions stop the work of Christ.

JESUS TEACHES ABOUT THE COST OF FOLLOWING HIM / 9:51-62 / *122*

With the phrase "Jesus resolutely set out for Jerusalem" (9:51
NLT), Luke began an extended section of his Gospel. This section

extends to either chapter 18 or chapter 19 and has as its theme Jesus' journey to Jerusalem (see 9:51; 13:31-35; 18:31-34). This section presents the teaching and parables of Jesus that, for the most part, focus on the cost of discipleship and the coming suffering that Jesus would endure—themes evident in 9:51-62; 10:1-20; 12:35-40; 14:25-35; 18:31-34. Jesus was preparing his disciples for the rejection, suffering, and death that he would experience.

As you read this passage (9:51-62) and the following chapters, think of Jesus as a man who knows he only has a number of months to live—he knows that he will face his own execution in Jerusalem and leave his disciples to continue his work. Through every word he says, he is trying to prepare his disciples to become leaders in spreading the gospel. In this passage, Jesus corrects his disciples about the nature of his ministry: he has not come in judgment but instead to offer the gospel message of salvation. At the same time, the way of salvation—following Jesus—is not easy. It requires extreme sacrifice—subordinating all other obligations to the cause of Christ. Jesus Christ does not ask for a couple of hours on Sunday; he desires all of a person's resources, talents, and time to be placed in his service. As Lord and Savior, he should be the top priority.

9:51 As the time approached for him to be taken up to heaven, Jesus resolutely set out for Jerusalem.^{NIV} Jesus knew that his time on earth was ending and that *the time approached for him to be taken up to heaven.* In other words, Jesus knew that he would soon die and that this death awaited him in Jerusalem. As if needing to arrive on time for a preplanned appointment, *Jesus resolutely set out for Jerusalem.*

DETERMINED
Although Jesus knew he would face persecution and death in Jerusalem, he was determined to go there. That kind of resolve should characterize believers' lives today. When God gives you a course of action, move steadily toward your destination, no matter what potential hazards await.

9:52-53 And he sent messengers on ahead, who went into a Samaritan village to get things ready for him; but the people there did not welcome him, because he was heading for Jerusalem.^{NIV} Jesus was journeying from Galilee to Jerusalem, so he had to travel south. Samaria lay between Galilee and Judea; thus he would have to travel through that region. The animosity between the Jews and the Samaritans was so great that many Jews would

go out of their way *not* to travel through Samaria, instead opting
to cross the Jordan River and travel on the other side until they
could recross. The animosity between the two races had begun
hundreds of years earlier. After Assyria had invaded Israel, the
northern kingdom, and had resettled it with its own people
(2 Kings 17:24-41), the mixed race that developed became
known as the Samaritans. "Purebred" Jews hated these "half-
breeds," and the Samaritans in turn hated the Jews. Jesus held no
such prejudices, so he *sent messengers on ahead* (probably a few
of his disciples) to go into a Samaritan village and *get things
ready for him* (presumably to secure lodging for Jesus and the
Twelve). Because the men were *heading for Jerusalem,* however,
the people in the Samaritan village refused to welcome him.

9:54-56 **When James and John heard about it, they said to Jesus,
"Lord, should we order down fire from heaven to burn them
up?" But Jesus turned and rebuked them. So they went on to
another village.**[NLT] When the messengers reported back that they
could not get everything ready in a certain Samaritan village
because they were refused a welcome, *James and John* were furious. The disciples had been told that if they faced rejection in a
certain town, they were to shake the dust from their feet as a testimony against the people (9:5). James and John did not want to
stop there—they asked Jesus if they should *order down fire from
heaven to burn them up.* Apparently these brothers had enough
love and loyalty for Jesus that they wanted to retaliate, and they
thought they had enough faith that they could actually do this.
They may have been thinking of Elijah, who had called fire down
from heaven on sinful people who mocked him (2 Kings 1:1-15).

RETALIATION
James and John wanted to retaliate on a village that would not
welcome Jesus by calling down fire from heaven on the people.
When feeling rejected or scorned, it is natural to feel like
retaliating and wishing to silence other groups with differing
methods and schools of thought. Remember that judgment
belongs to God. Do not expect him to use his power to carry
out your personal vendettas.

Jesus *rebuked* their suggestion. He had told the disciples that
when they were rejected, they should shake the dust from their
feet and move on. This was certainly a lot more mild than what
James and John were suggesting. But the point here was that the
villagers were not consciously rejecting Jesus; instead, they were
rejecting this group of thirteen or more because they were Jews

on their way to Jerusalem (9:53)—that was all. The disciples
were to take this rejection in stride and go *on to another village.*
Whether this other village was in Samaria is unknown. There was
no stopping Jesus—he continued resolutely toward Jerusalem.

9:57-58 **As they were going along the road, someone said to him, "I
will follow you wherever you go." And Jesus said to him,
"Foxes have holes, and birds of the air have nests; but the
Son of Man has nowhere to lay his head."**NRSV They had hoped
for lodging, but instead had to continue on their journey. Then
someone approached and wanted to follow Jesus. Matthew wrote
that this man was a scribe (teacher of the law, Matthew 8:19).
Most of the scribes became Jesus' enemies, but at least one apparently recognized Jesus' authority and wanted to be his disciple.
Jesus' reply, however, pointed out to the man the cost of becoming a disciple. Jesus did not grab on to disciples, eagerly taking
anyone who wanted to follow. Those who truly wanted to be his
disciples needed to understand that it would cost them something—they could not expect luxury or even a warm welcome (as
illustrated in the incident in 9:52-53). While most of God's creatures have warm places in which to live and to sleep, *the Son of
Man has nowhere to lay his head.*

To be Jesus' disciple, a person must willingly put aside worldly
security. To follow Jesus *wherever* he would go (as this scribe
said) would mean a willingness to give up home and security. In
the context of Jesus' present ministry, to follow him meant to be
constantly on the move, bringing his message to people in many
places. It is not known whether this scribe actually chose to follow, but the words are recorded for believers' benefit. Have you
counted the cost of following Jesus? Do you understand that following Jesus is far more valuable than anything this world offers?

9:59-60 **He said to another man, "Follow me." But the man replied,
"Lord, first let me go and bury my father." Jesus said to him,
"Let the dead bury their own dead, but you go and proclaim
the kingdom of God."**NIV The previous man came on his own to
Jesus (9:57-58); this time, however, Jesus asked another man to
follow him. But this man explained that he *first* needed to go and
bury his father. In ancient times, doing a proper burial of a dead
person was a sacred duty. The text does not report whether the
father was already dead or whether he was elderly or sick and
going to die soon. It is unlikely that the father was already dead
and the son was merely asking permission to finish the funeral
because, if that were the case, the son would have been nowhere
near Jesus—hardly on the road where Jesus was walking—
because he would have been at home with the mourners. More

likely, the man was asking for permission to wait until his father died—an indefinite delay.

PAYING THE PRICE
No great success comes without sacrifice. Ask champion athletes or concert musicians what they had to give up to attain their level of expertise. Ask a mother if she has had to forgo some of her own plans and desires in order to do what is best for her child, and she will tell you that she has. Nothing worthwhile comes without sacrifice, and that applies to Christian discipleship as well. Of course, there are incomparable benefits to having a living relationship with God, but they do not come without a price. Jesus said that he, the Son of Man, didn't even have a home, a place to call his own. What sacrifices has God asked you to make in view of the much greater privilege of following Jesus? Earthly success, possessions, and recognition must not deter us from serving others.

The reason is not given, but whatever it was, the man wanted to do it "first." Perhaps he was the firstborn son and wanted to be sure to claim his inheritance. Perhaps he did not want to face his father's wrath if he were to leave the family business. Whether his concern was fulfilling a duty, having financial security, keeping family approval, or something else, he did not want to commit himself to Jesus just yet. Jesus sensed this reluctance and challenged the man to consider that his commitment had to be complete, without reservation. If this man truly desired to follow Jesus, he would not wait until he had fulfilled all his traditional responsibilities. Jesus was not advising that children disregard family responsibilities. Rather, Jesus was responding to this disciple's qualifying use of "first." Jesus must always come "first," above all human loyalties. Jesus' directive was not heartless; it called the man to examine his primary loyalty.

Jesus' response (*"Let the dead bury their own dead"*) points out that those who want to follow him should count the cost and set aside any conditions they might have. "The dead" in Aramaic can also mean "the dying." So Jesus may have been saying, "Let the dying bury the dead." In other words, let those who are spiritually dying (those who have not responded to the call to commitment) stay home and handle responsibilities such as burying the dead. This may sound insensitive, but it had precedents. A high priest and those who had taken the Nazirite vow were required by the law to avoid the corpse of even a parent (Leviticus 21:11; Numbers 6:6-8). A later Jewish precedent says that if there were enough people in attendance, a student of the Torah should not stop his studying to bury the dead. Jesus placed commitment to

God even above these precedents. As God's Son, Jesus did not hesitate to demand complete loyalty. Even family loyalty was not to take priority over the demands of obedience to the command to *go and proclaim the kingdom of God.* Jesus' direct challenge forces believers to evaluate their priorities. They must not put off the decision to follow Jesus, even though other loyalties compete for attention. Like the first man, it is not known whether this man chose to follow Jesus or turned away.

A BETTER TIME?
Luke did not give the reason why this man said no to Jesus. But Jesus used the response to teach an important lesson. True discipleship requires instant action; the responsibilities of the kingdom cannot be put off until a "better time." Jesus did not teach people to forsake responsibilities to family, but he often gave commands to people in light of their real motives. Perhaps this man wanted to delay following Christ and used his father as an excuse. There is a cost to following Jesus, and each follower must be ready to serve, even when it requires sacrifice. Don't wait for a better time to follow and serve Jesus—he is calling you now.

9:61-62 Still another said, "I will follow you, Lord; but first let me go back and say good-by to my family." Jesus replied, "No one who puts his hand to the plow and looks back is fit for service in the kingdom of God."[NIV] A third person approached, and this one, like the first, expressed his desire to *follow* Jesus. However, this man too had something he wanted to do *first.* Jesus ascertained in this potential follower a sense of reluctance and an unfortunate willingness to put something else ahead of following Jesus. Who knows what might occur on his trek back to his family that would deter him from the task at hand. Who knows what this attitude might mean in the years to come if a precedent were set that service for the kingdom can be put off in pursuit of other matters. *"No,"* Jesus answered, for this was not the type of follower he needed.

The picture of a person putting a hand to the plow and looking back can be compared with Elijah's call of Elisha in 1 Kings 19:19-21. Elisha was called to be a prophet right in the middle of plowing a field—and he never looked back. In fact, he slaughtered the oxen so that they would not even be a temptation to return. Elisha then moved wholeheartedly into the ministry to which he had been called. Elisha was allowed to say good-bye to his father and mother, but the kingdom of God was not at hand then. Jesus explained that *service in the kingdom of God* was of such vital importance that his followers must make it their top priority. It had an even greater urgency than the Old Testament discipleship arrangement. They must step out in faith to serve him, without looking back.

What does Jesus want from his followers? Total dedication, not halfhearted commitment. His followers must accept the cross along with the crown, judgment as well as mercy. They must count the cost and be willing to abandon everything else that has given them security. Nothing should distract them from service for the kingdom.

LUKE 10

Luke is the only Gospel to record the sending out of seventy-two disciples. In this passage, Luke highlighted and anticipated the universal mission of Jesus—that the gospel would go to all people. Prior to this time, Jesus limited his mission to the Jews. The mission for Christians today is the same as for the seventy-two people who gathered around Jesus two thousand years ago. We must tell others about the coming of God's kingdom, the coming of Jesus to the world to save sinners. While Jesus' mission was to Israel, the mission of today's church encompasses the entire world, reaching out to all groups of people.

10:1 The Lord now chose seventy-two other disciples and sent them on ahead in pairs to all the towns and villages he planned to visit.[NLT] Far more than twelve people had been following Jesus. According to 1 Corinthians 15:6, Jesus had at least five hundred followers by the time he had finished his ministry. A group of 120 of these followers went to Jerusalem to begin the church there (Acts 1:15). Here Jesus designated a group of seventy-two to prepare a number of towns for his later visit. Even though Jesus was on his way to Jerusalem, knowing that death awaited him there, he did not stop his ministry of proclaiming the kingdom of God. As the Twelve had been sent out (9:1-6), so now Jesus *chose seventy-two other disciples and sent them on ahead.* Their ministry was much like that of the Twelve, preparing *the towns and villages* that Jesus was planning to visit.

The number "72" is found in the earliest Greek manuscripts. This number is significant for it was, according to Genesis 10, the traditional number of nations in the world, according to the Septuagint. Other Greek manuscripts read "70." This alternative reading may have been influenced by the Hebrew Old Testament, which lists seventy names in Genesis 10. By choosing and sending out seventy-two disciples, Jesus was symbolically showing that all nations in the world would one day hear the message. This would include the Gentiles—an important point for Luke's Gentile audience.

These disciples were not unique in their qualifications. They were not better educated, more capable, or of higher status than other followers of Jesus. What equipped the seventy-two for this mission was their awareness of Jesus' power and their vision to reach all the people. Christians should dedicate their skills to God's kingdom, but they should also be equipped with his power and have a clear vision of what he wants them to do.

THE VISION
While some disciples stayed back, these seventy-two went ahead to prepare for Jesus' visit to several towns. It was their turn to serve as missionaries, and no doubt their excitement was high. But most important, they were going in God's strength and with God's message. When you "go out"—to build schools, help with kids' camp, or whatever—go in prayer, trusting God for strength, to help people find their Savior.

10:2 He said to them, "The harvest is plentiful, but the laborers are few; therefore ask the Lord of the harvest to send out laborers into his harvest."^{NRSV} Jesus was sending thirty-six teams of two to reach the many towns and villages that he had not yet been able to visit. Jesus compared this work to a *harvest*—the gathering of new believers into his kingdom (see also John 4:35). To have a harvest, however, one must have *laborers* in the field. So many people need to hear the message ("the harvest is plentiful"), but there are so few laborers willing to gather it in ("the laborers are few"). Even as Jesus had sent the Twelve, and now seventy-two more, he told them to *ask the Lord of the harvest to send out laborers into his harvest.* These laborers should pray for more laborers—pray for more people to be willing to work in the harvest. In Christian service, there is no unemployment. God has work enough for everyone. No believer should sit back and watch others work because the harvest is great.

10:3 "Go! I am sending you out like lambs among wolves."^{NIV} The world into which these seventy-two were going was not a pleasant place. The harvest was going to involve intensive labor and possibly danger. Jesus commanded them to *go,* explaining that they were going out *like lambs among wolves.* The use of the word "lambs" refers to their vulnerability (see Isaiah 11:6; 65:25 where the image is also used). Just as Israel was a lamb among the hostile Gentile nations in the Old Testament, so the disciples would be in a hostile setting. But most important are the four words *I am sending you.* If Jesus were not sending them, then they would be attempting to go on their own plans, their own power, their own itinerary; being lambs among wolves would be like asking to be slaughtered. But because Jesus was sending them, they might face danger from the opposition. Their very defenselessness would cause them all the more to depend on God.

ROOKIE MISSIONARY
Jesus encouraged the disciples not just to do the work but also to pray for workers. Part of every missionary's job is to pray for new workers and to help newcomers learn the ropes. Whatever your role in God's work, pray today for more helpers. Believers are not always to work alone. God wants them to pray, recruit, and equip others to join them as they explore opportunities to serve Jesus. Some people, as soon as they understand the gospel, want to go to convert people immediately. Jesus gave a different approach: begin by mobilizing people to pray. And before praying for unsaved people, pray that other concerned disciples will join you in reaching out to them. God will lead you to an important responsibility, but prayer comes first.

10:4 "Don't take along any money, or a traveler's bag, or even an extra pair of sandals. And don't stop to greet anyone on the road."[NLT] These instructions are basically the same as those given to the Twelve in 9:3-4. The reason was the same—they were to travel light, spend no time preparing for the trip, and depend upon God and those to whom they ministered to meet their basic needs. Going without *money, traveler's bag, or even an extra pair of sandals* would seemingly make them that much more vulnerable to the "wolves" (10:3), but they are to trust God completely. So urgent is their task that they are not to *stop to greet anyone on the road.* Jesus did not mean for them to be impolite to people whom they passed, but rather that they were not to spend precious time on dallying by the wayside. They had to remain focused on their task (see also 2 Kings 4:29).

WOLVES
Jesus warned against opposition. Wolfish opposition comes in many forms. Some spiritual opponents will aggressively attack all religion, especially religion that respects patience, meekness, and chastity. Some opponents will appear to be spiritual, even more than you are.
     Serving God today requires courage under fire and discernment among counterfeits. Pray for growth in both virtues. Find a way to become better educated about the opposition you face.

10:5-6 **"Whatever house you enter, first say, 'Peace to this house!'**
And if anyone is there who shares in peace, your peace will
rest on that person; but if not, it will return to you."[NRSV] The
house that a pair of disciples would *enter* would be the home
from which they would receive hospitality during their stay in a
particular town. When they entered a house, they should give the
characteristic greeting of *peace.* But this greeting conveyed much
more. It represented the messianic peace promised in the Old Testament and stressed the authority based on power from God that
was behind the missionary. If the householder was one *who*
shares in peace (a person who had a proper attitude toward God),
then the greeting of *peace will rest on that person.* Such a person
will be open to the gospel message. But if the person did not
"share in peace," then he or she would not be open to the gospel
message; so the greeting *will return* to the one who had given it.
God's blessing of peace will return so that it can be redirected to
those who will appreciate it.

10:7 **"Remain in the same house, eating and drinking whatever**
they provide, for the laborer deserves to be paid. Do not move
about from house to house."[NRSV] Jesus had also directed the
Twelve to remain with their original hosts in any town (9:4). This
instruction avoided certain problems. For the two disciples to
move about from house to house could offend the families who
first took them in. Some families might begin to compete for the
disciples' presence, and some might think they weren't good
enough to hear their message. This instruction would also keep
them from sin caused by always looking for a better deal. If the
disciples appeared not to appreciate the hospitality offered them,
the town might not accept Jesus when he followed them there. In
addition, by staying in one place, the disciples would not have to
worry continually about getting good accommodations. They
could settle down and do their appointed task.

In addition, the disciples should willingly eat and drink what
their hosts provided, *for the laborer deserves to be paid.* Jesus told
his disciples to accept hospitality graciously because their work
entitled them to it. Ministers of the gospel deserve to be supported,
and it is believers' responsibility to make sure they have what they
need. There are several ways to encourage those who serve God in
his church. First, see that they have an adequate salary. Second, see
that they are supported emotionally; plan a time to express appreciation for something they have done. Third, lift their spirits with special surprises from time to time. Ministers deserve to know that
believers are giving to them cheerfully and generously. (See
1 Corinthians 9:3-18; 1 Timothy 5:18; 3 John 5-8.)

10:8-9 "When you enter a town and are welcomed, eat what is set
before you. Heal the sick who are there and tell them, 'The
kingdom of God is near you.'"ᴺᴵⱽ When the pairs of disciples
entered a town, received a *welcome,* and entered a home, Jesus told
them to *eat what is set before* them. It may well be that they would
be welcomed into non-Jewish homes where the meals might not satisfy all the ceremonial laws of the Jews. Jesus told them not to be
sidetracked about what they ate. Instead, they should do what they
came to do—*heal the sick* (which was a signal that the kingdom
had arrived) and proclaim to the people that *the kingdom of God is
near* (see also 10:11; 21:31). This "nearness" meant both "already
here" and "soon to come." The kingdom Jesus began on earth
would not overthrow Roman oppression and bring universal peace
right away. Instead, it was a kingdom that began in people's hearts
and was as near as people's willingness to make Jesus king over
their lives. One day Christ will return to set up his eternal kingdom
on earth—it may still be many years away, but it is certain to come,
and it is as near as accepting Jesus' sacrifice for salvation.

MISSIONARIES AND MONEY
Should missionaries ask for money? Should pastors consider
salary when thinking about a move?
 Simple faith and single-minded intensity are the twin foci of
this verse, not poverty or discourtesy. Disciples must trust God
for their needs and be devoted to their mission.
 Pastors usually try to live on a middle-range income
appropriate to the church they serve. Missionaries, on the other
hand, are normally considered rich by virtue of their having
shoes on their feet and books in their home. In neither case
must wealth be a motive. Serve God with a blind eye to
financial gain.

10:10-11 "But when you enter a town and are not welcomed, go into its
streets and say, 'Even the dust of your town that sticks to our
feet we wipe off against you. Yet be sure of this: The kingdom of
God is near.'"ᴺᴵⱽ Jesus also gave instructions if the disciples
should enter a town and not be welcomed. He made it clear that
they would face rejection in some places. But the rejection of their
message would not change the message. Even if the people refused
it, the kingdom of God was still near, but those who refused it
would miss it. Jesus repeated the instruction of shaking the dust of
that town from their feet "as a testimony against them" (9:5).

10:12 "The truth is, even wicked Sodom will be better off than such a
town on the judgment day."ᴺᴸᵀ Sodom was a *wicked* city that God
destroyed because of its great sinfulness (Genesis 19:24-28). The

city's name is often used to symbolize evil and immorality. Sodom will face God's wrath at Judgment Day, but cities that rejected the Messiah and his kingdom will face even worse wrath from God. A city as evil as Sodom would be *better off . . . on the judgment day* than these towns because they had been given the opportunity to believe the Messiah—they had seen great miracles and had the Good News preached to them—but they had turned away and had refused salvation. Their punishment would be severe.

AMAZING AUTHORITY
If respect goes to doctors and professors . . .
  If wealth goes to corporate chiefs and lawyers . . .
  If fame goes to sports and entertainment headliners . . .
  What do evangelists get?
  They get a message—
  the telling of which means eternal life,
  the rejecting of which separates from God forever,
  and there's no middle ground.
  If ever a job was important,
  needed doing, makes a difference—
  here it is.
  Your privilege and responsibility. Tell the message.

10:13-14 **"Woe to you, Chorazin! Woe to you, Bethsaida! For if the deeds of power done in you had been done in Tyre and Sidon, they would have repented long ago, sitting in sackcloth and ashes. But at the judgment it will be more tolerable for Tyre and Sidon than for you."**[NRSV] The word "woe" expresses deep sorrow as well as coming judgment (6:24). The mention of cities that might reject the Messiah (10:10-11) leads to a message of those who already had. *Chorazin* (also spelled Korazin) and *Bethsaida* were cities near Capernaum, at the north end of the Sea of Galilee. Jesus had concentrated his ministry in and around Capernaum, so he must have performed miracles in these cities *(deeds of power)*. These miracles are not recorded in the Gospels—there is much about Jesus' ministry that is unknown. *Tyre and Sidon* were pagan cities in Phoenicia, the territory north of Galilee. They had rebelled against God and had been judged and punished for their wickedness and opposition to God's people (see Isaiah 23:1-18; Jeremiah 25:22; 47:4; Ezekiel 26–28; Joel 3:4-8; Amos 1:9-10). Yet Jesus explained that, though these people were evil and rebellious, if he had come to them and had done miracles, *they would have repented long ago.* The mention of *sackcloth and ashes* depicts mourning and repentance. A person humbled himself or herself by wearing only this rough cloth made of goat hair and sitting in a pile of ashes. Tyre and Sidon had not had that opportunity, while Chorazin and Bethsaida had been visited by the Messiah, who had done miracles among them; yet they rejected him. The punishment these cities would suffer *at the judgment* would be far worse than what Tyre and Sidon experienced.

10:15 "And you, Capernaum, will you be lifted up to the skies? No, you will go down to the depths."^{NIV} Capernaum was Jesus' base for his Galilean ministry (Matthew 4:13; Mark 2:1). The city was located at an important crossroads used by traders and the Roman army, so a message proclaimed in Capernaum was likely to go far. Jesus had performed many miracles there, and apparently the people were feeling a certain amount of pride in their connection with Jesus. But many people of Capernaum did not understand Jesus' miracles or believe his teaching. Instead of being *lifted up to the skies* as they might have thought because Jesus chose to live among them, they would *go down to the depths* because they had seen the Messiah and rejected him. The language is reminiscent of Isaiah 14:12-15 where the prideful attitude of the king of Babylon is condemned. The Greek word translated "to the depths" is *Hades,* which is the opposite of heaven. Hades is the dwelling place of the condemned wicked people (16:23; Revelation 20:13-14), so it implied fiery judgment on this city that rejected Christ. Today the site of ancient Capernaum is desolate—a stunning picture of Jesus' words here.

10:16 Then he said to the disciples, "Anyone who accepts your message is also accepting me. And anyone who rejects you is rejecting me. And anyone who rejects me is rejecting God who sent me."^{NLT} Jesus' messengers are important people. They are sent with authority. In ancient times, when a person dealt with a messenger, it was the same as dealing with the person who had sent him (for example, see 7:3 and commentary). Therefore, people who accepted the message of Jesus' disciples were accepting Jesus. Likewise, people who rejected Jesus' disciples' message were rejecting Jesus. Because Jesus and God are one—*anyone who rejects [Jesus] is rejecting God* who sent him. These messengers could take their mission seriously because Jesus did—he was sending them out with his message and his authority.

THE SEVENTY-TWO MESSENGERS RETURN / 10:17-24 / **131**

This passage continues the theme of discipleship (started at 9:51). Here the seventy-two returned, rejoicing. Jesus rejoiced with them, praising God for the defeat of Satan and the fact that he had chosen to use these humble followers to advance his kingdom.

In the middle of this celebration, however, Jesus issued a strong warning: Don't take pride in what you have done or what God has done through you. Instead, rejoice in the fact that God has chosen you and has given you eternal life.

It is easy to start taking pride in your own accomplishments. But Jesus warns you to be careful not to forget from whom your abilities and strength come. Praise and gratitude always belong to God.

10:17 **The seventy-two returned with joy and said, "Lord, even the demons submit to us in your name."**[NIV] Some time had passed between 10:16 and 10:17. The seventy-two disciples completed their mission to various towns and villages (10:1) and *returned with joy.* They had seen tremendous results as they ministered in Jesus' name and with his authority. They were elated by the victories they had witnessed—that even the demons had submitted to them in Jesus' name. Probably they were able to heal demon-possessed people, and this thrilled them. Jesus shared their enthusiasm. He helped them get their priorities right, however, by reminding them of their most important victory—that their names were written in heaven (10:20). This honor was more important than any of their accomplishments. As we see God's wonders at work in and through us, we should not lose sight of the greatest wonder of all—our heavenly citizenship.

10:18-19 **He replied, "I saw Satan fall like lightning from heaven. I have given you authority to trample on snakes and scorpions and to overcome all the power of the enemy; nothing will harm you."**[NIV] The disciples noted in particular that demons had submitted to Jesus' authority through them (10:17). Jesus' reply is mysterious but may be understood in a couple of ways. It could be that Jesus *saw,* as in a vision, Satan falling *like lightning from heaven* (that is, from a place of power) during the ministry of these disciples—Satan suffered a notable defeat as these thirty-six pairs of men went around the countryside casting out demons.

Another view is that Jesus had seen his ultimate victory over Satan at the cross. John 12:31-32 indicates that Satan would be judged and driven out at the time of Jesus' death.

A third view says that Jesus was telling of the fall of Satan and was warning his disciples against pride. Perhaps he was referring to Isaiah 14:12-17, which begins, "How you have fallen from heaven, O morning star, son of the dawn!" (NIV). Some interpreters identify this verse with Satan and explain that Satan's pride led to his fall. Thus, some conclude that Jesus may have been giving this stern warning: "Your pride is the kind that led to Satan's downfall. Be careful!"

The first view is most preferred. Satan might attempt what he

could to discourage and harm Jesus' disciples, but when they were on this mission, nothing could harm them. Jesus
had given them *authority to trample on*
snakes and scorpions and to overcome
all the power of the enemy. This may

> The Devil's best ruse is to persuade us that he does not exist.
>
> *Charles Baudelaire*

allude to Psalm 91:13 where snakes are listed among dangerous
creatures from which God protects the people of Israel. See also
Deuteronomy 8:15 where scorpions and snakes are connected.
Indeed, nothing could harm them. They would be on a special
mission with special protection.

10:20 **"Nevertheless do not rejoice in this, that the spirits are subject
to you, but rather rejoice because your names are written in
heaven."**[NKJV] Such power and authority can be a heady experience,
so the disciples were warned not to rejoice in their mission and
their accomplishments and the fact that the evil spirits submitted
to them (10:17). The only reason to rejoice, Jesus explained, is
that *your names are written in heaven.* Their ministry was not to
become an experience of power leading to pride, but an experience
of servanthood out of love for God and out of the desire for more
people to join them in the kingdom, more names "written in
heaven." (See also Exodus 32:32-33; Daniel 12:1; Malachi 3:16;
Hebrews 12:23; Revelation 3:5; 20:12-15.)

JUST BECAUSE . . .
Much of what's done for Christ seeks results and rewards. Of
all that you do, what matters for its own sake and doesn't need
any further reward?
   . . . Students study hard to get grades to get . . . what?
   . . . Workers put in overtime to make money to get . . . what?
   . . . Disciples serve God . . . for what?
   The Bible tells of just a few steps God's people ought to take
just because they please God: loving people, keeping promises,
worshiping, telling others about Jesus. Can you add any? In all of
your efforts for Christ, take time to thank God that you have
eternal life.

10:21 **At that time Jesus, full of joy through the Holy Spirit, said,
"I praise you, Father, Lord of heaven and earth, because you
have hidden these things from the wise and learned, and
revealed them to little children. Yes, Father, for this was your
good pleasure."**[NIV] The seventy-two disciples returned, full of
joy at what God was doing (10:17). Jesus shared this joy and
praised God, for he could see God decisively at work—the effective ministry of the seventy-two disciples underscored this fact.

Jesus praised God, his *Father* who was also *Lord of heaven and earth,* for making spiritual truth available to the *little children.* Those who willingly submit themselves to God and do not depend upon their own wisdom will have the truth *revealed* to them. While many of life's rewards seem to go to the intelligent, the rich, the good-looking, or the powerful, the kingdom of God is equally available to all, regardless of position or abilities. Yet so often *the wise and learned* in this world refuse to submit themselves to God. They may not see their need for him, or they may think that their wisdom and learning have placed them in a separate class. These words of Jesus reveal God's sovereignty and initiative regarding who will receive divine truth. God has chosen to hide it from those who refuse and reject it (see 8:10), and instead reveals it to those who may not seem wise and learned but have trusting hearts (like little children, 9:47-48).

GOD'S CHOICE: YOU
How did you come to know about God? A typical Christian will answer: through reading the Bible or because someone witnessed to me. But the deeper reason (the explanation behind those immediate reasons) is that God chose you to know about himself.
    Why would God do that? Not because you're so kind to animals or anything else commendable. It was by grace, a gift entirely based on love from God to you.
    What should you do? Thank God in prayer; live each day for God; speak about God; and show God's love in generous concern for others. A great gift inspires a grateful response.

10:22 **"All things have been committed to me by my Father. No one knows who the Son is except the Father, and no one knows who the Father is except the Son and those to whom the Son chooses to reveal him."**[NIV] Jesus further identified his special and unique relationship with God the Father. So close and intimate, so completely trusting, that Jesus said, *"All things have been committed to me by my Father."* That is why Jesus spoke with such authority (4:32) and why he has absolute power over nature, demons, sickness, and death. The Father and the Son have an exclusive relationship that humanity at large cannot fathom. (Luke brought it up again in 20:41-44; 22:69; Acts 2:29-38.) However, Jesus did reveal God to some. His mission was to reveal God the Father to people. His words brought salvation down to earth. He explained God's love through parables, teachings, and, most of all, his life. By examining Jesus' actions, principles, and attitudes, those chosen by him are enabled to understand God more clearly. As used here, the word "chooses" does not refer to predestination; rather, it refers to Jesus' divine status and authority to reveal saving knowledge tó people. Only through Jesus can people come to know God; Jesus alone is our mediator; he is "the way, the truth, and the life" (John 14:6 NKJV). (See also John 10:15; 17:2.)

10:23-24 **Then turning to the disciples, Jesus said to them privately, "Blessed are the eyes that see what you see! For I tell you that many prophets and kings desired to see what you see, but did not see it, and to hear what you hear, but did not hear it."**NRSV Old Testament men of God such as David and the prophet Isaiah made many God-inspired predictions that Jesus fulfilled. As Peter later would write, these prophets wondered what their words meant and when they would be fulfilled (1 Peter 1:10-13). In Jesus' words, they *desired to see what you see, but did not see it, and to hear what you hear, but did not hear it.* Despite their privileged positions as part of God's people and God's plan, many *prophets and kings* were not as blessed as this little band of disciples or all the "simple" people who came in faith to Jesus.

THE PRIVILEGED FEW
The disciples had a fantastic opportunity—they were eyewitnesses of Christ, the Son of God. But for many months they took Jesus for granted, not really listening to him or obeying him. Believers today also have a privileged position, with knowledge of two thousand years of church history, availability of the Bible in hundreds of languages and translations, and access to many excellent pastors and speakers. Yet often Christians take these for granted. Remember, with privilege comes responsibility. Because you are privileged to know so much about Christ, you must be careful to follow him.

The prophets wanted to know more about what they were prophesying. They wondered about this Messiah, the circumstances that would surround his coming, what he would be like, what he would do, what their words of suffering and glory meant. Yet those who came to believe in Jesus—then and today—have the privilege of understanding the prophets' writings better than the prophets themselves understood them. The men at Jesus' side in those months were able to walk and talk with him, see his miracles, watch his life, and experience the emotions of his death and resurrection. They were indeed *blessed* at what they saw and heard. All of the predictions regarding the life, death, and resurrection of Jesus Christ were being completely fulfilled.

Although Christians since the first century have not been able to walk and talk with Jesus on earth, they have the records of prophecies fulfilled and the Gospel stories that tell all about Jesus. They also have the Holy Spirit, who fills their lives and speaks of the truth of the gospel message. They too have been blessed.

JESUS TELLS THE PARABLE OF THE GOOD SAMARITAN / 10:25-37 / **132**

Jesus had just praised God for hiding the secrets of the kingdom from the wise and learned (10:21). Next a learned lawyer in Old Testament law asked Jesus a question that revealed the lawyer's profound ignorance about central issues of the faith—eternal life and the basic command to love one's neighbor.

Jesus responded with the parable of the Good Samaritan. The story revolves around a surprising *reversal* (a theme that is found throughout Luke, see 1:52; 4:16-30; 7:20; 13:30). Jesus had just condemned the Jewish towns of Bethsaida and Capernaum and compared them with the pagan cities of Tyre and Sidon, cities known for evil. In this parable, Jesus contrasted the unloving actions of a priest and Levite with the loving actions of a Samaritan, a person who was considered irreligious by the Jews. By taking care of a wounded traveler, the Samaritan was obeying the central commandment of God's law—to love one's neighbor—while the priest and Levite, those who were meticulous about observing the law, were breaking it. This parable is not only a call to help those in need, it is a warning not to become self-satisfied in your own religiosity. The Word of God remains the standard of all conduct. Always be careful to measure your behavior by what it says.

10:25 On one occasion an expert in the law stood up to test Jesus. "Teacher," he asked, "what must I do to inherit eternal life?"NIV Apparently this question came in a teaching setting, for when this man addressed Jesus, he *stood up*. He was *an expert in the law,* a man who had made it his business to know and understand the details of the Jewish religion. He had studied the Scriptures (the Old Testament—the Law, the Psalms, and the Prophets). He also knew all the traditions. The fact that this man wanted to *test* Jesus does not necessarily indicate hostility; in fact, he did not so much want information as he wanted to find out what kind of answer the teacher would give. He wanted to know what he had to *do to inherit eternal life.* For this legal expert, "eternal life" meant life in God's kingdom, although he would not have understood it as a spiritual kingdom. For him, acceptance into that kingdom meant that he had to "do" something in order to receive it. He would not have understood divine grace.

10:26-28 **He said to him, "What is written in the law? What do you read there?" He answered, "You shall love the Lord your God with all your heart, and with all your soul, and with all your strength, and with all your mind; and your neighbor as yourself."**NRSV This expert in the law obviously would have known what was *written in the law.* In his answer, he quoted from Deuteronomy 6:5 and Leviticus 19:18. He correctly understood that the law demanded total devotion to God and love for one's neighbor. To "love the Lord your God with all your heart, and with all your soul, and with all your strength, and with all your mind" means that every area of a person's life should be focused on God. Nothing must be held back. The word for love is *agapao,* referring to totally unselfish love, a love of which human beings are capable only with the help of the Holy Spirit. God's Spirit helps us love him as we ought. While God wants his people to obey him, he also wants their love. The *heart (kardia)* is the center of emotions, desires, and affections; the *soul (psuche)* is a person's "being" and uniqueness; the *strength (ischus)* refers to the drive or will; the *mind (dianoia)* is the center of the intellect. These words are not used to divide up the human personality, but to show that love must be complete—the whole person must do the loving. To love God in this way is to fulfill completely all the commandments regarding one's "vertical" relationship.

But there's more, for another command from the law says to love *your neighbor as yourself.* This refers to "horizontal" relationships—among people. A person cannot maintain a good vertical relationship with God without also caring for his or her neighbor. The word "neighbor" refers to fellow human beings in general. The love a person has for himself or herself (in the sense of looking out for oneself, caring about one's safety, etc.) should be continued, but it should also be directed toward others. (See also Matthew 22:34-40 and Mark 12:28-34.)

The expert in the law had it right. **And He said to him, "You have answered rightly; do this and you will live."**NKJV Jesus explained that people only needed to obey these commands; in doing so, they would fulfill all the rest of them. But with these abrupt words, Jesus was subtly making the point that no one can obey these commands. *Do this and you will live* sounds simple— in reality, however, those commands are impossible to keep in our human strength alone. This would be the lifestyle of kingdom people—but they would not have to "do" it in order to be saved. Instead, they would be saved and then enabled by the Holy Spirit to obey these impossible demands. Jesus would show this to the man in the following story.

10:29 But wanting to justify himself, he asked Jesus, "And who is my neighbor?"NRSV Jesus had answered the expert's question—in fact, the expert had answered it himself. But the expert in the law would not leave the encounter there. He wanted to *justify himself.* It is unclear if he wanted to justify the question he had asked by asking the teacher to delve deeper into the topic, or whether he wanted Jesus to give an answer that he could then say he had fulfilled. He may have been attempting to pin down and limit the law's demand, thereby limiting his responsibility. So he pressed Jesus further, *"And who is my neighbor?"*

10:30 Jesus replied, "A man was going down from Jerusalem to Jericho, and fell into the hands of robbers, who stripped him, beat him, and went away, leaving him half dead."NRSV Jesus answered this legal expert by telling a story. The rest of his listeners could easily picture this *man* (obviously Jewish, but that is not mentioned here) who *was going down from Jerusalem to Jericho.* The distance was about seventeen miles on a road that descended over three thousand feet (thus he was going "down"). This road was notoriously dangerous because it curved through rocky and desolate terrain with many hiding places for robbers. As the listeners may have anticipated, the man in this story, who was traveling alone, *fell into the hands of robbers.* These robbers did more than just take his money, however; they *stripped him, beat him, and went away, leaving him half dead.* This man would surely die if he received no help.

10:31-32 "A priest happened to be going down the same road, and when he saw the man, he passed by on the other side. So too, a Levite, when he came to the place and saw him, passed by on the other side."NIV Jesus told a story about three different people, also traveling alone on this road. This *priest* served in the temple and probably offered sacrifices. That he was also "going down" means that he was traveling away from Jerusalem, presumably having finished his duties. The same goes for the *Levite,* another person who served in the temple.

Priests and Levites had to have come from the tribe of Levi. Exodus 28–29 gives some details about priests. The priests not only had to be Levites, but they also had to be in the line of Aaron, Israel's first high priest (Exodus 28:1-3). Priests and Levites had different jobs in and around the temple. Priests were authorized to perform the sacrifices. Levites were set apart to help the priests. They did the work of elders, deacons, custodians, assistants, musicians, movers, and repairmen. Priests and Levites were supported by Israel's tithes

WHO IS MY NEIGHBOR?

In the Bible, faith in and love for God always overflow into a love for one's fellow human beings, especially fellow believers. When believers love one another, they exemplify to others the love that God has shown to them. (Verse portions are quoted from the NLT.)

Reference	Faith in God	Love for neighbor
John 13:34-35	"So now I am giving you a new command-ment: Love each other. Just as I have loved you, . . ."	" . . . you should love each other. Your love for one another will prove to the world that you are my disciples."
John 15:10, 12	"When you obey me, you remain in my love. . . ."	"I command you to love each other in the same way that I love you."
Colossians 1:4-5	"We have heard that you trust in Christ Jesus . . ."	" . . . and that you love all of God's people."
1 Thessalonians 1:3	"As we talk to our God and Father about you, we think of your faithful work, . . ."	" . . . your loving deeds."
Philemon 1:5	"I keep hearing of your trust in the Lord Jesus . . ."	" . . . and your love for all of God's people."
1 Peter 2:17	" . . . Fear God."	"Show respect for every-one. Love your Christian brothers and sisters."
1 John 4:11	"Dear friends, since God loved us that much . . ."	" . . . we surely ought to love each other."

and by revenues from certain cities that had been given to them. Worship in the temple could not have taken place without the combined efforts of the priests and Levites. The Old Testament law demanded good deeds and caring for those who were hurt. Jesus' story highlights the shortcomings of the priest and the Levite because they were especially required to provide care.

Perhaps it was concern over defilement, for a Jew would become "unclean" if he came into contact with a dead body. This would render him unable to worship. The man on the road may have appeared dead, so they did not want to risk defilement if there were nothing they could do. Some argue, however, that these men would not have been so concerned about defilement because they were going away from Jerusalem and had already fulfilled their duties. Whatever their reasons, these two respected men who aided the nation in its worship *saw the man* and then *passed by on the other side*. They deliberately refused to help.

GENEROSITY
In this story, the Samaritan was extremely generous, and Jesus highlighted his helpful actions. Generosity inspired by God does more than

- cook the meal; it lights the candles.
- say grace; it prays God's blessing on each one present.
- pass the food; it draws people into convivial conversation.
- clear the table; it washes the dishes.

Extend yourself. When you see a job to do, go overboard. Do it to show just an ounce of what God's care for you is like. Do it with all the joy God has put in your heart.

10:33-34 **"But a Samaritan, as he traveled, came where the man was; and when he saw him, he took pity on him. He went to him and bandaged his wounds, pouring on oil and wine. Then he put the man on his own donkey, took him to an inn and took care of him."**[NIV] The audience listening to this story would surely have expected that the priest or the Levite would come to the aid of the helpless man. But that was not the case. Yet Jesus was not engaging in a "religious-leader-bashing" piece of propaganda, because the next person to come along was not a poor, common Jew who reached out to help the man. Instead, it was a hated *Samaritan*. Again, the question as to why a Samaritan would even be on this road takes away from the point of Jesus' story. Jews and Samaritans hated each other deeply (see 9:52-53). The Jews saw themselves as pure descendants of Abraham, while they saw the Samaritans as half-breeds because they descended from Jews from the northern kingdom who had intermarried with other peoples after Israel's exile. Jews hated Samaritans, so when Jesus introduced this Samaritan man into the story, the Jewish listeners would not have expected him to help a Jewish man. Even more, Samaritans were the main ones who beat and robbed Jews when they traveled through Samaria. But in great detail, Jesus described all that the Samaritan did for this man. He *took pity, bandaged his wounds* (perhaps with strips of cloth from his own clothing), *put the man on his own donkey* (meaning that he had to walk), *took him to an inn and took care of him.* The wine would have been used as a disinfectant and the oil as a soothing lotion. Apparently this Samaritan understood what it meant to help someone in need, to be a neighbor, regardless of racial tensions.

10:35 **"The next day he handed the innkeeper two pieces of silver and told him to take care of the man. 'If his bill runs higher than that,' he said, 'I'll pay the difference the next time I am here.'"**^{NLT} The Samaritan looked after the wounded man through the night. *The next day* he had to be on his way, but the wounded man was still in poor shape. So the Samaritan *handed the innkeeper two pieces of silver.* Other translations say "two denarii" (about two days' wages for a laborer), which probably purchased a few weeks' lodging for the wounded man. Even beyond that, the Samaritan agreed to pay any expenses that might run beyond the two silver pieces. He wanted the wounded man to have no worries and to be looked after carefully.

10:36-37 **"Now which of these three would you say was a neighbor to the man who was attacked by bandits?" Jesus asked. The man replied, "The one who showed him mercy." Then Jesus said, "Yes, now go and do the same."**^{NLT} Having finished the story, Jesus questioned the expert in the law, asking him who had been a neighbor to the wounded man—in essence, forcing the legal expert to answer his own question, "Who is my neighbor?" (10:29). Which of *these three*—that is, the priest, the Levite, or the Samaritan—had kept the law? The priest and Levite were obliged by the law to help the victim, but the law also told them not to touch a dead body. Perhaps they chose religious purity over service to a man in desperate need. They loved themselves more than their neighbor; they loved keeping the letter of the law over loving a person in need. In so doing, they broke the law. The Samaritan, unhampered by concerns over religious purity, was free to serve and did so. The legal expert had no choice but to answer that the man who *was a neighbor* to the wounded man was *the one who showed him mercy*—the Samaritan. The Samaritan traveler and the Jewish man were far apart in distance and spiritual heritage, but the Samaritan had loved his neighbor far better than the hurt man's own religious leaders. Jesus said that the legal expert had answered correctly and should *go and do the same.* Jesus taught that love is shown by action, that it must not be limited by its object, and that at times it is costly.

JESUS VISITS MARY AND MARTHA / 10:38-42 / **133**

This short story follows the parable of the Good Samaritan because it involves another reversal. Mary was sitting at Jesus' feet listening to his teaching, while Martha was busying herself fixing a meal. Although intently listening to Jesus was Mary's

A COLLECTION OF ATTITUDES

Confronting the needs of others brings out various attitudes. Jesus used the story of the good but despised Samaritan to make clear what attitude was acceptable to him. If most people are honest, they often will find themselves in the place of the expert in the law, needing to learn again who their neighbor is. Note these different attitudes toward the wounded man.

To the expert in the law, the wounded man was a subject to discuss.
To the robbers, the wounded man was someone to use and exploit.
To the religious men, the wounded man was a problem to be avoided.
To the innkeeper, the wounded man was a customer to serve for a fee.
To the Samaritan, the wounded man was a human being worth caring for and loving.
To Jesus, all of them were worth dying for.

---

way of expressing her love and devotion to God, in the first century, this would be quite unusual for a woman. Learning at a rabbi's feet was a privilege typically reserved for young men. Thus, Martha assumed that Jesus would honor her request that he rebuke Mary. Instead, Jesus commended Mary, welcoming her to learn from him.

As with Mary, the decision is often between what is good and what is best. Fixing and serving a meal wasn't intrinsically wrong, but it wasn't the best, at that moment. Jesus was there. Spending some time quietly listening to his words could empower Mary to serve many other days, to many other guests. She chose what was best. You too must choose what is best. Setting aside a time every day to listen to God, by reading the Bible and praying, is a start.

10:38 **As Jesus and the disciples continued on their way to Jerusalem, they came to a village where a woman named Martha welcomed them into her home.**^{NLT} The exact time and location of this event are left unknown, although John 11:1 explains that the *village* where these people lived was Bethany, located about two miles outside of Jerusalem. *Martha* had a sister named Mary (10:39, who was probably younger because this home is described as belonging to Martha) and a brother named Lazarus (whom Jesus later raised from the dead, John 11).

10:39-40 **She had a sister called Mary, who sat at the Lord's feet listening to what he said. But Martha was distracted by all the preparations that had to be made. She came to him and asked, "Lord, don't you care that my sister has left me to do the work by myself? Tell her to help me!"**^{NIV} Along with Martha's welcome of Jesus into her home, *preparations had to be made.* Jesus did not come alone— he had twelve disciples with him who all needed to have their feet washed, to be made comfortable, and to have a meal prepared for them—all of these a respectable hostess in the ancient world would do for her guests. The impression here, however, is that Martha was overdoing it. She wanted something extra special for the Master, but she let herself get to the point where she was *distracted,* overworked, and unable to enjoy these guests. In attempting to serve Jesus, she did not understand or attend to Jesus' reason for being there. Mary, however, *sat at the Lord's feet listening to what he said.* She was taking advantage of the opportunity to hear Jesus. In ancient Jewish times, women were not allowed to learn. Jesus changed all that, so here a woman

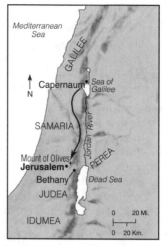

JESUS VISITS MARY AND MARTHA
After teaching throughout Galilee, Jesus returned to Jerusalem for the Feast of Tabernacles (John 7:2). He spoke in Jerusalem and then visited his friends Mary and Martha in the tiny village of Bethany on the slope of the Mount of Olives.

sits as a disciple would sit, at the feet of a rabbi. Mary wanted to learn all that she could while she had Jesus in their home.

WORKERS BEWARE
Hard workers beware. Note three potential problems:
   1. While asking for help (a legitimate request), you point to your own accomplishments (prideful).
   2. While calling Jesus "Lord" (certainly appropriate), you question his judgment with implied criticism that he is not directing his team effectively (suggesting you are a better chief than he).
   3. While acknowledging your relationship to another person (Martha referred to her sister), you criticize that person for failing to follow your lead (imposing your will as right and good just because it's productive).
   A better way:
   ▪ Never assume your own greatness.
   ▪ Support others in their special roles.
   ▪ Ask Jesus first; then get to work.

Martha, for her part, wanted to give her guests the royal treatment—and she should not be criticized for that. However, she allowed her concern and distraction to turn to irritation. She went to Jesus and asked him to tell Mary to get up and get to work. There is a touch of reproach in her words: *"Lord, don't you care?"* and *"Tell her to help me."*

10:41-42 And Jesus answered and said to her, "Martha, Martha, you are worried and troubled about many things. But one thing is needed, and Mary has chosen that good part, which will not be taken away from her."[NKJV] Jesus did not blame Martha for being concerned about preparing the meal, nor did he scold her for attempting to make him and his disciples welcome. But he did want her to understand that because she was *worried and troubled about many things,* she was not making time for what was most important—*that good part.* This "good part" is not defined, but it seems to be clearly shown in Mary's attitude. Jesus wanted Martha to rearrange her priorities. It is possible for service to Christ to degenerate into mere busywork that is no longer full of devotion to God. There was nothing wrong with Martha's desire to serve—after all, someone had to do it or no one would have eaten. Perhaps she could have laid out a less lavish feast so that she too could have had time to sit at Jesus' feet and digest his teaching. But Jesus was not going to send Mary away to attend to housework. She had chosen to be at Jesus' feet, and Jesus knew that he would not be on this earth forever. His time would be short, and he would not send away those who wanted to listen and learn.

SINGLE-MINDED
How quickly duties and demands rob us of our peace. Luke uses Mary and Martha's experience with Jesus to give us a timeless lesson in discipleship. Doing God's work in any of its phases of planning or implementation can distract us from reflecting on Jesus' teaching. Are you so busy working for him that you have no time to sit and listen at his feet? Jesus wants diligent service, but even more he desires that you relax, set aside worries and urgent responsibilities, and come to him in singleness of mind. Adjust your priorities. Take time to meditate on Jesus' life, his mercy, and his love.

LUKE 11

This passage highlights one of Luke's most prominent themes: prayer (see 1:9-10; 3:21; 6:12; 9:18, 28-29). Here the disciples asked Jesus about prayer—interestingly enough, it was after Jesus had been praying. Jesus gave them an example of a prayer and two stories that emphasize the importance of seeking God in prayer.

Jesus himself sought communion with God through prayer while on this earth; his followers were to do likewise. For those who ask, seek, and knock, God is more than willing to answer—even more willing than friends or an earthly father. But the believers' requests should be in line with Jesus' model prayer, asking for God's will to be done (11:2), necessities (11:3), forgiveness (11:4), and protection from all sorts of temptations (11:4). Set aside time each day to pray to your heavenly Father.

11:1 Once when Jesus had been out praying, one of his disciples came to him as he finished and said, "Lord, teach us to pray, just as John taught his disciples."^{NLT} Once again, Jesus had *been out praying.* Luke has presented several instances where Jesus was praying, making it clear that prayer was a regular part of his life (3:21; 5:16; 6:12; 9:18, 28-29; 18:1; 22:41, 44). Something about Jesus' prayer life prompted *one of his disciples* to approach him *as he finished.* This disciple wanted Jesus to teach them to pray, *just as John taught his disciples.* It was common for religious leaders to teach their followers how to pray. Being taught how to pray meant that the followers had a certain solidarity with their teacher and that their prayers were expressing the teacher's basic teachings. The disciples had been learning from and experiencing so much with Jesus. To be able to pray as their Master prayed would give them assurance of expressing themselves cor-

> When thou prayest, rather let thy heart be without words than thy words without heart.
>
> *John Bunyan*

rectly to God. The following verses focus on three aspects of prayer: its content (11:2-4), believers' persistence (11:5-10), and God's faithfulness (11:11-13).

LEARN TO PRAY
Prayer life seems easy enough. Find a quiet place and talk to God. It's like breathing; you just do it!

But even Jesus' disciples asked to be taught—suggesting a knowledge level they did not have, but wanted.

When was your last lesson in prayer?

Several organizations help churches organize and understand prayer. Locate, contact, and begin a movement in your church or small group to pray with greater effectiveness.

11:2 **So He said to them, "When you pray, say: Our Father in heaven, hallowed be Your name."**[NKJV] The prayer Jesus taught his disciples was not a formula prayer; rather, it was a "how to" prayer. These were not meant to be magical words prayed like an incantation over and over. Instead, he was giving the disciples a pattern. Luke's form of the Lord's Prayer is shorter than Matthew's (Matthew 6:9-13). Matthew has two extra petitions that Luke doesn't mention. Many scholars believe Matthew's version was older and therefore perhaps the original teaching, which Luke shortened. More likely they were two distinct prayers on two different occasions. Matthew's prayer was taught to a general audience in connection with the Sermon on the Mount. Luke's prayer was Jesus' response to the disciples' request for instruction. The differences in the prayers show that Jesus did not utter a rote prayer every time he prayed. Different occasions call for different utterances.

Notice the order in this prayer. First Jesus praised God; then he made his requests. The first-person plural pronouns indicate that the believers could pray this prayer corporately. The pattern of praise, intercession, and request helps believers understand the nature and purpose of their personal prayers in their relationship with their Father. Because Jesus taught it to his followers, it is a prayer pattern for believers today as well.

The phrase "Our Father in heaven" focuses on God as majestic and transcendent yet also personal and loving. His children desire to see his name *hallowed*. This refers to a commitment to honor God's holy name. Christians, God's children who bear his name, must be responsible to "hallow" God in every aspect of their lives. When believers pray for God's name to be "hallowed," they pray that the world will honor his name and look forward to the day when that will be a reality.

"Your kingdom come."^{NKJV} This "kingdom" refers to God's spiritual reign. God had announced his kingdom in the covenant with Abraham (see 13:28) and through the prophets (Isaiah 24:23; Zephaniah 3:15; Zechariah 14:9). Pious Jews were waiting for the day of the Lord to come (Psalm 96:13; Isaiah 13:9-10; Micah 1:3; Malachi 4:5). Jesus' followers recognize that the kingdom began with his arrival on earth. The kingdom is present in believers' hearts: "The kingdom of God is within you" (17:21 NIV). To say, "Your kingdom come," is to pray that more and more people will enter the kingdom; it is also a petition for all evil to be destroyed and for God to establish a new heaven and earth, thereby revealing his glory to all nations.

The phrase "your will be done on earth as it is in heaven" still appears here in Luke in the NKJV but is not in the earliest and best manuscripts. It was included in later manuscripts to match Matthew's version of this prayer.

11:3 "Give us each day our daily bread."^{NRSV} This is a request for a personal need to be met. "Bread" refers to food in general although it also could refer to spiritual "food." The word "daily" reveals that God's provision is daily and that believers do not need to worry from one day to the next. Christians cannot "store it up" and then cut off communication with God. And they dare not be self-satisfied. Instead, believers should live in a state of continual dependence on God. The Greek word translated "daily" is *epiousios,* an unusual word that occurs only in this prayer in its two places in the New Testament (see also Matthew 6:11). There have been three ways of translating it: (1) "necessary for existence," (2) "for this day," and (3) "for the following day." The word speaks of either what is necessary for existence or what supplies our day-to-day need. The meaning could be that just as God provided manna daily for the Israelites in the wilderness (Exodus 16:15-26), so God will meet his people's needs. It could also mean that God will provide what is necessary or sufficient but not necessarily above and beyond (although at times he may choose to do that). The request is that God will provide what is needed.

11:4 "Forgive us our sins, for we also forgive everyone who sins against us."^{NIV} As God's people need daily provision, they also need daily forgiveness. When Jesus taught his disciples to pray, he made forgiveness the cornerstone of their relationship with God. God has forgiven believers' sins; they must now forgive those who have wronged them. To remain unforgiving shows that the person has not understood that he or she deeply needs to be forgiven. The meaning of this sentence focuses on the true repen-

tance of a believer who understands the greatness of the forgiveness that he or she has received. This believer willingly extends
such forgiveness to others for their wrongs. To refuse to forgive
others can impede the forgiveness needed daily from God (see
6:37; Matthew 6:14-15; 18:23-35; Mark 11:25).

SHEDDING GRUDGES
Forgiving those who sin against you is very tough to do. Frank
has framed you, Sue has sacked you, and Chad has cheated
you. OK, Lou has lied to you too. Forgiving these people is
difficult. Yet Christ calls you to do it. Here's how you can start to
be more forgiving:
- Imagine how poorly you rate in view of God's holy standards. To forgive you, God must genuinely love you.
- Remember how disagreeable the people are who hate and
  hold grudges forever. You shun people like that. Don't
  become one.
- Recall that God, in charge of your life, can and will provide
  for your needs. To be cheated hurts; God will repair. To be
  lied to hurts; God will clean the wound with truth.
Now are you ready to forgive?

"And lead us not into temptation."[NIV] God doesn't *lead us . . .
into temptation,* for he does not tempt people to do evil (James
1:13). The Greek word translated "temptation" *(peirasmos)*
means "enticement" or "test" or "trial." In this context, it is a
request for spiritual protection from trials and temptations. There
are some interesting parallels between this prayer and Jesus'
prayer in the Garden of Gethsemane (22:39-46; Matthew 26:36-
46). The Lord's Prayer affirms the will of God ("your will be
done"), then asks for relief and delivery from trials. In the garden, Jesus asked the Father to remove the cup of trial while immediately declaring his willingness to cooperate with his Father's
will. Soon after, when Jesus discovered the disciples asleep, he
encouraged them to pray not to fall into temptation. Jesus knew,
however, that they would indeed fall and fail within moments.

This sentence in the Lord's Prayer is a reminder of the
importance of testing, even though believers seldom *desire* it.
Jesus, fully knowing that the Father will do what is best, both
taught and modeled a freedom in prayer that dared to ask
almost anything.

**11:5-6 And he said to them, "Suppose one of you has a friend, and
you go to him at midnight and say to him, 'Friend, lend me
three loaves of bread; for a friend of mine has arrived, and I
have nothing to set before him.'"**[NRSV] This parable points out,

with a touch of humor, that God's people must persist in their prayers and that God is always ready to give. It encourages believers to pray with confidence. Even friends will help us at inconvenience to themselves if the one asking is persistent. How much more will God, who loves his people, come to their aid when they persist in their prayers to him?

The setting is *midnight* in a small town in Palestine. A journeying friend *has arrived,* presumably unexpected. Social custom dictates that you provide food for that friend, but you and your family have eaten all the bread and you *have nothing to set before him.* Jewish customs of hospitality required that a guest be cared for lavishly and generously. You know that another friend in town has some bread (perhaps you know that he always has plenty, or did extra baking that day), so you go to him, knock on his door, and ask him to *lend* you *three loaves of bread.* These would be the small loaves; thus this would be enough for your guest.

11:7-8 **"And he answers from within, 'Do not bother me; the door has already been locked, and my children are with me in bed; I cannot get up and give you anything.' I tell you, even though he will not get up and give him anything because he is his friend, at least because of his persistence he will get up and give him whatever he needs."**NRSV The friend would not be happy to be interrupted at this late hour, having already gone to bed. These words depict a humble home, probably with only one room, in which the entire family slept on an elevated platform at one end. Sometimes the animals would sleep inside on the floor level. With his door locked, and his children with him in bed, the man was definitely settled for the night. To have to get up and get bread would mean disturbing the children, and probably the animals too. He would probably have to find a lamp and light it, so this would indeed be a genuine undertaking for him to get up and help out.

Jesus explained that although the friend might not get up for the sake of the friendship, he *will* do so because of the urgent request. *Because of [the] persistence* of the person who needs to feed the visiting friend, the man already in bed *will get up and give him whatever he needs.* Jewish laws of hospitality made two demands: (1) The man with a visitor must provide generously to his newly arrived guest. (2) The friend must help his neighbor with his request for bread. The Greek word for "persistence" occurs only

> God is perfect love and perfect wisdom. We do not pray in order to change His Will, but to bring our wills into harmony with His.
> *William Temple*

here in the New Testament—*anaideia;* it means both shameless-
ness and boldness. So it was nerve or audacity that required that
hospitality be met at midnight. There is some question as to whose
persistence Jesus was identifying—the knocker or the sleeper.
Because the focus was on the disciples and on persistence in
prayer, the interpretation should be that the boldness of the knocker
was in view here.

Boldness in prayer overcomes the praying person's apathy, not
God's perceived insensitivity. To practice persistence changes the
hearts and minds of those praying, and it helps them understand
and express the intensity of their need. Persistence in prayer
helps them recognize God's work. By praying persistently, believers are not trying to get a reluctant God to answer their prayers;
instead, they are showing that they are very serious about their
request.

11:9-10 **"So I say to you, ask, and it will be given to you; seek, and
you will find; knock, and it will be opened to you."**NKJV Highlighting the importance of persistent and consistent prayer, Jesus
encouraged his disciples, who wanted to be taught to pray (11:1),
to keep on asking, keep on seeking, and keep on knocking. Only
through prayer can believers stay in contact with God, know
what he wants them to do, and then have the strength to do God's
will in all areas of life. God will answer believers who persistently ask, seek, and knock. The verbs picture a faith that is willing to *ask* for something that only God can provide; to *seek*
something that has been lost or whose location is not known; and
to *knock* on a closed door in order to gain admittance. In all these
cases, God is accessible and willing to respond. Jesus promised,
**"For everyone who asks receives, and everyone who searches
finds, and for everyone who knocks, the door will be
opened."**NRSV God had told the prophet Jeremiah, "You will seek
me and find me when you seek me with all your heart" (Jeremiah
29:13 NIV). The three words (ask, seek, knock) combine to
emphasize the truth that those who bring their needs to God can
trust that they will be satisfied. All three actions are metaphors
for praying. Sometimes God does not answer Christians' prayers
immediately; sometimes they must keep on knocking, awaiting
God's answer. However, if we continue to trust God through
prayer, Jesus promised that we will receive, find, and have an
open door.

Believers must not take Jesus' words as a blank check, however; prayer is not a magical way to obtain whatever we want.
Requests must be in harmony with God's will, accepting his will
above our desires.

SEIZE THE DAY
Jesus encouraged us to be persistent in prayer. Prayer promotes a dynamic that separates passive sideliners from active participants. Prayer never makes the believer
- lethargic, unable to act
- dull, unable to feel
- indifferent, unable to dream
- cold, unable to love

Instead, prayer always makes the believer
- eager to grasp life, to seize the day
- ready to face the challenges
- courageous to expand his or her dreams
- passionate to share God's love

God does not ask you to pray so that you can blame him when life fails, but so that you will praise him when life opens to your knock.

11:11-13 **"Which of you fathers, if your son asks for a fish, will give him a snake instead? Or if he asks for an egg, will give him a scorpion? If you then, though you are evil, know how to give good gifts to your children, how much more will your Father in heaven give the Holy Spirit to those who ask him!"**[NIV] In Greek, both questions begin with a prefix *(e)* meaning, "or to put it another way." Jesus explained that his followers can depend on God to answer their prayers by arguing "from the lesser to the greater." In other words, if human beings who *are evil* would not think of giving a child a *snake* instead of a *fish,* or a *scorpion* instead of an *egg,* then how much more will a holy God acknowledge and answer Christians' requests? The snake was probably a water snake used as bait in fishing. When a scorpion rolls itself up, it would resemble an egg. A father who would do this would be playing a sadistic joke on his children. The phrase "you then, though you are evil" refers to what a cruel or uncaring parent would do. Even such parents can give good gifts.

In these words, Jesus revealed the heart of God the Father. God is not selfish, begrudging, or stingy; his followers don't have to beg or grovel when they come with their requests. He is a loving Father who understands, cares, comforts, and willingly gives *the Holy Spirit to those who ask him.* Because the Holy Spirit is God's highest gift and he will not refuse giving him to those who ask, believers can trust in God's provision for all their lesser needs as well. How much better the perfect heavenly Father treats his children! The most important gift he could ever give is the Holy Spirit (Acts 2:1-4), whom he promised to give all believers after his death, resurrection, and return to heaven (John 15:26).

JESUS ANSWERS HOSTILE ACCUSATIONS / 11:14-28 / **135**

While Mark's Gospel emphasizes the demonstration of Jesus' *power* in the miracles, Luke's emphasizes the various reactions to Jesus' miracles (7:29-30). In this passage, Luke underscores two different negative reactions: (1) those who reject Jesus, accusing him of being associated with the devil, and (2) those who sit on the fence, waiting for yet another sign.

Jesus confronted those who rejected him, by clearly asserting that his miracles were evidence of his connection to God. There is no middle ground, no room to withhold judgment. A person is either against him or for him. When an all-out battle is being waged, no one can stand in the middle of two armies, trying to mediate between the two. The same is true of spiritual warfare. A battle is being fought between God and Satan, between good and evil. You can't afford to *not* take sides. Jesus clearly says, "He who is not with me is against me" (11:23 NIV).

11:14-15 **Jesus was driving out a demon that was mute. When the demon left, the man who had been mute spoke, and the crowd was amazed. But some of them said, "By Beelzebub, the prince of demons, he is driving out demons."**NIV On another occasion, *Jesus was driving out a demon.* This was not an unusual or isolated event—Jesus and his disciples had already driven out many demons from people (see 4:35, 41; 8:2, 33; 9:1, 42; 10:17). In this instance, a demon had made a man unable to speak. Jesus drove out this *demon that was mute,* thus enabling the man to speak. As usually happened after these miraculous cures, *the crowd was amazed.* However, the text reveals that not everyone was overly awed by Jesus; in fact, *some* in the crowd were actively seeking to discredit him. They told the crowd that *by Beelzebub, the prince of demons, he is driving out demons.* A similar and possibly separate event is reported in Matthew 12:22-45 and Mark 3:20-30. The event described by Luke happened in Judea, while the other took place in Galilee. According to Luke, Jesus' accusers came from the crowds; Matthew and Mark pinpointed the Pharisees. In this situation these detractors may also have been religious leaders.

However, the accusation is an odd one for these people to make. The word "Beelzebub" occurs only in these parallel accounts in the Gospels and not in other Jewish literature. In Greek, the term is *beelzeboul.* The Vulgate and Syriac versions tried to clarify the term by changing it to *beelzebub,* the god of Ekron (see 2 Kings 1:2-3, 6, 16). The religious authorities may have invented the term by combining two Hebrew words: *ba'al* ("lord," Hosea 2:16) stood for the local Canaanite fertility god; and *zebul* ("exalted dwelling," 1 Kings 8:13). Most Jews would have understood this term as referring to Satan, the *prince* (or leader) *of demons.*

There are two common interpretations of these verses. (1) Some of the Pharisees and their followers drove out demons. Therefore, to accuse Jesus of being empowered by Beelzebub, the prince of demons (or Satan himself), because Jesus was driving out demons was also to say that the religious leaders were also doing Satan's work. (2) Another possibility is that the religious leaders were not driving out demons, and even if they tried, they did not succeed. Because Jesus was succeeding where they had failed, he must be doing so with the power of Satan himself. Jesus exposed the absurdity of this accusation.

11:16 Trying to test Jesus, others asked for a miraculous sign from heaven to see if he was from God.[NLT] Some wanted to make accusations, but others wanted *to test Jesus.* As if all the healings and miracles and sending demons from people were not enough, they *asked for a miraculous sign from heaven to see if he was from God.* If they thought that the exorcism just witnessed might be by the power of Satan, then they felt that they needed something "from heaven" as proof of Jesus' identity. The irony, of course, is that no matter what kind of sign Jesus might have given, they would have stubbornly refused to believe (see Matthew 12:38-42).

11:17-18 Jesus knew their thoughts and said to them: "Any kingdom divided against itself will be ruined, and a house divided against itself will fall. If Satan is divided against himself, how can his kingdom stand? I say this because you claim that I drive out demons by Beelzebub."[NIV] Jesus' first response was to the accusation recorded in 11:15. Apparently the accusation had not been said directly to him but had been whispered about in the crowd. However, Jesus *knew their thoughts,* so he answered the question they did not verbally ask. He explained that *any kingdom divided against itself will be ruined,* and likewise with *a house divided against itself.* If Jesus were driving out demons by Satan, then the conclusion would be that *Satan is divided against himself.* If that were true, it would mean civil war in the kingdom of evil. No king would throw his own soldiers out of his kingdom; neither would Satan throw his soldiers out of a person they had possessed. Such a kingdom could not stand. Because the people claimed that Jesus was driving *out demons by Beelzebub,* Jesus explained that it would be impossible for Satan to cast himself (or his demons) out of a person. Satan was not opposing himself, nor was he divided.

11:19-20 **"Now if I drive out demons by Beelzebub, by whom do your followers drive them out? So then, they will be your judges. But if I drive out demons by the finger of God, then the kingdom of God has come to you."**NIV Jesus was not the first person to exorcise demons. In the first century, exorcism was thriving as a business in both Jewish and pagan societies (Mark 9:38; Acts 19:13-14). Many Jewish exorcists were Pharisees. *"Now,"* says Jesus, *"if I drive out demons by Beelzebub, by whom do your followers drive them out?"* If it took Satan's power to drive out demons, then those Pharisees who drove out demons were also working under Satan's power. Those Pharisees who had performed exorcisms would act as *judges* regarding this allegation. Those accusers should go to those Pharisees and find out if they were working for Satan.

But if it isn't by Satan's power that demons were fleeing, then it had to be by the power of God. Jesus said, *"But if I drive out demons by the finger of God"* (the word "if" means "since"); then the obvious conclusion is that *the kingdom of God has come.* "Finger of God" refers to Exodus 8:19, a reference to when Egyptian magicians ascribed Moses' delivering the plagues as "the finger of God." It was a time of God's dynamic action to deliver the people of God from slavery in Egypt. Jesus' exorcisms were specific evidence of the presence of kingdom power. They showed that the hoped-for time of God's kingdom had come in the power of Jesus' authority. That Jesus was powerfully casting out demons and plundering Satan's kingdom revealed that the kingdom of God had begun.

11:21-22 **"When a strong man, fully armed, guards his own house, his possessions are safe. But when someone stronger attacks and overpowers him, he takes away the armor in which the man trusted and divides up the spoils."**NIV Jesus explained his words in 11:19-20 with a parable. Here Satan is *a strong man* who is *fully armed* with all kinds of demons, guarding *his own house.* As in Mark 3:27, this is the theme verse for Jesus' exorcism and the basis for the concept of the binding of Satan. What he possesses seems safe enough because few worldly powers can overtake him. This whole scene changes, however, *when someone stronger attacks and overpowers him,* as Jesus had just done in sending the demon out of the man (11:14, and had done many times previously). Satan cannot stand against God or against Christ. Jesus overpowers Satan. The fact that he *takes away the armor . . . and divides up the spoils* simply pictures a vanquished enemy (Isaiah

53:12). "Divides up the spoils" could refer to the claim Satan had on souls of people. Because he is a defeated enemy, Jesus' disciples will be able to reclaim them. The kingdom of God overthrows evil. Jesus may have been referring to Isaiah 49:24-26. Regardless of Satan's power, Jesus is stronger. He will bind Satan and dispose of him for eternity (see Revelation 20:2, 10).

11:23 **"Whoever is not with me is against me, and whoever does not gather with me scatters."**^{NRSV} The line has been drawn. There are two kingdoms—God's and Satan's. Satan is active and powerful in the world, but God's kingdom is far stronger and will eventually triumph. People cannot be neutral in this matter. Either they choose to side with God, or they do not. Those who choose not to side with God or simply attempt to remain neutral side with Satan. That is the meaning of Jesus' ominous words: *"Whoever is not with me is against me."*

The image of *"whoever does not gather with me scatters"* probably comes from Ezekiel 34:13: "I will bring them out from the nations and gather them from the countries, and I will bring them into their own land. I will pasture them on the mountains of Israel, in the ravines and in all the settlements in the land" (NIV). Ezekiel prophesied that the nation had been scattered because of their sins, but one day the true shepherd (the Messiah) would come. He would care for them and set up a kingdom of peace and justice (Ezekiel 34:22-31). In the final kingdom, God will gather his scattered flock. Jesus wants his followers to join in the task of "gathering." To not do so is again to be left with no middle ground—those who refuse to gather will be participating in the "scattering" and will be judged just as Israel's unfaithful leaders had been judged.

CROSSING THE LINE
In the movie *Hook,* a revived Peter Pan draws a line in the sand. Everyone who believes must cross. In the story of the Texas Alamo, Colonel Bowie does the same, asking defenders to commit to dawn's battle.

In neither case is it possible to stand on the line. If you're considering Jesus, weighing the options, exploring the possibilities—take the step, cross the line, trust God today. Your unanswered questions are still important. Seek and you shall find. Your doubts are still to be settled. Knock and the door of knowledge will open. Your unmet needs are vital. Ask and it will be given.

How does this verse relate to 9:50: "Whoever is not against you is for you"? In the earlier passage, Jesus was talking about a person who was driving out demons in his name. Those who fight evil, he was saying, are on the same side as one driving out demons in Jesus' name. Here, by contrast, he was talking about the conflict between God and the devil. In this battle, if a person is not on God's side, he or she is on Satan's. There is no neutral ground. Because God has already won the battle, why be on the losing side? If you aren't actively for Christ, you are against him.

11:24 **"When the unclean spirit has gone out of a person, it wanders through waterless regions looking for a resting place, but not finding any, it says, 'I will return to my house from which I came.'"**^{NRSV} To further illustrate the danger of attempting to be neutral about him, Jesus explained what can happen to such people. Unfilled and complacent people are easy targets for Satan. *The unclean spirit* was not "cast out" but for some reason had *gone out of a person.* The *waterless regions* (the desert) were believed to be the habitation of demons. Because demons need *a resting place* (that is, someone or something living that they can enter and torment), this demon returned to its former *house* when it could find nothing more suitable than the house it left. Jesus was making a serious point about people's spiritual destiny—they must make a decision about him.

11:25-26 **"When it comes, it finds it swept and put in order. Then it goes and brings seven other spirits more evil than itself, and they enter and live there; and the last state of that person is worse than the first."**^{NRSV} In the demon's absence, the "house" had been *swept and put in order,* but it is still empty. In fact, the accommodations are now so nice that the demon *goes and brings seven other spirits more evil than itself, and they enter and live there.* The "owner" of the "house" is now filled with eight demons instead of one; definitely, *that person is worse* off than before.

When the demon left, this person may have felt that he or she had conquered a problem or habit or had some sort of spiritual awakening. The attempt to clean up one's life without any sort of dependence on God, the Creator, is to invite disaster. Jesus was illustrating an unfortunate human tendency—personal desire to reform often does not last long, and attempts to take care of life end in disaster. It is not enough to be emptied of evil; the person must then be filled with the power of the Holy Spirit to accomplish God's new purpose in his or her life (see also Matthew 12:43-45; Galatians 5:22).

11:27-28 **As Jesus was saying these things, a woman in the crowd called out, "Blessed is the mother who gave you birth and nursed you." He replied, "Blessed rather are those who**

hear the word of God and obey it."ᴺᴵⱽ Jesus was speaking to people who highly valued family ties. Their genealogies guaranteed that they were part of God's chosen people. A man's value came from his ancestors, and a woman's value came from the sons she bore. Jesus' response to the woman meant that a person's obedience to God is more important than his or her place on the family tree (see 8:21). The patient work of consistent obedience is even more important than the honor of bearing a respected son. For more on the importance of hearing and doing, see 6:47; 8:15; James 1:22.

JESUS WARNS AGAINST UNBELIEF / 11:29-32 / 136

After admonishing his listeners to follow him (11:23), Jesus clearly described the consequences of not believing him. The request for a sign revealed wicked unbelief.

In his characteristic style, Luke once again highlighted the sayings of Jesus that contrasted the unbelief of the Jews with the faith of the Gentiles (another example of Luke's *reversals,* compare 4:24-27; 10:13-15). Jesus commended the pagan Queen of Sheba and the Gentile people of Nineveh for listening to God's messengers—Solomon and Jonah—while at the same time exhorting his Jewish listeners to follow their example and listen to him. By flatly refusing to give yet another sign, Jesus was stressing the importance of his message. It was more important than his miraculous signs, which only pointed to the truth of his message. That message is clearly laid out in the Bible. Just as Jesus confronted those who asked for a sign on that warm day in Galilee, every time you open Scripture, be ready to be confronted by Jesus' teaching. Let his words pierce your heart and soul, so that they can transform your life.

11:29-30 **As the crowds increased, Jesus said, "This is a wicked generation. It asks for a miraculous sign, but none will be given it except the sign of Jonah. For as Jonah was a sign to the Ninevites, so also will the Son of Man be to this generation."**ᴺᴵⱽ Here Jesus was responding to the request made in 11:16. The people had asked Jesus for a sign from heaven to prove that he was from God. Instead of giving a sign (beyond the miracles and healings he had performed), Jesus explained that no *miraculous sign* would be given *except the sign of Jonah.* God had asked Jonah to preach repentance to the Gentiles (non-Jews)—he had been sent by God to the Assyrian city of Nineveh (see the book of Jonah). Jonah preached to the city and saw it repent. With the words "as Jonah was a sign to the Ninevites, so also will the Son of Man be to this generation," Jesus was affirming Jonah's message. Salvation is not only for Jews but also for all people.

There are two possible meanings for "Jonah as a sign":

1. This may refer to a sign of judgment. God will not grant the sign the people asked for but will only point to their rejection of the message. In Jonah's day, Nineveh was capital of the Assyrian Empire, and it was as powerful as it was evil (Jonah 1:2). The wicked city repented at Jonah's preaching; by contrast, when Jesus came to his people, the Jews, they refused to accept him even though they had been looking for and expecting him.

2. The "sign" granted to them may refer to the Resurrection. Jesus' resurrection would prove that he was the Messiah. Three days after his death Jesus would come back to life, just as Jonah had been "brought back" to life after spending three days in the fish. Both had been delivered from death. Jonah's presence was a sign to the people of Nineveh; they repented at his teaching. Jesus' return to his people after his death would also be a sign to the people of his generation. Some would repent; many would not. This is the preferable meaning of the Son of Man being a sign to his generation.

THEY SEARCHED AND FOUND
The Ninevites and the Queen of the South had turned to God with far less evidence than Jesus was giving his listeners—and far less than people have today, with eyewitness reports of the risen Jesus, the continuing power of the Holy Spirit unleashed at Pentecost, easy access to the Bible, and knowledge of two thousand years of Christ's acts through his church. With all this available knowledge and insight, people today ought to respond completely and wholeheartedly to Christ. Jesus stands alone in his ultimate authority. Give him his proper place. Listen and respond to him.

11:31 **"The queen of the South will rise at the judgment with the people of this generation and condemn them, because she came from the ends of the earth to listen to the wisdom of Solomon, and see, something greater than Solomon is here!"**[NRSV] *The queen of the South* (also called the Queen of Sheba) had traveled from southern Arabia *(the ends of the earth)* to *listen to the wisdom of Solomon,* king of Israel (1 Kings 10:1-10). *Something greater than Solomon* was there with the people—the Messiah himself—but they refused to believe. As a result, this queen *will rise at the judgment . . . and condemn* the people of Jesus' generation because she, an unbelieving Gentile, had recognized true wisdom when it was presented to her, unlike Jesus' audience, who refused the truth and wanted signs instead. In fact, she had said to Solomon, "Praise be to the LORD your God, who has delighted in you and placed you on the throne of Israel. Because of the LORD's eternal love for Israel, he has made you king, to maintain justice and righteousness" (1 Kings 10:9 NIV).

11:32 "The people of Nineveh will rise up at the judgment with this generation and condemn it, because they repented at the proclamation of Jonah, and see, something greater than Jonah is here!"NRSV The cruel, warlike men of *Nineveh,* capital of Assyria, *repented at the proclamation of Jonah*—even though Jonah did not care about them. The pagan Queen of the South (Sheba) had praised the God of Israel when she had heard Solomon's wisdom, although Solomon was full of faults. By contrast, Jesus, the perfect Son of God, *something greater than Jonah,* had come to people whom he loved dearly—but they were rejecting him. Thus God's chosen people were making themselves more liable to judgment than either a notoriously wicked nation or a powerful pagan queen. And, like the Queen of the South (11:31), *the people of Nineveh will rise up at the judgment . . . and condemn* Jesus' generation. Compare this with 10:12-15, Jesus' statement that the evil cities of Sodom, Tyre, and Sidon would be judged less harshly than the cities in Judea and Galilee that had rejected Jesus' message.

JESUS TEACHES ABOUT THE LIGHT WITHIN / 11:33-36 / 137

After condemning the crowds in general as a "wicked generation," Jesus next exhorted each person to focus his or her eyes on the light: Jesus himself. The people had requested a sign (11:16, 29), but Jesus explained that the light of his perfect life should be enough of a sign. All who would focus their eyes on him and his teaching would be transformed by absorbing and reflecting the perfect light of God's truth. Jesus' command to "see to it, then, that the light within you is not darkness" (11:35 NIV) is also for you. Examine yourself, let the light of God's Word expose the inner darkness of your heart and transform you, so that you can live for him.

11:33 "No one lights a lamp and then hides it or puts it under a basket. Instead, it is put on a lampstand to give light to all who enter the room."NLT These words are very close to 8:16; however, in 8:16 the "lamp" that had been lit refers to the person who hears Jesus' message, responds to it, and spreads it to others. In this teaching situation, it seems that Jesus was describing his own ministry and message as lighting *a lamp* that was not hidden or put *under a basket,* but was done in public with a message available for all to accept. "All" refers to Jesus' mission to reach all the world, not just the Jews.

11:34 **"Your eye is the lamp of your body. When your eyes are good, your whole body also is full of light. But when they are bad, your body also is full of darkness."**[NIV] The "lamp" is Christ's message, and "light" is the truth of his revelation and guidance (11:33); the "eye" represents spiritual understanding and insight that are filtered through the "good" or the "bad" in a person. When eyes are *good,* that is, when they are operating properly, the illumination makes it easy for the body to function. Those with "good eyes" are those true disciples who listen and respond to Jesus' guidance. By contrast, when eyes are *bad,* that is, when they are not operating properly, the result is impaired functioning for the rest of the body. Those with "bad eyes" are those who reject Jesus' words; all they have is the darkness and futility of their own evil ways.

11:35-36 **"See to it, then, that the light within you is not darkness. Therefore, if your whole body is full of light, and no part of it dark, it will be completely lighted, as when the light of a lamp shines on you."**[NIV] To have the *light* that is *within* a person actually be *darkness* would be a sad state. That would mean that no goodness would be left, for even what might have been light would actually be dark—what good should have been there would actually be evil. But with Jesus, and with the infilling of the Holy Spirit, a person can have a *whole body . . . full of light, and no part of it dark.* This cannot happen from within—for the light does not originate there. It has an outside source, *as when the light of a lamp shines on you.*

SWITCHING ON THE LIGHT
Jesus is the light and we need his guidance. If your life seems pointless and without direction, empty and without love, boring and without purpose, common and without creativity, dull and without challenge, or transient and without hope . . .

Then switch on the light, God's Word. It will direct you toward a wonderful goal, it is full of love for you, it suggests lots of important work to challenge your gifts and talents, and it points to eternal life—God's generous promise to you.

JESUS CRITICIZES THE RELIGIOUS LEADERS / 11:37-54 / **138**

Placed after Jesus' teaching about the inner light is an example of those caught in darkness: the Pharisees and the scribes. These religious leaders had meticulously cleaned the outside of the "cup" but had not bothered to look at the filthiness of their souls. Jesus' words revolve around the central commandments of the law: to love God and one's neighbor (10:27), here described as "justice and the love of God" (11:42).

Jesus exposed the false religiosity of the Pharisees by pointing to their preoccupation with the external aspects of the law (tithing garden herbs), while they failed to give justice and mercy to the poor (11:42, 46). Jesus issues the same warning to all Christians, to all who consider themselves religious: Stop majoring on the minors! Evaluate your life according to the majors: Do you love God by listening to him and obeying what he says? Do you love your neighbor by pursuing justice in your community and showing compassion to those in need? Honest evaluation of your life in the searchlight of these two simple questions will reveal the inconsistencies—the petty envy, greed, and pride—that darken almost everyone's soul. A renewed commitment to live every moment of your life in light of these two principles will make you a shining light to others, a beacon of hope in the dark night of despair (11:33-36).

11:37-38 When Jesus had finished speaking, a Pharisee invited him to eat with him; so he went in and reclined at the table. But the Pharisee, noticing that Jesus did not first wash before the meal, was surprised.[NIV] Again Jesus was invited *to eat* with a Pharisee (see also 7:36). Again he is pictured as reclining at the table, a typical way of eating, as explained in the commentary at 7:36. Jesus offended his host, however, because he *did not first wash before the meal.* This washing was done not for health reasons but as a symbol of washing away any contamination from touching anything unclean. Not only did the Pharisees make a public show of their washing, but they also commanded everyone else to follow a practice originally intended only for the priests. This Pharisee *was surprised* that Jesus, a rabbi, would not follow the practice of ceremonial washing.

11:39-40 Then the Lord said to him, "Now you Pharisees clean the outside of the cup and of the dish, but inside you are full of greed and wickedness. You fools! Did not the one who made the outside make the inside also?"[NRSV] Luke didn't record that the Pharisee said anything to Jesus, but Jesus noted his surprise. Obsessed about ceremonial "purity," the Pharisees neglected their own internal defilement. They washed on the *outside,* like one would wash a *cup* or a *dish,* but they left the inside *full of greed and wickedness,* never bothering to deal with those sins. They were no more pure than a dirty cup. Jesus condemned the Pharisees and religious leaders for outwardly appearing saintly and holy but inwardly remaining full of corruption. Jesus accordingly castigated these Pharisees as *fools. The one* (referring to God) *who made the outside* of each person also made *the inside.* In other words, God is just as concerned with the inside as with the outside. He is concerned not only about what you do but also about who you are.

MASKS
Of the many masks used to hide hurt feelings, the mask of religion may be the most insidious. It projects an image of squeaky clean but hides an interior as rotten as maggots in a garbage can.
  Here Jesus invited a masked person to drop the pretense and confront the issue. The same invitation is for you.
  Admit your need and ask God to build you from the inside out. Masks are unnecessary. The real you, shaped and fashioned by God, is all the face you need.

11:41 **"But give what is inside the dish to the poor, and everything will be clean for you."**[NIV] The Pharisees loved to think of themselves as "clean," but their stinginess toward God and the poor proved that they were not as clean as they thought. This was reflected in their giving. This sentence has been interpreted in various ways. Some take "what is inside the dish" to refer to giving food *to the poor* rather than feasting themselves (these words are placed at a meal, 11:37). In other words, it is a "cleansing" act to so generously give. Others believe that the "dish" symbolizes possessions in general—that is, they should give generously of what they have. Jesus wanted to stress the importance of the inward over the outward, here focusing on the importance of a right attitude when giving to the poor. It should be a gift from the heart, not merely an outward gesture. The inner attitude must match the outward act in order for *everything* to be *clean.*

11:42 **"But woe to you Pharisees! For you tithe mint and rue and herbs of all kinds, and neglect justice and the love of God; it is these you ought to have practiced, without neglecting the others."**[NRSV] The word "woe" warns of judgment to come but also conveys a feeling of regret because Jesus knew that his listeners would refuse to repent. Jesus pronounced "woe" on the Pharisees because although they were keeping the tiniest details of law, ceremony, custom, and tradition, they were forgetting *justice and the love of God.* God's law contains no demand to tithe cooking herbs or medicinal spices, although the Israelites would tithe agricultural products such as fruit (Leviticus 27:30; Deuteronomy 14:22). Because these spices were edible, the scribes and Pharisees were carrying the law to its extreme and were tithing *mint and rue and herbs of all kinds.* Jesus did not condemn the practice of tithing, even of small amounts if one chose to do so. But this scrupulous accounting of even the tiniest of plants had robbed the joy of giving back to God. Jesus condemned the Pharisees for being scrupulous in less important matters while completely neglecting the larger issues that were far more important—such as dealing correctly and fairly with people and building a relationship with God. To concentrate on the trivial often means to overlook what is important. This Jesus condemned.

11:43 "Woe to you Pharisees! For you love to have the seat of honor in the synagogues and to be greeted with respect in the marketplaces."^NRSV Jesus pronounced another *woe* on the Pharisees, this time regarding their love of public importance and honor. The elders sat on the *seat of honor in the synagogues,* at the front, near the place where the scrolls of the Torah were kept. Those seats faced the congregation and were reserved for the most important people. *To be greeted with respect in the marketplaces* was a highly treasured honor. Greetings in the Near East, then and today, meant more than they do in the West. Custom called for those less learned to greet their superiors; thus, these religious leaders would receive many greetings. Jesus condemned the attitude that focused on the "perks" of position, while they forgot their responsibility to be teachers. The Pharisees loved to receive honor and deference from ordinary people, yet they did not love or desire to serve those people. Instead, they often showed contempt for them as "lower" than themselves.

11:44 "Woe to you! For you are like unmarked graves, and people walk over them without realizing it."^NRSV This third *woe* pictures the Pharisees, for all their ceremonial cleanliness, as actually typifying the worst sort of uncleanness. The Old Testament laws said a person who touched a grave was unclean (Numbers 19:16). Sometimes a body might be buried in an unmarked grave, causing an unwary traveler to become ceremonially unclean by walking over it. Jesus accused the Pharisees of actually being *unmarked graves* who made others unclean by their spiritual rottenness. Like unmarked graves hidden in a field, the Pharisees corrupted everyone who came in contact with them.

11:45-46 **One of the experts in the law answered him, "Teacher, when you say these things, you insult us also." Jesus replied, "And you experts in the law, woe to you, because you load people down with burdens they can hardly carry, and you yourselves will not lift one finger to help them."**NIV A certain lawyer had somehow assumed that Jesus' words were not directed at him and the other *experts in the law.* These men made it their profession to study the Old Testament law. While they were religious and usually also Pharisees, they were in a different profession. But then this man felt that Jesus was insulting him and his fellow lawyers. What in particular caused him to take insult is uncertain; something must have struck him as true.

Jesus did not back down from what was being taken as insults, nor did he leave these legal experts without condemnation—for they also deserved *woe.* Jesus condemned them for loading *people down with burdens they can hardly carry.* These "burdens" were the details the Pharisees had added to God's law. To the commandment, "Remember the Sabbath day by keeping it holy" (Exodus 20:8 NIV), for example, they had added instructions regarding how far a person could walk on the Sabbath, which kinds of knots could be tied, and how much weight could be carried. Healing a person was considered unlawful work on the Sabbath, although rescuing a trapped animal was permitted. Instead of teaching God's law so that people could love, understand, and obey the God who gave it, they turned the law into a confused maze of do's and don'ts that had become a burden to the people. The legal experts refused to *lift one finger to help* the people. As experts, they probably found all kinds of ways to get themselves out from under the burden. No wonder Jesus condemned them.

EXPERTS?
If you memorize every verse of every Bible version in your church library, but do not live by faith . . .
    If you trace all the cross-references in every center column of Bible text, but do not share with the poor . . .
    If you know the citations of every name of God in the Old and New Testament, but never tell a neighbor about Jesus . . .
    What are you? A religious expert. But what good is that?

11:47-48 **"Woe to you! For you build the tombs of the prophets whom your ancestors killed. So you are witnesses and approve of the deeds of your ancestors; for they killed them, and you build their tombs."**NRSV Jesus pronounced a second *woe* on the legal experts as he condemned them for murdering the prophets. The *tombs of the prophets* were revered. People even decorated the graves of those long dead who seemed worthy of such honor. Building tombs (sometimes marble monuments) over the graves of the martyrs was ironic because most of these prophets had been killed by the *ancestors* of this present religious establishment. In essence, these religious leaders were *witnesses* and were giving approval for the *deeds of [their] ancestors* in killing these prophets because they eagerly *build their tombs*. Jesus was saying that these leaders were no different from their ancestors who had killed God's messengers because, in a sense, they were simply completing their work. The attitude of hatred for God's messengers would carry through, and Jesus himself would face it as well.

LEARN . . . TO SERVE
With much knowledge comes great responsibility. Too casually do we

- buy Bible aids and commentaries.
- collect and listen to great cassettes of learning.
- seek a seminary education.
- spend weekends at big conferences.

Despite impressive educational credentials, the Bible experts in these verses were failures in Jesus' eyes. As you seek knowledge, also explore ways to share it, use it, and apply it—helping many others to find a closer relationship with God.

11:49-51 **"This is what God in his wisdom said about you: 'I will send prophets and apostles to them, and they will kill some and persecute the others.' And you of this generation will be held responsible for the murder of all God's prophets from the creation of the world—from the murder of Abel to the murder of Zechariah, who was killed between the altar and the sanctuary. Yes, it will surely be charged against you."**[NLT] God's prophets have been persecuted and murdered throughout history. But this generation was rejecting more than a human prophet—they were rejecting God himself. This quotation is not from the Old Testament. Jesus, the greatest Prophet of all, was directly giving them God's message.

Jesus gave two examples of martyrs in the Old Testament. Abel's death is recorded in Genesis 4:8—he was the first martyr, the first to die because of his faithfulness to God. Zechariah's death is recorded in 2 Chronicles 24:20-22 (the last book in the Hebrew canon). Zechariah is a classic example of a man of God who was killed by those who claimed to be God's people. The current religious establishment would be guilty of all of their deaths, for they would be guilty of murdering the Messiah and would face judgment for that act. The destruction of Jerusalem in A.D. 70 was a partial fulfillment of Jesus' words.

11:52 **"Woe to you experts in the law, because you have taken away the key to knowledge. You yourselves have not entered, and you have hindered those who were entering."**^{NIV} The *experts in the law* were effectively locking people out of God's kingdom. Their rejection of Jesus and emphasis on their petty demands had the effect of making them unable to enter the kingdom and then hindering those who might otherwise want to enter. Anyone who might have gotten in through a saving relationship with God was stopped short by their erroneous interpretations of Scripture and their added man-made rules. They made God's truth hard to understand and practice. They turned God's Word into a book of riddles and puzzles that only they could understand. Then, as they prided themselves in their "understanding," they themselves missed God's message. On top of that, these men were bad examples, arguing their way out of the demanding rules that they were placing on others. Caught up in a religion of their own making, they could no longer lead the people to God. They had closed the door of God's love to the people and had thrown away the keys.

INSIDE OUT

Jesus criticized the Pharisees and the experts in the law harshly because they (1) washed their outsides but not their insides, (2) remembered to give a tenth of even their garden herbs but were neglecting justice, (3) loved praise and attention, (4) loaded people down with burdensome religious demands, (5) would not accept the truth about Jesus, and (6) prevented others from believing the truth as well. They went wrong by focusing on outward appearances and ignoring the inner condition of their hearts. People do the same today when their service comes from a desire to be seen rather than from a pure heart and out of a love for others. People may sometimes be fooled, but God isn't. Don't be a Christian on the outside only. Bring your inner life under God's control, and your outer life will naturally reflect him.

11:53-54 **As Jesus finished speaking, the Pharisees and teachers of religious law were furious. From that time on they grilled him with many hostile questions, trying to trap him into saying something they could use against him.**^{NLT} It may come as no surprise that *as Jesus finished speaking, the Pharisees and teachers of religious law were furious.* He had challenged these professed experts, so they hoped to trip him up and arrest him for blasphemy, heresy, or lawbreaking. They were enraged by Jesus' words about them, but they couldn't arrest him for merely speaking words. They had to find a legal way to get rid of Jesus, so they *grilled him with many hostile questions, trying to trap him.* Jesus had pointed out the blatant hypocrisy of so much of Israel's leadership, and there would be no turning back. The opposition was mounting; Jesus had become a threat to the establishment. The questions were no longer out of interest or with a desire to learn more; they were merely ploys in an attempt to find *something they could use against him.*

EXPECT IT
As you witness to the truth of Jesus Christ, don't expect to always find happy, cheerful people crowded at your front door, smiling, grateful, and eager to learn more, or public-service awards for being a great person. It's more realistic to expect anything from quiet shunning to furious, scathing criticism. Jesus faced the latter but spoke the truth, and the fury has raged until this day. Expect to meet it, if you dare to be a channel for God's good news.

LUKE 12

After a passage denouncing the Pharisees and scribes for hypocrisy, follows a passage in which Jesus warns his disciples of the same pernicious problem. Perhaps they were being tempted by the popularity of Jesus—and, by extension, their own. With the limelight of fame shining on them, they were beginning to follow the Pharisees on a path of hypocrisy—acting religiously superior and judging others, while harboring jealousy, greed, and pride within their souls. This type of hypocrisy was utterly repugnant to Jesus. Parading a false religiosity in front of people, it completely ignores God. Those types of hypocrites claim to be close to God, when in fact they are far from him (11:52).

Jesus sternly warned his disciples of this yeast—this evil that spreads quickly among religious workers. But he also described a proper devotion to God, which trusts in his care (12:7). With the proliferation of radios and televisions today the allure of fame and popularity is just as dangerous as it was two thousand years ago, if not more so. Jesus' stern warning rings true: Be on guard against pride and hypocrisy. Be more concerned about your relationship with God than how you appear to others.

12:1 **Meanwhile, the crowds grew until thousands were milling about and crushing each other. Jesus turned first to his disciples and warned them, "Beware of the yeast of the Pharisees—beware of their hypocrisy."**NLT Even as Jesus began to infuriate the religious leaders, his popularity continued to grow, for Luke wrote that the *crowds grew until thousands were milling about and crushing each other.* As Jesus watched the huge crowds waiting to hear him, he warned his *disciples* against *hypocrisy*—trying to appear good when their heart was far from God. Just as *yeast* works its way through dough, so a small amount of evil can affect a large group of people. The *yeast of the Pharisees*—their hypocrisy—could permeate and contaminate society, leading the entire nation astray.

DON'T BE HYPOCRITICAL
Jesus warned against the spread of hypocrisy and its
destructive consequences. How do you avoid hypocrisy? Try
these suggestions:
- At the start of the day, ask God to lead you one step further—enough to challenge you.
- Find a small group that wants to talk honestly. Share your
  life with these people.
- Join a church where people can be who they are, a church
  that invites diversity in its membership and programs.
- Do Christian service in grateful response to God, and not
  as a scheme to gain anyone's approval.

12:2-3 **"For there is nothing covered that will not be revealed, nor hidden that will not be known. Therefore whatever you have spoken in the dark will be heard in the light, and what you have spoken in the ear in inner rooms will be proclaimed on the housetops."**NKJV Hypocrisy can happen when certain actions or attitudes are hidden. One day, however, everything will be *revealed, known, heard,* and *proclaimed.* The Pharisees could not keep their attitudes hidden forever. Their selfishness would act like "yeast" (12:1), and soon they would expose themselves for what they really were—power-hungry impostors, not devoted religious leaders. The time of this "revelation" could be the final Judgment Day when the true attitude of these hypocrites will be exposed (see Romans 2:16; 1 Corinthians 4:5).

12:4-5 **"I tell you, my friends, do not be afraid of those who kill the body and after that can do no more. But I will show you whom you should fear: Fear him who, after the killing of the body, has power to throw you into hell. Yes, I tell you, fear him."**NIV Here Jesus called his disciples "friends," meaning that he trusted them. He explained that they might face death for their faith in him, but he also told them to *not be afraid* of people who could kill them or even of death itself. Evil people may be able to *kill the body,* but they can *do no more.* Jesus knew that fear of opposition or ridicule could weaken their witness for him because the natural human tendency is to cling to peace and comfort, even at the cost of one's walk with God. Jesus said that there is only one whom all people *should fear*—God alone. He controls eternal consequences. It is more fearful to disobey God than to face martyrdom. The worst that people can do (kill the body) does not compare with the worst that God can do. While the Greeks believed that only the soul lived on after death, Jesus taught unmistakably that *hell* is a place of destruction for soul *and* body—the whole person.

HYPOCRISY
What are the signs of hypocrisy?
- *Hypocrisy is knowing the truth but not obeying it.*
Jesus repeatedly exposed the hypocritical attitudes of the religious leaders. They knew the Scriptures but did not live by them. They didn't care about *being* holy—just *looking* holy in order to receive the people's admiration and praise. Today, like the Pharisees, many people who know the Bible do not let it change their lives. They say they follow Jesus, but they don't live by his standards of love. People who live this way are hypocrites. Believers must make sure that their actions match their beliefs.
- *Hypocrisy is living a self-serving life.*
People desire positions of leadership not only in business but also in the church. It is dangerous when love for the position grows stronger than loyalty to God. This is what happened to the Pharisees and teachers of the law. Jesus is not against all leadership—Christian leaders are important—but against leadership that serves itself rather than others.
- *Hypocrisy is claiming Christ as Lord without following him.*
Jesus challenged society's norms. To him, greatness comes from serving—giving of yourself to help others. Service keeps believers aware of others' needs, and it stops them from focusing only on themselves. Jesus came as a servant. What kind of greatness do you seek?
- *Hypocrisy reduces faith to rigid rules.*
Being a religious leader in Jerusalem was very different from being a pastor in a secular society today. Israel's history, culture, and daily life centered around its relationship with God. The religious leaders were the best known, most powerful, and most respected of all leaders. Jesus made these stinging accusations because the leaders' hunger for more power, money, and status had made them lose sight of God, and their blindness was spreading to the whole nation.
- *Hypocrisy is outward conformity without inner reality.*
It's possible to obey the details of the laws but still be disobedient in general behavior. For example, a person could be very precise and faithful about giving 10 percent of his or her money to God, but refuse to give one minute of time in helping others. Tithing is important, but giving a tithe does not exempt a person from fulfilling God's other directives. The Pharisees strained their water so they wouldn't accidentally swallow a gnat—an unclean insect, according to the law. Meticulous about the details of ceremonial cleanliness, they nevertheless had lost their perspective on inner purity. Ceremonially clean on the outside, they had corrupt hearts. Jesus condemned the Pharisees and religious leaders for outwardly appearing saintly and holy but inwardly remaining full of corruption and greed. Living your Christianity merely as a show for others is like washing a cup on the outside only. When you are clean on the inside, your cleanliness on the outside won't be a sham.

The word translated "hell" here is *Gehenna*. The name was derived from the Valley of Hinnom, south of Jerusalem, where children had been sacrificed by fire to the pagan god Molech (see 2 Kings 23:10; 2 Chronicles 28:3; Jeremiah 7:31; 32:35). Later, during the reign of good king Josiah, the valley had become the city's garbage dump where fire burned constantly to destroy the garbage and the worms infesting it. *Gehenna*, hell, is the place of fire and punishment.

Those who love God must also "fear" him; they must respect his power and stand in awe of his greatness, never taking him for granted. He makes the final decisions; he holds the judgment that will determine each person's eternal destiny.

WORTHWHILE

Jesus taught how valuable each person was to God. How does a person assess his or her worth? A student's worth is measured by grade point average; a pitcher's by earned run average; a career professional's by salary; a salesclerk's by commission.

God measures your worth with no number, no calculation, no ratio.

You simply bear God's image.
Your life was worth God's Son.
Your future is in God's home.

Tomorrow, rise from your slumber as a person filled with value, known intimately by God, destined for greatness. Shed your silly inferiorities. You are a son or daughter of the Almighty.

12:6-7 **"What is the price of five sparrows? A couple of pennies? Yet God does not forget a single one of them. And the very hairs on your head are all numbered. So don't be afraid; you are more valuable to him than a whole flock of sparrows."**[NLT] While Jesus' followers should "fear" God because of his awesome power, they are not to *be afraid* of him because they are *more valuable to him than a whole flock of sparrows*. A person could buy *five sparrows* for a small amount of money; in economic terms, sparrows were not very valuable. They were the cheapest type of living food sold in the market; a penny was the smallest copper coin. Even so, *God does not forget a single one.* God loves his people so much that he cares about the smallest details of their lives—down to knowing the number of hairs on their heads. Jesus explained that because God is aware of everything that happens to sparrows and every tiny detail about each individual, his people need not be afraid. They are so valuable that God sent his Son to die for them (John 3:16). Because God places such value on his people, they need never fear personal threats or difficult trials. God, their Father, is in control.

A person's true value is God's estimate of that person's worth, not his or her peers'. Other people evaluate and categorize according to performance, achievement, or appearance. But God cares for all people, as he does for all of his creatures, because they belong to him. So they can face life without fear.

12:8-9 "And I tell you, everyone who acknowledges me before others, the Son of Man also will acknowledge before the angels of God; but whoever denies me before others will be denied before the angels of God."NRSV God sent his Son to die for people worldwide, and salvation is offered to all people. But individuals still must choose whether or not to accept God's offer. Jesus clearly explained, *"Everyone who acknowledges me before others* (that is, those who publicly confess their faith in and allegiance to him), *the Son of Man also will acknowledge before the angels of God."* The person who acknowledges faith in Jesus can trust that Jesus will acknowledge him or her as his own in heaven.

On the other hand, the person who *denies* his or her relationship to Jesus will, in turn, face denial by Jesus in heaven. These words refer to those whose lack of allegiance will be revealed under pressure. This will amount to apostasy (1 John 2:19). Most likely, this does not refer to an incident where lack of courage might cause a believer not to speak up, but rather to a person who totally rejects Christ and lives a life of denial. The astounding statement is that each person's standing before God is based on his or her relationship to Jesus Christ. He is the advocate whose intercession before God will depend on a person's faithfulness in acknowledging him.

DENY OR ACKNOWLEDGE?
Acknowledging Jesus demands our full allegiance to him. People deny Jesus when they hope that no one will think they are Christians, decide *not* to speak up for what is right, are silent about their relationship with God, blend into society, or accept their culture's non-Christian values.

By contrast, people acknowledge Jesus when they live moral, upright, Christ-honoring lives, look for opportunities to share their faith with others, help others in need, take a stand for justice, love others, acknowledge their loyalty to Christ, and use their lives and resources to carry out his desires rather than their own.

12:10 "And everyone who speaks a word against the Son of Man will be forgiven; but whoever blasphemes against the Holy Spirit will not be forgiven."NRSV While 12:8-9 deals with apostasy, 12:10

focuses on people outside of the faith who have not yet come to believe. These words mean that speaking against the person of Jesus can be forgiven because the insult may be based in ignorance of his true identity (before the Resurrection, not even Jesus' disciples completely understood who he was). But *whoever blasphemes against the Holy Spirit*—who continually rejects the Holy Spirit's message about Jesus and his convicting influence to believe in him—is beyond redemptive help. The rejection of the messenger (even of the Son himself) can be forgiven, but not the rejection of God himself through the Holy Spirit. The mighty works done by the Spirit were unmistakable announcements that the kingdom had arrived. Jesus said that those who blasphemed the Holy Spirit *will not be forgiven*—not because that sin is worse than any other, but because they will never ask for forgiveness. Whoever rejects the prompting of the Holy Spirit removes himself or herself from the only force that can lead anyone to repentance and restoration with God. Those who have seen the light and yet prefer the darkness blaspheme the Holy Spirit. That act has eternal consequences.

This sin of blasphemy against the Holy Spirit has worried many sincere Christians, so the meaning becomes very important to understand. The unforgivable sin means attributing to Satan the work that the Holy Spirit accomplishes. Thus the "unforgivable sin" is deliberate and ongoing rejection of the Holy Spirit's work and even of God himself. A person who has committed this sin has shut himself or herself off from God so thoroughly that he or she is unaware of any sin at all. John refers to this as the sin unto death (1 John 5:16). (See also Life Application Commentary discussion of Hebrews 6:4-6.) A person who fears having committed this sin shows by his or her very concern that he or she has not sinned in this way.

12:11-12 **"And when you are brought to trial in the synagogues and before rulers and authorities, don't worry about what to say in your defense, for the Holy Spirit will teach you what needs to be said even as you are standing there."**[NLT] The Holy Spirit will be every believer's helper (John 14:15-26). Jesus told the disciples that *when* (not "if") they would be *brought to trial in the synagogues and before rulers and authorities,* they need not *worry about what to say* in their own defense. Worry and fear would be normal responses to such a trial, for Jesus' fishermen-turned-disciples knew they would never be able to dominate a religious dispute with the well-educated Jewish leaders. Their fear might cause them to not acknowledge Jesus as they should. Nevertheless, they would not be left unprepared. Jesus promised that *the Holy Spirit* would supply the needed words at the very moment these words were needed. The disciples' testimony might not make them look impressive, but it would still point out God's work in the world through Jesus' life. We need to pray for opportunities to speak for God and then trust him to help us with our words. This promise of the Spirit's help, however, does not compensate for lack of preparation. Remember that these disciples had three years of teaching and practical application. Study God's Word; then God will bring his truths to mind when you most need them, helping you present them in the most effective way.

TIMELY DEFENSE
Public speaking creates more fear in people than any other normal activity. Surely making a public defense of your Christian faith sounds intimidating. But Jesus assures and advises:

- Don't worry—this is God's trial too.
- Don't bother with a scripted speech—your intelligence is not the issue.
- Don't fret if you stumble and stutter—all you say is a witness to God's truth.
- Take a deep breath, pray, and just be honest about all God has shown you. The Holy Spirit will do the rest.

JESUS TELLS THE PARABLE OF THE RICH FOOL / 12:13-21 / **140**

Perhaps because of Jesus' constant insistence on justice (11:42), a person from the crowd asked him to arbitrate a dispute. Instead of addressing the injustice, Jesus exposed the greedy motives of the man and revealed God's perspective on the foolishness of greed. The simple parable Jesus told describes a person who is solely concerned with himself—his welfare, pleasure, and security. He possessed no gratitude towards God or a willingness to share with those less fortunate. His ingratitude invoked God's anger and led to the man's downfall.

With every one of his teachings, Jesus gave a glimpse of heaven. Here, in vivid detail, can be seen God's reaction to the greedy—those who gather as much as they can for themselves. The Lord is appalled at their foolish ingratitude, and he rewards their hard work foolishly spent on themselves with severe judgment. If a person won't distribute his or her resources to others in this life, God will do it after the person's death. In effect, Jesus was telling this questioner to get his priorities straight—getting the "fair" amount of earthly inheritance might cost him his eternal inheritance. Jesus also calls you to reevaluate your attitude toward money and how you spend it. Get out your checkbook and look at your spending habits. Are you furthering God's kingdom with your money? Are you helping others with your money, showing generosity to people in need?

12:13 Someone in the crowd said to him, "Teacher, tell my brother to divide the family inheritance with me."NRSV The focus returned to *the crowd* (12:1). Then a person in the crowd appealed to Jesus as an authority. He wanted Jesus to settle a dispute over his *family inheritance.* The Old Testament laws covered most cases (see, for example, Numbers 26–27; 33:54; 36; Deuteronomy 21:17). But sometimes an issue would arise that needed intervention in order to make a decision. Problems like this were often brought to rabbis for them to settle (see 10:38-42).

This man apparently wanted Jesus to side with him in this dispute with his brother. Jesus' response, though not directly to the topic, was not a change of subject. Rather, Jesus was pointing to a higher issue—a correct attitude toward the accumulation of wealth. Life is more than material goods. Jesus put his finger on this questioner's heart. When we bring problems to God in prayer, he often does the same—showing us how we need to change and grow in our attitude toward the problem. This answer is often not the one we were looking for, but it is more effective in helping us trace God's hand in our lives.

GREED
Jesus warned against greed for possessions. Greed keeps track of every tool lent, every dime shared, every overtime minute worked, every check to charity grudgingly written.
   Jesus leads the way to generosity, a rare trait today. As God opens heaven to you, clutch less what you own and share more what you have been given.

12:14-15 Jesus replied, "Friend, who made me a judge over you to decide such things as that?" Then he said, "Beware! Don't be greedy for what you don't have. Real life is not measured by how much we own."NLT The word "friend" here is not used in the same sense as when Jesus spoke to his disciples in 12:4. Other translations use the informal "man." Jesus refused to intervene in this man's predicament. Perhaps the man had come with his problem, perceiving that Jesus had power and authority and that his decision could carry much weight. Jesus did not want to deal with inheritance issues—he had far more important work to do. Instead, he used the man's request as an opportunity to teach his listeners about the pitfalls of being *greedy.* "Greed" is the

excessive and consuming desire to have more possessions or
wealth. He explained that the good life has nothing to do with
being wealthy; *real life is not measured by how much we own.*
This is the exact opposite of what present-day society says.
Advertisers spend millions of dollars to entice people to think
that if they buy more and more products, they will be happier,
more fulfilled, and more comfortable. This man apparently
thought that the division of the inheritance would solve his problems. But Jesus wanted him to deal with deeper issues.

12:16-18 **And he gave an illustration: "A rich man had a fertile farm
that produced fine crops. In fact, his barns were full to overflowing. So he said, 'I know! I'll tear down my barns and
build bigger ones. Then I'll have room enough to store everything.'"**NLT Jesus proceeded to illustrate his point that life consists
of more than wealth and possessions. This story includes a man,
already *rich,* who had a productive year on his farm. So huge was
this bumper crop that *his barns were full to overflowing.* Wise
businessman that he was, the man simply tore down his barns and
built *bigger ones* so that he could *store everything.* While there
was nothing wrong with the man's rejoicing in his crop or building to make storage, his basic flaw was in focusing completely on
his wealth and on his own enjoyment. In Greek, this story
includes the word "my" four times and the word "I" eight times.
As this story reveals, the man's joy came from his things—but
things do not last forever.

MORE
The rich man in Jesus' story died before he could begin to use
what was stored in his big barns. Planning for retirement—
preparing for life *before* death—is wise, but neglecting life *after*
death is disastrous. If you accumulate wealth only to enrich
yourself, with no concern for helping others, you will enter
eternity empty-handed. Jesus challenges his people to think
beyond earthbound goals and to use what they have been
given for God's kingdom. Faith, service, and obedience are the
way to become rich toward God.

12:19-20 **"And I'll say to myself, 'You have plenty of good things laid
up for many years. Take life easy; eat, drink and be
merry.'"**NIV The rich man lived as though he had many years to
live (see James 4:13-17 for a similar thought). He had laid up
good things for himself; then he proceeded to spend it all on himself. He was concerned for no one else, and he had no care for
God. With no eternal perspective, the man's life was completely

focused on the temporal. His goal to *take life easy* and to *eat, drink and be merry* reveals his desire for mere self-indulgence. He thought that, with his barns storing up mountains of wealth for the future, he had everything completely under control. The future was his, so he thought. **"But God said to him, 'You fool! This very night your life will be demanded from you. Then who will get what you have prepared for yourself?'"**[NIV] The rich man had made a fatal flaw: he had forgotten to put God at the center of his life. Concerned for no one but himself, when the time came for him to stand before God, he was nothing more than a *fool.* He had counted on material wealth to sustain him. But God would take his life, and then who would get all his wealth? In addition, he would not have prepared himself for eternity, and that would be his most foolish mistake.

FOR THE FUTURE
Fully vested pension plans and adequate life insurance are practically synonymous with wise stewardship. Everyone should provide for older age and family survivors.

At the same time and with the same resolve because life is more than money, God wants you to share generously today with those who are poor. And, should wealth accumulate, never, never put your hope and pride in real estate, insurance, or mutual funds. God should be your security and joy.

Evaluate your financial plan. Ground it in active faith. Seek advice from growing Christians on matters of financial stewardship.

12:21 **"So it is with those who store up treasures for themselves but are not rich toward God."**[NRSV] The moral of the story: fools spend all their time storing up *treasures for themselves* but neglect to become *rich toward God.* The turning point is for whom the treasures are being accumulated. If for oneself, then the evils of wealth will be turned loose. Hoarding money without compassionate giving, regarding property as one's own not God's, or basing security on possessions rather than God's provisions are all examples of spiritual poverty (not being rich toward God). Being rich toward God means using wealth as he provides it to fulfill his priorities. (See also 12:33-34 where giving to the poor is the key to understanding God's kind of treasure.) People who are "rich" in this way love God and are filled with a passion to obey and serve him and to give to others. In this way, the "treasures" a person may gain in this life can be gladly handed back over to God for his use in furthering his kingdom. In Matthew 6:19-21, Jesus says, "Do not store up for yourselves treasures on earth, where moth and rust destroy, and where thieves break in and steal. But store up for yourselves treasures in heaven, where moth and rust do not destroy, and where thieves do not break in and steal. For where your treasure is, there your heart will be also" (NIV). (See also 1 Timothy 6:17-19 for more on generosity.)

JESUS WARNS ABOUT WORRY / 12:22-34 / **141**

Luke placed Jesus' teaching about believers and possessions right after the negative example of the rich fool (12:13-21). Instead of hoarding possessions, believers should give them away. Such generosity builds an eternal inheritance in God's kingdom. Christians should completely trust in God's loving provision for them; this should free them to show generosity.

Jesus calls his followers to raise their sights, to forget worrying about the pressures of this life—climbing the corporate ladder or *even* obtaining enough food—and instead to be concerned with developing character. If life's pressures are getting to you, take a moment to reflect on God's care for you in the past. Then, commit each one of your worries to him and refocus on doing his will.

12:22-23 Then He said to His disciples, "Therefore I say to you, do not worry about your life, what you will eat; nor about the body, what you will put on. Life is more than food, and the body is more than clothing."NKJV Jesus continued to highlight the priorities of those who want to follow him. Again, these words were directed not to the crowd in general but *to His disciples.* Just as their attitude toward money should differ from the world's (12:15), so their life view should be different. All the goals and worries in life can be entrusted to the loving heavenly Father who promises to meet every need. The command "do not worry" does not imply lack of concern, nor does it imply that people should be unwilling to work to supply their own needs and thus have to depend on others. Instead, Jesus was saying that worrying about *what you will eat* and *what you will put on* should never take priority over serving God. Food and clothes are less important than the life and body that they feed and cover. Worriers immobilize themselves and focus on their worries. They refuse to trust that God can supply their most basic needs.

Jesus' followers should not worry about their basic needs, but how can they avoid it? Only faith can free God's people from the anxiety caused by greed and covetousness. It is good to work and plan responsibly; it is bad to dwell on all the ways the plans could go wrong. Worry is pointless because it can't meet any needs;

worry is foolish because the Creator of the universe loves his people and knows what they need. He promises to meet all their real needs, but not necessarily all their desires. While working to supply money for food and clothing, believers must always remember that these ultimately come from God's hands. When the need arises, they need not worry, for they know that God will supply.

12:24 **"Consider the ravens, for they neither sow nor reap, which have neither storehouse nor barn; and God feeds them. Of how much more value are you than the birds?"**NKJV Jesus had already explained that God's care for the sparrows shows that he cares for his people (12:6-7). Here Jesus explained God's care for people's basic needs by asking the disciples to *consider the ravens.* The birds don't have elaborate farming systems by which to supply food for themselves; *God feeds them.* God makes sure that the birds, who do no worrying about their food supply, always have food to eat. The raven (or crow) was considered to be "unclean" (Leviticus 11:13-15), yet even unclean animals received God's care. The conclusion, of course, is that God's people are of *much more value . . . than the birds.* God's children can know that their Father will care for their needs as well.

OVERCOMING WORRY
Worry can be an important early warning device against foolish risk taking. It can also stunt your joy until you become a worry-impaired invalid. One of the world's richest men, Howard Hughes, took worry to pathological extremes and died a prisoner in his own bed. He needed, above all, the freedom that Jesus offers. Jesus declared worry to be useless effort. Instead, Christians' efforts to deal with their circumstances should be more productive.
Overcoming worry requires
- simple trust in God, your heavenly Father. This trust is expressed by praying to him rather than worrying.
- perspective on your problems. This can be gained by developing a strategy for addressing and correcting your problems.
- a support team to help. Find some believers who will pray for you to find wisdom and strength to deal with your worries.

12:25-26 **"And can any of you by worrying add a single hour to your span of life? If then you are not able to do so small a thing as that, why do you worry about the rest?"**NRSV Worry accomplishes nothing; it is wasted effort. It can actually be harmful because it creates a downward spiral in a person's emotions and increases the stress level. While worry cannot *add a single hour* to a person's life, it can damage that person's health, cause the object of worry to consume one's thoughts, disrupt productivity, negatively affect the way the person treats others, and reduce the ability to trust in God. In its essence, worry comes from not being able to control one's circumstances. Therefore, if people are not capable, by worrying, of adding a mere hour to their lives, then why do they worry at all? (For more on worry, see Life Application Commentary discussion on Philippians 4:6-7.)

12:27-28 **"Consider the lilies, how they grow: they neither toil nor spin; and yet I say to you, even Solomon in all his glory was not arrayed like one of these. If then God so clothes the grass, which today is in the field and tomorrow is thrown into the oven, how much more will He clothe you, O you of little faith?"**[NKJV] Like the ravens who do not store up food for themselves in barns, the *lilies* neither *toil* nor *spin* in order to array themselves. If God feeds the birds and clothes the earth with beauty that surpasses the fine garments of King *Solomon,* then will God not also clothe his people?

REVERSE
Jesus knew that many people worry about possessions and money. Most people base their decisions on getting and keeping money. Our society says money and possessions will buy a person security and make him or her happy. To reverse this pressure, try making decisions based on something other than money and security:

- Use your vacation for education rather than pleasure.
- Do a short-term mission assignment.
- Hire a homeless person and invest in his or her training.
- "Adopt" a child overseas, providing food and education.

These are acts of people who do not worry about stockpiling enough money for themselves. These are the acts of those who trust that God knows their needs.

Jesus was not condoning laziness while waiting for God to provide. He wanted his disciples to understand that they should place their lives in God's hands, refusing to worry about basic needs. It shows *little faith* to worry over what God has promised to provide. If he even *clothes the grass,* which is here today and *tomorrow is thrown into the oven,* he can also be trusted to clothe his people, who are of eternal value to him.

The phrase "thrown into the oven" could refer to the hot wind (called the sirocco) that would come off the desert southeast of Israel and wilt flowers. Also, in a land where wood was valuable and scarce, the dry and dead grass would be cut and used for fuel in the ovens when baking. See also 21:17-19 and Matthew 6:25-32.

12:29-30 **"And do not set your heart on what you will eat or drink; do not worry about it. For the pagan world runs after all such things, and your Father knows that you need them."**NIV Eating and drinking are necessary for survival, but God's people *do not set* their hearts on these things. They know that life is more than what they eat or drink, more than their clothing or possessions. If they *worry about* these things, they will find themselves motionless for God, accomplishing nothing for the kingdom. God's people are to be different. The *pagan world,* with its focus on self-indulgence, *runs after all such things.* Without an eternal focus, nothing remains except to chase what seems to satisfy the appetites. But believers have an eternal perspective that is focused on the kingdom to come; they trust their *Father* to know what they *need* for their time on the earth. Here Jesus, speaking to his disciples, called God their "Father."

12:31 **"But seek the kingdom of God, and all these things shall be added to you."**NKJV Clearly God's people should have different priorities from the "pagan world" (12:30) because they have the eternal perspective. Jesus told his disciples to *seek the kingdom of God.* The word "seek" is a present imperative, a command to fulfill a continuing obligation. To "seek the kingdom" means to submit to God's sovereignty today, to work for the future coming of his kingdom, to represent God here and now, and to seek his rule in our hearts and in the world. So many spend their time worrying about the basics of life, but Jesus says to seek the kingdom, and the basics *shall be added to you.* Christ's promise is not that kingdom seekers will get everything they desire but that the necessities for faith and service will be in abundance. When God's children have their priorities right, they can trust that God will always care for them. They may not become rich, but they will not lack what they need.

THY KINGDOM COME
Seeking the kingdom of God means making Jesus the Lord and King of your life. He must control every area—your work, play, money, plans, relationships. Is the kingdom only one of your many concerns, or is it central to all you do? Are you holding back any areas of your life from God's control? As Lord and Creator, he wants to help provide what you need as well as guide how you use what he provides.

12:32 **"Do not fear, little flock, for it is your Father's good plea-**
sure to give you the kingdom."^{NKJV} The kingdom is worth
seeking (12:31), for one day God the Father will *give* it to those
who faithfully follow him. The kingdom is a certain reality, so
God's people need not *fear.* Fear and worry will be constant
companions to those who devote their lives to getting, achieving, and protecting what they have. No bank and no medical
plan can protect a person from death or from present harm.
Only those whose true treasure is in heaven (12:33-34) can be
truly secure.

Here Jesus called his disciples *little flock,* picturing both their
helplessness and his protection as the Good Shepherd (John
10:11). This is the only place in the New Testament where the
term "little flock" is used for believers, whereas in the Old Testament, the word "flock" often described God's people (Psalm
77:20; Isaiah 40:11; Micah 4:8). Not only does God promise to
give believers his kingdom, but it is his *good pleasure* to do so.
God is always loving and merciful to his children. Christians
must not describe him as miserly or stingy. It pleases God to
bless his children. God the Father (12:30) wants to share his kingdom with them.

MONEY TRAP
Money seen as an end in itself quickly traps people and cuts
them off from both God and the needy. The key to using money
wisely is to see how much can be used for God's purposes, not
how much can be accumulated. Does God's love touch your
wallet? Does your money free you to help others? If so, you are
storing up lasting treasures in heaven. If your financial goals
and possessions hinder you from giving generously, loving
others, or serving God, sell what you must to bring your life into
perspective. Where do you put your time, money, and energy?
What do you think about most? How should you change the
way you use your resources in order to reflect kingdom values
more accurately?

12:33-34 **"Sell your possessions and give to the poor. Provide purses for**
yourselves that will not wear out, a treasure in heaven that will
not be exhausted, where no thief comes near and no moth
destroys. For where your treasure is, there your heart will be
also."^{NIV} Because of their eternal perspective (12:29-30) and
because of the future kingdom they will possess, God's people are
free to give. They can hold their possessions lightly. In fact, they
can *sell* them and *give to the poor.* In so doing, they will provide for
themselves *treasure* that cannot disappear, for it rests *in heaven.*

THE POOR

Jesus' example and attitude toward the poor gives believers a picture of how they ought to hold lightly to their worldly possessions, willingly sharing with those in need. (Verses quoted from the NIV.)

Luke 4:18, *"The Spirit of the Lord is on me, because he has anointed me to preach good news to the poor."*

We must not spiritualize away Jesus' concern for the poor. Jesus' ministry, as the promised Messiah, would focus on calling people back to God—those who saw their need, such as the poor, the outcasts, the disabled, and the Gentiles.

Luke 7:22, *"So he replied to the messengers, 'Go back and report to John what you have seen and heard: The blind receive sight, the lame walk, those who have leprosy are cured, the deaf hear, the dead are raised, and the good news is preached to the poor.'"*

The prophet Isaiah had prophesied that the "one to come" would do such miracles. See also 4:43; 8:1; Matthew 4:23; 9:35; Mark 1:14-15.-

Luke 11:41, *"But give what is inside the dish to the poor, and everything will be clean for you."*

It is a "cleansing" act to give generously. Jesus wanted to stress the importance of the inward over the outward, here focusing on the importance of a right attitude when giving to the poor. The inner attitude must match the outward act.

Luke 12:33, *"Sell your possessions and give to the poor. Provide purses for yourselves that will not wear out, a treasure in heaven that will not be exhausted, where no thief comes near and no moth destroys."*

Treasure in heaven far surpasses any accumulated treasure on earth. Why have abundance when others are starving? Why hoard when others could be helped?

Luke 14:13, 21, *"But when you give a banquet, invite the poor, the crippled, the lame, the blind. . . . The servant came back and reported this to his master. Then the owner of the house became angry and ordered his servant, 'Go out quickly into the streets and alleys of the town and bring in the poor, the crippled, the blind and the lame.'"*

When God's people can do good, without expectation of reward or repayment, they have truly served him unselfishly.

Luke 18:22, *"When Jesus heard this, he said to him, 'You still lack one thing. Sell everything you have and give to the poor, and you will have treasure in heaven. Then come, follow me.'"*

The task of selling possessions will not give anyone eternal life. But such obedience shows the desire to follow Jesus in complete commitment. Only when money is no longer lord of one's life can Jesus become Lord.

Luke 19:8, *"But Zacchaeus stood up and said to the Lord, 'Look, Lord! Here and now I give half of my possessions to the poor, and if I have cheated anybody out of anything, I will pay back four times the amount.'"*

Jesus took the initiative with Zacchaeus, and Zacchaeus took the initiative to follow wherever the path of obedience to Jesus might lead. Zacchaeus was able to give away his wealth in order to follow Jesus. This was the heart attitude Jesus was always looking for. When he perceived it in Zacchaeus, he lost no time in bringing this man the Good News.

Luke 21:2-3, *"He also saw a poor widow put in two very small copper coins. 'I tell you the truth,' he said, 'this poor widow has put in more than all the others.'"*

Jesus judged this woman's gift not by how much she gave but by how much she had left after giving. She gave *everything*. She could have kept back one coin, but she willingly gave both coins and trusted God to care for her. Jesus wanted the disciples to see this lesson in total surrender of self, commitment to God, and willingness to trust in his provision.

Jesus was not telling his followers to sell all their possessions, but rather to sell whatever they could to make giving to the poor possible. This "treasure" in heaven includes, but is not limited to, tithing money. Believers add to it as they bring others to Christ and act out their obedience to God. The "treasure" is the eternal value of whatever is accomplished on earth. Acts of obedience to God, stored in heaven, cannot be stolen, nor will they decay. Nothing can affect or change them; they are eternal.

"For where your treasure is, there your heart will be also" means that whatever occupies a person's thoughts and consumes his or her time—that is the person's "treasure." The heart will be with the treasure. A person who values self as treasure will acquire possessions; one who values others will help them. "Heart" refers to the mind, emotions, and will. What a person treasures most controls that person. Jesus explained to his disciples that their first loyalty should be to eternal matters. The person whose treasure is in heaven can hold loosely to whatever treasures God has given him or her in this world.

> We can hardly respect money enough for the blood and toil it represents. Money is frightening. It can serve or destroy man.
> *Michael Quoist*

JESUS WARNS ABOUT PREPARING FOR HIS COMING / 12:35-48 / **142**

The teaching about the end times in Luke does not entail a detailed description of what will occur but a secure conviction that the Son of Man *will* return in judgment. This knowledge should motivate Christians to be faithful servants or stewards, to do what God has commanded them to do, and to use their talents and resources effectively. Thus Luke placed Jesus' teaching about the end times right next to his teaching about the wise use of possessions. Good stewardship should grow out of a person's relationship with Christ, a fervent desire to obey him, and the knowledge that God will hold people accountable. Don't let the various theories and debates about the end times distract you from the ultimate significance of Christ's return. Jesus will return and will hold everyone accountable. You can be ready for his return by living in obedience to his commands.

12:35-36 **"Be dressed for action and have your lamps lit; be like those who are waiting for their master to return from the wedding banquet, so that they may open the door for him as soon as he comes and knocks."**[NRSV] The "seekers" of the kingdom (12:31) eagerly await the day when God the Father will give them the kingdom (12:32). Because of the certainty of its coming, and because it would be coming in the future, waiting for it requires both faith and vigilance. God's people must *be dressed for action* with their *lamps lit.* Faithful servants would stay awake while waiting for their master's return from a banquet. They are dressed so that they can do service for him should he require it. The lamps are lit so they can light his way into his room without any delay. No matter how late the master may come, the servants are prepared to open the door immediately upon his arrival. In the same way, God's people must be awaiting his arrival so they too can welcome him the moment he arrives. "Dressed for action" pictures a person who has tucked his long outer robe up into his belt or sash so he can be ready to run, travel, fight, or work.

12:37-38 **"It will be good for those servants whose master finds them watching when he comes. I tell you the truth, he will dress himself to serve, will have them recline at the table and will come and wait on them. It will be good for those servants whose master finds them ready, even if he comes in the second or third watch of the night."**[NIV] Servants who are *watching* for the master's arrival will be rewarded. Even more commendable is the fact that they are *ready* even *in the second or third watch of the night* (anytime between 9:00 P.M. and 3:00 A.M.). The master will be so pleased upon his arrival that, for these servants, *he will dress himself to serve, will have them recline at the table and will come and wait on them.* Such a reversal of roles likely will not happen in the world, but in God's kingdom such a welcome will await those who were ready. (For more on vigilance, see Life Application Commentary on Matthew 24:36-51.)

12:39-40 **"Know this: A homeowner who knew exactly when a burglar was coming would not permit the house to be broken into. You must be ready all the time, for the Son of Man will come when least expected."**[NLT] This story describes the need for constant vigilance as believers await the kingdom. A *homeowner* does not know when a burglar is coming to break into the house; if the homeowner did, he would be ready and *would not permit* it to happen. Likewise, God's people *must be ready all the time.* Jesus referred to himself as *the Son of Man* and left no doubt that he would be the one who *will come when least expected* (1 Thessalonians 5:2; 2 Peter 3:10; Revelation 16:15). God's people should be ready and waiting.

Christ's return at an unexpected time is not a trick by which God hopes to catch his people off guard. In fact, God is delaying his return so that more people will have the opportunity to follow him (see 2 Peter 3:9). Before Christ's return, believers have time to live out their beliefs and to reflect Jesus' love as they relate to others. Christians have time to bring more people with them into the kingdom.

READY AND WAITING
To be ready for Christ's coming means living in two worlds: one, the world of time and space where God's people care for God's creation; the other, a world made new at Jesus' coming for which the preparation includes prayer, worship, and Bible study. How can we be ready for Christ's return? People who are ready are not hypocritical, but sincere (12:1); not fearful, but ready to witness (12:4-9); not worried, but trusting (12:25-26); not greedy, but generous (12:33-34); not lazy, but diligent (12:37). May your life be more like Christ's so that when he comes, you will be ready to greet him joyfully.

12:41-42 **Peter asked, "Lord, are you telling this parable to us, or to everyone?" The Lord answered, "Who then is the faithful and wise manager, whom the master puts in charge of his servants to give them their food allowance at the proper time?"**[NIV] Peter wondered to whom Jesus was addressing the previous parable about being prepared for the kingdom's arrival—*to us* (meaning specifically the disciples) *or to everyone* (referring to the crowd). Perhaps Peter was wondering about the disciples' responsibilities. They still did not understand what this kingdom would be like. Peter wondered what their roles would be in comparison with the crowds in general.

Jesus answered Peter's question with another question that focused the disciples' attention on what it meant to be put in charge and what their roles should be as leaders. They should be like a *faithful and wise manager,* left in charge by *the master* to care for the rest of the *servants* in the household. In New Testament times, the steward was a servant (slave) placed in charge of the master's holdings. He was ordered to be in charge of the other servants and allocate the daily rations. In this story, there is one faithful steward (12:42-44) and three kinds of unfaithful ones (12:45-48).

Jesus further provides the answer in 12:47-48. Accountability and preparedness apply to all believers, yet the requirements are more severe for disciples in leadership, who have more awareness based on their privileged information and responsibility.

12:43-44 **"Blessed is that slave whom his master will find at work when he arrives. Truly I tell you, he will put that one in charge of all his possessions."**[NRSV] The *master* is Jesus, who would leave his servants in his household (the earth) to serve while he would be gone. All the slaves must work, although some are given more responsibility and thus more accountability (12:48). Those slaves who are hard at work when the master returns will be *blessed* and given more responsibility.

HEAVENLY REWARDS
Jesus promises a reward for those who have been faithful to the Master. While people sometimes experience immediate and material rewards for their obedience to God, this is not always the case. If so, they would be tempted to boast about their achievements and do good only for what they get. Jesus said that if they look for rewards now, they will lose them later (see Mark 8:36). Christians' heavenly rewards will be the most accurate reflection of what they have done on earth, and the rewards will be far greater than anyone can imagine. So serve God faithfully in the responsibilities he has given you.

12:45-46 **"But if that slave says to himself, 'My master is delayed in coming,' and if he begins to beat the other slaves, men and women, and to eat and drink and get drunk, the master of that slave will come on a day when he does not expect him and at an hour that he does not know, and will cut him in pieces, and put him with the unfaithful."**[NRSV] However, with the master gone, a slave might think to himself that he can do as he likes, taking advantage of his position of authority to *beat the*

other slaves . . . and to eat and drink and get drunk. This slave
abused his authority and position and did not give out the necessary food to the other servants so they could do their work. The
master would return unexpectedly, catch him in the act, and kill
him for being irresponsible to his task in the master's absence.
Some think that "cut him in pieces" is only an image of severe
punishment (as in "skin him alive"). This is only a story, but
Jesus' listeners understood that a master who owned a slave had
the authority of life and death over him. The master could kill a
slave if he chose to do so. The words "put him with the unfaithful" may be imagery that the slave wasn't killed but totally
rejected after his punishment. Thus, this phrase probably pictures
the end-time judgment, wherein the faithful enter God's kingdom
and the unfaithful are sent away (Matthew 25:31-46).

RESPONSIBLE
Jesus has told his followers how to live until he comes: they must
watch for him, work diligently, and obey his commands. Such
attitudes are especially necessary for leaders. Watchful and
faithful leaders will be given increased opportunities and
responsibilities. The more resources, talents, and understanding
a person has, the more that person is responsible to use them
effectively. God will not hold people responsible for gifts he has
not given them, but all believers have enough gifts and duties to
keep them busy until Jesus comes.

12:47-48 **"That slave who knew what his master wanted, but did not
prepare himself or do what was wanted, will receive a severe
beating. But the one who did not know and did what deserved
a beating will receive a light beating. From everyone to whom
much has been given, much will be required; and from the
one to whom much has been entrusted, even more will be
demanded."**[NRSV] Those who fail to do their duty can expect punishment. More responsibility, and thus more severe punishment,
however, will come to those who *knew what [the] master wanted*
but did not do it. Those who *did not know,* but still acted in such a
way as to deserve a beating, *will receive a light beating.* Each person is responsible to seek out God's will and to obey; however,
God will demand more from those who have been given many
gifts and entrusted with much responsibility for the kingdom.
Clearly, leadership in God's kingdom—no matter how small or
large one's responsibilities in comparison to others—is taken
very seriously by God. Those placed in positions where they will
guide, influence, and care for others have been *entrusted* with
much, and therefore God has high expectations for their moral,

spiritual, and ethical lives. They must show themselves to be
examples and must stay close to the Lord so he can guide them.
Their responsibilities involve the eternal destinies of others—a
job description that should cause them to be ever vigilant and
watchful of God's will.

JESUS WARNS ABOUT COMING DIVISION / 12:49-53 / *143*

These verses introduce a section in which Jesus calls the Jews to
accept him before their time runs out (12:54–13:8). It is a quick
summary of Jesus' earthly mission. Jesus came to earth to bring
division, not peace. That is because Jesus confronts everyone
with a choice. Will you side with him? There is no middle ground
(11:23). Or will you reject him? Such choices naturally cause
division. Jesus warns that such unrest and division are not necessarily a sign to abandon the truth. People who make a choice will
eventually have to take a stand. They will encounter opposition.
This should not be a reason to abandon one's stand but to stand
even more firm for the truth.

When you are confronted with opposition because of your
Christian faith, first evaluate whether the issue touches the core
beliefs of the Christian faith. If so, stand firm.

12:49-50 **"I have come to bring fire on the earth, and how I wish it
were already kindled! But I have a baptism to undergo, and
how distressed I am until it is completed!"**[NIV] "Fire" stands for
God's judgment and the coming of the Holy Spirit (see 3:16-17
for more on Jesus' baptism being one of Spirit and fire). Judgment is coming, and Jesus is the one to bring it. Jesus brought *fire*
to the earth because his arrival has caused upset and division
among people across the centuries. No one can sit on the fence
about Jesus; decisions have to be made to believe or not to
believe, inevitably dividing even families (see 12:51-53). Jesus
said that he wished *it were already kindled,* meaning that he
desired that God's purpose for the earth already be fulfilled. Judgment would come through Jesus, and after that he would reign.
But Jesus waits for God's timing.

Here Jesus anticipated the outworking of God's plan through
his *baptism,* which here refers to his coming suffering at the
cross. This passage gives a glimpse of Jesus' humanity as he
bares his feelings of distress at what must happen in order for the
fire to be *kindled.* Despite Jesus' distress, he anticipates this coming "baptism" because he knows that through it the work of salvation can begin in people's hearts.

12:51-53 "Do you think I came to bring peace on earth? No, I tell you, but division. From now on there will be five in one family divided against each other, three against two and two against three. They will be divided, father against son and son against father, mother against daughter and daughter against mother, mother-in-law against daughter-in-law and daughter-in-law against mother-in-law."[NIV] Jesus promises *peace,* but it is not the kind of peace the world gives or tries to give (John 14:27). Peace on earth, universal peace, will not come until Jesus' second coming when evil is destroyed and he reigns forever. Instead, Jesus' first coming and the time now as believers await his return is a time of *division* between God's forces and Satan's forces. There is no middle ground with Jesus. Because he demands a response, intimate groups may be torn apart when some choose to follow him and others refuse to do so. Loyalties must be declared and commitments made, sometimes to the point of severing relationships with those who reject Jesus or who try to substitute him with someone else.

Micah also prophesied about these kind of divisive conditions (Micah 7:6). Jesus explained the response to his call—conflict will arise between those who respond and those who do not. The reaction may be violent. In the early church, Jews who became Christians were excommunicated from the synagogues and often shunned by their families. Even today, the road is difficult for Jews or Muslims who turn to Christ. Their own family members become their worst enemies. Jesus did not come to make such divisions happen, yet his coming, his words, and his call inevitably will cause conflict between those who accept him and those who reject him.

FAMILY LOYALTY
In many parts of the world, becoming a Christian means severing all ties with family. Sometimes, these families have conspired with the government in the person's death sentence. In more tolerant countries, families may deeply resent converts, shunning them and disinheriting them.

In all circumstances, Jesus is Lord. Every other relationship comes after that. Are you willing to risk your family's disapproval in order to follow the Lord?

JESUS WARNS ABOUT THE FUTURE CRISIS / 12:54-59 / 144

"Hypocrites!" With this harsh word, Jesus tried to startle his listeners to the urgency of their plight. Their time was running out;

they were being led to debtor's prison, where daily beatings were common in the first century. Their spiritual plight was terrible. But Jesus, God's only Son, was offering them a way out—the free gift of salvation to all who believe in him. In effect, Jesus was saying, "Wake up! Destruction is around the corner. Come to me for salvation."

12:54-56 **Then Jesus turned to the crowd and said, "When you see clouds beginning to form in the west, you say, 'Here comes a shower.' And you are right. When the south wind blows, you say, 'Today will be a scorcher.' And it is."**NLT Jesus turned back *to the crowd* and spoke to them. For most of recorded history, the world's principal occupation has been farming. Farmers depend directly on the weather for their livelihood. They need just the right amounts of sun and rain—not too much, not too little—to make a living. Such people were skilled at interpreting natural signs. The people knew that clouds forming *in the west* over the Mediterranean Sea would bring rain. Wind blowing in from the desert to the south would bring hot weather. People interpreted these signs and then prepared themselves accordingly.

But these same people were ignoring the signs of the coming kingdom. Thus Jesus said, **"You hypocrites! You know how to interpret the appearance of earth and sky, but why do you not know how to interpret the present time?"**NRSV Jesus was announcing an earthshaking event that would be much more important than the year's crops—the coming of God's kingdom. Like a rainstorm or a sunny day, there were signs that the kingdom would soon arrive. While people could successfully discern the signs of the weather by watching the sky and predicting fair weather or storms, they were intentionally ignoring the signs of the times.

12:57-59 **"Why can't you decide for yourselves what is right? If you are on the way to court and you meet your accuser, try to settle the matter before it reaches the judge, or you may be sentenced and handed over to an officer and thrown in jail. And if that happens, you won't be free again until you have paid the last penny."**NLT With the signs of the kingdom around them and as Jesus stood among them, he asked his listeners, *"Why can't you decide for yourselves what is right?"* Why was it so difficult for them to recognize him? Why weren't they taking advantage of this opportunity to make peace with God? They ought to do so, for waiting could be disastrous, just as the man on his way to court would be wise to settle the matter beforehand. In Jesus' day, a person who couldn't pay a debt would be *thrown in jail* until he *paid the last penny.* A "penny" was one of the smallest

Roman coins, worth two-fifths of a cent. This shows that the debt had to be fully paid. Debts were repaid by selling property or going into contract as an indentured servant or slave. If the person had no way to earn money to pay back the debt, he or she could very well die in prison. How much better to attempt to settle the matter *on the way to court* (under Roman law, the plaintiff went with the defendant to court) than to wait for the judge's verdict to be handed down.

God's judgment is irreversible. Each person must decide what to do about Jesus. That decision should be made now.

LUKE 13

In Jesus' previous exhortation, he admonished the people to realize their predicament, that judgment was around the corner. Here Jesus took the sudden and terrifying deaths of some innocent people to illustrate their tragic situation. Still stunned by the grisly murders, the people were, in effect, told by Jesus that they faced a similar fate—eternal death, much worse than physical death.

Jesus used a contemporary event to drive home a point. The people were wondering whether those who had suffered so much were being specially judged by God. But Jesus forced them to consider whether they themselves were still under God's judgment, a fate even more horrifying than what happened to the people murdered by Pilate. Jesus often used this technique. He didn't let people sit back and analyze a subject; instead, he frequently confronted them, pressing them to reevaluate their lives in light of God's perfect law (see Jesus' answer to the lawyer in 10:25-37). Set aside a time to evaluate your speech, thought, and actions, according to God's standards. Leave enough time to confess your faults to Jesus and to receive the forgiveness you need to start anew.

13:1 About this time Jesus was informed that Pilate had murdered some people from Galilee as they were sacrificing at the Temple in Jerusalem.^{NLT} *Pilate* was last mentioned in 3:1. Pontius Pilate was the Roman governor of the province of Judea from A.D. 26 to 36. The city of *Jerusalem,* the site of the Jews' *Temple,* lay in his jurisdiction. Pilate, a harsh man, held only contempt for the Jews. Being stationed to rule such people in a far outpost of the Roman Empire probably hurt his pride and made the prospect of further promotion highly unlikely, so he took pleasure in demonstrating his authority over the Jewish people. At one point, he impounded money from the temple treasuries to build an aqueduct; another time, he insulted Jewish sensibilities by bringing imperial images into the city.

Pilate had a small contingent of soldiers, and his main duty was to keep the Pax Romana—the peace that ancient Rome imposed on all its conquered territories. While no other historical source refers to this incident where *some people from Galilee* were *murdered* at Pilate's orders, it is completely in character for this man. Galilee was a hotbed for fanatics who sought to bring down Rome by force. Galilee was out of Pilate's jurisdiction, but when some Galileans arrived in Jerusalem, they were murdered. Pilate may have heard that these people were plotting a revolt.

After being *informed* of this event, Jesus used it to teach a lesson about suffering and evil in the world.

13:2-3 **He asked them, "Do you think that because these Galileans suffered in this way they were worse sinners than all other Galileans? No, I tell you; but unless you repent, you will all perish as they did."**[NRSV] Jewish theology attributed individual suffering to individual sin. While the Pharisees would also have liked to see Israel freed from Roman control, they were against the use of force that many in Israel (such as a group called the Zealots) were advocating. Some people, such as the Pharisees and their followers, would have thought that these Galileans who were murdered must have been *worse sinners than all other Galileans* because they had *suffered in this way.* The Pharisees, who were opposed to using force to deal with Rome, would have said that the Galileans deserved to die for rebelling.

Jesus explained, however, that suffering has nothing to do with one's spiritual state. In fact, all people are sinful, and unless people repent, they *will all perish as they did.* This doesn't mean that everyone will be killed in such a manner. It could mean that death will be sudden with no second chance to repent, or it could mean that Jesus' listeners would suffer at the hands of the Roman conquerors (which the entire nation did in A.D. 70 when Jerusalem was destroyed and millions of Jews were killed).

13:4-5 **"And what about the eighteen men who died when the Tower of Siloam fell on them? Were they the worst sinners in Jerusalem? No, and I tell you again that unless you repent, you will also perish."**[NLT] Just as suffering is no indicator of one's spiritual state, neither is tragedy. The Pharisees would have seen the previous incident as God's judgment on the Zealots, but the Zealots would have seen this incident as God's judgment against those who had compromised with Rome. Again, popular thought would have concluded that the *eighteen men who died when the Tower of Siloam fell on them* must have been the eighteen *worst sinners in Jerusalem;* otherwise they would not have suffered such a fate. The Zealots, a group of anti-Roman terrorists, would have said that the aqueduct workers deserved to die for cooperating. The Zealots would have considered Jews working on a Roman project such as this as traitors and deserving of God's punishment.

Again Jesus explained that all people are sinners who must repent or they too will *perish*—spiritual death with eternal consequences. He said that neither the Galileans nor the workers should be blamed for their calamity. Instead of blaming others, everyone should consider his or her own day of judgment. People never know when they will die and be called to face their Maker. Just as believers should be ready for any moment when Christ will return, so they should be ready for any moment when they could be taken in death. Whether a person is killed in a tragic accident or miraculously survives is not a measure of righteousness. Everyone has to die; that's part of being human. But not everyone needs to stay dead. Jesus promised that those who repent of their sins and believe in him will not perish but have eternal life (John 3:16).

OF LIFE AND DEATH

Jesus dismissed ideas widespread in his day that accidents or human cruelties were God's judgment on especially pernicious sinners. Why else would some die and others live? Jesus did not answer that question but instead pointed to everyone's need for repentance.

Today some families will experience grief because of a car accident, airplane disaster, flood, tornado, or violent crime. They will ask why, and they will struggle to understand the unfairness of the loss. Jesus pointed to the only answer: God's grace. Accept Jesus as Lord and Savior today. When disaster strikes, God's promise will sustain you.

13:6-7 Then he told this parable: "A man had a fig tree planted in his vineyard; and he came looking for fruit on it and found none. So he said to the gardener, 'See here! For three years I have come looking for fruit on this fig tree, and still I find none. Cut it down! Why should it be wasting the soil?'"NRSV After highlighting the need for repentance, Jesus *told this parable* to show the people that while God is gracious in giving people time to repent, come to him, and grow in him, that patience will not go on forever. In the Old Testament, a fruitful tree was often used as a symbol of godly living (see, for example, Psalm 1:3 and Jeremiah 17:7-8). Jesus pointed out what would happen to the other kind of tree—the kind that took valuable time and space and still produced nothing for the patient gardener. In this way, Jesus warned his listeners that God would not tolerate forever their lack of productivity. (See 3:9 for John the Baptist's version of the same message.) A *fig tree* in the fertile soil of a *vineyard* should certainly have produced fruit—a tree that did not produce *for three years* was probably not going to produce at all. The farmer gave the command to *cut it down* so another, more fruitful tree could be planted in its place.

13:8-9 **"The gardener answered, 'Give it one more chance. Leave it another year, and I'll give it special attention and plenty of fertilizer. If we get figs next year, fine. If not, you can cut it down.'"**[NLT] The *gardener* intervened and asked the owner to *give [the tree] one more chance*. He even offered to give it *special attention* and *fertilizer.* Jesus had come to the nation; the time for repentance had come. The extra attention and love had been showered on the nation in the presence of their Messiah. God's judgment had been graciously held back. But if the people continued to refuse to "bear fruit" for God—if they continued to refuse to live for and obey him—the end would come. The tree would be cut down. There would be no more chances. God is merciful toward sinners. But for those who reject him, he will not be merciful forever. They will be punished.

GOD'S PATIENCE
God patiently allows more time. Do you suffer from an addiction that has spoiled your life for years? Lots of people have given up on you, but not God. Have you resisted coming to faith, forgiving your family, or admitting a crime—and the festering secret has spoiled friendships and jobs?

Maybe you've given up on yourself. But God has not given up on you. Give your problem to him. With the support of mature Christians, seek the help you need. Make the change today.

JESUS HEALS THE CRIPPLED WOMAN / 13:10-17 / 146

The story of healing this woman is unique to Luke. It reveals the unfruitfulness of the nation of Israel to which Jesus' parable of the unfruitful tree alludes (in the previous passage, see 13:6-8). Instead of finding love, justice, humility, and mercy among God's people, Jesus found an arrogance that didn't even allow healing a woman on the Sabbath, the day set aside for the God of mercy. The Jewish leaders had perverted God's law so much that they were using it as an excuse to squelch compassion and godliness, instead of as a tool to promote a love of God and others. Their hypocrisy was evident, and Jesus plainly said so (as he had previously, 12:56). Jesus exposes the same type of hypocrisy today. Christians should always be careful to never use religion as an excuse to judge others. Instead, Christians need to show love and mercy to other people, no matter who they are.

13:10-11 **One Sabbath day as Jesus was teaching in a synagogue, he saw a woman who had been crippled by an evil spirit. She had been bent double for eighteen years and was unable to stand up straight.**[NLT] As Luke has previously recorded, Jesus often could be found *teaching in a synagogue* on the Sabbath day, the Jewish day of worship (4:16, 31; 6:6). Jesus had already come into conflict with the religious leaders over how the Sabbath should be used. He consistently flouted their many laws, one of which was not to work on the Sabbath—meaning, to the Pharisees, not even doing a good deed such as healing a person (6:1-9). At this particular time, as Jesus looked over the crowd, *he saw a woman who . . . had been bent double for eighteen years.* The text explains that this was the work of *an evil spirit.* She may not have been demon possessed, because a demon didn't speak and Jesus did not cast out any demon. Instead, this woman's painful affliction is attributed to Satan's work in the world (see 13:16).

13:12-13 **When Jesus saw her, he called her forward and said to her, "Woman, you are set free from your infirmity." Then he put his hands on her, and immediately she straightened up and praised God.**[NIV] Jesus took the initiative in this healing, as he had for the man with the deformed hand (6:6-9). The woman did not ask; instead, Jesus *called her forward.* Jesus knew people's unasked needs, and clearly he wanted this woman to be *set free* from this horrible *infirmity.* Also, he had the power to do it. So *he put his hands on her* and she was *immediately* healed. She stood up straight for the first time in eighteen years (her age is not given—she may have been crippled that way for most of her life). No wonder her first response was to praise God!

13:14 **Indignant because Jesus had healed on the Sabbath, the synagogue ruler said to the people, "There are six days for work. So come and be healed on those days, not on the Sabbath."**[NIV] Jesus had performed a great miracle with God's power; a woman had been set free from years of suffering and was praising God! What better way to spend a Sabbath? What better teaching about God's compassion than this visual display for the crowds gathered there? The *synagogue ruler* (the leader who served as administrator) should have rejoiced. Instead, he was *indignant.* Why? Because *Jesus had healed on the Sabbath.* As noted in commentary on 6:1-2 and 6:6-7, the religious leaders had a written code of many actions that were forbidden on the Sabbath, including any type of work. The religious leaders regarded healing as part of a doctor's profes-

SEVEN SABBATH MIRACLES

Over the centuries, the Jewish religious leaders had added rule after rule to God's law. For example, God's law said the Sabbath is a day of rest (Exodus 20:10-11). But the religious leaders added to that law, creating one that said, "You cannot heal on the Sabbath 'because that is work.'" Seven times Jesus healed people on the Sabbath. In doing this, he was challenging these religious leaders to look beneath their rules to the true purpose of the rules—to honor God by helping those in need. Would God have been pleased if Jesus had ignored these people?

Jesus sends a demon out of a man . . . . Mark 1:21-28

Jesus heals Peter's mother-in-law . . . . Mark 1:29-31

Jesus heals a lame man by Bethesda Pool . . . . John 5:1-18

Jesus heals a man with a shriveled hand . . . . Mark 3:1-6

Jesus restores a crippled woman . . . . Luke 13:10-17

Jesus heals a man with dropsy . . . . Luke 14:1-6

Jesus heals a man born blind . . . . John 9:1-16

---

sion, and practicing one's profession on the Sabbath was prohibited. The synagogue ruler, who was addressing his remarks *to the people* and not to Jesus, could not see beyond the law to Jesus' compassion in healing this crippled woman. He simply concluded that if Jesus wanted to heal people, he should reserve his healings for the other six days, not the Sabbath. For Jesus to do that, however, would mean endorsing the many petty laws that had grown up around God's basic laws regarding Sabbath observance. Jesus did not need to abide by those laws, for they did not fulfill God's intention for the Sabbath and were burdensome on the people. Jesus had already explained, at another Sabbath healing, that he was Lord of the Sabbath (6:5).

13:15-16 But the Lord answered him and said, "You hypocrites! Does not each of you on the sabbath untie his ox or his donkey from the manger, and lead it away to give it water? And ought not this woman, a daughter of Abraham whom Satan bound for eighteen long years, be set free from this bondage on the sabbath day?"NRSV Jesus shamed this synagogue ruler and the other leaders by pointing out their hypocrisy. They would untie their animals and care for them on the Sabbath. Yet these same people refused to see that care for humans is far more important. They were such *hypocrites,* willing to help animals but not willing to help a human being, a *woman, a daughter of Abraham.* What "work" had Jesus done? He had merely reached out and touched her—not even as much work as leading an *ox* or *donkey* to water.

Yet these hypocrites could not see past their laws. They hid behind their own set of laws to avoid love's obligations. People today can use the letter of the law to rationalize away their obligation to care for others (for example, by tithing regularly and then refusing to help a needy neighbor). But people's needs are more important than rules and regulations. Take time to help others, even if doing so might compromise your public image.

Jesus attributed the woman's illness to *Satan* and *bondage* by him. In this fallen world, disease and disability are common. Their causes are many and often multiple—inadequate nutrition, contact with a source of infection, lowered defenses, and even direct attack by Satan. Whatever the immediate cause of an illness, its original source is Satan, the author of all the evil in the world. The good news is that Jesus is more powerful than any devil or any disease. He often brings physical healing in this life; and when he returns, he will put an end to all disease and disability.

OPEN TO CARING
Religious do-goodism had so infected Israel's leadership that, by some twist of religious logic, they had come to see the Lord's Sabbath as a day when compassion was illegal. Jesus would have no part of it.

Today, well-meaning Christians have allowed purely human rules to intrude on the church's welcome to "outsiders." Dress codes, hair codes, behavior codes, and language codes give many churches a pharisaic feel. Let Jesus remove all such barriers to people finding God's love. Let compassion be your guide; let the rules that hinder it be forgotten.

13:17 When he said this, all his opponents were humiliated, but the people were delighted with all the wonderful things he was doing.[NIV] When Jesus made this point, *the people were delighted.* They probably appreciated a rabbi who stood up for them against the burdensome laws that the religious leaders had placed on them in every area of life. Jesus' *opponents were humiliated.* What more could they say? Jesus had called them hypocrites, and the people were delighted with him and his miracles. This humiliation would cause such intense hatred that they would plot to kill him.

JESUS TEACHES ABOUT THE KINGDOM OF GOD / 13:18-21 / 147

First-century Jews expected the kingdom of God to come all at once, in great glory and power. But Jesus corrected their perception, by the illustrations of the mustard seed and yeast. Both are small; but one grows into a huge tree and the other eventually permeates an entire loaf.

Jesus did not want his listeners to be deceived by appearances. His ministry was small—healing the sick only in Israel—but the ministry of the gospel would eventually grow to cover the entire globe (a story Luke begins to tell in the book of Acts). The kingdom of God had come upon them whether they realized it or not (11:20). Two thousand years later, God's kingdom has continued to grow, spreading to every nation. Christians all over the world are awaiting Jesus' second coming, when he *will* come in glory, compelling everyone to bow before him.

13:18-19 **He said therefore, "What is the kingdom of God like? And to what should I compare it? It is like a mustard seed that someone took and sowed in the garden; it grew and became a tree, and the birds of the air made nests in its branches."**NRSV Jesus used a variety of parables to describe what the *kingdom of God* is *like*. Nothing on earth can completely explain the kingdom or give us an adequate picture of it, for the kingdom will be far beyond anything we could ever imagine. Jesus took this parable to explain that his kingdom would have a small beginning. The general expectation among Jesus' hearers was that the Messiah would come as a great king and leader, freeing the nation from Rome and restoring Israel's former glory. But Jesus said that his kingdom was beginning quietly. The *mustard seed* was so small that it would take almost twenty thousand seeds to make one ounce.

From one tiny seed would grow a large shrub—the largest shrub among all the herbs that the farmer would plant in his *garden*. A mustard shrub could grow ten to twelve feet in just a few weeks. No other seed so small produced such a large plant. While that is not technically a "tree," Jesus used its rapid growth to stress both the insignificance and magnificence of the kingdom. Like the tiny mustard seed that becomes a large plant, the kingdom of God would eventually push outward until the whole world would be changed.

Jesus' mention of *birds of the air* added color and showed how large the shrub could become, but it probably had no allegorical meaning. Some commentators, however, think the birds may represent the Gentiles becoming part of God's kingdom (see prophecies such as Ezekiel 17:22-24; 31:6).

13:20-21 **He also asked, "What else is the Kingdom of God like? It is like yeast used by a woman making bread. Even though she used a large amount of flour, the yeast permeated every part of the dough."**NLT Another symbol of something small producing something much larger occurs with *yeast* added to *flour* in making *dough*. In some Bible passages, "yeast" is used as a symbol of evil or uncleanness (12:1). Here it pictures positive growth. While the mustard seed grows, the yeast permeates and transforms, providing another picture of *the Kingdom of God*. Although yeast looks like a minor ingredient (only a small amount is used), it is responsible for the dough's rising. Although God's kingdom had small beginnings, it would grow to have a great impact on the world.

Jesus made it clear that his kingdom would not be a political coup overthrowing Roman oppression. Instead, the kingdom would steadily grow in people's hearts, making a difference in people's lives and preparing them for life to come in that eternal kingdom.

PLANT LIFE
Chances are you have never planted a mustard seed, never watched mustard grow, never measured the mass of a full-grown plant against its original seed. No matter.

Next spring, take any seed—most are small. It represents your life with God. Plant it. Care for it. Each time you check it, praise God for your growing faith. It may be slow and quiet, but it's sprouting and bearing and reaching for the sun. When you water that plant, water your life with God's Word. When you weed around that plant, eliminate activities that stunt your spiritual growth. As you watch it grow and blossom, thank God for his personal love and care for you.

JESUS TEACHES ABOUT ENTERING THE KINGDOM / 13:22-30 / **153**

A key theme of Luke comes into sharp focus: salvation (1:69, 71, 77; 2:30; 3:6; 7:50; 9:24; 19:10). Jesus answered a person who asked whether only a few would be saved. Jesus turned this theoretical question into a practical question. Instead of letting the questioner analyze who would be entering heaven and, by implication, judge the process and then those who would enter, Jesus asked that person, "Are *you* saved?"

Jesus didn't divulge how many people would be in heaven; instead, he encouraged the people to "make every effort" to be saved (13:24 NIV). Clearly Jesus wasn't implying "salvation by works," for entry into the narrow gate is controlled by the owner of the house (a reference to Jesus himself). Entry into the gate is dependent on whether the person knows the owner. In the same way, salvation is guaranteed by knowing Jesus, believing in him, and obeying his instructions. Don't let yourself be distracted by worrying about who will and who will not be in heaven. This is ultimately God's righteous decision, which should not be questioned by any person. Instead, focus on yourself, making sure your heart is humbly devoted to Christ.

13:22 And He went through the cities and villages, teaching, and journeying toward Jerusalem.^{NKJV} This is the second reminder that Jesus was intentionally *journeying toward Jerusalem* (the other time is in 9:51). Jesus knew he was on his way to die, but he continued traveling *through cities and villages, teaching* the crowds. The prospect of death did not deter Jesus from his mission.

FINDING SALVATION
Many people react negatively to the concept of a narrow door or of Jesus being the only way. Behind their reaction may be the desire that the door of their choosing be the right way to God. The point of Jesus' story was not to keep people out or to make it difficult to enter but to stress that the narrow door was still open for a short time. God opens the door, not people. He makes salvation available. People do not custom-design their own salvation. All people must come to God on his terms, not their own.

It's difficult to submit and surrender to God. It's difficult to accept someone else's terms, even God's. It's difficult to give up control.

Don't let your ego keep you from God.

13:23-24 Someone asked him, "Lord, will only a few be saved?" He said to them, "Strive to enter through the narrow door; for many, I tell you, will try to enter and will not be able."^{NRSV} The question about whether *only a few* or many people would *be saved* was a topic of debate and much speculation among the rabbis. Jesus refused to be drawn into taking a side in this argument; instead, he urged his listeners to be among those who would be saved, no matter what the final number might be. He told his audience to *strive to enter through the narrow door.* The word "strive" means to put one's whole self into the task of listening and responding. Finding salvation requires concentrated effort. Obviously people cannot save themselves—there is no way to "work" into God's favor. This "striving" means earnestly desiring to know Christ and diligently following him whatever the cost. Jesus did not explain "the narrow" door, but the picture is of a way that one must seek out and then enter into while it is still open. Keeping the law or simply being Jewish will not earn salvation; only by entering the door through faith can anyone be saved. At other times, Jesus said,

"I am the gate" (John 10:9 NRSV) and "I am the way" (John 14:6). Jesus explained that although many people know something about God, only a few have acknowledged their sins and accepted his forgiveness. Just listening to Jesus' words or admiring his miracles is not enough—all must turn from sin and trust in God for salvation. Regardless of how many would be saved, Jesus said that *many . . . will try to enter and will not be able.* The time for decision would pass them by, and it would be too late, as Jesus described in the following parable.

13:25-27 **"Once the owner of the house gets up and closes the door, you will stand outside knocking and pleading, 'Sir, open the door for us.' But he will answer, 'I don't know you or where you come from.' Then you will say, 'We ate and drank with you, and you taught in our streets.' But he will reply, 'I don't know you or where you come from. Away from me, all you evildoers!'"**[NIV] Familiarity with Jesus will not count when God's kingdom arrives and people rush to be a part of it. When the door is closed, the time for salvation will have passed, and they will "not be able" to enter (13:24). While many will claim to have eaten with him and listened to his teaching, they had not turned to him in faith for salvation. Such people will be utterly rejected, for Jesus will simply say, *"I don't know you."* Such words will be the final pronouncement of rejection on those who rejected him. They will be sent *away* from God, the kingdom, and all that is good—sent to be among *evildoers.* Only two groups will be at the final judgment—those who by faith accepted the salvation Jesus offered, and those who rejected it.

TRUE FAITH
How could those who have known Jesus be rejected by him? Jesus makes clear that the way of salvation is open to all. No one is excluded by birth or background (13:29). Yet salvation does not happen merely because of loose association with Jesus. Jesus said in 5:32, "I have not come to call the righteous, but sinners to repentance" (NIV). We must come to Jesus on his terms, not our own. Jesus requires action, namely repentance, from those who desire to be his followers. As we present Christ to others, we must stress the importance of repentance. As we deal with those who have been in the church for many years, we must help them see that associating with Christians will not substitute for true faith and repentance.

13:28 **"And there will be great weeping and gnashing of teeth, for you will see Abraham, Isaac, Jacob, and all the prophets within the Kingdom of God, but you will be thrown out."**[NLT]

Apparently many of these "evildoers" and outcasts will be Jews who had expected that, by virtue of their nationality, they would be in God's kingdom. When the door is shut and they are sent away, there will be intense sorrow *(weeping and gnashing of teeth).* Jesus pictured them looking in the windows at the ancestors on whom they had depended for their salvation—the patriarchs *Abraham, Isaac, and Jacob.* They will also see *all the prophets,* many of whom had been slain for speaking God's messages. Such people will be feasting in *the Kingdom of God* because they had loved and obeyed him. These men had not had the opportunity to see the Messiah, but they had loved God, believed his promises, and trusted that he would accomplish what he said. Thus, they received places in the kingdom. By contrast, many of these Jewish people, who *did* have the opportunity to eat and drink with and then listen to the teachings of the Messiah himself (13:26), subsequently rejected him. For such rejection they would be *thrown out* of the kingdom.

13:29-30 "People will come from east and west and north and south, and will take their places at the feast in the kingdom of God. Indeed there are those who are last who will be first, and first who will be last."[NIV] God's kingdom will include people from every part of the world. Israel's rejection of Jesus as Messiah would not stop God's plan. True Israel includes all people who believe in God. Jesus promised that *people will come from east and west and north and south, and will take their places at the feast* (see Isaiah 49:12). The inclusion of Gentiles in God's kingdom had been prophesied, but it still would have astounded Jesus' Jewish audience to hear of the Gentiles' being involved in God's kingdom at all. This was an important fact for Luke to stress because he was directing his Gospel to a Gentile audience (see also Romans 4:16-25; Galatians 3:6-9). Even worse for these Jews, however, was the statement that some of them might *not* have places at the feast.

In addition, there will be many surprises in God's kingdom. Some who are despised now will be greatly honored then; some influential people here will be left outside the gates. Many "great" people on this earth (in God's eyes) are virtually ignored by the rest of the world. What matters to God is not a person's earthly popularity, status, wealth, heritage, or power, but his or her commitment to Christ. How do your values match what the Bible tells you to value? Put God in first place, and you will join people from all over the world who will take their places at the feast in the kingdom of heaven.

FIRST-PLACE FINISHERS
If nations grow by war and conquest, God's kingdom grows
slowly and quietly. If successful people fight to the top,
successful Christians enjoy the bottom.
   Someday, all the strategies for greatness the world has
devised will be dismantled as God's kingdom fully emerges.
The poor, ordinary, faithful believer will be honored as first; the
powerful pagan will be relegated to last. Don't be troubled by
your ordinary life today. Faithfully follow Jesus. At history's
finish line, you will be a champion.

JESUS GRIEVES OVER JERUSALEM / 13:31-35 / 154

Luke placed Jesus' grieving over Jerusalem right after a discussion about salvation, those being first (the Jews who were chosen
by God) being placed last (or excluded from God's heavenly
kingdom). Jesus mourned Jerusalem's rejection of God's message
and salvation. He used an intimate image of a hen and her chicks
to describe his love for the Jews and the tragedy of their rejection. God has that same type of love for everyone (John 3:16;
Romans 5:8). He loved his people when they were still sinners,
even willing to give up his Son for their sins.

13:31 **At that time some Pharisees came to Jesus and said to him,
"Leave this place and go somewhere else. Herod wants to
kill you."**NIV The motives of these *Pharisees* remain unknown—
they may have been concerned for Jesus. Given the general
attitude of most of the Pharisees, however, it is more likely that
they weren't interested in protecting Jesus from danger. Perhaps they were simply trying to get him out of their area, wanting him to *go somewhere else*. They thought that telling Jesus
of Herod's plan (whether true or not) would cause Jesus to be
afraid and run. This was the same *Herod* who had killed John
the Baptist and who had been perplexed about who Jesus was
(9:7-9). It is highly possible that he did want to kill Jesus. But
Jesus' life, work, and death were not to be determined by Herod
or the Pharisees. His life was planned and directed by God himself, and his mission would unfold in God's time and according
to God's plan.

13:32 **He said to them, "Go and tell that fox for me, 'Listen, I am
casting out demons and performing cures today and tomorrow, and on the third day I finish my work.'"**NRSV Jesus was
hardly going to run in fear of Herod; in fact, the message he
sent to him was filled with contempt, calling Herod *that fox*. To

call someone a "fox" showed that Jesus saw Herod as without honor, without greatness befitting one who was king, filled with slyness mixed with evil. He had clearly shown that in his dealings with John the Baptist. In Jesus' day, a "fox" was also someone who was considered insignificant. That Jesus told the Pharisees to *go and tell* Herod this message could point to Jesus' understanding that they were actually in league with Herod. Jesus clearly explained that Herod would have absolutely no control of Jesus' life and ministry. Jesus would continue *casting out demons and performing cures.* Jesus also understood, however, that his earthly ministry would not go on forever. There would be an end. "The third day I finish my work" could refer to his plan for leaving Herod's jurisdiction and moving on, or it could refer to the work of redemption that he would soon accomplish through his death.

ON GOD'S TERMS
Often it appears that life unfolds by accident, by someone's power-decision, or by luck. Jesus knew that life unfolds by God's guidance and control. Herod could hunt for him, but God alone controlled Jesus' future.
Likewise for you. Don't worry about threats or accidents or evil catching up with you. Your life is God's to guide. Don't be afraid. You will fulfill the purpose God has for you.

13:33-34 **"In any case, I must keep going today and tomorrow and the next day—for surely no prophet can die outside Jerusalem!"**NIV Jesus had definite purpose—he knew exactly what he was supposed to do, and absolutely followed God's plan. Jesus knew that he *must keep going* in his ministry until the very moment appointed for his death. The words "surely no prophet can die outside Jerusalem" have a stinging sound—Jesus knew he was to die and he knew he would die in Jerusalem. The city of God, Jerusalem, was Israel's largest city and the nation's spiritual and political capital. Jews from around the world visited it frequently. Jesus had visited the city on previous occasions, going to the annual festivals. But Jerusalem had a history of rejecting God's prophets (1 Kings 19:10; 2 Chronicles 24:19-21; Jeremiah 2:30; 26:20-23), and it would reject the Messiah just as it had rejected his forerunners. Thus Jesus mourned for the city, **"O Jerusalem, Jerusalem, the one who kills the prophets and stones those who are sent to her! How often I wanted to gather your children together, as a hen gathers her brood under her wings, but you were not willing!"**NKJV Jesus' emotional words reveal his compassion and love for the people to whom he had come. Like a mother *hen* who *gathers her brood under her wings,* Jesus would have gathered his people under *wings* of love and protection. Several places in the Old Testament picture the loving God protecting his people under his "wings" (see Ruth 2:12; Psalms 17:8; 36:7; 57:1; 61:4; 63:7; 91:4). But they *were not willing* to be sheltered; they were not willing to accept their Savior's love. Instead, they rejected him and sealed their fate.

FULL RANGE OF EMOTION
Jesus was clearly saddened by Israel's resistance to God's message. His compassion for people included love's full range of emotions.
So should yours. When love gets exuberant, let it show. When love must weep, don't hide your emotion under a stalwart, phony front.
Jesus was "real." He spoke about his feelings. He voiced the reasons for his sadness. Follow his permission to do likewise.

13:35 **"Look, your house is left to you desolate. I tell you, you will not see me again until you say, 'Blessed is he who comes in the name of the Lord.'"**[NIV] "House" could refer to the city itself or to its temple. The nation had rejected their promised Messiah and invited the final result of such rejection. They would be *desolate* (or forsaken). Jesus may have been referring to Jeremiah 12:7: "I will forsake my house, abandon my inheritance; I will give the one I love into the hands of her enemies" (NIV). Jeremiah had prophesied the coming destruction of the temple by the Babylonians. The nation's sin had sealed their punishment, and God's presence had left the temple. When Jesus Christ came, God himself again stood in the temple. But the people's refusal to accept him would have severe consequences, for he would leave again. The temple stood for the people's relationship with God; a "desolate" temple meant separation from God (see Matthew 23:38).

The Jews understood their temple to be the dwelling place of God on earth. The city was intended to be the center of worship of the true God and a symbol of justice to all people. No wonder Jesus loved the city and grieved over it. But the people had become blind to God. They had killed the prophets and would put to death the one about whom the prophets had testified. In that very city, the Messiah would be rejected and put to death (13:33). God's presence would leave what was supposed to have been the holy city. The city would not see him again until the words of Psalm 118:26 would be fulfilled: *"Blessed is he who comes in the name of the Lord."* While some take this to refer to Jesus' triumphal entry, Matthew recorded these same words as being spoken after the Triumphal Entry (Matthew 23:39). The solemn prediction of desolation would come true, but as always, God would have compassion. A day would come when some of God's people would recognize him as their Messiah (Romans 11:25-26).

LUKE 14

To illustrate how Israel rejected Jesus (13:31-35), Luke recorded an example of the Pharisees' opposition to Jesus (see 14:7-24). Here again is a miracle performed on the Sabbath (see 13:10-17), a direct confrontation with the Pharisees and their understanding of the nature of the Sabbath. These confrontations between Jesus and the Pharisees on the Sabbath highlight the hard-heartedness of the Israelites, especially their religious leaders. In the face of repeated miracles, the Pharisees stood stone-faced. They did not rejoice with the man healed of dropsy; instead, they accused and condemned Jesus for having compassion and doing good. Don't let official religion harden you to the needs of people around you. Break the invisible social barriers of your community, church, or school, and reach out to the needy. Reflect Jesus' love in your life.

14:1 One Sabbath, when Jesus went to eat in the house of a prominent Pharisee, he was being carefully watched.NIV Earlier Jesus had been invited to a Pharisee's home for dinner (7:36). This time a prominent Pharisee (literally "ruler of the Pharisees") invited Jesus to his home, but Jesus *was being carefully watched.* It may be surprising to see Jesus on the Pharisees' turf after he had denounced them so many times. Perhaps this *prominent Pharisee* actually wanted to learn from Jesus or was interested in a discussion with him. But the fact that Jesus was being watched, and the fact that he addresses several Pharisees and teachers of the law (14:2-3), makes it seem that there was more behind this meal than a simple discussion. Evidently the religious leaders at this meal were hoping to trip up Jesus. Because it was another *Sabbath,* perhaps they again hoped to find Jesus violating their Sabbath rules.

14:2-3 There in front of him was a man suffering from dropsy. Jesus asked the Pharisees and experts in the law, "Is it lawful to heal on the Sabbath or not?"NIV It seems quite suspicious that a man *suffering from dropsy* happened to be *there in front of* Jesus at a meal with a group of religious leaders who were carefully watching him (14:1). This certainly makes one wonder if this man were not there on purpose—as a plant by the religious leaders so they could again catch Jesus in the act of healing on the Sabbath. It is also possible that the man was an outsider who came in near Jesus, as had the woman who had anointed Jesus' feet at another Pharisee's house (7:37-38). Luke, the physician, identified this man's disease as "dropsy" (also called edema), an abnormal accumulation of fluid in bodily tissues and cavities causing swelling. It may have been related to a heart condition.

Jesus knew what his "watchers" were thinking, so he asked them the question that had caused friction between him and them before: *"Is it lawful to heal on the Sabbath or not?"* That was the crux of the matter. Under any normal circumstances, a person would say that it would be perfectly all right to heal another human being on the Sabbath. Yet because the Pharisees had added so many rules regarding Sabbath observance, and because they allowed the rules to occupy their lives, they would have answered Jesus' question in the negative. Their oral tradition said that it was only lawful to heal on the Sabbath if it was a life-threatening situation. But Jesus would heal on the Sabbath no matter what the Pharisees thought, for he was Lord of the Sabbath. (For more on Sabbath healings, see commentary on 6:1-9; 13:10-17.)

SORTING RIGHT FROM WRONG
Sometimes matters of right and wrong can get very complicated, as they had here concerning "lawful" Sabbath activities. Jesus cut through all the complications with a simple appeal to love.

Is your faith in gridlock (like the Pharisees) because of overlapping and conflicting regulations that hardly seem to make sense? With each action ask yourself—what does love require?

Love will always respect God's rules (the Ten Commandments, for example) and will always serve people's best interests. Often a simple appeal to love will cut through the fog and clarify a plan of action.

14:4-6 When they refused to answer, Jesus touched the sick man and healed him and sent him away. Then he turned to them and asked, "Which of you doesn't work on the Sabbath? If your son or your cow falls into a pit, don't you proceed at once to get him out?" Again they had no answer.NLT The religious leaders *refused to answer* Jesus' question. Why didn't they respond? Why didn't they explain that it was not lawful and then patiently tell him why? Because they knew Jesus would heal the man and because they were hoping to use it against him. The men had no more concern for their rules at this moment than Jesus did. The rules did not serve the purpose, so they refused to answer. So Jesus *touched the sick man and healed him and sent him away.* Just as he had done with the crippled woman (13:10-17), Jesus did no more than touch the man. The Pharisees' rules and regulations did not ban touching another person. In fact, Jesus explained that when it served their purposes, they *did* work on the Sabbath. They could go pull a son or a cow out of a pit if need be, but they were ready to condemn Jesus for touching a man and healing him from a disease. Jesus pointed this out to them, but *they had no answer.*

JESUS TEACHES ABOUT SEEKING HONOR / 14:7-14 / 156

Jesus wasn't one to mince words; he didn't wait for a discreet time to teach and preach. In the midst of his enemies (the Pharisees were carefully watching him to see if they could trap him in any way), Jesus admonished them for their arrogance. The Pharisees possessed great social power in first-century Israel, and they were jockeying with each other for the greater position (similar to the disciples, whom Jesus also rebuked, 9:46-48). Jesus' rebuke is clear: Don't exalt yourself. Instead humble yourself—even to the extent of being willing to serve the poor, the crippled, the lame, and the blind. Jesus was encouraging the people to refocus their sights, from exalting themselves to exalting and serving others. Jesus calls Christians today to do the same. Humble yourself before the Lord and seek to serve others. Whom can you help this week?

ON YOUR HONOR
Here's practical advice on avoiding embarrassment and practicing the love that serves others:
- If you desire to be elected deacon in your church, nominate and support someone else.
- If you want to be regarded as a great student of the Bible, be an avid learner and an infrequent expositor.

Direct your ambition for honor toward someone else's gain. Then if honor comes to you, it will not be due to self-promotion.

14:7-9 **When he noticed how the guests chose the places of honor, he told them a parable. "When you are invited by someone to a wedding banquet, do not sit down at the place of honor, in case someone more distinguished than you has been invited by your host; and the host who invited both of you may come and say to you, 'Give this person your place,' and then in dis-**

grace you would start to take the lowest place."ᴺᴿˢⱽ In Jesus' day, Jewish custom at a dinner was to arrange couches in a U shape with a low table in front of them. Guests reclined on the left elbow, and they would be seated according to status, with the place of honor being the seat at the center of the U. The seats would decline in status the farther away from that seat of honor. If arrivals had placed themselves in the *places of honor,* and then *someone more distinguished* arrived, they would be asked to move to lower seats. By then, the only seat that would still be open would be the *lowest place.*

This may seem like an odd bit of social manners given by Jesus, but his meaning went much deeper. This *wedding banquet* pictures the Messiah's kingdom. Those who seek honor for themselves will be disgraced. Jesus explains that honor cannot be taken; it must be given by God. He will not honor those who seek to honor themselves.

TRULY HUMBLE
Who are those who exalt themselves? They are the arrogant people. They're the ones who, in any group of people, would rather talk than listen, dominating the conversation with their own thoughts and ideas. They consistently think everyone else is far less intelligent than they are. They treat people in service occupations as inferior and meant to serve only them.

Who, then, are the humble people? Unfortunately, some people try to give the appearance of humility in order to manipulate others. Still others think that humility means putting themselves down. Truly humble people compare themselves only with Christ, realize their sinfulness, and understand their limitations. They also recognize their gifts and strengths and are willing to use them as Christ directs. Humility is not self-degradation; it is realistic assessment and commitment to serve.

14:10-11 **"But when you are invited, go and sit down at the lowest place, so that when your host comes, he may say to you, 'Friend, move up higher'; then you will be honored in the presence of all who sit at the table with you. For all who exalt themselves will be humbled, and those who humble themselves will be exalted."**ᴺᴿˢⱽ Jesus explained that people should *go and sit down at the lowest place.* This would show that the person had not overestimated his or her own importance. Then, the host may ask that person to *move up higher,* to a seat of higher honor. Then, instead of being disgraced, the person would be *honored.* The principle would be true in that situation and in the kingdom of God—*all who exalt themselves will be humbled, and*

those who humble themselves will be exalted. The *host,* God himself, will make the final seating arrangements in his kingdom.
People dare not presume upon their own importance; how much
better to be honored by God. They must approach that banquet in
great humility before the host. He alone will decide who deserves
honor.

14:12-14 **Then he turned to his host. "When you put on a luncheon or
a dinner," he said, "don't invite your friends, brothers, relatives, and rich neighbors. For they
will repay you by inviting you back.
Instead, invite the poor, the crippled,
the lame, and the blind. Then at the
resurrection of the godly, God will
reward you for inviting those who
could not repay you."**[NLT] While guests
ought not presume upon their importance in the eyes of their host (14:7-11),
hosts should not be exclusive about
whom they invite. Jesus explained that
they shouldn't invite only people who
can pay them back. Instead, they should
*invite the poor, the crippled, the lame,
and the blind.* When God's people can
do good, without expecting reward or
repayment, they will have truly served
him unselfishly. *God will reward* those
who so willingly serve him. The reason? Because their generosity mirrors
God's. While God offers his kingdom
to everyone, those who accept are often
the ones who seem of so little value to
this world. Yet no one at God's banquet, no matter what their status or power on this earth, can possibly *repay* what God has done.
The *resurrection of the godly* is the resurrection of those who
have trusted Jesus Christ for salvation; their judgment will be one
of rewards for their service for God's kingdom.

> Humility does not mean thinking less of yourself than of other people, nor does it mean having a low opinion of your own gifts. It means freedom from thinking about yourself one way or the other at all. . . . The humility which consists in being a great deal occupied about yourself, and saying you are of little worth, is not Christian humility. It is one form of self-occupation and a very poor and futile one at that.   *William Temple*

JESUS TELLS THE PARABLE OF THE GREAT FEAST / 14:15-24 / **157**

The tie between this parable and the previous one is the resurrection. The host who invites the poor, the crippled, the lame, and
the blind will be rewarded at the resurrection. Jesus went on to

explain that God himself, the heavenly host of the messianic banquet, would offer the same invitation.

WHO SIGNS THE BILL?
Jesus constantly showed concern for the poor and encouraged his followers to do the same. But some people cannot pay. Who volunteers to pay for them? They cannot pay their own way. How amazing that God offers to pick up their bill, eventually. Your helping them now is merely a loan against God's account. Try this:
- Give 10 percent of your entertainment budget toward world hunger relief.
- Adopt a foreign child through a responsible Christian agency.
- Widen your circle of friends to include people who clearly do not earn your income.

Jesus wants his people to show generosity toward others, even those who cannot improve one's social standing or bring someone financial gain.

The parable describes those who were initially invited by God (the Israelites) turning down his offer because they were distracted by the cares of life—buying and selling, marrying and giving in marriage. The irate host orders his servants to go out in the streets, inviting the poor, the blind, the crippled, the lame, and even strangers on the highways to the banquet. They come. This indicates that the Gentiles will come to salvation (a fact recorded in Acts 10), while many Israelites will be excluded. Thus, the first will be last, and the last will be first. This is the great reversal highlighted throughout Luke's Gospel (2:32; 7:1-10). Today most of the Christian church is Gentile. As Romans 9–11 states, this means that Gentile Christians should never take for granted their position in Christ. Salvation is never achieved by one's parents or the church one attends; it is a free gift of God through faith in Jesus. Each person has to accept that gift and not spurn it, as many of the first-century Israelites did.

14:15 **When one of those at the table with him heard this, he said to Jesus, "Blessed is the man who will eat at the feast in the kingdom of God."**[NIV] Jesus' words about the resurrection sparked a comment from *one of those at the table* (apparently a Pharisee or teacher of the law, 14:1-3). The concept of a *feast in the kingdom of God* comes from the Old Testament (see Isaiah 25:6-8), and this Pharisee assumed that he and his fellow Pharisees and other leaders would be *blessed* as part of that celebration. They counted on their ancestry and their law keeping to have reserved places for them (and probably places of highest honor) at this feast. Jesus would shatter this preconception. Those to be "blessed" would be those who humbly accepted the offer of salvation given through Jesus Christ.

JOIN THE FEAST
This chapter gives Jesus' words against seeking status, and in favor of hard work and even suffering. Don't lose sight of the end result of your humility and self-sacrifice—a joyous banquet with the Lord! God never asks his people to suffer for the sake of suffering. He never asks you to give up something good unless he plans to replace it with something even better. Jesus is calling his people to join him not in a labor camp but in a feast—the wedding supper of the Lamb (Revelation 19:6-9), when God and his beloved church will be joined forever. Have you accepted the invitation? Will you be there?

14:16-17 **Jesus replied with this illustration: "A man prepared a great feast and sent out many invitations. When all was ready, he sent his servant around to notify the guests that it was time for them to come."**ᴺᴸᵀ It was customary to send two invitations to a party—the first to announce the event. Thus, this man *prepared a great feast and sent out many invitations.* It does not appear that anyone had declined, so the man made final preparations in order to have enough for everyone. The second invitation told the guests that everything was ready. In this case, the man's *servant* personally notified all the guests that *it was time for them to come.* This custom made perfect sense in a time frame of no telephones, watches, or assured timing for preparation of a huge meal. So the second invitation helped everyone to know exactly when to come.

14:18-20 **"But they all alike began to make excuses. The first said, 'I have just bought a field, and I must go and see it. Please excuse me.' Another said, 'I have just bought five yoke of oxen, and I'm on my way to try them out. Please excuse me.' Still another said, 'I just got married, so I can't come.'"**ᴺᴵⱽ The guests in Jesus' story insulted the host by making *excuses* when he issued the second invitation telling them that everything was ready. The guests decided that other matters were more important at the time—*a field, five yoke of oxen,* and even a spouse. The host was being snubbed. These were lame excuses. Rarely would a person buy a field without already having seen it, or five yoke of oxen without already having tried them out. These answers were the result of preoccupations with material possessions. The wedding was not a surprise to the man between the first and second invitations. He would have known about this commitment, and his intervening marriage would not have rendered him unable to come. This was no more than an excuse.

Business and relationships are certainly vital to people's lives. But they must never substitute for God's invitation and never become an excuse to put off joining God's kingdom. All pursuits, no matter how valid they seem, can rob people of the great celebration with Jesus. Let nothing stand in the way of following Christ.

14:21-23 **"The servant came back and reported this to his master. Then the owner of the house became angry and ordered his servant, 'Go out quickly into the streets and alleys of the town and bring in the poor, the crippled, the blind and the lame.' 'Sir,' the servant said, 'what you ordered has been done, but there is still room.' Then the master told his servant, 'Go out to the roads and country lanes and make them come in, so that my house will be full.'"**NIV Upon learning how his invitations had been snubbed, the master of the house *became angry.* But his banquet was ready; the food had been prepared. Instead of abandoning the whole prospect, he sent his servant *into the streets and alleys of the town* to bring into the banquet hall *the poor, the crippled, the blind and the lame* (see also 14:13). This done, the servant reported back that *there is still room.* So the master again dispatched the servant to go throughout the *roads and country lanes* and fill the house. This story would seem scandalous to Jesus' audience. No ancient wealthy person would ever invite the poor. This startling statement told Jesus' hearers that God's kingdom is especially for the poor. The words "make them come" do not mean to use force, but rather to not take no for an answer. Surely such people would need to be compelled to accept such an invitation; they were not used to being wanted at such an occasion. Not a morsel of food was to go to waste. If the previously invited guests would not accept the hospitality of the master, then he would invite those who would.

TOO LATE
In Jesus' story, many people turned down the invitation to the banquet because the timing was inconvenient. People today can also resist or delay responding to God's invitation, and their excuses may sound reasonable—work duties, family responsibilities, financial needs, and so forth. Nevertheless, God's invitation is the most important event in life, no matter how inconveniently it may be timed. Are you making excuses to avoid God's kind and generous invitation? Jesus said that the time will come when God will withdraw his invitation and offer it to others—then it will be too late to get into the banquet.

14:24 **"'For none of those I invited first will get even the smallest
taste of what I had prepared for them.'"**^{NLT} In Israel's history,
God's *first* invitation came from Moses and the prophets; the second came from his Son. Jesus' listeners, the religious leaders,
accepted the first invitation. They believed that God had called
them to be his people. But they insulted God by refusing to
accept his Son. They would miss the banquet completely because
they refused to accept the Son's invitation—they would not *get
even the smallest taste of* what had been prepared for them. And
there would be no second (or third) chance. Thus, just as the master in the story sent his servant into the streets to invite the needy
to his banquet, so God was sending his Son to the whole world of
needy people (Jews and Gentiles) to tell them that his kingdom
had arrived and was ready for them.

JESUS TEACHES ABOUT THE COST OF BEING A DISCIPLE / 14:25-35 / *158*

This collection of Jesus' teachings about discipleship suggests a
turning point in Luke's narrative of "the journey to Jerusalem"
begun at 9:51. From this point to the end of this "Jerusalem section" around chapter 18, the Gospel contains materials that focus
on discipleship.

A large crowd had been following Jesus, perhaps because of
the great miracles he had performed—raising people from the
dead (7:14-15) and giving food to thousands (9:12-17)—or
because he had courageously confronted the religious authorities
(13:17). For whatever reason, they were following him. Jesus
turned around and told them flatly what it meant to *truly* follow
him. They would have to give up everything, even the most treasured relationships with their families, to put Jesus first in their
lives. Jesus not only warned them of the difficulties they would
encounter, he also gave each of them the option to rid themselves
of any obligation to him. Jesus was not a salesman. He did not try
to sell Christianity by telling people the benefits they would
receive, the wonderful experiences they would have, and the reasons they should follow him. Instead, he told them the costs, the
hardships, and the difficulties they would experience, and he
encouraged them to carefully evaluate the costs before they followed him.

14:25-26 **Now large crowds were traveling with him; and he turned
and said to them, "Whoever comes to me and does not hate
father and mother, wife and children, brothers and sisters,
yes, and even life itself, cannot be my disciple."**^{NRSV} Jesus was

still *traveling* toward Jerusalem, and *large crowds* had joined him. Perhaps all these casual followers considered themselves "disciples" of this popular teacher. Perhaps they thought he was the Messiah and wanted to be there when he inaugurated his kingdom. But Jesus needed to explain that following him did not mean receiving goodies, like so many children. He wanted to explain what it meant to truly be his disciple. So *he turned* and spoke to them. His disciples had to *hate father and mother, wife and children, brothers and sisters, yes, and even life itself.* Certainly this caused a stir among the people. Who would possibly ask his followers to hate their family members and life itself?

Yet remember that God never contradicts himself. Never has Jesus advocated "hatred"—in fact, he even commanded his followers to love their enemies (6:27, 35). In these words, therefore, Jesus was not going against his own commands of love, or the fifth commandment to honor father and mother (Exodus 20:12). Nor was he attempting to subvert the natural love that exists among family members, which is a blessing from God. Instead, the word "hate" is a Semitic hyperbole—an obvious exaggeration to make a point (see Genesis 29:30-33; Proverbs 13:24). Their love for Jesus should be so complete and wholehearted that their love for family members, and for life itself would pale in comparison, to the point of being like hatred. In first-century Jewish family settings, deciding for Jesus could mean alienation from the family. Jesus warned the would-be disciples that they must be clear about their true allegiance. Jesus' point was that those who wanted to be his followers would have demands placed upon them. The task would not be easy. Sometimes relationships would be severed, and his followers would have to turn away and remain with Jesus (12:51-53). Those who cannot make that kind of commitment *cannot be [his] disciple.*

CASUAL DISCIPLESHIP
Is your interest in living for God halfhearted? The time may come for you to make hard choices because God doesn't take fourth priority for long. If you make career your idol, or sports or wealth, perhaps you should reevaluate. You will have to decide: to what are you really devoted? to whom are you really loyal? Following Jesus must be your first priority.

14:27 "Whoever does not carry the cross and follow me cannot be my disciple."NRSV Besides being willing to love Jesus more than any others and more than life itself, the true disciple must be ready to *carry the cross and follow* (see also 9:23 and commen-

tary there). Jesus' audience was well aware of what it meant to
"carry the cross." When the Romans led a criminal to his execution site, the criminal would be forced to carry the cross on which
he would die. This showed submission to Rome and warned ob-
servers that they had better submit too. Jesus gave this teaching
to get the crowds to think through their enthusiasm for him. He
encouraged those who were superficial either to go deeper or to
turn back. Following Christ means total submission to him—
perhaps even to the point of death.

14:28-30 **"But don't begin until you count the cost. For who would
begin construction of a building without first getting estimates and then checking to see if there is enough money to
pay the bills? Otherwise, you might complete only the foundation before running out of funds. And then how everyone
would laugh at you! They would say, 'There's the person who
started that building and ran out of money before it was finished!'"**NLT Jesus gave two examples of what people should consider before joining his band of followers. There is a cost in
following Jesus. It is not a joyride, nor is it a passage to health
and wealth. Jesus promised his followers a kingdom, but he also
said that they would face difficulty and suffering because of their
faith. He did not paint an unrealistic picture for his followers.
Those on the fence needed to *count the cost*. When a builder
doesn't count the cost or estimates it inaccurately, his building
may be left half-completed. What are those "costs" to believers?
Christians may face loss of social status or wealth. They may
have to give up control over their money, time, or career. They
may be hated, separated from their family, and even put to death.
Following Christ does not mean living trouble-free. All people
must carefully count the cost of becoming Christ's disciple so
that they will know what they are getting into and won't be
tempted to turn back when the going gets tough.

14:31-32 **"Or what king would ever dream of going to war without
first sitting down with his counselors and discussing
whether his army of ten thousand is strong enough to defeat
the twenty thousand soldiers who are marching against
him? If he is not able, then while the enemy is still far away,
he will send a delegation to discuss terms of peace."**NLT In
this second example, Jesus described a wise king's decision to
consider whether his *ten thousand* soldiers could defeat twice
that number coming against him. He has to act, but should he
fight or *send a delegation to discuss terms of peace?* To rush
out with his soldiers, without first discussing the options,
would invite disaster for his nation. Far better to think it

through beforehand. So those who want to follow Jesus should carefully consider their decision.

EASY DECISION?
If you made a decision sometime in the past to trust Christ for salvation but since then you haven't paid much attention to your devotion and discipleship, you may be one of those followers who hasn't counted the cost.

A decision to trust Christ means that God Almighty is now your Lord and Savior. You had better listen to him, read his Word, follow his teaching. To "walk the aisle" and then drift along is no decision at all. If you have trusted Christ, show you mean it by doing what God commands.

14:33 **"So no one can become my disciple without giving up everything for me."**^{NLT} The cost to be counted is a willingness to give up *everything* for Jesus. For some, this may be literal, such as the rich young man in 18:18-23 and many of Jesus' early followers; for others it may be a willingness to hold loosely to material possessions. To be preoccupied with money or possessions is to miss the demands and joys of true discipleship, as with the people who refused the host's invitation to the kingdom (14:18-20). Again Jesus painted no rosy picture of a high-paying job with all the benefits. He said that the way would be rough and would be a way of self-sacrifice. Oddly enough, however, this is the only way to true fulfillment and satisfaction. Unfortunately, too many refuse to count the cost or, having counted, decide it is too high. They do not count the cost to God—the life of his Son—or the immense treasures awaiting all disciples in the kingdom. Jesus does not ask anyone to give anything up without having given it up himself. Jesus' promise is: "And everyone who has left houses or brothers or sisters or father or mother or children or fields for my sake will receive a hundred times as much and will inherit eternal life" (Matthew 19:29 NIV).

14:34-35 **"Salt is good; but if salt has lost its taste, how can its saltiness be restored? It is fit neither for the soil nor for the manure pile; they throw it away. Let anyone with ears to hear listen!"**^{NRSV} In the ancient world, *salt* was used as a seasoning and as a preservative. The salt came mostly from salt marshes in the area southwest of the Dead Sea. This impure salt was susceptible to deterioration and could lose its flavor, leaving only useless crystals *fit neither for the soil nor for the manure pile.* Such salt was simply thrown away. Jesus' question *"How can its salti-*

ness be restored?" did not require an answer—for once salt has deteriorated, nothing is left but worthless residue.

Many Christians blend into the world and avoid the cost of standing up for Christ. But Jesus says if Christians lose their distinctive *saltiness,* they become worthless. Just as salt flavors and preserves food, Christ's disciples are to preserve the good in the world, help keep it from spoiling, and bring new flavor to life. This requires careful planning, willing sacrifice, and unswerving commitment to Christ's kingdom. Being "salty" is not easy, but if Christians fail in this function, they fail to represent Christ in the world. The person *with ears* should be able to understand these words and apply them.

LUKE 15

This passage of Luke begins with the opposition of the Pharisees, just like the previous section (14:1). Here the Pharisees grumbled about Jesus consorting with "sinners," as they had done before (5:30; 7:39).

In this introductory material, Luke placed three parables together that speak of the joy of God at the repentance of a single sinner: the parable of the lost sheep, the lost coin (15:8-10), and the lost son (15:11-32). Each is an implicit rebuke of the Pharisees' attitude and an invitation to rejoice in the restoration of sinners to God, instead of grumbling about Jesus' association with them. For Christians today, this parable of the lost sheep is not only an invitation to rejoice with God at the repentance of sinners but also a reminder to follow Jesus' example in searching for the lost. Join God in his search for the lost by telling one of your acquaintances about Jesus today.

15:1-2 **Tax collectors and other notorious sinners often came to listen to Jesus teach. This made the Pharisees and teachers of religious law complain that he was associating with such despicable people—even eating with them!**NLT Jesus' association with the *despicable people* in the eyes of the Pharisees has already been documented (5:30; 7:34). *Tax collectors* were Jews who worked for the Roman Empire in collecting Rome's taxes from their countrymen—often charging more than was required, keeping the difference, and vastly enriching themselves (3:12-13). Tax collectors were considered traitors and so were outcasts from Jewish society. The *other notorious sinners* were probably people whose lifestyles were less than pristine and who thus also had become outcasts. Yet these people *came to listen to Jesus teach.* These were the very people Jesus had come to reach—those who needed help. At another time when Jesus was *eating* with such notorious people, Jesus had explained to the *Pharisees and teachers of the law* that "it is not the healthy who need a doctor, but the sick. I have not come to call the righteous, but sinners to repentance" (5:31-32 NIV). The religious leaders had hardened their hearts against Jesus and his message, but the "despicable" people were coming to listen.

In that culture, sitting down and having a meal with a person showed a certain amount of identification and welcome. If Jesus was eating with such horrible people, then he was guilty by association. The Pharisees would not even go near such people, not even to teach them the law or point them to God. They retreated into their holy facade and spent time on their own attempts at righteousness rather than helping others toward God. They were always careful to stay "clean" according to Old Testament law. In fact, they went well beyond the law in their avoidance of certain people and situations and in their ritual washings. By contrast, Jesus took their concept of "cleanness" lightly. He risked defilement by touching those who had leprosy and by neglecting to wash in the Pharisees' prescribed manner, and he showed complete disregard for their sanctions against associating with certain classes of people. He came to offer salvation to sinners, to show that God loves them. Jesus didn't worry about the accusations. Instead he continued going to those who needed him, regardless of the effect on his reputation. Jesus had come to bring the Good News and could scarcely do it if he were to allow his holiness (which was true holiness, not like the Pharisees' attempts at it) to stand in the way of his ministry with sinful people. To teach them, he had to be among them.

GUILT BY ASSOCIATION
There is wisdom in choosing friends wisely. Sports stars are told not to hang out with gamblers. A teenager who runs with druggies stands a good chance of becoming one. In big cities, caring parents forbid youngsters any contact with street gangs.

In Jesus' case, however, time spent with sinners was part of a mission to spread the Good News to all people. Churches today should be like an oasis in the jungle for sinners of all notorious types. Instead, they often care only for the clean-shaven and well-healed.

Investigate this week what your church might do to help different, overlooked, and disreputable people hear and believe God's message.

15:3-5 **So he told them this parable: "Which one of you, having a hundred sheep and losing one of them, does not leave the ninety-nine in the wilderness and go after the one that is lost until he finds it? When he has found it, he lays it on his shoulders and rejoices."**NRSV The grumbling Pharisees wanted to demonstrate their disapproval of Jesus' actions, but Jesus didn't say a word in his own defense; instead, he chose to speak a *parable*. The religious leaders were to picture themselves as shepherds (in reality, as leaders of the nation, they should have been serving as shepherds of God's people). Each shepherd has one hundred sheep—a typical number for the average flock of sheep. Shepherds counted their sheep every night, for sheep would easily stray away and get lost. When this shepherd counted, he was missing one sheep. Jesus used the shepherd's concern for each sheep to set up the question: *"Which one of you . . . does not leave . . . and go after the one that is lost until he finds it?"* The answer was obvious to these listeners—any caring shepherd would do so. He would search, find the lost sheep, carry it back to the flock, and rejoice.

It may seem foolish for the shepherd to leave ninety-nine sheep to go search for just one. But the shepherd knew that the ninety-nine were safe, whereas the lost sheep was in danger. (Most likely the other sheep were left in the care of a fellow shepherd in a makeshift wilderness corral or shelter.) Because each sheep was of high value, the shepherd knew that it was important to search diligently for the lost one.

God's love for each individual is so great that he seeks each one out and rejoices when he or she is "found." Jesus associated with sinners because he wanted to bring the lost sheep—people considered beyond hope—the good news of God's kingdom. Just as the shepherd took the initiative to go out and find the sheep, so Jesus actively seeks lost souls. These tax collectors and sinners (15:1) with whom Jesus was associating were like sheep who had strayed away from God and needed to be returned. More than that, they needed the salvation that Jesus offered.

SEARCHLIGHT
It may be easy to understand God forgiving sinners who had come to him for mercy. But God, who tenderly searches for sinners and then joyfully forgives them, must possess an extraordinary love! This love prompted Jesus to come to earth to search for lost people and save them. This is the kind of extraordinary love that God has for you. If you feel far from God, don't despair. He is searching for you.

15:6-7 **"And when he comes home, he calls together his friends and neighbors, saying to them, 'Rejoice with me, for I have found my sheep that was lost.' Just so, I tell you, there will be more joy in heaven over one sinner who repents than**

**over ninety-nine righteous persons who need no repen-
tance."**^NRSV The shepherd did not rejoice alone. He even called
his friends and neighbors to rejoice with him that he found his
lost sheep. Then Jesus explained that *there will be more joy in
heaven over one sinner who repents than over ninety-nine righteous persons who need no repentance.* In reality, the shepherds
would not have had a party over one found sheep. Jesus used
this element in the story to stress his kingdom's reality and the
value of one lost person. God rejoices when "lost" sinners are
"found" and brought into the kingdom. He rejoices over you!
When a sinner repents—turns from sin and accepts the forgiveness Jesus offers—heaven rejoices. While there is certainly joy
over those already safe in the kingdom, there is "more joy" for
each changed life (see 15:10).

LOST AND FOUND
The Bible is full of gladness when lost valuables are found: the
Prodigal Son, the lost coin, and, here, a lost sheep.
   Picture yourself in both roles. As the lost sheep, you need a
Shepherd-Savior to bring you home. As a shepherd, you have
a job to do, and all heaven rejoices when you find a lost
person, just as heaven did when you were found.
   In the shepherd's role, take a step beyond your comfort zone
today. Start a conversation with a stranger, greet a neighbor on
the other side of the block, cross a standard dividing line that
separates you from others.
   And if you're better cast in the lost-sheep role today, follow
the Savior's voice home without delay or detour.

JESUS TELLS THE PARABLE OF THE LOST COIN / 15:8-10 / *160*

In this parable, Jesus portrays God's love for people who fall into
a life of sin. They are lost, disconnected from their true owner,
God himself. But their owner (the Creator of the universe)
doesn't give up on people. Instead, he compassionately searches
for them, freely offering them forgiveness through his Son, Jesus
Christ. He reaches out to them. And when they accept his offer, a
noisy celebration breaks out in the heavens. A sinner has come
home; a person has been reconciled with his or her Creator.
Today God still reaches out to sinners. Through the preaching of
the gospel, he offers salvation.

15:8-9 **"Or suppose a woman has ten valuable silver coins and
loses one. Won't she light a lamp and look in every corner**

of the house and sweep every nook and cranny until she
finds it? And when she finds it, she will call in her friends
and neighbors to rejoice with her because she has found her
lost coin."[NLT] Palestinian women would often receive ten silver
coins as a wedding gift. Besides their monetary value, these
coins held sentimental value like that of a wedding ring; to lose
one would be extremely distressing. Each coin was of great
value. The ten coins could have been this woman's life savings,
meant to support her in a time of need. One coin would have
been a tenth of that nest egg. Upon discovering that one of the
coins was missing, the woman would *light a lamp* in order to
see into the dark corners, and *sweep* every part of the dirt-
packed floor in hope of finding it. Although the woman still
had nine coins, she would not rest until the tenth was retrieved.
Her search was rewarded—*she finds it.* Like the shepherd, she
shared her joy with *her friends and neighbors* so they could
rejoice with her.

15:10 **"In the same way, I tell you, there is rejoicing in the presence
of the angels of God over one sinner who repents."[NIV]** Just as a
shepherd would rejoice over finding a lost sheep and a woman
would rejoice at finding her lost coin, so all heaven rejoices over
a repentant sinner. Each individual is precious to God. He
rejoices whenever one of his children is found and brought into
the kingdom. He actively seeks those lost ones, and when they
are found, *there is rejoicing in the presence of the angels of God.*
Through these two parables, Jesus was explaining to his detractors that, while they were not pleased with him, God was pleased
that Jesus was seeking the lost souls and bringing them the good
news of the kingdom.

JESUS TELLS THE PARABLE OF THE LOST SON / 15:11-32 / **161**

The previous two parables—the one of lost sheep and the lost
coin—build up to the climax, the parable of the lost son, a parable that is unique to Luke. Through the parable of the lost son,
Jesus presents a vivid illustration of God and his mercy for repentant sinners.

The parable describes the passion of a caring father for his run-
away son. Day after day, the father had been scanning the hori-
zons for any sign of his lost son. Although in the first century a
father would typically wait until a son showed some sign of
respect before addressing him, here the father threw all social
conventions aside. He couldn't wait to see his son. He started

walking toward him. With open arms, he embraced his son, pulling him tightly to himself.

God is like this loving father. He wants to welcome sinners back home with open arms. This parable is a picture of God's grace. Thank him for showing that type of compassion to you.

15:11-12 **To illustrate the point further, Jesus told them this story: "A man had two sons. The younger son told his father, 'I want my share of your estate now, instead of waiting until you die.' So his father agreed to divide his wealth between his sons."**^{NLT} Jesus continued with another parable *to illustrate the point further*—that God rejoices when lost sinners repent and find forgiveness. *A man had two sons,* the younger of whom wanted his share of his father's *estate* (inheritance). This would have been one-third of the total estate, with the older son receiving two-thirds, a double portion of the other as prescribed by the law (Deuteronomy 21:17). In most cases the son would have received this at his father's death, although fathers sometimes chose to divide up their inheritance early and retire from managing their estates. What is unusual is that the younger son initiated the division of the estate. This showed arrogant disregard for his father's authority as head of the family.

15:13-14 **"A few days later this younger son packed all his belongings and took a trip to a distant land, and there he wasted all his money on wild living. About the time his money ran out, a great famine swept over the land, and he began to starve."**^{NLT} Within just *a few days,* the younger son was on his way—indicating that this had been his plan when he had asked for his inheritance in the first place. He *packed all his belongings* and got as far away from his family as possible, traveling *to a distant land.* The listeners would have understood that the young man had traveled outside Jewish territory, since he later ended up with pigs (15:15-16)—animals Jews did not own because they were considered unclean. The young man apparently had wanted to live his own way, be his own master, get out from under the rules of his home and his father. Money was his ticket out, so he took it and ran.

In this distant land, he *wasted all his money on wild living.* Apparently this "wild" life and the freedom he thought went with it had also been part of his plan. So he lived on the wild side for a while, spending freely on whatever he chose. But then *his money ran out.* The inheritance, whatever amount it was, sustained him for a time, but it was not an endless supply. It dried up, and then, to make matters worse, *a great famine swept over the land* and the boy did not even have money for food.

YOUNG ADULTS
Young people need to plan for the future while they're still young. Two more years of school now, painful as it may appear, could mean a career they would not otherwise have. Plan for the unexpected even when your immediate needs seem immense. The young son in this story wasted his money just before a famine.

Thinking ahead is a Christian's duty, yet many treat it as a useless hindrance to moving on. Wild living may offer short-term thrills, but it's all a waste. Your treasure and time are God's gifts. Use them for him.

15:15-16 **"So he went and hired himself out to a citizen of that country, who sent him to his fields to feed pigs. He longed to fill his stomach with the pods that the pigs were eating, but no one gave him anything."**NIV The young man became so desperate that *he went and hired himself out* to work for a *citizen of that country, who sent him to his fields to feed pigs.* According to Moses' law, pigs were unclean animals (Leviticus 11:2-8; Deuteronomy 14:8). This meant that pigs could not be eaten or used for sacrifices. To protect themselves from defilement, Jews would not even touch pigs. For a Jew to stoop to feeding pigs would have been a great humiliation, and for this young man to desire to eat food that the pigs had touched was to be degraded beyond belief. The *pods* were the seeds of the carob tree, which grows around the Mediterranean Sea. That *no one gave him anything* shows that he was neglected and insignificant; he had truly sunk to the depths.

15:17-19 **"When he finally came to his senses, he said to himself, 'At home even the hired men have food enough to spare, and here I am, dying of hunger! I will go home to my father and say, "Father, I have sinned against both heaven and you, and I am no longer worthy of being called your son. Please take me on as a hired man." ' "**NLT When reality finally hit him, the son *finally came to his senses.* Sitting among pigs that were better fed than he was, he reflected on life back home. He realized that at home *even the hired men have food enough to spare.* With no money, no dignity, and, so he thought, no claim to sonship in his father's household, he decided to go *home to [his] father,* confess his sin, and ask to be taken on *as a hired man.* At least there he would not go hungry.

While his motivation at first seems to have been his hunger, he could have saved his pride by never going back. He could have searched for a job as a hired hand anywhere (although his present experience showed him that not all hired hands were treated as well as those on his father's estate). He could have avoided his older brother's inevitable scorn over what he had done by staying away. Instead, this young man chose to go home. The key lies in the words that he planned to say to his father: *"I have sinned against both heaven and you."* He wanted to tell his father he was sorry. He wanted to repent of his selfishness that had sent him away and spent all the money that his father had set aside for his future. Even if it meant living as a hired man in his own home, he would return there in order to say these things to his father.

COMING TO ONE'S SENSES
The younger son, like many who are rebellious and immature, wanted to be free to live as he pleased, and he had to hit bottom before he came to his senses. It often takes great sorrow and tragedy to cause people to look to the only one who can help them. For this young man, coming to his senses meant reconnecting his life to those who loved him. He had had his fill of individualistic adventure, and he realized his best prospect was to reconnect with family and friends.

Youth loves freedom and needs a growing portion of it. But youth needs family, friends, and community too—the solid base that provides identity and support. Are you trying to live your own way, selfishly pushing aside any responsibility or commitment that gets in your way? Stop and look before you hit bottom. You will save yourself and your family much grief. In your young adult years, reach high but keep connections strong.

15:20-21 **"So he returned home to his father. And while he was still a long distance away, his father saw him coming. Filled with love and compassion, he ran to his son, embraced him, and kissed him. His son said to him, 'Father, I have sinned against both heaven and you, and I am no longer worthy of being called your son.'"**^{NLT} The son *returned home to his father,* not knowing what to expect—the best he could anticipate was a cold shoulder, a halfhearted welcome, but in hopes of being hired to work for his father.

The father, however, seemed to have cast his eyes on the horizon many times since his son had left, hoping one day to see him returning. Finally, *his father saw him coming* even while he was far away. The father ran, embraced, and kissed his son. He was *filled with love and compassion* at the sight of his son who had come home. For the patriarch of the family to run was to lose all caution and dignity. The father went beyond normal forgiveness and showed incredible love. The son began to give his father the speech he had prepared (15:19), but he didn't even get to the part about asking to be hired, for the father wanted to welcome his son back into his home with a grand celebration.

In the two preceding stories, the seeker actively looked for the sheep and the coin, which could not return by themselves. In this story, the father watched and waited. He was dealing with a human being with a will, but he was ready to greet his son if he returned. In the same way, God's love is constant and patient and welcoming. He will search and give people opportunities to respond, but he will not force them to come to him. Like the father in this story, God waits patiently for people to come to their senses.

This father's love and compassion picture the love God has always shown to his wayward people. The psalmist wrote:

As a father has compassion on his children, so the LORD has compassion on those who fear him. (Psalm 103:13 NIV)

Jeremiah the prophet wrote:

"So there is hope for your future," declares the LORD. "Your children will return to their own land. I have surely heard Ephraim's moaning: 'You disciplined me like an unruly calf, and I have been disciplined. Restore me, and I will return, because you are the LORD my God. After I strayed, I repented; after I came to understand, I beat my breast. I was ashamed and humiliated because I bore the disgrace of my youth.' Is not Ephraim my dear son, the child in whom I delight? Though I often speak against him, I still remember him. Therefore my heart yearns for him; I have great compassion for him," declares the LORD. (Jeremiah 31:17-20 NIV)

Clearly God's love reaches out to sinners who, repenting of their sin, run to him for forgiveness. They can be assured of a warm welcome from the one who has been watching for them to come.

ADMIT YOUR MISTAKES

When the wayward son returned home, he apologized to his father. Though his father loved him anyway, the son needed to apologize in order to heal his own relationship with his father. When you have offended someone, don't apologize indirectly or halfheartedly. Say it and mean it.

When you have made a mistake, don't blame bad luck or bad friends. Admit it, and prepare to go on.

When you are embraced by those you have hurt, don't refuse the forgiveness they offer. Guilt will ruin your recovery. When forgiven, accept the gift and let the past go.

15:22-24 **"But his father said to the servants, 'Quick! Bring the finest robe in the house and put it on him. Get a ring for his finger, and sandals for his feet. And kill the calf we have been fattening in the pen. We must celebrate with a feast, for this son of mine was dead and has now returned to life. He was lost, but now he is found.' So the party began."**NLT The father immediately restored this destitute and humbled young man as his son, directing the servant to bring *the finest robe* (generally given to a guest of honor), *a ring* (signifying authority, as a son, not a servant), *and sandals* (only slaves and the very poor went barefoot). Then the *calf* that was being fattened up for the time when a special feast should be prepared was to be killed—the father could think of no more fitting celebration. His son had been as good as *dead* to him but now had *returned to life.* He had been *lost* but now was *found.* As the shepherd celebrated upon finding the lost sheep (15:6), and the woman upon finding her lost coin (15:9), so this father celebrated at "finding" his "lost" son.

FORGIVE AND FORGET
This father restored his wayward son and celebrated his return. In this reconciliation, the father absorbed the hurt and financial loss and was willing to adjust his hopes and dreams for his child. People are not perfect; your life will not unfold according to blueprints; your children will not develop according to your specifications. You can harbor resentment if you choose, but when it comes to relationships, that choice is always self-defeating.

Joy embraces others; stubbornness shuns them. Peace forgives others; pride prolongs the separation. Love cleans the slate of hurts recorded; self-pity smudges the record until nobody remembers who is at fault or why.

When the lost relationship is found, when apology is genuine, when reconciliation is sought, forgive and forget, absorb the loss and the cost, and let the party begin!

15:25-27 **"Meanwhile, the older son was in the fields working. When he returned home, he heard music and dancing in the house, and he asked one of the servants what was going on. 'Your brother is back,' he was told, 'and your father has killed the calf we were fattening and has prepared a great feast. We are celebrating because of his safe return.'"**NLT The elder brother, according to tradition, would have received a double inheritance. He probably had continued to be under his father's authority, working on the estate. While he would inherit it, this would not take place until his father's death. So he *was in the fields working,* being responsible to do the work that he should do, patiently following the typical plan for passing on the family inheritance. But as the verses below indicate, he also may not have been content with his situation; he just had not acted upon his desires as his brother had.

Imagine this other brother's surprise at returning from a day of hard work to the sound of a grand celebration going on in the house. Naturally he wondered *what was going on.* The servant simply replied with the facts—the wayward brother had returned, the calf had been killed, the feast had been prepared, and everyone was celebrating the brother's *safe return.*

15:28-30 **"The older brother became angry and refused to go in. So his father went out and pleaded with him. But he answered his father, 'Look! All these years I've been slaving for you and never disobeyed your orders. Yet you never gave me even a young goat so I could celebrate with my friends. But when this son of yours who has squandered your property with prostitutes comes home, you kill the fattened calf for him!'"**[NIV] At the report of the news, the older brother *became angry and refused to go in* to join the celebration. The father's response is contrasted with the older brother's. The father forgave because he was filled with love. The son refused to forgive because he was bitter about what he saw as injustice. The older son's resentment rendered him just as lost to the father's love as his younger brother had been.

The older son was quite reasonable in his list of complaints. He reviewed his résumé and argued from experience. The father could have consented, pacifying his older son with additional gifts and rewards. But relationships prosper on love, not on fairness. Love is the dynamic that sweeps "reasonable claims" into secondary concerns here. When relationships need love, we often must let fairness take a second seat.

While the resentment of this older brother is easy to understand, his volley of words reveals the same sort of self-righteousness that afflicted the religious leaders of Jesus' day. The key to understanding this story is found in the context of 15:1-2. The younger son stands for the tax collectors and sinners, the waiting father is God, and the older brother represents the religious leaders. The younger son had lived as a notorious sinner, so the brother wanted nothing to do with him. Yet the loving father, who had gone out to meet his younger son, also *went out* to plead with his elder one. Instead of humbly accepting his father's words, however, the older son let out a torrent of pent-up anger and frustration, describing that he had *been slaving* away for his father, never getting any special favors. He did not take a moment to understand that he would inherit everything that he was working for and that he was dearly loved by his father. He only felt angry that his father was celebrating "your son's" (not "my brother's") return home. Why should there be a celebration for an irresponsible person, when the model son got nothing comparable?

The religious leaders, ever claiming how hard they "slaved" for God, were attempting to keep myriad rules and regulations, many of which God never even demanded. They had the Father's love but had chosen to reject it in favor of hard work and self-denial. So when God eagerly welcomed the sinful, common people into the kingdom, the religious leaders were refusing to join the celebration. But God rejoiced that these sinful people had come "home," and he invited even these religious leaders to join the party. But they will retort with only anger and resentment that they who tried so hard should not get the party.

YOUNGER BROTHERS
It was hard for the older brother to accept his younger brother when he returned, and it is just as difficult to accept "younger brothers" today. People who repent after leading notoriously sinful lives are often held in suspicion; churches are sometimes unwilling to admit them to membership. Instead, we should rejoice like the angels in heaven when an unbeliever repents and turns to God. Like the father in the parable, accept repentant sinners wholeheartedly and give them the support and encouragement that they need to grow in Christ.

15:31-32 **"His father said to him, 'Look, dear son, you and I are very close, and everything I have is yours. We had to celebrate this happy day. For your brother was dead and has come back to life! He was lost, but now he is found!'"**ᴺᴸᵀ The father spoke kindly to his overheated son; he explained that what the older son had been experiencing in the interim was far better than a one-day celebration. The older son had not been displaced as the first-born—he had his relationship with his father (who obviously loved him very much), and he still had his inheritance. The younger son had squandered his and had gone through great suffering before coming to his senses. The wild life the younger son had sought had brought him only to ruin, and he returned home with no inheritance, humbled from having suffered some hard knocks. The older son needed to get his perspective, be grateful that he had not had to go through such pain, and *celebrate this happy day* of his brother's safe return. The father repeated the words he had spoken to the servants—the younger son had been dead and was now alive; he had been lost and was found! The father got back his son; he wanted his elder son to rejoice at getting back his brother. This celebration was the right action to take—it was truly a joyful time in the life of this family.

Desperate sinners, notorious outcasts, difficult people—all have been offered salvation. God's people must not stand aside and above, but they must join in heaven's celebration when those who were lost have been found, when those who were "dead to sin [become] alive to God in Christ Jesus" (Romans 6:11 NIV).

 NO PLACE FOR ANGER
In Jesus' story, the older brother represents the Pharisees, who were angry and resentful that sinners were being welcomed into God's kingdom. "After all," the Pharisees must have thought, "we have sacrificed and done *so much* for God." How easy it is to resent God's gracious forgiveness of others considered to be far worse sinners than oneself.

LUKE 16

This passage of Luke begins a section dealing with the wise use
of one's possessions. People often try to acquire possessions to
secure their future and to live comfortably in the present. Here
Jesus used the example of a shrewd manager to reveal the foolishness of hoarding earthly riches. The lesson of this parable
revolves around the shrewd manager realizing his own predicament, that he would be judged for the dishonest way he had handled his master's possessions. In light of that fact, he tried to
obtain friends who would provide for his welfare later, by
decreasing what was owed to his master. His shrewd action
would guarantee his future welfare.

With this parable, Jesus was pointing out that everyone, fully
warned of the coming divine judgment, should follow this manager's example. All people are in a worse predicament than this
manager because their eternal destinies hang in the balance. Instead
of frantically holding on to possessions that soon will disappear,
people should give possessions away, especially to those in need
(12:33). Money will not last, but people, God's Word, and his kingdom will. Will your investments reap eternal dividends?

**16:1-2 Then Jesus said to the disciples, "There was a rich man who
had a manager, and charges were brought to him that this
man was squandering his property. So he summoned him and
said to him, 'What is this that I hear about you? Give me an
accounting of your management, because you cannot be my
manager any longer.'"**NRSV This parable is one of the most difficult to interpret, but a careful study reveals Jesus to be a master
storyteller. This parable of the shrewd manager explains how
Jesus' followers ought to use worldly wealth.

The parable begins with a *rich man who had a manager*. This
"manager" handled financial matters for the rich man. Sometimes
called a "steward," such managers would handle the business
affairs of a household, an estate, or even a city. Their responsibilities and authority could vary, but in this case, the manager had

extensive authority over the rich man's financial affairs, even the ability to make contracts in the master's name. A person in such a position should have complete integrity. Unfortunately, this manager did not. He had mismanaged the funds, *squandering* ("wasting," as in 15:13) the rich man's *property,* siphoning off money for his own high living.

Having been informed of the problems, the rich man *summoned* the manager and demanded an *accounting of [his] management.* As a consequence, the rich man would strip the manager of his authority, but first he required that the steward prepare the documents. This would take some time, and the manager used this time to his advantage.

MONEY POWER
Money provides a good test of the lordship of Christ. Use your resources wisely because they belong to God, and not to you. Money can be used for good or evil; use yours for good. Money has a lot of power, so you should use it carefully and thoughtfully. Use your material goods in a way that will foster faith and obedience (see 12:33-34).

16:3-4 "The manager said to himself, 'What shall I do now? My master is taking away my job. I'm not strong enough to dig, and I'm ashamed to beg—I know what I'll do so that, when I lose my job here, people will welcome me into their houses.'"[NIV] The manager just lost his livelihood, but he had a window of time because his boss wanted him to "give an accounting" (16:2). So the manager thought about how best to handle his coming unemployment. Having been a manager, he did not want to *dig* (become a laborer), he had too much pride to *beg,* and his mismanagement of his master's funds would cause no one else to hire him for such a position. So he came up with a plan whereby others would take care of him. "Welcome me into their houses" reveals the heart of his plan. By plying upon the code of reciprocity, the manager could find food and housing and possibly a job from those whose debts were reduced.

16:5-7 "So he invited each person who owed money to his employer to come and discuss the situation. He asked the first one, 'How much do you owe him?' The man replied, 'I owe him eight hundred gallons of olive oil.' So the manager told him, 'Tear up that bill and write another one for four hundred gallons.' 'And how much do you owe my employer?' he asked the next man. 'A thousand bushels of wheat,' was the reply. 'Here,' the manager said, 'take your bill and replace it with one for only eight

hundred bushels.'"[NLT] Much discussion has arisen around exactly what this money manager was doing in this situation. Some commentators suggest that what the manager was doing was removing the interest and his own earnings from each of the debts. Jews were not supposed to charge interest to fellow Jews, so those commentators think that interest may have been hidden in the charges either by the rich man or by this steward, who was going to enrich himself with it. Thus the reductions in the debts would not hurt the master any; they would only have served to leave the manager without any income on any of the debts. That did not matter, however, for he had already figured that this would serve his future. The manager also would have appeared to have been acting on the master's behalf, so this would enhance the master's reputation as a kind and generous man. The manager anticipated his future need and took aggressive action.

More likely, this manager was acting very shrewdly in figuring out a way to put his master's debtors in his own debt. The debts here involved are very high; thus these probably would have been commercial transactions—perhaps involving lease arrangements on pieces of land. The manager summoned all his master's debtors and reduced their debts by a substantial amount. In this fraudulent way, the manager earned their goodwill. Once the debts had been dishonestly reduced, the master could do nothing, but social custom would require these debtors to reciprocate such kindness to the manager. Only two examples were cited, but the manager handled all his master's debtors in this way, reducing each debt by a certain amount depending on the commodity owed. The debtors may not have known the extent of it at the time, but when the manager reduced their debt to the master, they were becoming indebted to the manager—who would need their reciprocal kindness that very day when he would be out of work.

SEIZE THE DAY
In this story, the manager used the time and opportunity he had. Don't let time run out before you deal with the most important realities of life. Use the opportunities God gives you. Perhaps you worked late every night when your family was young, and now, with savings and security, your son isn't a Little Leaguer anymore. You missed it.

Perhaps you always wanted to tell your mom what she meant to you, how much you love her. But she died last year, before you ever said it.

Perhaps you always intended to get right with God, to confess your sins, to worship, to serve the Lord. Do it now.

16:8-9 **"The master commended the dishonest manager because he had acted shrewdly. For the people of this world are more shrewd in dealing with their own kind than are the people of the light. I tell you, use worldly wealth to gain friends for yourselves, so that when it is gone, you will be welcomed into eternal dwellings."**[NIV] The commendation received by the *dishonest manager* raises questions. Why would dishonesty be commended? This is the best example of Jesus twisting a story so as to make a point. No master in history has ever commended the shrewdness of a crook. Instead, the master throws the crook in jail. The manager had cut down the debts, legally made them binding with a third party, and indebted others to him. Thus, there was nothing left for the master to do than to commend the manager for his shrewdness. He had solved his problem—albeit at further expense to his master. The commendation seems odd, unless the master was simply appreciating the farsightedness of the plan.

STRATEGIC PLANNING
Jesus applauded the steward who had assessed the situation clearly, planned bold and decisive action that would benefit others, and executed the plan effectively. This steward was nobody's fool. Yet many Christians act without skill or finesse when it comes to financial matters compared to their secular counterparts. Many downplay budget, investing, and business principles as though they are unspiritual issues for the church. Should Christians take action strategically? Should they seize opportunities with discernment? Should they find ways to do more with their finances? Jesus commended those who did.

Actually, Jesus did not want his listeners to focus on the details as much as on the lesson to be learned, which he includes here: *For the people of this world are more shrewd in dealing with their own kind than are the people of the light.* "People of the world" refers to unbelievers, who are committed neither to God nor to his eternal standards. "People of the light" refers to the disciples and followers of Jesus. The shrewd manager sized up his situation, made some decisions, came up with a strategy, and did what was needed. Jesus was not commending dishonesty, but rather the manager's foresight and diligence to follow through and make friends. The manager did not profit directly in reducing the debts, but he used the principle of reciprocity to gain favor with the debtors. By doing a favor for them, the manager could require a favor *from* them. The debtors would be indebted to the manager.

Then Jesus added, *"I tell you, use worldly wealth to gain friends for yourselves, so that when it is gone, you will be welcomed into eternal dwellings."* Believers are to make wise use of their financial opportunities, not to earn heaven, but to use their resources to make friends by helping the poor. Literally, "they will welcome you" refers to the poor who have been helped. Their welcome will be the believers' reward in heaven. If believers use their money to help those in need or to help others find Christ, their earthly investment will bring eternal benefit. Those who obey God will find that the unselfish use of their possessions will follow. Soon Jesus would spell out some of the applications for gaining friends (16:10-13).

16:10-12 **"Whoever can be trusted with very little can also be trusted with much, and whoever is dishonest with very little will also be dishonest with much. So if you have not been trustworthy in handling worldly wealth, who will trust you with true riches? And if you have not been trustworthy with someone else's property, who will give you property of your own?"**^{NIV} How people handle their *worldly wealth* shows their trustworthiness. If a person can be trusted with a little bit, if he or she maintains integrity even in small matters, where a little slip might not show up, then that person has proven trustworthiness for large matters. The reverse is also true—the one who would willingly steal a dollar may also be willing to steal thousands. Trustworthiness goes to a person's very core and will emerge in all situations—whether small or big, insignificant or important. Every penny of "worldly wealth" comes from God. If someone has *not been trustworthy in handling* even that wealth, how can God trust that person with *true riches*—the endless treasures of heaven? If someone has not been trustworthy with *someone else's property* (that is, earthly possessions that actually belong to God), then how can he give heaven as the eternal possession?

MONEY MATTERS
Integrity often meets its match in money matters. God calls his people to be honest even in small details that could easily be rationalized away. Heaven's riches are far more valuable than earthly wealth. But those who are not trustworthy with money here (no matter how much or little) will be unfit to handle the vast riches of God's kingdom. Don't let your integrity slip in small matters, and it will not fail you in crucial decisions either.

16:13 **"No one can serve two masters. For you will hate one and love the other, or be devoted to one and despise the other. You cannot serve both God and money."**^{NLT} Money often takes the place of God in people's lives. How a person handles money indicates how much mastery money has attained in that person's life. Jesus explained that *no one can serve* (be a slave to, belong to) *two masters.* From a spiritual standpoint, all people will serve someone or something; here Jesus spoke of two choices, God and money. People can choose to serve money—in essence, this means serving themselves and all the pleasure and power money can buy—or they can choose to serve God. But no one can do both, for the two choices are diametrically opposed. No one can seek selfish pleasure and be able to give money away. When money is one's master, there can be no room for God, who requires single-hearted obedience and devotion.

Avoid mistaken judgments here. Many rich people are genuine, mature Christians. Wealth is not the issue. Many mature Christians work hard and expect to be paid. That's not the issue either. Money for these people is only a means to an end. Yet some people tragically have made wealth an end in itself—the thing to serve, their god. For Christians, money is always a means of service, never an ultimate goal. Money is God's loan to you for smart stewardship, never a measure of your real worth.

MASTER MONEY
Money can easily take God's place in your life. It can become your master. How can you tell if you are a slave to money? If you answer yes to most of these questions, you have a problem.

- Do you think and worry about it frequently?
- Do you give up doing what you should do or would like to do in order to make more money?
- Do you spend a great deal of your time caring for your possessions?
- Is it hard for you to give money away?
- Are you in debt?

Money is a hard master and a deceptive one. Wealth promises power and control but often cannot deliver. Great fortunes can be made—and lost—overnight, and no amount of money can provide health, happiness, and eternal life. Instead, let God be your Master. His servants have peace of mind and security, both now and forever.

16:14-15 **The Pharisees, who dearly loved their money, naturally scoffed at all this. Then he said to them, "You like to look good in public, but God knows your evil hearts. What this world honors is an abomination in the sight of God."**[NLT]
Because the Pharisees *loved their money,* they *scoffed* at Jesus' teaching. They may not have thought that they were serving

money (16:13), but their laughing at Jesus' words shows that
Jesus had touched a sensitive area. The Pharisees acted piously to
get praise from others, but *God* knew what was in their *hearts*—
and he considered it *evil*. They considered their wealth to be a
sign of God's approval. God detested their wealth, however,
because it caused them to abandon true spirituality. Though prosperity may earn praise, it must never substitute for devotion and
service to God because *what this world honors is an abomination
in the sight of God.* People, like these religious leaders, who
focus their lives on outward appearance and impressing others
(and wealth accomplishes both) serve the wrong master and therefore cannot serve God. Such actions are an "abomination" (something abhorred, loathed, detested) in his sight.

16:16-17 **"The Law and the Prophets were proclaimed until John.
Since that time, the good news of the kingdom of God is being
preached, and everyone is forcing his way into it. It is easier
for heaven and earth to disappear than for the least stroke of
a pen to drop out of the Law."**NIV Jesus emphasized that his
kingdom fulfilled the *Law;* it did not cancel it (Matthew 5:17).
And his arrival marked the fulfillment of the words of the *Prophets.* "The Law and the Prophets" was a way of referring to the
entire Old Testament. This was not a new system but the culmination of the old. The same God who had worked through Moses
was working through Jesus. Therefore, not *the least stroke of a
pen* would *drop out of the Law;* it would all be fulfilled.

John the Baptist's ministry was the dividing line between the
Old and New Testaments (John 1:15-18). Up until his time, the
only revelation of God available to people came through the Law
and the Prophets. But *since that time,* that is, since John's and
Jesus' arrival, *the good news of the kingdom of God is being
preached.* Yet, that Good News was the culmination of all that
the Law demanded and the Prophets foresaw. Nothing had
changed with Jesus' coming, and those who recognized his true
identity realized that the kingdom had come and were *forcing*
their way into it, so desiring to be part of it.

This verse continues from 16:14-15 as a condemnation to the
Pharisees. For all their knowledge of the Law and the Prophets,
these religious men were missing the kingdom of God.

16:18 **"Anyone who divorces his wife and marries another woman
commits adultery, and the man who marries a divorced
woman commits adultery."**NIV Jesus had just made the point that
his coming fulfilled the Law and the Prophets. That did not
mean, however, that the law was no longer valid. In fact, in many
cases, Jesus took the law and required even higher standards for

those who would follow him (Matthew 5:21-22, 27-28, 33-35, 38-39, 43-44). Divorce was a hot topic of debate among the Shammai and Hillel schools of the Pharisees. The followers of Rabbi Hillel said a man could divorce his wife for almost any reason, even finding another woman more attractive than his wife. The followers of Rabbi Shammai believed that a man could divorce his wife only if she had been unfaithful to him. Matthew recorded Jesus' words about divorce when the Pharisees, trying to trick Jesus, brought him a question. Jesus focused on God's original plan, however, so his words about divorce went beyond what Moses had taught (Deuteronomy 24:1-4). For more information on marriage and divorce, see Life Application Commentary on Matthew 19:1-12 and Mark 10:1-12.

MARRIAGE, SEX, AND DIVORCE
Sex is a wonderful human experience, yet its attraction and power can spoil a marriage. This especially applies to men who are barraged daily with media messages delivered by sumptuously beautiful women.

Like Old Testament kings, today's men often have concubines and harems, too—on screen. Sometimes, a married man believes he has found a more satisfying real-life partner, leaves his wife, and seeks his happiness with another. That's wrong.

Treasure your wife. Love her as God's gift to you. When the beauty of another turns your head, make sure your heart and your pleasure long for only one.

Stricter than any of the then-current schools of thought, Jesus' teachings shocked his hearers (see Matthew 19:10) just as they shake today's readers. Jesus stated in no uncertain terms that marriage is a lifetime commitment, and he explained that divorce dissolves a divinely formed union. He also explained that marriage after divorce is *adultery*. (Matthew 19:9 gives one exception: marital unfaithfulness.) While the application of Jesus' words requires interpretation to specific situations, one truth is inescapable: God created marriage to be a sacred, permanent union and partnership between husband and wife. Anyone who takes this lightly forgets God's law and his plan for marriage from the very beginning.

Through this statement about divorce, Jesus was showing the unbelieving religious leaders that his words do not violate the law. He also wanted to point out to them their hypocrisy in attempting to keep the letter of the law while failing to fulfill its moral obligations.

Kingdom standards are built upon that foundation and are, in many cases, even higher than the demands of the law. That is because kingdom people do not have to obey the standards in order to get in; they merely need to trust in Jesus and allow the Holy Spirit to work in their lives. Then they can grow to become the people God wants them to be.

JESUS TELLS ABOUT THE RICH MAN AND THE BEGGAR / 16:19-31 / *163*

Once again, Luke's Gospel highlights a reversal (see this theme in 1:48, 51-53; 4:18; 6:20, 24-26; 16:19-31). In Jesus' parable of a rich man and a poor man, their fortunes were exactly reversed at death: the poor man went to paradise, while the rich man suffered in hell. In agony, the rich man cried out for help, asking Abraham to send Lazarus to warn his brothers of this tragic, irreversible fate. Abraham's reply is instructive. The brothers had access to the truth through the Old Testament, which sufficiently warned them of the coming judgment. Even raising Lazarus from the dead would not melt their cold hearts.

But as the readers of Luke would have known, Jesus had already raised a man from the dead (7:14-15), would raise a man named Lazarus from the dead (John 11:41-43), and would himself rise from the dead—not dying again but ascending to heaven (24:1-52). There was abundant evidence for the Jews to believe—in addition to the healings of the sick and the exorcisms of demons—but they still rejected him, seeking not only his death but Lazarus's as well (John 12:9-10). Abraham was right! Their evil way of life was not a result of a lack of information but was instead due to their stony hearts. They were rejecting Jesus because they wanted to persist in their wickedness.

Don't be deceived, like the Pharisees. Don't let your heart grow hard, continually resisting the promptings of the Holy Spirit and the truth of God's Word. Consistently set aside time to soften your heart by reading the Bible and humbling yourself before God in prayer.

16:19-21 Jesus said, "There was a certain rich man who was splendidly clothed and who lived each day in luxury. At his door lay a diseased beggar named Lazarus. As Lazarus lay there longing for scraps from the rich man's table, the dogs would come and lick his open sores."^NLT Finally, regarding the Pharisees' attitude toward money (they "dearly loved" it, 16:14), Jesus gave an illustration that vividly portrays the value of money in light of future judgment. This *Lazarus* should not be confused with the

Lazarus whom Jesus raised from the dead in John 11. Incidentally, this is the only person in any of Jesus' stories who is given a
name. Some have argued from this point that because Jesus
didn't say the story was a parable, this was an actual historical
event. To do this would give stronger validity to the teaching
about the afterlife found in the story. Most likely, however, it was
an illustration-story, like that of the Good Samaritan (10:30-37)
and the rich fool (12:13-21), rather than a historical event.

The *rich man* in this parable lived out the lifestyle afforded to
the wealthy who lived in the Roman Empire. Splendid clothing,
delicious food of all types, and days lived in *luxury* could be had
by those with enough money.

In contrast, there is a poor *diseased beggar.* Ancient Rome had
no middle class—there were the very rich and the very poor.
Often the poor were reduced to begging in order to survive. This
man, Lazarus, was sick, hungry, and abandoned, so he *lay* at the
rich man's door, *longing for scraps from the rich man's table.*
Leftovers were all he desired, and the rich man could easily have
shared from his extravagance by sending a servant out with a
plateful. But the rich man chose to spend his money on himself,
refusing to share, probably not even taking notice of the poor
man at his door. His wealth was not sinful, but his selfishness
was. While he had everything he could possibly want, Lazarus
lay hungry with even the *dogs* licking *his open sores.* The beggar's name, Lazarus, means "the one God helps," showing that
he alone had status with God.

HARD-HEARTED HOARDING
The Pharisees considered wealth to be a proof of a person's
righteousness. Jesus startled them with this story where a
diseased beggar is rewarded and a rich man is punished. The
rich man did not go to hell because of his wealth but because
he was selfish, refusing to feed Lazarus, take him in, or care for
him. The rich man was hard-hearted despite his great
blessings. The amount of money a person has is not as
important as the way he or she uses it. What is your attitude
toward your money and possessions? Do you hoard them
selfishly, or do you use them to help others?

16:22-23 **"The time came when the beggar died and the angels carried
him to Abraham's side. The rich man also died and was buried. In hell, where he was in torment, he looked up and saw
Abraham far away, with Lazarus by his side."**[NIV] In time, both
the rich man and Lazarus died, for death takes everyone regardless of social station or wealth. Jesus revealed nothing of their

spiritual state, but it can be assumed that the wealthy man was bankrupt spiritually due to his complete self-absorption when need was at his doorstep. This verse reveals the truth of that assumption as the rich man ended up *in hell* and *in torment.* The Greek word is *Hades,* the place for departed spirits, the realm of the dead, the destiny of those who have refused to believe. The "torment" is described in 16:24 as "flames." Added to the torment was the rich man's ability to see paradise, with Abraham and Lazarus in peace and luxury. The role reversal is obvious—as Lazarus once lay in pain outside the door of the rich man's house watching him feast, so here the rich man was in torment watching the joy far away in heaven.

> Hell was not prepared for man. God never meant that man would ever go to hell. Hell was prepared for the devil and his angels, but man rebelled against God and followed the devil. . . . Hell is essentially and basically banishment from the presence of God for deliberately rejecting Jesus Christ as Lord and Savior.   *Billy Graham*

In contrast, Lazarus must have been a God-fearing man, despite the fact that God had not allowed him an easy or pleasant lifetime on earth. Yet when Lazarus died, *the angels carried him to Abraham's side*—another way of describing the kingdom feast at the banquet table. Lazarus shared the privilege of the highest Old Testament saints—an angelic escort accompanied his death.

A theology of heaven and hell should not be based on Jesus' words here. Pressing the details too much will take us away from the main point of the illustration, which is to teach about the danger of pursuing wealth, as well as the finality of God's judgment.

16:24-25 **"He called out, 'Father Abraham, have mercy on me, and send Lazarus to dip the tip of his finger in water and cool my tongue; for I am in agony in these flames.'"**NRSV Not only could the rich man in this story see into heaven's bliss from his torment, but he could call out to those in paradise as well. He spoke to *Father Abraham,* a title any Jew would use for Abraham, the father of their nation (John 8:39). The request for Abraham to *send Lazarus to dip the tip of his finger in water* should be taken as understatement. The rich man was actually requesting enough water to drink and assuage his thirst.

Yet the rich man's basic attitude had not changed. For all his deference to Abraham, he still thought of Lazarus as no more than a messenger who could be sent by Abraham to do the rich man a favor.

"But Abraham said, 'Child, remember that during your lifetime you received your good things, and Lazarus in like manner evil things; but now he is comforted here, and you are in agony.'"^{NRSV} Abraham sent an answer, but not the one that the rich man wanted or even expected. The rich man may have thought there was a mistake. He had been rich, and if wealth was a sign of God's blessing, why would he be in agony?

Abraham gave the answer, calling the rich man *child,* a sign of compassionate sorrow for one who had chosen so poorly. The rich man had received all manner of *good things* during his lifetime. Jesus called them *your* good things—they had been the rich man's choice. He could have enjoyed his wealth and also chosen other "good things," such as helping the poor within his reach (such as Lazarus). Instead, the only "good things" he had chosen were for his own personal pleasure. Lazarus, however, had received only *evil things.* Jesus did not say "his" evil things; in other words, the evil that Lazarus had experienced came not as a result of his sin or his own foolish choices.

The roles for eternity would be reversed. Lazarus went from pain and hunger to comfort; the rich man went from pleasure and merriment to *agony.* This would have unnerved the Pharisees who were listening to this parable. To them, wealth was a sign of God's blessing, poverty a sign of God's disfavor. So they enjoyed their wealth and did not attempt to bridge the chasm that separated them from the "disfavored ones." But Jesus was explaining that another chasm would develop, and they would find themselves on the wrong side.

USE IT!
Wealth is not wrong; not all rich people are bound for hell. But the temptation is very great to use what God has given on one's own pleasures. Jesus was making the point that a person's possessions, no matter how many or how few, and that person's wealth, no matter how vast, have been entrusted by God to be used on his behalf. Believers are to use what God has given them to further his kingdom and to help needy brothers and sisters. You are merely a steward of what God has given. God wants you to share with others what he has given you.

16:26 **"'And besides all this, between us and you a great chasm has been fixed, so that those who want to go from here to you cannot, nor can anyone cross over from there to us.'"**^{NIV} Abraham explained to the rich man that he couldn't send Lazarus because between them and him *a great chasm has been fixed* and no one can cross over. The ultimate fates cannot be changed. God's decision upon death is final. There is only one life on this earth, and that is the time of decision. People cannot wait until eternity to make their relationship right with God. For it will be too late. The judgment will have been made on the basis of their choices, and it will be irreversible.

16:27-29   **"Then the rich man said, 'Please, Father Abraham, send him to my father's home. For I have five brothers, and I want him to warn them about this place of torment so they won't have to come here when they die.' But Abraham said, 'Moses and the prophets have warned them. Your brothers can read their writings anytime they want to.'"**[NLT] The rich man still thought Lazarus could be sent on messenger duty. If Lazarus could not come to help him, then he wanted Lazarus sent to warn his *five brothers* about the *place of torment* so they wouldn't have to go there when they died. Apparently the rich man did have some concern for those of his own family. He thought

> God has no need of marionettes. He pays men the compliment of allowing them to live without him if they choose. But if they live without him in this life, they must also live without him in the next.
> *Leon Morris*

that his brothers would surely believe a messenger who had been raised from the dead. Abraham simply explained that they could read the words of *Moses and the prophets* (that is, the Old Testament) and there find the warnings about the place of torment. If those brothers hadn't heeded the major message of God in his Word, they would not heed a minor messenger.

16:30-31   **"'No, father Abraham,' he said, 'but if someone from the dead goes to them, they will repent.' He said to him, 'If they do not listen to Moses and the Prophets, they will not be convinced even if someone rises from the dead.'"**[NIV] Perhaps the rich man knew his brothers only too well. The suggestion that they read God's Word (or listen to it read in the synagogue) met with a *no*. It just wouldn't happen—probably for the same reasons that the rich man himself never had heeded the warnings therein. So the rich man begged that *someone from the dead* go back to them. Surely, then, they would *repent*. He seems to think that if he had been accorded such a message, he would not be where he was.

Abraham answered that if these brothers did not *listen to Moses and the Prophets* (that is, if they did not believe what was written in Scripture, which includes all the warnings about the place of torment and the many words about their responsibility to care for the needy), then *they will not be convinced even if some-one rises from the dead* and appears to them.

Notice the irony in Jesus' statement; on his way to Jerusalem to die, he was fully aware that even when he had risen from the dead, most of the religious leaders would not accept him. They were set in their ways, and neither Scripture nor God's Son himself would shake them loose.

HARD-CORE SKEPTIC

In his life, the rich man refused to listen to God's command to be generous to the poor. Honest and difficult questions about God will always tug at the minds and hearts of honest searchers who are open and curious and do not regard questions as threats or sins.

Hard-core skeptics reject such questions as unsolvable and therefore unimportant. Their minds are resolved to avoid matters of faith, God, and eternity.

If you have questions, that's good. Keep looking for answers. If you have given up, take this story's warning. The serious pursuit of good questions is our human responsibility; an uncaring disposition erects a high wall between you and truth. One day all must give an account for rejecting God.

LUKE 17

After the parable of the rich man and Lazarus, Luke collected
four of Jesus' teachings that involve discipleship (a theme that
Luke also developed in 9:23-27, 57-62; 18:24-30). In these teachings, Jesus addressed his followers' relationship with each other
and their relationship with God. They are sharp words of truth
from the Savior—a firm prod to reevaluate all of life in light of
these principles.

Jesus warned his disciples against causing the downfall of
other believers and holding grudges against them. He also encouraged them to place their complete trust in God and to serve him
with joy. In these four short teachings, Jesus gave his disciples
the keys to an effective Christian life. Christians need to make it
a priority to encourage each other to live godly lives and to forgive the lapses of fellow believers. At the same time, they should
cultivate a true faith in God that wholeheartedly trusts in his plan
and a humble spirit that seeks to serve God instead of self.

**17:1 Jesus said to his disciples: "Things that cause people to sin
are bound to come, but woe to that person through whom
they come."**[NIV] Since 16:14, Jesus had been focusing his comments toward the Pharisees. The following samples of teaching,
whether chronological or not, were focused toward *his disciples*.
Because people are sinful and because people live in relationship
with one another, they will *cause* each other *to sin*. The Greek
word *skandala* used here denotes any hindrance that causes
another person to fall into sin, whether through temptation or
false teaching. Jesus explained that this was *bound* to happen, but
it did not excuse *that person through whom* the temptation came.
Jesus may have been referring to the religious leaders who taught
their converts their own hypocritical ways (see Matthew 23:15).
These leaders were perpetuating an evil system through their
false teaching. A person who teaches others has a solemn responsibility (James 3:1). Like physicians, a teacher should keep this
ancient oath in mind: "First, do no harm."

17:2 **"It would be better for you if a millstone were hung around your neck and you were thrown into the sea than for you to cause one of these little ones to stumble."**^{NRSV} Leading another person astray is very serious. Jesus explained that the consequences were so severe that it would be *better* to have *a millstone* tied around one's neck and be *thrown into the sea* than for a person to face God after causing others to stumble. A "millstone" was a heavy, flat stone used to grind grain. This large stone would be connected to an ox or donkey that would walk in a circle, causing the stone to roll and crush the grain. To have a millstone tied around the neck and be dumped into the sea pictured a horrifying death by drowning. Even such a death would be minor, however, compared to what this person would face in eternity.

Jesus used the term "little ones" to refer not just to children but to his followers. This pictures children who are trusting by nature. As children trust adults, and as adults prove to be trustworthy, the children's capacity to trust in God grows. God holds parents and other adults who influence young children accountable for how they affect these little ones' ability to trust God. "Woe to that person" (17:1) who would turn people away from him; he or she will receive severe punishment.

THE LITTLE ONES
Jesus warned about God's wrath for those who offend, abuse, or lead astray the little ones. Jesus warns off any predators who would hurt children in any way. How appropriate such a warning is in this day when corruption enters our homes every day in many television programs. While Christians must guard against physical abuse, they also must be aware of and work against the mental and spiritual corruption that unfiltered TV viewing can bring.

But Jesus' warning envisions an additional group. The "little ones" can be new disciples. Indifference to the training and treatment of new Christians can leave them theologically vulnerable. Make the follow-through care of recent converts and new members a high priority in your church.

17:3-4 **"Be on your guard! If another disciple sins, you must rebuke the offender, and if there is repentance, you must forgive. And if the same person sins against you seven times a day, and turns back to you seven times and says, 'I repent,' you must forgive."**^{NRSV} Careful leadership is important for Jesus' followers, but so is constant forgiveness. When there is sin among God's people, they are responsible to *rebuke* one another. To "rebuke" does not mean to point out every sin, for Jesus also warns against being judgmental (6:37). To "rebuke" (always in love) means to bring sin to a person's attention with the purpose of restoring that person to God and to fellow humans. In context here, this refers to sin that could pull that person or others away from God and thus result in the horrible judgment Jesus spoke of in 17:2. When a person feels that he or she must rebuke another Christian for a sin, it is wise for that person to check his or her attitudes and motivations first. Unless rebuke is tied to forgiveness, it will not help the sinning person. Jesus explained, in fact, that if the other person repents, the rebuker *must forgive.* And that forgiveness extends constantly (seven times a day simply means "all the time") because, after all, that is how God deals with every person. Because God has forgiven all believers' sins, they should not withhold forgiveness from others. Realizing how completely Christ has forgiven should produce a free and generous attitude of forgiveness toward others. Those who don't forgive others set themselves outside and above Christ's law of love. (See Life Application Commentary on Matthew 18:15-18 for the three steps of church discipline.)

EFFECTIVE CONFRONTATION
Rebuking a fellow believer requires care. Finding fault and expressing it effectively are delicate proceedings. People are easily offended. In a first-time confrontation, try these six steps:
  1. Pray for God's help in getting your concern across without generating antagonism or defensiveness.
  2. Approach the other person as a friend, not an adversary.
  3. Imagine the most innocent possible reason for the other's fault, not the most insidious or repulsive.
  4. Make your approach a series of gradual and mutual agreements: "Could I speak to you?" "I'm having trouble with something. May I ask you about it?"
  5. State your case once clearly. Repetition becomes the pounding of a sledgehammer.
  6. Express gratitude for the conversation, confidence in the friendship, and cordial expectations for the future. Show that you harbor no doubt that the matter has been solved.

17:5-6 **The apostles said to the Lord, "Increase our faith!" The Lord replied, "If you had faith the size of a mustard seed, you could say to this mulberry tree, 'Be uprooted and planted in the sea,' and it would obey you."**[NRSV] Perhaps as a result of the commands Jesus had given to those who would live in his kingdom (such as not causing others to stumble, and always being willing to forgive), the apostles (referring to the Twelve) asked Jesus to *increase [their] faith.* The disciples' request was genuine; they wanted the faith necessary for such radical forgiveness. But Jesus didn't directly answer their question because the amount of faith is not as important as its genuineness. What is faith? It is total dependence on God and a willingness to do his will.

A *mustard seed* is small, but it is alive and growing. Like a tiny seed, a small amount of genuine faith in God will take root and grow. Almost invisible at first, it will begin to spread, first under the ground and then visibly. Although each change will be gradual and imperceptible, soon this faith will have produced major results that will uproot and destroy competing loyalties. The apostles didn't need more faith; a tiny seed of faith would be enough, if it were alive and growing.

Jesus pointed to a nearby *mulberry tree* and said that even small faith could uproot it and send it into the sea. Mulberry trees grow quite large (as high as thirty-five feet). Matthew's Gospel records similar teaching when Jesus said that a mountain could be told to throw itself into the sea (Matthew 21:21). It is the power of God, not faith, that uproots trees and moves mountains, but faith must be present for God to work. Even a small "seed" of faith is sufficient. There is great power in even a little faith when God is there. It is not the amount of faith that matters; rather, it is the power of God available to anyone with even the smallest faith.

17:7-10 **"When a servant comes in from plowing or taking care of sheep, he doesn't just sit down and eat. He must first prepare his master's meal and serve him his supper before eating his own. And the servant is not even thanked, because he is merely doing what he is supposed to do. In the same way, when you obey me you should say, 'We are not worthy of praise. We are servants who have simply done our duty.'"**^{NLT} When Jesus' followers obey, they have only done their duty and should regard it as a privilege. They should not expect thanks, for they were only doing what they were supposed to do. Jesus used the example of a slave who renders service and does not expect to be thanked; the slave is merely doing his or her required social obligation. Obedience is not something extra done for God; it is the duty of anyone who desires to be Christ's follower. "Don't be selfish; don't live to make a good impression on others. Be humble, thinking of others as better than yourself. Don't think only about your own affairs, but be interested in others, too, and what they are doing" (Philippians 2:3-4 NLT). Before God, all people are sinners, saved only by God's grace, but believers *are* saved and therefore have great worth in God's kingdom. They must lay aside selfishness and treat others with respect and common courtesy.

With these words, Jesus was not rendering service as meaningless or useless, nor was he doing away with rewards. He was

attacking unwarranted self-esteem and
spiritual pride—perhaps such as many
of the religious leaders were exhibiting,
or what the disciples themselves might
be tempted to fall into as they would
seek to serve God. Jesus' followers
focus their eyes on God with their goal
only to serve and please him. They
don't work for recognition or rewards

> A Christian man is the
> most free lord of all,
> and subject to none; a
> Christian man is the most
> dutiful servant of all, and
> subject to everyone.
> *Martin Luther*

or even for God to praise them for their hard work. They understand that their duty is to serve the Master.

A SERVANT'S WAGES
Everyone in Jesus' day understood the role of a slave. That
person did the duty he or she was purchased to perform. The
owner owed no thanks for work done, and a slave wouldn't
expect it. So many people want recognition and appreciation
for every small step they take to help or serve. Loyalty and
obedience are merely the beginning of a believer's obligation.
When believers seek praise and reward, they serve themselves
and not God. Examine your motives. What do you expect when
you serve others?

JESUS HEALS TEN MEN WITH LEPROSY / 17:11-19 / 169

Ten lepers were healed, but only one leper—a Samaritan—returned
to thank Jesus. This story, unique to Luke, highlights the faith of a
foreigner in Israel. One of the major themes of Luke is the remarkable faith of Gentiles. Although many of the Jewish religious leaders rejected Jesus, a number of foreigners wholeheartedly placed
their trust in him (7:1-10). This theme is continued in the book of
Acts, where Luke wrote how the gospel message spread to the Gentiles after the initial rejection of it by many of the Jews (see Acts
1:8; see also Cornelius's conversion in Acts 10).

17:11 **Now on his way to Jerusalem, Jesus traveled along the border
between Samaria and Galilee.**^{NIV} Jesus was still *on his way to
Jerusalem,* knowing that he had an "appointment" there in order
for his ministry to be completed (9:51; 13:22). Jesus was traveling *along the border between Samaria and Galilee.* Galilee was
Jewish; Samaria was occupied by Samaritans, who were despised
by the Jews (see the commentary on 9:52-53). The exact location
is unknown, but that Jesus was near the border accounts for a
Samaritan (a "foreigner," 17:16, 18) in the group of lepers.

17:12-13 **As he entered a village there, ten lepers stood at a distance,
crying out, "Jesus, Master, have mercy on us!"**^{NLT} People who
had leprosy (called lepers) were required to try to stay away from
other people and to announce their presence if they had to come
near (see the commentary on 5:12-13). Thus these *ten lepers* were
standing at a distance, outside the city, and they were *crying out*
to Jesus for mercy. They called Jesus *Master*—they knew who he
was and what he could do for them. They did not try to get close,
however, perhaps because of the crowd that was probably still following Jesus (14:25).

ON THE PERIPHERY
Ten lepers cried out for mercy. On the edges of our lives, at a
distance, but within shouting range stand needy people whom
Jesus loves. What can you do to reach them?

- A street kid in Brazil, courted by druggies.
- A prostitute in Bangkok, her youth spoiled.
- A refugee in Zaire, undernourished and without work.
- A homeless drifter a mile from your home, a block from your church.

Their cry is barely audible, "Christian, have mercy. . . ."

How easy it is for believers to go on with "business as usual"
in their daily lives when so many people live in desperate need,
poverty, and suffering. Because there are so many needs and
so few resources, believers must ask God for direction and
depend upon his resources. Work through your church and
actively seek some way you can help.

17:14 **He looked at them and said, "Go show yourselves to the
priests." And as they went, their leprosy disappeared.**^{NLT} Sometimes leprosy would go into remission. If a leper thought his leprosy had gone away, the leper was supposed to present himself to
a priest, who could declare him clean (Leviticus 14). Jesus sent
the ten lepers to the priest before they were healed, for *as they
went, their leprosy disappeared.* Jesus did not touch these men or
even speak words of healing as he had done for most of his healings. This time he simply gave them the command to *go . . . to
the priests.* Jesus was asking the men to respond in faith that, by
their obedience, what they desired would happen. All the men
responded in faith, and Jesus healed them on the way. Consider
your own trust in God. Is your faith so strong that you act on
what he says even before you see evidence that it will work?

17:15-16 **One of them, when he saw that he was healed, came back to
Jesus, shouting, "Praise God, I'm healed!" He fell face
down on the ground at Jesus' feet, thanking him for what he
had done. This man was a Samaritan.**^{NLT} Jesus healed all ten

lepers, but only *one of them, when he saw that he was healed,* returned to thank him. It is possible to receive God's great gifts with an ungrateful spirit—nine of the ten men did so. Only the thankful man, however, learned that his faith had played a role in his healing, and only grateful Christians grow in understanding God's grace. God does not demand that his people thank him, but he is pleased when they do so. And he uses their responsiveness to teach them more about himself.

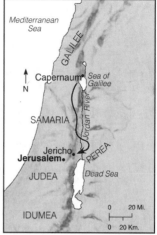

The grateful man returned to Jesus, praised God, *fell face down,* and thanked Jesus. Luke added, almost as a parenthesis, that, by the way, *this man was a Samaritan.* As noted in the commentary at 9:52-53, the Samaritans were a race despised by the Jews as idolatrous half-breeds. The surprise of this story is that this Samaritan,

LAST TRIP FROM GALILEE
Jesus left Galilee for the last time—he would not return before his death. He passed through Samaria, met and healed ten men who had leprosy, and continued on to Jerusalem. He spent some time east of the Jordan (Mark 10:1) before going to Jericho (Luke 19:1).

used to being despised by Jews (except perhaps for his fellow lepers), would dare to go to this Jewish healer and prostrate himself before him. But this man's faith went deep enough that he saw God's hand in the healing. Once again Luke was pointing out that God's grace is for everybody. The Samaritan not only portrayed the same trust that Jesus brought to the story of the Good Samaritan (10:30-37) but also set the stage for Jesus' mission to all people (see Acts 8:4).

17:17-19 Jesus asked, **"Didn't I heal ten men? Where are the other nine? Does only this foreigner return to give glory to God?" And Jesus said to the man, "Stand up and go. Your faith has made you well."**[NLT] Jesus had been distressed many times with his own people's lack of acceptance and faith (7:9; 8:25; 12:28). This time was no different. *Ten men* had been healed, but only one, the *foreigner* (referring to the man from Samaria), came back to *give glory to God.* Jesus was not so much concerned about being thanked as he was about the men's understanding of what had happened. The other nine went off, free from leprosy but not necessarily free from sin through the salvation Jesus could offer. This one man was freed, so Jesus sent him on his way with the knowledge that his *faith* had made him well. He not only had a restored body, his soul had been restored as well.

FAITH AND HEALING
Jesus' miracles of healing provide wonderful encouragement, for they reveal his power and his compassion. The difficulty comes from applying these accounts today. How should believers pray for themselves and loved ones who are sick or terminally ill? How should they believe? This story provides not all the answers but some insights into Jesus' healing of the sick.
- These lepers recognized Jesus' authority. They did not demand that he heal them. They called out for Jesus to have mercy on them (17:13).
- Jesus emphasized the necessity of faith (17:19). Just as in the parable of the mustard seed (13:18-19), it is not the size of faith but the presence of genuine faith that is important.
- Jesus stressed public testimony. He directed the lepers to go to the priests (17:14) to demonstrate what God had done. Believers also must be prepared to give God the credit when they are healed.
- Jesus highlighted the need for gratitude and praise to God (17:18). Will your attitude be grateful to God despite the outcome of your prayer? Can you trust fully in God's care each day, living or dying?

Christians should always be the ones who return to Jesus and thank him for his mercy and power.

JESUS TEACHES ABOUT THE COMING OF THE KINGDOM OF GOD / 17:20-37 / **170**

Here Luke placed a series of Jesus' teachings about the kingdom of God in order to present a concise summary of it. This passage, plus 21:15-38, parallels the Olivet discourse of Matthew 24 and Mark 13. In answering the Pharisees' question about the kingdom, Jesus pointed out that the kingdom was already "among" them (17:21 NLT). With his ministry, Jesus had already inaugurated the kingdom of God. He was preaching to the poor, healing the sick, and freeing people from the grip of evil. The kingdom of God was already among them as manifest in Jesus' teaching and miracles.

But Jesus also warned his disciples (17:22) that the complete realization of the kingdom of God was still in the future. They had to be prepared, for without warning, the kingdom would come. Jesus cited the sudden judgment that fell on the people of Noah's time and the inhabitants of Sodom and Gomorrah as vivid examples of the coming judgment of God.

The way to be prepared for this coming judgment is to give away your life to Jesus—and in service to others—instead of centering your efforts around yourself (17:33). The kingdom of God is already here—in the spread of the gospel throughout the world. Prepare yourself for the full revelation of the kingdom of God by allying yourself with it now.

> In Jesus the service of God and the service of the least of the brethren were one.
> *Dietrich Bonhoeffer*

17:20-21 Once Jesus was asked by the Pharisees when the kingdom of God was coming, and he answered, "The kingdom of God is not coming with things that can be observed; nor will they say, 'Look, here it is!' or 'There it is!' For, in fact, the kingdom of God is among you."NRSV Up to this point in the chapter, Jesus was explaining how his followers should live. From 17:20 to 18:8, as a response to a question brought by the Pharisees, Jesus discussed *when the kingdom of God was coming.* The Pharisees were expecting an altogether different kind of kingdom than what Jesus would bring. They may have thought, since Jesus had claimed to be the Messiah, that he would soon inaugurate his kingdom. They may also have been testing him since they had not seen him doing what a king would do to prepare himself for a takeover. They wondered when this kingdom he kept talking about was going to arrive.

The Pharisees did not understand that the kingdom of God had already arrived with Jesus. Jesus had made this clear in 11:20. In 19:11-27, he will explain that the full expression of God's kingdom is yet to come (and is still to come). These are the days "between"—the kingdom has arrived in Jesus Christ, yet it has not arrived in its fullness. Believers are waiting for it, as Jesus has already described (12:35-48), knowing that it could come at any moment. So Jesus' words here explain the nature of the kingdom now.

Jesus explained that the kingdom *is not coming with things that can be observed;* in other words, no one can project when it will come by looking for supernatural signs. Nor will anyone be able to point to anything that proves that the kingdom is *here* or *there.* The kingdom of God *was among* the people because Jesus was among them. Some translations say, "The kingdom of God is within you." When Jesus returned to heaven, the kingdom remained and continues today, with the work of God's Spirit in people's lives and in relationships. Still, today, believers must resist looking to institutions or programs for evidence of the progress of God's kingdom. Instead, they should look for what God is doing in people's hearts. Rather than looking for signs or trying to figure out timetables, each person should look into his or her own heart to be sure to be ready. When the kingdom arrives, will you be ushered in or sent away?

17:22 **Then he said to the disciples, "The days are coming when you will long to see one of the days of the Son of Man, and you will not see it."**NRSV Jesus turned his attention back to his disciples and explained that days would come when they would *long to see one of the days of the Son of Man,* but they would not see it. We are not certain whether this longing on the disciples' part would be for the return of the days when Jesus was among them physically (for he would soon be gone physically), or if their longing looked ahead to the "days" of the end times when the kingdom would arrive and Jesus would return. Most likely their "longing" would be looking ahead for what had been promised (because the following verses concern the Second Coming). The phrase "you will not see it" means that they would not see his arrival in their lifetimes. There would be an intervening time between Jesus' first and second comings.

17:23-24 **"They will say to you, 'Look there!' or 'Look here!' Do not go, do not set off in pursuit. For as the lightning flashes and lights up the sky from one side to the other, so will the Son of Man be in his day."**NRSV In these intervening days, after Christ has returned to heaven and as his followers await his return, there will be much speculation. Some will attempt to pinpoint exactly when Jesus will return; others will attempt to mock believers' expectations. Some will claim to be the Messiah; others will say that Jesus has returned—and people will believe them. Jesus warned believers never to take such reports seriously, no matter how convincing they may sound. If someone says the Messiah has come, *do not set off in pursuit.* When Jesus returns, his power and presence will be evident to everyone, like *lightning* that *lights up the sky from one side to the other.* No one will need to spread the message because all will see for themselves.

17:25 **"But first the Son of Man must suffer terribly and be rejected by this generation."**NLT Before this great return occurs, however, Jesus would return to heaven from earth. In order for that to occur, he would *suffer terribly and be rejected,* and then be crucified. This would happen soon, for it would be *this generation* who would do it, specifically this generation of religious leaders, who would arrange for Jesus to be put to death (9:21-27, 37-44; 18:31-34).

17:26-27 **"Just as it was in the days of Noah, so also will it be in the days of the Son of Man. People were eating, drinking, marrying and being given in marriage up to the day Noah entered the ark. Then the flood came and destroyed them all."**[NIV] To illustrate the suddenness of his return, Jesus used two examples, the first being the Flood (see Genesis 6–7). In the days before the Flood, life went on as usual for most people. With the exception of *Noah,* who had been building a huge boat for many years, the rest of mankind had been *eating, drinking, marrying and being given in marriage.* With no impending danger, life went on as usual *up to the day Noah entered the ark.* Then, it began to rain, *the flood came,* and everyone drowned.

Jesus was warning against false security. Although life will continue as usual until the day of Christ's return, believers must always be ready to go at a moment's notice. When Christ returns, there will be no second chances. Some will be taken to be with him; the rest will be left behind.

AS THE WORLD SPINS
In every age, it has been easy to assume that life goes on, never spending a second thought on God's promised intervention. For most people, everything seems normal—your grocery store has fresh produce, your doctor is doing physicals, your mail is delivered, and the corner deli is open for business.

But don't think God has forgotten. One day soon all of God's glory and fury will burst into view. The kingdom that grew slowly—at your neighborhood church, in your small-group Bible study, at youth-group outings, and in prayer with friends—will explode into plain sight, and God's truth will be known by all. Reach out to those yet untold of Christ's love and mercy. Help them be prepared for Christ's return.

17:28-29 **"And the world will be as it was in the days of Lot. People went about their daily business—eating and drinking, buying and selling, farming and building—until the morning Lot left Sodom. Then fire and burning sulfur rained down from heaven and destroyed them all."**[NLT] The second example of the suddenness of Christ's return is the destruction of the city of Sodom (recorded in Genesis 18–19). Sodom, along with the nearby city of Gomorrah, was destroyed by God because of its great wickedness. *Lot,* Abraham's nephew, had chosen to settle in the city of Sodom (Genesis 13:11-13). The people of Sodom, wicked as they were, *went about their daily business.* Then, *the morning Lot left Sodom,* the city was destroyed. The destruction came so suddenly that only Lot and his family escaped. Angels came and spared Lot and his family from the *fire and burning sulfur.*

In the time between Christ's first and second comings, some may be lulled into complacency by the fact that life continues with its normal activities. Many today see life moving ahead with no interruptions. But Jesus made it clear that judgment would come, unexpectedly, without warning, in the middle of what would begin as a routine day.

GET READY!
Christ will return with no warning. Most people will be going about their everyday tasks, indifferent to the demands of God. They will be as surprised by his return as the people in Noah's day were by the Flood (Genesis 6–8) or as the people in Lot's day were surprised by the destruction of Sodom (Genesis 19). No one knows when Christ will return, but his return is certain. He may come today, tomorrow, or centuries in the future. Whenever Jesus comes, believers must be morally and spiritually ready. Live as if Jesus were returning today.

17:30-32 **"It will be just like this on the day the Son of Man is revealed. On that day no one who is on the roof of his house, with his goods inside, should go down to get them. Likewise, no one in the field should go back for anything."**^{NIV} *It will be just like* the day when the Flood came, or the day when fire rained down on Sodom *on the day the Son of Man is revealed.* When Christ returns, there will be no time to return home for anything. Houses in Bible times had flat roofs with an outside staircase. The roof was often used as an additional living area. When Christ returns, material possessions will no longer matter. Those on their roofs should not go back inside to try to get anything; those working out in the fields should not return to the city. Jesus exhorted his listeners to **"remember what happened to Lot's wife!"**^{NLT} When the angels led Lot and his family out of the city, the angels warned them not to look back (Genesis 19:17). Surely the sound of destruction would reach their ears, but they were not to turn around. "But Lot's wife looked back, and she became a pillar of salt" (Genesis 19:26 NIV). Clinging to the past, she was unwilling to completely leave the evil of the city and the comfort of her possessions.

The time for deciding about Christ will pass in a single moment. Those who were waiting and longing to see that day (17:22) will rejoice at its arrival. Those who did not believe it would happen will not have time to do anything about it. It will be too late.

17:33 **"Whoever clings to this life will lose it, and whoever loses this life will save it."**ᴺᴸᵀ Christ's return will cause great upheaval and danger. This is described in other prophecies regarding the end times, such as chapter 21 and the book of Revelation. The person looking for the kingdom will be able to run with joy to welcome it, willingly forfeiting home and possessions in order to have eternal life. However, *whoever clings to this life will lose it,* for nothing in this life will remain. When God's kingdom comes, everything will change. Clinging to this world is foolish, for it will pass away. Clinging to life is foolish, for it too will pass away. Jesus said much the same thing in 9:24 (see commentary there). (See also Matthew 10:39; 16:25; Mark 8:35; John 12:25.)

LOSING LIFE TO SAVE IT
Those clinging to this life are those seeking to escape physical persecution. Those who live for themselves display these common attitudes:

- *Materialism*—I want it and work hard to get it. All that I see is real. Unseen things are merely ideas and dreams.
- *Individualism*—I work hard for me, and you work hard for you. I may make it; you may not. That's your problem, not mine.
- *Skepticism*—Anything I'm not convinced about can't be important. Everything important to know I can figure out.

Those who have these attitudes may protect themselves, but they will lose the spiritual dimension to their lives. Keep your commitment to Christ at full strength. Then you'll be ready when he returns.

17:34-36 **"That night two people will be asleep in one bed; one will be taken away, and the other will be left. Two women will be grinding flour together at the mill; one will be taken, the other left."**ᴺᴸᵀ The sudden return of Christ and the sudden end of all chances to change one's decision about him will result in sudden separation of his followers from those who chose not to follow. People may be close enough in this world—even sleeping in the same bed or working together at the same job. Note: The best manuscripts do not include 17:36, although the ɴᴋᴊᴠ includes it as another separation scenario: **"Two men will be in the field: the one will be taken and the other left."**

While these people may have looked no different from the outside, one difference will separate them forever. When Jesus returns, he will take his followers to be with him. The apostle Paul wrote:

*For since we believe that Jesus died and rose again, even so,
through Jesus, God will bring with him those who have died.
For this we declare to you by the word of the Lord, that we
who are alive, who are left until the coming of the Lord, will by
no means precede those who have died. For the Lord himself,
with a cry of command, with the archangel's call and with the
sound of God's trumpet, will descend from heaven, and the
dead in Christ will rise first. Then we who are alive, who are
left, will be caught up in the clouds together with them to meet
the Lord in the air; and so we will be with the Lord forever.
(1 Thessalonians 4:14-17* NRSV*)*

"We who are alive . . . will be caught up in the clouds together"
refers to those who have accepted the salvation Jesus offers. Only
they will go with Christ when he returns. Those who have not
accepted him will be surprised to find that their companions have
been *taken away* and that they are *left* behind.

WILL YOU BE TAKEN?
When God's kingdom comes, will you be included? You can be
sure of it! Accept Jesus Christ as your Savior today. In a prayer,
admit your need, ask for pardon from your sin, and thank God
for welcoming you into his family. Live for your Lord today. Help
someone overcome a problem. Give someone an encouraging
word from the Bible. Pray for someone in trouble.

17:37 **"Where, Lord?" they asked. He replied, "Where there is a
dead body, there the vultures will gather."**NIV Those listening to
Jesus' words of warning wanted to know *where* all of this would
take place. To answer the disciples' question, Jesus quoted a
familiar proverb. One vulture circling overhead does not mean
much, but a gathering of vultures means that a dead body is
nearby. Likewise, one sign of the end may not be significant, but
when many signs occur, the Second Coming will be near.

LUKE 18

This parable, unique to Luke, illustrates the importance of prayer
for Christians (a theme of Luke's, see 5:16; 6:12; 11:1-13). In the
same way as the widow, Christians should not give up praying to
God even when facing indifference and powerful opposition. If
an unjust judge will eventually give justice to a painfully persistent widow, then the Lord will surely answer his people's prayers.
This short parable concludes the preceding section, which
addresses the coming of the kingdom of God. The appropriate
response to the delay of Jesus' coming is to not give up on prayer.
Instead believers need to place their hopes even more in Jesus'
coming, the time when he will establish truth and righteousness
forevermore.

**18:1 Then Jesus told his disciples a parable to show them that they
should always pray and not give up.**NIV The following *parable*
and the injunction to *pray and not give up* should be interpreted
in light of the preceding chapter and its focus on the coming kingdom. Jesus had been discussing with his listeners the aspects of
the "in-between" time as they lived in a sinful world and awaited
the kingdom. The problem of evil and suffering and the need for
justice would plague Jesus' followers as they experienced pain
and awaited vindication. As they wrestled with these difficulties,
they could know that their heavenly Father listened and understood. In light of God's ultimate victory over evil and the coming
kingdom where "there will be no more death or mourning or crying or pain" (Revelation 21:4 NIV), Christ's followers can know
that the answer to their prayers for relief and justice is coming in
his time.

Continual prayer would have been a new idea for the Jews,
who said that it was best to pray three times a day so as not to
weary God. To persist in prayer and not give up does not mean
endless repetition or painfully long prayer sessions. Always praying means keeping one's requests constantly before God as one
lives for him day by day, believing he will answer. Living by

faith means not giving up. God may delay answering, but his delays always have good reasons. Christians must not be discouraged by God's delays.

PRAY HARD
Jesus taught his disciples about persistent prayer. A T-shirt reads: "Life is short. Pray hard." How does a person pray hard? Do not approach prayer like work. Hard work means sweat, fatigue, and muscle strain. Instead, persistent prayer involves

- *Faith.* Unbelievers may succumb to anger, resentment, or despair when they face problems. But you believe God has a solution for you. Prayer builds faith.
- *Hope.* Life ends, sometimes tragically, but it always ends. God promises eternal life in his Word to those who trust him. When you pray often, you reactivate your trust in future life with God. Constant prayer generates hope.
- *Love.* To be concerned primarily about yourself, your needs, and your problems is normal. To care about someone other than yourself contradicts your instincts. God wants you to learn to love and to express love to others. Remember, prayer nurtures love.

When life is hard, prayer provides a way for you and God to face it together.

18:2-5 **"There was a judge in a certain city," he said, "who was a godless man with great contempt for everyone. A widow of that city came to him repeatedly, appealing for justice against someone who had harmed her. The judge ignored her for a while, but eventually she wore him out. 'I fear neither God nor man,' he said to himself, 'but this woman is driving me crazy. I'm going to see that she gets justice, because she is wearing me out with her constant requests!'"**NLT Jesus was not comparing God to this unjust and contemptuous judge, as though he would treat believers in this manner. Instead, this parable shows that if even an evil man can be made to deal justly by a persistent woman, how much more would God, who loves his people, care for their requests.

The scene pictures a *judge* who is *godless* and contemptuous. He was probably not a Jew, but a Gentile who served as a local administrator for the Jews who could not take their particular cases to their religious leaders. As a judge, he should have been championing those who needed justice (2 Chronicles 19:4-6), but when *a widow* came for help, he *ignored her.* Widows and orphans were among the most vulnerable of all God's people, and both Old Testament prophets and New Testament apostles insisted that these needy people be properly cared for. (See, for example, Exodus 22:22-24; Isaiah 1:17; 1 Timothy 5:3; James

1:27.) So here's a helpless widow up against a contemptuous judge who chooses to ignore her. She has little hope of gaining the justice she seeks, so she uses the only weapon she has—persistence. Without anything to lose, she makes herself an irritant to the judge, willing to drive him crazy *with her constant requests.* Even this contemptuous man grows tired of her. Even worse, she is hurting his reputation, embarrassing him with her pounding persistence. So, to get rid of her, he sees that *she gets justice.*

HOW MUCH MORE
Does prayer ever feel as though you are talking to an empty room when nobody's listening? Do you wonder if your requests are an exercise in auto-suggestion? Is prayer a waste of time because God has more important things to do?

Jesus used the "how much more" argument to demonstrate that God is not indifferent or inattentive. Do not attribute those qualities to him. God hears your prayers eagerly and compassionately. God acts on your behalf and for your best. God cares about you personally.

When you pray, remember God's promise to hear your prayer.

18:6-8 **And the Lord said, "Listen to what the unjust judge says. And will not God bring about justice for his chosen ones, who cry out to him day and night? Will he keep putting them off? I tell you, he will see that they get justice, and quickly. However, when the Son of Man comes, will he find faith on the earth?"**[NIV] If an unjust judge will respond to constant pressure, how much more will a great and loving God respond to his people? They know he loves them; they can believe he will hear their cries for help. They can trust that one day God will *bring about justice for his chosen ones, who cry out to him day and night.* God's people, his followers (described here as "chosen ones") who persist in prayer (18:1) as they seek to be obedient in this sinful world, can know that God will not *keep putting them off.* It may seem for a time that their cries go unheard. But one day, God *will see that they get justice, and quickly.* (This quickness was described in 17:24-35.) But Christ has not yet returned. Jesus had made it clear that there would be an intervening time. This would be the church age, the present time. During these years, God's people help others find the kingdom and are themselves strengthened in their faith. Their needs cause them to be on their knees constantly, knowing that God alone is their help. Jesus gave no indication of how long this intervening time would last or when he would return. Indeed, he said no one knows (Matthew 24:36), so believers are always to be ready. But Jesus asked, *"When the Son of Man comes, will he find faith on the earth?"* Will people have persisted in faith? Will they be ready and waiting when he comes?

JESUS TELLS THE PARABLE OF TWO MEN WHO PRAYED / 18:9-14 / *172*

After encouraging the disciples to be persistent in prayer (18:1-8), Jesus taught them, with a parable, how to pray. This parable sharply contrasts the prayer of a Pharisee with that of a tax collector. The first prayer was essentially a personal eulogy, while the other prayer was a heartfelt plea for mercy. Jesus commended the tax collector for his humility before God. Then he ended the parable with his familiar saying that the exalted would be humbled and the humble exalted (see 1:52-53; 6:20-26; 14:11 for similar teachings). The lesson is clear: When you come to God in prayer, humble yourself before him. Then he will not only forgive your sin but also empower you and lift you up.

18:9-10 **To some who were confident of their own righteousness and looked down on everybody else, Jesus told this parable: "Two men went up to the temple to pray, one a Pharisee and the other a tax collector."**NIV Prayer is important (18:1-8), but the attitude of prayer is vitally important. The people *who were confident of their own righteousness and looked down on everybody else* were the Pharisees and other religious leaders who saw themselves as the only ones righteous enough to be acceptable to God. To these people, Jesus told a parable about *two men* who went to the temple to pray. The people who lived near Jerusalem often would go *to the temple* for times of prayer (either public or private) because the temple was the center of their worship. These two men were as different as could be: the one was a law-keeping and religious *Pharisee* (for more on Pharisees, see commentary on 5:17), and the other was *a tax collector* (for more on tax collectors, see commentary on 5:27). Immediately Jesus established a dichotomy in the minds of his listeners. Unsure of what this parable would be about, at first they would have pictured a godly Pharisee and a traitorous tax collector. The fact that this outcast tax collector had come *to pray* added interest to this story. They would expect to see the Pharisee praying there, but not the tax collector.

18:11-12 **"The proud Pharisee stood by himself and prayed this prayer: 'I thank you, God, that I am not a sinner like everyone else, especially like that tax collector over there! For I never cheat, I don't sin, I don't commit adultery, I fast twice**

a week, and I give you a tenth of my income.'"^{NLT} This Pharisee's actions and his prayer provide a picture of his life and occupation—he was a separatist, but his separatism and desire to remain clean before God had hardened

> No man can really at one and the same time call attention to himself and glorify God.   *Louis Benes*

into a lifestyle of self-righteousness. He *stood by himself* and prayed. This would be typical for anyone who prayed at the temple.

The words of this prayer, however, while probably true, were not prayed in the correct attitude of humility before God. It was as if this Pharisee were trying to trade his good deeds for God's grace. First of all, he thanked God that he was *not a sinner like everyone else.* While the Pharisee was probably not like everyone else in a lot of ways, he erred in thinking that he was "not a sinner." This Pharisee knew that he was far better than the tax collector he saw praying across the way. Tax collectors were not noted for their honesty, so this Pharisee compared himself favorably, telling God that he himself had never cheated or sinned or committed adultery. And, by the way, he also fasted *twice a week* and tithed from his income. Fasting was mandatory for the Jewish people once a year, on the Day of Atonement (Leviticus 23:32). The Pharisees fasted twice a week, on Mondays and Thursdays. While fasting has great spiritual value, the religious leaders had turned it into a way to gain public approval. For more on tithing, see commentary on 11:42. (Old Testament references about fasting include Judges 20:26; 1 Samuel 7:6; Ezra 8:21; Esther 4:16. References about tithing include Leviticus 27:30-33; Numbers 18:12; Deuteronomy 12:6-9; 14:22-29; 26:12-15; Nehemiah 10:37-38; 12:44; 13:5; Malachi 3:8, 10.)

This Pharisee was confident of himself and his righteousness, while at the same time despising this other man, even though he too was in the temple praying to the same God. The Pharisee did not welcome the tax collector who may have been seeking God; instead, the Pharisee gloated that he was so much more righteous.

LOOK AT ME! I'M PRAYING!
The Pharisee went to the temple to use prayer as an announcement about how good he was. We all know that God was not impressed. Neither are we.

Prayer that recites our accomplishments is nothing more than pious conceit. When you pray, recite God's accomplishments instead—all that God has done for you and others. That kind of prayer directs praise to the right mailbox.

18:13-14 **"But the tax collector stood at a distance. He would not even look up to heaven, but beat his breast and said, 'God, have mercy on me, a sinner.' I tell you that this man, rather than the other, went home justified before God. For everyone who exalts himself will be humbled, and he who humbles himself will be exalted."**[NIV] The focus shifted to the tax collector who was *at a distance* from the praying Pharisee. Whether either heard the other was not the point, for this is merely a story of attitudes. In this parable, the tax collector had come to the temple and seems to have known full well the extent of his sin. He felt so low that he did not think he could *even look up to heaven* into God's face; instead he *beat his breast* (a sign of sorrow), praying for God to have mercy on him. He recognized himself as *a sinner.* He had been convicted of his sin and had come to the one place where he could find forgiveness. He had come to God, humbly recognizing that he did not deserve mercy.

Surprisingly enough, only the tax collector *went home justified before God.* The word "justified" means God's act of declaring people "not guilty" of sin. Only the tax collector recognized his sin; therefore, he was the only one God justified. The self-righteous Pharisee had said that he had no sin; therefore, there was nothing for God to justify for him. He returned home no different than when he had entered. His prayer had not touched heaven, for it was merely a self-congratulatory speech. But having thrown himself on God's mercy, the tax collector *went home justified.*

The principle is that no one has anything of value to bring to God in order to deserve salvation, mercy, justification, or even a second glance from God. Those who exalt themselves *will be humbled;* those who humble themselves before God *will be exalted.* Acceptance before God cannot be achieved by actions, good deeds, piety, or any amount of self-proclaimed righteousness.

DEEP DOWN INSIDE
Today, guilt is unpopular; feeling "good about myself" is much more in fashion. Anyone found beating his breast in guilt is sent for counseling until such negative behavior is corrected. It's not healthy to feel guilt. Humbling oneself is likewise not in vogue. The papers are full of advice that self-asserting behavior and affirming oneself are the means to success.

But God's grace cannot be found without humility. It is essential to receiving mercy. That's the point of Jesus' parable in 18:13-14.

Do you want to be free of guilt? First confess your sins before God with remorse and repentance. Then accept God's gift to you—the forgiveness that Jesus Christ offers.

JESUS BLESSES LITTLE CHILDREN / 18:15-17 / **174**

Jesus used a child's humility as a striking picture of the appropriate attitude with which to approach God. That type of humility was demonstrated by the tax collector in the previous parable (18:9-14). In the next passage (18:18-30), the rich ruler is an example of a person who refuses to humble himself. Jesus' words forcefully confront hearers today. Do they receive the kingdom of God with childlike humility?

18:15 One day some parents brought their little children to Jesus so he could touch them and bless them, but the disciples told them not to bother him.^NLT In the first century, Jewish households were patriarchal—men came first, followed by women and children. Adult men were the key members of society, women quite secondary, and children were to be seen but not heard. It was customary, however, for parents to bring their children (the Greek word for "children" is *paidia,* meaning children ranging in age from babies to preteens) to an elder or a scribe *so he could touch* (or lay hands on) *and bless them.* This was often done on the eve of the Day of Atonement (Yom Kippur). Nonetheless, the disciples apparently viewed these *parents* and *little children* as an intrusion and a drain of time and energy. So they *told them not to bother* Jesus.

HE WELCOMED THEM
It was customary for a mother to bring her children to an elder or scribe for a blessing, and that is why these mothers gathered around Jesus. The disciples, however, thought the children were unworthy of the Master's time—less important than whatever else he was doing. But Jesus welcomed them because little children have the kind of faith and trust needed to enter God's kingdom. Does your church give slight attention and resources to the Sunday school children's program or to the youth program? Keep these ministries as priorities. It is important to approach Jesus with childlike attitudes of acceptance, faith, and trust, and to introduce children to Jesus so that they can do so as well.

18:16-17 Then Jesus called for the children and said to the disciples, "Let the children come to me. Don't stop them! For the Kingdom of God belongs to such as these. I assure you, anyone who doesn't have their kind of faith will never get into the Kingdom of God."^NLT Instead of being too busy for children, Jesus *called for* them and wanted them to come to him. No one should be stopped from coming to Jesus, no matter how young or old. Jesus explained that *the Kingdom of God belongs to such as* *these,* not meaning that heaven is only for children, but meaning that people need childlike attitudes of trust in God. The receptiveness of little children was a great contrast to the stubbornness of the religious leaders, who let their education and sophistication stand in the way of the simple faith. Anyone of any age who exhibits childlike faith and trust is promised access to Jesus and to the kingdom. In fact, *anyone who doesn't have their kind of faith will never get into the Kingdom of God.* Childlike faith means trusting God no matter what, always knowing that he has your best in mind. You love him because he loves you. You trust completely because the one you trust is completely trustworthy.

THEIR KIND OF FAITH
How does someone have a child's kind of faith, as emphasized by Jesus? It means having the simple, trusting attitude that children show to adults on whom they depend. Jesus wants his people to
- enjoy prayer by delighting in his company.
- find ways in a busy day to read the Bible enthusiastically.
- seek God's help in any problem and rely on him for guidance.
- above all, trust explicitly in his promises.

Children do all that with adults who love them. How much more should believers have that attitude toward Jesus, who loves them.

JESUS SPEAKS TO THE RICH YOUNG MAN / 18:18-30 / 175

A ruler stopped Jesus with a perfectly legitimate question: "What must I do to inherit eternal life?" Jesus told the man what he needed to hear instead of what he wanted to hear. The young man wanted to have another possession in his expansive collection—eternal life. He wanted to have the kingdom of God, but as it turned out, he wasn't ready.

This episode with the rich young man differs greatly with Jesus' blessing of children in the previous section. The children are an example of innocent faith and trust. The rich young man thought he could gain eternal life by what he did, only to find that he could not have it.

18:18 **A certain ruler asked him, "Good teacher, what must I do to inherit eternal life?"**NIV In Matthew 19:22, this person is called a "young man" (Mark 10:22 says he had great wealth), so he apparently was a relatively wealthy young man of prominent social standing (hence, he is called a *ruler*). He addressed Jesus as *good teacher* (not the more common "rabbi") and eagerly asked a question about what he should *do to inherit eternal life.* He viewed eternal life as something that a person could achieve or earn through certain works or good deeds, and he wanted to make sure that he did everything necessary.

BUSINESS SENSE
This young "ruler" had business sense. Getting rich was no problem, but he knew that someday he was going to die. What's the use of money if you can't keep it?

Sometimes people come to Jesus for life insurance—they would rather not lose everything at death. But Jesus' call is one step deeper, beyond possessions to the real self.

Are you God's child, whatever you own? Are you Jesus' disciple, whatever the cost? Becoming a Christian means happily surrendering the best of earth for the brightest of heaven. Have you placed your possessions and wealth fully under God's control?

18:19 "Why do you call me good?" Jesus asked him. "Only God is truly good."^{NLT} Instead of answering the young man's question, Jesus first took issue with the way the man addressed him as "good teacher" (18:18). This may have been no more than a flippant attempt at flattery, but Jesus forced the young man to think about it. Because *only God is truly good,* the young man had made a statement about Jesus that he probably did not even realize. By asking this question, Jesus was saying, "Do you really know the one to whom you are talking?" Jesus did not deny his deity but instead confirmed it by these words. The young man was correct in calling Jesus good, for he was good and also God.

18:20-21 "But as for your question, you know the commandments: 'Do not commit adultery. Do not murder. Do not steal. Do not testify falsely. Honor your father and mother.'" The man replied, "I've obeyed all these commandments since I was a child."^{NLT} Regarding the young man's question about what he needed to *do* to inherit eternal life, Jesus at first pointed him back to the *commandments* (meaning the Ten Commandments). Jesus listed only five of them—those dealing with human relationships. He did not list any of the first four commandments that deal with a person's relationship to God. All of the ones listed could be easily identified—the man probably could honestly say that he had not committed adultery or murder, had not stolen or lied, and had honored his parents. To keep the letter of these laws would be relatively easy for a wealthy young Jewish man. So he responded that he had *obeyed* all those commandments since childhood, yet he still felt strongly that something was lacking in his life. So he asked if there were more he should do. The point is that even *if* a person could keep all these commandments perfectly, which this man claimed to have done, there would *still* be a *lack* of assurance of salvation, for this man needed such assurance. Keeping the commandments perfectly cannot save anyone. Jesus would reveal to this man what he lacked.

18:22-23 **When Jesus heard this, he said to him, "There is still one thing lacking. Sell all that you own and distribute the money to the poor, and you will have treasure in heaven; then come, follow me." But when he heard this, he became sad; for he was very rich.**NRSV The young man saying that he had kept all the commandments led Jesus to focus on the man's relationship to his material possessions (alluding to the last commandment not to covet) and on his relationship to God (the first four commandments that Jesus had not mentioned). Jesus perceived an area of weakness—his wealth—and so gently told the young man that it was the money itself that was standing in the way of his reaching eternal life. So Jesus told him to *sell* everything he owned, give away his money *to the poor,* and then *follow* him. This challenge exposed the barrier that would keep this young man out of the kingdom: his love of money. Money represented the young man's pride of accomplishment and self-effort. Ironically, his attitude made him unable to keep the first commandment, one that Jesus did not quote: "You shall have no other gods before me" (Exodus 20:3). The young man did not love God with his whole heart as he had presumed. In reality, his many possessions were his god. If he could not give these up, he would be violating the first and greatest commandment.

The task of selling every possession would not, of itself, give the man eternal life. But such radical obedience would be the first step. The emphasis was not so much on "selling" as on "following." Jesus' words to this rich young man were a test of his faith and his willingness to obey. The man thought he needed to *do* more; Jesus explained that there was plenty more he could do but not in order to obtain eternal life. Instead, he needed an attitude adjustment toward his wealth; only then could he submit humbly to the lordship of Christ. By putting his *treasure in heaven* and following Jesus along the road of selflessness and service to others, the man could be assured of his eternal destiny. But the young man *became sad* when he heard this. He wanted to do good deeds and stay rich. He did not expect such an answer from Jesus, so he realized that what Jesus said he needed to do was exactly what he could not do. Jesus asked him to become a disciple, to follow him. Tragically, the man refused.

Jesus does not ask all believers to sell everything they have. He does ask each person, however, to get rid of anything that has become more important than God. If your basis for security has shifted from God to what you own, you may need to get rid of those possessions.

UNTIL JESUS IS ALL
Jesus told the young man to sell his possessions and give the money to the poor. For true disciples, wealth can be dangerous. Money and possessions can make people
- care more about money than about their role in God's kingdom.
- worry more about comfort than about their neighbor's needs.
- shop more for possessions to make them happy; search less for answers to life's big questions.
- anchor happiness in their accomplishments, not in God's Word.
- cling more to the tangibly immediate, less to the promised future.

To have the treasure in heaven that Jesus promises requires letting go of attachment to earthbound riches. How easy it is to rationalize away Jesus' teaching. If Jesus visited present-day churches, many believers would be told the same truth. Yet Jesus requires even more. It is not enough to be indifferent to money or be willing to give it up. Jesus demands that his followers actively give to the poor.

18:24-25 Jesus watched him go and then said to his disciples, "How hard it is for rich people to get into the Kingdom of God! It is easier for a camel to go through the eye of a needle than for a rich person to enter the Kingdom of God!"NLT Offered discipleship, the young man chose to return to his possessions. Jesus sadly pointed out to his disciples that it is *hard* for rich people to get into God's kingdom. This was contrary to conventional wisdom. Most Jews believed that wealth was a sign of God's blessing on people. Here Jesus explained that riches can often prove to be a stumbling block. Rich people often don't feel the deep spiritual hunger needed to seek out and find God. They can use their money to buy possessions, trips, and helpers so that they don't perceive any needs in their lives. With all their advantages and influence, the rich often find it difficult to have the attitude of humility, submission, and service required by Jesus. Because money represents power and success, the rich often miss out on the fact that power and success on earth cannot provide eternal salvation. Even if they use their money to help good causes, they can still miss out on God's kingdom.

Jesus used a well-known Jewish proverb to describe the difficulty faced by the rich; he said that *it is easier for a camel to go through the eye of a needle than for a rich person to enter the Kingdom of God.* Some commentators have suggested that the "needle" may refer to a certain gate in the wall of Jerusalem, a gate that was too low for camels to get through without removing everything from their backs. The Greek word, however, refers to a needle used with thread. Futhermore, the Needle's Eye Gate didn't exist in Jesus' day. It was put in later when the city was rebuilt after its destruction by the Romans. Jesus' image, therefore, was for hyperbolic effect. The camel, the largest animal in Palestine, could get through the eye of a sewing needle easier than a rich person could get into God's kingdom. These are indeed sobering words for those whose money and possessions are extremely important to them. Those very things cannot give eternal life and may, in fact, cause a person to miss eternal life just as they caused this young man to miss being with Jesus.

RICHES
Jesus taught that it was nearly impossible for a rich person to enter the kingdom of God. Because money represents power, authority, and success, often it is difficult for wealthy people to realize their need and their powerlessness to save themselves. The rich in talent or intelligence suffer the same difficulty. Unless God reaches into their lives, they will not come to him. Jesus surprised some of his hearers by offering salvation to the poor; he may surprise some people today by offering it to the rich. It is difficult for a self-sufficient person to realize his or her need and come to Jesus, but what is impossible with people is possible with God. If God has blessed you with wealth, make sure you give to the poor as Jesus taught. Then your testimony may be the best way to reach others who are wealthy.

18:26-27 Those who heard it said, "Then who can be saved?" He replied, "What is impossible for mortals is possible for God."NRSV Because the Jewish people saw riches as a sign of God's special blessing, they were astounded when Jesus said that riches actually worked against people finding God. So they asked, *"Then who can be saved?"*

Jesus answered that *what is impossible for mortals is possible for God.* People cannot save themselves, no matter how much power, authority, or influence they buy. Salvation comes from God alone. Both rich and poor can be saved, and human impossibilities are divine possibilities. The rich will need to loosely hold their riches, remembering that every penny comes from God. And they should willingly use what God has given to advance his kingdom. This does not come easily for anyone, rich or poor. Money can be a major stumbling block, but God can change anyone.

18:28-30 **Peter said to him, "We have left all we had to follow you!" "I tell you the truth," Jesus said to them, "no one who has left home or wife or brothers or parents or children for the sake of the kingdom of God will fail to receive many times as much in this age and, in the age to come, eternal life."**[NIV] Peter and the other disciples had paid a high price—leaving their homes and jobs—to follow Jesus. The Greek word *aphekamen* is in the aorist tense, signifying a once-for-all act. They had done what the rich young man had been unwilling to do. They had abandoned their former lives.

Jesus reminded Peter that following him has its benefits as well as its sacrifices. Any believer who has had to give up something to follow Christ will be paid back in this life as well as in the next. For example, if you must give up a secure job, you will find that God offers a secure relationship with himself now and forever. If you must give up your family's approval, you will gain the love of the family of God. The disciples had begun to pay the price of following Jesus, and Jesus said they would be rewarded—they would have *eternal life.* This is what the young man had wanted to be sure of—eternal life (18:18). The answer lies in setting aside your life in order to live wholly for Christ. For the rich young man that meant giving up money as his idol. For each person the sacrifice may be different, though no less difficult. No matter how much or how little you have, no matter how difficult the sacrifice may be, are you willing to do whatever it takes to have eternal life? Are you willing to listen to God and obey him in all areas of life? You can never outgive God. When you obey and follow, you will receive rewards without measure—that's his promise.

> I never made a sacrifice. We ought not to talk of "sacrifice" when we remember the great sacrifice which he made who left his Father's throne on high to give himself for us.
>
> *David Livingstone*

Believers are saved by God through Christ's faithful work in dying on the cross. Believers receive mercy and forgiveness by accepting God's kindness through trusting in him. But the Bible teaches that all people will be held accountable for their lives. For believers, there will be rewards for service. The Bible teaches that Jesus Christ has been given authority to judge all the earth (Romans 14:9-11; Philippians 2:9-11). There is a future final judg-

MESSIANIC PROPHECIES AND FULFILLMENTS

For the Gospel writers, one of the main reasons for believing in Jesus was the way his life fulfilled the Old Testament prophecies about the Messiah. Following is a list of some of the main prophecies.

	Old Testament Prophecies	*New Testament Fulfillment*
1. Messiah was to be born in Bethlehem	Micah 5:2	Matthew 2:1-6; Luke 2:1-20
2. Messiah was to be born of a virgin	Isaiah 7:14	Matthew 1:18-25; Luke 1:26-38
3. Messiah was to be a prophet like Moses	Deuteronomy 18:15, 18-19	John 7:40
4. Messiah was to enter Jerusalem in triumph	Zechariah 9:9	Matthew 21:1-9; John 12:12-16
5. Messiah was to be rejected by his own people	Isaiah 53:1, 3; Psalm 118:22	Matthew 26:3-4; John 12:37-43; Acts 4:1-12
6. Messiah was to be betrayed by one of his followers	Psalm 41:9	Matthew 26:14-16, 47-50; Luke 22:19-23
7. Messiah was to be tried and condemned	Isaiah 53:8	Luke 23:1-25; Matthew 27:1-2
8. Messiah was to be silent before his accusers	Isaiah 53:7	Matthew 27:12-14; Mark 15:3-4; Luke 23:8-10
9. Messiah was to be struck and spat on by his enemies	Isaiah 50:6	Matthew 26:67; 27:30; Mark 14:65
10. Messiah was to be mocked and insulted	Psalm 22:7-8	Matthew 27:39-44; Luke 23:11, 35
11. Messiah was to die by crucifixion	Psalm 22:14, 16-17	Matthew 27:31; Mark 15:20, 25
12. Messiah was to suffer with criminals and pray for his enemies	Isaiah 53:12	Matthew 27:38; Mark 15:27-28; Luke 23:32-34
13. Messiah was to be given vinegar and gall	Psalm 69:21	Matthew 27:34; John 19:28-30
14. Others were to cast lots for Messiah's garments	Psalm 22:18	Matthew 27:35; John 19:23-24
15. Messiah's bones were not to be broken	Exodus 12:46	John 19:31-36
16. Messiah was to die as a sacrifice for sin	Isaiah 53:5-6, 8, 10-12	John 1:29; 11:49-52; Acts 10:43 13:38-39
17. Messiah was to be raised from the dead	Psalm 16:10	Matthew 28:1-10; Acts 2:22-32
18. Messiah is now at God's right hand	Psalm 110:1	Mark 16:19; Luke 24:50-51

ment when Christ returns, and everyone's life will be reviewed and evaluated. While believers' destiny is secure, Jesus will look at how they handled gifts, opportunities, and responsibilities in order to determine their heavenly rewards. The greatest reward will be eternal life. Beyond that, believers do not know all that Christ has in mind for his people. (See also 19:24-27; 22:28-30.)

NO LOSS SO GREAT
Jesus promised much to his followers. Nothing you lose threatens the love, joy, and peace God promises to all his children.

- Not your home. Tornadoes may flatten it.
- Not your job. Stingy bosses may cancel it.
- Not your spouse. Cancer may snatch him or her away.
- Not your friends. They may shun "religious types."

Your life's losses will add up as years go by, but God's presence in you and promise to you is all the greater a share of your heart's real treasure. No loss is so great that God does not fill the void.

JESUS PREDICTS HIS DEATH THE THIRD TIME / 18:31-34 / 177

For the third time, Jesus predicted his death; this time, he graphically described his rejection by the religious leaders and even predicted his own resurrection. While Mark placed the three predictions relatively close together (see Mark 8:31-32; 9:30-32; 10:32-34), Luke placed these predictions within his long section that recounts Jesus' "journey to Jerusalem." He placed the first two predictions at the beginning of the journey (9:22, 43-45) and this third prediction toward the end, showing that Jesus was heading to Jerusalem to fulfill these predictions (see 12:50; 13:32-33; 17:25). The disciples still did not understand what Jesus was talking about and would continue in their ignorance until Jesus himself explained how he had fulfilled the Old Testament (on the Emmaus road in 24:13-32 and in Jerusalem in 24:33-48).

18:31 Gathering the twelve disciples around him, Jesus told them, "As you know, we are going to Jerusalem. And when we get there, all the predictions of the ancient prophets concerning the Son of Man will come true."[NLT] Here Jesus told his disciples for the third time about his coming death (see also 9:21-27, 44-45). He had already set his face toward Jerusalem, knowing that he had to be there for the Passover, knowing that he had to die (9:51). As a warning to his disciples, he gathered them in around him and explained that when they arrived in Jerusalem *all the predictions of the ancient prophets concerning the Son of Man will come true.* Some of those predictions about what would happen to Jesus are in Psalm 41:9 (betrayal); Psalm 22:16-18; Isaiah 53:4-7 (crucifixion); and Psalm 16:10 (resurrection). The disciples still may have been hoping that Jesus would become the military leader; perhaps they still held out hope that somehow his words of death were allegorical, not factual. Jesus here explained, however, that the plans had already been in place for thousands of years and soon would be fulfilled.

18:32-34 **"He will be handed over to the Gentiles. They will mock him, insult him, spit on him, flog him and kill him. On the third day he will rise again."**[NIV] The first time Jesus told of his impending death, he focused on his rejection by Israel's leaders (9:21-27); the second time, he added the element of betrayal (9:44-45). Here Jesus mentioned the foretelling of these events by the prophets and the involvement of the *Gentiles* who would *mock, insult, spit on, flog,* and *kill him.* While the Jewish leaders would reject Jesus (as reported in 9:21-27), they had to submit to Rome's authority in cases of capital punishment. They could punish lesser crimes, but only Rome could call for and enact an execution. "The Gentiles" refers primarily to Pilate, the Roman governor, who represented Rome in Palestine. The mocking, insults, and flogging all came true, just as Jesus predicted here (see chapter 23; also Matthew 27:27-31; Mark 15:16-20).

So sad were these words that it seems the disciples didn't even hear the last sentence—on the third day, he would *rise again.* However, **The disciples did not understand any of this. Its meaning was hidden from them, and they did not know what he was talking about.**[NIV] Perhaps they again thought this was some sort of allegory they didn't yet understand. Most likely, their ignorance and blindness were simply because they could not grasp the scope of God's plan in Jesus. The disciples didn't understand Jesus, apparently because they were focusing on what he said about his death. This "hiddenness" was mentioned earlier (9:45) and would not be illuminated until later. Even though Jesus spoke plainly, they would not grasp the significance of his words until they had seen the risen Christ face-to-face (see 24:13-35).

JESUS HEALS A BLIND BEGGAR / 18:35-43 / 179

The healing of the blind man is the last miracle before the Passion Week. On his approach to Jerusalem, Jesus went through Jericho. Here a blind man, a person considered insignificant by others, cried out for mercy. The crowd tried to silence him, but he cried even louder, calling Jesus "the Son of David." By using this well-known messianic title, the blind man was expressing his faith in Jesus as the Messiah who could save him. This type of bold faith was rewarded. The blind man was healed and ended up leading others in praising God. He believed, not because of the clarity of his sight, but because of what he had heard.

AGAINST THE CROWD

When did you last reject the pressure to conform and just did it your own way? The crowd here wanted even-tempered decorum, but Bartimaeus wanted Jesus' attention. He broke a lot of social rules to get it.

What normal social patterns would you have to break to find Jesus? What if your office likes Sunday morning golf, but you want to worship? What if your colleagues' language is crisp with profanity, and you respect Jesus' name? What if joking about sexual exploits is common at work, but you believe sex is too special for such calloused treatment?

Add to the list, and bring it to a small group for discussion. Together pray for strength to break through this week, getting closer to Jesus and conforming less to "normal" expectations.

18:35-36 As they approached Jericho, a blind beggar was sitting beside the road. When he heard the noise of a crowd going past, he asked what was happening.[NLT] Continuing on their journey toward Jerusalem, Jesus and the disciples *approached Jericho.* The Old Testament city of Jericho had been destroyed by the Israelites (Joshua 6:20), but during his rule over Palestine, Herod the Great had rebuilt the city (about a mile south of the original city) as a site for his winter palace. Jericho was a popular and wealthy resort city not far from the Jordan River, about eighteen miles northeast of Jerusalem.

They came upon a *blind beggar* who was *sitting beside the road.* Beggars often waited along the roads near cities because that was where they were able to contact the most people. Usually disabled in some way, beggars were unable to work for a living. Medical help was not available for their problems, and people tended to ignore their obligation to care for the needy (Leviticus 25:35-38). Thus, beggars had little hope of escaping their degrading way of life. This blind beggar, however, hearing the great crowd going past him, realized that someone of great importance had come. So he naturally called out to someone in the crowd to answer and tell him *what was happening.*

This story in Matthew spoke of two blind men, while Mark

and Luke mention only one, probably the more vocal of the two. Mark gave his name as Bartimaeus (Mark 10:46).

18:37-39 **They told him that Jesus of Nazareth was going by. So he began shouting, "Jesus, Son of David, have mercy on me!" The crowds ahead of Jesus tried to hush the man, but he only shouted louder, "Son of David, have mercy on me!"**NLT The answer caused the blind man's heart to skip a beat. He had obviously heard of Jesus of Nazareth, for Jesus' reputation as a great teacher and healer had preceded him. Jesus, the man who could heal anything, was right there among the crowd. This was an opportunity not to be missed, so the blind man shamelessly cried out for Jesus' attention. He called Jesus, *Son of David,* a title for the Messiah (Isaiah 11:1-3). This means that the blind man understood Jesus to be the long-awaited Messiah.

The crowds *tried to hush the man,* perhaps trying to keep Jesus from being harassed by beggars. But that only made the blind man more persistent. He would not miss this opportunity to receive mercy and healing from Jesus.

DO THIS FOR ME
Jesus asked the blind man, "What do you want me to do for you?" What do you want Jesus to do for you? Make a list of six responses you might make to Jesus' question. Avoid clichés and "safe" items (such as "make me a better Christian"). Get personal and specific. Often the healing that Jesus brings begins with identifying our spiritual needs and having the desire to change. Don't hesitate to ask for what others label as impossible. Like Bartimaeus, you need Jesus' help today. Ask for it.

18:40-41 **When Jesus heard him, he stopped and ordered that the man be brought to him. Then Jesus asked the man, "What do you want me to do for you?" "Lord," he pleaded, "I want to see!"**NLT Any normal human being, heading toward certain death, would be extremely preoccupied and probably not necessarily in the mood to help others. But Jesus, in his humanity, was perfect, and his perfect mercy and compassion did not ebb and flow with his feelings or his schedule. He did not reject the man as the crowd had done. He *heard* the man's persistent cries, *stopped,* and *ordered that the man be brought to him.* Jesus knew that the man had to be brought, and he would have known from looking at the man what he needed. But Jesus asked him to voice his request. What did he want Jesus to do? The man replied unhesitatingly, *"Lord . . . I want to see!"* How many times in his life had he voiced that desire? Probably thousands. But here he stood before the one person in the universe who could actually make his desire a reality. And he would not have asked if he had not believed that it could be so.

18:42-43 **Jesus said to him, "Receive your sight; your faith has healed you." Immediately he received his sight and followed Jesus, praising God. When all the people saw it, they also praised God.**[NIV] Jesus recognized the man's faith. As a result of such faith, Jesus healed him. All Jesus did was speak the words, and *immediately he received his sight.* The man immediately joined the crowd of followers, staying with Jesus and *praising God.* This was also the response of the people in the crowd. There were no healings of the blind recorded in the Old Testament, so the Jews believed that such a miracle would be a sign that the messianic age had begun (Isaiah 29:18; 35:5). Jesus healed other blind people as well, so these people knew something special was happening. A poor and blind beggar could see that Jesus was the Messiah, and the crowds understood that God was to be praised for such miracles. But the religious leaders who saw his miracles were blinded to his identity and refused to recognize him as the Messiah.

NAME IT AND CLAIM IT?
Many preachers today urge people to a "name it and claim it" type of faith. They advocate this view of faith in healing based on Jesus words: "Your faith has healed you." Therefore, they teach that anyone who has sufficient faith will be automatically healed. However, more than faith operates in healing. In this event, it was Jesus' powerful words, "receive your sight," and his merciful will that healed this man. Jesus desired wholeness for people, and this man was instantaneously and completely healed, resulting in his salvation and praise to God. This man's faith and persistence got him through the crowd to Jesus. Faith is the means by which we come to Jesus for healing, but beware of believing or teaching that we can demand healing from Christ.

LUKE 19

In Jericho, Jesus invited himself to the home of Zacchaeus, the chief tax collector. Many in the town would have considered him the "chief sinner," for tax collectors were despised for their association with Rome. Because their salary was gleaned from the additional money they collected from others, many tax collectors were tempted to charge more.

Apparently Zacchaeus was one of these corrupt tax collectors. Although he was despised and hated, he became an impressive example of a rich man coming to salvation. The rich ruler, who was satisfied with his own religiosity and did not want to give up what he owned, could not be saved (see 18:23-27). He depended on his own accomplishments and possessions, instead of God. The young man's attitude made it impossible for him to enter the kingdom of God. But with Zacchaeus, Jesus accomplished the impossible. He sought out a wealthy sinner and called him to repentance and salvation. In fact, Jesus' earthly mission was "to seek and to save what was lost" (19:10 NIV). Imitate Zacchaeus's attitude: be eager to listen to Jesus and willing to repent and turn from your sin.

19:1-2 Jesus entered Jericho and was passing through. A man was there by the name of Zacchaeus; he was a chief tax collector and was wealthy.[NIV] After healing a blind man outside the city (18:35-43), *Jesus entered Jericho* (see also 18:35-36). Again the scene shifts, this time to a man named Zacchaeus who was the *chief tax collector* and, thus, *was wealthy.* To finance their great world empire, the Romans levied heavy taxes on all nations under their control. The Jews opposed these taxes because they supported a secular government and its pagan gods, but they were still forced to pay. Some of their own countrymen became tax collectors, lured by the wealth such a position promised. Luke has presented stories of several tax collectors and their dealings with Jesus (see 3:12; 5:27-30; 7:29; 15:1; plus a parable in 18:10-13). As the "chief" tax collector, Zacchaeus was apparently in charge over others. Matthew had been a tax collector, but Zacchaeus was chief of his region. Matthew had been well off; Zacchaeus was very wealthy.

19:3-4 **He tried to get a look at Jesus, but he was too short to see over the crowds. So he ran ahead and climbed a sycamore tree beside the road, so he could watch from there.**^{NLT} Zacchaeus, like the rest of the people in Jericho, was curious to see this man whose healings and teachings had been astounding people all over the country. Moments earlier, a blind man sitting on the side of the road had been healed (18:42-43). The news had spread, and Zacchaeus wanted to *get a look at Jesus*. The text reveals another detail about this wealthy tax collector; he was *short*—so short, in fact, that he could not see over the people in the crowd. Zacchaeus would not be put off. He ran on down the road and *climbed a sycamore tree*. The sycamore tree was easy to climb, like an oak tree with wide lateral branches.

LOVE FOR ALL
Tax collectors were among the most unpopular people in Israel. Jews by birth, they chose to work for Rome and were considered traitors. Besides, it was common knowledge that tax collectors were making themselves rich by gouging their fellow Jews. No wonder the people muttered when Jesus went home with the head tax collector Zacchaeus, a man who was good at being bad. Despite the fact that Zacchaeus was a cheater and a turncoat, Jesus loved him; in response, the little tax collector was converted. In every society, certain groups of people are considered outcasts because of their political views, immoral behavior, or lifestyle. Don't give in to social pressure to avoid these people. Jesus loves them, and they need to hear his Good News.

19:5-7 **When Jesus came by, he looked up at Zacchaeus and called him by name. "Zacchaeus!" he said. "Quick, come down! For I must be a guest in your home today." Zacchaeus quickly climbed down and took Jesus to his house in great excitement and joy.**^{NLT} Up in the tree, Zacchaeus watched the approaching crowd. He wanted to see Jesus, and apparently Jesus wanted to see him. Many places in Luke reveal Jesus having knowledge of people's inner thoughts and needs (see 5:22; 6:8; 7:39-40; 8:46; 9:47). As always, every act of Jesus was part of a divine plan—he said, *"I must go to your home."* Jesus knew Zacchaeus's heart, and he took the initiative, calling Zacchaeus *by name* and inviting himself over. Far from being embarrassed or put out, Zacchaeus climbed down *quickly* and took Jesus home *in great excitement and joy.*

But why Zacchaeus? In fact, many in the crowd were unhappy with Jesus' choice of hosts: **But the crowds were displeased. "He has gone to be the guest of a notorious sinner," they grumbled.**^{NLT} The religious leaders often complained about the ones to whom Jesus ministered (see 15:2). Luke recorded Jesus' words: "I have not come to call the righteous, but sinners to repentance" (5:32 NIV). Zacchaeus must have been a pretty bad character, for the crowd reacted with great displeasure that Jesus would have chosen him out of everyone. No one else in the crowd could have known that Jesus' visit would change this tax collector's life.

TAKING THE INITIATIVE
Jesus took the first step in reaching out to Zacchaeus. He cut through the exclusivity of the Jews and approached this outsider. Often the first step in making a friend is the most difficult one. Take the initiative.
- Avoid prejudgments based on appearance or social status.
- Learn something about the other person before you approach.
- Let your overture be open and your demeanor engaging. Don't demand friendship; offer it.
- Spend time. Listen attentively and share something personal.

19:8 But Zacchaeus stood up and said to the Lord, "Look, Lord! Here and now I give half of my possessions to the poor, and if I have cheated anybody out of anything, I will pay back four times the amount."^{NIV} Some grumbled, but Jesus knew that Zacchaeus was ready for a change in his life. After Jesus took the initiative with him, Zacchaeus took the initiative to follow wherever the path of obedience to Jesus might lead. The rich young ruler had come asking and had gone away empty, unable to give up his money and possessions (18:18-23). Zacchaeus, however, was able to give away his wealth in order to follow Jesus. This is the heart attitude that Jesus was looking for. Perceiving it in Zacchaeus, he quickly brought this man the Good News.

Zacchaeus himself lost no time, for

> It was to *save* sinners that Christ Jesus came into the world. He did not come to help them to save themselves, nor to induce them to save themselves, nor even to enable them to save themselves. He came to *save* them.
> *William Hendriksen*

immediately (the verb is in the present tense) he said he would *give half* of all that he owned to the poor. The words "if I have cheated anybody" imply that he surely had—most tax collectors did cheat others, so a wealthy tax collector most certainly did. So eager was Zacchaeus to rid himself of the shackles of wealth that he said he would *pay back four times the amount* of the overage that he had charged people. The Old Testament law for restitution required returning the amount plus one-fifth (see Leviticus 5:16; Numbers 5:7). Zacchaeus went far beyond the law's requirements in righting the wrongs he had done. His attitude was correct, and his actions showed his inner desire to obey. Zacchaeus was setting his priorities right, and he would be ready for the kingdom.

FAITH AND ACTION
Judging from the crowd's reaction to him, Zacchaeus must have been a very crooked tax collector. But after he met Jesus, he realized that his life needed straightening out. By giving to the poor and making restitution—with generous interest—to those he had cheated, Zacchaeus demonstrated inward change by outward action. It is not enough to follow Jesus in your head or heart alone. You must show your faith by changed behavior. Has your faith resulted in action? What changes do you need to make?

19:9-10 **Jesus said to him, "Today salvation has come to this house, because this man, too, is a son of Abraham. For the Son of Man came to seek and to save what was lost."**[NIV] This tax collector was perceived as a traitor by his people, so they would not have considered him a *son of Abraham.* Yet, by opening his heart to Jesus, he proved himself to be not only a son of Abraham in the sense of a Jew looking for the kingdom but also a son of Abraham in the truest sense of the word because he had *today* experienced *salvation.* Salvation came to Zacchaeus, not because he did good deeds, but because he truly believed in Jesus and set aside anything that might get in the way of obeying him. Whether Zacchaeus continued as a tax collector is unknown. If he did, certainly he would have been the most honest tax collector around, doing just what John the Baptist had recommended to the tax collectors who had come to him to be baptized: "Don't collect any more than you are required to" (see 3:12-13 NIV).

When Jesus said Zacchaeus was a son of Abraham and yet was lost, he must have shocked his hearers in at least two ways. They would not have acknowledged that this unpopular tax collector was a fellow son of Abraham, and they would not have thought that sons of Abraham could be lost. A person is not saved by a good heritage or condemned by a bad one; faith is more important than genealogy. To the grumblers, detractors, and self-righteous, to those who thought they were saved simply because they were descendants of Abraham, Jesus explained his mission—*the Son of Man came to seek and to save what was lost.*

JESUS TELLS THE PARABLE OF THE KING'S TEN SERVANTS / 19:11-27 / *181*

Because the crowd was expecting the coming kingdom of God, Jesus told them a parable that corrected their misunderstanding about the nature of the kingdom. Here, as in 12:35-40 (the parable of the servants waiting for their master), Jesus tied responsible stewardship of resources to the coming kingdom of God. The first parable emphasized the importance of being alert and watchful, for the master may return suddenly and at any time. This parable encourages listeners to wisely use their resources for the master's benefit. The implication is clear. Christians are accountable to Jesus for the way they use their time, money, and abilities. In essence, all of these are gifts from God and should be used for his glory. Take some time to reevaluate your life in light of Jesus' coming. What resources are you wasting, instead of using for God's kingdom?

19:11 **The crowd was listening to everything Jesus said. And because he was nearing Jerusalem, he told a story to correct the impression that the Kingdom of God would begin right away.**[NLT] The people still hoped for a political leader who would set up an earthly kingdom and get rid of Roman domination. The fact that Jesus had been steadily heading toward Jerusalem fueled speculation among *the crowd* that he was going there, in essence, to "take over" and begin *the Kingdom of God.* So Jesus *told a story* to correct this wrong impression. Jesus' parable showed that his kingdom would not take this form right away. First he would go away for a while, and his followers would need to be faithful and productive during his absence. Upon his return, Jesus would inaugurate a kingdom more powerful and just than anything they could expect.

This story showed Jesus' followers what they were to do during the time between Jesus' departure and his second coming. Because believers today live in that time period, it applies directly to them as well. Christians have been given excellent resources to build and expand God's kingdom. Jesus expects them to use these talents so that the kingdom grows. He asks each believer to account for what has been done with his or her gifts. While awaiting the coming of the kingdom of God in glory, Christians must do Christ's work.

ALERT LISTENING
The crowd did well to listen to Jesus, but clearly they were hearing, not his message, but their own wishes for a leader to send Roman troops packing. How easy it is to project one's own needs and expectations onto Jesus.

When you hear God's Word preached or taught, do you
- immediately interpret it based on your own agenda?
- screen out items that don't match your personal desires?
- take notes but file them away without applying them to your life?

God will challenge and change your life, but you must listen and learn. Don't put God's Word in your file drawer; use it to reorganize all your files. Alert listening means hearing God despite our "earplugs" of prejudice and self-assurance. It requires a willingness to act.

19:12-13 **He said: "A man of noble birth went to a distant country to have himself appointed king and then to return. So he called ten of his servants and gave them ten minas. 'Put this money to work,' he said, 'until I come back.'"**[NIV] In the world of the Roman Empire, when a man was going to become king, he would go to Rome to receive the appointment and then return to his land to begin his rule. Herod the Great had followed this prescribed plan. When Herod divided up his kingdom among his sons, each of them also had to go to Rome to receive confirmation of their positions as king.

This *man of noble birth went to a distant country to have himself appointed king.* Any territory under the rule of an empire often had a king appointed by the empire. To travel all the way to Rome and back usually required several months, so the king in this parable made sure that his financial situation did not become stagnant while he was gone. He gathered *ten of his servants* (obviously men he trusted) and gave them *ten minas,* each servant receiving one mina. A mina was worth two hundred denarii; a denarius was a day's wage for a laborer. So each servant received about six months' worth of wages. The servants' job was to put their master's money to work while he was gone—making it earn more money through some kind of business venture or investment.

In these words, Jesus was making it clear that there would be a time interval between his presence with them and the time when he would come to set up his kingdom. Like this king, he would go away to a distant country (heaven) and would be gone for an undetermined amount of time. In the meantime, his servants here would be given responsibilities to handle. As believers wait for their King to *come back,* they are to be busy with what he has given them, investing it for the future of his kingdom.

19:14-15 "But his subjects hated him and sent a delegation after him to say, 'We don't want this man to be our king.' He was made king, however, and returned home. Then he sent for the servants to whom he had given the money, in order to find out what they had gained with it."ᴺᴵⱽ The historical background to this story provides a further link to what Jesus was saying in this parable and how his listeners would have understood exactly what was happening. As noted above, rulers had to go to Rome to officially receive their appointments. The visit there by one of Herod the Great's sons, Archelaus, provided the setting for this parable. Archelaus was an evil man who had murdered three thousand Jews at the first Passover after becoming their ruler. Truly *his subjects hated him.* So when he went off to Rome, the Jews *sent a delegation* to plead for him not to be given the title. The emperor gave Archelaus the authority to rule but did not give him the title of "king" until he would prove himself worthy. Unfortunately, he never improved, so he never received the title. The fact that this was told near Jericho makes the Archelaus connection even more interesting, for Archelaus had built a beautiful palace in that city.

The king in this parable had subjects who hated him and did not want him made king. *He was made king, however, and returned home.* After his return, he called for his ten servants to give an accounting for what they had done with the money he had given them, *what they had gained with it.* He fully anticipated that they had made more money with his money through wise business and investments.

The parable continues with Jesus having rebel subjects, although with Archelaus they were fully justified in their rebellion. Not so, however, with Jesus, for he was, is, and always will be the perfect king.

19:16-17 "The first servant reported a tremendous gain—ten times as much as the original amount! 'Well done!' the king exclaimed. 'You are a trustworthy servant. You have been faithful with the little I entrusted to you, so you will be governor of ten cities as your reward.'"ᴺᴸᵀ The first servant came and *reported a tremendous gain*—he took the money entrusted to him and made *ten times* the original amount. The king, knowing that his servant had been trustworthy and wise with that fairly small amount of money, told this servant he would be entrusted with far more responsibility. So the king made him *governor of ten cities.* The servant would share in his master's rule, all because he had shown faithfulness with the *little* that had been *entrusted* to him (see also 16:10).

A time of accounting will come for all believers. Christians can know they are saved and will be with God in his kingdom, but they will be judged for how they have used what God has entrusted to them during his absence and their time on earth. God will reward faithful servants.

19:18-19 **"The next servant also reported a good gain—five times the original amount. 'Well done!' the king said. 'You can be governor over five cities.'"**[NLT] The second servant also had a gain—not as much as the first, but still he had done a fine job and was commended by the king. This servant also was rewarded in proportion to his ability.

19:20-21 **"But the third servant brought back only the original amount of money and said, 'I hid it and kept it safe. I was afraid because you are a hard man to deal with, taking what isn't yours and harvesting crops you didn't plant.'"**[NLT] We are not told of the other seven servants, but this third servant received mention because of his failure to do what his master had expected of him. There would have been only two groups: those who used the master's money well (the amount they made seems to have been inconsequential), and those who did nothing, as this servant here who *brought back only the original amount.* He had not stolen it; in fact, he *hid it and kept it safe* (literally, "put away in a face cloth"). Some might think that should have been enough—but his motivation for doing so was wrong. Actually, burying the money in the ground would have been considered even more secure. This servant was *afraid* of the master, and that fear had led him to inactivity. He was only thinking of himself and playing it safe. Afraid of a risky investment, this servant did not invest at all. He was afraid that his master expected too much, so he did nothing at all. Perhaps there was a bit of anger that he had to do all the work, while the master took the profits—*taking what* wasn't his and *harvesting crops* that he *didn't plant.*

RISK TAKING
The problem with Mr. One Talent was his giving lip service to doing his master's will (he agreed to do it), but he did not make the necessary effort. This manager's cover-up for his laziness and disobedience was "I played it safe." Christ will not reprimand his followers for risk taking and failure, but for unfaithfulness. Do you seek the safe and secure solution to the demands of discipleship? Christ was the great risk taker; he forsook all to be your Lord. In your service for Christ, playing it safe may amount to squandering your opportunity.

GOSPEL ACCOUNTS FOUND ONLY IN LUKE

19:22-23 **"His master replied, 'I will judge you by your own words, you
wicked servant! You knew, did you, that I am a hard man,
taking out what I did not put in, and reaping what I did not
sow? Why then didn't you put my money on deposit, so that
when I came back, I could have collected it with interest?'"**[NIV]
The master became very angry at this servant, whom he would
judge with the very anger the servant had feared. If the servant
had been so afraid, he should have at least put the money in the
bank in order for it to earn some interest. There were several reasons for his failure and for the king's anger. The king punished
the man because he didn't share his master's interest in the kingdom; he didn't trust his master's intentions; his only concern was
for himself; and he did nothing to use the money.

Like the king in this story, God has given you gifts to use for
the benefit of his kingdom. Some people, like this servant, don't
mind being identified in a nominal way with Jesus, but when
given responsibility or expectations, they refuse to do anything
and do not want to be made accountable to God. Do you want the
kingdom to grow? Do you trust God to govern it fairly? Are you
as concerned for others' welfare as you are for your own? Are
you willing to use faithfully what he has entrusted to you? The
results, the "earnings," are ultimately in God's hands, but believers are responsible to use what they have to glorify God. While
the king's anger need not be attributed to Jesus, what is learned

here is the seriousness of flouting God's commands. Even the "smallest" gift must be put to use for the kingdom.

19:24-27 **"Then turning to the others standing nearby, the king ordered, 'Take the money from this servant, and give it to the one who earned the most.' 'But, master,' they said, 'that servant has enough already!'"**[NLT] The king took the money away from the faithless servant and gave it to the one who had proved to be responsible with it. Although the others standing around wondered why the king would give more to the one who already had the most, the king was acting wisely in giving more resources to the most effective servant. He says, **"'I tell you, to all those who have, more will be given; but from those who have nothing, even what they have will be taken away. But as for these enemies of mine who did not want me to be king over them—bring them here and slaughter them in my presence.'"**[NRSV] Those who have much—because they make wise use of what they have been given—will be given more abundance so they can continue to produce. Those who have nothing—because they refuse to take advantage of any opportunities they have—will end up losing even what they had been given.

ACTIVE FAITH
Jesus' parable teaches the importance of investing for the kingdom. Unused resources and opportunities disappear. Undeveloped relationships and ideas fall by the wayside. For Jesus' faithful servants, faith is not being passive while others are active, waiting while others are busy, or stalling while others are problem solving.

Instead, faith makes maximum use of talents and resources, operates freely without worry and self-centeredness, energetically pursues God's mission in the world, and shows increasing love for people on the fringes. Are you a faithful and productive servant for Christ?

God's people dare not sit idly by, not using their God-given gifts. The excuses are many. Some may not feel "ready." Others may not feel that they can use what they have been given on a large enough scale or make a big enough difference. Others may think, pridefully, that they ought to be able to share some of the glory instead of giving it all to God. Others may be afraid that if they cannot produce "ten times as much," then they do not want to produce at all. If they cannot receive an A+, then they do not want to try. Others may see people with the same gift who seem to use it so much better with better results, so let *them* do it. Others do not feel needed. Still others do not seek out opportunities, expecting people to come to them. But to sit idly by will mean to eventually lose that gift, that "mina" that God has given. (For more on rewards, see the chart in Life Application Commentary, Matthew 16:27, and discussion on Matthew 18:29-30.)

The parable ends with the ultimate judgment on those who had actively rebelled against the king. They would be slaughtered. When Jesus returns, his enemies will be judged and sentenced to eternity without him.

JESUS RIDES INTO JERUSALEM ON A DONKEY / 19:28-44 / *183*

Until this point, Luke presented a sampling of Jesus' ministry—his teaching and his miracles. But with this description of Jesus' final entry into Jerusalem, Luke, just like the other Gospel writers, slowed down his narrative, taking time to present the powerful details of Jesus' final week leading up to the Cross.

The crowd that accompanied Jesus into Jerusalem was made up of his followers and pilgrims on their way to the Passover celebration. When Jesus mounted a donkey, perhaps some hoped that this would be his time to declare his political intentions. Many of them broke out into praise, following him into Jerusalem. But Luke is the only Gospel writer who recorded what Jesus was feeling at the time—he was grieved for Jerusalem (19:41-44). He saw through all the excitement; he knew that within a few days, many of the people of Jerusalem would reject him. Although the blind man of Jericho had seen Jesus' true identity (see 18:35-43), many of these people would remain blind to who was with them: God incarnate. Don't be blind to the spiritual realities around you, like the Jewish religious leaders of Jesus' day.

The parallel accounts of the Triumphal Entry provide a good example of the benefits of having four biographies of Jesus. Matthew and John were eyewitnesses of these events; Mark and Luke recorded others' eyewitness accounts. Matthew highlighted the prophetic fulfillment by noting a second donkey, the colt's mother. Jesus didn't ride her, nor is she essential to the story. But she provides a detail of fact. Her calming presence also explains the handling of an unbroken colt. In contrast, John's recollection of the colt is almost incidental. Perhaps he wasn't involved in the errand to fetch it. John was more concerned to indicate to his readers that the disciples understood little of what was happening at the time (John 12:16). While John viewed the Triumphal Entry in light of its impact on the disciples themselves, Matthew highlighted the crowd's responses, pointed to Jesus as the Messiah, and kept the story in the temple area to show Jesus' authority over Judaism. Further, Mark reported the events in storyteller fashion. Luke focused on Jesus' state of mind. Each of the views helps to form a complete picture.

Each of the Gospels presents a variation of the Triumphal Entry. Overall, the Gospel accounts are seldom identical. The differences usually have to do with perspective and priorities. Under the inspiration of the Holy Spirit, each writer told his story. The Gospels maintain a balance between shared similarities and independent entries. The similarities in language indicate that the later writers were aware of and used material from the earlier ones and that they were all writing about the same life. The dissimilarities show that they wrote independently and that each one had a slightly different purpose and audience in mind while composing his version of the events.

19:28-31 After telling this story, Jesus went on toward Jerusalem, walking ahead of his disciples. As they came to the towns of Bethphage and Bethany, on the Mount of Olives, he sent two disciples ahead.NLT Jesus continued *on toward Jerusalem,* which we already know to have been his ultimate destination (9:51). They approached Bethphage and Bethany, two towns about one mile apart, situated *on the Mount of Olives* to the east of Jerusalem. Bethany was the home of his friends Mary, Martha, and Lazarus, whom Jesus had visited before (10:38; see also John 11:1). When Jesus spoke these words, they were probably in Bethphage. *He sent two disciples ahead* to Bethany, telling them, **"Go into that village over there," he told them, "and as you enter it, you will see a colt tied there that has never been ridden. Untie it and bring it here. If anyone asks what you are doing, just say, 'The Lord needs it.'"**NLT By this time Jesus was extremely well known. Everyone coming to Jerusalem for Passover had heard of him, and, for a time, the popular mood was favorable toward him. *"The Lord needs it"* was all the disciples had to say, and the colt's owners gladly turned their animal over to them. Jesus had walked all the way from Galilee, so this switch to riding a colt the last mile into Jerusalem was a deliberate gesture, filled with meaning for the Jews. The specification that this be a colt *that has never been ridden* is significant in light of the ancient rule that only animals that had not been used for ordinary purposes were appropriate for sacred purposes (Numbers 19:2; Deuteronomy 21:3; 1 Samuel 6:7).

19:32-35 So those who were sent departed and found it as he had told them. As they were untying the colt, its owners asked them, "Why are you untying the colt?" They said, "The Lord needs it." Then they brought it to Jesus; and after throwing

**their cloaks on the colt, they
set Jesus on it.**^{NRSV} The two disciples did as they were told, and
found the colt exactly as they
were told. As Jesus had warned
them, they were indeed asked by
the owners why they were taking
the colt. Donkeys and colts were
valuable; what the disciples did
amounted to coming along and
taking someone's car. But they
said what Jesus told them to say.
Mark wrote that Jesus also said
the colt would be returned (Mark
11:3). The owners let the colt go,
and the disciples brought it to
Jesus.

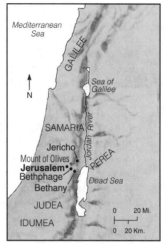

LAST WEEK IN JERUSALEM
*As they approached Jerusalem
from Jericho (19:1), Jesus and the
disciples came to the villages of
Bethany and Bethphage, nestled
on the eastern slope of the Mount
of Olives, only a few miles outside
Jerusalem. Jesus stayed in Bethany during the nights of that last
week, entering Jerusalem during
the day.*

In Matthew, a donkey and a
colt are mentioned (Matthew
21:2), while the other Gospels
mention only the colt. This was
the same event, but Matthew
focused on the prophecy in Zechariah 9:9, which indicates a donkey and a colt, thus affirming
Jesus' royalty. The disciples then
threw their *cloaks* over the colt,
making a seat for Jesus. With this act of entering Jerusalem on a
donkey's colt, Jesus was fulfilling prophecy and affirming his
messianic royalty. He came in royal fashion, not as a warring
king on a horse or in a chariot, but as a gentle and peaceable king
on a donkey's colt.

19:36-37 **Then the crowds spread out their coats on the road ahead of
Jesus. As they reached the place where the road started
down from the Mount of Olives, all of his followers began to
shout and sing as they walked along, praising God for all
the wonderful miracles they had seen.**^{NLT} The custom of
spreading coats on the ground ahead of a royal personage can
also be seen in 2 Kings 9:12-13. This was Sunday of the week
that Jesus would be crucified, and the great Passover festival
was about to begin. Jews would come to Jerusalem from all
over the Roman world during this weeklong celebration to
remember the great Exodus from Egypt (see Exodus 12:37-51).
Many in the crowd had heard of or had seen Jesus and were

hoping he would come to the temple (John 11:55-57). People lined the roads, and Jesus already had a crowd of followers who, when they saw what he was doing, *began to shout and sing as they walked along.* According to the other Gospels, many others joined the celebration of praise. The Gospel of John (12:13) also describes the people cutting down branches from the trees, probably from olive or fig trees, to wave in welcome.

Jesus approached Jerusalem fearlessly, knowing what awaited him there: death at the hands of people who should have recognized his true identity. This glorious celebration was temporary, and few understood its meaning. Most wanted to believe that liberation from Rome was at hand. Any who had heard Jesus' parables should have understood that time would elapse between his first and second comings; the disciples should have remembered what he told them about going to Jerusalem to die. At this point, however, Jesus clearly fulfilled prophecy and showed himself to be the Messiah.

19:38 Saying: "'Blessed is the King who comes in the name of the LORD!' Peace in heaven and glory in the highest!"NKJV The expression "Blessed is the King who comes in the name of the LORD" may have been recited as part of the Passover tradition—as a blessing given by the people in Jerusalem to the visiting pilgrims (see Psalm 118:25-26). The people lined the road, praising God, waving branches, and throwing their cloaks in front of the colt as it passed before them. "Long live the King" was the meaning behind their joyful shouts because they knew that Jesus was intentionally fulfilling prophecy. The people who were praising God for giving them a king had the wrong idea about Jesus. They expected him to be a national leader who would restore their nation to its former glory; thus they were deaf to the words of their prophets and blind to Jesus' real mission. When it became apparent that Jesus was not going to fulfill their hopes, many would turn against him.

THE STONES WILL CRY OUT
Jesus confronted these Pharisees who rejected his authority. They had political interests to protect, so any praising and confessing of Jesus as the Messiah threatened their position. Today, believers still face pressures that make them uncomfortable when they should witness for Jesus. If you truly know who Jesus is and love him as God's true Messiah, speak out for him.

19:39-40 **And some of the Pharisees called to Him from the crowd,
"Teacher, rebuke Your disciples." But He answered and said
to them, "I tell you that if these should keep silent, the stones
would immediately cry out."**NKJV The Pharisees thought that the
crowd's words were sacrilegious and blasphemous. They didn't
want someone challenging their power and authority, and they
didn't want a revolt that would bring the Roman army down on
them. So they asked Jesus to keep his people quiet. But Jesus said
that if the people were quiet, *the stones would immediately cry
out* (see Habakkuk 2:11). Habakkuk had prophesied the judgment
of God upon Judah just before the fall of Jerusalem to the Babylonians in 586 B.C. He had said, "The stones of the wall will cry
out" (NIV) concerning all the sins the people rebelling against
God had done. So Jesus' words may have a double meaning.
Praise for the true Messiah could not be repressed, and the stones
of the wall would bear witness to the city's rejection of him.

19:41-42 **As he approached Jerusalem and saw the city, he wept over it
and said, "If you, even you, had only known on this day what
would bring you peace—but now it is hidden from your
eyes."**NIV Only Luke recorded this lament by Jesus as he *approached
Jerusalem and saw the city.* In contrast to the great joy of the
crowd, the man on the donkey *wept* at the sight of the city. The
name of the city has "peace" as part of its meaning (Hebrews 7:2),
but the people of the city did not know what would bring them
peace. The "city of peace" was blind to the "Prince of Peace"
(Isaiah 9:6). If the people had known *on this day* what was truly
happening and had recognized it for what it was, they could have
found peace. But the Jewish leaders had rejected their Messiah
(19:39, 47); they had refused God's offer of salvation in Jesus
Christ when they were visited by God himself. Now the truth
would be *hidden,* and soon their nation would suffer.

ON THIS DAY
Christian faith often seems like a long, long process. God's
Word had been delivered to the inhabitants of Jerusalem for
many centuries. Jesus wept because the people of Jerusalem
had failed to see God's truth. Those who delay their commitment to Christ make the same mistake. Encourage others not
to postpone Christ as if he were second priority. Their acceptance of the Savior is of utmost importance, and their service to
his kingdom is needed.
   People highly desire this peace that only Christ can give.
Share with others the good news of God's gift to them. Urge
them to accept the gift before the opportunity passes.

19:43-44 **"The days will come upon you when your enemies will build an embankment against you and encircle you and hem you in on every side. They will dash you to the ground, you and the children within your walls. They will not leave one stone on another, because you did not recognize the time of God's coming to you."**ᴺᴵⱽ About forty years after Jesus said these words, they came true. In A.D. 66, the Jews revolted against Roman control. Three years later Titus, son of the emperor Vespasian, was sent to crush the rebellion. Roman soldiers attacked Jerusalem and broke through the northern wall but still couldn't take the city. Finally they laid siege to it, and in A.D. 70 they were able to enter the severely weakened city and burn it. Six hundred thousand Jews were killed during Titus's onslaught. This would occur as judgment *because* though some of the people believed (such as the disciples and other faithful followers), most *did not recognize the time of God's coming to* them. But God did not turn away from the Jewish people who obeyed him. He continues to offer salvation to both Jews and Gentiles.

JESUS CLEARS THE TEMPLE AGAIN / 19:45-48 / *184*

Jesus directly confronted those who dared to try to make an exorbitant profit in the very temple of God. He had expelled these peddlers and money-mongers during a previous visit (see John 2:12-25). Here Jesus again stood for what was right, confronting those who dared to participate in wickedness under the guise of religiosity.

19:45-46 **Then Jesus entered the Temple and began to drive out the merchants from their stalls. He told them, "The Scriptures declare, 'My Temple will be a place of prayer,' but you have turned it into a den of thieves."**ᴺᴸᵀ This is the second time that Jesus cleared the temple (see John 2:13-17). Jesus entered Jerusalem and *entered the Temple.* Always on a divine mission, Jesus went to the temple for a specific reason—*to drive out the merchants from their stalls.* These "merchants" were the people who sold goods to worshipers. People came to the temple in Jerusalem to offer sacrifices. The temple was run by the high priest and his associates. All adult male Jews were required to go to Jerusalem for three annual celebrations: Passover in late spring, the Feast of Tabernacles (or Booths) in the fall, and the Feast of Weeks in early summer. God had originally instructed the people to bring sacrifices from their own flocks (Deuteronomy 12:5-7). The religious leadership, however, had established four markets on the Mount of Olives where such animals could be purchased. Some people did not bring their own animals and planned to buy one at the market. Others brought their own animals, but when the priests managed to find the animal unacceptable in some way (it was supposed to be an animal without defect, Leviticus 1:2-3), worshipers were forced to buy another.

Then a marketplace was set up in the temple area itself, in the Court of the Gentiles, the huge outer court of the temple. The Court of the Gentiles was the only place where Gentile converts to Judaism could worship. They could go no farther into the temple because they were not "pure" Jews. But the market filled their worship space with merchants so that these foreigners, who had traveled long distances, found it impossible to worship. Because both those who bought and those who sold were going against God's commands regarding the sacrifices, Jesus drove them out.

Jesus told them, in no uncertain terms, why he was so angry and why he acted as he did in throwing these merchants out of the temple. He quoted from Isaiah 56:7, explaining God's purpose for the temple: *a place of prayer.* The merchants had turned it into *a den of thieves.* Their treatment of pilgrims who had traveled and needed to count on them for service, their exorbitant rates, and their cheating of the customers had made them no better than thieves hiding out together in a "den." But this "den" was God's temple—no wonder Jesus was angry.

HOUSE OF PRAYER
Jesus said that the temple was to be a place of prayer. How do people describe your church?
- Great youth group, exciting missions trips?
- Superb counseling and a terrific singles group?
- Wonderful music and sound system?
- What about a place of prayer?

Has busyness or neglect turned your church away from its mission to pray? What can you do to understand prayer better? practice prayer more regularly? lead others in the church toward prayer as a priority?

19:47-48 Every day he was teaching in the temple. The chief priests, the scribes, and the leaders of the people kept looking for a way to kill him; but they did not find anything they could do, for all the people were spellbound by what they heard.[NRSV] During his last week on earth, Jesus was still busy—*every day he was teaching in the temple.* He traveled into the city each morning, then retired out to the environs, perhaps to the home of Mary, Martha, and Lazarus in Bethany (Matthew 21:17; Mark

11:11). Jesus had many enemies who *kept looking for a way to kill him.* These enemies were the Jewish religious leaders themselves—the people who, above everyone else, should have been the first to recognize and rejoice in the arrival of their Messiah. Luke has already recorded some of Jesus' confrontations with the chief priests (usually Pharisees) and the scribes (or teachers of the law) (see 5:21, 30; 6:7; 11:53; 15:2). The *leaders of the people* probably included wealthy leaders in politics, commerce, and law. They had several reasons for wanting to get rid of Jesus. He had damaged business in the temple by driving the merchants out. In addition, he was preaching against injustice, and his teachings often favored the poor over the rich. Further, his great popularity was in danger of attracting Rome's attention, and the leaders of Israel wanted as little as possible to do with Rome.

Despite their plans, however, these people could not do anything. The man they wanted to kill came daily to the temple, but he was far too popular with the people. His teaching held the people *spellbound.* Much of this teaching is recorded in Luke 20–21.

LUKE 20

With Jesus' entrance into Jerusalem (19:28-44), Luke began an
extended section (19:45–21:4) that highlights the growing contro-
versy between Jesus and the Jewish religious leaders. In this first
clash after Jesus' cleansing of the temple, the representatives of
the Sanhedrin struck at the heart of the issue between them: Who
had the authority? The Roman government had granted the Sanhedrin authority over the temple of God. The Sanhedrin could
even order the instant execution of any Gentile who entered the
temple's inner courts. But with Jesus' expulsion of the money
changers from the temple (most likely from the temple's outer
court), Jesus was implicitly asserting his own authority over the
temple, a challenge to the Sanhedrin's power.

Jesus' question to his opponents revealed their duplicity. They
really did not care under whose authority Jesus was acting,
whether divine or human. They only wanted to force him to say
something incriminating.

20:1-2 **One day as he was teaching the people in the temple courts
and preaching the gospel, the chief priests and the teachers of
the law, together with the elders, came up to him. "Tell us by
what authority you are doing these things," they said. "Who
gave you this authority?"**NIV Soon after Jesus' cleansing of the
temple (according to Matthew this occurred the next day), Jesus
returned to the temple to teach and preach. While he was there, a
delegation of *chief priests, teachers of the law,* and *elders*
stopped Jesus. These were representative of the three groups that
made up the Sanhedrin, the Jewish ruling council (Jesus already
had predicted that the Jewish religious authorities would reject
him, see 9:22). Apparently the Sanhedrin had met after the clear-
ing of the temple, enraged by Jesus actions, but unable to decide
how to handle him. They then sent this representative group to
question Jesus regarding his actions, hoping he would say something treasonous or blasphemous. They demanded to know *by
what authority* he had thrown out the merchants from the temple

and who had given him that authority. The innuendo is that Jesus had not been authorized by them (the religious leaders of Jerusalem) and therefore was perceived to be a rebel.

The questions the priests and teachers of the law asked were legitimate questions, but they didn't really want to know the source of Jesus' authority. They were simply looking for a reason to accuse or disregard him. While the people were delighted and amazed by Jesus' authoritative preaching and actions, the Pharisees were enraged. With their great learning and wealth, the religious teachers, Pharisees, and scribes held a great deal of authority over the people. But Jesus challenged their authority, pointing out their hypocrisy, pride, and greed. The delegation knew that Jesus hadn't obtained his authority from the Sanhedrin or the Romans. The questioners hoped that if Jesus had acted without the proper authority, his actions would discredit him before the people. If he claimed to have acted on the authority of God, they could prosecute him for blasphemy (a crime deserving the death penalty, Leviticus 24:10-23). If he were to answer that he was his own authority, they could safely dismiss him as a fanatic and trust that the crowds would eventually see it as well.

WHOSE AUTHORITY?
In an individualistic and self-centered society such as our own, the individual has become increasingly his or her own authority. Instead of looking to religious teachers, people are encouraged to look within themselves for religious direction. Just as Jesus confronted the arrogant religious authorities of Israel two thousand years ago, Jesus confronts today's arrogance and hypocrisy. Will you reject his authority and hate him, like the religious leaders of Jesus' day? Or will you accept his authority and live by his commands?

20:3-4 **"Let me ask you a question first," he replied. "Did John's baptism come from heaven, or was it merely human?"**[NLT] Jesus countered the Jewish religious teachers' question with a question, a common debate technique for both Jewish scribes and Greek philosophers in the first century. By answering this way, Jesus was reshaping the query to arrive at the truth. The real question was not upon whose authority Jesus was acting, but whether the religious leaders had accepted John's call to repentance and had prepared their hearts for the coming of God.

Jesus knew that the religious leaders' attitude toward John the Baptist would reveal their attitude toward him. With this question, Jesus was implying that his authority came from the same source as John the Baptist's. John had called the people to repentance, and the people had expressed their repentance through baptism, a symbol of the cleansing of one's sins. So Jesus asked these religious leaders what they thought: *Did John's baptism come from heaven* [thus, from God], *or was it merely human?* By this question Jesus was exposing the leaders' inconsistencies, a fact that they quickly understood as seen in the discussion to follow.

20:5-8 They discussed it with one another, saying, "If we say, 'From heaven,' he will say, 'Why did you not believe him?' But if we say, 'Of human origin,' all the people will stone us; for they are convinced that John was a prophet." So they answered that they did not know where it came from. Then Jesus said to them, "Neither will I tell you by what authority I am doing these things."NRSV Here Luke recorded a private discussion of the religious teachers that reveals with clarity their hypocrisy. They weren't interested in Jesus' authority or in the truth. They really didn't want an answer; instead, they wanted to trap Jesus. But they found themselves looking completely foolish. Their only desire was to save face at this point. If they answered that John's baptism had come *from heaven* (with God's authority), then they would be incriminating themselves for not listening to John. The people knew that their religious leaders were ambivalent about Herod's murder of John. If they accepted John's authority, however, they would be accepting his criticism of them as a "brood of vipers" who refused to repent (see 3:7-9; Matthew 3:7-10). They would also then have to accept the one John had pointed them to—and that was Jesus.

On the other hand, if they rejected John as having any divine authority and said that his baptism was *of human origin,* they would infuriate the crowd, who saw the truth in John's message—and by extension Jesus' message—and might be driven to stone them on the spot. So they remained silent, but their silence spoke volumes.

Because they refused to answer, Jesus said that he too would refuse to answer their question. By his silence, Jesus had already answered. His authority was the same as John the Baptist's. John was clearly a prophet of God, and Jesus also was commissioned by God to call all who would listen to him. All who were willing to humble themselves before God, instead of silencing the truth, would know beyond a shadow of a doubt that Jesus was from God.

While some in the crowd may have understood and believed, the religious leaders had already rejected Jesus because he was challenging their authority. Are you willing to submit to Jesus' authority, to acknowledge your own sinfulness and repent? It was the religious leaders' arrogance that kept them from seeing what the crowd already saw: Jesus' divine authority.

A TIME FOR SILENCE
In this argument, Jesus refused to answer the leaders' question (20:8). When you engage someone in a discussion of matters of faith, you will find out fairly quickly whether that person is truly interested in what you have to say or only interested in arguing. If the person is interested, take as much time and effort as you can in giving him or her answers and information. If the person merely wants a debate, don't oblige. It is pointless to give intellectual responses to issues of the heart. The real battleground for that person is not in the mind but in the heart. Until the person has an open heart, as well as an open mind, intellectual discussions will likely only serve to harden his or her disbelief. Save your breath . . . and wait until God prepares the heart.

JESUS TELLS THE PARABLE OF THE WICKED TENANTS / 20:9-19 / **191**

After his confrontation of the Jewish religious leaders, Jesus told a parable that revealed the spiritual realities behind his conflict with them. In the parable of the wicked farmers, Jesus used a strong image of judgment from the Old Testament (see Isaiah 5:1-7). Isaiah's ancient poem about the wicked farmers incriminated Jerusalem by name. The religious leaders immediately saw the connection and knew that Jesus was charging them. They were the tenant farmers who thought they could steal the land and renounce the true owner, when all the while they were making themselves liable to his dreadful judgment.

20:9 Now Jesus turned to the people again and told them this story: "A man planted a vineyard, leased it out to tenant farmers, and moved to another country to live for several years."NLT Jesus told a parable that indirectly answered the religious leaders' question about his authority, showed them that he knew about their plan to kill him, and revealed the judgment that awaited them for rejecting their Messiah.

The characters in this story are easily identified. Even the religious leaders understood it. The owner of the vineyard is God; the vineyard is Israel; the tenant farmers are the religious leaders; the servants are the prophets and priests God sent to Israel; the son is the Messiah, Jesus; and the others are the Gentiles. The comparison of Israel to a vineyard is common in the Old Testament (Psalm 80:8-13; Isaiah 5:1-7; Jeremiah 12:10; Hosea 10:1). It pictures God's work (someone has to plant a vineyard) and patient care in tending and caring for his people.

Jesus described a common business method of the time—an absentee owner who hired tenant farmers to care for the fields and crops. Much land was dedicated to grape vineyards, with wine being one of the major exports of Galilee. The tenant farmers paid their "rent" by giving a portion of the crop to the landowner, who would send servants at harvesttime to collect it. Tensions often arose; records exist of bitter disputes between landowners and their tenants.

GIVE BACK TO GOD
Have you ever given a child a gift—a toy, perhaps, or a stuffed animal—and then asked to have it back just for a moment? If so, you may have met with a less-than-positive response. In fact, the child may have become downright nasty: "Mine! My toy!" The fact that you gave it to her means nothing to her. All she cares about is her own immediate desire to have the thing she wants. Everyone can see what is wrong with acting that way; hopefully, most people outgrow such behavior. And yet how childish people can be when God is the giver and they are the recipients of his benevolence! Like the ungrateful farmers in this parable, they selfishly cling to those things he has given them and resent it when they are asked to give back to him some measure of his gifts. God, like the owner, expects a return. Has God given you a gift—money, abilities, opportunities—that you are clutching tightly to yourself, refusing to use for his purposes? Learn a lesson from a bunch of agricultural ingrates: give back to God freely and gratefully.

20:10-12 **"At grape-picking time, he sent one of his servants to collect his share of the crop. But the farmers attacked the servant, beat him up, and sent him back empty-handed. So the owner sent another servant, but the same thing happened; he was beaten up and treated shamefully, and he went away empty-handed. A third man was sent and the same thing happened. He, too, was wounded and chased away."**[NLT] *At grape-picking time* (that is, when the grape harvest came), the absentee landowner *sent one of his servants* to collect the "rent"—namely, *his share of the crop.* Generally this amounted to a quarter to a half of the crop, probably in the form of wine, not grapes. The "servants" represented the prophets and priests whom God had sent over the years to the nation of Israel. The picture of angry farmers beating the landowner's servants and sending them on their way without any "rent" pictured the religious leaders who were entrusted with the care of the vineyard. Instead of listening to the prophets (God's "servants"), they had mistreated them, *treated* them *shamefully* and sent them away, stubbornly refusing to listen. "Servants" refers to the prophets who had been sent to Israel over the centuries. Some had been beaten (Jeremiah 26:7-11; 38:1-28), some had been killed (tradition says that Isaiah was killed; John the Baptist had been killed, Matthew 14:1-12), and some had been stoned (2 Chronicles 24:21). Jesus was reminding the religious leaders that God's prophets often had been ridiculed and persecuted by God's people.

SEIZE THE INHERITANCE?
What person in his right mind would think that he could kill someone and then ask to have the victim's inheritance given to him? Yet that is precisely the situation described by Jesus in the parable of the vineyard owner and the tenants. Jesus said that the vicious, unruly tenants actually went so far as to kill the owner's son, thinking they could then seize the inheritance. Jesus' listeners must have been shocked. But, ironically, Jesus was referring to how Israel had treated God's prophets and how they would treat God's Son yet still thought they could have God's inheritance.
    American culture today is also guilty of benefiting from a Christian heritage—the "inheritance"—while people try to kill off any connection to Jesus. Society wants the positive results without crediting the cause of them. What else explains the universal celebration of Christmas while trying to outlaw public displays of manger scenes? That's like having a birthday party and telling the guest of honor he's not welcome. Where did the notion of love, peace, and family unity come from? The Bible teaches that people reap what they sow. Make sure you aren't benefiting from our Christian legacy while your life denies Christ.

20:13 "Then the owner of the vineyard said, 'What shall I do? I will send my son, whom I love; perhaps they will respect him.'"^{NIV} The fact that this landowner had not already punished the farmers for their treatment of his servants shows a man of great patience. This pictures God, who has been very patient with his people over the centuries, even when they stubbornly refused to listen to his messages through the prophets. So the landowner sent his *son,* whom he loved. This cherished son was sent to the tenant farmers to collect the fruit of the vineyard in hopes that the farmers would give him due honor and respect. This "son" refers to Jesus (see also 3:22; 9:35). With these words, Jesus implicitly answered the religious leaders' question regarding the source of his authority (20:2). Like the son in this parable, Jesus had been sent on behalf of the Father. He was acting with God the Father's authority. The Son had been sent to the stubborn and rebellious nation of Israel to win them back to God.

20:14-16 **"But when the tenants saw him, they talked the matter over. 'This is the heir,' they said. 'Let's kill him, and the inheritance will be ours.' So they threw him out of the vineyard and killed him."**[NIV] The historical situation behind this section reflects the law that property would go to anyone in possession of it when the master died. The tenants probably thought that the arrival of the son *(the heir)* meant that his father (the landowner) had died. They reasoned, therefore, that if they killed the son, they could claim the property *(the inheritance)* as their own. So they killed the son. With these words, Jesus was revealing to the religious leaders his knowledge of their desire to kill him.

"What then will the owner of the vineyard do to them? He will come and kill those tenants and give the vineyard to others." When the people heard this, they said, "May this never be!"[NIV] In Greek, "owner" is *kurios,* meaning "master"; it was also a title for God (the Lord). In using this word, Jesus was giving a deliberate hint about who the "owner" represented. Jesus asked his listeners what they thought the *owner of the vineyard* would do to his tenant farmers when he found out that they had killed his son. The answer: *He will come and kill those tenants.* Over hundreds of years, Israel's kings and religious leaders had rejected God's prophets—beating, humiliating, and killing them. Most recently, John the Baptist had been rejected as a prophet by Israel's leaders. Finally Jesus, the beloved Son of God, already rejected by the religious leaders, would be killed. Jesus explained that the Jewish leaders would be punished for his death because in rejecting the messengers and the Son, they were rejecting God himself.

Jesus added that not only would the wicked tenant farmers be killed but that the owner would *give the vineyard to others.* God's judgment on the Jewish people who rejected him would result in the transfer of the privileges of ownership "to others," namely, the Gentiles. In Romans 11:25-32, the apostle Paul explained that "a hardening has come upon part of Israel, until the full number of the Gentiles has come in" (Romans 11:25 NRSV). In this parable Jesus was speaking of the beginning of the Christian church among the Gentiles. God would not totally reject Israel; in ancient times he always preserved a remnant of true believers (see, for example, 1 Kings 19:18). Yet the religious leaders—who should have recognized the Messiah, rejoiced at his arrival, and led the people to him—instead would put him to death. Jesus' question forced the religious leaders to announce their own fate.

The people sensed the horror of the story but did not understand its immediate application in the light of Jesus himself—the

Son who came but would be killed. The religious leaders understood it all too well, and it infuriated them (20:19).

BROKEN OR CRUSHED?
The word "broken" conjures up uniformly negative images: broken bones, broken hearts, broken toys. You don't want something you value to be broken. Conversely, in God's dictionary, brokenness is not only good but also essential. He uses only people whose hearts, volition, and pride have been broken. Jesus gives a double warning: those who "fall on that stone"—himself—will be broken to pieces, while those "on whom it falls" will be crushed. God offers a choice of "brokennesses." Those who cast themselves on Jesus, submitting their wills and all that they are to him, will be broken by him of arrogance, hard-heartedness, self-centeredness. It is not a pleasant process but an absolutely necessary one. For those who do not submit to him, he will ultimately "fall on them," an experience that can only be described as "crushing." The choice is yours: broken before him, or crushed by him.

20:17-18 **But he looked at them and said, "What then does this text mean: 'The stone that the builders rejected has become the cornerstone'? Everyone who falls on that stone will be broken to pieces; and it will crush anyone on whom it falls."**NRSV
Quoting Psalm 118:22, Jesus showed the unbelieving leaders that even their rejection of the Messiah had been prophesied in Scripture. Psalm 118 was a key part of the Passover service—all the pilgrims coming to Passover would recite 118:25-26 as they came to Jerusalem. The religious leaders had been reciting this passage for years without understanding or applying it (see John 5:39-40). In Jesus' quotation, the "son" of the parable became the *stone* of this prophecy; the "tenant farmers" of the parable became the *builders.* Rejecting the *cornerstone* was dangerous. A person could be tripped or crushed (judged and punished).

Jesus used this metaphor to show that one stone can affect people different ways, depending on how they relate to it (see Isaiah 8:14-15; 28:16; Daniel 2:34, 44-45). Ideally they will build on it; many, however, will trip over it. Although Jesus had been rejected by many of his people, he would become the "cornerstone" of his new building, the church (see Acts 4:11 and 1 Peter 2:6-7, where it is clear that Peter was impressed with this vivid image of Jesus being the rejected stone). Although Jesus had been rejected and defeated by his own people, the Jews, God would raise him from the dead and seat him at his own right hand. Nothing can thwart God's purpose. At the Last Judgment, God's enemies will be crushed by it. At that time, Christ, the

"building block," will become the "crushing stone." He offers
mercy and forgiveness now, and he promises judgment later. Are
you taking Christ seriously enough?

**20:19 When the teachers of religious law and the leading priests
heard this story, they wanted to arrest Jesus immediately
because they realized he was pointing at them—that they
were the farmers in the story. But they were afraid there
would be a riot if they arrested him.**NLT This delegation that had
been sent to demand answers from Jesus (20:1-2) realized that
they had been insulted and condemned by Jesus' parable. *They
realized he was pointing at them—that they were the farmers in
the story* (the evil tenant farmers who had killed the son, 20:14-
16). They would have arrested Jesus on the spot, but he was still
surrounded by crowds of eager listeners, and *they were afraid
there would be a riot.* They really had no grounds on which to
arrest Jesus except that they were angered at his parable. In addition, a riot would also make them look bad in the eyes of the
Roman government to whom they were accountable for keeping
the peace. There was nothing to do but go away to gather new
ideas and think of new questions to try to trap Jesus.

RELIGIOUS LEADERS QUESTION JESUS ABOUT PAYING TAXES / 20:20-26 / *193*

Although the religious leaders had been outwitted by Jesus once
(20:1-8), they did not give up. They returned with another carefully thought-out question to trap him. This new question related
to taxation: to pay or not to pay taxes to Rome. If Jesus answered
in the affirmative either way, he would be in a predicament. His
support from the people would decline if he endorsed paying
taxes. But if he implied that Jews should not pay taxes to Rome,
the Roman governor could prosecute him for sedition. It was a
perfect trap, or so the Pharisees thought.

Where the religious teachers saw an impossible conflict, however, Jesus described parallel duties. The people were to fulfill
their legitimate obligations to all human authorities, while at the
same time surrendering their ultimate allegiance to God. How
does the way you spend your money, time, and talents reflect
your ultimate allegiance to the Lord?

**20:20 Keeping a close watch on him, they sent spies, who pretended
to be honest. They hoped to catch Jesus in something he said
so that they might hand him over to the power and authority
of the governor.**NIV The religious leaders may not have been able
to arrest Jesus, but that did not stop them from *keeping a close*

watch and continuing in their attempts to *catch Jesus in something he said so that they might hand him over.* Luke explains
that *they sent spies, who pretended to be honest.* These men
addressed Jesus as if he were a mediator, inviting him to settle
their dispute. Their true purpose, however, was to discredit Jesus.
They thought they could *catch* him on one of the horns of a
dilemma: to pay or not to pay taxes to Caesar. The word translated "catch" is found only here in the New Testament and was
used for catching a wild animal in a trap. These two groups, on
different sides of religious and political issues, hoped to get an
answer from Jesus that would trap him.

Jesus turned his enemies' attempt to trap him into a powerful
lesson: God's followers have legitimate obligations to both God
and the government. But it is important to keep priorities straight.
When the two authorities conflict, a believer's duty to God
always must come before his or her duty to the government.

LISTENER OR CRITIC?
There is a story about the comedian W. C. Fields (never noted
for his Christian beliefs) reading the Bible on his deathbed.
"Getting religious at the eleventh hour?" someone asked him.
"No," Fields replied. "Just checking for loopholes." There are
different reasons for investigating Jesus' life and works. People
can come to him openly and honestly, sincerely wanting to
know what he is all about and what it means to be his follower.
Or they can come to him like the spies, only looking for
something to criticize. God knows everyone's heart. He knows
whether a person comes to him as a seeker or a cynic. Ask him
to give you an open, receptive heart to hear his truth.

20:21-22 **So they asked him, "Teacher, we know that you are right in
what you say and teach, and you show deference to no one,
but teach the way of God in accordance with truth. Is it lawful for us to pay taxes to the emperor, or not?"**NRSV Pretending
to be honest men (20:20), these spies flattered Jesus before asking him their trick question, hoping to catch him off guard. But
Jesus knew what they were trying to do and stayed out of their
trap. They asked him a question that was a hot topic in Palestine
at the time: *Is it lawful for us to pay taxes to the emperor, or not?*
This was a loaded question. Obviously it was lawful according to
Caesar, but was it lawful according to God's law? The Jews hated
having to pay taxes to Rome, thus supporting the pagan government, pagan religion, and the luxurious lifestyles of Rome's
upper class. There were three basic types of taxes: (1) a land or
produce tax took one-tenth of all grain and one-fifth of all fruit

(or wine); (2) a head or poll tax was collected when a census was taken—one day's wages—and was paid by everyone aged fourteen to sixty-five; and (3) a custom tax was collected at ports and city gates as toll for goods transported—rates were 2 to 5 percent of the value of the goods. This question may have focused on the poll tax or on taxes in general. Luke's Gentile readers knew all about the various forms of heavy taxation from Rome—all the taxes generally totaled over one-third of a person's income.

The Jews hated the system that allowed tax collectors to charge exorbitant rates and keep the extra for themselves. If Jesus said they should pay taxes, they would call him a traitor to their nation and their religion. But if he said they should not, the religious leaders could report him to Rome as a rebel. The crowd waited expectantly for Jesus' answer. Jesus' questioners thought they had him this time, but he outwitted them again.

DON'T STRETCH IT
These scribes and priests were confusing self-interest with piety. They seemed to pursue God's law as their first love, but they were really protecting their money. They hated to pay the tax, so they wanted to rationalize that God was against it. Are people guilty of the same today? Do they stretch the truths of the Bible about freedom to justify not obeying the government?

20:23-25 **He saw through their duplicity and said to them, "Show me a denarius. Whose portrait and inscription are on it?" "Caesar's," they replied. He said to them, "Then give to Caesar what is Caesar's, and to God what is God's."**[NIV] Jesus knew this was a trick—he knew that they were baiting him to give an answer that would condemn him either way he answered. Jesus asked someone in the crowd to show him *a denarius,* a silver coin that was the usual pay for one day's work. It was a silver coin with a *portrait* of the reigning Caesar on it, probably Tiberius Caesar, who reigned A.D. 14–37. The tax paid to Rome was paid in these coins. The *inscription* referred to Caesar as divine and as "chief priest." The Caesars were worshiped as gods by the pagans, so the claim to divinity on the coin itself repulsed the Jews. In addition, Caesar's

> We must give Caesar his dues. They can be paid in the coin of earth's mintage; but he has no claim on our conscience, faith, love. These bear the mint-mark of God, and to God they must be rendered. Ah, soul! Thou belongest to the great King; thou art stamped with his image and superscription! Give him thyself!   *F. B. Meyer*

image on the coins was a constant reminder of Israel's subjection to Rome.

Jesus' answer surprised everyone. Since Caesar's portrait and inscription were on the coins, he said, *"Give to Caesar what is Caesar's, and to God what is God's."* Having a coin meant being part of that country, so citizens should acknowledge the authority of Caesar and pay for the benefits accorded to them by his empire (for example, peace and an efficient road system). They would lose much and gain little if they refused to pay Caesar's taxes (see Romans 13:1-7; 1 Timothy 2:1-6; 1 Peter 2:13-17).

Paying the taxes, however, did not have to mean submission to the divinity claimed by the emperor through the inscription on the coins. Caesar had the right to claim their tax money, but he had no claim on their souls. The Jews had a responsibility to give to God what was his. While they lived in the Roman world, the Jews had to face the dual reality of subjection to Rome and responsibility to God. Jesus explained that they could do both if they kept their priorities straight. The tax would be paid as long as Rome held sway over Judea, but God had rights on eternity and on their lives.

IN HIS IMAGE
The nation holds an election, and the results are broadcast virtually simultaneously all over the country and even around the world. In the information age, there is little doubt as to who has power in the nation. But in the ancient world, there was no CNN, no satellite uplinks, no fax machines or digital cellular technology. How did people know who their king or emperor was and where his territory extended? One way was through the money of the realm. Coins were printed with the image of the emperor on them, and wherever that money was used, the person whose image was on the coin ruled. When Jesus asked for a coin, he knew whose image it bore. His point was that just as the coin bore the image of Caesar, each human being bears the stamp of his or her ultimate sovereign: God himself. God has placed his stamp of ownership and authority on each believer. Do you give him what is due him in terms of your allegiance, time, abilities, and money?

20:26 So they failed to trap him in the presence of the people. Instead, they were amazed by his answer, and they were silenced.[NLT] In his reply, Jesus did not show rebellion against Caesar, nor did he show any disloyalty to God and his law. This answer *amazed* and *silenced* Jesus' questioners. Their amazement showed that Jesus had been victorious over his opponents. They had tried to trap him, but he stayed one step ahead of them (see also 20:39-40).

RELIGIOUS LEADERS QUESTION JESUS ABOUT THE RESURRECTION / 20:27-40 / *194*

Jesus had already evaded two traps laid by the Jewish religious leaders—one involving his authority and then one on Roman taxation. They were determined to embarrass Jesus. The challenge by the Sadducees in this section indicates that the religious leaders were getting desperate. This time, the Sadducees used a standard theological question they had often used to discredit the idea of a resurrection, which was a belief of the Pharisees. If Jesus was not able to answer this question, his image as a great religious teacher would be tarnished.

Jesus rose to this occasion, as well, and he exposed the Sadducees' ignorance of the Scripture and of God's infinite power. He didn't let their clever philosophical puzzle distract people from what was truly important. The question the Sadducees should have asked was whether they would be able to participate in the resurrection of the righteous (20:35), not whether there was a resurrection.

20:27 Then some Sadducees stepped forward—a group of Jews who say there is no resurrection after death.NLT No sooner had one delegation withdrawn from Jesus in amazement than another appeared to take up the cause. The religious leaders were determined to eliminate Jesus, so *some Sadducees stepped forward.* The Sadducees were a group of conservative Jewish religious leaders who honored only the Pentateuch—Genesis through Deuteronomy—as Scripture. They did not believe in a resurrection of the dead because they could find no mention of it in those books.

The political party of the Sadducees was mostly made up of the wealthiest and most prominent among the Jews. They dominated the Sanhedrin, the Jewish ruling council. Under Roman rule, the Council had received a certain amount of independence and authority, yet Rome could also take away their property rights and privileged positions if it so desired. It served the Sadducees' best interests, therefore, to cooperate with Rome. The Sadducees enjoyed wealth, comfort, and power. *Resurrection after death* was a future dream for the poor masses to hold on to, but the Sadducees did not believe in it.

FAITH OR WISHFUL THINKING?
"Life after death? That's just escapism. Why don't Christians face the truth and quit living in a fantasy world?" Have you ever heard that kind of objection to the Christian doctrine of resurrection? The Sadducees were first-century skeptics who did not believe in life after death. Undoubtedly they considered themselves hard-nosed realists, compared to Jesus and his followers, who believed strongly in the resurrection. The Christian belief in an afterlife is hardly a nice, escapist notion. The thought that after death people are called to give an account of their lives before a righteous, holy God is not a comforting fantasy—it's a call to live holy lives before such a God. People will die, and then face judgment. Are you ready for that hard, cold reality? Take some time to take stock of your life and make sure that you're prepared.

20:28 **They posed this question: "Teacher, Moses gave us a law that if a man dies, leaving a wife but no children, his brother should marry the widow and have a child who will be the brother's heir."**[NLT] The Sadducees, handicapped by their unbelief in the resurrection, thought they had a thorny problem from God's Word that would make the very idea of life beyond death ludicrous. They decided to try their hand at tricking Jesus, so they brought him a question that had always stumped the Pharisees. In the Law, Moses had written that if a man died without a son, his unmarried brother (or nearest male relative) should marry the widow and produce children. The first son of this marriage would be considered the heir of the dead man (Deuteronomy 25:5-6). The main purpose of the instruction was to produce an heir and guarantee that the family would not lose their land. The book of Ruth gives an example of this law in operation (Ruth 3:1–4:12; see also Genesis 38:1-26). This law, called "levirate" marriage, protected the widow (in that culture, widows usually had no means to support themselves) and allowed the family line to continue.

20:29-33 **"Well, there were seven brothers. The oldest married and then died without children. His brother married the widow, but he also died. Still no children. And so it went, one after the other, until each of the seven had married her and died, leaving no children. Finally, the woman died, too. So tell us, whose wife will she be in the resurrection? For all seven were married to her!"**[NLT] In order to show what they perceived as the absurdity of believing in the resurrection, the Sadducees offered a hypothetical situation in which the same woman married and outlived seven brothers but never had any children. Resurrection was pictured by some Jews in the intertestamental period as a continuation of life on earth. This particular woman would have had a real problem because when she and her seven husbands would be resurrected, the Sadducees asked, *whose wife will she be?* Their problem lay in their view of resurrection and the God who, throughout Scripture, promised it. The Sadducees had brought God down to their level and decided that because they could not make sense out of resurrection life, God couldn't raise the dead. They did not consider for a moment that God, Creator and Sustainer of all life, could not only raise the dead but also create entirely new lives that would be different from what people had on this earth. It will be far more glorious than any human being can imagine.

HOME IS WHERE THE HEART IS
What are your hopes for the future? A better job, bigger office, nicer house, more money? Those things are fine—but very transient. The Christian's ultimate hope is heaven. People in affluent circumstances, including Christians, tend to forget that. Their lives are very comfortable here, so they tend to focus on enjoying it to the neglect of setting their sights on eternity. The Sadducees were guilty of this, as well. Life was very comfortable for them, so they weren't concerned with the afterlife. Their question about the woman and her seven husbands wasn't a serious inquiry about resurrection; it was designed to show the ridiculousness of the whole idea of resurrection. The same is true today—rich people don't write many great spirituals. Where is your heart—on the good things of this world or on the eternal things of the world to come?

20:34-36 Jesus replied, **"The people of this age marry and are given in marriage. But those who are considered worthy of taking part in that age and in the resurrection from the dead will neither marry nor be given in marriage, and they can no longer die."**[NIV] Jesus pointed out that there are differences between life in this age and life in the age to come. The resurrection life in heaven will not be merely a continuation of life on this earth. Here in this world, people *marry and are given in marriage.* However, those who do get to heaven, the saved—*those who are considered worthy of taking part in that age and in the resurrection from the dead*—will find that their lives are not merely extended into eternity, but that everything is different. They won't be marrying or being given in marriage (as per the Sadducees' question); in fact, everything will be different. And *they can no longer die.* How horrible it would be to have a resurrection into a continuation of this life—filled with sin, death, grief, sorrow, unhappiness. Instead, believers anticipate the resurrection that brings eternal life—new and different; it is a resurrection to a life of no more tears or sorrow (Revelation 21:4).

In the new heaven and new earth, marriage will no longer be needed. Inheritance laws and property rights will be irrelevant. It is important to human beings in this world, but it will not be a needed feature of the kingdom. In addition, marriage is needed in this world in order to produce children and thereby continue the human race. This also will not be needed in the kingdom because no one can die there. Death will have been banished and will not affect people in the kingdom (Revelation 20:14).

NO MARRIAGE IN HEAVEN?
Many people are jolted at the prospect of eternal life without marriage with their partner on earth and the physical relationship that goes along with it because it is one of earth's greatest pleasures. At first reading, Jesus seems to imply as much here.

At its very best, sexual activity creates a great sense of oneness between lovers, a superb moment of intense intimacy, and wonderful physical feelings. Lovers wish their excitement would last and last, but too quickly life returns to normal.

People who ponder eternity (and who doesn't?) are right to hope that the freedom, intensity, and intimacy they experience now will be transformed, expanded, and made utterly glorious in new life with God in heaven, where joys last and last, and never grow old.

Christians don't know what God has planned, but they trust in his love. The beauty and excitement they feel now is not a trick but a foretaste of an even better experience.

In the new heaven and new earth, the relationships among all Christian brothers and sisters will be so intense, so filled with love, that earthly marital bliss will seem shallow by comparison.

"For they are like the angels. They are God's children, since they are children of the resurrection."[NIV] Believers *will be like the angels* regarding marriage. Believers do not become angels because angels were created by God for a special purpose. Angels do not marry or propagate; neither will glorified human beings who are *God's children . . . children of the resurrection.* Having been raised to new life, those in heaven will no longer be governed by physical laws but will be "like the angels"; that is, believers will share the immortal and exalted nature of angels, living above physical needs.

Jesus was not teaching that people will not recognize their spouses in heaven, thereby dissolving the eternal aspect of marriage. Nor was he doing away with sexual differences or teaching that people will be asexual beings after death. Nor was he teaching that the angels are asexual. Little can be learned about sex and marriage in heaven from this one statement by Jesus. His point was simply that people must not think of the next life as an extension of life as they now know it. Relationships in this life are limited by time, death, and sin; in the new heaven and new earth they will be different from here and now. The same physical and natural rules will not apply. Jesus was showing that because there would be no levirate marriage in the resurrection or new marriage contracts, the Sadducees' question was completely irrelevant. But their assumption about the resurrection that lay behind their question still needed a definitive answer, and Jesus would give it.

TRICKY QUESTIONS
The Sadducees came to Jesus with a trick question. Not believing in the resurrection, they wanted Jesus to say something they could refute. Even so, Jesus did not ignore or belittle their question. He answered it, and then he went beyond it to the real issue. When people ask you tough religious questions—"How can a loving God allow people to starve?" "If God knows what I'm going to do, do I have any free choice?"—follow Jesus' example. First answer the question to the best of your ability; then look for the real issue—hurt over a personal tragedy, for example, or difficulty in making a decision. Often the spoken question is only a test, not of your ability to answer hard questions, but of your willingness to listen and care.

20:37-38 **"But now, as to whether the dead will be raised—even Moses proved this when he wrote about the burning bush. Long after Abraham, Isaac, and Jacob had died, he referred to the Lord as 'the God of Abraham, the God of Isaac, and the God of Jacob.' So he is the God of the living, not the dead. They are all alive to him."**NLT After addressing their question about marriage, Jesus answered the Sadducees' assumption about the resurrection—*as to whether the dead will be raised*—that was the issue behind the prolonged story about the woman and her many husbands. Jesus based his answer on the writings of Moses, an authority the Sadducees respected. *"Even Moses proved this,"* Jesus said. Moses understood that the resurrection of the dead was a reality, for *when he wrote about the burning bush,* he wrote of the patriarchs as though they were still alive (Exodus 3:6), referring to the Lord as *the God of Abraham, the God of Isaac, and the God of Jacob.* Thus, from God's perspective, they were alive. God had a continuing relationship with these men because of the truth of the resurrection. In Matthew and Mark, the entire quote from Exodus 3:6 is used, with God saying, "I am the God of . . ."—with the argument being that God, speaking in the present tense, was affirming his continuing relationship with these men. Therefore *he is the God of the living, not the dead.* God could not have a relationship with dead beings. Although men and women have died on earth, God continues his relationship with them because *they are all alive to him.* Death separates people from their loved ones on earth, but it cannot separate believers from God.

20:39-40 **"Well said, Teacher!" remarked some of the teachers of religious law who were standing there. And that ended their questions; no one dared to ask any more.**^{NLT} The teachers of the law (Pharisees), who also had been attempting to trick Jesus, had to congratulate Jesus on this answer to the Sadducees. This question had probably stumped the Pharisees for some time, and at last the Sadducees had been duly silenced. At this time, the questions ended, for *no one dared to ask any more.* Once again, the trap failed (see also 20:26). The various groups tried to stump Jesus on issues of politics and theology. But Jesus' wisdom prevailed. Jesus' victory over them was complete. His enemies would have to resort to another strategy to stop him.

RELIGIOUS LEADERS CANNOT ANSWER JESUS' QUESTION / 20:41-44 / 196

Jesus had already emerged victorious over his opponents on three separate occasions (20:1-8, 20-26, 27-40). They had asked the questions, and Jesus had responded. But here Jesus took the offense, challenging his opponents with a question of his own: Who is the Son of David? With this question, Jesus identified the weakness of the religious teachers' thinking. They had not sufficiently examined what the Scripture said about the coming Messiah.

"The Son of David" was a commonly known first-century title for the Messiah. But was the Messiah only David's son? Was there more to be said about him, since David himself had called the Messiah his Lord? Most first-century Jews thought the Messiah would be a political figure, a conquering king who was a descendant of King David (Psalm 2:4-12). But Jesus was pushing them to broaden their understanding of the Messiah. The Messiah would suffer as Isaiah prophesied (compare Jesus' predictions of his suffering in 9:22; 17:25 to Isaiah 53:1-12) and would be raised to the right hand of God to exercise divine authority and power (Psalm 110:1; see Peter's explanation of this prophecy in Acts 5:31).

Take Jesus' implicit rebuke of the Jewish religious teachers to heart. Reevaluate your thinking about Jesus in light of God's Word.

20:41 **Then Jesus said to them, "How is it that they say the Christ is the Son of David?"**NIV The Pharisees and Sadducees had asked their questions. Then Jesus turned the tables and asked them a question that went right to the heart of the matter—what they thought about the Messiah's identity. The central issue of life is what people believe about Jesus. Other spiritual questions are irrelevant unless they first decide to believe that Jesus is who he claimed to be. The Pharisees and Sadducees could not do this. They remained confused over Jesus' identity. The Pharisees knew that the Messiah would be a Son (or descendant) of David, but they did not understand that he would be more than a human descendant—he would be God in the flesh. So Jesus turned to the book of Psalms and asked, *"How is it that they say the Christ is the Son of David?"* He used this question, which he will answer, to make them think about the true meaning of these prophetic words.

OFFENSE VS. DEFENSE
When discussing their faith with others, Christians often find themselves on the defensive: answering objections, giving reasons for their beliefs, communicating what often seems incommunicable. No wonder many believers are uncomfortable witnessing to others. They may be able to give reasons for their faith (1 Peter 3:15), but there is also a place for putting the skeptic on the defensive. Sometimes it may be difficult to give answers for one's faith, but it is even more difficult to defend a lack of belief or outright cynicism. Jesus turned the tables in such a fashion. After meeting the challenges of the Pharisees, the Sadducees, and the scribes, Jesus asked them some penetrating questions, designed to expose the shallowness of their unbelief. Defense, as any championship sports team will tell you, is crucial, but so is the ability to put the other team on the defensive. Are you knowledgeable enough about your beliefs to go on the offensive? If not, consider taking a class in apologetics or reading good books on theology.

20:42-43 **"Now David himself said in the Book of Psalms: 'The LORD said to my Lord, "Sit at My right hand, till I make Your enemies Your footstool."'"**NKJV Jesus was quoting from Psalm 110:1 to show that David knew the Messiah would be both human and divine. The Pharisees expected only a human ruler to restore Israel's greatness as in the days of David and Solomon. So Jesus quoted these words, explaining what the religious leaders should have understood:

- David said, "The *Lord.*" This first "Lord" is *Yahweh,* the Hebrew name for God the Father.
- The second "Lord" in Hebrew is *Adonai* (in Greek, *Kurios*) and refers to David speaking of the coming Messiah as his "Lord."
- "Sit at My right hand" means that the Messiah would sit at the right side of God's throne, the place of highest honor and authority in God's coming kingdom. In ancient royal courts, the right side of the king's throne was reserved for the person who could act in the king's place.
- "Till I make Your enemies Your footstool" describes the final conquering of sin and evil. In ancient Oriental battles, the conquered ruler would be forced to put his neck under the foot of the triumphant ruler, showing defeat and subjection.

20:44 "Since David called him Lord, how can he be his son at the same time?"[NLT] There is an inherent problem in the prophecy because it makes no sense that David would call the Messiah "Lord" when the Lord was also his son. The only way to understand this is to see the Messiah as more than a mere human being (see Romans 1:2-4). David himself didn't think the Messiah would be just one of his descendants; instead, David, under the inspiration of the Holy Spirit, said that the Messiah would be God.

The answer to Jesus' question is that David was clearly saying the Messiah was his *Lord.* By this statement, Jesus was revealing his divine identity. The divine Messiah had, indeed, come in human form; he was standing among them.

JESUS WARNS AGAINST THE RELIGIOUS LEADERS / 20:45-47 / 197

Luke, like the other Synoptic writers (see Matthew 23:1-12; Mark 12:38-40), concluded this section, which describes the confrontation between Jesus and the religious leaders (19:45–21:4), with Jesus' severe condemnation of the teachers of the law. Their concern for outward appearances over the condition of their own hearts, especially their total inattention to justice and mercy, was despicable in God's eyes. As you read this scathing attack on the Pharisees and Sadducees, sincerely evaluate your own life. Where have you allowed arrogance, hypocrisy, and greed to grow?

20:45-47 Then, with the crowds listening, he turned to his disciples and said, "Beware of these teachers of religious law! For they love to parade in flowing robes and to have everyone bow to them as they walk in the marketplaces. And how they love the seats of honor in the synagogues and at banquets. But they shamelessly cheat widows out of their property, and then, to cover up the kind of people they really are, they make long prayers in public. Because of this, their punishment will be the greater."[NLT] The teachers of the law loved the benefits associated with their position, and they sometimes cheated the poor in order to get even more benefits. Every job has its rewards, but gaining rewards should never become more important than doing the job faithfully. God will punish people who use their position of responsibility to cheat others. Thus Jesus warned his followers, *with the crowds listening,* to *beware of these teachers of religious law.* They were supposed to be just what their title implied—teachers who led people into the truth of God; instead, they loved the "perks" of their position and did just the opposite. They led people away from God.

The reference to parading in *flowing robes* and being bowed to in the marketplaces pictured these religious leaders who went through the market in their long robes, often white to symbolize purity, receiving bows of respect from everyone. The white robes were supposed to be worn for religious duties; however, the religious leaders had taken to wearing them in public, such as to the marketplaces, for attention. The white robes singled them out and thus caused the people to recognize them as authorities and to greet them respectfully. These actions were motivated by vanity.

They loved the *seats of honor in the synagogues and at banquets* because those seats were reserved for the most important people. In the synagogue, the seats of honor were situated in front of the box containing the scrolls, facing the general congregation. At banquets, such seats were generally the closest to the host. Those seated there received special treatment during the meal.

The accusation of cheating widows out of their property pictured the teachers' abuse of their trusted position. Because they received no pay for their services, they depended on the hospitality of devout Jews. It was considered an act of piety for people to help the scribes. But some of these religious men were using their position to defraud the gullible. Some people would even go so far as to place all their finances in the scribe's control (especially widows who trusted them). As the nation's lawyers, scribes were often employed in handling the money a widow received from her father's dowry. Some abused their trusted positions by supposedly obtaining the dowry for the temple and then keeping it themselves. They were in a position to exploit people, cheating the poor out of everything they had and taking advantage of the rich. How could they deserve anything but condemnation!

Their lengthy public prayers, Jesus said, amounted to no more than a cover-up. Their long prayers were not conversations with the Lord but were merely ploys to make people think they were especially holy. Through their pious actions they hoped to gain status, recognition, and respect.

The punishment for these scribes would be especially severe because as teachers they were responsible for shaping the faith of the people. But they saddled people with petty rules while they, themselves, lived greedily and deceitfully. Their behavior gave a pretense of piety, while they oppressed and misled the very people they were supposed to lead. Jesus solemnly announced, *"Their punishment will be the greater."* These words certainly must have affected the disciple James, for he later wrote, "Not many of you should become teachers . . . for you know that we who teach will be judged with greater strictness" (James 3:1 NRSV).

THE LEADERS' TRAP

Jesus chastised these religious leaders for their contrived self-importance, love of popularity, and desire for acclaim. Every person in leadership—preacher, professor, speaker, writer, Sunday school teacher, or office holder in a Christian organization—needs to guard against these pitfalls of hypocrisy:

- "Love to parade in flowing robes." Do you love to be seen in the right places? Do you insist on titles, positioning, and symbols of authority? Do you dress for effect and to display your success? Do you engage in "name-dropping"?
- "Love to have everyone bow to them." Are you more motivated by service or by receiving attention and adulation?
- "Love the seats of honor." Are you oversensitive to recognition and slights? Do you seek exposure to enhance your influence?
- "Make long prayers in public." Have your sermons or lectures become pretense designed for public effect rather than service for God?

Seek to serve others, not to impress them. Keep your public profession and inner attitude in control. Avoid the hypocrisy of the Pharisees.

LUKE 21

After warning his disciples about the greed of the teachers of the law (20:46), Jesus pointed out a poor widow as an example of extraordinary faith. Although her two small coins could not compare to the much larger gifts of the rich, she had given it out of her poverty. She had used all she owned to serve the Lord, trusting God to supply her needs. The teachers of the law were devouring "widows' houses" (20:47), but this widow was looking for opportunities to give to God. Evaluate your giving in light of Jesus' commendation of this poor widow.

21:1-2 **As he looked up, Jesus saw the rich putting their gifts into the temple treasury. He also saw a poor widow put in two very small copper coins.**[NIV] Jesus spent much time during his last week on earth in the temple, teaching, preaching, and dealing with religious leaders (19:45–20:47). At some point during one of his days there, Jesus *looked up* and watched people put donations into the temple treasury. Jesus was in the area of the temple called the Court of Women. The treasury was there or in an adjoining walkway. Seven boxes were in this area. Worshipers could deposit their temple tax in these boxes. In addition, six boxes more collected freewill offerings like the one this woman gave. A lot of money came into the temple treasury during Passover.

The rich people (probably obvious by their apparel) put their gifts into the treasury—large gifts that may have made a lot of noise as the coins clattered into the boxes. Then *a poor widow* came and dropped in *two very small copper coins.* Her status as a widow may also have been revealed through her dress, or Jesus may have known this by his divine knowledge. As a widow, she had few resources for earning money and may have been without financial support. Jesus watched as she gave her gift, coins that amounted to no more than a fraction of a penny. Two lepta were the smallest coins in use, valued at about one-eighth of a penny or one-hundredth of the average daily wage. Yet these were put in the freewill-offering box, meaning that this was not a required tax but a gift.

BEYOND CONVENIENCE
This widow gave all she had to live on, in contrast to the way most people handle their money. Those who consider giving a certain percentage of their income to be a great accomplishment resemble those who gave out of their wealth. Here in 21:1-2, Jesus was admiring generous and sacrificial giving. Believers should consider increasing their giving—whether of money, time, or talents—to a point beyond convenience, comfort, or safety.

21:3-4 "I assure you," he said, "this poor widow has given more than all the rest of them. For they have given a tiny part of their surplus, but she, poor as she is, has given everything she has."NLT Jesus judged the poor woman's gift not by how much she gave but by how much she had left after giving. The rich did well to give out of their abundance, but they had plenty left, having given *a tiny part of their surplus.* Yet she gave *everything* and therefore had *given more than all the rest of them.* The widow could have kept back one coin, but she willingly gave both coins. She gave everything and trusted God to care for her. Jesus wanted the disciples to see this lesson in total surrender of self, commitment to God, and willingness to trust in God's provision. For more on giving, see 1 Corinthians 16:1-4; 2 Corinthians 8:1-5.

TRUE GIVING
How do you react when you see the offering plate coming toward you? Annoyance, yawning, resignation? Would it change your attitude toward giving of your money to the work of the ministry in your church if you knew that God could do great things with little contributions? That's the message of Luke 21:3-4. The poor widow's offering far outclassed all the others because she gave sacrificially, while the others gave recreationally. It is obvious which kind of giving God honors. Which kind does yours resemble?

*JESUS TELLS ABOUT THE FUTURE / 21:5-24 / **201***

A disciple's casual remark concerning the splendor of the temple gave Jesus the opportunity to make an alarming prophecy about the temple and the end times. This section, along with 17:20-37, parallels the Olivet discourse given in Matthew 24:1-25 and Mark 13:1-23. Unlike many "prophecy experts" today, Jesus did not prophesy about the future in order to

impress others. Instead, he spoke of the end times in order to
realign his disciples' priorities and to caution them about being
deceived. The disciples were impressed with the external
appearance of the temple, but Jesus admonished them to focus
not on the building itself but, instead, on God to whom the
building was dedicated. The temple would eventually be
destroyed, but God's Word (which pointed to Jesus himself,
21:12-18, 33) would remain. Jesus sternly warned his disciples
not to be deceived by false messiahs or to lose hope. No matter
what situation they found themselves in, they were to stand
firm on the truth of God's Word.

21:5-6 **When some were speaking about the temple, how it was
adorned with beautiful stones and gifts dedicated to God, he
said, "As for these things that you see, the days will come when
not one stone will be left upon another; all will be thrown
down."**^{NRSV} Jesus and the disciples would leave Jerusalem every
evening of that final week and walk the couple of miles back to

Bethany. As they
left the city on one
of those evenings,
some of the disci-
ples commented
on the beauty of
the temple itself.
The temple that
the disciples were
admiring was not
Solomon's
temple—that had
been destroyed by
the Babylonians in
the seventh cen-
tury B.C. This
temple had been
built by Ezra after
the return from
exile in the sixth
century B.C., dese-
crated by the
Seleucids in the
second century
B.C., reconsecrated
by the Maccabees
soon afterward,

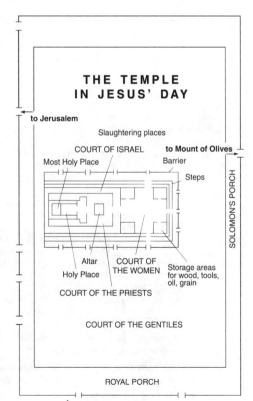

**THE TEMPLE
IN JESUS' DAY**

to Jerusalem

Slaughtering places

COURT OF ISRAEL   to Mount of Olives

Most Holy Place   Barrier

Steps

SOLOMON'S PORCH

Altar   COURT OF
Holy Place THE WOMEN   Storage areas
                        for wood, tools,
                        oil, grain

COURT OF THE PRIESTS

COURT OF THE GENTILES

ROYAL PORCH

and enormously expanded by Herod the Great over a forty-six-year period. It was a beautiful, imposing structure with a significant history. Although no one knows exactly what it looked like, it must have been magnificent, for in its time it was considered one of the architectural wonders of the world.

The temple was impressive, covering about one-sixth of the land area of the ancient city of Jerusalem. It was not one building, but a majestic mixture of porches, colonnades, separate small edifices, and courts surrounding the temple proper (see the map, "The Temple in Jesus' Day," on page 471). Next to the inner temple, where the sacred objects were kept and the sacrifices offered, was a large area called the Court of the Gentiles (this was where the money changers and merchants had their booths). Outside these courts stretched long porches. Solomon's porch was 1,562 feet long, and the royal porch was decorated with 160 columns stretching along its 921-foot length. The disciples gazed in wonder at marble pillars 40 feet high, each one carved from a single solid stone. The temple's foundation was so solid that it is believed that some of the original footings remain to this day. The Jews were convinced of the permanence of this magnificent structure, not only because of the stability of construction, but also because it represented God's presence among them.

PEOPLE, NOT BUILDINGS
"A church was burned last night in another case of suspected arson. . . ." These kinds of headlines, unfortunately becoming all too common, are misleading. No one can "burn down" a church; only the buildings are susceptible to destruction by arson. The church is people, not buildings. Even Jesus' disciples lost sight of the truth at times. They admired the great beauty of the restored and expanded temple in Jerusalem, commenting to one another about its magnificence. Jesus gave them a rather startling lesson on perspective: "The days will come when not one stone will be left upon another." It must have grieved the disciples, steeped as they were in Jewish tradition, to know this. And yet the church, the people of God—the true temple—would not only survive but also grow and flourish and ultimately conquer hell itself. Buildings are great tools, but people are the church. It's all right to appreciate a place of worship. Just don't confuse it with the church.

Jesus used the disciples' comments about the temple to give them a prophetic statement about the fate of the temple: *"As for these things that you see, the days will come when not one stone will be left upon another; all will be thrown down."* Jesus prophesied that Jerusalem and the beautiful temple would again be completely destroyed. This happened only a few years later when the Romans sacked Jerusalem in A.D. 70. The Romans fulfilled Jesus' words to the letter. After fire raged through the temple, Emperor Titus ordered the leveling of the whole area so that no part of the original walls or buildings remained. Titus considered this as punishment for the Jewish rebellion in A.D. 66. The temple has never been rebuilt, and the stones that we can see today, commonly called the "wailing wall," are part of the foundation. Truly the temple was leveled.

21:7-8 **"Teacher," they asked, "when will all this take place? And will there be any sign ahead of time?" He replied, "Don't let anyone mislead you. For many will come in my name, claiming to be the Messiah and saying, 'The time has come!' But don't believe them."**[NLT] Mark wrote that the inner circle of disciples (this time with Andrew added—Andrew was Peter's brother; James and John were brothers) came to Jesus privately (Mark 13:3-4). Matthew and Luke did not distinguish the four. Probably all the disciples heard Jesus' answer. They wanted to understand what Jesus meant and when this terrible destruction would happen.

The disciples' question had two parts. They wanted to know (1) *When will all this take place?* (referring to the destruction of the temple) and (2) *Will there be any sign ahead of time?* They expected the Messiah to inaugurate his kingdom soon, and they wanted to know the sign that it was about to arrive. They probably thought the destruction of the temple would merely involve removing the old temple in order to make room for the glorious temple of God's kingdom. The true meaning of Jesus' words escaped them. That the Jews' temple would be destroyed would have been unthinkable to the Jews of that day.

Jesus first answered the disciples' second question about the end of the age and the coming kingdom. The disciples wondered what sign would reveal these things, but Jesus warned them against false messiahs: *"Don't let anyone mislead you. For many will come in my name, claiming to be the Messiah."* Jesus knew that if the disciples looked for signs, they would be susceptible to deception. Many false prophets would display counterfeit signs of spiritual power and authority. Jesus predicted that before his return, many believers would be misled by false teachers coming in his name—that is, claiming to be Christ. In the first century, there were false messiahs pretending to have authority. Many messianic movements sprung up, especially before the destruction of Jerusalem. Second Thessalonians 2:3-10, which describes a man of lawlessness who will lead people astray, reflects the teaching of this passage. The first century saw many such deceivers arise (see Acts 5:36-37; 8:9-11; 2 Timothy 3; 2 Peter 2; 1 John 2:18; 4:1-3).

Many individuals have claimed to be the Christ or to know exactly when Jesus will return—even some in our own generation. Jesus warned us about them and said clearly, *"Don't believe them."* Obviously, no one else has been Christ, and no one has been right about the timing of the Second Coming. According to Scripture, the one clear sign of Christ's return will be his unmistakable appearance in the clouds that will be seen by all people (Matthew 24:30; Revelation 1:7). In other words, believers never have to wonder whether a certain person is the Messiah. When Jesus returns, believers will know beyond a doubt because he will be evident to all.

Jesus did not leave his disciples unprepared for the difficult years ahead, but he made it clear that there would be a length of time between his first and second comings and that during that time his people would face difficulties. He warned them about false messiahs, natural disasters, and persecutions; but he assured them that he would be with them to protect them and make his kingdom known through them. In the end, Jesus promised that he would return in power and glory to save them. Jesus' warnings and promises to his disciples also apply to believers today as they look forward to his return.

THE END IS NEAR!
Have you heard anyone declare: "The Rapture will happen on September 6, 1999"? There have been countless predictions in regard to eschatology, the study of the last times, throughout the history of the church. Every generation of Christians has believed it would be the last. So far, they all have been wrong. Does that mean that Christians should not study passages like Luke 21 or that these passages are of lesser importance? No, if it's in the Bible, it's worth studying. Each verse is beneficial. But believers should approach prophecy with humility, not arrogance and dogmatism. Whatever your beliefs about the end times, realize that you may not have the whole picture and that others may have helpful insights to offer you. If you have been dogmatic about your views, repent and ask God to give you a teachable spirit.

21:9 "When you hear of wars and revolutions, do not be frightened. These things must happen first, but the end will not come right away."[NIV] Just as false messiahs and religious frauds come and go (21:8), so do political and natural crises. *Wars and revolutions . . . must happen first* as part of God's divine plan; however, these do not signal *the end* (the end of the world). The disciples probably assumed that the temple would only be destroyed at the end of the age as part of God establishing his new kingdom. Jesus taught that horrible events would happen, but the end *will not come right away.* Believers should *not be frightened.* God will not lose control of his creation, and his promises will come true.

21:10-11 **Then he said to them: "Nation will rise against nation, and kingdom against kingdom. There will be great earthquakes, famines and pestilences in various places, and fearful events and great signs from heaven."**NIV Jesus' words indicated that there would be a span of time before the end of the age and the coming kingdom—the kingdom would not come that week or immediately upon Jesus' resurrection or even right after the destruction of Jerusalem. First, much suffering would occur as a part of life on earth, including wars, fighting among nations and kingdoms, and many natural disasters. These, along with *fearful events and great signs from heaven,* will mean only that history is moving toward a single, final, God-planned goal—the creation of a new earth and a new kingdom (Revelation 21:1-3). Today we must guard against preoccupation with signs such as frequency of earthquakes, etc. Instead, we must focus on doing God's will.

21:12 **"But before all this occurs, they will arrest you and persecute you; they will hand you over to synagogues and prisons, and you will be brought before kings and governors because of my name."**NRSV Without hesitation, Jesus explained that his followers would not escape suffering. Before *all this* (referring to the end times) *occurs,* these followers would be arrested and persecuted. These persecutions soon began; Luke recorded many of them in the book of Acts. "They will arrest you" refers to fellow Jews who would turn against the disciples for believing in Jesus and *hand [them] over to synagogues and prisons.* This refers to the local Jewish courts held in the synagogues (smaller versions of the Sanhedrin in Jerusalem). Jesus didn't say it, but the disciples would learn that loyalty to Christ meant separation from Judaism. Two of the disciples listening to Jesus (Peter and John, see Mark 13:3) faced the Sanhedrin not long after

> The Church is called to follow her Lord. No easier path than his may she choose. Where there is no outward suffering, there may be the inner cross and the death to all that the soul had once prized. Jesus has always stood beside his own wherever they have been called to witness for the truth; and the testimony given by his witnesses has reached the great ones of the earth and reverberated through courts and palaces.
>
> *F. B. Meyer*

PERSEVERE TO THE END

Luke 21:19, "By standing firm, you will gain life" (NIV).	*PERSEVERANCE GROWS OUT OF COMMITMENT TO JESUS CHRIST.* Standing firm is not the way to be saved but the evidence that a person is really committed to Jesus. Endurance is not a means to earn salvation; it is the by-product of a truly devoted life.
2 Timothy 4:5, "But you should keep a clear mind in every situation. Don't be afraid of suffering for the Lord. Work at bringing others to Christ. Complete the ministry God has given you" (NLT).	*GOD WILL MAKE BELIEVERS' PERSEVERANCE WORTHWHILE.* He will help his people complete whatever work he has called them to do: He will help them draw others into the kingdom.
Hebrews 3:6, "But Christ, the faithful Son, was in charge of the entire household. And we are God's household, if we keep up our courage and remain confident in our hope in Christ" (NLT).	*PERSEVERANCE KEEPS BELIEVERS COURAGEOUS AND HOPEFUL BECAUSE THEY CAN TRUST CHRIST.* Because Christ lives in Christians, and because he is completely trustworthy to fulfill all his promises, believers can remain courageous and hopeful.
Revelation 14:12, "This calls for patient endurance on the part of the saints who obey God's commandments and remain faithful to Jesus" (NIV).	*BELIEVERS' ABILITY TO PERSEVERE IS RELATED TO THE QUALITY OF THEIR RELATIONSHIP WITH GOD.* The secret to perseverance is trust and obedience. Trust God to give you the patience to endure even the small trials you face daily. The fact of God's ultimate triumph can encourage believers to remain steadfast in their faith through every trial and persecution.

Jesus' resurrection (Acts 4:1-12; see also Acts 12:1-2). At that time, they certainly remembered these words. Not only would Jesus' followers be in trouble with Jews, they would also find themselves standing trial before Gentile *kings and governors.* The reason? Because of the disciples' belief in Jesus *(because of my name).*

21:13-15 "This will give you an opportunity to testify. So make up your minds not to prepare your defense in advance; for I will give you words and a wisdom that none of your opponents will be able to withstand or contradict."NRSV These trials in the synagogues and before Gentile rulers would give the disciples *an opportunity to testify.* They were not to worry about defending themselves; instead, they were to concentrate on proclaiming the

gospel. Standing before the Jewish leadership, Roman procon-
suls, or governors would be intimidating, but Jesus explained that
they did not need to laboriously prepare their defense; instead,
they could trust him to give them *words and a wisdom* that would
astound their opponents. Notice that Jesus did not guarantee
acquittal. James, one of the disciples here listening to Jesus,
would be killed because of his faith (Acts 12:1-2).

GETTING PREPPED
The pastor stood up to preach and realized to his horror that he
had left his notes at home. "I don't have my notes this morning,
ladies and gentlemen," he said nervously, "I guess I'll just have
to trust the Holy Spirit for what I'm going to say. But don't
worry—this will never happen again." Should Christians
prepare sermons, Bible studies, and Sunday school lessons—
or simply trust God to provide the words to say at the right
time? Other Scriptures make it clear that it is appropriate to
study God's Word in preparation for preaching and teaching
(see Psalm 119 or 2 Timothy 2:15). But Jesus also promises
that when his followers are called on unexpectedly to give
testimony to their faith or speak up for the cause of Christ, he
will himself give them the words to say. What great words of
comfort and assurance! When you are able to prepare ahead
of time, you should; when you aren't, he will prepare for you.
Walk confidently.

21:16-19 **"You will be betrayed even by parents and brothers, by relatives and friends; and they will put some of you to death. You
will be hated by all because of my name."**NRSV Jesus warned that
in the coming persecutions his followers would be betrayed by
their family members and friends. Christians of every age have had
to face this possibility. Some were even *put . . . to death* and forever
hated— again *because of [Jesus'] name* (also 21:12). As noted
above, one of the disciples sitting there, James, would soon be put
to death because of his faith in Jesus (Acts 12:1-2).

   Not only would the disciples face hatred from religious and
civil leaders as well as their own families, they also would be
hated by all. For Jews to convert to Christianity would soon
become very dangerous because they would be hated and ostracized. Jesus' words also looked forward to the time when hatred
of Christians would again occur. Jesus gave a promise however:
**"But not a hair of your head will perish. By standing firm you
will gain life."**NIV For believers, to believe in Jesus and stand
firm to the end will take perseverance because their faith will be
challenged and opposed. Severe trials will sift true Christians
from fair-weather believers. *Standing firm* to *gain life* does not

mean that standing firm earns salvation; instead, it marks those who are already saved. Assurance of salvation will keep believers going through the times of persecution.

PAYING THE PRICE
Has following Christ cost you? Have you lost friendships, business associates, promotions, or even relationships with family members because of your Christian faith and lifestyle? You are not alone. Throughout history, God's people have suffered great losses for the sake of their beliefs. Jesus even predicted that these things would happen. Of course, it hurts to be ridiculed and outright hated for what you believe. But if that is your experience, remember: you are in good company with countless of other Christians and with Jesus himself. Take the rejection of the world as a confirmation of your acceptance by the Lord.

What assurance was Jesus giving in light of the eventual martyrdom of James and Peter? Some have taken the reality of the words about being put to death (21:16) and not a hair of one's head perishing to mean that some will be taken and others will be preserved. But this seems to nullify the whole tone of assurance. Most likely, "not a hair of your head will perish" refers to ultimate deliverance and salvation in Christ's kingdom. Some will suffer and some will die, but none of Jesus' followers will suffer spiritual or eternal loss. On earth, everyone will die, but believers in Jesus will be saved for eternal life. It is reassuring to know that even when you feel completely abandoned, the Holy Spirit will stay with you. He will comfort you, protect you, and give you the words you need. This assurance can give you the courage and hope to stand firm for Christ no matter how difficult the situation.

21:20 **"When you see Jerusalem being surrounded by armies, you will know that its desolation is near."**NIV Luke 21:20-24 refers not to the end times (the warning for that is recorded in 17:30-36) but to the coming destruction of the city of Jerusalem that would occur in A.D. 70. Some have taken these words to have been written after the event happened, dating Luke after the destruction of Jerusalem. But we can accept these words as Jesus' prophecy of what was soon to come. The verb "being surrounded" pictures the coming siege of the city. Jesus' words in the next verses explain what the people should do quickly before the city would be completely surrounded and put under siege.

For an ancient city to be "surrounded" generally meant that the enemy army was putting it under siege. This usually spelled *deso-*

lation for the city because a siege meant that no one could enter
or leave the city. Usually a walled city got its food from the fields
outside the city, so as the enemy army waited them out, the
people in the city eventually would surrender or starve to death.

**21:21-22 "Then let those who are in Judea flee to the mountains, let
those in the city get out, and let those in the country not enter
the city. For this is the time of punishment in fulfillment of all
that has been written."**NIV With the armies coming to surround
the city, the people who are outside should *flee to the mountains,*
those in the city should *get out,* those in the country should not
attempt to *enter the city.* This was the opposite of the usual
advice—generally, in time of war, the people outside would go to
the city for protection. But not this time. *The time of punishment*
will have arrived; the city would face the full punishment for its
history of unfaithfulness and rebellion against God.

HANG ON
On July 4, 1952, Florence Chadwick attempted to do
something no woman had ever done before: swim the
twenty-one-mile channel from Catalina Island to the California
coast. For almost sixteen hours she valiantly fought the chilly
waters, fog, and even sharks, but then gave up . . . a half-mile
from the shore. If she had known how close she was to her
destination, she could have hung on and made it. Jesus tells us
that by standing firm, his followers will gain life. No matter what
the obstacles, no matter how vicious the opposition, keep
trying. Florence Chadwick did—two months after her first
attempt, she tried again and made it. You can do it, too. You
may be closer to the shore than you think. Get a brother or
sister to help you through the tough times and to hold you
accountable, and press on.

Many of Jesus' followers would live to see this happen. The
Jewish historian Josephus wrote that from A.D. 66, Jewish Zealots
clashed with the Romans. Many people realized that rebellion
would bring the wrath of the Empire, so they fled to Pella, a town
located in the mountains across the Jordan River. As Jesus had
said, this proved to be their protection, for when the Roman army
swept in, the nation and its capital city were destroyed.

**21:23-24 "How dreadful it will be in those days for pregnant women
and nursing mothers! There will be great distress in the land
and wrath against this people. They will fall by the sword and
will be taken as prisoners to all the nations. Jerusalem will be
trampled on by the Gentiles until the times of the Gentiles are
fulfilled."**NIV Jesus expressed sympathy and concern for those

who would have difficulty fleeing because they were *pregnant* or had small children. These people literally would be running for their lives from the *great distress* and *wrath against this people.* If they didn't get away, they would *fall by the sword* or *be taken as prisoners to all the nations.* According to the historian Josephus, ninety-seven thousand people were taken prisoner during the war and over one million were killed.

Jerusalem, the Holy City, *will be trampled on by the Gentiles until the times of the Gentiles are fulfilled.* These would have been horrifying words to any Jew. The "times of the Gentiles" began with Babylon's destruction of Jerusalem in 586 B.C. and the exile of the Jewish people. No longer an independent nation, Israel was under the control of Gentile rulers. In Jesus' day, Israel was governed by the Roman Empire, and a Roman general would "trample" the city in A.D. 70. Jesus was saying that the domination of God's people by his enemies would continue until God decided to end it. The "times of the Gentiles" refers not just to the repeated destructions of Jerusalem but also to the continuing and mounting persecution of God's people until the end.

BAD NEWS
Jesus' prophecy of the destruction of Jerusalem by the Gentiles must have sounded like something out of a nightmare to his listeners. Jerusalem—the Holy City—being desecrated by filthy Gentiles? That would be like Americans seeing Washington, D.C., captured and razed by foreign terrorists, only worse. Very few Americans consider Washington a holy city. Why would God allow such a catastrophe to occur? It's the universal question of why God allows bad things to happen to "good people." No one knows why, but everyone can know the one who knows. Perhaps eventually people will understand why they went through a period of suffering and trial. Whatever the case, trust that God sees your pain, your fears, and your losses and that he cares. God did not abandon Jerusalem forever, and he will not abandon you.

JESUS TELLS ABOUT HIS RETURN / 21:25-33 / 202

After predicting Jerusalem's destruction, Jesus described his second coming (21:27). It will be accompanied by all kinds of cosmic signs, instilling terror in those who are unprepared for the end but inspiring hope in those who are anticipating his return. Don't be caught unprepared; commit yourself to follow Jesus wholeheartedly and to pray fervently (21:34-36).

21:25 **"There will be signs in the sun, moon and stars. On the earth, nations will be in anguish and perplexity at the roaring and tossing of the sea."**^{NIV} The disciples had asked if there would be a sign (21:7); here Jesus gave the answer, but he went well beyond what they had asked. The original question focused on the destruction of the temple and the devastation of the nation. In his answer, Jesus spoke of his return in full glory without any of the limitations he had taken on by becoming human. Jesus was speaking not of his immediate resurrection but of his eventual, glorious return. Some of the signs would be in nature, for nature itself would experience change. As taught in Romans 8 and 2 Peter 3, the entire universe had become involved in humanity's fallen predicament; thus, the entire universe will be changed when humanity is changed. There will be a variety of changes—the *sun* going dark, the *moon* not being seen, *stars* falling, heavenly bodies being shaken (see Matthew 24:29). The "roaring sea" shows that nature will be chaos from one end of the earth to the other (see Psalm 46:2-4; Isaiah 17:12). These words also recall the words of the prophets (Isaiah 13:10; Joel 2:10-11). What Jesus described here, John saw in his vision of the end times recorded in Revelation: "I watched as he opened the sixth seal. There was a great earthquake. The sun turned black . . . , the whole moon turned blood red, and the stars in the sky fell to earth. . . . The sky receded like a scroll, rolling up" (Revelation 6:12-14 NIV).

21:26 **"People will faint from fear and foreboding of what is coming upon the world, for the powers of the heavens will be shaken."**^{NRSV} Persecutions and natural disasters will cause great sorrow in the world—*people will faint from fear and foreboding.* When believers see these events happening, they should realize that the return of their Messiah is near and that they can look forward to his reign of justice and peace. Rather than being terrified by what is happening in the world, believers should confidently await the Lord's return, an event that will shake the very heavens.

21:27 **"Then everyone will see the Son of Man arrive on the clouds with power and great glory."**^{NLT} The signs will occur, and afterwards *everyone will see the Son of Man arrive on the clouds with power and great glory.* Jesus' return will be unmistakable. Jesus had already explained that his coming would be known by all (17:22-24). The "clouds" will bring him from heaven to earth in the Second Coming, just as they had taken him (Acts 1:9-11). To the Jews, clouds signified divine presence (Exodus 13:21; 19:9; Psalm 97:1-2; Daniel 7:13). Jesus will return as the powerful, glorious, and divine Son of Man. There will be no doubt as to his identity. With *power and great glory* he will defeat Satan and all evil and establish his eternal reign.

21:28 **"When these things begin to take place, stand up and lift up your heads, because your redemption is drawing near."**[NIV] The picture of the coming persecutions and natural disasters is gloomy, but ultimately it should cause, not worry, but great joy. When believers see these events happening, they will know that the return of their Messiah is near, and they can look forward to his reign of justice and peace. Rather than being terrified by what is happening in the world, believers should confidently await Christ's return to bring justice and restoration to his people.

UPLIFTED
Watch what happens when someone wins a gold medal in an athletic competition: she throws her hands in the air and lifts up her face. It is so universal that it almost seems part of being human. Victory, or celebration of any kind, causes people to lift up their heads. Conversely, defeat or sorrow makes one's countenance fall. Jesus said that these signs of the times would be reason to "stand up and lift up your heads, because your redemption is drawing near." As frightful as some of those signs will be, Christians need not cower and feel cast down. The signs merely indicate that the King is returning. Does your faith cause you to walk around with your head lifted up, or your face downcast? If you belong to Jesus, hold your head up. He's coming back for you.

21:29-30 **Then he gave them this illustration: "Notice the fig tree, or any other tree. When the leaves come out, you know without being told that summer is near."**[NLT] Here Jesus answered the disciples' other question about "when" the events would occur (21:7); again, however, he answered the question more fully by talking about his second coming, not the destruction of Jerusalem. People knew when summer was coming by looking at *the fig tree* (or, for that matter, *any other tree*). Seeing the dry, brittle branches becoming tender, filled with sap, and beginning to bud, people knew *without being told that summer is near.*

21:31 **"So you also, when you see these things happening, know that the kingdom of God is near."**[NKJV] Just as people can interpret the seasons by watching the signs in nature, so they can know that when they *see these things happening . . . the kingdom of God is near.* The second coming of Jesus is both certain and near. The fulfillment of Jesus' prophecy would assure the disciples that the other prophecies he had given regarding the end times would also come true.

21:32 "I tell you the truth, this generation will certainly not pass away until all these things have happened."ᴺᴵⱽ "I tell you the truth" indicates that what Jesus was going to say would be very important. Jesus explained that *this generation will certainly not pass away until all these things have happened.* There are three main views of the meaning of this verse: (1) It refers only to those alive at the time Jesus spoke and who still would be alive at the destruction of Jerusalem; (2) it refers only to those who would experience the end times; (3) it refers both to the destruction of Jerusalem and the end times—the destruction of Jerusalem contains within itself the elements of the final end times and thus serves a precursor.

Jesus singled out *this generation.* The Greek word for "generation" is *genea;* it refers both to those living at a given time as well as to race or lineage (therefore, Jesus would have been speaking of the Jewish race). This makes the third view most likely.

21:33 "Heaven and earth will pass away, but My words will by no means pass away."ᴺᴷᴶⱽ Everything may change, and eventually everything will *pass away.* But one truth is absolutely, eternally certain: Jesus' words *will by no means pass away.* Everything he said will come true.

ETERNAL OR TEMPORAL?
Political trends come and go. Office seekers keep a close watch on each day's opinion polls. Fashions have a very short life expectancy. A life's savings can be lost or squandered. Music groups and other entertainers are the rage one day and forgotten the next. Every certainty that the world values so highly is temporal at best. Contrast them with Jesus' words: "Heaven and earth will pass away, but My words will by no means pass away." If your beliefs, values, and philosophy of life are not based on Christ's supremacy and his authoritative words, you are headed for eventual collapse. Your life's work will die when you do.

JESUS TELLS ABOUT REMAINING WATCHFUL / 21:34-38 / **203**

Jesus concluded his teaching on the end times (21:5-38) with a grave warning to his disciples. They were to guard against letting the worries of this life or the pleasures of the world distract them from the truth—especially the truth that the Son of Man would return, in judgment. They were to be always prepared for his return. They could be fully prepared by praying that God would help them persevere in faith until Christ's return.

21:34-35 **"Be careful, or your hearts will be weighed down with dissipation, drunkenness and the anxieties of life, and that day will close on you unexpectedly like a trap. For it will come upon all those who live on the face of the whole earth."**[NIV] Across the centuries, Christians have wondered when Jesus would return. Jesus had just said that his words would never pass away (21:33), and believers have taken that to heart, knowing that he *will* indeed return. But because no one knows when this great event will occur (Matthew 24:36), Jesus told his followers to *be careful* and not let the temptations or worries of this life distract them from watching and being ready for his return. (See 12:13-31, 35-48; 17:26-37 where Jesus warned against materialism and indulgence.) That day will come *unexpectedly,* and it will *come upon* everyone—no exceptions. There will be no opportunity for last-minute repentance or bargaining. The choice that each person has already made will determine his or her eternal destiny.

READY TO MOVE
Jesus told the disciples to keep a constant watch for his return. Although nearly two thousand years have passed since he spoke these words, their truth remains: Christ is coming again, and believers need to watch and be spiritually fit. This means working faithfully at the tasks God has given them. Don't let your mind and spirit be dulled by careless living, drinking, or the foolish pursuit of pleasure. Don't let life's anxieties overburden you. Be ready to move at God's command and welcome his return. "For you know quite well that the day of the Lord will come unexpectedly, like a thief in the night" (1 Thessalonians 5:2 NLT, see also Revelation 16:15).

21:36 **"Be always on the watch, and pray that you may be able to escape all that is about to happen, and that you may be able to stand before the Son of Man."**[NIV] For Jesus' followers to *be always on the watch, and pray* pictures an attitude toward life that seeks to stay away from evil and to follow and obey Jesus. Both watching and praying are volitional actions—as believers await Jesus' return, they work to further his kingdom. Only with a focus on him can believers *escape all that is about to happen,* and only through obedience to him will they *be able to stand before the Son of Man* when he returns. All believers must be ready and alert for Jesus' return, working for the kingdom, both because they know of the certainty of Christ's return and because they don't know *when* that return will happen. Being prepared demonstrates believers' faith and wholehearted obedience. For more on vigilance, see Life Application Commentary on Matthew 24:36-51. For more on prayer, see 18:1-8; Romans 8:26-39; Ephesians 6:18; Philippians 4:6-7; Hebrews 13:17-18.

WHEN SUFFERING STRIKES
Only days after telling the disciples to pray that they might escape persecution, Jesus asked God to spare him the agonies of the cross, if that was God's will (22:41-42). It is abnormal to *want* to suffer, but Jesus' followers should be willing to suffer if by doing so they can help build God's kingdom. Two wonderful promises help believers during suffering: God will always be with them (Matthew 28:20), and he will one day rescue them and give them eternal life (Revelation 21:1-4). Trust him for ultimate deliverance no matter what you may experience.

21:37-38 **Every day Jesus went to the Temple to teach, and each evening he returned to spend the night on the Mount of Olives. The crowds gathered early each morning to hear him.**[NLT] During this final week on the earth, Jesus went *every day* to the temple to teach the people (samples of that teaching have been recorded in chapters 20–21). He left the city in the evening and spent the night on the Mount of Olives, probably in the city of Bethany (Matthew 21:17). He returned the next morning, and already crowds of people had gathered to hear him.

LUKE 22

Luke began the final section of his Gospel (22:1–24:53) with a
short statement of the evil intentions of the chief priests and the
teachers of the law. They were diligently looking for an opportunity to have Jesus arrested and executed. Ironically, they were
plotting murder at the time of the Passover and the Festival of
Unleavened Bread, a time when Jews commemorated God's
deliverance of the Israelites from Egyptian slavery and the angel
of death.

The Jewish religious leaders had opposed Jesus from the beginning (6:7; 7:29-30; 11:53; 19:47), and their opposition had grown
more fierce in the last couple of days (see 20:1-8, 20-26, 27-40).
But here the plot thickened. Judas struck a deal with the Sanhedrin to betray Jesus for money.

Take special note that Satan was involved in this deception
(22:3). The Betrayal and eventually the Crucifixion involved more
than the jealous ambitions of a few religious leaders and the disillu-
sionment of one disciple; it involved a cosmic battle between God
and Satan, a battle in which Satan was completely defeated (as indicated by Jesus' resurrection, see 24:1-12; Colossians 2:15).

**22:1 The Festival of Unleavened Bread, which begins with the
Passover celebration, was drawing near.**ᴺᴸᵀ All Jewish males
over the age of twelve were required to go to Jerusalem for Passover. This would be followed by a seven-day festival called the
Festival of Unleavened Bread (Exodus 12:15-20). For these festivals, Jews from all over the Roman Empire would converge on
Jerusalem to celebrate one of the most important events in their
history. Passover took place on one night and at one meal, but the
Festival of Unleavened Bread would continue for a week. The
Passover celebration commemorated the night the Israelites were
freed from Egypt (Exodus 12) when God "passed over" homes

marked by the blood of a lamb. This was the last great plague on Egypt; in the unmarked homes the firstborn sons died. After this horrible disaster, Pharaoh let the Israelites go.

The *Festival of Unleavened Bread* recalled the Israelites' quick escape from Egypt when, because they wouldn't have time to let their bread rise, they baked it without leaven (yeast). Eventually the eight days (the day of Passover and the week of the Festival of Unleavened Bread) came to be called the Passover. Passover was celebrated on the fourteenth day of the Jewish month of Nisan (by our calendar, the last part of March and the first part of April).

22:2 The chief priests and the scribes were looking for a way to put Jesus to death, for they were afraid of the people.NRSV The religious leaders' opposition to Jesus had grown to such a point that they *were looking for a way to put Jesus to death.* There is a certain irony in seeing these leaders celebrating the Exodus while plotting to kill one of their own at the same time. But they had a problem: *they were afraid of the people.* Jesus was a popular teacher, and there were many Galileans in the city who would have rioted if Jesus had been taken captive. The religious leaders felt that they had to kill him because of his growing popularity (20:19; 22:6). They had been planning to do it all along (19:47-48). They first tried to trap him, but Jesus answered all their questions; then they, in turn, were publicly embarrassed because they could not answer Jesus' questions. The chief priests and scribes really had nothing against Jesus except their own sore egos for his having insulted them. So they continued to look for a way to get rid of Jesus. The Pharisees had been Jesus' main opponents, but here the ones who actually had political power to do something, *the chief priests,* took over. The *scribes* were the legal experts who doubtless were needed as the leaders attempted to build their case against Jesus.

22:3-4 Then Satan entered into Judas Iscariot, who was one of the twelve disciples, and he went over to the leading priests and captains of the Temple guard to discuss the best way to betray Jesus to them.NLT The leaders' opportunity to get to Jesus came in a manner they least expected. One of Jesus' closest followers, *one of the twelve disciples,* came to them willing to act as betrayer and accuser. Luke explained that *Satan entered into Judas Iscariot* (see also John 12:6; 13:2, 27). Satan's part in the betrayal of Jesus does not remove any of the responsibility from Judas. Disillusioned because Jesus was talking about dying rather than about setting up his kingdom, Judas may have been trying to force Jesus' hand and make him use his power to prove he was the Messiah. Or perhaps Judas, not understanding Jesus' mission, no longer believed that Jesus was God's chosen one. Whatever Judas thought, Satan assumed that Jesus' death would end Jesus' mission and thwart God's plan. Like Judas, Satan did not know that Jesus' death and resurrection were the most important parts of God's plan all along.

At the bottom line, Judas accepted money for his betrayal. Matthew recorded that Judas went to the leaders and said, "What will you give me if I betray him to you?" (Matthew 26:15 NRSV). Judas realized that his greedy desire for money could not be fulfilled if he followed Jesus, so he betrayed him in exchange for money from the religious leaders. Discovering a traitor among Jesus' followers greatly pleased the religious leaders. They had been having difficulty figuring out how to arrest Jesus, so when an offer of help came from this unexpected source, they took advantage of it. The *captains of the Temple guard* were officers in charge over a contingent of soldiers (probably Jews) who served in and around the temple complex.

BETRAYAL
Judas decided to betray Jesus, and thereby Judas became one of the worst villains in history. No one names a baby boy Judas today. His name has become synonymous with treachery, betrayal, and untrustworthiness. Yet, every believer has to face the ugly reality that there is a potential Judas in each person. Put in the right (or wrong) circumstance, facing the right amount of pressure, everyone is capable of betrayal, even betraying the Messiah. It's easy to feel contempt for Judas. It may be more helpful, and more honest, to ask God for the grace to never betray Jesus. Your task is to remain faithful to Jesus and not be Satan's pawn.

22:5-6 They were greatly pleased and agreed to give him money. So he consented and began to look for an opportunity to betray him to them when no crowd was present.NRSV Naturally these leaders, who had been looking for a way to kill Jesus (22:2), *were greatly pleased* at this unexpected defection from Jesus' ranks. Matthew alone recorded the exact amount of *money* Judas accepted to betray Jesus—thirty pieces of silver, the price of a slave (Exodus 21:32; Matthew 26:15). The religious leaders had planned to wait until after the Passover to take Jesus, but with Judas's unexpected offer, they accelerated their plans. Judas, in turn, *began to look for an opportunity to betray him to them* when there would be no Passover crowds to prevent Jesus' capture and no possibility of a riot.

DISCIPLES PREPARE FOR THE PASSOVER / 22:7-13 / 209

Jesus and the disciples were one group out of thousands looking for a place to celebrate the Passover meal in Jerusalem. Jesus' instructions to Peter and John reveal God's complete control over all the events surrounding Jesus' final days on earth. The room where the disciples would celebrate the Last Supper had been prepared (22:12), and Jesus knew every detail, even how Peter and John would find the room (22:10).

22:7-8 Then came the day of Unleavened Bread, on which the Passover lamb had to be sacrificed. So Jesus sent Peter and John, saying, "Go and prepare the Passover meal for us that we may eat it."NRSV Jesus and his disciples had been together long enough to celebrate Passover several times. Disciples often ate this celebratory meal with their teacher, so it was not unusual for Jesus to send Peter and John to prepare this Passover meal for him and his disciples.

The Passover meal included the sacrifice of a lamb because of the association with the Jews' exodus from Egypt. Before the Exodus, when the Jews were getting ready to leave, God told them to kill a lamb and put its blood on the doorframes of their houses. Then, they were to prepare the meat for food. As part of the Passover celebration, all the Jews killed the *Passover lamb* and prepared this special meal on the same day. *Peter and John* were given the responsibility of getting everything ready. They would have had to buy and prepare the lamb, as well as the unleavened bread, herbs, wine, and other ceremonial food.

This was either Wednesday night (the day before Passover) or Thursday of Jesus' last week (the night of the Passover meal). The highlight of the festival was the Passover meal, a family feast with the main course of lamb. The sacrifice of a lamb and the spilling of its blood commemorated Israel's escape from Egypt when the blood of a lamb painted on their doorposts had saved their firstborn sons from death. They then were to prepare the meat for food and eat it in their traveling clothes.

Scholars wonder whether this Last Supper was a Passover meal. Most likely it was. In the Gospel of John, Jesus seems to have had this meal on the evening before Passover. But Mark and Luke both identify this as a Passover meal (22:7-16; Mark 14:12-16). Certain descriptions in the Gospels indicate that this was a Jewish seder:

- A traditional Passover contains a hand-washing ceremony that could have been the opportunity for the foot washing (John 13:1-11).

- The use of bread and wine in the seder provided a natural way for Jesus to present the new covenant.
- The dipping of the unleavened bread into the preparation of bitter herbs comes from Passover (Mark 14:20; John 13:26).

Another question concerns whether this meal took place on Wednesday or Thursday. Traditionally, the Passover went from sundown (6:00 P.M.) on Thursday to sundown on Friday, the fifteenth day of the month of Nisan. Matthew, Mark, and Luke seem to indicate that Jesus and the disciples celebrated the Last Supper on Thursday evening. Several verses in John, however, suggest that the Last Supper occurred on a Wednesday (see John 13:1, 29; 18:28; 19:14, 31, 42).

The following three attempts have been made to solve this apparent problem:

1. There were two calendars being used to determine the day of Passover. The official calendar that the Pharisees and Sadducees followed was lunar. Jesus and the disciples followed a solar calendar, possibly used at Qumran (a monastic community by the Dead Sea). The two calendars differed by one day, so Jesus would have eaten the Passover meal one full day before the Jerusalem Passover. There have been no conclusive historic arguments to support this theory.
2. Jesus and his disciples had the Passover meal one day early in anticipation of Passover. This view explains John 18:28 and allows Jesus to be the Passover Lamb—crucified at the same time as the Passover lambs were slaughtered. If Jesus can heal on the Sabbath because he is the Lord of the Sabbath, he certainly could authorize eating the Passover meal one day early. This view is the best (though not perfect) harmony of the chronologies of all the Gospel writers. It allows for a full three-day period when Jesus was in the grave—not just part of Friday, all of Saturday, and part of Sunday—but from Thursday evening to Sunday morning.
3. Jesus and the disciples did eat the meal on the official day of Passover. In A.D. 30 (the year of Jesus' crucifixion), the Passover was celebrated on Thursday evening (the fourteenth of Nisan) and was immediately followed by the Feast of Unleavened Bread, which lasted from the fifteenth of Nisan (Friday) to the twenty-first of Nisan. During each day of this celebration, special meals *(chaggigah)* were eaten. According to this view, the other references in John are to the Feast of Unleavened Bread, not the Passover meal (John 13:29; 18:28; 19:14). In John 13:29, after the Passover meal, Judas went out to betray Jesus, while the disciples thought he went out to buy

provisions for the upcoming feast. In John 18:28 the Pharisees did not want to make themselves unclean by entering Pilate's palace and thereby be unable to partake of the feast. In John 19:14 "the preparation for the Passover" was not for the Passover meal but for the whole week that followed, which in New Testament times was called both the Passover and the Feast of Unleavened Bread.

SACRIFICE
The first Passover took place in Egypt, as the people of Israel prepared to receive God's protection from the slaying of the firstborn son and God's deliverance from bondage. The first Lord's Supper, the new covenant counterpart to Passover, took place in an upper room in Jerusalem, as the disciples prepared to witness the death of God's "firstborn" and the deliverance he purchased from the bondage of sin. In reading the Old Testament, it is disturbing how often the people of Israel forgot all that God did for them in the Exodus and in bringing them to the Promised Land. Do believers today do a better job of remembering and showing their gratitude as God's new covenant people? Take some time today to thank God for the incomparable gift of your redemption and salvation.

22:9-11 **"Where do you want us to prepare for it?" they asked. He replied, "As you enter the city, a man carrying a jar of water will meet you. Follow him to the house that he enters, and say to the owner of the house, 'The Teacher asks: Where is the guest room, where I may eat the Passover with my disciples?'"**NIV Peter and John needed to know *where* they should go to *prepare* the Passover meal. They would need a location big enough for Jesus and the twelve disciples. As out-of-towners from Galilee, they needed some direction. Jesus' answer indicates that he had, in advance, made many of these preparations. It was not left to chance. Jesus knew that he needed safety and security in order to avoid being taken prematurely. The time in the upper room was a precious time for Jesus and his disciples, as the record of the conversation and teaching shows (recorded in John 13–17).

A prearranged signal, for safety and security purposes, would lead Peter and John to the home where they could set up and prepare the Passover meal. As they entered Jerusalem, they would see *a man carrying a jar of water.* Ordinarily women, not men, went to the well and brought home the water. So this man would have stood out in the crowd. They should follow this man to his house, and the owner of that house would show them to the room where they would eat together. This private location kept the plans secret—even Judas would not know their destination until they arrived.

Tradition says that this may have been Mark's home (the writer of the Gospel). If this speculation is true, the owner of the house would have been Mark's father and one of Jesus' followers. He knew exactly who *the Teacher* was and probably knew the disciples by sight. The disciples did as Jesus directed and made preparations for the others.

22:12-13 **"He will show you a large upper room, all furnished. Make preparations there." They left and found things just as Jesus had told them. So they prepared the Passover.**^{NIV} The owner of the house to which Peter and John would be led would *show [them] a large upper room, all furnished.* Many homes had large upstairs rooms, sometimes with stairways both inside and outside the house. This room was large enough to accommodate Jesus and his twelve disciples for a banquet at a large table with reclining couches. It seems that Jesus had prearranged this because he already knew what the room looked like—it was large, furnished, and ready. Again this indicates a prearrangement on Jesus' part to have security and privacy during this last supper with his disciples.

As before, when two disciples went to get the donkey for Jesus to ride into Jerusalem (19:29-32), these two disciples *found things just as Jesus had told them.* The preparations for the Passover would have included setting the table, buying and roasting the Passover lamb, and making the unleavened bread, sauces, and other ceremonial food and drink that were a traditional part of every Passover meal.

JESUS AND THE DISCIPLES HAVE THE LAST SUPPER / 22:14-30 / **211**

Although the Gospel of John goes into great detail recounting what Jesus said and did during his last Passover meal (see John 13:1–17:26), Luke's Gospel merely highlights Jesus' institution of the Lord's Supper (22:17-20), his prediction of his betrayal (22:21-23), his teaching on service (22:24-27), and his prediction of Peter's denial (22:31-34).

This was Jesus' final meal with his disciples; he clearly tells them this (see 22:15-16). But instead of trying to learn as much as they could from him, the disciples were arguing about who was the greatest (an argument they had had before, see 9:46). Jesus encouraged them to change their thinking. Instead of trying to be the greatest, they needed to strive to serve (22:26). At this last meal with them, Jesus physically demonstrated his own willingness to serve the disciples, by stooping to wash their feet (see John 13:1-17).

22:14 When the hour came, Jesus and his apostles reclined at the table.^{NIV} Peter and John had been sent ahead to prepare the meal; then at the appointed time to eat, *Jesus and his apostles* arrived and assumed their seats at the table. The Passover meal was supposed to be eaten in Jerusalem after sunset and finished before midnight. The disciples and Jesus took their places on the reclining couches around the table. During such an important meal as the Passover, everyone would recline at the table, symbolizing the freedom the people had gained after the very first Passover and their subsequent release from slavery in Egypt.

THE ALREADY AND THE NOT YET
Jesus' last supper with his disciples is a poignant picture of something all Christians experience: the fulfillment of their present relationship with him and the longing for their future completion in him. Jesus "eagerly desired" to share the Passover meal with his closest friends, the disciples; at the same time Jesus looked forward to its ultimate fulfillment at his return. Believers today live an in-between life as followers of Christ. They already experience the peace, forgiveness, and satisfaction, that come from knowing Jesus. Yet they also long for the consummation of their faith, that day when believers will be perfected and completed in his presence. Do you sometimes feel that tension? If so, don't worry. It is the normal experience of God's people awaiting the return of Christ.

22:15-16 And he said to them, "I have eagerly desired to eat this Passover with you before I suffer. For I tell you, I will not eat it again until it finds fulfillment in the kingdom of God."^{NIV} Jesus had *eagerly desired* this quiet time with his disciples. We know from John's Gospel that a great deal was said during the Passover meal. These would be Jesus' "last words"—thus words of vital importance to these to whom he was entrusting the carrying on of his work. Jesus knew that his time to *suffer* would soon come and that he would not celebrate this event again until *it finds fulfillment in the kingdom of God.* The mention of "fulfillment" reveals the complete and ultimate significance of the entire Passover celebration. While Passover commemorated a past event (i.e., Israel's escape from Egypt when the blood of a lamb painted on their doorframes saved their firstborn sons from death), it also foreshadowed Jesus' work on the cross. As the spotless Lamb of God, his blood would be spilled in order to save his people from the penalty of death brought by sin. At that time, *in* *the kingdom of God* (see 22:18), those who belong to Christ will sit down at a glorious banquet (see 13:29; 14:15-24; Isaiah 25:6-8; Revelation 19:7-9). Jesus will not celebrate Passover until God's plan is complete.

22:17-18 **After taking the cup, he gave thanks and said, "Take this and divide it among you. For I tell you I will not drink again of the fruit of the vine until the kingdom of God comes."**NIV This Gospel mentions two cups of wine, while Matthew and Mark mention only one. The reason for the difference may be that Matthew and Mark were speaking only of the final cup of wine drunk in this special Passover meal—the cup whereby Jesus instituted the new covenant. This cup of wine probably would have been different from those drunk during the Passover celebration. Luke may have been speaking of another cup of wine—perhaps the fourth cup.

In the traditional Passover meal, the wine is served four times, symbolizing the four-part promise of redemption found in Exodus 6:6-7. (1) "I will bring you out"; (2) "I will rescue you from their bondage"; (3) "I will redeem you"; and (4) "I will take you as My people, and I will be your God" (NKJV).

There was a traditional program for the meal. First would come a blessing of the festival and the wine, followed by drinking the first cup of wine (this also made the meal special because water was usually served with meals). Next, the food would be brought out. Then the youngest son would ask why this night was distinguished from others. The father would answer with the story of the Exodus and would point to each item on the table as he explained its symbolic significance (for example, bitter herbs symbolized the bitter bondage of slavery in Egypt). This would be followed by praise to God for past and future redemption (taken from the first part of the Hallel in Psalms 113–114). Then the second cup of wine would be drunk. After the second cup, the bread would be blessed, broken, distributed, and then eaten with bitter herbs and a fruit-paste dish.

This would be followed by eating the meal. The Passover meal included roasted lamb that had been sacrificed in the temple. At the end of the meal, the father would bless a third cup of wine, which would be followed by singing the second part of the Hallel (from Psalms 115–118). A fourth cup of wine would conclude the meal.

Jesus made the vow to abstain from wine before the fourth cup, which traditionally was drunk after the recitation of these words: "I will take you as My people, and I will be your God." Jesus reserved the drinking of this cup for the future restoration. This powerful scene is accented by Jesus' taking the third cup, saying, "I will redeem you," sharing the cup with the disciples, and then pledging that together they would finish this celebration in the kingdom of God (see also 14:15; Isaiah 25:6; Revelation 3:20; 19:6-9). Because Jesus would be raised, so his followers will be raised. One day all believers will be together again in God's new kingdom (see 11:2) "The kingdom of God" refers to the time of the complete fulfillment of the rule of God. The *fruit of the vine* in the kingdom will be new like Jeremiah's new covenant (Jeremiah 31:31-34). When Jesus celebrates with his people, all God's promises, power, and authority will be fully realized.

IN REMEMBRANCE
In a memorial service, words are spoken or actions taken to pay tribute to the deceased. People may say, "I'm doing this because I know that's the way John would have wanted it." Think how inappropriate it would be for someone to clearly go against the deceased's wishes or principles. When Christians celebrate Communion, they do more than hold a memorial service. The Savior who died is alive and well, and he is present and involved in Communion. How much more, then, should believers want to conduct themselves—actions, attitudes, thoughts, and words—in a manner consistent with the love and compassion of Jesus. The next time you participate in the Lord's Supper, give serious consideration to how you will live "in remembrance of him."

22:19 And He took bread, gave thanks and broke it, and gave it to them, saying, "This is My body which is given for you; do this in remembrance of Me."NKJV Jesus *took* the loaf of unleavened *bread, gave thanks and broke it.* Because bread was considered a gift from God, it was irreverent to cut bread with a knife, so bread would be torn (or broken) with the hands. Jesus gave the bread to the disciples to eat with the sauce. As he did so, he gave this Passover practice an entirely new meaning. Just as the Passover celebrated deliverance from slavery in Egypt, so the Lord's Supper celebrates deliverance from sin by Christ's death. Jesus told the disciples: *"This is My body which is given for you."* Jesus used literal terms to describe a figurative truth. Just as he had so many times said, "I am" the door, the bread, the light, the vine, so the bread symbolized Jesus' work of salvation on behalf of humanity. His words "this is My body" symbolize the spiritual nourishment believers obtain from a personal relationship with the Savior. It was Jesus' pledge of his personal presence with all his disciples whenever they would partake of this meal. That his body would "be given" pictures the cross on which Jesus gave his body in death, allowing it to be broken so that believers could receive life.

Jesus told the disciples to eat the broken bread *in remembrance of Me.* He wanted them to remember his sacrifice, the basis for forgiveness of sins, and also his friendship that they could continue to enjoy through the work of the Holy Spirit.

Christians differ in their interpretation of the meaning of the commemoration of the Lord's Supper. There are three main views: (1) the bread and wine actually become Christ's body and blood; (2) the bread and wine remain unchanged, yet Christ is spiritually present by faith in and through them; (3) the bread and wine, which remain unchanged, are lasting memorials of Christ's sacrifice. No matter which view they favor, all Christians agree that the Lord's Supper commemorates Christ's death on the cross for their sins and points to the coming of his kingdom in glory. When Christians partake of it, they show their deep gratitude for Christ's work on their behalf. And through the Lord's Supper, their faith is strengthened.

Although the exact meaning of Communion has been strongly debated throughout church history, Christians still take bread and wine in remembrance of their Lord and Savior, Jesus Christ. Do not neglect participating in the Lord's Supper. Let it remind you of what Christ did for you.

> The real teaching of the Bible is that in the atoning death of his Son, instead of laying the punishment of guilty man upon an innocent third person, God took the shame and suffering due to man upon himself; and so far from that being unjust and cruel, it is amazing grace!
>
> *R. A. Torrey*

PAYMENT
Imagine that you are in an upscale jewelry store when a child walks in and intentionally destroys a very valuable item. The store owner, understandably outraged, demands that the child come up with a way to pay for what he has done. The child, holding out his empty pockets, says he doesn't have the money to pay for it, and that his allowance is only a dollar a week. He'll never be able to pay off his debt. Into this impasse a man steps forward and says, "I have the money, and I'll pay the boy's debt. Is that acceptable?" That is, in effect, what Christ did when he enacted the new covenant. Under the old covenant with its system of sacrifices, sins were "atoned for" by animal sacrifice. But it was never enough, and it wasn't permanent. The new covenant, however, has been ushered in by the blood of Christ—the ultimate, completely sufficient, and final payment for sin. How do you respond to God's gracious offer—with grateful acceptance, or callous indifference?

22:20 **Likewise He also took the cup after supper, saying, "This cup is the new covenant in My blood, which is shed for you."**[NKJV] This Gospel records two cups of wine, while Matthew and Mark mention only one. As noted above, in a traditional Passover meal, wine is served four times. Most likely the cup mentioned in this verse was the third cup; the words of 22:17-18 were spoken about the fourth and final cup that Jesus did not drink, vowing first to complete his mission before drinking again of wine. Jesus took this cup and explained, *"This cup is the new covenant in My blood, which is shed for you."*

RESPONSIBILITY
People have argued for centuries about whether or not Judas was to blame for what he did, or whether he merely played the part God had written out for him. While there can be no doubt that what Judas did was part of God's sovereign plan of redemption, Luke 22:22 also makes it clear that Judas was responsible. How easy it is for people to blame their sins on others—even God! They use his sovereignty and his omnipotence as an excuse for their own moral and spiritual failures. Is there a sin or lack of obedience in some area in your life that you need to face and for which you need to take responsibility? Stop making excuses. Confess, repent, and let God forgive you and restore your relationship with him.

In Old Testament times, God agreed to forgive people's sins if they brought animals for the priests to sacrifice. When this sacrificial system was inaugurated, the agreement between God and sinful humanity was sealed with the blood of animals (Exodus 24:8). But animal blood did not in itself remove sin (only God can forgive sin), and animal sacrifices had to be repeated day by day and year after year. Jesus instituted a "new covenant," or agreement, between humans and God. Under this new covenant, Jesus would die in the place of sinners. Unlike the blood of animals, his blood would be "shed for" his people and would truly remove the sins of all who put their faith in him. This event foreshadowed Jesus' work on the cross. As the spotless Lamb of God, his blood would be spilled in order to save his people from the penalty of death brought by sin.

22:21 **"But see, the one who betrays me is with me, and his hand is on the table."**[NRSV] Verses 3-6 reveal that the betrayer was Judas Iscariot. Although the other disciples were confused by Jesus' words, Judas knew what he meant. The betrayer was there among them, joining them in the meal, one of Jesus' chosen twelve disciples. Jesus' words allude to Psalm 41:9: "Even my close friend, whom I trusted, he who shared my bread, has lifted up his heel against me" (NIV).

22:22 "For the Son of Man is going as it has been determined, but woe to that one by whom he is betrayed!"^{NRSV} Jesus death' was part of the divine purpose; Jesus recognized that, saying, *"The Son of Man is going as it has been determined."* But this does not remove responsibility from *that one by whom he is betrayed.* Judas allowed his desires to place him in a position where Satan could manipulate him (22:3). In betraying Jesus, Judas made the greatest mistake in history. But the fact that Jesus knew Judas would betray him doesn't mean that Judas was a puppet of God's will. Judas made the choice. God knew what that choice would be and confirmed it. Judas didn't lose his relationship with Jesus; rather, he had never found Jesus in the first place. Jesus pronounced "woe" on him, meaning divine judgment was coming. It was an expression of grief for the consequences that Judas would bring upon himself. Judas was "doomed to destruction" (John 17:12 NIV) because he was never saved. He, by his own choice, betrayed God's Son into the hands of soldiers (22:48). Jesus knew that Judas's life of evil would not change; he was a devil (John 6:70) and a thief (John 12:4-6). Judas's betrayal of Jesus was part of God's sovereign plan (Psalm 41:9; Zechariah 11:12-13; Matthew 20:18; 26:20-25; Acts 1:16, 20).

It must be remembered that while Judas betrayed him, all the disciples fled, and Peter even denied ever knowing Jesus. But all those disciples came to Jesus for forgiveness; Judas never took that opportunity. Instead, he killed himself (Matthew 27:3-5).

22:23 Then the disciples began to ask each other which of them would ever do such a thing.^{NLT} Apparently Judas was not obvious as the betrayer. After all, he was the one the disciples were trusting to keep the money (John 12:4-6). So *the disciples began to ask each other which of them would ever do such a thing.* Matthew wrote that even Judas asked this question: "Then Judas, the one who would betray him, said, 'Surely not I, Rabbi?'" (Matthew 26:25 NIV). Jesus answered Judas, "You yourself have said it." This answer was not understood by the disciples as identifying Judas as the betrayer; if it was, they would have stopped him from going out. Only Judas knew that Jesus had identified him as the betrayer. Judas had been able to keep his treachery a secret from everyone, except the one he would betray.

22:24 A dispute also arose among them as to which one of them was to be regarded as the greatest.^{NRSV} The most important event in human history was about to take place, and the disciples were still arguing about their prestige in the kingdom! Reading about this *dispute,* you may say, "This was no time to worry about status." But the disciples, wrapped up in their own concerns, did not perceive what Jesus had been trying to tell them about his approaching death and resurrection. The disciples had already had this discussion (9:46), and Jesus had told them that they should be like children— the least among them would be the greatest (9:48). As before, they were either ignoring his words about his death or wondering who would take over when Jesus died.

In this private moment with Christ, first Judas, then the rest of the disciples portrayed the two pitfalls the church has to face. The first pitfall involves betrayal, defection, and apostasy—as portrayed by Judas's betrayal of Jesus. The second pitfall is individual striving for power—as exemplified in the disciples seeking promotion, recognition, and self-acclaim. To avoid these pitfalls, Christians must stay loyal to Christ and serve him sacrificially and humbly.

TRUE GREATNESS
Most people occasionally dream of being great in the eyes of the world. In those dreams, they imagine themselves as famous, wealthy, powerful, sought-after. Perhaps they see themselves having meetings with presidents and prime ministers, shielding their eyes from the glare of the television cameras, capturing the attention of the world through their accomplishments and reputation. There is nothing wrong about having such dreams, of course, but Jesus' definition of greatness has very little to do with any of that. Jesus said greatness is defined in terms of servanthood and humility— quite a contrast from the world's idea. If by God's grace you attain any greatness in the eyes of the world, thank him for it. But never forget that those who are great in God's eyes are those who forget about themselves and give themselves away to others in Jesus' name.

22:25-26 But he said to them, "The kings of the Gentiles lord it over them; and those in authority over them are called benefactors. But not so with you; rather the greatest among you must become like the youngest, and the leader like one who serves."NRSV The world's system of leadership varies greatly from leadership in God's kingdom. Worldly leaders are often selfish and arrogant as they claw their way to the top. *Benefactor* was a title used in the Greek and Roman societies for princes, Roman emperors, and the gods. It was a reciprocal relationship in that the clients who received support from the benefactors were required to recognize their authority and give public adulation to the benefactor. But among Christians, the *leader* is to be the one who *serves* best. There are different styles of leadership—some lead through public speaking, some through administering, some through relationships. Whatever the style, every Christian leader needs a servant's heart.

Jesus immediately corrected their attitudes, for they would be unable to accomplish their mission if they did not love and serve one another. There would be a big difference between the kingdoms they saw in the world and God's kingdom, which they had not yet experienced. In Gentile kingdoms of the world, people's greatness depended on their social standing, place in the family line (such as being the eldest), or family name. Jesus explained, however, that his kingdom would be like nothing they had ever experienced.

LEADERSHIP
Who do you think of as being a great leader? A political figure, perhaps, or a military general or head coach of a sports team? No doubt there are many in those fields who command people's respect and attention. But Jesus said that leadership is not primarily a matter of getting people to jump when ordered. Instead, he said a leader is to be a servant. It's true that not everyone will respect or even understand servant leadership, but Jesus never promised that faithfulness to God would be popular—only rewarded. What is your leadership style? Do you expect those under your authority to serve you, or do you serve them? Jesus' model is clear: true leadership is servant leadership.

22:27 "For who is greater, the one who is at the table or the one who serves? Is it not the one at the table? But I am among you as one who serves."NRSV The answer to Jesus' question is obvious— *the one who is at the table* is greater than *the one who serves*. But Jesus turned everything upside down. He was by far the greatest, for he was God himself. But he did not come to sit at the table and be served; he came *as one who serves*. Greatness is determined by servanthood. The truly great leader places his or her needs last, as Jesus exemplified: "Just as the Son of Man came not to be served but to serve, and to give his life a ransom for many" (Matthew 20:28 NRSV, see also Matthew 23:8-12; Mark 10:45). Jesus was the Son of God, but his glory was hidden in the form of a servant who would pay the ultimate price to serve others: He would give his life.

Because Jesus served, his disciples must also seek to serve, not seek to occupy better positions. Being a "servant" did not mean occupying a servile position; rather, it meant having an attitude of life that freely attended to others' needs without expecting or demanding anything in return. An attitude of service brings true greatness in God's kingdom.

22:28-30 **"You are those who have stood by me in my trials. And I confer on you a kingdom, just as my Father conferred one on me, so that you may eat and drink at my table in my kingdom and sit on thrones, judging the twelve tribes of Israel."**NIV The disciples had *stood by* Jesus throughout the three years of ministry and the hardships it often entailed (9:58). They had been willing to be servants, sharing the gospel message and healing people through Jesus' power (9:1-6). The words "I confer on you a kingdom" refer to Jesus' promise that because of their faith in him, they would enjoy the promised messianic banquet with him, able to *eat and drink at [his] table in [his] kingdom.* This would happen, not immediately, but in due time. They would receive all that he had promised.

In addition, they would also *sit on thrones, judging the twelve tribes of Israel.* The "thrones" and "tribes" can be understood in different ways.

- If taken literally, the twelve apostles will rule the tribes of Israel at Christ's return (although this leaves open the question of Judas's betrayal, the addition of Matthias as a disciple to replace Judas, and the role of Paul's apostleship). The exact time and nature of that role is not specified.
- If not taken literally, then the disciples will oversee the church, which will have a prominent place in God's plan.
- This may be a promise to Jesus' closest disciples (probably Paul would be included), who will have a special place of authority in God's kingdom. But the entire church, meaning all believers, is included.

The second understanding (the disciples will oversee the church) seems likely. Jesus Christ gave the kingdom to the new Israel, his church—all faithful believers. His coming ushered in the kingdom of God with all believers as its citizens. God may allow persecution to continue for a while, but the destiny of his followers is to possess the kingdom and live with him forever. The apostles, and all believers, can trust that Jesus will surely accomplish all that he promised.

JESUS PREDICTS PETER'S DENIAL / 22:31-38 / *212*

After describing the disciples' glorious roles in the kingdom of God (22:29-30), Jesus turned to the immediate trials they would face. First, Jesus warned Peter of his future denial. Second, Jesus warned them all to prepare themselves for the coming troubles, by rhetorically commanding them to keep their purses, bags, and swords. Peter and the disciples' response appears to be commendable. Peter enthusiastically reaffirmed his commitment to Jesus, even if it meant death or imprison- ment. The disciples were preparing themselves to withstand the enemy. But in all their enthusiasm and energy, they should have taken a clue from what Jesus was doing: he was praying. He had already prayed for Peter (22:32), and he would soon spend the entire night in prayer (22:39-46).

22:31-32 **"Simon, Simon, Satan has asked to sift you as wheat."**NIV Luke alone recorded these solemn words to *Simon* (Peter) and described Satan's role in the upcoming difficulties all the disciples (the word "you" is plural), but especially Peter, were soon to face. Satan *asked to sift* Peter *as wheat,* meaning a severe trial. These words recall when Satan asked God for permission to test Job (Job 1:7; 2:2). Satan wanted to crush Simon Peter and the other disciples like grains of wheat. He hoped to find only chaff and blow it away. But Jesus assured Peter that although his faith would falter, it would not be destroyed, for he said, **"But I have prayed for you that your own faith may not fail; and you, when once you have turned back, strengthen your brothers."**NRSV Jesus had intervened on Peter's behalf, asking that Peter's *faith may not fail.* Jesus prayed for faith, not the removal of the test. Apparently he knew that Peter would fail; otherwise, there would be no need for Peter to "turn back." Yet Jesus was confident of this turning back and also understood that, having faced this trial, Peter would be able to *strengthen* his *brothers* (that is, his fellow disciples, and later his fellow believers). Indeed, the book of 1 Peter deals entirely with encouragement for believers who are undergoing trials and difficulties. Peter became a source of strength to many who needed it.

RESTORED
Peter was certainly no stranger to failure. But Jesus made sure that Peter didn't wallow in it. He prayed for Peter and encouraged him to "bounce back" and be a source of strength to the other disciples. The Bible and church history reveal that Peter did indeed come back from his failure to lead the early church. Satan attempts to destroy believers by accusing them of disloyalty and lack of integrity. Whatever your failure(s), learn a lesson from Peter. Remember that Jesus intercedes for you. Focus on your love for Jesus and your desire to do his will. Keep in the forefront of your mind that people need your example and leadership.

22:33 **But he said to Him, "Lord, I am ready to go with You, both to prison and to death."**[NKJV] Peter seemed to ignore Jesus' words regarding intercession on his behalf and simply answered with bravado, *"Lord, I am ready to go with You, both to prison and to death."* Peter considered his loyalty to exceed anyone's, for he declared that suffering and death could not dissuade him.

22:34 **Then He said, "I tell you, Peter, the rooster shall not crow this day before you will deny three times that you know Me."**[NKJV] Peter surely wanted to believe that his loyalty to Jesus would be strong, but Jesus already knew that Satan had asked to sift Peter and that Peter would initially fail the test. Instead of being the only loyal disciple, Peter would, in fact, prove to be more disloyal than the other ten. Not only would he desert Jesus, but he would also *deny three times* that he even knew Jesus. And this would happen in the space of the next few hours. Before the night was over (i.e., before the rooster crowed at dawn's first light), Peter would deny the Master to whom he claimed such loyalty. This was supernatural knowledge—why Jesus chose to tell this to Peter is unknown. But despite knowing about it, Peter did not stop it from happening. He did deny his Lord, just as Jesus had said.

22:35 **Then Jesus asked them, "When I sent you out to preach the Good News and you did not have money, a traveler's bag, or extra clothing, did you lack anything?" "No," they replied.**[NLT] Here Jesus would reverse his earlier advice regarding how to travel (9:3). Before, Jesus had sent the disciples out without extra resources, wanting them to depend on God and on other believers to meet their basic needs. The disciples remembered that they did not *lack anything* during that preaching tour.

A PRACTICAL FAITH

Trust God and keep your powder dry. That dusty piece of wisdom, dating from the Revolutionary War era, says that believers should do whatever they reasonably can to fend for themselves, and then place their faith in God. Jesus gave similar advice to the disciples (22:35-36). Once before he had sent them out to preach, telling them not to worry about pedestrian things like a change of clothes or money with which to buy food. And that trip had worked out just fine, as the disciples well remembered. But now—with his death looming just over the horizon—now it was time to think of more pragmatic concerns. Are you facing a significant decision or even a crisis? Do whatever you can legally, morally, and ethically to prepare yourself, and then trust God's gracious provision for you.

22:36 **He said to them, "But now, the one who has a purse must take it, and likewise a bag. And the one who has no sword must sell his cloak and buy one."**NRSV *But now,* Jesus explained, the situation was different. His followers needed to be prepared—taking along a purse, a bag, and a sword. They were to take full provisions. These words have caused much question. How can these words be reconciled with Jesus' previous instructions in 9:3 and his apparent call for bearing a weapon, with his condemnation of its use when he rebuked the use of the sword against the high priests's servant (22:49-51)? Most likely these words were meant to be taken as Jesus' explanation of a time of impending crisis. Difficult days lay ahead. No longer would they be able to count on the kind of reception they had gotten, as recorded in 9:1-5 and 10:1-9. They would need to take care of themselves. Surely the sword was for protection rather than aggressive action. The church maintained a stance of nonviolence when faced with persecution (see Acts 4:25-31; 8:1-3; 9:1-2; 12:1-5). They would need courage more than they would need their cloaks (a clothing item of great importance).

22:37 **"It is written: 'And he was numbered with the transgressors'; and I tell you that this must be fulfilled in me. Yes, what is written about me is reaching its fulfillment."**NIV Jesus quoted from Isaiah 53:12 and said that those very words were about to be *fulfilled* in him. Jesus was explaining that the words of Isaiah 53, the suffering Servant, were written about him. Jesus would be *numbered with the transgressors,* pointing to his death for sinners. His would be a substitutionary death; Jesus would take the place of transgressors, taking their punishment for them. Because of all that was about to happen to Jesus, the disciples would be in danger too.

22:38 **"Lord," they replied, "we have two swords among us." "That's enough," he said.**NLT The disciples did not understand. The "fulfillment" of which Jesus spoke referred to his death, but the disciples were busy checking for arms with which to defend themselves. They came up with *two swords* among them, hardly enough to defend them all. But Jesus said, *"That's enough,"* meaning either that this was not the time to think of using swords or that he'd had enough of their discussion. In either case, mention of a sword vividly communicated the trials they soon would face.

JESUS AGONIZES IN THE GARDEN / 22:39-46 / **223**

Throughout his Gospel, Luke highlighted Jesus' consistent prayer life (3:21; 5:16; 6:12; 9:18, 28-29; 11:1; 18:1-14; 22:32). This section provides an intimate look at Jesus' dependence on prayer, right before his greatest hour of need. For Jesus, prayer was not an escape, but a respite; not a way to avoid difficulty, but a way to strengthen himself to endure it. Neither was Jesus' prayer devoid of feeling; he laid out his heart before the Lord. But in the end, he submitted to God's perfect will (22:42). The importance that Jesus gave to prayer is clearly revealed in his profound disappointment with the disciples. They had fallen asleep, instead of spending the entire night praying. Their foolish actions would make them more vulnerable to temptation, when they faced the troubles that were coming.

Evaluate your schedule in light of Jesus' attitude toward prayer. Are you spending enough time in prayer?

PRAY FOR STRENGTH
Is there someone in your life who has demonstrated his or her love for you over and over again, to the point where you know beyond doubt that this person is for you and has your best interests at heart? If so, be very thankful, and ask yourself: would you intentionally do something to hurt that person, cause him or her grief, or bring shame or disgrace on him or her? You would never want to treat such a person that way. That's why Jesus told the disciples that the way to overcome temptation was through prayer. Communing with God is the most powerful motivation believers have to keep his will and honor his name. Are you experiencing intense temptation, perhaps sexually, financially, legally, or ethically? When that temptation shows its seductive face, look past it and into the eyes of the one who loves you enough to die for you—and do what honors him the most.

22:39 Then, accompanied by the disciples, Jesus left the upstairs room and went as usual to the Mount of Olives.^NLT The disciples and Jesus finished the Passover meal and the lengthy teaching recorded in John (John 13:31–17:26); then they *left the upstairs room and went as usual to the Mount of Olives.* Apparently this was a favorite place for Jesus and the disciples. Up to this point, Jesus and the disciples had been returning each night to Bethany; but this time, Jesus only went as far as the Mount of Olives, located just to the east of Jerusalem. Jesus went up the southwestern slope to an olive grove called Gethsemane, which means "oil press." That Jesus went to a "usual" location shows his determination that his time had come. He could have been secretive, as he was in planning for the Passover meal, so that Judas would not know his destination ahead of time. But to go to the Mount of Olives meant that Judas would know right where to find him. Jesus went there to pray and to await his arrest.

TO NOT BE OVERCOME BY TEMPTATION

Scripture explains what to do to not be overcome by temptation.

Reference	Lesson about temptation
Genesis 3	Satan wants to see all believers stumble and will actively work to make it happen.
Genesis 39	When you are tempted, focus on your relationship with God and obey him.
2 Samuel 11:2-4	Temptation will come at weak spots and unexpected times.
Psalm 51:4	Temptation can lead to sin and its consequences.
Proverbs 7:1-5	Avoid temptation by storing up God's commands in your heart.
Matthew 4:1-11	Combat temptation by using the Word of God.
Matthew 6:13	God doesn't lead us into temptation, but sometimes he allows believers to be tested by it.
Matthew 8:7-9	Being tempted is not a sin, but you must not let temptation lead you into sin.
Matthew 26:40	Watch and pray to avoid falling into sin.
1 Corinthians 10:13	God will not allow temptations you cannot handle.
1 Timothy 6:11-12	To avoid temptation, you must fight as in a battle.
2 Timothy 2:22	At times you may need to turn and run from temptation.
Hebrews 2:16-18	Because Jesus Christ was tempted, he understands how you feel and knows how to help you resist.
James 1:12-16	You sometimes cause your own temptations.
James 4:7-8	Submit to God; resist the devil.

22:40 **There he told them, "Pray that you will not be overcome by temptation."**[NLT] Jesus asked the disciples to pray that they would *not be overcome by temptation* because he knew that he would soon be leaving them. Jesus also knew that they would need extra strength to face the temptations ahead—temptations to run away or to deny their relationship with him. They were about to see Jesus die. Would they still think he was the Messiah? The disciples' strongest temptation would undoubtedly be to think that they had been deceived.

22:41-42 **He withdrew about a stone's throw beyond them, knelt down and prayed, "Father, if you are willing, take this cup from me; yet not my will, but yours be done."**[NIV] During his life on earth, Jesus prayed constantly to his Father (5:16; 6:12; 9:28; 11:1; 18:1; 22:32). This night, Jesus again *prayed* to his Father, and Luke recorded the content of his prayer as he struggled with the task that lay before him. He

> Success is never final, failure is never fatal. It is courage that counts.
> *Winston Churchill*

withdrew about a stone's throw beyond them, knelt down and prayed. Jesus exposed his dread of the coming trials, but he also reaffirmed his commitment to do what God wanted. In deep anguish, he asked the Father to let the mission be accomplished some other way not requiring the agony of crucifixion, when he would become sin and be separated from the Father. The *cup* he spoke of meant the terrible agony he knew he would endure—not only the horror of the crucifixion but, even worse, the total separation from God that he would have to experience in order to die for the world's sins. The "cup" in the Old Testament could be a symbol of blessing (Psalms 16:5; 23:5) or of cursing (Psalms 11:6; 75:8). A whole nation could "drink a cup" of either blessings or curses (Isaiah 51:22; Jeremiah 25:15; 49:12; Ezekiel 23:31-33).

"I DON'T WANT TO, LORD"
Following Jesus may put believers in situations where they confront tough choices, where doing right will cost them physically, emotionally, or financially. At a time like that, you may tell God, "I don't want to do what you want me to do here. I do not want to pay the price." Jesus had a horrible choice in front of him: go to the cross and redeem fallen mankind, or avoid the suffering and death and let mankind be lost. He knew what was right, and he didn't want to go through with it. But he obeyed his Father. Are you in a crisis of obedience right now? It's all right to tell God you don't want to obey. He understands. Just be sure you do what he tells you in spite of your reluctance.

With the words "if you are willing, take this cup from me," Jesus was expressing his true feelings as a human being, but he was not denying or rebelling against God's will. Jesus knew about the coming suffering, isolation from God, and death he would have to endure to atone for the sins of the world. Jesus recoiled from sin, yet part of his task would be to take the sins of the whole world upon himself. This was the cup that he didn't want to drink. As God's Son, Jesus knew constant fellowship with the Father. Yet for a time on the cross he would have to be deprived of that fellowship. This, too, was a cup he hated to drink. The physical suffering would be horrible enough, but what

God's Son feared most was the cup of spiritual suffering—taking on sin and being separated from God (Hebrews 5:7-9).

Jesus was not trying to get out of his mission, however. He reaffirmed his desire to do what God wanted by saying, *"Yet not my will, but yours be done."* Jesus' human will was distinct from God's will, but it did not oppose God's will. His prayer reveals his terrible suffering, but he willingly placed himself in his Father's hands.

22:43-44 **Then an angel appeared to Him from heaven, strengthening Him. In his anguish he prayed more earnestly, and his sweat became like great drops of blood falling down on the ground.**[NKJV] This portion, known as "the bloody sweat passage," is often bracketed and/or noted in most modern English versions because it does not appear in many of the earliest manuscripts. The debate about the genuineness of this passage has focused on what view one takes concerning whether or not Jesus needed to have been strengthened by angels during his trial in the Garden of Gethsemane. Some have said that the passage was excised because certain Christians thought that the account of Jesus overwhelmed with human weakness was incompatible with his sharing the divine omnipotence of the Father. Others have argued that the passage was an early (second century) interpolation, added from an oral tradition concerning the life of Jesus.

> Spread out your petition before God, and then say, "Thy will, not mine, be done." The sweetest lesson I have learned in God's school is to let the Lord choose for me.
> *Dwight L. Moody*

Angels appear in Luke's narrative many times: with Zechariah (1:11), Mary (1:26), shepherds (2:9), the women at the tomb (24:4, 23). Jesus spoke often of angels (9:26; 12:8-9; 15:10; 16:22; 20:36). Matthew 4:11 reveals that angels came and ministered to Jesus after his temptation by Satan. Here an angel appears from heaven, *strengthening* Jesus. Angels are God's emissaries, sent to do his bidding, ministering to people on earth. God sent an angel to be with Jesus in this horrible time of fear, and perhaps even temptation far worse than what Satan tried. In his humanity, Jesus suffered terribly during this night, battling what he knew had to be. Jesus was in extreme agony; his prayer reveals his terrible suffering. Luke was speaking metaphorically. Jesus did not sweat blood, but rather the emotional agony he felt caused the perspiration to fall like clotted blood. The focus of this prayer was probably not so much on the painful death but on the agony of being separated from God. The sinless Son of God became sin to save his people from suffering and separation:

- "God made him who had no sin to be sin for us, so that in him we might become the righteousness of God" (2 Corinthians 5:21 NIV).
- "He himself bore our sins in his body on the tree, so that we might die to sins and live for righteousness; by his wounds you have been healed" (1 Peter 2:24 NIV). Jesus went ahead with the mission for which he had come.

God did not take away the "cup," for the cup was his will. Yet he did take away Jesus' extreme fear and agitation. Jesus moved serenely through the next several hours, at peace with God, knowing that he was doing his Father's will.

22:45 **At last he stood up again and returned to the disciples, only to find them asleep, exhausted from grief.**ᴺᴸᵀ Jesus got up *at last* from praying—how long he struggled in prayer is not revealed, but the hour was late. Matthew wrote that Jesus went back and forth three times between praying and checking on the disciples, each time finding them asleep (Matthew 26:40-45). Jesus needed his friends to support him with their prayers, but they were *asleep, exhausted from grief.* It had been a long day, and the reality of Jesus' impending death left them emotionally exhausted. They were sleeping instead of praying. This proved to be their undoing—for in the coming time of difficulty, no one stood strong. They all fled.

22:46 **"Why are you sleeping?" he asked. "Get up and pray. Otherwise temptation will overpower you."**ᴺᴸᵀ Jesus told the disciples that this was the time to *get up and pray,* for very soon they would face the temptation to run away or to deny their relationship with him. They would need extra strength so that these temptations would not *overpower* them. The word "temptation" can mean testing or trial. Jesus wanted his disciples to pray for strength to go through the coming ordeal. The disciples were about to see Jesus die. Would they still think he was the Messiah? The disciples would soon face confusion, fear, loneliness, guilt, and the temptation to conclude that they had been deceived.

JESUS IS BETRAYED AND ARRESTED / 22:47-53 / 224

Despite all of Jesus' warnings about the coming trouble, the disciples were unprepared for it when the moment arrived. Judas, formerly one of them, appears and betrays Jesus with a kiss. The disciples attempt to defend Jesus, and then flee, as Jesus gives himself over to an illegal arrest.

22:47 **But even as he said this, a mob approached, led by Judas, one of his twelve disciples. Judas walked over to Jesus and**

greeted him with a kiss.^{NLT} Even as Jesus spoke the words about
not being overcome by temptation (22:46), *a mob approached.*
The leader was *Judas,* who had gone to the Jewish religious leaders in order to betray Jesus (22:3-4). He was at the Last Supper
with Jesus and the other disciples (Matthew 26:25) and then had
abruptly left, apparently to let the leaders know where to find
Jesus (John 13:27). Luke reminded readers that Judas was *one of
[Jesus'] twelve disciples.* The betrayer came from among Jesus'
closest followers.

Judas and a mob arrived. Matthew tells us that they were
armed with swords and clubs (Matthew 26:47). There were also
chief priests, officers of the temple guard, and elders in the crowd
(22:52). Then Judas came up to Jesus *and greeted him with a
kiss.* Judas had told the crowd to arrest the man whom he would
kiss (Matthew 26:48). This would be an arrest by religious leaders, not by Roman soldiers under Roman law. Judas pointed Jesus
out because Jesus was hard to recognize in the dark and because
Judas had agreed to be the formal accuser in the trial.

EMPTY GESTURE
A kiss is the traditional greeting among men in certain parts of
the world. In this case, it was also the agreed-upon signal to
point out Jesus. It is ironic that a gesture of greeting would be
the means of betrayal. It was a hollow gesture because of
Judas's treachery. In a sense, people can still betray Christ
when their acts of service or giving are insincere or carried out
merely for show.

22:48 **But Jesus said to him, "Judas, are you betraying the Son of
Man with a kiss?"**^{NKJV} With this kiss of greeting, Judas showed
himself to be the ultimate traitor. He had eaten with Jesus only
hours before, and here he used a sign of friendship and affection
in his betrayal. Apparently Jesus understood that this greeting had
been designated as a signal; this was no benign greeting. Jesus
asked, *"Judas, are you betraying the Son of Man with a kiss?"*
This was the height of disloyalty and hypocrisy.

22:49-50 **When Jesus' followers saw what was going to happen, they
said, "Lord, should we strike with our swords?" And one of
them struck the servant of the high priest, cutting off his
right ear.**^{NIV} Apparently the arrival of the mob had awakened
the sleeping disciples, and they came fully awake and ready to
fight. The light of the lanterns and torches coming toward them
in the middle of the night made them aware of *what was going
to happen.* In 22:36-38, Jesus had told them to take up swords,

so Peter was ready to act. Apparently not waiting for an answer, *one of them struck the servant of the high priest, cutting off his right ear.* The Gospel of John reveals that the man who cut off the servant's ear was Peter and that the servant's name was Malchus (John 18:10).

22:51 But Jesus answered, "No more of this!" And he touched the man's ear and healed him.NIV Peter may have thought that this was the time to fight, the time to defend themselves, but Jesus told Peter, *"No more of this."* Peter should put away his sword and allow God's plan to unfold. Jesus' time of prayer had made him serene in God's will. He would comply with God's plan. So *he touched the man's ear and healed him.* Even as Jesus was being led away to face what would be the most difficult of trials, he first stopped to care for this member of the mob, restoring his ear.

PEOPLE OF THE NIGHT
Sometimes a crime is described as having happened "in broad daylight." It's always said with an air of amazement that anyone would have the audacity to do something like that without waiting for nightfall. There's a reason that most crimes and other illicit activities take place in the darkness: Those who engage in them don't want anyone else to see. They don't want to get caught, and they wish to hide under the cover of darkness. Jesus told his accusers that they were people of the night in 22:52-53: "This is your hour—when darkness reigns" (NIV). What a shameful allegation and equally undeniable. Is there anything in your life that cannot stand the light of day or the light of truth right now? Confess it and expose it to the light of God's grace, and let him remove its shadow from you.

22:52-53 Then Jesus said to the chief priests, the officers of the temple guard, and the elders, who had come for him, "Am I leading a rebellion, that you have come with swords and clubs? Every day I was with you in the temple courts, and you did not lay a hand on me. But this is your hour—when darkness reigns."NIV Apparently many of the religious leaders had come together to take part in this arrest. Jesus pointed out the ridiculous picture of all these men coming after him *with swords and clubs* as though he had an armed battalion and was *leading a rebellion.* Twelve peaceful men in a garden, most of them asleep, would hardly prove to be much of a threat, but apparently the leaders were taking no chances.

Jesus also pointed out the basic cowardice in their actions. He had been among them every day *in the temple courts,* but they had not laid a hand on him. We know from 20:19 and 22:2 that they had not arrested Jesus in the temple for fear of a riot. Instead, they came secretly at night, under the influence of the prince of darkness, Satan himself. This was their *hour.* Although it looked as if Satan was getting the upper hand and that *darkness* was in control, everything was proceeding according to God's plan. It was time for Jesus to die.

PETER DENIES KNOWING JESUS / 22:54-65 / 227

Peter was a Galilean; his strong accent gave it away. Huddled around the fire in the high priest's courtyard, his accent had become a liability, something that associated him with Jesus of Nazareth. Peter's confidence and courage had wilted under pressure. Only several hours before, he had courageously asserted that he would follow Jesus to prison—or even to death. At this point, however, he was repeatedly denying any association with Jesus. Each denial distanced Peter further from him: First, he denied being with Jesus in any way; second, he denied being one of Jesus' followers; third, he fiercely denied even knowing Jesus. Then the rooster crowed, and Jesus gave him a look that he could not bear. The deep sorrow in Jesus' eyes made him run from the courtyard, weeping bitterly.

The best part of this sad story is that it did not end here. Peter did not have to live the rest of his life with a heavy burden of sorrow and regret. Instead Jesus reinstated him and asked him to become a leader of the church (see John 21:15-21). With genuine sorrow and repentance, Peter learned from his past mistakes and mustered the courage and integrity to take a leadership role in the early church (see Acts 1:15; 2:14; 4:13; 11:4; 15:7). The same should be true of every believer. Learn from your past mistakes and courageously serve Jesus.

22:54 So they arrested him and led him to the high priest's residence, and Peter was following far behind.[NLT] Jesus did not resist arrest, his disciples had turned and run (Mark 14:50), so Jesus was led away *to the high priest's residence,* even though it was not yet daylight. The Jewish leaders were in a hurry because they wanted to complete the execution before the Sabbath and get on with the Passover celebration. The high priest's residence was a palace with outer walls enclosing a courtyard. That this trial should occur here was unprecedented. Normally the Sanhedrin would meet in a large hall in the temple area. They could have met there because during the Passover, the temple opened at midnight rather than at dawn. This meeting at Caiaphas's home may have been to aid in a hasty assembly; however, they still could just as easily have met in a normal location. Most likely, it was their desire to avoid a riot that led them to this more private setting.

First Jesus was questioned by Annas, the former high priest and father-in-law of Caiaphas, the ruling high priest. Annas had been Israel's high priest from A.D. 6 to 15, when he had been deposed by Roman rulers. Then Caiaphas had been appointed high priest. He held that position from A.D. 18 to 36/37. According to Jewish law, the office of high priest was held for life, but the Roman government had taken over the process of appointing all political and religious leaders. Caiaphas served for eighteen years, longer than most high priests, suggesting that he was gifted at cooperating with the Romans. Caiaphas was the first to recommend Jesus' death in order to "save" the nation (John 11:49-50). Many Jews, however, still considered Annas to be the high priest. Annas may have asked to question Jesus after his arrest and then been given permission to do so. This hearing is described in John 18:12-24. Annas and Caiaphas undoubtedly lived near each other, perhaps even sharing this same large residence in Jerusalem. Thus Jesus could easily have been questioned by both of them in a short amount of time.

Peter, disheartened by Jesus' words against his attempt to help out, was not arrested despite his attack. He probably was safe because of Jesus' intervention, but still curious. He followed the mob from *far behind.* He was the only one who acted with courage. The others were cowering behind closed doors (John 20:19).

22:55 The guards lit a fire in the courtyard and sat around it, and Peter joined them there.[NLT] As mentioned above, this *courtyard* was probably in a central area of the buildings that made up the high priest's residence. In the courtyard, *the guards lit a fire,* around which the servants and soldiers were warming themselves against the early morning chill. Although most of the disciples had fled when the soldiers arrested Jesus, two of them, Peter and another disciple (perhaps John), were also there (John 18:15). After securing permission to enter the courtyard, Peter joined the others as they warmed themselves around the fire. Peter's experiences in the next few hours would revolutionize his life. He would change from an impulsive follower to a repentant and wiser disciple, and finally to the kind of person Christ could use to build his church.

22:56-57 A servant girl noticed him in the firelight and began staring at him. Finally she said, "This man was one of Jesus' followers!" Peter denied it. "Woman," he said, "I don't even know the man!"[NLT] John wrote that this *servant girl* was acting as a guard at the gate to the inner courtyard (John 18:16). "The other disciple" had secured permission for Peter to enter. She apparently looked him over and noticed *in the firelight* that he looked familiar, so she *began staring at him.* Then the girl realized where she had seen Peter before—he was *one of Jesus' followers.* Where she had seen him is unknown—perhaps in the temple or somewhere on the streets of Jerusalem. In any case, she recognized him.

This put Peter in a difficult position. Standing among the soldiers and servants right there in enemy territory, Peter did not necessarily want to be identified with the man held in an upstairs room, on trial for his life. So Peter made a natural and impulsive response—he lied, *"Woman . . . I don't even know the man!"* It didn't matter that Peter had arrived soon after Jesus did or that he was there in the courtyard for an unknown reason at this early morning hour. He simply denied even knowing who Jesus was. Temptation came when Peter least expected it. This serves as a warning to all believers to be prepared. Peter had been ready to fight with a sword, but not to face the accusations of a servant girl.

STAYING CLOSE

How could Peter deny Jesus before a servant girl and two other bystanders? After all, this was the same man who only hours earlier had showed considerable courage by drawing a sword and trying to defend Jesus in front of armed soldiers. Perhaps the lesson is that temptation and compromise are most powerful when they do not come in obvious ways. But an even better lesson is this: as long as Peter was with Jesus, he was bold and aggressive. Left on his own, he wasn't. Stay close to Jesus in your devotions, Bible study, and worship. Anyone is capable of denying the Lord and selling him out when he or she stands alone.

22:58 A little later someone else, on seeing him, said, "You also are one of them." But Peter said, "Man, I am not!"NRSV Peter could run, but he couldn't hide. He got away from the questioning servant girl only to run into *someone else* who also recognized him as *one of them* (one of Jesus' followers). But Peter again denied it.

22:59-60 About an hour later another asserted, "Certainly this fellow was with him, for he is a Galilean." Peter replied, "Man, I don't know what you're talking about!" Just as he was speaking, the rooster crowed.NIV This time, another bystander also recognized Peter. John wrote that this last person to question Peter was "one of the servants of the high priest, a relative of him whose ear Peter cut off" (John 18:26 NKJV). He heard

Peter's Galilean accent, which was closer to Syrian speech than to that of the Judean servants in the Jerusalem courtyard. Thus the group concluded that Peter must have been with the Galilean on trial inside the palace. Peter again replied in the negative, claiming to not even know what they were talking about. These three denials did not occur quickly, one immediately after another. Time elapsed in between, yet Peter could not escape his own fear. As he spoke these words of his third denial, *the rooster crowed,* signaling the early morning hour. The period of the night from midnight to about 3:00 A.M. was known as "cockcrowing." A rooster would crow first at about 12:30 A.M., then again at about 1:30 A.M.

THE SPREAD OF SIN

Sin, like cancer, has a way of growing if unchecked. Notice the progression of Peter's denials: In 22:57, he denied knowing Jesus; in 22:58, he denied being one of his followers; in 22:60, he denied even knowing what they were talking about. Sin has a way of spreading. As it does, the cover-up gets bigger as well. The time to get a grip on sin and its cancerous effects is in the very beginning, before it has time to multiply its poisons in your life. Better yet, kill it before it even begins. Confess your sins or your desire to sin to the Lord, and ask his help to avoid Peter's mistakes.

22:61-62 And the Lord turned and looked at Peter. Then Peter remembered the word of the Lord, how He had said to him, "Before the rooster crows, you will deny Me three times." So Peter went out and wept bitterly.^{NKJV} Peter's denials fulfilled Jesus' words to him (22:34). When Peter heard the rooster crowing and then saw Jesus turn and look at him (either from the upper story where the trial was being held or as he passed through the courtyard between visits with Annas and Caiaphas), *Peter remembered* what Jesus had said to him earlier (12:9). Peter had indeed denied Jesus three times before the rooster crowed.

Peter *went out and wept bitterly.* His bitter tears were not only because he realized that he had denied his Lord, the Messiah, but also because he had turned away from a very dear friend, a person who had loved and taught him for three years. Peter had said that he would go to prison or even death for Jesus (22:33-34; Mark 14:29-31). When frightened, however, he went against all he had boldly promised. Unable to stand up for his Lord for even twelve hours, he had failed as a disciple and as a friend.

Fortunately, the story does not end there. Peter's tears were of true sorrow and repentance. Later, Peter would reaffirm his love for Jesus, and Jesus would forgive him (see Mark 16:7; John 21:15-19).

22:63-65 **Now the guards in charge of Jesus began mocking and beating him. They blindfolded him; then they hit him and asked, "Who hit you that time, you prophet?" And they threw all sorts of terrible insults at him.**[NLT] After the preliminary meeting in Caiaphas's house, the men adjourned to await daybreak and the arrival of the entire Sanhedrin for the more formal meeting in the temple. Matters had really already been decided during the night, but the full trial would be held early in the morning to satisfy a law that allowed trials only during the daytime. This would be a formality to carry out the sentence that already had been decided.

THE MEETING OF THE EYES
Peter experienced overwhelming guilt and shame. After denying his Lord three times, Peter had to undergo the pain and shame of looking Jesus in the eyes. Imagine the stinging, choking remorse and regret Peter must have felt! No wonder he "went out and wept bitterly." Peter may very well have wished he could die. Yet Jesus wasn't through with Peter. He still had a role for Peter to play, a ministry for him to fulfill. In spite of Peter's sin and faithlessness, Jesus still loved him and used him greatly in leading the early church. When you face trials, remember the warnings of Jesus and use the strength and preparation he has provided for you.

Apparently Jesus was left in the care of *guards,* who proceeded to mock and beat him. Evidently the charge of Jesus being a prophet had come up, so the guards took advantage of their prisoner by playing on this claim. *They blindfolded him . . . hit him and asked* that he say who had hit him. This was a form of a child's game where one child was blindfolded and had to guess who hit him from among other playmates. The children would use papyrus husks to strike the blindfolded person. In this case with Jesus, the striking was used more as mockery than torture. In addition, they *threw all sorts of terrible insults at him.* Matthew and Mark wrote that these guards were only following the example of the religious leaders themselves, who had already beaten and insulted Jesus (Matthew 26:67-68; Mark 14:65). None of this surprised Jesus. He had already told his disciples, "They will mock him, insult him, spit on him" (18:32 NIV).

JESUS' TRIAL

Jesus' trial was actually a series of hearings, carefully controlled to accomplish his death. The verdict was predetermined, but certain "legal" procedures were necessary. A lot of effort went into condemning and crucifying an innocent man. Jesus went through an unfair trial so that his people would not have to face a fair trial and receive the well-deserved punishment for their sins.

Event	Probable reasons	References
Trial before Annas (powerful ex-high priest)	Although no longer the high priest, he still may have wielded much power	John 18:13-23
Trial before Caiaphas (the ruling high priest)	To gather evidence for the full Council hearing to follow	Matthew 26:57-68; Mark 14:53-65; Luke 22:54, 63-65; John 18:24
Trial before the Council (Sanhedrin)	Formal religious trial and condemnation to death	Matthew 27:1; Mark 15:1; Luke 22:66-71
Trial before Pilate (highest Roman authority)	All death sentences needed Roman approval	Matthew 27:2, 11-14; Mark 15:1-5; Luke 23:1-6; John 18:28-38
Trial before Herod (ruler of Galilee)	A courteous and guilt-sharing act by Pilate because Jesus was from Galilee, Herod's district	Luke 23:7-12
Trial before Pilate	Pilate's last effort to avoid condemning an obviously innocent man	Matthew 27:15-26; Mark 16:6-15; Luke 23:13-25; John 18:39–19:16

THE COUNCIL OF RELIGIOUS LEADERS CONDEMNS JESUS / 22:66-71 / **228**

Luke's presentation of Jesus' trial before the Sanhedrin is much shorter than Matthew's or Mark's (see Matthew 26:57-68; Mark 14:53-65). In retelling the story of the trial, Luke's clear purpose was to get at the heart of the matter: Who is Jesus? Peter had already confessed that Jesus was the Messiah when he was among the disciples (see 9:20). Ironically, by this time, Peter was denying that he even knew Jesus (22:60-62). Yet when all of Jesus' followers deserted him, Jesus fearlessly and publicly affirmed his true identity: Jesus was the Son of God, the one who would eventually sit at the right hand of God, judging all people. Although Jesus' confession was completely true, the chief priests considered it as blasphemy and redoubled their efforts to have Jesus executed.

22:66 At daybreak the council of the elders of the people, both the chief priests and teachers of the law, met together, and Jesus was led before them.^{NIV} As stated above, the *council of the elders of the people* (the Sanhedrin) had to hold the trial during the day in order for it to be legal. So they met immediately *at daybreak*. (It is ironic that they kept such trivialities of the law while holding a trial that was completely illegal.) This was the entire group—*the chief priests and teachers of the law*—no one wanted to miss this particular meeting. Jesus had been a topic of discussion for weeks, and here was their opportunity to deal with him. The accused, Jesus, *was led before them.*

22:67-69 "If you are the Christ," they said, "tell us." Jesus answered, "If I tell you, you will not believe me, and if I asked you, you would not answer. But from now on, the Son of Man will be seated at the right hand of the mighty God."^{NIV} They already knew what they planned to do with Jesus, so this meeting was merely a formality. They asked him to tell them if he was *the Christ.* This title, not in common use, referred specifically to the Messiah—thus they were asking if Jesus was claiming to be the Messiah. What could Jesus say? To answer in the affirmative would be to incriminate himself—that was what the Council wanted. Jesus had already made it clear that he was indeed the Messiah, so they knew his answer. To answer in the negative would have been to lie.

SELF-INCRIMINATION
What a scene—the trial of the Son of God! Not surprisingly, Jesus' accusers found it difficult to make their case against him. After all, he was sinless; what charge could they possibly make stick? In what must have been their last desperate attempt to pin something on him, they asked him to incriminate himself: "If you are the Christ, tell us." They were asking for a confession— and they got it, although not quite the way they expected. Jesus willingly incriminated himself, when the Council couldn't do it on their own. What amazing love and submission! His willingness to go to the cross knew no bounds. He gave his all for us. What are we willing to give for him?

Jesus knew this too, for he said, *"If I tell you, you will not believe me."* The Council had already proven that they had no intention of believing Jesus to be their Messiah. Even if he were to say that he was "the Christ," their understanding of who "the

Christ" was and what he would do was still so skewed that they would not have believed him. They had not stopped looking for the military leader/king who would restore David's kingdom on earth and rid them of Roman domination.

Jesus also knew that if he questioned them, they *would not answer* (as already seen in 20:1-8). Jesus was in a no-win situation. Jesus told them the truth, *"From now on, the Son of Man will be seated at the right hand of the mighty God."* To say this was to say that yes, he was the Messiah. To say this was to boldly claim his own exaltation to the place of highest honor in heaven. "The Son of Man" stood for Jesus' role as the divine agent appointed by God to carry out judgment. In Psalm 110:1, the Son is given the seat of authority at the right hand of God. "Seated at the right hand of the mighty God," Jesus would one day come to judge his accusers, and they would have to answer to him (Revelation 20:11-13). These words represent the highest possible claim to deity; Jesus was declaring his royalty in no uncertain terms.

THE AMAZING CLAIM
Many non-Christians object, "But Jesus never claimed to be the Son of God. That's just something his followers made up later on." Next time you hear that, point your nonbelieving friend to Luke 22:70. Jesus clearly claimed divinity for himself; that's the real reason the Council voted to put him to death. It certainly wasn't for teaching rebellion or for healing people. Jesus drew the wrath of the religious leaders because he claimed to be the Son of God. He still draws strong reactions over that claim. How do you respond to his claim to be deity? That is still the question every person must answer for himself.

22:70-71 They all shouted, "Then you claim you are the Son of God?" And he replied, "You are right in saying that I am."NLT The religious leaders understood exactly what Jesus was saying. He was indeed claiming to be the Son of God—but they needed him to be a bit more clear. So they asked again. Jesus agreed, saying, *"You are right in saying that I am."* Jesus identified himself with God by using a familiar title for God found in the Old Testament: "I AM" (Exodus 3:14). **Then they said, "What further testimony do we need? We have heard it ourselves from his own lips!"**NRSV The Council recognized Jesus' claim and realized that they needed no further testimony. He had accused himself. Their accusation against him was blasphemy—claiming equality with God (Matthew 26:65; Mark 14:64). For any other human this claim would have been blasphemy, but in this case it was true. Blasphemy, the sin of claiming to be God or of attacking God's authority and majesty in any way, was punishable by death. The Jewish leaders had the evidence they wanted. Under Jewish law, a person who committed blasphemy was to be stoned (Leviticus 24:16). The Council could condemn Jesus to death, but they could not carry out the death penalty under Roman law. The Romans would have to condemn him. So Jesus was led to trial before the local Roman leader—Pontius Pilate.

LUKE 23

Early that morning, Jesus' accusers rushed him to Pilate. What they heard from Jesus the night before made them more determined than ever to bring about his demise. For them, Jesus' claim to have access to God was not only blasphemy but also a threat to their own religious authority (22:69-70). To the high priests and the teachers of the law, Jesus was very dangerous. He simply had to be eliminated. Therefore, they did not shrink from presenting completely false charges against Jesus (see 20:20-26).

Pilate saw through their blatant lies. He knew Jesus was innocent. But the religious leaders would not give up; they pressured Pilate with a threat of a riot. Pilate didn't appreciate their manipulative tactics, but he couldn't see any way out of his predicament. A riot would jeopardize his leadership of the region. To delay the decision, he hurried Jesus off to Herod for examination.

23:1 Then the entire council took Jesus over to Pilate, the Roman governor.^{NLT} The Jewish Council had already decided that Jesus should die, but they could not, under Roman law, carry out the death penalty. Jesus would have to be tried and convicted in a Roman court. Thus, *the entire council took Jesus over to Pilate, the Roman governor.* Pilate was the governor of Judea, where Jerusalem was located. Pilate's normal residence was in Caesarea on the Mediterranean Sea, but he happened to be in Jerusalem because of the Passover festival. With the large crowds who had flocked to the city for that celebration, Pilate and his soldiers came to help keep the peace. He stayed in his headquarters, called the Praetorium.

There is much behind this simple statement, for the Jews hated the Romans in general and Pilate in particular. (For more on Pontius Pilate, see commentary on 13:1.) He, in turn, had contempt for his subjects. Pilate seemed to take special pleasure in harassing the Jews. As Pilate well knew, such acts could backfire. If the people were to lodge a formal complaint against his administration, Rome might remove him from his post. Pilate was already feeling insecure in his position when the Jewish leaders brought Jesus to trial. Would he continue to badger the Jews and risk his political future, or would he give in to their demands and condemn a man who, he was quite sure, was innocent?

23:2 **And they began to accuse him, saying, "We have found this man subverting our nation. He opposes payment of taxes to Caesar and claims to be Christ, a king."**[NIV] The Jewish leaders wanted Jesus executed on a cross, a method of death that they believed brought a curse from God (see Deuteronomy 21:23). They wanted the death to appear Roman-sponsored so that the crowds wouldn't blame them. The Jewish leaders had arrested Jesus on theological grounds—blasphemy—but because this charge would be thrown out of a Roman court, they had to come up with a political reason for executing Jesus. Their strategy was to present him as a rebel who told the people not to pay their taxes and who claimed to be a king and thus a threat to Caesar. The charges against Jesus in the Roman court were rebellion and treason.

The irony is that the first accusation, that Jesus was *subverting the nation,* was completely unfounded. The second accusation, that Jesus opposed *payment of taxes to Caesar,* was an outright lie (see 20:20-26). The third charge, that he was claiming *to be Christ, a king,* was absolutely true, yet Jesus' accusers never had listened long enough to understand what kind of king he was. They had *wanted* a king who would lead a rebellion; in fact,

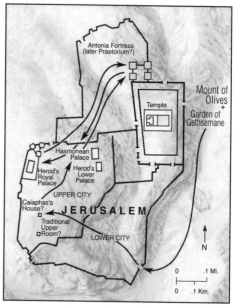

JESUS' TRIAL
Taken from Gethsemane, Jesus first appeared before the Jewish Council, which had convened at daybreak at Caiaphas's house. From there he went first to Pilate, the Roman governor; then to Herod, tetrarch of Galilee, who was visiting in Jerusalem; then back to Pilate, who sentenced Jesus to die.

that was what they expected their Messiah to be. When Jesus did not fulfill this, they went to Pilate and used their disappointed expectation as an accusation against Jesus.

23:3-4 So Pilate asked him, "Are you the King of the Jews?" Jesus replied, "Yes, it is as you say."^{NLT} Pilate focused on the accusation about Jesus claiming to be a king, for that could amount to treason and be grounds for a death sentence. So *Pilate asked* the prisoner, *"Are you the King of the Jews?"* This question is identical in all four Gospels, and in all four the word "you" is emphatic. The question comes as a sort of surprise that the religious leaders could have been worried about this solemn rabbi, who didn't look like much of a king at that moment. Yet Jesus answered the question, *"Yes, it is as you say."* To have said otherwise would have been to lie. Jesus was a king, but his kingship was not a threat to Pilate or to Caesar. (It was a threat to Herod, who considered himself "King of the Jews.")

REACTIONS TO JESUS
You can walk into any room in this country and say, "I believe in God," and the majority of people in that room will respond positively. But if you then add, "And I believe that Jesus of Nazareth was his one and only Son, and the only way to God," you will quickly find yourself in the minority. Jesus provokes a reaction in people. He did then, and he does now. People are not neutral about Jesus. Next time you find yourself in a heated discussion with a nonbeliever who objects to the exclusive nature of Jesus' claims, ask the person why he or she feels so strongly about it. If Jesus is wrong, after all, he should simply be dismissed and forgotten like all of history's other false prophets. If he's right, then he deserves to be worshiped and obeyed. Either way, he provokes a response.

Jesus didn't appear to be a king, and he didn't look like a revolutionary either; Pilate had seen enough of those to recognize the anger in the eyes. Pilate also realized the obvious irony of the Jews bringing to him a man suspected of rebellion or treason. So Pilate refused to take their bait. At some point, he realized that there was nothing behind this except the religious leaders' desire to get rid of this man. **Then Pilate said to the chief priests and the crowds, "I find no basis for an accusation against this man."**^{NRSV} Pilate's reluctance to prosecute Jesus was undoubtedly due more to his contempt for the Jews than for any particular consideration of Jesus.

23:5 Then they became desperate. "But he is causing riots everywhere he goes, all over Judea, from Galilee to Jerusalem!"^{NLT}

The Jews' plan was unraveling. Pilate wasn't playing into their hands as they had hoped, and *they became desperate.* So they came up with more trumped-up charges—also completely untrue. Jesus was never *causing riots everywhere.* Again it is ironic that these leaders would attribute such influence to Jesus—that he could cause such disturbances all over the land. But because Pilate was mainly charged with keeping peace, he would be interested in dealing with a man who was causing riots. If this charge were true, however, Pilate would have heard about Jesus long before this.

JESUS STANDS TRIAL BEFORE HEROD / 23:6-12 / 231

Herod was ecstatic that he would be able to see Jesus. He had heard so much about this mysterious, miracle-working man from Galilee. But Herod was severely disappointed. Jesus remained silent. He would not answer Herod's questions, much less perform any miracles. His silence was met with ridicule. Chained and bruised, Jesus was a pathetic-looking king. He appeared to be powerless before Herod. But the time had not come for Jesus to reveal his true power. That day, reserved for his second coming when he will judge all of his enemies, would come soon enough (Acts 17:31).

23:6-7 When Pilate heard this, he asked whether the man was a Galilean. And when he learned that he was under Herod's jurisdiction, he sent him off to Herod, who was himself in Jerusalem at that time.^{NRSV} When the religious leaders mentioned that Jesus had been in Galilee, *he asked whether* Jesus *was a Galilean.* Jesus had grown up in Nazareth and later had made Capernaum his base; he was indeed *under Herod's jurisdiction.* Herod, also called Herod Antipas, *was himself in Jerusalem* that weekend for the Passover celebration, mainly as a tactic to please his subjects. A trial usually would be held in the place where the offense was committed, although it could be held in the place where the accused had lived. Pilate saw the mention of riots in Galilee as filling both possibilities, so he hoped to pass Jesus off on Herod.

This was the Herod who had killed John the Baptist. (For more about Herod, see commentary on 3:19-20; 9:7-9.) Herod had had opportunity to talk to John the Baptist and surely had heard the message that he needed to repent and believe (Mark 6:20). Herod had killed John the Baptist as a party favor, but he had become concerned when reports about Jesus had begun to circulate. When he had heard about Jesus, he thought that John had come back from the dead. So Herod was very interested in meeting Jesus (9:7-9).

23:8-9 Herod was delighted at the opportunity to see Jesus, because he had heard about him and had been hoping for a long time

to see him perform a miracle. He asked Jesus question after
question, but Jesus refused to answer.^{NLT} Herod may have been
delighted to finally *see Jesus,* but he had already closed his window of opportunity to hear the message. John had spoken to him;
Herod had killed John. Herod's motivation here was only to see
Jesus *perform a miracle.* He apparently saw Jesus as no more
than an amazing traveling sideshow. When Jesus was brought
before him, Herod asked him questions, *but Jesus refused to
answer.* Herod is the only person to whom Jesus said nothing at
all. Herod had not listened to John; Jesus had nothing to add to
what John had said. Cold and cruel, Herod had a hard heart. Jesus
knew this and remained silent.

A DEAFENING SILENCE
People often approach the Christian faith with questions. There
is nothing wrong with that; honest questions lead to honest
faith. Often, however, the inquirer's questions are merely
"smoke screens." When that happens, it is pointless to try to
answer the objections. That person isn't interested in answers;
he or she is merely interested in excuses not to believe. When
you are in a situation like that, save your breath. Just as Jesus
didn't dignify Herod's superficial inquiries (Luke 23:8-9),
Christians should refuse to engage anyone in such empty
chatter. Sometimes the best answer you can give is silence.

**23:10 And the chief priests and scribes stood and vehemently
accused Him.**^{NKJV} The religious leaders were getting upset. This
whole trial idea was not going as they had anticipated. They had
hoped for a quick sentence from Pilate, so they could return to
their religious duties during this important Passover celebration.
But they had already had to trek with Jesus from Pilate's residence over to Herod's palace, and now Herod was wasting more
time. So they *stood and vehemently accused Him,* probably with
more of the same kinds of lies (23:2, 5). They hoped their accusations would sway Herod, so they would get an accusation from
him that would be as good as one from Pilate.

**23:11-12 Now Herod and his soldiers began mocking and ridiculing
Jesus. Then they put a royal robe on him and sent him back
to Pilate. Herod and Pilate, who had been enemies before,
became friends that day.**^{NLT} With this prisoner refusing to
answer, and looking very little like a great miracle worker, *Herod
and his soldiers began mocking and ridiculing Jesus.* Angry at
Jesus' refusal to even answer questions for him, Herod resorted to
making a mockery of this man who was supposedly such a great
prophet, teacher, and miracle worker. To make fun of Jesus' claim

to be a king (probably Pilate had sent along this information when he sent Jesus to Herod), Herod *put a royal robe on him,* probably a purple color with fine workmanship. Herod did not even take the charge seriously. So he neither released the prisoner nor made a judgment about his guilt. He simply *sent him back to Pilate.*

Herod and Pilate had a rather tenuous relationship. Herod was the part-Jewish ruler of Galilee and Perea. Pilate was the Roman governor of Judea and Samaria. Those four provinces, together with several others, had been united under Herod the Great. But when Herod the Great died in 4 B.C., the kingdom was divided among his sons, each of whom was called "tetrarch" (meaning "ruler of a fourth part of a region"). Archelaus, the son who had received Judea and Samaria, was removed from office within ten years, and his provinces were then ruled by a succession of Roman governors, of whom Pilate was the fifth.

Herod Antipas had two advantages over Pilate: he had come from a part-Jewish monarchy, and he had held his position much longer. But Pilate had two advantages over Herod: he was a Roman citizen and an envoy of the emperor, and his position was created to replace that of Herod's ineffective half brother. It is not surprising that the two men were uneasy around each other. Jesus' trial, however, brought them together. Because Pilate had recognized Herod's authority over Galilee, Herod had stopped feeling threatened by the Roman politician. And because neither man knew what to do in this predicament, their common problem united them.

PILATE HANDS JESUS OVER TO BE CRUCIFIED / 23:13-25 / **232**

According to the Roman custom of releasing a criminal during the Passover season, Pilate presented Jesus to the people. Pilate did not want to bear the responsibility of putting an innocent man to death. But the crowd insisted on Barabbas's freedom, the release of a known murderer. That Jesus literally died in Barabbas's place vividly illustrates the ultimate significance of Jesus' death. He took the place of not only Barabbas but also all who stand condemned before God's perfect standard and trust in Christ for salvation.

23:13-14 Pilate then called together the chief priests, the leaders, and the people, and said to them, "You brought me this man as one who was perverting the people; and here I have examined him in your presence and have not found this man guilty of

any of your charges against him."NRSV Pilate thought he had gotten rid of his problem, only to have Jesus sent back. The decision still rested on his shoulders. So he attempted to let this innocent man go by telling Jesus' accusers that he had *examined him* and *not found this man guilty of any* of their charges—including subversion, refusal to pay taxes, causing riots, or *perverting the people.* He didn't even find Jesus guilty of being the king he claimed to be. Pilate may have incorrectly thought that Jesus was just a poor, deluded man; he did know, however, that Jesus was innocent.

DO WHAT'S RIGHT
When the stakes are high, it is difficult to stand up for what is right, and it is easy to see opponents as problems to be solved rather than as people to be respected. Had Pilate been a man of real courage, he would have released Jesus regardless of the consequences. But the crowd roared, and Pilate buckled. People are like Pilate when they know what is right but decide not to do it. When you have a difficult decision to make, don't discount the effects of peer pressure. Realize beforehand that the right decision could have unpleasant consequences: social rejection, career derailment, public ridicule. Then think of Pilate and resolve to stand up for what is right no matter what other people pressure you to do.

23:15 **"Herod came to the same conclusion and sent him back to us. Nothing this man has done calls for the death penalty."**NLT Pilate could back up his decision with Herod's conclusion about Jesus. Herod had mocked Jesus but apparently had sent back word to Pilate that he could find nothing worthy of the *death penalty.* Jesus was tried a total of six times, by both Jewish and Roman authorities, but he was never convicted of a crime. Even when condemned to execution, he had been convicted of no felony. Today, no one can find fault in Jesus. Just like Pilate, Herod, and the religious leaders, however, many still refuse to acknowledge him as Lord.

23:16 **"Therefore, I will punish him and then release him."**NIV The word "punish" here may not indicate the severe flogging that Jesus received after being sentenced, prior to his crucifixion (as noted in Matthew 27:26; Mark 15:15), although John 19:1 reports Jesus being flogged and then brought before the crowd. Pilate may have hoped that the flogging would appease the crowd, and they would pity the man and let him go. Pilate was planning to *release* Jesus, but first he would *punish* him—to pacify the Jews and teach the prisoner a lesson to stay out of trouble in the future.

RIDING THE FENCE

Pilate knew that Jesus had done nothing deserving punishment, and certainly not the death penalty. Even so, he didn't have the courage or the decency to release Jesus; he tried to find a middle position that would allow Jesus to live and still appease the chief priests and the Jewish rulers. He failed, and Pilate is known forever as the man who ordered the crucifixion of the Son of God. Where do you stand? Have you made up your own mind about Jesus, whether to follow him as Lord and Messiah, or to dismiss him as a misguided martyr? There is no middle ground, no way to ride the fence when it comes to Jesus. You must either embrace him as Lord or reject him as a fraud.

23:17 (For it was necessary for him to release one to them at the feast).^{NKJV} This verse does not exist in most modern English versions because it does not appear in any of the earliest Greek manuscripts. It may have been added later, perhaps picked up from Mark 15:6 to make a smoother transition between what is recorded in verses 16 and 18. This information helps the reader understand why the Jews called for the release of a prisoner in 23:18. But the text without 23:17 reads just as well; Pilate's statement about releasing Jesus (23:16) is followed (23:18) by an immediate plea from the crowd to release Barabbas instead.

Each year at Passover, Pilate had made it a custom to release any prisoner the people requested. He may have instituted this custom to be on good terms with them as well as to help cover his many wrongful acts toward them. In any case, it became expected. So, according to the people, *it was necessary for him to release* a prisoner *to them at the feast.*

23:18-19 With one voice they cried out, "Away with this man! Release Barabbas to us!" (Barabbas had been thrown into prison for an insurrection in the city, and for murder.)^{NIV} The suggestion that Pilate was going to release Jesus (23:16) sent the leaders into a frenzy. Pilate had wanted to release Jesus as the Passover gift (Mark 15:8-9). This had been a public announcement, so many people in the crowd cried out *with one voice* that Jesus must be put to death. The prisoner they wanted set free was a man named *Barabbas.* Oddly enough, Barabbas *had been thrown into prison for an insurrection.* Barabbas may have been somewhat of a hero among the Jews for his acts of rebellion against Rome, but he was on death row in a Roman prison. He was a true rebel and revolutionary and had even committed *murder.* The religious leaders had tried to pin this accusation on Jesus in order to have him put to death, but they chose a man who had done such acts and wanted him set free. Clearly their actions followed no logic. They merely wanted Jesus put to death and would go to any lengths to make sure it happened.

Who was Barabbas? Jewish men had names that identified them with their fathers. Simon Peter, for example, was called Simon, son of Jonah (Matthew 16:17). Barabbas is never identified by his given name, and this name, "Bar-abbas," simply means "son of 'Abba'" (or "son of daddy"). He could have been anybody's son—and that makes for interesting commentary in that he represents all sinners. Barabbas, son of an unnamed father, committed a crime. Because Jesus died in his place, this man was set free. All people too, are sinners and criminals who have broken God's holy law. Like Barabbas, they deserve to die. But Jesus has died in their place, for their sins, and, by faith, they have been set free.

THE DEBT
If you were heavily in debt—to the point where you could never pay it off on your own—and someone offered to pay your debt for you, what would you say? Or if you were sentenced to life in prison, and someone offered to serve your sentence for you, how would you respond? That is what Jesus has done for believers in his death on the cross. He has paid a debt that they could never repay; he has served a sentence that they deserved. Jesus was sentenced to death by crucifixion, a horrible form of death normally reserved for slaves and non-Roman citizens. In addition, the Old Testament taught (Deuteronomy 21:23) that anyone who died by hanging on a tree was cursed. His death atoned for our sins and fulfilled the requirements for breaking the covenant with God. How do you respond toward the one who has done all that for you? The only appropriate response is to live a life of gratitude and obedience before him.

23:20-21 Wanting to release Jesus, Pilate appealed to them again. But they kept shouting, "Crucify him! Crucify him!"[NIV] Pilate really wanted to *release Jesus*. Matthew recorded that even Pilate's wife had experienced a dream about Jesus and had urged Pilate to let Jesus go (Matthew 27:19). Pilate must have been in a tight spot, because for some reason he put himself in the position of bargaining with the crowd. He had the authority to let Jesus go and then get on with his day; instead, he *appealed to them again* but to no avail. They wanted Jesus to be crucified.

This was, in itself, an amazing request. Crucifixion was the

Roman penalty for rebellion and abhorrent to the Jews. They thought that Jesus' crucifixion would demonstrate that his life and message had been under God's curse, for Deuteronomy 21:23 says, "Anyone who is hung on a tree is under God's curse" (NIV). This is just what the Jewish religious leaders wanted. If Jesus were to be executed, it would be by crucifixion. He would die the death of a rebel and slave, not the death of the king he claimed to be. The crucifixion, from the Jewish perspective, was meant to brand Jesus as cursed by God; the crucifixion, from the Christian perspective, pictures Jesus as taking God's curse against sin upon himself and allowing his people to be set free from sin.

TAKING A STAND
What are the nonnegotiables in your life? What are those core principles and bedrock beliefs that you will not compromise or sell out no matter what? Consider this question before you are in a crisis whereby your principles and beliefs are put to the test. Pilate seems to have had no such convictions. He knew Jesus was innocent and undeserving of punishment, yet he yielded to pressure from his political enemies to sacrifice him. Like Pilate, most people are put in positions where they have to decide where they will stand. Unlike Pilate, Christians must decide to stand firm on the truth revealed to them by God. Where do you stand?

23:22 **For the third time he spoke to them: "Why? What crime has this man committed? I have found in him no grounds for the death penalty. Therefore I will have him punished and then release him."**NIV Pilate tried for the *third time*. He could not fathom why the crowd so badly wanted this man's death. Jesus had not committed any crime; there were *no grounds for the death penalty.* Pilate repeated what he had said in 23:16. He would have Jesus *punished and then release him.*

There are two reasons why Luke stressed these three attempts Pilate had made to release Jesus. First, Luke wanted to show through his Gospel the innocence of Jesus before Roman law. Luke was giving evidence to prove the acceptability of Christianity to his Gentile readers. Second, he was establishing the Jewish guilt for Jesus' death. In Acts, this is the basis of the evangelistic sermons to the Jews—you killed him; he died for you and rose again; now repent and be converted (Acts 2:36-38; 3:13-16; 13:26-41).

23:23-24 **But the crowd shouted louder and louder for Jesus' death, and their voices prevailed. So Pilate sentenced Jesus to die as**

they demanded.ᴺᴸᵀ Pilate wanted to release Jesus, but the crowd *shouted louder and louder for Jesus' death . . . so Pilate sentenced Jesus to die.* No doubt Pilate did not want to risk losing his position, which may already have been shaky, by allowing a riot to occur in his province. As a career politician, he knew the importance of compromise, and he saw Jesus more as a political threat than as a human being with rights and dignity.

23:25 **He released the man who had been thrown into prison for insurrection and murder, the one they asked for, and surrendered Jesus to their will.**ᴺᴵⱽ Pilate did not want to give Jesus the death sentence. He thought the Jewish leaders were simply jealous men who wanted to get rid of a rival. When they threatened to report Pilate to Caesar (John 19:12), however, Pilate became frightened. Historical records indicate that Pilate had already been warned by Roman authorities about tensions in this region. The last thing he needed was a riot in Jerusalem at Passover time when the city was crowded with Jews from all over the Empire. So Pilate *released* Barabbas, *the man who had been thrown into prison for insurrection and murder,* and then *surrendered Jesus to their will.* One must wonder if Pilate ever questioned himself later—why he had allowed a mob to convince him to set a murderer free and execute an innocent man. Clearly Pilate was a man of little conviction and even less courage. But don't forget the responsibility of these Jewish leaders who demanded that Jesus die— Matthew recorded that they accepted

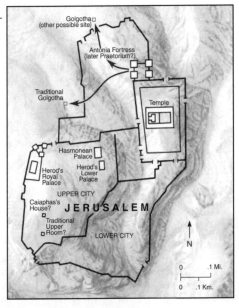

JESUS IS LED AWAY TO DIE

As Jesus was led away through the streets of Jerusalem, he could no longer carry his cross. Simon of Cyrene was given the burden. Jesus was crucified, along with common criminals, on a hill outside Jerusalem.

WHAT DOES THE CROSS MEAN?

The Cross is . . .	Reference
A place of ransom—Jesus made the payment for believers' debt of sin.	Mark 10:45; 1 Timothy 2:6; Hebrews 9:15
A place of substitution—Jesus took the punishment that everyone deserves.	John 6:51; Romans 8:3; 2 Corinthians 5:21
A place of propitiation—Jesus' perfect sacrifice removed God's punishment from those who believe.	Romans 3:25
A place of victory—Jesus' sacrifice defeated Satan's hold on humanity.	John 3:14-15; 8:28; 12:31-32; 18:32
A place of beginning—Jesus' shed blood began the church.	Acts 20:28
A place of ending—Jesus' sacrifice ended all other sacrifices for sin.	Hebrews 8–10
A place of separation—Jesus' death is the basis on which God sets apart a people to be a holy community.	1 Peter 1:2, 18-25; 2:1-11
A place of mediation—Jesus became mediator between sinful humanity and holy God.	Galatians 3:13, 19-20
A place of reconciliation—Jesus reconciled God and sinners, and reconciled Jews and Gentiles.	Romans 5:8-11; 2 Corinthians 5:20-21; Ephesians 2:11-22; Colossians 1:21-22; 2:11-15
A place of justification—Jesus' death makes it possible for God to declare believers righteous before him.	Romans 3:21-31

the responsibility, stating that Jesus' blood could remain on them and on their children (Matthew 27:25).

Matthew's Gospel explains that Pilate took water and washed his hands in front of the crowd to symbolize his innocence in condemning Jesus (Matthew 27:24), but this act was no more than self-deception. Jesus may have been surrendered to the will of the mob, but this was still a purely Roman execution. Pilate had to command it in order for it to happen. After releasing Barabbas, Pilate did allow Jesus to be flogged (Matthew 27:26; Mark 15:15) as part of the Roman legal code that demanded flogging before a capital sentence was carried out. The Romans did it to weaken the prisoner so that he would die more quickly on the cross. Jesus had predicted that he would be flogged (18:32).

JESUS IS LED AWAY TO BE CRUCIFIED / 23:26-31 / 234

Severely beaten and worn out from last night's ordeal, Jesus could not carry his cross to the crest of Golgotha. So Simon was drafted to carry Jesus' cross. The image of Simon shouldering the cross graphically pictures what every follower of Christ should be willing to do: to take up his or her own cross daily to serve Christ (see 14:27).

23:26 As they led Jesus away, Simon of Cyrene, who was coming in from the country just then, was forced to follow Jesus and carry his cross.^{NLT} Jesus was led away from Pilate and out to the place where he would be executed. Condemned prisoners had to carry the crossbeam of their own cross on their shoulders through the streets of Jerusalem and to the execution site outside the city. Jesus started to carry his cross, but, weakened from the beatings he had received, he was physically unable to carry it all the way. A man named Simon from the country of Cyrene was coming into the city. *Cyrene* was in northern Africa (see Acts 2:10). He may have been a Jew coming on a pilgrimage to the city for the Passover, or he may have been from Cyrene but resided in Palestine. Soldiers were free by law to coerce citizens at any time. The soldiers were probably experienced in these matters. They knew how to read the crowd's reaction. A staggering criminal could be hated and humiliated by the crowd, but one completely unable to shoulder his cross might stir up the sympathy of the same people. Through public executions, Rome showed that it meant business. Criminals were not to be pitied. So a stranger *was forced to follow Jesus and carry his cross.*

CARRYING THE CROSS
In some ways, Simon is unique in all of human history. He was forced to do something that everyone else does (or does not do) by choice: carry the cross for Jesus. Simon had no real choice—he either carried the cross or faced the displeasure of the Roman soldiers. People today, on the other hand, are given the incredible compliment by God of having a choice, to follow Jesus on his way to Calvary or not. As Simon surely discovered, it was difficult and painful work; it still is. G. K. Chesterton said: "It is not that Christianity has been tried and found wanting. It has been found difficult and left untried." The work of being Jesus' fellow crossbearer is the most difficult—and most important—work anyone can ever do. What's your choice?

23:27-28 **A large number of people followed him, including women who mourned and wailed for him. Jesus turned and said to them, "Daughters of Jerusalem, do not weep for me; weep for yourselves and for your children."**[NIV] Luke alone wrote of the Jewish women shedding tears for Jesus while he was being led through the streets to his execution. Not everyone wanted Jesus to die—only those whom the religious leaders had been able to sway in the mob outside of Pilate's palace. Others were saddened that Jesus had been condemned to die. Seeing him on his way to be executed caused many, especially women along the way, to mourn and wail for him. Jesus told them not to weep for him but to weep for themselves and for their children. He knew that in only about forty years they would face great suffering and would then mourn, weep, and wail, for at that time Jerusalem and the temple would be destroyed by the Romans. This was Jesus' third lament for the city of Jerusalem (see also 13:34-35; 19:41-44).

23:29-31 **"For the days are surely coming when they will say, 'Blessed are the barren, and the wombs that never bore, and the breasts that never nursed.' Then they will begin to say to the mountains, 'Fall on us'; and to the hills, 'Cover us.' For if they do this when the wood is green, what will happen when it is dry?"**[NRSV] That *the days are surely coming* indicates a key time in God's judgment about to unfold (21:23). While being *barren* was normally a curse, the coming days in Jerusalem would be so difficult that it would be considered a blessing not to have had children. Punishment would be so great that people would want the *mountains* and *hills* to fall on them and kill them. Death would be preferred to the judgment that they will face and its accompanying misery.

This proverb about the green wood and dry wood is difficult to interpret. Some think it means that if the innocent Jesus (green wood) suffered at the hands of the Romans, what would happen to the guilty Jews (dry wood)? The "green wood" is hard to burn, so if fire burns it up, what chance has dry wood? If God did not spare Jesus, his beloved Son, he certainly won't spare the rebellious, hard-hearted Jewish nation from judgment. Thus, Jesus expressed his grief over the nation for the last time.

JESUS IS PLACED ON THE CROSS / 23:32-43 / 235

Even during the final hours of Jesus' life, when he struggled in agony for his last gasp of air, people reacted to him in a variety of ways. Although some mourned for Jesus, many taunted him openly. The teachers of the law gloated over their success: they had finally eliminated this troublemaker from Galilee. Even the two men who were being crucified with Jesus had starkly different reactions to Jesus. One joined the crowd, throwing taunts and insults at him, while the other recognized Jesus' complete innocence. There was no reason for Jesus to suffer their fate. While one thief went to his death ridiculing Jesus, the other one woke up to the spiritual realities behind this gruesome event: the innocent, godly King was dying for his sins. The man's humble plea for mercy did not go unanswered. Jesus forgave this dying criminal, just as he had forgiven all of those involved in his crucifixion (23:34).

23:32-33 Two others, both criminals, were led out to be executed with him. Finally, they came to a place called The Skull. All three were crucified there—Jesus on the center cross, and the two criminals on either side.^{NLT} Jesus was not the only "criminal" executed that morning. *Two others,* who truly deserved to be called *criminals* (Matthew 27:38), were also led out to be crucified. In his death, Jesus truly was numbered among transgressors (22:37; Isaiah 53:12).

The place called *The Skull,* or Golgotha, was probably a hill outside Jerusalem along a main road. The familiar name "Calvary" is derived from the Latin *calvaria* (also meaning "skull"). Thus, it became known as "The Skull"—although some say its name was derived from its appearance, a hill with a stony top that may have looked like a skull. Golgotha may have been a regular place of execution. It was prominent, public, and outside the city along a main road. Executions held there served as examples to the people and as deterrents to criminals.

The words are direct, but the full meaning was horrific: *all three were crucified there.* Crucifixion was a hellish method of killing. It caused the greatest possible amount of pain to the victim before his inevitable death. Instituted by the Romans, crucifixion was a feared and shameful form of execution. It was designed to prolong the gruesome pain. There were several shapes of crosses and several different methods of crucifixion. Neither Matthew, Mark, nor Luke mentions Jesus' being nailed to the cross, although it is suggested in Luke 24:40 that at least his hands were nailed (see also John 20:25; Colossians 2:14). Nailing would have increased the pain but also hastened death through the loss of blood. In both cases, death would come by suffocation as the person would lose strength and the weight of the body would make breathing more and more difficult. Crucifixion was the harshest form of capital punishment in the ancient world.

THE WAY OF THE CROSS
When James and John asked Jesus for the places of honor next to him in his kingdom, he told them that they didn't know what they were asking (Mark 10:35-39). Here, as Jesus was preparing to inaugurate his kingdom through his death, the places on his right and on his left were taken by dying men—criminals. As Jesus explained to his two position-conscious disciples, a person who wants to be close to Jesus must be prepared to suffer and die. The way to the kingdom is the way of the cross. Are you prepared to follow him to the fullest extent, with your life?

23:34 **Then Jesus said, "Father, forgive them; for they do not know what they are doing."** NRSV Jesus spoke only a few times from the cross, and his prayer of forgiveness was the first thing he said. (See page 545 for the chart "The Seven Last Words of Jesus on the Cross.") Some early manuscripts do not include this sentence, yet other reliable manuscripts do include it. These words ought to be accepted as genuine, for this was Jesus' reason for dying. He asked his Father to forgive them. Jesus lived and died by the words he preached: "Love your enemies" (6:27-28). The church continued in Jesus' message and example of nonviolence (Acts 3:17; 13:27; 17:20). "For they do not know what they are doing" refers most likely to the Jews, not the Roman soldiers, although all who participated in Jesus' death were included in his prayer for forgiveness. The Jews made a serious mistake, for they failed to realize God's plan for their nation. If they had known what they were doing, they would not have done it. Paul later wrote, "But the rulers of this world have not understood it; if they had, they would never have crucified our glorious Lord" (1 Corinthians 2:8 NLT). Yet this forgiveness needed to be accepted in order for anyone to obtain salvation. And some would do so. In Peter's sermon at Pentecost, he pointed to his fellow Jews and said, "You nailed him to the cross and murdered him" (Acts 2:23 NLT). That day three thousand people from that audience were added to the church (Acts 2:41). Those who accepted Christ's forgiveness were saved.

And they cast lots to divide his clothing. NRSV Roman soldiers customarily would divide up the clothing of executed criminals among themselves. When they *cast lots* for Jesus' clothes, they fulfilled the prophecy in Psalm 22:18. Jesus was crucified naked. John recorded that four soldiers divided the garments (John 19:23). The clothes were meager, however, so they made a game out of casting lots to see who got what. Casting lots was a way of making a decision by chance, like throwing dice or drawing straws.

23:35 The people stood watching, and the rulers even sneered at him. They said, "He saved others; let him save himself if he is the Christ of God, the Chosen One."NIV These men, hanging in extreme pain and humiliation on their crosses, provided hours of grisly entertainment for spectators. People stood around *watching*. Some were sorrowful; others sneered. Luke pointed specifically at *the rulers* who had accomplished what they wanted. They had followed Jesus to the execution site, had watched him be crucified, and now *sneered at him*. Jesus had gone about the countryside healing people, but he could not *save himself*. They assumed that if he truly had God's divine favor as he had claimed, then he would be able to get himself out of his present predicament. Jesus' position there on the cross proved to them that he was not any kind of Messiah. Unfortunately, they missed the fact that this entire episode had been prophesied (Psalm 22:6-8) and was all proceeding exactly as God had planned.

FORGIVE THEM
What is the most amazing thing you have ever seen or heard? For many, it was watching a man land on the moon; for others, perhaps it was witnessing the birth of a child. Life is filled with astounding events, personal and public. But the twelve most amazing words ever spoken are found in Luke 23:34: "Father, forgive them; for they do not know what they are doing." Jesus was suffering the most horrible, painful death ever devised by sinful man, and he looked at the people responsible for his suffering and prayed for their forgiveness. Amazing, astounding, unbelievable—choose your adjective. Then choose to live for this remarkable Savior and to extend his grace, mercy, and compassion to others.

23:36-37 The soldiers also mocked him, coming up and offering him sour wine, and saying, "If you are the King of the Jews, save yourself!"NRSV The *soldiers* (presumably the Roman soldiers who had carried out the execution) had the duty that day of sitting and waiting until the men on the crosses died. They had already divided up the clothing, and then began mocking the man on the cross who had claimed to be a king. These may have been the same soldiers who had mocked him earlier (Matthew 27:27-31; Mark 15:16-20). Jesus had been offered drugged wine early in the crucifixion (Matthew 27:34; Mark 15:23) that was supposed to deaden some of the pain—Jesus had refused it. Right before he died, he cried out that he was thirsty and was given some vinegar (or cheap wine, John 19:29). Only Luke wrote of this offer of sour wine as part of the soldiers' mockery. They too called up to him to *save* himself, if he were indeed *the King of the Jews.*

The mockery of the soldiers, the sign on the cross (23:38), and the insult of the criminal on the cross (23:39) all serve as ironic witnesses or unintended fulfillment of prophecies about Jesus. The Resurrection would meet their challenge and prove that Christ is indeed the "King of the Jews."

23:38 A signboard was nailed to the cross above him with these words: "This is the King of the Jews."NLT This *signboard* stated the condemned person's crime and was placed on the cross as a warning. According to John, Pilate wrote this sign in three languages: Aramaic, Latin, and Greek. The religious leaders protested the sign, wanting it to say, instead, that this man had "claimed" to be king of the Jews. But Pilate refused to change what he had written (John 19:19-22). The three languages meant that people of any nationality passing that way would be able to read the sign. Because Jesus was never found guilty, the only accusation placed on his sign was the "crime" of calling himself king of the Jews. Perhaps this was another way for Pilate to show contempt for the Jews—here was their king, stripped and executed in public view.

It seemed to most onlookers that day that a poor, deluded man had been executed without good reason. But on that Friday, a huge spiritual battle was being waged unseen. Satan rejoiced that Jesus was going to die—he surely thought he had won a sound victory. The angels in heaven looked on in sorrow, held back from intervening by the hand of God. God himself looked away from his Son as the sins of the world descended upon him. But Jesus was actually gaining a huge victory. His death and resurrection would strike the deathblow to Satan's rule and would establish Christ's eternal authority over the earth. Few people reading the sign that bleak afternoon understood its real meaning, but the sign was absolutely true. All was not lost. Jesus is King of the Jews—and the Gentiles, and the whole universe.

23:39 One of the criminals who hung there hurled insults at him: "Aren't you the Christ? Save yourself and us!"NIV Matthew and Mark recorded that both criminals taunted Jesus. It may have begun that way, but apparently one had a change of heart. They also *hurled insults at him,* even though the three of them were facing the same horrible deaths. One of them seems to have picked up on the taunts of the religious leaders: if Jesus were indeed *the Christ,* then he should *save* himself and them. Obviously these

words were no more than barbed sarcasm. All three were beyond
hope, beyond the point of being saved—physically.

PERSPECTIVE
Have you ever listened to two people describe an event from
completely different perspectives—a car accident, perhaps, or
a political debate? Their descriptions sound so divergent that
you may wonder if they are talking about the same thing. Luke
recorded something like that in 23:39-41: two criminals, dying
the same horrifying death, on opposite sides of the cross of
Christ. One saw another failed opportunity to get himself off the
hook; the other saw and understood that the way of salvation
was opening up for himself and the whole world. The first man
(apparently) died in his sins; the second received forgiveness,
salvation, and eternal life. Perspective makes all the difference.
Ask God to help you get or maintain proper perspective in your
walk with him—that of a forgiven sinner made clean by the
grace of God.

23:40-43 **But the other criminal rebuked him. "Don't you fear God,"**
he said, "since you are under the same sentence? We are pun-
ished justly, for we are getting what our deeds deserve. But
this man has done nothing wrong."NIV
One criminal *rebuked* the other criminal—pointing out that they deserved
their sentence, but Jesus did not. They
were being *punished justly,* but Jesus
had *done nothing wrong.* How this one
criminal understood this truth is
unknown; perhaps the truth of Jesus'
innocence was far more widespread
than the religious leaders believed.
There, on the cross, receiving punish-

> If there be ground for you
> to trust in your own
> righteousness, then all
> that Christ did to
> purchase salvation, and
> all that God did to
> prepare the way for it is in
> vain.   *Jonathan Edwards*

ment for what his deeds deserved, this criminal faced himself,
feared God, and turned to Jesus: **Then he said, "Jesus, remem-**
ber me when you come into your Kingdom." And Jesus
replied, "I assure you, today you will be with me in para-
dise."NLT The dying criminal had more faith than all the rest of
Jesus' followers put together. Although the disciples continued to
love Jesus, their hopes for the kingdom had been shattered. Most
of them had gone into hiding. As one of his followers would
sadly say two days later, "We had hoped that he was the one who
was going to redeem Israel" (24:21 NIV). By contrast, the criminal looked at the man who was dying next to him and said,
"Jesus, remember me when you come into your Kingdom." By
all appearances, the kingdom was finished. How awe inspiring is

the faith of this man who alone saw beyond the present shame to the coming glory!

Jesus assured him that *today*—that very day, after they breathed their last—the criminal would be *with [him] in paradise.* The criminal may have lived an evil, lawbreaking life that had resulted in execution, but as he faced death, he turned to and believed in Jesus. This powerful, startling conversation is perfect proof of Jesus' purpose to seek and save the lost (19:10). The assurance of immediate paradise was probably more than he even expected. The word "paradise" is a Persian loanword meaning "garden"—used in the Old Testament to refer to the Garden of Eden. This place would be one of beauty, joy, and rest (see 2 Corinthians 12:4; Revelation 2:7).

NEVER TOO LATE
As this criminal was about to die, he turned to Christ for forgiveness, and Christ accepted him. This shows that deeds don't save—faith in Christ does. It is never too late to turn to God. Even in his misery, Jesus had mercy on this criminal who decided to believe in him. People's lives will be much more useful and fulfilling if they turn to God early, but even those who repent at the very last moment will be with God in paradise. Help others see that "today" is the time of opportunity. Bring them to Christ for his forgiveness.

JESUS DIES ON THE CROSS / 23:44-49 / *236*

Around noon, the sky darkened. The earth shook (Matthew 27:51). The curtain that separated the Most Holy Place from the Holy Place was torn in two, from top to bottom. The dark sky was pierced by an anguished cry: "My God, my God, why have you forsaken me?" (Matthew 27:46; Mark 15:34 NLT). Then Jesus said, "Father, I entrust my spirit into your hands!" (23:46 NLT). And finally, "It is finished!" (John 19:30 NLT).

What was the meaning of all this? Most of the people who gathered left with heavy hearts. The inexplicable incidents that surrounded Jesus' death filled them with terror. But one of the centurions realized that Jesus wasn't just an ordinary man dying for the evil he had done on this earth. He was the sinless Son of the living God.

23:44 By this time it was noon, and darkness fell across the whole land until three o'clock.^{NLT} Jesus had been placed on the cross at nine o'clock in the morning. Three hours had passed, hours of excruciating pain and physical agony. Then, *it was noon,* and at

the height of the day, an eerie *darkness fell across the whole land*
for three hours. How this darkness occurred is unknown, but it is
clear that God caused it to happen. Some suggest an eclipse, but
Passover was held at a full moon, a time when a solar eclipse is
not possible. It was probably some kind of natural event with
supernatural timing. All nature seemed to mourn over the stark
tragedy of the death of God's Son. The darkness was both physical and spiritual—for while nature mourned, this was also the
time when darkness reigned (22:53).

SAVING FAITH
Sometimes churches or individual believers give the impression
that becoming a Christian is a complicated process. You must
ascribe to a certain set of beliefs, join a particular church, give
a prescribed amount of money, and read a specific translation
of the Bible. Contrast that with the simple cry of a dying thief:
"Jesus, remember me when you come into your Kingdom." And
with those words, the man received a response that has
brought comfort and relief to countless men and women ever
since: "Today you will be with me in paradise." Such simplicity
in those words, and yet such power! Christians should study,
be faithful church members, and read God's Word—and never
forget how simple salvation really is.

**23:45 Then the sun was darkened, and the veil of the temple was
torn in two.**[NKJV] Obviously the darkness that covered the land
meant that somehow the sun had been *darkened.* Luke did not
explain it, but clearly God controlled these events. Most significant and symbolic was an event that occurred in the city of Jerusalem, in the beloved temple, right in the inner area called the
Holy Place.

The temple had three parts: the courts for all the people; the
Holy Place, where only priests could enter; and the Most Holy
Place, where the high priest alone could enter once a year to
atone for the sins of the people (Leviticus 16:1-34). In the Most
Holy Place, the ark of the covenant and God's presence with it
rested. As Jesus suffered on the cross and as darkness covered the
land, *the veil of the temple was torn in two.* The veil (curtain) that
was torn was the one that closed off the Most Holy Place from
view. Symbolically, that curtain separated holy God from sinful
people. There are several views about the significance of this tearing, and even each Gospel writer who mentioned it may have had
something different in mind. Some see the tearing of the veil as a
prophetic foreshadowing of the destruction of the temple, which
occurred forty years later, in A.D. 70. Thus, this was showing

God's judgment on the temple. Others see it as signifiying the end of the old covenant making way for the new. The writer of Hebrews saw it as God's way of removing the barrier between himself and humanity. Now sinful people could approach the holy God directly through Christ (Hebrews 9:1-14; 10:19-22). From then on, God would not reside behind a curtain in the temple; he would take up residence in his people.

ULTIMATE COMMITMENT
It's one thing to be committed to God when life is going well. It's a different matter to trust in him when everything is coming apart and death itself rears its dark visage. To be able to trust God in those circumstances takes a gutsy, gritty kind of faith, one rarely seen. But Luke wrote that this was the kind of faith Jesus had in his Father. As Jesus drew his last breaths on the cross, surrounded by spiritual and physical darkness like no one else has ever experienced, it would have been understandable for him to cry out in anguish and bitterness against God the Father. Instead, Jesus submitted to the Father in perfect obedience. Life turns dark and bitter for everyone from time to time, and death comes to all. When you "walk through the valley of the shadow," remember the Lord and his example. Trust God even in the dark times, even in the final moments. He will see you through and meet you on the other side.

23:46 Jesus called out with a loud voice, "Father, into your hands I commit my spirit." When he had said this, he breathed his last.NIV That Jesus had a *loud voice* at all shows his tremendous will. But these were Jesus' very last words from the cross. In committing his spirit to the Father, Jesus died, fulfilling the words of Psalm 31:5. Jesus did not faint; he did not become unconscious only to be revived later—he *breathed his last.* Jesus died as a human being—voluntarily, sacrificially, in the place of sinners.

23:47 The centurion, seeing what had happened, praised God and said, "Surely this was a righteous man."NIV Matthew, Mark, and Luke all point to the head Roman soldier, *the centurion,* who had apparently been in charge of carrying out this execution. A centurion had authority over one hundred men. He may have mocked Jesus earlier (23:36-37), but upon *seeing what had happened,* he realized that Jesus had been no ordinary person. Presumably this centurion had carried out other such executions, but never had he experienced what he did at this one. Besides the three hours of darkness at midday (23:44), an earthquake shook and many dead people came back to life (Matthew 27:51-53). The centurion may have even heard Jesus' words of forgiveness (23:34). This Gentile sol-

THE SEVEN LAST WORDS OF JESUS ON THE CROSS

The statements that Jesus made from the cross have been treasured by all who have followed him as Lord. They demonstrate both his humanity and his divinity. They also capture the last moments of all that Jesus went through to gain forgiveness for believers. (Verses are from NIV.)

"Father, forgive them, for they do not know what they are doing." . . . . Luke 23:34

"I tell you the truth, today you will be with me in paradise." . . . Luke 23:43

Speaking to John and Mary: "Dear woman, here is your son. . . . Here is your mother.". . . . . John 19:26-27

"My God, my God, why have you forsaken me?" . . . . Matthew 27:46; Mark 15:34

"I am thirsty." . . . . John 19:28

"It is finished." . . . . John 19:30

"Father, into your hands I commit my spirit." . . . . Luke 23:46

dier understood something that most of the Jewish nation had missed: *Surely this was a righteous man.* The Greek word *dikaios* can also be rendered "innocent" (see Matthew 23:35; 27:19). If so, the centurion had probably reflected on Pilate's verdict of Jesus' innocence (23:22). More likely, "righteous" is the best meaning because a Roman would not have praised God for Jesus' innocence. Matthew recorded him as calling Jesus "the Son of God" (Matthew 27:54; see also Mark 15:39). It is likely that the soldier did say, "Surely this was the Son of God" and meant it as a title of honor and respect. Luke used the word "righteous" in a way that his Gentile audience could understand. The centurion did not necessarily mean it as believers would now understand it. But he was declaring that Christ was righteous above all others, worthy of God's recognition and man's praise. The centurion understood that Jesus was innocent and had not deserved what he received, yet Jesus had borne it all with dignity, courage, and even words of forgiveness. The centurion saw him as a man who could correctly be considered righteous. While the Jewish religious leaders were celebrating Jesus' death, a Gentile soldier was the first to proclaim Jesus as the Son of God after his death. This pointed forward to the coming days of the evangelism and missionary effort in the church, when God would draw people from all nations.

23:48 And when the crowd that came to see the crucifixion saw all that had happened, they went home in deep sorrow.NLT
Miracles had occurred out there on the hill—darkness, an earth-

quake, dead people walking, and the torn curtain in the temple that no one had probably heard about yet. Perhaps the crowd expected, through all that, to see Jesus come down off the cross and yet be their Messiah. But he didn't. He died. The onlookers in the crowd, who had come to see the spectacle of this execution, *went home in deep sorrow.* Many were deeply affected by Jesus' death.

23:49 **But all his acquaintances, including the women who had followed him from Galilee, stood at a distance, watching these things.**NRSV Jesus' friends and family who had stayed near the cross could hardly believe what had happened. Jesus was dead. No one yet understood what that meant. *The women who had followed him from Galilee* are named in 8:2-3. John wrote that besides himself, Jesus' mother was also there, as well as others (John 19:25-26). Perhaps Jesus' mother, watching *at a distance,* finally understood Simeon's words from years before: "A sword will pierce your own soul" (2:35 NIV). Among Jesus' disciples, only John was at the cross.

JESUS IS LAID IN THE TOMB / 23:50-56 / **237**

Jesus was dead. It was all over (but see 24:1-12). Sometimes the worst circumstances bring out the best in people. In this case, two secret disciples—Joseph of Arimathea and Nicodemus (according to John 19:38-39)—openly expressed their allegiance to Jesus. Joseph was a member of the Sanhedrin, and Nicodemus was a Pharisee. Their colleagues had mercilessly opposed Jesus from the start and had plotted his murder. At Jesus' death, these two came out of hiding and provided for his burial. Associating themselves with Jesus at this time would have been dangerous, but through Jesus' death, Joseph and Nicodemus had become convinced of his complete innocence. They had to stand for the truth, no matter what the cost.

It is never too late to stand for the truth. If you are faced with a situation where you have compromised your witness for Jesus, don't be paralyzed by fear or sorrow. Determine to stand for the truth today, and pray for the strength to do so.

23:50-51 **Now there was a good and righteous man named Joseph. He was a member of the Jewish high council, but he had not agreed with the decision and actions of the other religious leaders. He was from the town of Arimathea in Judea, and he had been waiting for the Kingdom of God to come.**NLT The scene shifts away from the cross to a man, *a member of the Jewish high council* who *had not agreed with the decision and* *actions of the other religious leaders.* Apparently the death sentence for Jesus had not been a unanimous vote. Joseph had been against it, as had another member of the Council named Nicodemus (John 3:1; 19:38-42). Both of these men came to bury Jesus' body. Their commitment to Jesus forced them out of hiding.

Joseph *was from the town of Arimathea,* about twenty-two miles northwest of Jerusalem. This town was the birthplace of Samuel, and its older name was Ramathaim (1 Samuel 1:1). Joseph was a wealthy and honored member of the Jewish Council, and a secret disciple of Jesus (John 19:38) who was *waiting for the Kingdom of God to come* (suggesting that he was a Pharisee, not a Sadducee). The disciples who had publicly followed Jesus had fled, but Joseph boldly took a stand that could cost him dearly. He cared enough about Jesus to ask for his body so he could give it a proper burial.

23:52 He went to Pilate and asked for Jesus' body.^{NLT} Joseph had to go *to Pilate* to ask if he could have *Jesus' body* in order to give it a proper burial. Apparently Pilate alone could give this permission, and this may not have been an easy thing to do—going back to Pilate, who was already furious at the Jewish leaders. Mark recorded that Pilate was surprised that Jesus was already dead and asked the centurion for verification (Mark 15:44-45).

NONCONFORMITY
In every organization, every institution, every society, there is an "inner circle," a privileged few who seem to have disproportionate power and influence over others in that field. Most long to be in that "inner circle" and to have the power and enjoy the prestige that come with it. Unfortunately, some will do almost anything to become a part of it and, once in, almost anything to stay in it. Contrast this with Joseph of Arimathea, a member of the Jewish Council and a secret believer in Jesus. He was a member of the "inner circle," yet he risked giving it all up when he asked to be given Jesus' body for burial. This must have put Joseph at odds with the other Council members and possibly even caused them to ostracize him. He was willing to risk it all for Jesus. How much are you willing to risk for the one who gave his life for you?

23:53 Then he took it down, wrapped it in linen cloth and placed it in a tomb cut in the rock, one in which no one had yet been laid.^{NIV} Joseph had to hurry; Sabbath was fast approaching. Fortunately he had help. John wrote that Nicodemus, another member of the Sanhedrin, brought spices for the burial. Probably along with the help of several servants, Jesus' body was carefully taken down from the cross, washed, wrapped in layers of *linen cloth* with the spices in between, and laid in a tomb. Jesus was given a burial fit for a king.

The *tomb* was likely a man-made cave cut out of one of the many limestone hills in the area around Jerusalem. Such a tomb was large enough to walk into. Some caves were large enough to hold several bodies, but this tomb had never been used—in fact, it was owned by Joseph himself (Matthew 27:60). Such tombs were for wealthy people. So Jesus had a proper burial. After Jesus' burial, a large stone was rolled across the entrance to the tomb (John 20:1).

23:54 It was Preparation Day, and the Sabbath was about to begin.NIV Friday of every week was *Preparation Day,* the day when people prepared for the Sabbath—all necessary work had to be completed before Sabbath began at sundown on Friday. Sabbath ended at sundown on Saturday. Jesus died just a few hours before sundown on Friday. Joseph had to hurry in order to complete this burial before the Sabbath began.

If Jesus had died on the Sabbath when Joseph was unavailable, his body would have been taken down by the Romans. An executed man lost all dignity—it was common to simply leave the body to rot away. Remains would be thrown into a common grave. Had the Romans taken Jesus' body, no Jews could have confirmed his death, and opponents could have disputed his resurrection.

23:55-56 The women who had come with him from Galilee followed, and they saw the tomb and how his body was laid. Then they returned, and prepared spices and ointments. On the sabbath they rested according to the commandment.NRSV The Galilean women who had been at the cross followed Joseph to the tomb. This way, they would know exactly where to find Jesus' body when they would return after the Sabbath with their *spices and ointments.* Anointing a body was a sign of love, devotion, and respect. Bringing spices to the tomb would be like bringing flowers to a grave today. Since bodies were not embalmed in Israel, perfumes were normally used. The women undoubtedly knew that Joseph and Nicodemus had already wrapped the body in linen and spices. They were probably going to do a simple external application of the fragrant spices. After seeing where the body was laid, they went home and *rested according to the commandment* for the Sabbath, planning to return at first light on Sunday morning.

DO WHAT YOU CAN
These women could not do "great" things for Jesus—they were not permitted to stand up before the Jewish Council or the Roman governor and testify on his behalf—but they did what they could. They stayed at the cross when most of the disciples had fled, and they got ready to anoint their Lord's body. Because of their devotion, they were the first to know about the Resurrection. Believers may feel that they can't do much for Jesus. But they must take advantage of the opportunities given to them by doing what they can do and not worrying about what they cannot do.

LUKE 24

Jesus' awful death on the cross was not the end of the story. Within three days, Jesus rose from the tomb. The women who visited the empty tomb were surprised; the disciples were astonished; Thomas doubted (John 20:24-28). Even though Jesus had predicted his own resurrection (9:22; 18:32-33), no one believed it would happen. The disciples even labeled talk of his resurrection as nonsense (24:11). The Resurrection was a complete surprise. Yet it was this pleasant surprise that motivated the disciples to become fearless witnesses to the truth. They would see Jesus with their own eyes (24:36-40); he would teach them from the Scripture (24:25-27). Knowing that Jesus was still alive inspired them to withstand all kinds of hardships, beatings, and even death to tell others about him.

Today Jesus still lives, at the right hand of God the Father (Acts 2:33). The Resurrection still stands as the foundation of the Christian faith. Christians can have complete confidence that Christ is alive, guiding the church and individual Christians through the Holy Spirit. His own resurrection is a guarantee of the future resurrection; death has already been conquered. Moreover, the same power that brought Christ's body back from the dead is available to every Christian today, bringing each spiritually dead person back to life (1 Corinthians 15:12-28).

24:1-2 On the first day of the week, very early in the morning, the women took the spices they had prepared and went to the tomb.^{NIV} *The first day of the week* was not the Sabbath. The women had to wait until then to bring their gifts to the tomb. Jesus had died on Friday; Joseph had taken his body and had prepared it for burial just before the Sabbath began at sundown on Friday. The women had stayed at the cross and had followed Joseph to the tomb, so they knew where Jesus had been laid. The Sabbath had ended at sunset on Saturday, so the women ventured out at first light on Sunday morning. (They are listed in 24:10.) They brought *spices* to the tomb, just as people today would bring flowers—as a sign of love and respect. They had planned to enter the tomb and do a simple

WHY IS THE RESURRECTION SO IMPORTANT?

The resurrection of Jesus from the dead is the central fact of Christian history. On it, the church is built; without it, there would be no Christian church today. Jesus' resurrection is unique. Other religions have strong ethical systems, concepts about paradise and afterlife, and various holy Scriptures. Only Christianity has a God who became human, literally died for his people, and was raised again in power and glory to rule his church forever.

- Because Christ was raised from the dead, Christians know that the kingdom of heaven has broken into earth's history. The world is now headed for redemption, not disaster. God's mighty power is at work destroying sin, creating new lives, and preparing believers for Jesus' second coming.
- Because of the Resurrection, Christians know that death has been conquered and that they, too, will be raised from the dead to live forever with Christ.
- The Resurrection gives authority to the church's witness in the world. Look at the early evangelistic sermons in the book of Acts: The apostles' most important message was the proclamation that Jesus Christ had been raised from the dead!
- The Resurrection gives meaning to the church's regular feast, the Lord's Supper. Like the disciples on the Emmaus Road, believers break bread with their risen Lord, who comes in power to save them.
- The Resurrection helps Christians find meaning even in great tragedy. No matter what happens in their walk with the Lord, the Resurrection gives them hope for the future.
- The Resurrection assures Christians that Christ is alive and ruling his kingdom. He is not legend; he is alive and real.
- God's power that brought Jesus back from the dead is available to believers so that they can live for him in an evil world.

Christians can look very different from one another, and they can hold widely varying beliefs about politics, lifestyle, and even theology. But one central belief unites and inspires all true Christians—Jesus Christ rose from the dead! (For more on the importance of the Resurrection, see 1 Corinthians 15:12-58.)

---

application of the fragrant spices to the body. Mark records that as they were on their way, they discussed who was going to move the large stone for them (Mark 16:3). But they need not have worried. When they arrived, **they found the stone rolled away from the tomb.**[NKJV] In the Jewish reckoning of time, a "day" included any part of a day; thus, Friday was the first day, Saturday was the second day, and Sunday was the third day. When the women arrived at daybreak, Jesus had already risen. Matthew records how the stone was moved (it was a huge stone that was rolled down into an entrance and would have been difficult to remove). There was an earthquake, and an angel of the Lord had descended from heaven, had rolled back the stone, and had sat on it (Matthew 28:2). The stone was not rolled away so that Jesus could get out, for he was already gone. It was rolled aside so others could get in and see for themselves that Jesus had indeed risen from the dead, just as he had said he would.

24:3 So they went in, but they couldn't find the body of the Lord Jesus.^{NLT} The stone had been rolled back, and the women went in expecting to accomplish their task with the spices. Many tombs were large enough to walk into, so these women went into the tomb, *but they couldn't find the body of the Lord Jesus.* Of course, the body was not there because Jesus had been raised, just as he said. But Jesus' followers did not expect this. They had been told at least three times, but they had not come to truly believe (9:21-27, 44-45; 18:31-34).

HE LIVES!
The two angels (appearing as "men in clothes that gleamed like lightning") asked the women why they were looking in a tomb for someone who was alive. People often look for God among the dead. They study the Bible as a mere historical document and go to church as if going to a memorial service. But Jesus is not among the dead—he lives! He reigns in the hearts of Christians, and he is the head of his church. Do you look for Jesus among the living? Do you expect him to be active in the world and in the church? Look for signs of his power—they are all around you.

24:4 While they were wondering about this, suddenly two men in clothes that gleamed like lightning stood beside them.^{NIV} Matthew and John reveal that these two men in gleaming clothes were angels. When angels appeared to people, they looked like humans. Matthew and Mark wrote that one angel met the women at the tomb, while Luke mentioned *two men.* Each Gospel writer chose to highlight different details as he explained the same story, just as eyewitnesses to a news story may each highlight a different aspect of an event. Matthew and Mark probably emphasized only the angel who spoke. The unique emphasis of each Gospel shows that the four accounts were written independently. All four Gospels are true and reliable.

The men's clothing *that gleamed like lightning* revealed that they were not mere humans, but angels making a visitation at this remarkable event. "Gleamed like lightning" also described Jesus' clothes at the Transfiguration (9:29) and recalls Moses' glory after being with God (Exodus 34:29-35). Two angels dressed this way were also present at Jesus' ascension (Acts 1:10). They had been sent to these women to give them an important message.

EVIDENCE THAT JESUS ACTUALLY DIED AND AROSE

This evidence demonstrates Jesus' uniqueness in history and proves that he is God's Son. No one else was able to predict his own resurrection and then accomplish it.

Proposed Explanations for the Empty Tomb	Evidence against These Explanations	References
Jesus was only unconcious and later revived.	A Roman soldier told Pilate that Jesus was dead.	Mark 15:44-45
	The Roman soldiers did not break Jesus' legs because he had already died, and one of them pierced Jesus' side with a spear.	John 19:32-34
	Joseph of Arimathea and Nicodemus wrapped Jesus' body and placed it in the tomb.	John 19:38-42
The women made a mistake and went to the wrong tomb.	Mary Magdalene and Mary the mother of Joses saw Jesus placed in the tomb.	Matthew 27:59-61; Mark 15:47; Luke 23:55
	On Sunday morning, Peter and John also went to the same tomb.	John 20:3-9
Unknown thieves stole Jesus' body.	The tomb was sealed and guarded by Roman soldiers.	Matthew 27:65-66
The disciples stole Jesus' body	The disciples were ready to die for their faith. Stealing Jesus' body would have been admitting that their faith was meaningless.	Acts 12:2
	The tomb was guarded and sealed.	Matthew 27:66
The religious leaders stole Jesus' body to produce it later.	If the religious leaders had taken Jesus' body, they would have produced it to stop the rumors of his resurrection.	None

24:5-7 In their fright the women bowed down with their faces to the ground, but the men said to them, "Why do you look for the living among the dead? He is not here; he has risen! Remember how he told you, while he was still with you in Galilee: 'The Son of Man must be delivered into the hands of sinful men, be crucified and on the third day be raised again.'"NIV

These men at the tomb surprised the women, and their dazzling appearance frightened them. The women reacted in humility, bowing *with their faces to the ground* before these men (probably in fear and respect, but not in worship, for the angels would not have accepted any form of worship).

The angel asked the obvious question, *"Why do you look for the living among the dead?"* Why would these women come to a tomb to find someone who had promised to be alive—and, indeed, was alive? Then one angel spoke the words that have thrilled every believer since that first Resurrection morning: *"He is not here; he has risen!"*

HE REALLY IS ALIVE
People who hear about the Resurrection for the first time may need time before they can comprehend this amazing story. Like the disciples, they may pass through four stages of belief. (1) At first, they may think it is a fairy tale, impossible to believe. (2) Like Peter, they may check out the facts but still be puzzled about what happened. (3) Only when they encounter Jesus personally will they be able to accept the fact of the Resurrection. (4) Then, as they commit themselves to Jesus and devote their lives to serving him, they will begin fully to understand the reality of his presence with them. As you witness, accept people's need to think through. Allow them time to wonder.

The angels then reminded the women that Jesus had accurately predicted all that had happened to him—how he would be *delivered into the hands of sinful men, be crucified and on the third day be raised again.* Jesus had made these exact predictions regarding himself—the *Son of Man*— in 9:21-27, 44-45; 18:31-34.

Luke stressed God's divine initiative and control in all Christ's predictions (see 24:26, 44). In three elements, "to be delivered," "to be crucified," and "to be raised again," God's plan was fully stated and explained the empty tomb to these women.

24:8-9 Then they remembered his words, and returning from the tomb, they told all this to the eleven and to all the rest.NRSV These women must have been among Jesus' faithful followers and had heard Jesus' predictions of his death, for Luke says *they remembered [Jesus'] words* to them, and suddenly everything came together. It *had* all occurred just as Jesus had said, and he now had been raised on the third day, just as he had tried to tell them. So these women left the tomb and *told all this to the eleven* (disciples, minus Judas Iscariot) *and to all the rest* of Jesus' followers, who may have been in hiding since the Crucifixion. Matthew and Mark say that the angel told them to go and tell the disciples what had happened. The women obeyed, running with the great news to the sorrowing and bewildered disciples.

24:10-11 **The women who went to the tomb were Mary Magdalene, Joanna, Mary the mother of James, and several others. They told the apostles what had happened, but the story sounded like nonsense, so they didn't believe it.**^NLT The women are named here, probably because some of the later believers may have known them or about them. *Mary Magdalene* had been a loyal follower—Jesus had cast seven demons out of her (8:2). All the Gospels place her at the cross and at the tomb. Jesus' first appearance to any human after his resurrection was to this woman (Mark 16:9; John 20:11-16). *Joanna* was previously mentioned among the women who followed Jesus (8:3). *Mary the mother of James* is also mentioned in Mark 15:40; 16:1 (she may be "the other Mary" of Matthew 28:1). The *several others* include Salome (Mark 16:1) and other unnamed persons—all women.

They brought their story back to *the apostles*—giving them the message that the angel had told them: "He has risen from the dead and is going ahead of you into Galilee. There you will see him" (Matthew 28:7 NIV). The fact that the message was carried by women gives credibility and persuasive force to Luke's account. No ancient person making up such a story would have women as the official witnesses. By Jewish law, women could not do so.

Amazingly, the disciples did not believe it—*the story sounded like nonsense.* Apparently Jesus' words about dying and rising again had gone past all of them, or they somehow had interpreted the words figuratively rather than literally. Jesus' arrest and death had stunned them all; their disloyalty to him had humiliated them. Their last two days had been spent together in hiding as they tried to sort through what had happened. Peter must have told them about his experience in the high priest's courtyard and his blatant denials. Judas had killed himself. Jesus had been executed. Had they been completely duped? What was going on? Then these women arrived on the scene, sounding as though they had gone over the edge—empty tomb? angels? Perhaps these women hoped too much. Perhaps they merely had gone to the wrong tomb. It should not be surprising, then, that the eleven men *didn't believe it.* And they certainly were not going to make the trip to Galilee on the words of these women who supposedly had received the message from two men at the tomb who looked like angels!

Many skeptics have tried to write off the Resurrection as a story made up by a group of overzealous disciples. But here the opposite occurred. The disciples were not anxiously looking for any reason to believe that Jesus had risen; in fact, they were not anticipating it. When told of the Resurrection, they refused to believe without concrete evidence. Even a missing body was not enough to convince them.

A PRESENT DARKNESS

Have you ever had an experience, or maybe even a series of experiences, that at the time seemed to make no sense and, in fact, seemed contrary to God's will? That was certainly the case with the men on the way to Emmaus. They had hoped for Jesus to be the promised Messiah, the one who would save his people, but he had died a horrible, public death, thus putting an end to their hopes and dreams. Or so it seemed . . . until Jesus himself came to them as they walked and opened their hearts and minds to the truth. If you are going through a dark time when nothing seems to make sense, and right and wrong seem to have changed jerseys—hold on. Keep walking faithfully, and wait for God to open your heart and mind. He will. Then you will perhaps understand the purpose of the darkness.

24:12 Peter, however, got up and ran to the tomb. Bending over, he saw the strips of linen lying by themselves, and he went away, wondering to himself what had happened.[NIV] John 20:3-4 reveals that another disciple ran to the tomb with Peter. That other disciple was almost certainly John, the author of the fourth Gospel. When Peter arrived at the tomb, he bent over and looked in. *He saw the strips of linen lying by themselves.* John's Gospel says, "He saw the strips of linen lying there. . . . The cloth was folded up by itself, separate from the linen" (John 20:6-7 NIV). The graveclothes, the linen that had been wrapped around Jesus' body, had been left as if Jesus had passed right through them. The headpiece was rolled up separately from the other wrappings. A grave robber couldn't possibly have made off with Jesus' body and left the linens as if they were still shaped around it. The neatness and order indicated that there was not a hasty removal of Jesus' body. No wonder Peter *went away, wondering to himself what had happened.*

JESUS APPEARS TO TWO BELIEVERS TRAVELING ON THE ROAD / 24:13-35 / *243*

Luke was the only Gospel writer who described in detail Jesus' encounter with the two disciples on the road to Emmaus (Mark briefly mentioned this encounter in Mark 16:12-13). Perhaps Luke chose to emphasize this story because it identified the major error of the disciples at this time. First they did not know the Scripture that well, and second they were slow to believe.

Jesus sternly admonished the two disciples for these two faults and proceeded to explain to them how his life, death, and resurrection had fulfilled the prophecies of Scripture.

IN OUR MIDST

The two disciples returning to Emmaus at first missed the significance of history's greatest event because they were too focused on their disappointments and problems. In fact, they didn't recognize Jesus when he was walking beside them. To compound the problem, they were walking in the wrong direction—away from the fellowship of believers in Jerusalem. Christians are likely to miss Jesus and withdraw from the strength found in other believers when they become preoccupied with their dashed hopes and frustrated plans. Only when looking for Jesus in their midst will believers experience the power and help he can bring. Be alert to his presence in every aspect of daily living.

24:13-14 That same day two of Jesus' followers were walking to the village of Emmaus, seven miles out of Jerusalem. As they walked along they were talking about everything that had happened.^{NLT} This event occurred on Sunday, the *same day* as the Resurrection. Two followers of Jesus were leaving Jerusalem and walking the seven miles to *the village of Emmaus.* Little is known of these disciples—one was named Cleopas (24:18). The other was not one of the eleven disciples, as noted by 24:33.

During their walk, *they were talking about everything that had happened.* As *Jesus' followers,* they may have taken in the Triumphal Entry, and they may have heard the crowds call for Jesus' death. They may have witnessed Jesus' final walk through Jerusalem or seen his execution. They were discussing these events as they left the city. Jesus had died; they were returning home.

HOPE LOST AND REGAINED

God seems to specialize in allowing our dreams to die, only to bring them back around again in rather surprising ways. Job's fortunes and even his family were restored to him many times over. Abraham and Sarah were blessed with a child long after nature would have made that impossible. And the ultimate example is the death and resurrection of Jesus himself. The hopes of many, including the two dejected pilgrims on the way to Emmaus, seemed to have died on the cross with him. Little did they understand that even the Cross was all part of God's sovereign plan to make a way of salvation for everyone. Have you lost hope in God's deliverance and even his goodness? Learn a lesson from these two believers: Wait for the Lord to redeem your situation and give you hope once more.

24:15-16 **While they were talking and discussing, Jesus himself came near and went with them, but their eyes were kept from recognizing him.**^{NRSV} The two followers were deep in discussion as they walked along the road away from Jerusalem toward Emmaus. Apparently a man walking in the same direction drew up beside them (they knew he had been in Jerusalem, 24:18). This man was *Jesus himself . . . but their eyes were kept from recognizing him.* In other appearances after the Resurrection, Jesus was also not recognized at first (John 20:14; 21:4). Here, God prevented these people from seeing Jesus until Jesus was ready to reveal himself to them (24:30-31). God's divine sovereignty kept them from understanding until the full reality of the bodily resurrection of Jesus could be understood.

24:17 **He asked them, "What are you discussing together as you walk along?" They stood still, their faces downcast.**^{NIV} Jesus, who had walked up behind them during their intense discussion, asked what they had been talking about. The verb "discussing" refers to an exchange of ideas. In their bewilderment over all that had happened during that weekend, these disciples were talking back and forth about what they had learned, heard, and understood— and what it all meant in light of the latest development, Jesus' death. At Jesus' question, *they stood still, their faces downcast.* Apparently in their discussion they had been unable to come to any understanding, so they were still sad and upset about what had occurred.

Then one of them, whose name was Cleopas, answered him, "Are you the only stranger in Jerusalem who does not know the things that have taken place there in these days?"^{NRSV} Jesus had apparently walked up behind the two believers, so they assumed that he too was a pilgrim traveling home from Jerusalem. If he had been in Jerusalem, how could he not have known what had happened there? The news about Jesus' crucifixion had spread throughout the city.

ON THE ROAD TO EMMAUS
After Jesus' death, two of his followers were walking from Jerusalem back toward Emmaus when a stranger joined them. After dinner in Emmaus, Jesus revealed himself to them and then disappeared. They immediately returned to Jerusalem to tell the disciples the good news that Jesus was alive.

Because this was Passover week, Jewish pilgrims visiting the city from all over the Roman Empire would have known about his death. This was not a small, insignificant event, affecting only the disciples—the whole nation was interested.

LIVING WITNESS
These disciples knew that the tomb was empty, but they didn't understand that Jesus had risen, and they were filled with sadness. Despite the women's witness, which was verified by other disciples, and despite the biblical prophecies of this very event, they still didn't believe. Today the Resurrection still catches people by surprise. In spite of two thousand years of evidence and witness, many people refuse to believe. What more will it take? For these disciples it took the living, breathing Jesus in their midst. For many people today, it takes the presence of living, breathing Christians. Are you willing to be that witness to others?

24:19 "What things?" he asked. "About Jesus of Nazareth," they replied. "He was a prophet, powerful in word and deed before God and all the people."^{NIV} Jesus asked *what things* had occurred. They answered that much had happened to a man named *Jesus of Nazareth.* The two followers described him as *a prophet, powerful in word and deed before God and all the people.* They had heard Jesus teach and had seen him perform miracles of healing; they understood him to be a "prophet" (see commentary on 24:44-45). They thought he was much more— the one who would "redeem Israel" (24:21). But, as far as they knew, he had died like all the other prophets before him.

BAFFLED?
The world has not changed its values: a suffering Servant is no more popular today than two thousand years ago. But there is not only the witness of the Old Testament prophets; the witness of the New Testament apostles and the history of the Christian church all point to Jesus' victory over death. Step outside the values of your culture and put your faith in Jesus. Don't foolishly continue to be baffled by his Good News!

24:20 "But our leading priests and other religious leaders arrested him and handed him over to be condemned to death, and they crucified him."^{NLT} The telling item in this statement is that these two disciples knew who was responsibile for Jesus' death. The Romans may have actually done the executing, but the Jews' (they said *our*) *leading priests and other religious leaders* *arrested him and handed him over.* If all of Jerusalem knew what had happened, then the religious leaders' plan to try to blame the execution on the Romans had failed. Everyone knew the leaders' role in Jesus' death.

24:21 **"But we were hoping that it was He who was going to redeem Israel. Indeed, besides all this, today is the third day since these things happened."**^{NKJV} The disciples from Emmaus had been *hoping* that Jesus could redeem Israel—that is, that he would rescue the nation from its enemies. The words "redeem" and "redemption" have deep roots in Israel's history. To "redeem" someone meant to pay a price for his or her freedom. Most Jews believed that the Old Testament prophecies pointed to a military and political Messiah who would free the nation from Roman tyranny. Jesus had come to redeem, however, and had indeed paid a huge price—his life. No one comprehended this yet. They didn't realize that the Messiah had come to redeem people from slavery to sin. When Jesus died, therefore, they lost all hope. They didn't understand that Jesus' death offered the greatest hope possible. Instead, they hoped, but at his death, their hopes were dashed. Their report that *today is the third day since these things happened* reveals a bit of expectation at Jesus' promises regarding the "third day" after his death. As far as they knew, however, nothing had changed.

> The gospel is light but only the Spirit can give sight.   *A. W. Tozer*

24:22-24 **"Then some women from our group of his followers were at his tomb early this morning, and they came back with an amazing report. They said his body was missing, and they had seen angels who told them Jesus is alive! Some of our men ran out to see, and sure enough, Jesus' body was gone, just as the women had said."**^{NLT} Another insight found in this statement is that these two followers had left Jerusalem, hopeless and downcast, *after* having heard *an amazing report.* The women who had been to the tomb and heard the angels' words went and told the disciples (and apparently other followers as well) that Jesus' *body was missing* and that angels had said *Jesus is alive.* Then some men (Peter and John, 24:12; John 20:3-4) verified what the women had said and found that, *sure enough, Jesus' body was gone.* Yet there was still gloom, as noted by these disciples, who had all this information but had left the city still believing that all their hopes in Jesus had been dashed. Their reaction typifies the human tendency even of disciples to ignore the law of God and to doubt in spite of clear evidence.

PUZZLED?
After the two disciples had explained their sadness and confusion, Jesus responded by going to Scripture and applying it to his ministry. When you are puzzled by questions or problems, you too can go to Scripture to find authoritative help. If you, like these two disciples, do not understand what the Bible means, you can turn to other believers who know the Bible and have the wisdom to apply it to your situation.

24:25-27 **He said to them, "How foolish you are, and how slow of heart to believe all that the prophets have spoken! Did not the Christ have to suffer these things and then enter his glory?" And beginning with Moses and all the Prophets, he explained to them what was said in all the Scriptures concerning himself.**NIV Why did Jesus call these disciples *foolish?* Even though they well knew *all that the prophets have spoken,* they failed to understand that Christ's suffering was his path to glory. The prophets had said that Christ would have to *suffer these things and then enter his glory.* The disciples could not understand why God did not intervene to save Jesus from the cross. They were so caught up in the world's admiration of political power and military might that they were unprepared for the reversal of values in God's kingdom—that the last will be first and that life grows out of death.

Beginning with the promised offspring in Genesis (Genesis 3:15) and going through the suffering Servant in Isaiah (Isaiah 53), the pierced one in Zechariah (Zechariah 12:10), and the messenger of the covenant in Malachi (Malachi 3:1), Jesus reintroduced these disciples to the Old Testament. Christ is the thread woven through all the Scriptures, the central theme that binds them together. Following are several key passages Jesus may have mentioned on this walk to Emmaus: Genesis 3; 12; Psalms 22; 69; 110; Isaiah 53; Jeremiah 31; Zechariah 9; 13; Malachi 3. Jesus pointed out the authority of God's Word and the error of treating it selectively. Jesus spoke from *Moses* (the Law—the books of Genesis through Deuteronomy) and *all the Prophets,* pointing out *what was said in all the Scriptures concerning himself.* Unlike the religious leaders, who had spent their lifetimes studying Scripture and conveniently disregarding the concept of a "suffering Servant," Jesus pointed out all the Scriptures and how what had happened to Jesus had fulfilled everything that had been prophesied regarding the Messiah. While several texts in the Old Testament are specific prophecies regarding the Messiah, Jesus' conversation with the two followers probably took them through the entire Old Testament history and story line, pointing out the problem of sin and how it would have to be solved through the sacrificial death of God's own Son.

JESUS' STYLE OF WITNESSING
Christians can learn better ways to reach friends and neighbors with the gospel by studying the Lord's methods on the road to Emmaus. (1) Jesus walked with them, joining them in their activity and context. (2) Jesus talked with them, inquiring about their discussion. (3) Jesus utilized the truth of Scripture to deal with their unbelief. (4) Jesus shared a meal with them for the sake of friendship.

24:28-29 **As they approached the village to which they were going, Jesus acted as if he were going farther. But they urged him strongly, "Stay with us, for it is nearly evening; the day is almost over." So he went in to stay with them.**[NIV] They approached Emmaus and the journey's end for the two travelers. Jesus would not have stayed with them if he had not been invited. But they were impressed with all that Jesus had been telling them—probably answering many of the questions the two of them had been discussing before this man had joined them. They wanted to talk further, so they invited Jesus to stay.

As it was *nearly evening,* it would have been dangerous to travel farther after dark. So interest and common laws of hospitality caused them to invite this man to stay both for a meal and for overnight lodging. *So he went in to stay with them.*

When he was at the table with them, he took bread, blessed and broke it, and gave it to them. Then their eyes were opened, and they recognized him; and he vanished from their sight.[NRSV] At the meal, Jesus *took bread, blessed and broke it, and gave it to them.* This was probably not a Communion meal but, rather, simply a fellowship meal. Usually the host would break the bread at the beginning of the meal, but Jesus took this task upon himself. When he did so, *their eyes were opened, and they recognized him.* These two disciples had not been at the Last Supper, so this was not what sparked recogni-

> *"Peace Be unto You."* Jesus himself is here! We need nothing else when we are terrified and afraid. You may be fearing the consequences of your sin; fearing the approach of your enemy; fearing the future with its unknown contingencies; but Jesus himself is the antidote of fear. He keeps the soul that trusts him within the double doors of peace.   *F. B. Meyer*

tion. This was the exact time God wanted them to recognize Jesus. God had kept them from understanding (24:16), and now he opened their eyes through the teaching of the Word (24:27) and the breaking of the bread. His mission accomplished with these two disciples, Jesus *vanished from their sight.*

24:32 **They said to each other, "Were not our hearts burning within us while he was talking to us on the road, while he was opening the scriptures to us?"**^{NRSV} Jesus had vanished as quickly as he had come, and the two disciples were left to discuss how they had felt something different in their hearts as Jesus had talked with them and had opened the Scriptures to them. Jesus' presence had almost imperceptibly changed their mood from despair to *hearts burning within.* They experienced relief and tremendous excitement as Jesus walked them through the Scriptures. Only when they realized who he was did they realize what he had done, not only with his logical explanations, but also in their inner beings, in their hearts. Their hope had been confirmed; their doubts dispelled.

HEARTS AFLAME
One of the marks of true conversion is the way a person's heart is changed by the indwelling Christ. Truth and events that once seemed unimportant or even irrelevant take on new significance, new meaning. A cold, dead heart that was completely wrapped up in self-centered pursuits begins to thaw and warm to the realities of the Spirit and the needs of others. John Wesley described it by saying his heart was "strangely warmed"; the Emmaus-bound disciples asked, "Were not our hearts burning within us while he was talking to us on the road, while he was opening the scriptures to us?" Does your heart burn for the realities of God? Has it grown cold due to neglect or sin? Only by spending time in the presence of the living Christ can you reverse the cooling process. Make a commitment to spend some time with him—today.

24:33-34 **And within the hour they were on their way back to Jerusalem, where the eleven disciples and the other followers of Jesus were gathered. When they arrived, they were greeted with the report, "The Lord has really risen! He appeared to Peter!"**^{NLT} Evening may have been coming on (24:29), but their news was too exciting to wait until morning. *Within the hour* the two disciples *were on their way back to Jerusalem.* They knew where to find *the eleven disciples and the other followers* because they had apparently left that gathering that morning (24:22-24). When they got there, they found that Jesus had

JESUS' APPEARANCES AFTER HIS RESURRECTION

1. Mary Magdalene	Mark 16:9-11; John 20:10-18
2. The other women at the tomb	Matthew 28:8-10
3. Peter in Jerusalem	Luke 24:34; 1 Corinthians 15:5
4. The two travelers on the road	Mark 16:12-13; Luke 24:13-35
5. Ten disciples behind closed doors	Luke 24:36-43; John 20:19-25
6. All eleven disciples (including Thomas)	Mark 16:14; John 20:26-31; 1 Corinthians 15:5
7. Seven disciples while fishing on the Sea of Galilee	John 21:1-14
8. Eleven disciples on a mountain in Galilee	Matthew 28:16-20; Mark 16:15-18
9. A crowd of 500	1 Corinthians 15:6
10. Jesus' brother James	1 Corinthians 15:7
11. Those who watched Jesus ascend into heaven	Mark 16:19-20; Luke 24:50-53; Acts 1:3-9

already *appeared to Peter,* and this caused them to know that *the Lord has really risen!*

Paul also mentioned that Jesus appeared to Peter alone (1 Corinthians 15:5). This appearance is not further described in the Gospels. Jesus showed individual concern for Peter because Peter felt completely unworthy after denying his Lord. But Peter repented, and Jesus approached him and forgave him. Soon God would use Peter in building Christ's church (see the first half of the book of Acts).

24:35 Then the two told what had happened on the way, and how Jesus was recognized by them when he broke the bread.[NIV] The two disciples then told their story of how Jesus had appeared and talked to them and how they had recognized him *when he broke the bread.* Why Jesus chose certain people to whom to appear at first and not others is unknown. Peter apparently needed an extra personal encounter; Mary Magdalene's love and devotion accorded her the opportunity to see Jesus first. Whatever the reason for Jesus to have spent a lengthy time with these two disappointed followers on the road to Emmaus, the story stands as a beautiful treasure of Jesus' compassion and love for those who, when discouraged and confused, needed his presence and wisdom to comfort them.

JESUS APPEARS TO THE DISCIPLES BEHIND LOCKED DOORS / 24:36-43 / **244**

The disciples, who had gathered in Jerusalem, were already talking with excitement about what had occurred. The tomb was empty. Jesus had appeared to Peter and to two of them on the way to Emmaus (24:33-35). In the excitement and confusion of it all, Jesus appeared in the room, wishing them "peace." Suddenly the room became deathly still. They sat in stunned silence; they couldn't believe their eyes. It was Jesus! The wounds on his hands and feet could be clearly seen. He was real. He was alive. Even the doubters, such as Thomas, eventually were persuaded by the evidence. After seeing Jesus alive, Thomas cried, "My Lord and my God." His confession should be on believers' lips today (John 20:26-29).

PEACE
People everywhere search for peace. Some seek it through artificial means like alcohol and other chemicals; some through temporary thrills like sex or diversions like shopping; and some through self-improvement schemes like transcendental meditation or positive-thinking techniques. Sooner or later— usually sooner—the inadequacy and spiritual bankruptcy of all these things show through, leaving the seeker more troubled and less hopeful than before. Where can peace be found? Jesus said, "Peace be with you." How could Jesus pronounce peace in what had to be an excruciatingly turbulent time? Simply because he was there. As the old saying goes, "Know Jesus, know peace; no Jesus, no peace." If you would have peace, you must know Jesus. In his presence you find the calm, quiet assurance that he is in fact working all things together for your good (Romans 8:28). Have you spent time with him lately?

24:36 **While they were talking about this, Jesus himself stood among them and said to them, "Peace be with you."**NRSV As Jesus' followers discussed his recent appearances, suddenly *Jesus himself stood among them.* He appeared among them behind locked doors (John 20:19). Jesus could do this because his resurrection and glorification had altered his bodily form. In this new body he was able to transcend all physical barriers.

Jesus' first words to the group of disbelieving and bewildered followers and disciples, all of whom had deserted him in his time of greatest need, were: *"Peace be with you."* This was a standard Hebrew greeting, but here it was filled with greater meaning. Jesus brought a greeting of peace, and his presence brought peace.

They were startled and frightened, thinking they saw a ghost. He said to them, "Why are you troubled, and why do doubts rise in your minds? Look at my hands and my feet. It is I myself! Touch me and see; a ghost does not have flesh and bones, as you see I have."[NIV] These people in the locked room were still wrestling with

> Faith does not operate in the realm of the possible. There is no glory for God in that which is humanly possible. Faith begins where man's power ends.
> *George Mueller*

the fact that Jesus' body was missing, and then they heard amazing stories of his appearances to several people of their group. Suddenly the missing body was there among them; they had not yet even begun to consider, *if* Jesus really was alive, what his body would be like. Jesus appeared among them suddenly, and *they were startled and frightened, thinking they saw a ghost.* But Jesus' body wasn't a figment of the imagination; they weren't seeing a ghost. Jesus encouraged them to look and touch. He had *flesh and bones* and could even eat food (24:43). On the other hand, his body wasn't a restored human body like Lazarus's (John 11)—he was able to appear and disappear. Jesus' resurrected body was immortal.

LET JESUS TEACH YOU
Jesus opened these people's minds to understand the Scriptures. The Holy Spirit does this in believers' lives today as they study the Bible. Have you ever wondered how to understand a difficult Bible passage? Besides reading surrounding passages, asking other people, and consulting reference works, pray that the Holy Spirit will open your mind to understand, giving you the needed insight to put God's Word into action in your life.

24:40-43 **As he spoke, he held out his hands for them to see, and he showed them his feet. Still they stood there doubting, filled with joy and wonder. Then he asked them, "Do you have anything here to eat?" They gave him a piece of broiled fish, and he ate it as they watched.**[NLT] Jesus showed them *his hands* and *his feet* so as to reveal the wounds inflicted by the nails that had held him to the cross (see John 20:25). His resurrected body still bore these wounds as a testimony to his followers that this was the same man whom they had loved, followed, and seen die. This was too good to be true—and they experienced the conflicting emotions of disbelief, doubt, joy, and wonder that any person would have when a most desired, but seemingly most impossible, wish actually comes true. Jesus stood there among them, alive, even eating *a piece of* *broiled fish* to show that he was not a ghost. He was real; he came back to life just as he had told them he would.

JESUS APPEARS TO THE DISCIPLES IN JERUSALEM / 24:44-49 / **249**

Jesus did not come back to Jerusalem after his resurrection to provide a spectacular show or to seek revenge on his enemies. Instead, he returned to teach his disciples. He had already instructed them while he was with them, but they had not completely understood him (see 9:45; 18:34). During his final days, he taught them again. This time, he opened their minds, so that they could understand the truth: his life, death, and resurrection all fulfilled Scripture. He taught them so they could teach others, telling what they had seen Jesus do and heard him say. They were to be Jesus' witnesses (a theme Luke continued in the book of Acts, see Acts 1:4-5, 7-8).

REPENTANCE AND FORGIVENESS
"If you want to build a church that appeals to today's culture, you can't talk about stuff like sin, repentance, and judgment. People don't want to hear about that. Just tell them about the good stuff, like forgiveness, grace, and heaven. That's what they want to hear." In some circles, this kind of talk actually takes place among those who want to see big, growing churches. A growing church is a good goal—but not if growth comes at the expense of truth. Jesus said that the gospel message is one of repentance (turning away from our sins) and forgiveness (being cleansed from our sins) through faith in him. This is the message that Christians are to preach in their churches and to live out in their relationships. Is your church faithfully proclaiming this message? Are you?

24:44-45 **He said to them, "This is what I told you while I was still with you: Everything must be fulfilled that is written about me in the Law of Moses, the Prophets and the Psalms." Then he opened their minds so they could understand the Scriptures.**[NIV] Many days may have elapsed between 24:43 and 24:44 because Jesus and his followers traveled to Galilee and back before he returned to heaven (Matthew 28:16; John 21). Acts, Luke's second book, reveals that Jesus spent forty days with his disciples between his resurrection and ascension.

As he had already done with the two on the road to Emmaus, Jesus *opened their minds so they could understand the Scriptures* and explained how everything that had been written about the coming Messiah had been fulfilled in him. "The Law of Moses,

the Prophets and the Psalms" is a way to describe the entire
Old Testament. In other words, the entire Old Testament points
to the Messiah. For example, Jesus' role as prophet was foretold in Deuteronomy 18:15-20; his sufferings were prophesied
in Psalm 22 and Isaiah 53; his resurrection was predicted in
Psalm 16:9-11 and Isaiah 53:10-11.

24:46-48 **He told them, "This is what is written: The Christ will suffer
and rise from the dead on the third day, and repentance and
forgiveness of sins will be preached in his name to all nations,
beginning at Jerusalem. You are witnesses of these things."**[NIV]
Not only had the Old Testament Scriptures been fulfilled in Jesus'
life, death, and resurrection, but the Old Testament went much further—speaking of *repentance and forgiveness of sins* that would *be
preached . . . to all nations.* Luke was writing to the Greek-speak-
ing world. He wanted them to know that Christ's message of God's
love and forgiveness should go to all the world—and that this had
been God's plan from the very beginning. Christ's gospel has a
worldwide scope. God wants all the world to hear the good news of
salvation. The apostle Paul, a former Pharisee and student of the
Old Testament, later testified: "I am saying nothing beyond what
the prophets and Moses said would happen—that the Christ would
suffer and, as the first to rise from the dead, would proclaim light to
his own people and to the Gentiles" (Acts 26:22-23 NIV). Isaiah had
written:

> As the soul does not live idly in the body, but gives motion and vigour to every member and part, so the Spirit of God cannot dwell in us without manifesting himself by the outward effects.   *John Calvin*

- "I, the LORD, have called you in righteousness; I will take hold of your hand. I will keep you and will make you to be a covenant for the people and a light for the Gentiles" (Isaiah 42:6 NIV).
- "It is too small a thing for you to be my servant to restore the tribes of Jacob and bring back those of Israel I have kept. I will also make you a light for the Gentiles, that you may bring my salvation to the ends of the earth" (Isaiah 49:6 NIV).
- "Nations will come to your light, and kings to the brightness of your dawn" (Isaiah 60:3 NIV).

God's covenant with Abraham had stated, "All peoples on
earth will be blessed through you" (Genesis 12:3 NIV). His covenant with David said, "I will raise up your offspring to succeed
you, who will come from your own body, and I will establish his
kingdom. He is the one who will build a house for my Name, and

I will establish the throne of his kingdom forever" (2 Samuel 7:12-13 NIV). Jesus probably explained the worldwide sweep of what he had accomplished as he told his disciples that his name would be preached to all nations. They would begin right where they were—in Jerusalem—and then be *witnesses of these things* throughout the world (see Acts 1:8).

WAITING FOR THE POWER
Trying to drive a car without the keys, operating a power tool without electricity, a hydroelectric plant without any water source—all of these futile actions make as much sense as trying to minister to others without the power of the Holy Spirit. Believers can do nothing good without his power, yet how often they try! Christians schedule revival as if God ran on their schedule, they launch evangelistic efforts without praying that God will prepare people's hearts, and they run churches and ministries as if God were more interested in marketing and management techniques than people's souls. How tragic—and how foolish! Take a page from the first church's strategy for growth: wait for the power from on high. Does your church need to go back to basics like this?

24:49 **"I am going to send you what my Father has promised; but stay in the city until you have been clothed with power from on high."**NIV This task of being witnesses to salvation through Jesus Christ was not to be carried out in the disciples' own strength. Obviously these followers, hiding behind locked doors in fear of the Jews right there in Jerusalem, hardly seemed like the kind of people who could take the message across the world. But Jesus was not expecting them to do it on their own—he would send what his Father had promised—the Holy Spirit (John 14:15-27; 16:5-15). Jesus said, *"I am going to send."* This shows his power and authority as mediator of the Holy Spirit. Jesus instructed them to *stay in the city* (that is, in Jerusalem) until they were *clothed with power from on high.* Jesus promised them the power (the Spirit in them), which would enable them to be witnesses (Acts 1:8). After his exaltation at his ascension, the power would be given to them (Acts 2:1-4). "Clothed with" refers to the equipping and enabling that the Spirit would bring.

JESUS ASCENDS INTO HEAVEN / 24:50-53 / **250**

Luke concluded his Gospel with a brief account of Jesus' ascension. In Acts, he provided a more complete description of it (see Acts 1:6-11).

After watching Jesus ascend into heaven, the disciples returned to Jerusalem to praise God in the temple (just as Simeon and Anna had done when Jesus was an infant, see 2:25-32, 36-38). Luke ended his account with the disciples praising God, the only appropriate response to Jesus' glorious life and his message of salvation.

24:50 Then he led them out as far as Bethany, and, lifting up his hands, he blessed them.NRSV Jesus took his followers out of Jerusalem *as far as Bethany,* the village only a couple miles away on the slopes of the Mount of Olives. Jesus lifted his hands and *blessed* his followers. At this time, he would leave them, never to return until the time of the Second Coming. They would never be able to walk and talk with him physically as they had been able to do during those three years of ministry. But they would soon receive the Holy Spirit, who would fill them and be with them always.

24:51 While he was blessing them, he left them and was taken up to heaven.NLT In the act of blessing his followers, Jesus *left them and was taken up to heaven.* Jesus' physical presence left the disciples (Acts 1:9), but the Holy Spirit soon came to comfort them and empower them to spread the gospel of salvation (Acts 2:1-4). Today Jesus' work of salvation is completed, and he is sitting at God's right hand, where he has authority over heaven and earth.

THIS SAME JESUS
As the disciples stood and watched, Jesus began rising into the air, and soon he disappeared into heaven. Seeing Jesus leave must have been frightening, but the disciples knew that he would keep his promise to be with them through the Holy Spirit. This same Jesus, who lived with the disciples, who died and was buried, and who rose from the dead, loves you and promises to be with you always. You can get to know him better through studying the Scriptures, praying, and allowing the Holy Spirit to make you more like Jesus.

24:52-53 And they worshiped him, and returned to Jerusalem with great joy; and they were continually in the temple blessing God.NRSV The sight of Jesus returning to glory in heaven called for a response of worship from those who watched. Then they *returned to Jerusalem with great joy.* There was no more sorrow, no more bewilderment, no more wonder about what was going on with this Jesus. Instead, the disciples understood and were filled with joy. As yet, they did not separate themselves from their Jewish roots but *were continually in the temple blessing God.* There were no more closed and locked doors for these followers. Jesus told them to stay in Jerusalem, so they did. Acts 1 gives some idea of their activity as they awaited the promised Holy Spirit. But they openly went to the temple to praise God for all that he had done.

Luke's Gospel portrays Jesus as the perfect example of a life lived according to God's plan—as a child living in obedience to his parents and yet amazing the religious leaders in the temple, as an adult serving God and others through preaching and healing, and finally as a condemned man suffering without complaint. This emphasis was well suited to Luke's Greek audience, who placed high value on being an example and improving oneself, and who often discussed the meaning of perfection. The Greeks, however, had a difficult time understanding the spiritual importance of the physical world. To them, the spiritual was always more important than the physical. To help them understand the God-man who united the spiritual and the physical, Luke emphasized that Jesus was not a phantom human but a real human being who healed people and fed them because he was concerned with their physical health as well as the state of their souls.

Believers today, living according to God's plan, should obey their Lord in every detail as they seek to restore people's bodies and souls to the health and salvation God has in store for them. To know how to live a perfect life, look to Jesus as the perfect example.

CELEBRATION
Pick the word or words from the following that describe worship services in your church: solemn, quiet, reverent, somber, or joyful, warm, uplifting, celebrative. Biblical worship doesn't have to be an either/or proposition. It can be both dignified and uplifting. But if there isn't an overriding element of joy, it isn't true worship, and it isn't worthy of the risen Lord. Dignified doesn't have to mean dour, and celebration doesn't have to be synonymous with superficial. It is possible to have both aspects of worship present at the same time. What is worship like in your church? If it leans too heavily toward the solemn and the somber, your congregation needs to get in touch with all the reasons they have to be glad in the Lord.

---

250 EVENTS IN THE LIFE OF CHRIST/ A HARMONY OF THE GOSPELS

All four books in the Bible that tell the story of Jesus Christ—Matthew, Mark, Luke, and John—stand alone, emphasizing a unique aspect of Jesus' life. But when these are blended into one complete account, or harmonized, we gain new insights about the life of Christ.

This harmony combines the four Gospels into a single chronological account of Christ's life on earth. It includes every chapter and verse of each Gospel, leaving nothing out.

The harmony is divided into 250 events. The title of each event is identical to the title found in the corresponding Gospel. Parallel passages found in more than one Gospel have identical titles, helping you to identify them quickly.

Each of the 250 events in the harmony is numbered. The number of the event corresponds to the number next to the title in the Bible text. When reading one of the Gospel accounts, you will notice, at times, that some numbers are missing or out of sequence. The easiest way to locate these events is to refer to the harmony.

In addition, if you are looking for a particular event in the life of Christ, the harmony can help you locate it more rapidly than paging through all four Gospels. Each of the 250 events has a distinctive title keyed to the main emphasis of the passage to help you locate and remember the events.

This harmony will help you to better visualize the travels of Jesus, study the four Gospels comparatively, and appreciate the unity of their message.

I. BIRTH AND PREPARATION OF JESUS CHRIST

	Matthew	Mark	Luke	John
1 Luke's purpose in writing			1:1–4	
2 God became a human being				1:1–18
3 The ancestors of Jesus	1:1–17		3:23–38	
4 An angel promises the birth of John to Zechariah			1:5–25	
5 An angel promises the birth of Jesus to Mary			1:26–38	
6 Mary visits Elizabeth			1:39–56	
7 John the Baptist is born			1:57–80	
8 An angel appears to Joseph	1:18–25			
9 Jesus is born in Bethlehem			2:1–7	
10 Shepherds visit Jesus			2:8–20	
11 Mary and Joseph bring Jesus to the temple			2:21–40	
12 Visitors arrive from eastern lands	2:1–12			
13 The escape to Egypt	2:13–18			
14 The return to Nazareth	2:19–23			
15 Jesus speaks with the religious teachers			2:41–52	
16 John the Baptist prepares the way for Jesus	3:1–12	1:1–8	3:1–18	
17 John baptizes Jesus	3:13–17	1:9–11	3:21, 22	
18 Satan tempts Jesus in the desert	4:1–11	1:12, 13	4:1–13	
19 John the Baptist declares his mission				1:19–28

	Matthew	*Mark*	*Luke*	*John*
20 John the Baptist proclaims Jesus as the Messiah				1:29–34
21 The first disciples follow Jesus				1:35–51
22 Jesus turns water into wine				2:1–12

II. MESSAGE AND MINISTRY OF JESUS CHRIST

	Matthew	*Mark*	*Luke*	*John*
23 Jesus clears the temple				2:12–25
24 Nicodemus visits Jesus at night				3:1–21
25 John the Baptist tells more about Jesus				3:22–36
26 Herod puts John in prison			3:19, 20	
27 Jesus talks to a woman at the well				4:1–26
28 Jesus tells about the spiritual harvest				4:27–38
29 Many Samaritans believe in Jesus				4:39–42
30 Jesus preaches in Galilee	4:12–17	1:14, 15	4:14, 15	4:43–45
31 Jesus heals a government official's son				4:46–54
32 Jesus is rejected at Nazareth			4:16–30	
33 Four fishermen follow Jesus	4:18–22	1:16–20		
34 Jesus teaches with great authority		1:21–28	4:31–37	
35 Jesus heals Peter's mother-in-law and many others	8:14–17	1:29–34	4:38–41	
36 Jesus preaches throughout Galilee	4:23–25	1:35–39	4:42–44	
37 Jesus provides a miraculous catch of fish			5:1–11	
38 Jesus heals a man with leprosy	8:1–4	1:40–45	5:12–16	
39 Jesus heals a paralyzed man	9:1–8	2:1–12	5:17–26	
40 Jesus eats with sinners at Matthew's house	9:9–13	2:13–17	5:27–32	
41 Religious leaders ask Jesus about fasting	9:14–17	2:18–22	5:33–39	
42 Jesus heals a lame man by the pool				5:1–18
43 Jesus claims to be God's Son				5:19–30
44 Jesus supports his claim				5:31–47
45 The disciples pick wheat on the Sabbath	12:1–8	2:23–28	6:1–5	
46 Jesus heals a man's hand on the Sabbath	12:9–14	3:1–6	6:6–11	
47 Large crowds follow Jesus	12:15–21	3:7–12		
48 Jesus selects the twelve disciples		3:13–19	6:12–16	
49 Jesus gives the Beatitudes	5:1–12		6:17–26	
50 Jesus teaches about salt and light	5:13–16			
51 Jesus teaches about the law	5:17–20			
52 Jesus teaches about anger	5:21–26			
53 Jesus teaches about lust	5:27–30			
54 Jesus teaches about divorce	5:31, 32			
55 Jesus teaches about vows	5:33–37			
56 Jesus teaches about retaliation	5:38–42			
57 Jesus teaches about loving enemies	5:43–48		6:27–36	
58 Jesus teaches about giving to the needy	6:1–4			
59 Jesus teaches about prayer	6:5–15			
60 Jesus teaches about fasting	6:16–18			
61 Jesus teaches about money	6:19–24			
62 Jesus teaches about worry	6:25–34			
63 Jesus teaches about criticizing others	7:1–6		6:37–42	
64 Jesus teaches about asking, seeking, knocking	7:7–12			
65 Jesus teaches about the way to heaven	7:13, 14			
66 Jesus teaches about fruit in people's lives	7:15–20		6:43–45	
67 Jesus teaches about those who build houses on rock and sand	7:21–29		6:46–49	
68 A Roman centurion demonstrates faith	8:5–13		7:1–10	
69 Jesus raises a widow's son from the dead			7:11–17	
70 Jesus eases John's doubt	11:1–19		7:18–35	
71 Jesus promises rest for the soul	11:20–30			
72 A sinful woman anoints Jesus' feet			7:36–50	
73 Women accompany Jesus and the disciples			8:1–3	
74 Religious leaders accuse Jesus of being under Satan's power	12:22–37	3:20–30		

	Matthew	Mark	Luke	John
75 Religious leaders ask Jesus for a miracle	12:38–45			
76 Jesus describes his true family	12:46–50	3:31–35	8:19–21	
77 Jesus tells the parable of the four soils	13:1–9	4:1–9	8:4–8	
78 Jesus explains the parable of the four soils	13:10–23	4:10–25	8:9–18	
79 Jesus tells the parable of the growing seed		4:26–29		
80 Jesus tells the parable of the weeds	13:24–30			
81 Jesus tells the parable of the mustard seed	13:31, 32	4:30–34		
82 Jesus tells the parable of the yeast	13:33–35			
83 Jesus explains the parable of the weeds	13:36–43			
84 Jesus tells the parable of hidden treasure	13:44			
85 Jesus tells the parable of the pearl merchant	13:45, 46			
86 Jesus tells the parable of the fishing net	13:47–52			
87 Jesus calms the storm	8:23–27	4:35–41	8:22–25	
88 Jesus sends the demons into a herd of pigs	8:28–34	5:1–20	8:26–39	
89 Jesus heals a bleeding woman and restores a girl to life	9:18–26	5:21–43	8:40–56	
90 Jesus heals the blind and mute	9:27–34			
91 The people of Nazareth refuse to believe	13:53–58	6:1–6		
92 Jesus urges the disciples to pray for workers	9:35–38			
93 Jesus sends out the twelve disciples	10:1–16	6:7–13	9:1–6	
94 Jesus prepares the disciples for persecution	10:17–42			
95 Herod kills John the Baptist	14:1–12	6:14–29	9:7–9	
96 Jesus feeds five thousand	14:13–21	6:30–44	9:10–17	6:1–15
97 Jesus walks on water	14:22–33	6:45–52		6:16–21
98 Jesus heals all who touch him	14:34–36	6:53–56		
99 Jesus is the true bread from heaven				6:22–40
100 The Jews disagree that Jesus is from heaven				6:41–59
101 Many disciples desert Jesus				6:60–71
102 Jesus teaches about inner purity	15:1–20	7:1–23		
103 Jesus sends a demon out of a girl	15:21–28	7:24–30		
104 The crowd marvels at Jesus' healings	15:29–31	7:31–37		
105 Jesus feeds four thousand	15:32–39	8:1–10		
106 Religious leaders ask for a sign in the sky	16:1–4	8:11–13		
107 Jesus warns against wrong teaching	16:5–12	8:14–21		
108 Jesus restores sight to a blind man		8:22–26		
109 Peter says Jesus is the Messiah	16:13–20	8:27–30	9:18–20	
110 Jesus predicts his death the first time	16:21–28	8:31–9:1	9:21–27	
111 Jesus is transfigured on the mountain	17:1–13	9:2–13	9:28–36	
112 Jesus heals a demon-possessed boy	17:14–21	9:14–29	9:37–43	
113 Jesus predicts his death the second time	17:22, 23	9:30–32	9:44, 45	
114 Peter finds the coin in the fish's mouth	17:24–27			
115 The disciples argue about who would be the greatest	18:1–6	9:33–37	9:46–48	
116 The disciples forbid another to use Jesus' name		9:38–41	9:49, 50	
117 Jesus warns against temptation	18:7–9	9:42–50		
118 Jesus warns against looking down on others	18:10–14			
119 Jesus teaches how to treat a believer who sins	18:15–20			
120 Jesus tells the parable of the unforgiving debtor	18:21–35			
121 Jesus' brothers ridicule him				7:1–9
122 Jesus teaches about the cost of following him	8:18–22		9:51–62	
123 Jesus teaches openly at the temple				7:10–31
124 Religious leaders attempt to arrest Jesus				7:32–52
125 Jesus forgives an adulterous woman				7:53–8:11
126 Jesus is the light of the world				8:12–20
127 Jesus warns of coming judgment				8:21–30
128 Jesus speaks about God's true children				8:31–47
129 Jesus states he is eternal				8:48–59
130 Jesus sends out seventy-two messengers			10:1–16	
131 The seventy-two messengers return			10:17–24	
132 Jesus tells the parable of the Good Samaritan			10:25–37	
133 Jesus visits Mary and Martha			10:38–42	
134 Jesus teaches his disciples about prayer			11:1–13	
135 Jesus answers hostile accusations			11:14–28	
136 Jesus warns against unbelief			11:29–32	

		Matthew	Mark	Luke	John
137	Jesus teaches about the light within			11:33–36	
138	Jesus criticizes the religious leaders			11:37–54	
139	Jesus speaks against hypocrisy			12:1–12	
140	Jesus tells the parable of the rich fool			12:13–21	
141	Jesus warns about worry			12:22–34	
142	Jesus warns about preparing for his coming			12:35–48	
143	Jesus warns about coming division			12:49–53	
144	Jesus warns about the future crisis			12:54–59	
145	Jesus calls the people to repent			13:1–9	
146	Jesus heals the crippled woman			13:10–17	
147	Jesus teaches about the kingdom of God			13:18–21	
148	Jesus heals the man who was born blind				9:1–12
149	Religious leaders question the blind man				9:13–34
150	Jesus teaches about spiritual blindness				9:35–41
151	Jesus is the Good Shepherd				10:1–21
152	Religious leaders surround Jesus at the temple				10:22–42
153	Jesus teaches about entering the kingdom			13:22–30	
154	Jesus grieves over Jerusalem			13:31–35	
155	Jesus heals a man with dropsy			14:1–6	
156	Jesus teaches about seeking honor			14:7–14	
157	Jesus tells the parable of the great feast			14:15–24	
158	Jesus teaches about the cost of being a disciple			14:25–35	
159	Jesus tells the parable of the lost sheep			15:1–7	
160	Jesus tells the parable of the lost coin			15:8–10	
161	Jesus tells the parable of the lost son			15:11–32	
162	Jesus tells the parable of the shrewd manager			16:1–18	
163	Jesus tells about the rich man and the beggar			16:19–31	
164	Jesus tells about forgiveness and faith			17:1–10	
165	Lazarus becomes ill and dies				11:1–16
166	Jesus comforts Mary and Martha				11:17–37
167	Jesus raises Lazarus from the dead				11:38–44
168	Religious leaders plot to kill Jesus				11:45–57
169	Jesus heals ten men with leprosy			17:11–19	
170	Jesus teaches about the coming of the kingdom of God			17:20–37	
171	Jesus tells the parable of the persistent widow			18:1–8	
172	Jesus tells the parable of two men who prayed			18:9–14	
173	Jesus teaches about marriage and divorce	19:1–12	10:1–12		
174	Jesus blesses little children	19:13–15	10:13–16	18:15–17	
175	Jesus speaks to the rich young man	19:16–30	10:17–31	18:18–30	
176	Jesus tells the parable of the workers paid equally	20:1–16			
177	Jesus predicts his death the third time	20:17–19	10:32–34	18:31–34	
178	Jesus teaches about serving others	20:20–28	10:35–45		
179	Jesus heals a blind beggar	20:29–34	10:46–52	18:35–43	
180	Jesus brings salvation to Zacchaeus's home			19:1–10	
181	Jesus tells the parable of the king's ten servants			19:11–27	
182	A woman anoints Jesus with perfume	26:6–13	14:3–9		12:1–11
183	Jesus rides into Jerusalem on a donkey	21:1–11	11:1–11	19:28–44	12:12–19
184	Jesus clears the temple again	21:12–17	11:12–19	19:45–48	
185	Jesus explains why he must die				12:20–36
186	Most of the people do not believe in Jesus				12:37–43
187	Jesus summarizes his message				12:44–50
188	Jesus says the disciples can pray for anything	21:18–22	11:20–26		
189	Religious leaders challenge Jesus' authority	21:23–27	11:27–33	20:1–8	
190	Jesus tells the parable of the two sons	21:28–32			
191	Jesus tells the parable of the wicked tenants	21:33–46	12:1–12	20:9–19	
192	Jesus tells the parable of the wedding feast	22:1–14			
193	Religious leaders question Jesus about paying taxes	22:15–22	12:13–17	20:20–26	
194	Religious leaders question Jesus about the resurrection	22:23–33	12:18–27	20:27–40	
195	Religious leaders question Jesus about the greatest commandment	22:34–40	12:28–34		
196	Religious leaders cannot answer Jesus' question	22:41–46	12:35–37	20:41–44	

	Matthew	Mark	Luke	John
197 Jesus warns against the religious leaders	23:1–12	12:38–40	20:45–47	
198 Jesus condemns the religious leaders	23:13–36			
199 Jesus grieves over Jerusalem again	23:37–39			
200 A poor widow gives all she has		12:41–44	21:1–4	
201 Jesus tells about the future	24:1–25	13:1–23	21:5–24	
202 Jesus tells about his return	24:26–35	13:24–31	21:25–33	
203 Jesus tells about remaining watchful	24:36–51	13:32–37	21:34–38	
204 Jesus tells the parable of the ten bridesmaids	25:1–13			
205 Jesus tells the parable of the loaned money	25:14–30			
206 Jesus tells about the final judgment	25:31–46			

III. DEATH AND RESURRECTION OF JESUS CHRIST

	Matthew	Mark	Luke	John
207 Religious leaders plot to kill Jesus	26:1–5	14:1, 2	22:1, 2	
208 Judas agrees to betray Jesus	26:14–16	14:10, 11	22:3–6	
209 Disciples prepare for the Passover	26:17–19	14:12–16	22:7–13	
210 Jesus washes the disciples' feet				13:1–20
211 Jesus and the disciples have the Last Supper	26:20–30	14:17–26	22:14–30	13:21–30
212 Jesus predicts Peter's denial			22:31–38	13:31–38
213 Jesus is the way to the Father				14:1–14
214 Jesus promises the Holy Spirit				14:15–31
215 Jesus teaches about the vine and the branches				15:1–17
216 Jesus warns about the world's hatred				15:18–16:4
217 Jesus teaches about the Holy Spirit				16:5–15
218 Jesus teaches about using his name in prayer				16:16–33
219 Jesus prays for himself				17:1–5
220 Jesus prays for his disciples				17:6–19
221 Jesus prays for future believers				17:20–26
222 Jesus again predicts Peter's denial	26:31–35	14:27–31		
223 Jesus agonizes in the garden	26:36–46	14:32–42	22:39–46	
224 Jesus is betrayed and arrested	26:47–56	14:43–52	22:47–53	18:1–11
225 Annas questions Jesus				18:12–24
226 Caiaphas questions Jesus	26:57–68	14:53–65		
227 Peter denies knowing Jesus	26:69–75	14:66–72	22:54–65	18:25–27
228 The council of religious leaders condemns Jesus	27:1, 2	15:1	22:66–71	
229 Judas kills himself	27:3–10			
230 Jesus stands trial before Pilate	27:11–14	15:2–5	23:1–5	18:28–37
231 Jesus stands trial before Herod			23:6–12	
232 Pilate hands Jesus over to be crucified	27:15–26	15:6–15	23:13–25	18:38–19:16
233 Roman soldiers mock Jesus	27:27–31	15:16–20		
234 Jesus is led away to be crucified	27:32–34	15:21–24	23:26–31	19:17
235 Jesus is placed on the cross	27:35–44	15:25–32	23:32–43	19:18–27
236 Jesus dies on the cross	27:45–56	15:33–41	23:44–49	19:28–37
237 Jesus is laid in the tomb	27:57–61	15:42–47	23:50–56	19:38–42
238 Guards are posted at the tomb	27:62–66			
239 Jesus rises from the dead	28:1–7	16:1–8	24:1–12	20:1–9
240 Jesus appears to Mary Magdalene		16:9–11		20:10–18
241 Jesus appears to the women	28:8–10			
242 Religious leaders bribe the guards	28:11–15			
243 Jesus appears to two believers traveling on the road		16:12, 13	24:13–35	
244 Jesus appears to the disciples behind locked doors			24:36–43	20:19–23
245 Jesus appears to the disciples including Thomas		16:14		20:24–31
246 Jesus appears to the disciples while fishing				21:1–14
247 Jesus talks with Peter				21:15–25
248 Jesus gives the Great Commission	28:16–20	16:15–18		
249 Jesus appears to the disciples in Jerusalem			24:44–49	
250 Jesus ascends into heaven		16:19, 20	24:50–53	

BIBLIOGRAPHY

Bock, Darrell L. *Luke*. The IVP New Testament Commentary Series. Downers Grove, Ill.: InterVarsity Press, 1994.

———. *Luke. Vol. 1*. Baker Exegetical Commentary on the New Testament. Grand Rapids: Baker Books, 1994.

———. *Luke. Vol. 2*. Baker Exegetical Commentary on the New Testament. Grand Rapids: Baker Books, 1996.

Douglas, J. D., ed. *The New Greek-English Interlinear New Testament*. Robert K. Brown and Philip W. Comfort, trans. Wheaton, Ill.: Tyndale House Publishers, 1990.

Evans, Craig A. *Luke*. The New International Biblical Commentary Series; W. Ward Gasque, New Testament ed. Peabody, Mass.: Hendrickson Publishers, 1990.

Green, Joel B., and Scot McKnight, eds. *Dictionary of Jesus and the Gospels*. Downers Grove, Ill.: InterVarsity Press, 1992.

Liefiled, Walter. "Luke" in *The Expositor's Bible Commentary;* Frank Gaebelein, ed. Grand Rapids: Zondervan Publishing House, 1984.

Miller, Donald G. *Luke*. The Layman's Bible Commentary. Atlanta: John Knox Press, 1959.

Morris, Leon. *Luke*. Tyndale New Testament Commentaries. Grand Rapids: Eerdmans, 1988.

Nolland, John. *Luke 1–9:20*. Word Biblical Commentary. Dallas: Word Books, 1989.

———. *Luke 9:21–18:34*. Word Biblical Commentary. Dallas: Word Books, 1993.

———. *Luke 18:35–24:53*. Word Biblical Commentary. Dallas: Word Books, 1993.

Osborne, June, and Chris Sugden. *Luke*. Bible Study Commentary. Fort Washington, Penn.: Christian Literature Crusade, 1987.

Stein, Robert H. *Luke* The New American Commentary, vol. 24. Nashville: Broadman Press, 1992.

INDEX

Garden of Gethsemane, 505–513
Gentiles
Jesus' ministry to, 171–176
part in Jesus' death, 424
application for today, 172
Gerasenes, 212
Gifts/Talents, 433–439
application for today, 436, 438, 451, 470
God
his mercy and love, 159
nothing impossible for, 22, 420–421
Chart: As God Is Merciful, 160
Chart: God's Unusual Methods, 8
application for today, 16, 159, 340, 369, 423
God's Will
application for today, 40, 63, 97, 136, 185
Golden Rule, 158
Greed
parable of the rich fool, 317–321
application for today, 318, 319
Guidance
application for today, 39, 77, 350, 477
Healing
disciples given power to do, 229–230
of a bleeding woman, 219–224
of a blind beggar, 424–427
of a crippled woman, 340–343
of a man with dropsy, 353–355
of a man with leprosy, 116–120
of a man's ear, 511–512
of a man's hand, 140–144
of a paralyzed man, 120–128
of Peter's mother-in-law, 103–106
of other people, 105–106, 150, 181
of ten men with leprosy, 399–402
application for today, 104, 402, 427
Hearts
salvation brings change of, 11–12
application for today, 11
Hell, 312, 314
Herod Antipas, 61–62, 73, 233–235, 349–350, 526–528
Herod, King (the Great)
as king of Judea, 5
Herodias, 73
History
as theme of Luke's Gospel, *xxii*
Holy Place
in the temple, 7–8

Holy Spirit
as theme of Luke's Gospel, *xxiv*
blasphemy of, 315–316
filled Elizabeth, 24
filled Jesus, 74–76, 83–85, 91, 275–276
filled Simeon, 49–50
filled Zechariah, 31–35
part in Jesus' birth, 21–22
promise of, 10–11, 70–72, 293, 316–317
application for today, 24, 71, 85, 567, 570, 571
Honor
Jesus teaches about, 355–357
application for today, 355
Hope
application for today, 50, 225, 227, 558
Humility
parable about, 355–357
application for today, 356
Hypocrisy, 311–317, 342–343
application for today, 312, 313
Incense
its use in the temple, 7–8
Isaiah, the prophet, 65–66, 93–94
Jairus, 220–221, 224–227
James (son of Alphaeus), 148
James (son of Zebedee), 115–116, 146–147, 248, 261–263
Jealousy
of disciples, 258–259
application for today, 259
Jericho, 425, 429
Jerusalem, 48, 56, 260, 349–352, 439–446, 478–480
Jesus Christ
ancestors of, 76–82
as bridegroom, 133
as theme of Luke's Gospel, *xxii*
ascension, 570–572
betrayal of, 510–513
called "Christ the Lord," 45
his birth told to Mary, 18–21
holy, 21–22
is born, 40–48
is God, 273, 276–277
his childhood, 54–59
Lord of the Sabbath, 139
resurrection, 551–570
significance of his name, 18–19
Savior, 44–45
"Son of David," 465–466